Portfolio

of Accounting Systems

for Small and Medium-Sized

Businesses

Portfolio of

for Small

Prentice-Hall, Inc.

VOLUME **I**

Accounting Systems and Medium-Sized Businesses

National Society of Public Accountants

Marjorie D. James, Editor

Englewood Cliffs, New Jersey

Portfolio of Accounting Systems for Small
and Medium-Sized Businesses
by NSPA

© 1968, by
PRENTICE-HALL, INC.
Englewood Cliffs, N.J.

Library of Congress
Catalog Card Number: 68-18738

Second Printing..... March, 1969

PRINTED IN THE UNITED STATES OF AMERICA
X

PORTFOLIO OF ACCOUNTING SYSTEMS
FOR SMALL AND MEDIUM-SIZED BUSINESSES

This *Portfolio* comprises an encyclopedia of accounting systems for small and medium-sized businesses never before gathered into an accounting publication.

Much that has been said about big business is presumed to apply as well to smaller enterprises. But the small and medium-sized businesses fundamental to the economy of the United States have their own problems and peculiarities which must be solved and handled in ways distinctively applicable to them.

For this reason the authors of the chapters are members of the National Society of Public Accountants, the representative of local practitioners and the voice of independent accountants everywhere. The authors knowingly place emphasis upon unusual features of the businesses about which they write and upon explanation of procedures unique to these enterprises, and the resolving of problems inherent in them.

The *Portfolio* is intended as a practical tool for experienced accountants unfamiliar with a particular business or profession, so that they may design, revise, install, and put into effect a system especially adapted to each client. It is not just another book of accounting elements and fundamentals.

Each chapter is built upon a standard outline, contrived to insure equal coverage and comprehensiveness for each business. While special situations have caused a departure from this outline, each chapter was based upon the following principal sections:

1. Characteristics of the business or profession that affect the accounting system.
2. Functional organization.
3. Principles and objectives of the accounting system.
4. Classification of accounts and books of accounts.
5. Peculiarities of procedures for: sales-receivables cycle; purchases-payables cycle; cash receipts and disbursements.
6. Time and payroll system.
7. Cost accounting and departmental accounting, if applicable.
8. Time-saving ideas.
9. Reports to management.

If nothing of special mention is apparent under a particular topic in the outline, the author has omitted the topic or indicated that ordinary methods and procedures would be followed. Explanations of tax techniques have been deleted except in the case where a tax is unique to a particular business. Fundamentals familiar to accountants and common to all businesses were deliberately avoided.

No specific manner of coding for the charts of accounts is prescribed nor any rigid standardization of terminology. Each author has been allowed to follow his accustomed practice.

Throughout these sections almost 600 forms and diagrams have been reproduced. Filled-in forms have been shown when more complete clarification was desired. Discussions of methods and procedures are supported by the charts of accounts.

The outline arrangement allows the reader to locate more easily the various phases of discussion, compare similarities or differences, and approach the problem of reference and research with some degree of optimism. He is able to employ ideas from the variety of fields in adapting to new situations, or in acquiring a background of knowledge concerning the business before interviewing a prospective client.

MARJORIE DIEHL JAMES

ACKNOWLEDGEMENTS

The NATIONAL SOCIETY OF PUBLIC ACCOUNTANTS sincerely thanks the vast team of business associates, advisors, associations, organizations, manufacturers and designers of forms for their help and cooperation.

Commendation is due the chapter authors listed in the Board of Contributors. The *Portfolio* would not have been possible without their diligence, their time, and their unfailing courtesy, even during the frenetic days of the annual tax season.

The Board of Contributors and the National Society extend recognition to the 45 accountants listed below who served as critics in authenticating content and evaluating procedures. Certain reviewed as many as four chapters. The painstaking efforts and ready cooperation of all are respectfully acknowledged.

Joseph G. Abod, Chicago, Illinois
George C. Akins, Sacramento, California
Paul S. Allen, Westfield, Massachusetts
Guy S. Balser, Long Beach, California
Charles Bauer, Washington, D.C.
Sidney C. Becker, Chicago, Illinois
John K. Berry, Washington, D.C.
Chester J. Borelli, Denver, Colorado
Eugene P. Cornett, Indianapolis, Indiana
Thomas Deluzio, Washington, D.C.
Edward D. Dery, Washington, D.C.
James P. Dunn, Rochester, New York
Stuart W. Frankford, Detroit, Michigan
William J. Franz, Cleveland, Ohio
R. P. Goodwin, Pittsburgh, Pennsylvania
Robert Grille, Falls Church, Virginia
Kenneth R. Hancock, Endicott, New York
Mary P. Hayes, Newport News, Virginia
John G. Herbst, St. Louis, Missouri
Eugene E. Hines, Washington, D.C.
A. M. Hunt, Midland, Michigan
Gil Johnson, White Bear Lake, Minnesota
Col. Laurence T. King, Wilbraham, Massachusetts
Cora Lanphear, El Paso, Texas
Ralph W. Larrabee, Lynnwood, Washington
S. C. Levin, Des Moines, Iowa
Harry Malin, Washington, D.C.
Harold L. Mills, Millen, Georgia
Anthony J. Nicolella, Springfield, Pennsylvania
R. J. Passero, Rochester, New York

Harry C. Perry, Jr., Washington, D.C.
Harry J. Phelan, San Francisco, California
A. Clyde Rohrs, Kansas City, Missouri
Roy B. Rollins, Sr., Charleston, West Virginia
Donald C. Rosenthal, Washington, D.C.
Joseph Y. Rosenzweig, Chicago, Illinois
David Schectman, Pittsburgh, Pennsylvania
Basil W. Seguin, Lewiston, Maine
William N. Tanner, Jr., Philadelphia, Pennsylvania
William A. Vasiliou, Middletown, Connecticut
Robert T. Violett, Hyattsville, Maryland
Rocco Volpi, Denver, Colorado
Sidney L. Weinberg, Baltimore, Maryland
Alfred F. Yaude, Charlotte, North Carolina
Peter Yosinoff, Providence, Rhode Island.

The Editor is grateful to Officers, District Governors, and State Directors of the National Society whose recommendations were helpful in bringing together the 65 authors who have made the *Portfolio* a material contribution to the accounting profession.

Proofreading help from NSPA staff members is deeply appreciated.

The Editor is especially indebted to Stanley H. Stearman, NSPA Executive Director, whose counsel, guidance, assistance, and support have been invaluable.

BOARD OF CONTRIBUTORS

Louis F. Math, Casper, Wyoming

Martha Melekov, Gardena, California

E. W. Moore, Alva, Oklahoma

Richard D. Nivison, Clare, Michigan

John B. Owens, Atlanta, Georgia

Arthur W. Pagano, Albany, New York

Theodore Panagiotis, Providence, Rhode Island

Carl M. Pereira, New Bedford, Massachusetts

Claude H. Reitz, Agawam, Massachusetts

Edward J. Rohter, Chicago, Illinois

J. Waldo Rost, Holdrege, Nebraska

Edward J. Schlitzer, Rochester, New York

Stanley S. Schuman, Newark, New Jersey

S. Arthur Seidman, Baltimore, Maryland

Donna H. Sharkey, Columbus, Ohio

W. F. Shelton, Louisburg, North Carolina

Milton R. Simon, Rochester, New York

Ezra E. Stevens, San Mateo, California

Ben Stoner, Springfield, Missouri

Floyd L. Swanson, Arcadia, California

William N. Tanner, Jr., Philadelphia, Pennsylvania

James Ten Hoeve, Paterson, New Jersey

William J. Tibbetts, Medford, Massachusetts

A. Whitmer Weigel, Corning, New York

John J. Welch, Boca Raton, Florida

Georg Wernmark, The Dalles, Oregon

Paul L. Williams, Fort Smith, Arkansas

Jean Yott, Detroit, Michigan

CONTENTS

1

Introduction to Systems

BY WILLIAM N. TANNER, JR.

Certified Public Accountant, Philadelphia, Pennsylvania; Editor of the "Accountants Forum" column of The National Public Accountant magazine

The late Dr. Alfred J. Cardall, one of the few nationally prominent psychologists with actual business experience, frequently stated, "Wherever there is a systems problem, you have a personnel problem."

Perhaps the first axiom in systems work is "Will they use it?", for unless a system is accepted by the people who use it, it will not work.

As a professional consultant, you are in an enviable position. Your opinion is respected. Your word carries authority. You are bringing to your client a new viewpoint. It may not be a better viewpoint; only time will prove how well your system works.

The experienced systems man is a good listener. As he listens, he watches. The lowliest clerk can give you an idea which may make a modification in your whole plan worthwhile. Or a word of explanation from you may make a whole operation acceptable to the man who uses it every day and win his enthusiastic support to insure the success of your entire system.

In the ensuing chapters you will find systems designed by accountants who are specialists in their fields. Each of their chapters presents a model for a

1

particular business. It has worked in that business enough times to be considered standard but, for your client's needs, it is up to you to custom tailor the system, so that it fits your client's business.

Are there any people more familiar with the problems a system must solve than those performing the work? It takes their ideas to make your system work well. You are not a roughshod "expert" who inflicts upon an unwilling user a pattern which chafes and irritates. You are the catalyst; you are the tailor who snips here and trims there; you discard the chaff and settle the kernel into a smooth-working operation.

So much for you and the people who will make—or break—your system. Keep an open mind. Be flexible. Be ready to change a little here and there but always to meet a specific situation. There are times to move quickly and decisively, but the really successful systems man is the one adroit enough to persuade the workers and management that it is their system rather than his. He leaves behind him an operation (system) that will make him long remembered as "the best in the world."

The next important point in systems work is to know where to stop. Accounting is only worthwhile when it produces information useful in the conduct of the business. A system which produces more than the owner (manager) can or will use in making decisions is ordinarily too cumbersome or too expensive to consider. The cost of a system, no matter how effective it is, must not be greater than the results it produces for a particular business.

There is the story of the erudite accountant who undertook design of a system for a public stenographer. He came up with multicolumn journals which distributed every penny spent or taken in. The poor girl spent almost as much time bookkeeping as she did typing. The accountant froze to his there-is-only-one-right-way-to-do-it theory and refused to modify his design. His successor substituted a simple, daily record of billings and expenses which related her production and total costs and took but minutes a day to handle. It was all she needed to control her small business.

Sometimes a psychological block will make a system useless. A printer friend, 20 years after his father's death, was still using the old system. This friend worried for days when I suggested triplicate invoices be prepared to eliminate the laborious copying into a daybook and into a separate customer's jacket. He finally concluded that I was expert and, therefore, probably right, but he just would not be happy with the change. Today, some 10 years later, he is still spending most of his evenings and many weekends copying in a vain effort to "catch up" on his bookkeeping. But it is worth it to him and until he is ready to accept change, no other system will work.

Sometimes a step at a time is more advisable than a whole new system. In one furniture store, a partner balked at a $3,000 investment in a cash register installment accounting setup. A potential $3,000 annual salary saving was not convincing. We compromised on a hand-posting setup which required an initial investment of about $250. It saved so much time and created so much customer satisfaction that a year later the money-conscious partner urged its replacement by the machine-posting setup we originally suggested. Meanwhile the slower hand method had effectively trained the salesmen and office personnel, so the machine system came in with less commotion than had it been the original installation. The key here was to design the hand forms so that practically without change they could be used in the machine.

Do not hesitate to spend money, but make sure that (1) the investment will not overtax the firm's cash position and (2) will be more than recovered by the savings the change creates.

I recall local businessmen who organized a department store and spent most of their cash installing an elaborate pneumatic tube system in a rented building to connect their sales stations with the cashier. When invoices for merchandise came due, there were no funds. The expensive pneumatic system reverted to the landlord, and the stockholders lost every dime they had invested. The store closed forever less than a year after it opened.

This is an extreme case, but each of you who have been in practice for 10 years has seen many pieces of almost new equipment out of use in the basement.

In systems, as in love, it is not the first cost but the upkeep that counts. If equipment is to be purchased, a good rule of thumb is to ask yourself: (1) Can the business afford it? and (2) How long will it take for the savings the new equipment makes to pay for it? If the cost will be recovered within a reasonable period of time by a business which can afford the investment, there is no reason for hesitation in buying it.

A fine example for accountants to remember is the electric adding machine. The motor may double the cost of the machine, but it eliminates so much fatigue and saves so much time that any volume of adding requires the electrically operated adder.

A good systems man will not hesitate to recommend the best method or the best equipment which is economical for his client to use. The test is not its selling price but the value of the equipment to the proper performance of its function for your client.

Often the investment to be made is in printing rather than in machines. Will a form save time or provide essential information otherwise apt to be overlooked? Is the form easily read and designed to provide a natural flow of work? Or does the user have to interrupt his work to explore the form to find the next information he needs? Will an extra carbon copy save time or expedite the transmission of information? Is the information on it necessary? Is it being used? Are other data needed?

A familiar example of a useless form, in many cases, is the stub of a checkbook. If your client keeps his checkbook in the office, why have the girl write out a stub and copy it into a Cash Disbursement book? How much simpler it is to use the Cash Disbursement book as a replacement for the check stub!

The most expensive work in an office is a task continued after its usefulness is ended. Too often a form, such as a check stub, is faithfully continued as a part of the work routine long after its use has been duplicated by the introduction of some other record. Too often, a report needed for some temporary emergency continues to be produced, even though it is not read, years after the emergency is over.

A word on typewriters in form design will be helpful. The two principal type faces are pica, 10 letters to an inch, and elite, 12 letters to an inch. Each has six lines of type to the inch. These type faces are standard on all makes of machines.

Lines and spacing on forms must conform exactly with the line spacing on the typewriter used to complete the form. Aside from time losses and hard-to-read data created by overlooking this precaution, the untidy work which results from lack of synchronization generates sloppy performance throughout the system.

A dot, so small as to be unnoticeable to anyone but the typist and printed on the form where a line such as an address is to begin, is a valuable time-saver which insures the information being placed where it is needed.

Most accountants are familiar with the use of carbon paper in pegboard systems. Its use in other applications should not be overlooked. Two, three, or more snap-out copies, collated, are long familiar in billing operations and have many other uses. A check, for example, which carries application of remittance data may also provide a carbon copy which eliminates the Cash Disbursement book, while a third copy may be used as the outstanding check list for bank reconciliations. Many such applications are the basis of so-called "bookless bookkeeping systems" and may easily replace a tediously written record. Labor is always more expensive than printing.

The new carbonless copy papers produce excellent copies and are cleaner to use than carbon paper. Another new idea is carbon-interleaved, padded second sheets. The typist merely selects the number of copies she requires, places a letterhead on top and inserts them in the typewriter. The one-time carbons provide excellent copies at a considerable time saving at no increase in material cost.

Consult your sources of supply. In the course of a year, the local stationer sees many more office operations than do you. His ideas can be valuable.

He may not be as adept as the forms company at design, but he does have catalogs from most manufacturers which will give you ideas. His experience in many offices and plants can be most useful to you.

Large printers whose principal business is forms production employ specialists in form design who are ready and willing to help you. Manufacturers of machines and equipment are as much interested as are you in having the machine best fitted for your client's need set up in his office. The specialists will help you in selection and use of equipment which will effect the maximum return for the client.

All of these people are interested in keeping you informed of new developments in their field. After all, a recommendation from an accountant is a fine entry for their salesmen. A well-informed accountant keeps in continuous touch with such sources of information. It is a good way to save money for your client and to create fees for yourself.

As you design his system, keep in mind the growth potential of your client and his business. Will he require more accounts or higher capacity equipment next year or the year after? If so, an extra column in today's form may save a new plate next year or the discarding of unused printed forms.

Is your chart of accounts flexible enough to accommodate the normal expansion of the business? Will it permit the use of tabulating equipment or computers? Your client may never own a computer, but next year you may want to recommend a computer or tabulator service bureau for him.

How well does your chart of accounts accommodate itself to published data, particularly the reporting services of the client's business associations? The American Institute of Laundering and many other associations regularly publish financial data on operations of members in their industry. It will be most helpful to your client if his financial reports are comparable to those of his industry. Comparison gives him not only a measure of his performance but delineates where his operation is above or below that of the other members of his association doing a similar volume of business. The more use he is able to make of the data your system provides for him, the more valuable it is to him.

Another source of operating data is the various Federal Reserve Banks each of which regularly publishes a survey of business. A request to the Federal Reserve Bank in your district will put you on their mailing list.

Returning to charts of accounts, a numerical system of coding accounts conforming to widely followed principles will reduce the amount of trial and error in usage, lower the number of errors, and be easily recognized and remembered by the clerks using it. A code based on basic machine operations, fits into manual operation without difficulty. In this way your client can at any time switch to mechanical operations without retraining his staff. Likewise, such a code is applicable to any business.

A commonly used code applicable to most accounting systems consists of four digits, 0000. In use, left-hand zeros are eliminated; thus 0100 is written as 100. Numbers with right-hand zeros are held in reserve and are not assigned to ledger accounts until capacity requires it.

The first thousand accounts, 0000 to 0999, are assigned to balance sheet accounts; the remainder, 1000 to 9999, to income and expense accounts. The bookkeeper knows instantly from the account number where an account belongs in the ledger.

Numbers are assigned to major groupings of ledger accounts as required in somewhat the following fashion:

BALANCE SHEET ACCOUNTS.

ASSETS	LIABILITIES
100 Current assets	500 Current liabilities
200 Other assets	600 Fixed liabilities
300 Fixed assets	700 Other liabilities
400 Intangible assets	800 Available for assignment
	900 Net worth

In a partnership the 900 accounts might be used as:

911 Capital—Mr. Jones	921 Personal account—Mr. Jones
912 Capital—Mr. Smith	922 Personal account—Mr. Smith
913 Capital—Mr. Taylor	923 Personal account—Mr. Taylor

In a corporation the 900 accounts might be assigned as:

900 Preferred Stock	940 Treasury Stock
920 Common Stock	970 Retained Earnings

If the number of accounts available permits, it is good coding practice to leave space between the numbers assigned, for future expansion. Using 920 instead of 901 or 910 for common stock leaves 19 accounts available for future issues of new classes of preferred stock before it is necessary to revamp the chart of accounts.

INCOME AND EXPENSE ACCOUNTS.

1000 Sales	5000 Administrative expenses
2000 Sales returns and allowances	6000 Office expenses
3000 Cost of goods sold	8000 Other income
4000 Selling expenses	9000 Other expenses

Space does not permit providing a complete chart of accounts, nor would two of your clients use identically the same chart of accounts. Illustrating two typical sections of a chart of accounts will give you an insight into the principles of coding which you can apply to the situations which develop in your system.

Current assets, No. 0100, will be used as the first illustration. The 01 is the major control, which would probably be broken down into intermediate controls (the next digit), along these lines:

0100	Cash on Hand	0140	Inventories
0110	Cash in Bank	0150	Deferred Charges
0120	Notes Receivable	0190	Miscellaneous Current Assets
0130	Accounts Receivable		

The right-hand or minor control comprises 10 accounts, 0 to 9. The 9 ordinarily is used for miscellaneous items for the sake of uniformity, while the 0 is not used until the other eight numbers have been assigned to accounts.

Where the same title appears in several intermediate controls, the assignment of the same number to all of its minor control accounts will facilitate coding data and reduce coding errors. For example, if your checking account in the First National Bank is coded 0111, then your note payable to the First National Bank should be coded 0501 if the number is available.

Similarly, recurring expense accounts should be assigned the same number. For instance, 2001, 3001, 4001, and 5001 might all be salary or wage accounts.

A four-digit code allows considerable flexibility. The second, third, and fourth digits in the illustrated income and expense section, for example, are all available for use in denoting territories, products, or type of account:

11—	Sales, Store No. 1		
111–	do	—meats	
1111	do	— do	—wholesale (or beef)

41—	Selling Expenses, Store No. 1		
411–	do	do	—meats
4111	do	do	—salaries
4112	do	do	—payroll
4113	do	do	—payroll expense
4114	do	do	—travel and entertainment
4115	do	do	—advertising
4116	do	do	—depreciation
4117	do	do	—rent
4118	do	do	—telephone
4119	do	do	—other sales expenses.

In summary, a chart of accounts should provide a flow of work designed to assemble data quickly and accurately in as much detail as is useful for the control of the business and no more. It should facilitate the condensation of detail into easily read and quickly prepared summaries so that operating data are available to executives with a minimum of delay.

A numerical code should be used where it aids in accomplishing these purposes and reduces the cost of recording the data. The code should be easily understood and designed to prevent errors in rapidly handling data.

To those who enjoy working with people and are fascinated by new problems, the design and installation of accounting systems offer a satisfying challenge and the opportunity for real achievement. Enter it without rigid rules as to how things must be done; apply the rule of reason to every decision and stay within the principles of sound operation, and you will make a real contribution to your client's progress. Good luck to you!

2

Accountants
(Private Practice)

BY DON C. McVAY

**Certified Public Accountant;
Partner, Weyl, McVay & Wickline, Columbus, Ohio**

Characteristics of the Profession That Affect the Accounting System

"Physician, heal thyself" is a saying that has lived for centuries. This adage could well be adopted by practicing accountants. Many businessmen are their own worst customers—they do not practice what they preach. The plumber has leaking faucets at home, and the electrician has overloaded circuits. Likewise, many an independent accountant has an inadequate accounting system to do for himself what he strives to do for his clients; namely, to install an accounting system directed toward efficient management, rather than toward a mere history book of the business.

The practitioner's first area of endeavor is to provide records, reports, and tax returns for his clients. Equally important is his advice to management in the use of these reports for planning and decision making, for use with various lending institutions, and in settlement of tax liabilities with Federal, state, and local taxing authorities.

9

Many practicing accountants are also engaged in the areas of estate planning, assist in establishment of pension and profit-sharing plans, and provide management services. It is to their advantage to put these very experiences to work for themselves. Should not the practicing accountant be his own best client?

FUNCTIONAL CHARACTERISTICS OF THE PROFESSION

Independent accountants, like their professional counterparts in medicine or law, conduct business as individual proprietors or as partnerships but also, where permitted by state law, as professional service corporations. Records of the vast majority of businesses operated as proprietorships or partnerships are kept on a calendar-year basis. Therefore, the natural business year is not generally a factor in the accounting system discussed in this chapter.

The profession of public accounting does not have competition as it is generally understood in the business world. The cooperation that exists between practitioners, individually and collectively, makes for a healthy environment in which to work and benefits the general public.

PRINCIPAL ACCOUNTING PROBLEMS

The principal accounting problem is that of billing for services rendered. How much to bill? Is it too much? Too little? Can the rates used be justified in arriving at the amount of the fee charged? Facets of this many-sided problem concern timekeeping, time analysis, compilation of hourly overhead costs, and showing how this information can provide management tools to increase efficiency and to achieve personal goals. The system to be described is fully adaptable by a single practitioner, a partnership, or a firm with various departments such as auditing, tax, management services, etc. With variations this system can be used by small, medium-sized, or large firms. It is also fully adaptable to manual or electronic data processing.

Functional Organization

A firm of accountants in private practice may be organized under a number of logical plans. One such plan would specify that all auditing be performed by a certain segment of the staff with a partner in charge of the department. The tax return preparation for all clients would be performed by the tax department with a partner responsible for its operation. Other departments, each with a partner in charge, could be established to service "small business" clients; to conduct research for all of the other departments; to operate pension and profit-sharing plans, management services, internal operations, or other aspects, depending upon the size of the firm.

Another plan specifies that each partner or senior accountant be assigned certain clients. The individual would be responsible for all phases of the services performed for those clients whether it be auditing, taxes, or business planning.

Principles and Objectives of the Accounting System

The purpose of this chapter is not only to explain how to set up a system of accounts for accountants serving the public but to expand upon some of the shortcomings of the ordinary system so that realization of the reasons for being in business may be achieved.

The primary objective of a good accounting system is to make the business more effective in its operations, not only from its service to the public but also in its service to its own internal financial stability. A fully integrated accounting system, such as this one, is necessary to obtain and maintain a satisfactory level of income for the staff and for the accountants themselves. It can also provide a vital by-product—higher proficiency as a practicing accountant.

Classification of Accounts and Books of Accounts

The chart of accounts for a public accounting firm, shown below, is standard for all departments. If desired, the department number may be prefixed to these codes.

While on the surface this chart of accounts appears to be in no way unusual, closer examination will reveal several areas that are different. It is these differences which require further comment. It is understood that the account numbers could be changed, depending on the use of the various data processing centers, or of certain manual accounting procedures.

BALANCE SHEET ACCOUNTS.

ASSETS	LIABILITIES
Current assets	*Current liabilities*
101 Cash in Bank	202 Notes Payable
106 Petty Cash	212 Accounts Payable
107 Postage Meter	224 Payroll Taxes Withheld
108 Accounts Receivable	NET WORTH
Fixed assets	271 Partner A, Investment
145 Automobiles	272 Partner A, Withdrawals
146 Accumulated Depreciation	273 Partner A, Advances
149 Furniture and Fixtures	274 Partner B, Investment
150 Accumulated Depreciation	275 Partner B, Withdrawals

276 Partner B, Advances
277 Partner C, Investment
278 Partner C, Withdrawals

279 Partner C, Advances
297 Net Profit or Loss

INCOME AND EXPENSE ACCOUNTS.

INCOME

301 Accounting Fees
315 Less: Direct Client Supplies

EXPENSES

501 Wages—Productive
502 Wages—Nonproductive
503 Subcontract
504 Rent
506 Telephone and Telegraph
507 Licenses
508 Insurance
509 Interest
510 Office Supplies
511 Postage
512 Bank Charges
513 Legal

514 Dues and Subscriptions
518 Data Processing
519 Tax Services
521 FICA Tax
522 Unemployment Taxes
523 Personal Property Taxes
525 Other Taxes
533 Depreciation—Auto
535 Depreciation—Furniture and Fixtures
540 Auto Expenses
544 Maintenance and Repairs
551 Promotional
553 Traveling
557 Clients' Expenses Paid
559 Prorated Expenses
560 Miscellaneous

ACCOUNTS PECULIAR TO THE PROFESSION

Postage Meter. Account No. 107 contains the standard amount that is maintained in the postage meter. On the last day of each month, or other accounting period, a check is written to bring the meter back to this standard amount, so that the books will reflect actual postage expense for the accounting period involved.

Accounts Receivable and Accounts Payable. Most independent accountants keep their books and report their income on a cash basis rather than on an accrual basis. However, merely by accruing the Accounts Receivable (No. 108) and Accounts Payable (No. 212) and entering the offsetting entry to Net Worth, the balance sheet can be much more meaningful in analyzing the business operations.

Partner's Withdrawals. The proprietor's or partner's withdrawal (Nos. 272, 275, or 278) should be an account to which his regular "salary" drawings are charged. In this way he knows what he has withdrawn in earnings as if he were an employee.

Partner's Advances. Account Nos. 273, 276, or 279 would be charged with all items of fringe benefits that the accountant has paid for through the business. These would include such items as hospitalization premiums, the percentage of expenses for personal auto usage, and the like.

Direct Client Supplies. Often a practicing accountant will purchase and pay for supplies for his clients. These disbursements are charged to Account No. 315, which indicates total disbursements for clients' supplies. When the client pays for these expenses with his regular accounting fee, it is not necessary to break down the payment but merely to credit the total amount to the Accounting Fees account (No. 301). The amount in "Total Income" will be the net receipts for services rendered.

Wages—Productive and Nonproductive. One of the great problems in the field of public accounting is that of knowing the payroll cost of productive and nonproductive time of employees (Nos. 501 and 502). Through the time and payroll cost explained in later paragraphs, it will be shown how these amounts are computed and how they fit into the overall system.

Promotional. Occasionally a client, a business associate, or someone directly associated with the firm may be hospitalized or become deceased. Flowers and cards in such circumstances would be charged to Promotional Expense (No. 551). Any business lunches for clients, staff members, etc., would likewise be charged to this account.

Clients' Expenses Paid. There are times when it is proper for a practitioner to pay a penalty or interest that is legally the client's expense but morally the accountant's. This can happen when it is necessary to secure an extension of time to file a tax return because of problems in the accountant's office. The interest would be a charge to this account, No. 557. There should be a zero balance in the account; but the unexpected can happen, and the client should not be penalized by having to pay this interest.

Prorated Expenses. Certain expenses in a departmentalized firm of public accountants cannot be allocated directly to each department, or it is not economically feasible to do so. Therefore, these expenses are prorated to each department or partner on a predetermined basis. It may be on the basis of productive hours, gross income, or some other equitable plan. The expenses are charged to a separate statement of expenses and allocated to each department by a charge to Prorated Expenses (No. 559).

BOOKS AND FORMS PECULIAR TO THE PROFESSION

A customary double entry system is the best method of accounting because of the built-in checks and balances. Cash Receipts can be as simple as a duplicate deposit slip, assuming that all receipts are deposited into the bank account; or Cash Receipts may be more elaborate by use of a columnar

STATEMENT OF ACCOUNT

John Any Client
123 Main Street
Anytown, U.S.A.

2101

Weyl, McVay & Wickline
Public Accountants
Park Towers
First Floor - 1620 East Broad Street
Columbus, Ohio 43203
Phone 252-1171

Date	Reference	Charges	Payments	Balance	Date	Reference	Charges	Payments	Balance
19__									
2-28	653	175.00		175.00					
3-15			175.00	-o-					
3-31	731	195.00		195.00					
4-18			195.00	-o-					
4-30	866	192.50		192.50					
5-12			192.50	-o-					
5-31	910	162.50		162.50					
6-30	995	185.00		347.50					

* Courtesy of Weyl, McVay & Wickline, Public Accountants, Columbus, Ohio.

Figure 1: Statement of Account

journal. The latter may be desirable where a breakdown of income between departments or partners is needed.

All invoices and collections should be posted to an individual Accounts Receivable sheet for each client (Figure 1). This Statement of Account can serve as a history of the client's paying pattern, and the total billing for each client. It can also be used as a convenient means of making a statement merely by photocopying the form and sending it to the client.

Proper alignment will permit the folding of the statement to fit a window envelope. In this way no envelopes need be addressed, and typing errors are

WEYL, McVAY & WICKLINE
PUBLIC ACCOUNTANTS
PARK TOWERS — 1620 EAST BROAD STREET
COLUMBUS, OHIO 43203

25-3 / 412

DATE June 30, 19___   CHECK NO.   *   2042

Pay
TO THE ORDER OF

INSURED 8N17454 21 DOLS 85 CTS $**21.85

WEYL, McVAY & WICKLINE

Petty Cash

SPECIMEN * NOT NEGOTIABLE
By_____

⑆0412⑈0003⑆ 17⑆6425 6⑊

WEYL, McVAY & WICKLINE — Columbus, Ohio 43203

| PERIOD ENDING | HOURS | | | EARNINGS | | | | DEDUCTIONS | | | | |
	REG.	O.T.	TOTAL	REGULAR	OVERTIME	OTHER	TOTAL	F.I.C.A.	WITHHOLD-ING TAX	STATE TAX		NET PAY

INVOICE DATE	INVOICE NUMBER	DESCRIPTION	OUR REFERENCE NO.	AMOUNT OF INVOICE	DEDUCTIONS	NET AMOUNT
				Dr.	Cr.	21.85
		Petty Cash Reimbursement	1551	2.10		
		as of June 30, 19___	2551	3.25		
			3551	2.75		
			1511	5.00		
			2553	2.25		
			3510	4.50		
			2540	2.00		
			1101		7.10	
			2101		7.50	
			3101		7.25	

REMITTANCE STATEMENT
DETACH THIS STATEMENT BEFORE DEPOSITING CHECK

* COURTESY OF WEYL, McVAY & WICKLINE, PUBLIC ACCOUNTANTS, COLUMBUS, OHIO.

Figure 2: Triplicate Check

avoided. A numerical file of all invoices provides further control to help avoid the loss of an invoice. Thus there is filed at all times an exact copy of any invoice to which reference may be made if it is necessary to know exactly what was stated on that invoice.

Ordinary checks, three to a page, are good because they provide adequate space for description of the disbursement. Duplicate and voucher-type checks are being used more and more, and have certain features that lend themselves well to this system. A triplicate voucher check (Figure 2) will not only pay the bill but also provide a numerical, chronological file of an exact copy of the check to serve as a check stub. The third copy of the check, attached to the paid bill and filed for reference, provides exact date, check number, address, and description of the transaction. Such data can be essential in case of a disputed payment.

The checks can be coded with the proper account number, not only for the debit but also for the credit. It can be seen that multiple debit or credit breakdowns are possible whether it be for a single proprietor or for a larger firm. The duplicate and voucher checks may then be entered in the customary Cash Disbursements journal. Without further effort on the accountant's part, they are ready to be key punched for data processing, along with other information of receipts and adjusting journal entries. The computer then prepares the accounting reports (balance sheet and income statement, including operating percentages), the General ledger, and a chronological listing of all entries during the accounting period.

Other than a General journal for a manual accounting system, there are no books or forms that are peculiar to this particular system that are not described or referred to in this chapter.

Time and Payroll System

Daily Time Sheet. The heart of the system of keeping time is the Daily Time Sheet (Figure 3). All a practicing accountant has to sell is time. The type of work performed, the knowledge and experience of the accountant performing the services *must* be considered in setting the rate to be charged for this time. The more knowledge and experience—the more valuable the service—the higher the rate to be charged. It makes little difference how the amount of the bill is determined. It may be on a straight-time basis, on a flat-fee system, or by retainer. The primary consideration in arriving at the fee is TIME.

The Daily Time Sheet provides for the employee or proprietor's name, the date, classification of the person preparing the time sheet, the starting and stopping time for three periods during the work day, and the total time worked.

Every client is assigned a number so that the office secretary can readily post the time. The number can also be used for client identification in the processing of the client's accounting records, either by a manual or a data processing method. If the accountant's time system is automated, use of the number helps to avoid errors.

The month number column indicates the month for which the work is being done. The work may be performed in June but cover accounting for May; therefore, the number 5 would be inserted in this space.

Time is entered in either the Accounting or the Tax Department column by use of the decimal system. For example, 1.5 hours or 3.2 hours in place of 1 hour, 30 minutes or 3 hours, 12 minutes, respectively.

The column to the far right lists any direct client expenses, such as travel, meals, or special delivery fees. Such information is entered regardless of whether the client can be charged for the expense. This expense ties into the total cost of doing the client's work.

At the end of the day the individual makes an analysis of his time at the bottom of the Daily Time Sheet to indicate his productive time and non-productive time for the day, as well as any time spent outside the office. These data can be helpful for insurance purposes where a record of outside time is required to keep insurance coverage in force. The individual then certifies the accuracy of the Daily Time Sheet with his signature.

WEYL, McVAY & WICKLINE – PUBLIC ACCOUNTANTS – COLUMBUS, OHIO 43203

DAILY TIME SHEET

Name_____Partner B_____

Title_____Partner_____ Date___June 15, 19___

Worked from___8.0____to___12.3___; from___1.3___to___5.4___; from___7.0___to___9.0___
                    4.3   4.1   2.0
              Total time worked___10.4___

CLIENT NUMBER	CLIENT NAME	MONTH NUMBER	WORK PERFORMED	ACCOUNTING DEPARTMENT	TAX DEPARTMENT	DIRECT CLIENT EXPENSE
2101	John Any Client	5	Monthly Audit for May	7.7		Lunch $ 4.50
						Mileage 100 @ 10¢ = $ 10.00
2209	Tom Any Client	6	Telephone Call on income tax case		.2	

* COURTESY OF WEYL, McVAY & WICKLINE, PUBLIC ACCOUNTANTS, COLUMBUS, OHIO.

Figure 3: Daily Time Sheet (front)

CLIENT NUMBER	CLIENT NAME	MONTH NUMBER	WORK PERFORMED	ACCOUNTING DEPARTMENT	TAX DEPARTMENT	DIRECT CLIENT EXPENSE

	1	2	3		9	Totals
Accounting Department		7.7				7.7
Tax Department		.2				.2
Total Productive		7.9				7.9
Non-Productive		2.5				2.5
OUTSIDE TIME		10.4				10.4
7.7 Totals						

I certify that the above is correct and that I have worked the time indicated.

Partner   B

Signature _____

* COURTESY OF WEYL, McVAY & WICKLINE, PUBLIC ACCOUNTANTS, COLUMBUS, OHIO.

Figure 3: Daily Time Sheet (reverse)

Nomenclature plays a large part in the communication of ideas. It should be pointed out that the account description of Wages—Productive (No. 501) and Wages—Nonproductive (No. 502) could also be called Wages—Chargeable and Wages—Nonchargeable. The amount of chargeable time would normally be that amount of time which produces income for the firm. Nonproductive time covers time used in corrections of work performed or training time for which a client cannot be charged. It also includes staff meetings, time spent on the firm's business, nonchargeable research time, and lost time. The discussion in this chapter will follow the first terminology.

Client Cost Report. The time, date, and direct client expenses are then posted to the Client Cost Report (Figure 4). Here are accumulated data for the billing period to permit accurate invoicing of the client. At the bottom of the report are columns for amounts at standard billing rates, at standard cost rates, and the actual billing. The result is the accumulated profit (or loss) for the current calendar year to date.

Monthly Time Analysis. The report shown in Figure 5 is kept for each person in the firm. Especially interesting is the rate of productivity of a particular individual which is provided by the monthly and year-to-date totals. Computation of percentages can be enlightening in discovering employee potential in the field of public accounting and whether any help can be given to make an employee a better worker. Measurement of a person's effectiveness is quite important. Too often nonproductive or nonchargeable time has been the back breaker of an organization.

The person's total salary for the month is divided by the number of hours worked to arrive at his effective hourly rate. This rate is multiplied by the number of productive and nonproductive hours to determine payroll cost. Costs totaled for all employees are the breakdown for the payroll entry to Wages—Productive (No. 501) and Wages—Nonproductive (No. 502). No special employee payroll sheet is required. However, the use of tables that combine the Social Security, Medicare, and income withholding taxes is recommended as a time saver in computing the payroll and in balancing the employee payroll sheet.

Hourly Cost Analysis. Figure 6 is the culmination of all the record keeping described thus far. The Hourly Cost Analysis is used to compute total cost per productive hour for each classification of worker in the firm. This figure shows how much the accountant's cost is, and from this amount can be determined how much should be charged per productive hour for each person in the firm including the proprietor or partner.

Note that on line 12, the partner's (or proprietor's) hourly cost rate is

CLIENT COST REPORT

Name: John Any Client   No. 2101   Month & Year May 19___

Assignment: Monthly Audit for May

Date 19___	PRINCIPAL A	T	SENIOR A	T	SEMI-SR. A	T	JUNIOR A	T	Travel Expense	OUTSIDE SERVICES Description	Amount
6–10	.2										
6–15	7.7				7.7				100 miles @ 10¢ = 10.00	3 lunches	4.50
6–17							1.2				
6–22	.3										

	Hours	Standard Billing	Standard Cost	BILLING
Principal	8.2	$ 106.60	$ 52.32	
Seniors				
Semi-Sr.	7.7	69.30	38.50	
Juniors	1.2	8.40	5.40	
Sub-Total	17.1	$ 184.30	$ 96.22	
Travel Expense		10.00	10.00	
Outside Services		4.50	4.50	
Total		$ 198.80	$ 110.72	
Previous year to-date	63.2	750.00	425.00	Current $ 185.00
Grand Total to-date	80.3	$ 948.80	535.72	Previous 725.00
Year to-date Profit (Loss)		$ (38.80)	$ 374.28	Total $ 910.00

* COURTESY OF WEYL, McVAY & WICKLINE, PUBLIC ACCOUNTANTS, COLUMBUS, OHIO.

Figure 4: Client Cost Report

John Doe, Semi-Senior Accountant   MONTHLY TIME ANALYSIS

Date 19__	Productive Time	Nonproductive Time	Total Time			
June 1	6.3	2.2	8.5			
2	2.6	6.4	9.0			
3	6.8	1.5	8.3			
4	3.5	.5	4.0			
6	5.7	3.0	8.7			
7	6.2	2.7	8.9			
8	5.9	2.4	8.3			
9	7.0	2.1	9.1			
10	6.6	1.4	8.0			
11	3.3	.8	4.1			
13	5.7	2.9	8.6			
14	6.0	2.8	8.8			
15	7.7	.5	8.2			
16	6.3	1.7	8.0			
17	6.2	1.9	8.1			
18	2.5	1.5	4.0			
20	4.9	3.3	8.2			
21	7.1	1.0	8.1			
22 -	7.2	1.1	8.3			
23	6.9	1.1	8.0			
24	5.6	3.0	8.6			
25	2.5	1.7	4.2			
27	6.3	1.7	8.0			
28	2.4	5.8	8.2			
29	1.6	6.5	8.1			
30	2.1	6.2	8.3			
Month Total	134.9	65.7	200.6			
Effective Hourly Rate			$ 2.991			
Payroll	$ 403.50	$ 196.50	$ 600.00			
Time Through Last Month	750.0	400.0	1150.0			
Time Year To Date	884.9	465.7	1350.6			
Time Ratios	65.52%	34.48%	100.0%			

* COURTESY OF WEYL, McVAY & WICKLINE, PUBLIC ACCOUNTANTS, COLUMBUS, OHIO.

Figure 5: Monthly Time Analysis

21

125 percent of the staff senior's cost rate. The percentage is strictly arbitrary; it could very well be any percent that is felt to be reasonable and proper. Hourly cost rates are used on the Client Cost Report (Figure 4) in determining total costs. A notation of these hourly costs by classification is most helpful to the accountant when he makes quotations to clients regarding fees for his services.

Recomputation and updating of the Hourly Cost Analysis (Figure 6) should be done on a quarterly basis to keep cost figures as current as possible. In doing so, the amounts for a full 12-month period should be used. To use any one quarter would make the resulting figures misleading because of extra-heavy hours, or unusually high expenses in one time segment. The Hourly Cost Analysis can be a real eye-opener. If properly used this analysis is a very real producer of added earnings for the public accountant who employs it.

Partnership Accounting

The system described in this chapter can readily be adapted for use in an accounting system for public accounting partnerships. The chart of accounts would remain the same except that the code number would be prefixed with a number for that partner. For example: Cash in Bank 101 would become 1101, 2101, and 3101 for a three-partner firm. If there are firm accounts in which all partners share in the earnings, then the next thousand series of numbers would be used. Indication of the breakdown of disbursements on voucher checks is simplified and highly accurate as reflected in Figure 2. Here again, data processing can be utilized very well in letting the computer sort all of the entries by account number to arrive at individual balance sheets and income statements for each partner. The Time Analyses (Figures 4, 5, and 6) can be expanded easily to include the breakdown of each person's time not only by productive and nonproductive phases but also to emphasize the area of responsibility of each partner.

Allocation of income and costs between partners in this manner can help avoid the possibility of dissatisfaction between partners and benefit the long life of the firm. The partner who works longer hours or who has an unusually profitable billing will receive credit for his proper share of the firm's earnings.

WEYL, McVAY & WICKLINE

HOURLY COST ANALYSIS

For the period April 1, 19___ to March 31, 19___

1 – Total Expenses $ 38,750.

2 – Less: Productive Payroll $ 18,850.

3 –   Subcontract   500.

4 –   Data Processing   1,200.

5 – Total Productive Labor Cost – Lines 2, 3 and 4   20,550.

6 – Overhead Costs – Line 1 less Line 5 $ 18,200.

7 – Divide by Productive Hours   9,100

8 – Overhead Cost Per Productive Hour – Line 6 ÷ Line 7 $ 2.00

	A Partners	B Seniors	C Semi-Seniors	D Juniors	E Total
9 – Productive Hours	2,600	1,300	2,600	2,600	9,100
10 – Productive Payroll	————	$ 4,550.	$ 7,800.	$ 6,500.	$ 18,850.
11 – Employee's Hourly Rate Line 10 ÷ Line 9	————	$ 3.50	$ 3.00	$ 2.50	$ ————
12 – Partner's Hourly Cost Rate, Column B Line 11 X 125%	$ 4.38	– – –	– – –	– – –	– – –
13 – Overhead Rate – Line 8 Above	2.00	2.00	2.00	2.00	– – –
14 – Total Cost Per Productive Hour Lines 11, 12 & 13	$ 6.38	$ 5.50	$ 5.00	$ 4.50	$ – – –

* Courtesy of Weyl, McVay & Wickline, Public Accountants, Columbus, Ohio.

Figure 6: Hourly Cost Analysis

Reports to Management

The reports provided by this system will give the independent accountant a fine set of tools with which to manage his practice. These are the balance sheet; income statement including operating percents; analyses of the time, cost, standard, and actual billing, and the profit (or loss) by client; analysis of time and payroll cost per employee; and an analysis of the actual cost per productive hour by employee classification (proprietor, partner, senior accountant, etc.).

Summary

This chapter is not intended as a cure-all for the operation of a public accounting practice. It is intended to bring about creative thinking to improve accountants' practices. The discussion is designed to provide an awareness of tools to be created with a little effort, tools that can and will make practicing accountants more efficient, more helpful to clients, and more capable of earning higher material rewards. Many of the items treated in this chapter can be applied to other businesses, particularly those offering service. These items can also be applied to departmental operations in a similar manner as applied to partners. In short, when accountants help themselves first, they are in a better position to help their clients.

3

Advertising Agencies

BY CORNELIUS E. COUGHLIN

**Public Accountant and Auditor,
West Acton and Acton,
Massachusetts**

Characteristics of the Business That Affect the Accounting System

Advertising is that portion of published information, whether seen or heard, the cost of which is borne by businesses that expect to gain by the spread of the ideas expressed. This specialized service for business is often best performed by an advertising agency. The agency may, in the beginning, operate in the general field of supplying advertisers with the following services: Art work, copywriting services, media selection and insertion, market research, and direct mail. Usually as time passes, the agency will specialize in one or more of these services and will confine its endeavors to the broad classification of industrial or retail advertisers.

FUNCTIONAL CHARACTERISTICS OF THE BUSINESS

Agencies may operate as partnerships or corporations; smaller agencies sometimes function as individual proprietorships. The latter method of operations is usually superseded by the partnership or corporation as the agencies

25

increase in size. This is a natural outgrowth stemming from the increased business of these service organizations and their need to attract creative and talented personnel. In the financial world of today, these people are not only interested in good salaries but desire a share in the profits of the enterprise and wish to participate further in the long-term growth through stock ownership by means of stock option or purchase plans.

As service organizations, records are usually kept on a calendar year basis. It is not uncommon to find, though, that some agencies will adopt a fiscal year common to the industrial or retail field in which they may specialize. In either case the business year does not present a problem in the accounting system discussed here.

PRINCIPAL ACCOUNTING PROBLEMS

The principal source of agency income in twofold: Fees received for such services as copywriting, art preparation, and marketing research; and commissions earned for media selection and insertion. The latter present no complicated accounting problem, since in most cases the same rate of commission has come to be used for most types of general media.

On the other hand, the billing of fees for services performed warrants and demands an accounting system that will provide management with the data necessary to set just fees. These fees should cover not only direct costs but overhead as well as profit. Therefore, the system is charged with the responsibility of providing adequate and accurate timekeeping and analysis and the proper allocations of expense items to both direct client costs and overhead items.

Lastly, no accounting system is sufficient alone as a means of collecting or assembling data but must be capable of supplying management with concise, accurate, and timely reports for their evaluation and analysis.

The accounting system to be described will provide for the accurate and concise collection of data to be presented in report form for all types of business organizations—proprietorships, partnerships, or corporations. It is relatively simple to install and allows for further in-depth breakdown and analysis as management may desire. It is also designed to allow for maximum ease for conversion to data processing either directly or through the utilization of a service bureau.

Functional Organization

Agencies, in their inception, may departmentalize by account but usually will departmentalize, at a later date, by advertising function. In the first instance the agencies have a complete staff of technicians who spend all of their time preparing and placing the advertising for a single client. In the latter instance the preparation and placing of each advertisement, no matter who the client is, passes through all departments necessarily involved.

The nomenclature for this service organization is peculiar to it and thus it is appropriate to run quickly through the normal operation. The agency executive who contacts the advertiser is called the account executive. He serves as liaison between the agency and the client and is responsible for seeing that the agency staff performs to the client's satisfaction. In most agencies a planning board, composed of the heads of the various departments, decides on the basic strategy of the advertising. Then the Copy Department writes the copy; the Art Department prepares the illustrations; the layout man puts the two together; the typographer specifies type; the Production Department sees that a plate, a mat, or the necessary engravings for printing are made; and the Media Department decides where the ad will be published.

Subject to their size and specialization, agencies will have all or some of the departments just indicated.

Principles and Objectives of the Accounting System

The purpose of this chapter is to provide an accounting system that will enhance the opportunity for profits for the advertising agencies following the principle of management by the exception. Guided by this specific goal, a few of the specific objectives can be enumerated:

1. Daily Financial Operations Report
2. Monthly Profit and Loss Statements
3. Monthly Departmental Expense Reports
4. Weekly Wage and Hour Analysis
5. Ease of access to data for analysis of problem areas.

Classification of Accounts and Books of Accounts

The chart of accounts listed below is standard and needs little explanation. The coding process is simple to allow for expansion of new accounts, further in-depth departmentalization (for example, No. 621.11 Indirect Labor —Art Department), and future conversion to electronic data processing, either by use of the service bureaus or by direct installation.

BALANCE SHEET ACCOUNTS.

ASSETS

100 *Current assets*

102 Cash in Bank
112 Petty Cash
116 Notes Receivable
124 Accounts Receivable
128 Allowance for Doubtful
    Accounts
134 Advances to Employees
136 Advances to Officers
138 Travel Advances
160 Inventory—Unbilled
    Client Costs
170 Prepaid Insurance
171 Prepaid Interest
172 Prepaid Expenses—Other

200 *Fixed assets*

202 Land
203 Buildings
204 Accumulated Depreciation
205 Furniture and Fixtures
206 Accumulated Depreciation
207 Equipment
208 Accumulated Depreciation
209 Motor Vehicles
210 Accumulated Depreciation
211 Leasehold Improvements
212 Allowance for Depreciation

LIABILITIES

300 *Current liabilities*

302 Notes Payable
314 Accounts Payable—Trade

315 Accounts Payable—Other
316 Client Advance Payments
320 Withheld Tax—Federal
322 Withheld Tax—FICA
323 Withheld Tax—State
324 Withheld Tax—City
330 Sales Tax Payable
331 Accrued Payroll Taxes
332 Accrued Salaries and Wages
333 Accrued Expenses

400 *Noncurrent liabilities*

401 Mortgage Payable
402 Long-Term Notes Payable
403 Officers' Loans
430 *Reserves*
431 Allowance for Federal and State
    Income Taxes

NET WORTH

Corporation
451 Common Stock
452 Preferred Stock
453 Treasury Stock
454 Paid-In Surplus
455 Retained Earnings

Partnerships

460 Capital _____
461 Capital _____
466 Withdrawal _____
467 Withdrawal _____

Proprietorship

470 Proprietor Capital
471 Proprietor Withdrawal

INCOME AND EXPENSE ACCOUNTS.

INCOME

500 Income—Media
501 Income—Copywriting
502 Income—Consulting

503 Income—Other
600 *Cost of services*
601 Direct Labor—Media
602 Direct Labor—Art

603 Direct Labor—Copywriting
604 Direct Labor—Production
605 Direct Labor—Other
606 Direct Purchases—Client
607 Applied Overhead Costs

620 *Overhead costs*

621 Indirect Labor
622 Utilities
623 Insurance
624 Telephone
625 Equipment Rental
626 Rent
627 Payroll Taxes
628 Depreciation
629 Miscellaneous

EXPENSES

700 *Selling expenses*

701 Account Executive Salaries
702 Clerical Salaries
703 Commissions
704 Advertising
705 Travel and Entertainment
722 Utilities
723 Insurance
724 Telephone
725 Equipment Rental
726 Rent

727 Payroll Taxes
728 Depreciation
729 Miscellaneous

800 *General and Administrative*

801 Officers' Salaries
802 Office Salaries
803 Office Supplies
804 Postage
805 Travel and Entertainment
806 Professional Fees
807 Officers' Life Insurance
808 Dues and Subscriptions
822 Utilities
823 Insurance
824 Telephone
825 Equipment Rental
826 Rent
827 Payroll Taxes
828 Depreciation
829 Miscellaneous

OTHER INCOME

881 Purchase Discounts
882 Miscellaneous

OTHER EXPENSES

891 Sales Discounts
892 Interest

BOOKS AND FORMS PECULIAR TO THE BUSINESS

The accounting system described in this chapter is readily adaptable to a manual, mechanical, electromechanical, or electronic data processing method of processing the data. The exact method used will certainly depend upon the present size and future growth of the agency and the demands it imposes upon its accounting system.

With the exception of the Cash Receipts and the Cash Disbursements journals, there are no ledgers or journals recommended other than those discussed in this chapter.

ACCOUNTS PECULIAR TO THE BUSINESS

Inventory—Unbilled Client Costs (No. 160) is charged and credited each month through the General journal. Debited for the current month are labor and purchase costs (from the 600 series of accounts through No. 607). Costs which have been billed to the client are credited for the current month.

Client Advance Payments (No. 316). Credits to this account come from such items as advance payments for media advertising. Posting to No. 316 is through the Accounts Receivable journal as payments are made. Charges

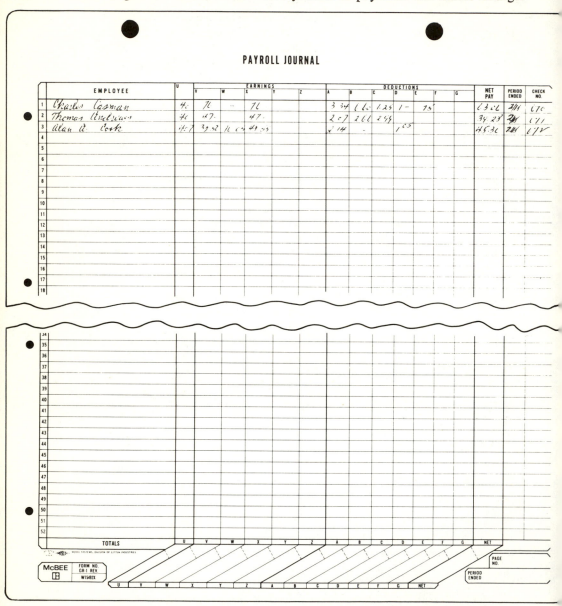

* COURTESY OF MCBEE SYSTEMS, A DIVISION OF LITTON INDUSTRIES, GREENWICH, CONNECTICUT.

Figure 1: Payroll Journal

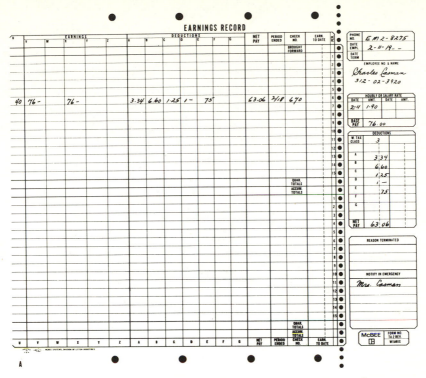

Figure 2: Earnings Record

Figure 3: Payroll Check in One-Write System

arrive out of invoices received for services indicated above. Posting to this account is made through the Accounts Payable journal as each invoice is entered.

Direct Purchases—Client (No. 606). Client posting to this account is done when the agency makes a direct purchase for the client for such items as envelopes, postage, contest prizes, etc. It would originate through the Accounts Payable journal as each invoice is entered.

Applied Overhead Costs (No. 607) is charged each month from monthly journal entries made in the General journal. The computation is made on the basis of either direct labor hours or dollars accumulated during the month.

All other accounts are relatively standard and need no explanation.

Time and Payroll System

Figure 1 illustrates the Payroll journal, Figure 2 the Earnings record, and Figure 3 the payroll check.

WEEKLY TIME AND DISTRIBUTION REPORT

EMPLOYEE NAME AND NUMBER				WEEK ENDING		JOB CLASS. Drafting			SHIFT ✓				
James Smith				1-28-19--		PROJECT OR DEPT. Art			1	2	3		
									x				

	JOB NO. OR DESCRIPTION	TYPE OF WORK		HOURS WORKED BY DAYS							TOTAL HOURS	RATE	AMOUNT	
		ACCOUNT	SUB ACCT.	1	2	3	4	5	6	7				
1	Jones Mfg.	602		8		8		8			24	3 00	72 00	
2	Smith Co.	602			8						8	3 00	24 00	
3	Cline Mfg.	602					8				8	3 00	24 00	

	JOB NO. OR DESCRIPTION	ACCOUNT	SUB ACCT.	1	2	3	4	5	6	7	TOT.HRS.	RATE	AMOUNT	
4														
5														
6														

EMPLOYEE														GROSS PAY
James Smith			8	8	8	8	8			40	3 00	120 00		120 00
SUPERVISOR	WEEK ENDING	PROJECT OR DEPT.	F.I.C.A. A	WITH. TAX B	A C	B D	C E	D F	E G					NET PAY
1-28-19-	Art		5 28	11 00	2 72									101 00

FORM LC-58

Figure 4: Weekly Time and Distribution Report

* COURTESY OF McBEE SYSTEMS, A DIVISION OF LITTON INDUSTRIES, GREENWICH, CONNECTICUT.

The use of a McBee posted board and their one-write system will allow the completion of the payroll check, the Earnings record, and the Payroll journal in one writing.

Figures 4 and 5 illustrate the forms used for the accumulation of labor charges both by labor breakdown and by client. The Weekly Time and Distribution Report (Figure 4) is to be used for both hourly and salaried personnel. It is filled out by each employee on a daily basis and is turned into

NAME John Smith DATE January 25,19--

1	CLIENT	Jones Mfg.	EXPENSE #606 $10.00
	DETAIL	reviewed copyright material with client, discussed	TIME
		media advertising method	
		lunch with client- see expense charge	2.5
2	CLIENT	Cline Mfg. January 25,19--	EXPENSE
	DETAIL	went over art work and copyright work	TIME 1.5
3	CLIENT		EXPENSE
	DETAIL		TIME

NAME DATE

4	CLIENT		EXPENSE
	DETAIL		TIME
5	CLIENT		EXPENSE
	DETAIL		TIME
6	CLIENT		EXPENSE
	DETAIL		TIME

NAME DATE

7	CLIENT		EXPENSE
	DETAIL		TIME
8	CLIENT		EXPENSE
	DETAIL		TIME

* Courtesy of McBee Systems, A Division of Litton Industries, Greenwich, Connecticut.

Figure 5: Time and Expense Record

```
TNT ADVERTISING

               ACCOUNT DISTRIBUTION VOUCHER

                              To:_____
                                 _____
Approvals             Initial    _____
F.O.B. Checked        _____
                                 Invoice No. or
Terms Approved        _____      Reference              _____

Price Approved        _____    Due Date                 _____

Extensions Verified   _____    Discount %               _____

Frt. Bill No.         _____    Terms                    _____

Frt. Amount           _____    Voucher No.              _____

Material Rec'd        _____

Services Complete     _____    Invoice Amount                  _____

Material Approved     _____    Less - Adjustments

Payment Approved      _____        Credits      _____

                                     Discount     _____        _____

                                 Check Amount                    _____

                                 Date Paid                       _____

                                 Check No.                       _____
- - - - - - - - - - - - - - - - - - - - - - - - - - - - - - - - - -
Remarks:
```

Figure 6:   Account Distribution Voucher

the appropriate department head for approval. The report is then forwarded to the Personnel Department where it is used as a basis of making out the payroll for the period. The form is in triplicate and is carbon spotted on the back of each part. This unique feature allows for separation of the second and third parts into six distinct charge slips which are accumulated and posted to each client cost record through the General Journal. Time should be charged on the basis of 15-minute intervals. The top sheet is kept in the Payroll Department which is equivalent to a time card for payroll recording purposes.

The Time and Expense Record (Figure 5), filled out by the account and officer executives, is used much in the same manner but is more appropriate to the executive level. It should be kept on the basis of 30-minute intervals, if possible. The accumulation of time on this basis will allow for proration of the executive's fixed monthly or weekly salary to the proper accounts and client accounts.

Cost Accounting

The Account Distribution Voucher (Figure 6) is used to account for each client cost with the exception of payroll. As the invoices are entered on the Accounts Payable journal, this voucher is created in triplicate. The original and one copy of this voucher are filed by due date until time for payment, assuring that all discounts will be taken. The third copy of this voucher is filed in the client cost folder.

The same procedure is followed in the posting of overhead expense in the General journal at the end of each accounting period. Since advertising agency charges are compiled primarily on the basis of time and actual purchased items (such as media advertising), this accumulation of purchased client costs and the method of accumulating time will give rise to proper billing.

TNT ADVERTISING FINANCIAL OPERATIONS REPORT

DATE_____________

Cash

Balance Forward as @ ________
Deposits from _____ to _____ ________
Total
Disb. from _____ to _____ ________
Balance this date ________

- -

Accounts Receivable

Balance as @ ________
Billings from _____
to _____ ________
Total
Payments from _____
to _____ ________
Balance this date ________

Aging

Current ________
Past Due 30 days ________
Past Due 60 days ________

Cash Flow

	Receipts	Disbur.
Balance as @	________	________
Flow from _____ to _____	________	________
Totals as @	________	________

Sales

Balance as @ ________
Add-Billings from _____
to _____ ________
Less-Credits from _____
to _____ ________
Balance as @ ________

- -

Accounts Payable

Balance as @ ________
Purchases from _____
to _____ ________
Total ________
Payments from _____
to _____ ________
Balance this date ________

Aging

Current ________
Past Due 30 days ________
Past Due 60 days ________

Purchase Commitments

Current Month ________
Due in 30 days ________
Due in 60 days ________
Due in 90 days ________
Held for Release ________
Total ________

Backlog

To be billed current month ________
To be billed following month ________
Billings with longer completion ________
Total ________

Figure 7: Daily Financial Operations Report

Of further importance, the prompt review of each client's fee by the appropriate account executive will correct for improper fee charges.

Reports to Management

This system will produce a multitude of summary or detail reports subject only to time and imagination. The following reports are suggested: Daily, a

Month This Year	TNT ADVERTISING	TO – Date This Year
	Income	
	Media	
	Copywriting	
	Consulting	
	Other	
	Total Income	
	Cost of Services	
	Gross Profit	
	Less – Operating Expenses	
	Selling Expenses	
	General and Administrative	
	Total Operating Expenses	
	Net Profit	
	Add – Other Income	
	Total	
	Less – Other Expenses	
	Net Profit	
	Less – Provision for Taxes	
	Net Profit After Taxes	

Figure 8: Departmental Expense Statement

financial operations report (Figure 7); monthly, a balance sheet; a profit and loss statement; a departmental expense statement; and a client cost review.

The financial operations report is taken from the summary of the daily transactions affecting each item; for example, the totals from the Accounts Receivable journal would be posted to the Accounts Receivable section of the report. This report is designed to put into an executive's hands a capsule picture of a few of the major items of interest and concern.

TNT ADVERTISING

Wk. or Mo. Ending	Description	Labor	Purchases	Overhead	Total	Media	Consulting
1/28/19--	Art Dept.	72.00					
	W. Brown Account Executive	15.00	15.00				

Jones Mfg. Co. — Costs / Billings

Figure 9: Client Cost Review

The balance sheet, the profit and loss statement, and the departmental expense statements are taken directly from the General ledger. These reports can then be entered onto preprinted forms as indicated in Figure 8. Utilizing the pegboard technique, these reports can be so spread as to compare figures to date vs. figures a year ago, or month to date vs. previous month or the same month of previous year.

The Client Cost Review (Figure 9) is updated monthly and reviewed as indicated earlier with the appropriate account executive. Copies of this review should be forwarded to the chief executive responsible for the marketing effort of the agency.

This chapter is presented as a guide, rather than as an absolute rule to solve the problems of setting up and installing an accounting system for the advertising agency. The system itself would have to be tailored both to the specific agency and to the needs of agency management.

4

Architects

BY THOMAS J. KIERNAN

Public Accountant, Staten Island,
New York

Characteristics of the Profession That Affect the Accounting System

The practice of architecture is a blending of aesthetic and scientific knowledge into a profession. The basic services of the architect include design of all elements of the project, incorporating the structural, electrical, plumbing, heating, and air conditioning systems and other required equipment or "built-in" materials. The architect selects and employs consultants whenever necessary or desirable to supplement his own forces in performing adequate and proper services for his client; and he maintains prime professional control over the various aspects of each project.

The services of the architect generally consist of four basic phases: (1) Schematic Design. Through conferences with the client, the building scope and program are determined, (2) Design Development. Following the owner's approval of the schematic design, the architect proceeds with the development sketches, the building plan, and the exterior treatment, (3) Construction Documents. This phase involves the preparation of detailed working drawings and specifications in the final form, (4) Construction Contract Administration. Primarily, this point involves supervision of the project during construction.

FUNCTIONAL CHARACTERISTICS OF THE PROFESSION

Architects usually conduct their practice as individual proprietors or as partners. Records of the vast majority operating as proprietorships or partnerships are kept on a calendar-year basis. The natural business year is not a factor in this type of operation.

The profession of architecture does not experience competition as it is generally understood in the business world because an architect does not compete with another architect on a basis of professional charges, nor is he permitted to use paid advertising.

In addition, there is a shortage of qualified people in this field. This situation will exist for some years to come, because of the strict licensing requirements, a benefit to the general public.

PRINCIPAL ACCOUNTING PROBLEMS

Like most professional men, architects must be sold on the necessity of an adequate accounting system. Once an architect has experienced the efficient management of this type of operation, he will never go back to the old slipshod methods.

The principal technical accounting problem of the profession is that of billing for services rendered. Architects' fees are based on the type of job involved and are quite standardized and justified.

The architect employs one of two methods in charging the client for his services: A fixed percentage of construction cost *or* a fee for his personal services plus the payroll cost of technical personnel plus the proportionate amount of office overhead. This "cost-plus" fee may be a percentage of the construction cost but not less than one-third the applicable basic rate. Overhead charges amount to 100 percent or more of payroll cost. The architect may require a retainage (usually 5 percent of his estimated total fee) at the time he enters into an agreement with a client. Such retainage is, of course, credited against partial payment or payments as they become due, until the retainage has been expended. The architect is entitled to payment by the 10th of each month for services performed through the last day of the preceding month.

Under the cost-plus arrangement, or when the fee is otherwise related to time and expenses involved, monthly payments should cover the full fee earned to date as calculated by the method agreed upon.

Under the percentage or lump-sum arrangement, the amount of monthly partial payments should be based on the architect's estimate of the time and expenses incurred by him to date in comparison with those required to complete his full basic services. As an aid in making an equitable determination of the portion of fee earned at various stages of the work, the following should be considered the percentage of fee earned upon completion of subsequent phases: Schematic Design—15 percent. Design Development—35 percent. Bidding and Award Phase (Construction Documents)—80 percent. Construction Phase—20 percent.

Functional Organization

A firm of architects may be organized under a number of logical plans. In a firm operated as an individual proprietorship, the office staff is in charge of the senior draftsman or office manager, who in turn is responsible directly to the architect. This plan is flexible, but since all work must be approved by the architect-owner or owners, it is not feasible to handle this function another way.

Principles and Objectives of the Accounting System

The architect operating as an individual is primarily interested in a simple accounting system that can be handled with a minimum of detail and forms. The system must be adaptable to use by the owner or one of his assistants. Billing and follow-up are generally handled by the office secretary. However, since total cost is not known until completion of the job, an architect wants to know specific costs.

The simplest formula for determining a cost-plus factor to be applied to overhead is: Indirect salaries plus Indirect Partners' or Proprietors' Time plus General Operating Expenses divided by Direct Salaries plus Direct Partners' or Proprietor's Time.

A complicated, unwieldy system defeats the main objective. The system to be described is adaptable by including time sheets for compilation of hourly overhead costs by a simple job time memorandum suited to the firm's use.

Classification of Accounts and Books of Accounts

The chart of accounts for a firm of architects, shown below, has been used by small business firms with success.

BALANCE SHEET ACCOUNTS.

ASSETS

Current assets
101 Cash in Bank
102 Petty Cash
103 Securities
108 Accounts Receivable

Fixed assets

145 Automobiles
146 Allowance for Depreciation
149 Furniture and Fixtures
150 Allowance for Depreciation

LIABILITIES

Current liabilities
202 Notes Payable
212 Accounts Payable
224 Federal Payroll Taxes
225 State Payroll Taxes

NET WORTH

271 Proprietor's Investment
272 Proprietor's Withdrawals
273 Proprietor's Advances
297 Net Profit or Loss

INCOME AND EXPENSE ACCOUNTS.

INCOME

301 Architects' Fees

EXPENSES

501 Salaries—Draftsmen—Direct
502 Salaries—Clerical—Indirect
504 Rent
506 Telephone and Telegraph
507 Licenses
508 Insurance
509 Interest
510 Photostats and Blueprints
511 Notary Fees
512 Office Supplies
513 Postage
514 Bank Service Charges

515 Legal
516 Accounting
517 Dues and Subscriptions
521 FICA Tax
522 Unemployment Taxes
523 Personal Property Taxes
525 Other Taxes
533 Automobile Depreciation
535 Furniture and Fixtures
      Depreciation
540 Auto Expenses
544 Maintenance and Repairs
      (Office)
551 Promotional
553 Traveling
560 Miscellaneous

The net worth accounts can easily be changed as required by a partnership.

ACCOUNTS PECULIAR TO THE PROFESSION

Accounts Receivable (No. 108) and Accounts Payable (No. 212). The majority of architects keep their books and report their income on a cash basis rather than on an accrual basis because of the tax advantage. However, for the purpose of analyzing the business or securing additional capital, these Accounts Receivable and Payable can be accrued, and the offsetting entry posted to net worth.

Proprietor's Withdrawal (No. 272). Regular salary is charged to this account. In this way the architect knows what he has withdrawn in earnings as if he were an employee. The same would apply to a Partner's Withdrawal account.

THE AMERICAN INSTITUTE OF ARCHITECTS

AIA Document A101

Standard Form of Agreement Between Owner and Contractor

where the basis of payment is a
STIPULATED SUM

Use only with AIA Document A201, General Conditions of the Contract for Construction, Tenth Edition, dated Sept. 1966

AGREEMENT

made this   day of   in the year of Nineteen
Hundred and

BETWEEN

the Owner, and

the Contractor.

The Owner and the Contractor agree as set forth below.

AIA DOCUMENT A101 • OWNER-CONTRACTOR AGREEMENT • SEPTEMBER 1966 EDITION   1
AIA® © THE AMERICAN INSTITUTE OF ARCHITECTS, 1735 NEW YORK AVENUE, N.W., WASH., D.C. 20006

* PERMISSION TO PUBLISH THIS DOCUMENT IN THIS BOOK HAS BEEN GRANTED BY THE AMERICAN INSTITUTE OF ARCHITECTS.

Figure I: Owner, Contractor Agreement Form

Proprietor's Advances (No. 273). In the same manner, hospitalization premiums, personal taxes, insurance, percentage of expenses for personal auto usage, etc., should be charged to this account.

Promotional (No. 551). Proper charges here are flowers, cards, business lunches for clients and staff members, etc.

ARTICLE 1

THE CONTRACT DOCUMENTS

The Contract Documents consist of this Agreement, Conditions of the Contract (General, Supplementary and other Conditions), Drawings, Specifications, all Addenda issued prior to execution of this Agreement and all Modifications issued subsequent thereto. These form the Contract, and all are as fully a part of the Contract as if attached to this Agreement or repeated herein. An enumeration of the Contract Documents appears in Article 8.

ARTICLE 2

THE WORK

The Contractor shall perform all the Work required by the Contract Documents for
(Here insert the caption descriptive of the Work as used on other Contract Documents.)

ARTICLE 3

ARCHITECT

The Architect for this Project is

ARTICLE 4

TIME OF COMMENCEMENT AND COMPLETION

The Work to be performed under this Contract shall be commenced

and completed
(Here insert any special provisions for liquidated damages relating to failure to complete on time.)

AIA DOCUMENT A101 • OWNER-CONTRACTOR AGREEMENT • SEPTEMBER 1966 EDITION
AIA® © THE AMERICAN INSTITUTE OF ARCHITECTS, 1735 NEW YORK AVENUE, N.W., WASH., D.C. 20006   2

Figure I: Owner, Contractor Agreement Form (cont.)

BOOKS AND FORMS PECULIAR TO THE PROFESSION

A customary double-entry system is the best method of accounting because of the built-in checks and balances. Cash receipts are posted to a
columnar journal and deposited. All invoices and collections should be

---

ARTICLE 5

CONTRACT SUM

The Owner shall pay the Contractor for the performance of the Work, subject to additions and deductions by Change Order as provided in the Conditions of the Contract, in current funds, the Contract Sum of

(State here the lump sum amount, unit prices, or both, as desired.)

ARTICLE 6

PROGRESS PAYMENTS

Based upon Applications for Payment submitted to the Architect by the Contractor and Certificates for Payment issued by the Architect, the Owner shall make progress payments on account of the Contract Sum to the Contractor as provided in the Conditions of the Contract as follows:

On or about the   day of each month   per cent of the proportion of the Contract Sum properly allocable to labor, materials and equipment incorporated in the Work and   per cent of the portion of the Contract Sum properly allocable to materials and equipment suitably stored at the site or at some other location agreed upon in writing by the parties, up to the   day of that month, less the aggregate of previous payments in each case; and upon Substantial Completion of the entire Work, a sum sufficient to increase the total payments to   per cent of the Contract Sum, less such retainages as the Architect shall determine for all incomplete Work and unsettled claims.

(Here insert any provisions made for limiting or reducing the amount retained after the Work reaches a certain stage of completion.)

AIA DOCUMENT A101 • OWNER-CONTRACTOR AGREEMENT • SEPTEMBER 1966 EDITION
AIA® © THE AMERICAN INSTITUTE OF ARCHITECTS, 1735 NEW YORK AVENUE, N.W., WASH., D.C. 20006

Figure 1: Owner, Contractor Agreement Form (cont.)

ARTICLE 7

FINAL PAYMENT

Final payment, constituting the entire unpaid balance of the Contract Sum, shall be paid by the Owner to the Contractor _____ days after Substantial Completion of the Work unless otherwise stipulated in the Certificate of Substantial Completion, provided the Work has then been completed, the Contract fully performed, and a final Certificate for Payment has been issued by the Architect.

ARTICLE 8

MISCELLANEOUS PROVISIONS

8.1 Terms used in this Agreement which are defined in the Conditions of the Contract shall have the meanings designated in those Conditions.

8.2 The Contract Documents, which constitute the entire agreement between the Owner and the Contractor, are listed in Article 1 and, except for Modifications issued after execution of this Agreement, are enumerated as follows:

(List below the Agreement, Conditions of the Contract (General, Supplementary, other Conditions), Drawings, Specifications, Addenda and accepted Alternates, showing page or sheet numbers in all cases and dates where applicable.)

Figure 1: Owner, Contractor Agreement Form (cont.)

This Agreement executed the day and year first written above.

OWNER _____   CONTRACTOR _____

Figure 1:   Owner, Contractor Agreement Form (cont.)

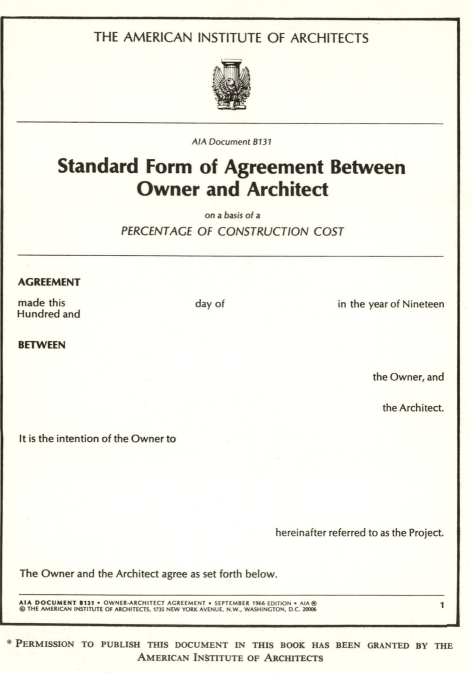

THE AMERICAN INSTITUTE OF ARCHITECTS

AIA Document B131

Standard Form of Agreement Between Owner and Architect

on a basis of a

PERCENTAGE OF CONSTRUCTION COST

AGREEMENT

made this   day of   in the year of Nineteen
Hundred and

BETWEEN

the Owner, and

the Architect.

It is the intention of the Owner to

hereinafter referred to as the Project.

The Owner and the Architect agree as set forth below.

AIA DOCUMENT B131 • OWNER-ARCHITECT AGREEMENT • SEPTEMBER 1966 EDITION • AIA ®
© THE AMERICAN INSTITUTE OF ARCHITECTS, 1735 NEW YORK AVENUE, N.W., WASHINGTON, D.C. 20006   1

* PERMISSION TO PUBLISH THIS DOCUMENT IN THIS BOOK HAS BEEN GRANTED BY THE
AMERICAN INSTITUTE OF ARCHITECTS

Figure 2: Owner, Architect Agreement Form

I. THE ARCHITECT shall provide professional services for the Project in accordance with the Terms and Conditions of this Agreement.

II. THE OWNER shall compensate the Architect, in accordance wtih the Terms and Conditions of this Agreement, as follows:

a. *FOR THE ARCHITECT'S BASIC SERVICES,* as described in Paragraph 1.1, a Basic Fee computed at the following percentages of the Construction Cost, as defined in Article 3, for portions of the Project to be awarded under

A Single Stipulated Sum Contract	per cent (%)
Separate Stipulated Sum Contracts	per cent (%)
A Single Cost Plus Fee Contract	per cent (%)
Separate Cost Plus Fee Contracts	per cent (%)

b. *FOR THE ARCHITECT'S ADDITIONAL SERVICES,* as described in Paragraph 1.3, a fee computed as follows:

Principals' time at the fixed rate of   dollars ($) per hour. For the purposes of this Agreement, the Principals are:

Employees' time computed at a multiple of   (   ) times the employees' Direct Personnel Expense as defined in Article 4.

Additional services of professional consultants engaged for the normal structural, mechanical and electrical engineering services at a multiple of (   ) times the amount billed to the Architect for such additional services.

c. *FOR THE ARCHITECT'S REIMBURSABLE EXPENSES,* amounts expended as defined in Article 5.

d. *THE TIMES AND FURTHER CONDITIONS OF PAYMENT* shall be as described in Article 6.

AIA DOCUMENT B131 • OWNER-ARCHITECT AGREEMENT • SEPTEMBER 1966 EDITION • AIA ®
© THE AMERICAN INSTITUTE OF ARCHITECTS, 1735 NEW YORK AVENUE, N.W., WASHINGTON, D.C. 20006   2

Figure 2:   Owner, Architect Agreement Form (cont.)

TERMS AND CONDITIONS OF AGREEMENT BETWEEN OWNER AND ARCHITECT

ARTICLE 1

ARCHITECT'S SERVICES

1.1 BASIC SERVICES

The Architect's Basic Services consist of the five phases described below and include normal structural, mechanical and electrical engineering services.

SCHEMATIC DESIGN PHASE

1.1.1 The Architect shall consult with the Owner to ascertain the requirements of the Project and shall confirm such requirements to the Owner.

1.1.2 The Architect shall prepare Schematic Design Studies consisting of drawings and other documents illustrating the scale and relationship of Project components for approval by the Owner.

1.1.3 The Architect shall submit to the Owner a Statement of Probable Construction Cost based on current area, volume or other unit costs.

DESIGN DEVELOPMENT PHASE

1.1.4 The Architect shall prepare from the approved Schematic Design Studies, for approval by the Owner, the Design Development Documents consisting of drawings and other documents to fix and describe the size and character of the entire Project as to structural, mechanical and electrical systems, materials and such other essentials as may be appropriate.

1.1.5 The Architect shall submit to the Owner a further Statement of Probable Construction Cost.

CONSTRUCTION DOCUMENTS PHASE

1.1.6 The Architect shall prepare from the approved Design Development Documents, for approval by the Owner, Working Drawings and Specifications setting forth in detail the requirements for the construction of the entire Project including the necessary bidding information, and shall assist in the preparation of bidding forms, the Conditions of the Contract, and the form of Agreement between the Owner and the Contractor.

1.1.7 The Architect shall advise the Owner of any adjustments to previous Statements of Probable Construction Cost indicated by changes in requirements or general market conditions.

1.1.8 The Architect shall assist the Owner in filing the required documents for the approval of governmental authorities having jurisdiction over the Project.

BIDDING OR NEGOTIATION PHASE

1.1.9 The Architect, following the Owner's approval of the Construction Documents and of the latest Statement of Probable Construction Cost, shall assist the Owner in obtaining bids or negotiated proposals, and in awarding and preparing construction contracts.

CONSTRUCTION PHASE—ADMINISTRATION OF THE CONSTRUCTION CONTRACT

1.1.10 The Construction Phase will commence with the award of the Construction Contract and will terminate when final payment is made by the Owner to the Contractor.

1.1.11 The Architect shall provide Administration of the Construction Contract as set forth in Articles 1 through 14, inclusive of the General Conditions of the Contract for Construction, AIA Document A201, Tenth Edition dated September 1966, and the extent of his duties and responsibilities and the limitations of his authority as assigned thereunder shall not be modified without his written consent.

1.1.12 The Architect, as the representative of the Owner during the Construction Phase, shall advise and consult with the Owner and all of the Owner's instructions to the Contractor shall be issued through the Architect. The Architect shall have authority to act on behalf of the Owner to the extent provided in the General Conditions unless otherwise modified in writing.

1.1.13 The Architect shall at all times have access to the Work wherever it is in preparation or progress.

1.1.14 The Architect shall make periodic visits to the site to familiarize himself generally with the progress and quality of the Work and to determine in general if the Work is proceeding in accordance with the Contract Documents. On the basis of his on-site observations as an Architect, he shall endeavor to guard the Owner against defects and deficiencies in the Work of the Contractor. The Architect shall not be required to make exhaustive or continuous on-site inspections to check the quality or quantity of the Work. The Architect shall not be responsible for construction means, methods, techniques, sequences or procedures, or for safety precautions and programs in connection with the Work, and he shall not be responsible for the Contractor's failure to carry out the Work in accordance with the Contract Documents.

1.1.15 Based on such observations at the site and on the Contractor's Applications for Payment, the Architect shall determine the amount owing to the Contractor and shall issue Certificates for Payment in such amounts. The issuance of a Certificate for Payment shall constitute a representation by the Architect to the Owner, based on the Architect's observations at the site as provided in Subparagraph 1.1.14 and on the data comprising the Application for Payment, that the Work has progressed to the point indicated; that to the best of the Architect's knowledge, information and belief, the quality of the Work is in accordance with the Contract Documents (subject to an evaluation of the Work as a functioning whole upon Substantial Completion, to the results of any subsequent tests required by the Contract Documents, to minor

AIA DOCUMENT B131 • OWNER-ARCHITECT AGREEMENT • SEPTEMBER 1966 EDITION • AIA ®
© THE AMERICAN INSTITUTE OF ARCHITECTS, 1735 NEW YORK AVENUE, N.W., WASHINGTON, D.C. 20006   3

Figure 2: Owner, Architect Agreement Form (cont.)

deviations from the Contract Documents correctable prior to completion, and to any specific qualifications stated in the Certificate for Payment); and that the Contractor is entitled to payment in the amount certified. By issuing a Certificate for Payment, the Architect shall not be deemed to represent that he has made any examination to ascertain how and for what purpose the Contractor has used the moneys paid on account of the Contract Sum.

1.1.16 The Architect shall be, in the first instance, the interpreter of the requirements of the Contract Documents and the impartial judge of the performance thereunder by both the Owner and Contractor. The Architect shall make decisions on all claims of the Owner or Contractor relating to the execution and progress of the Work and on all other matters or questions related thereto. The Architect's decisions in matters relating to artistic effect shall be final if consistent with the intent of the Contract Documents.

1.1.17 The Architect shall have authority to reject Work which does not conform to the Contract Documents. The Architect shall also have authority to require the Contractor to stop the Work whenever in his reasonable opinion it may be necessary for the proper performance of the Contract. The Architect shall not be liable to the Owner for the consequences of any decision made by him in good faith either to exercise or not to exercise his authority to stop the Work.

1.1.18 The Architect shall review and approve shop drawings, samples, and other submissions of the Contractor only for conformance with the design concept of the Project and for compliance with the information given in the Contract Documents.

1.1.19 The Architect shall prepare Change Orders.

1.1.20 The Architect shall conduct inspections to determine the Dates of Substantial Completion and Final Completion, shall receive written guarantees and related documents assembled by the Contractor, and shall issue a final Certificate for Payment.

1.1.21 The Architect shall not be responsible for the acts or omissions of the Contractor, or any Subcontractors, or any of the Contractor's or Subcontractors' agents or employees, or any other persons performing any of the Work.

1.2 PROJECT REPRESENTATION BEYOND BASIC SERVICES

1.2.1 If more extensive representation at the site than is described under Subparagraphs 1.1.10 through 1.1.21 inclusive is required, and if the Owner and Architect agree, the Architect shall provide one or more Full-time Project Representatives to assist the Architect.

1.2.2 Such Full-time Project Representatives shall be selected, employed and directed by the Architect, and the Architect shall be compensated therefor as mutually agreed between the Owner and the Architect as set forth in an exhibit appended to this Agreement.

1.2.3 The duties, responsibilities and limitations of authority of such Full-time Project Representatives shall be set forth in an exhibit appended to this Agreement.

1.2.4 Through the on-site observations by Full-time Project Representatives of the Work in progress, the Architect shall endeavor to provide further protection for the Owner against defects in the Work, but the furnishing of such project representation shall not make the Architect responsible for the Contractor's failure to perform the Work in accordance with the Contract Documents.

1.3 ADDITIONAL SERVICES

The following services are not covered in Paragraphs 1.1 or 1.2. If any of these Additional Services are authorized by the Owner, they shall be paid for by the Owner as hereinbefore provided.

1.3.1 Providing special analyses of the Owner's needs, and programming the requirements of the Project.

1.3.2 Providing financial feasibility or other special studies.

1.3.3 Providing planning surveys, site evaluations, or comparative studies of prospective sites.

1.3.4 Making measured drawings of existing construction when required for planning additions or alterations thereto.

1.3.5 Revising previously approved Drawings, Specifications or other documents to accomplish changes not initiated by the Architect.

1.3.6 Preparing Change Orders and supporting data where the change in the Basic Fee resulting from the adjusted Contract Sum is not commensurate with the Architect's services required.

1.3.7 Preparing documents for alternate bids requested by the Owner.

1.3.8 Providing Detailed Estimates of Construction Costs.

1.3.9 Providing consultation concerning replacement of any Work damaged by fire or other cause during construction, and furnishing professional services of the type set forth in Paragraph 1.1 as may be required in connection with the replacement of such Work.

1.3.10 Providing professional services made necessary by the default of the Contractor in the performance of the Construction Contract.

1.3.11 Providing Contract Administration and observation of construction after the Contract Time has been exceeded by more than twenty per cent through no fault of the Architect.

1.3.12 Furnishing the Owner a set of reproducible record prints of drawings showing significant changes made during the construction process, based on marked up prints, drawings and other data furnished by the Contractor to the Architect.

1.3.13 Providing services after final payment to the Contractor.

1.3.14 Providing interior design and other services required for or in connection with the selection of furniture and furnishings.

1.3.15 Providing services as an expert witness in connection with any public hearing, arbitration proceeding, or the proceedings of a court of record.

1.3.16 Providing services for planning tenant or rental spaces.

Figure 2: Owner, Architect Agreement Form (cont.)

ARTICLE 2

THE OWNER'S RESPONSIBILITIES

2.1 The Owner shall provide full information regarding his requirements for the Project.

2.2 The Owner shall designate, when necessary, a representative authorized to act in his behalf with respect to the Project. The Owner or his representative shall examine documents submitted by the Architect and shall render decisions pertaining thereto promptly, to avoid unreasonable delay in the progress of the Architect's work.

2.3 The Owner shall furnish a certified land survey of the site giving, as applicable, grades and lines of streets, alleys, pavements and adjoining property; rights of way, restrictions, easements, encroachments, zoning, deed restrictions, boundaries and contours of the site; locations, dimensions and complete data pertaining to existing buildings, other improvements and trees; and full information concerning available service and utility lines both public and private.

2.4 The Owner shall furnish the services of a soils engineer, when such services are deemed necessary by the Architect, including reports, test borings, test pits, soil bearing values and other necessary operations for determining subsoil conditions.

2.5 The Owner shall furnish structural, mechanical, chemical and other laboratory tests, inspections and reports as required by law or the Contract Documents.

2.6 The Owner shall furnish such legal, accounting and insurance counselling services as may be necessary for the Project, and such auditing services as he may require to ascertain how or for what purposes the Contractor has used the moneys paid to him under the Construction Contract.

2.7 The services, information, surveys and reports required by Paragraphs 2.3 through 2.6 inclusive shall be furnished at the Owner's expense, and the Architect shall be entitled to rely upon the accuracy thereof.

2.8 If the Owner observes or otherwise becomes aware of any fault or defect in the Project or non-conformance with the Contract Documents, he shall give prompt written notice thereof to the Architect.

2.9 The Owner shall furnish information required of him as expeditiously as necessary for the orderly progress of the Work.

ARTICLE 3

CONSTRUCTION COST

3.1 Construction Cost to be used as a basis for determining the Architect's Fee for all Work designed or specified by the Architect, including labor, materials, equipment and furnishings, shall be determined as follows, with precedence in the order listed:

3.1.1 For completed construction, the total cost of all such Work;

3.1.2 For work not constructed, the lowest bona fide bid received from a qualified bidder for any or all of such work; or

3.1.3 For work for which bids are not received, (1) the latest Detailed Cost Estimate, or (2) the Architect's latest Statement of Probable Construction Cost.

3.2 Construction Cost does not include the fees of the Architect and consultants, the cost of the land, rights-of-way, or other costs which are the responsibility of the Owner as provided in Paragraphs 2.3 through 2.6 inclusive.

3.3 Labor furnished by the Owner for the Project shall be included in the Construction Cost at current market rates. Materials and equipment furnished by the Owner shall be included at current market prices, except that used materials and equipment shall be included as if purchased new for the Project.

3.4 Statements of Probable Construction Cost and Detailed Cost Estimates prepared by the Architect represent his best judgment as a design professional familiar with the construction industry. It is recognized, however, that neither the Architect nor the Owner has any control over the cost of labor, materials or equipment, over the contractors' methods of determining bid prices, or over competitive bidding or market conditions. Accordingly, the Architect cannot and does not guarantee that bids will not vary from any Statement of Probable Construction Cost or other cost estimate prepared by him.

3.5 When a fixed limit of Construction Cost is established as a condition of this Agreement, it shall include a bidding contingency of ten per cent unless another amount is agreed upon in writing. When such a fixed limit is established, the Architect shall be permitted to determine what materials, equipment, component systems and types of construction are to be included in the Contract Documents, and to make reasonable adjustments in the scope of the Project to bring it within the fixed limit. The Architect may also include in the Contract Documents alternate bids to adjust the Construction Cost to the fixed limit.

3.5.1 If the lowest bona fide bid, the Detailed Cost Estimate or the Statement of Probable Construction Cost exceeds such fixed limit of Construction Cost (including the bidding contingency) established as a condition of this Agreement, the Owner shall (1) give written approval of an increase in such fixed limit, (2) authorize rebidding the Project within a reasonable time, or (3) cooperate in revising the Project scope and quality as required to reduce the Probable Construction Cost. In the case of (3) the Architect, without additional charge, shall modify the Drawings and Specifications as necessary to bring the Construction Cost within the fixed limit. The providing of this service shall be the limit of the Architect's responsibility in this regard, and having done so, the Architect shall be entitled to his fees in accordance with this Agreement.

AIA DOCUMENT B131 • OWNER-ARCHITECT AGREEMENT • SEPTEMBER 1966 EDITION • AIA ®
© THE AMERICAN INSTITUTE OF ARCHITECTS, 1735 NEW YORK AVENUE, N.W., WASHINGTON, D.C. 20006   **5**

Figure 2: Owner, Architect Agreement Form (cont.)

ARTICLE 4

DIRECT PERSONNEL EXPENSE

4.1 Direct Personnel Expense of employees engaged on the Project includes architects, engineers, designers, job captains, draftsmen, specification writers and typists, in consultation, research and design, in producing Drawings, Specifications and other documents pertaining to the Project, and in services during construction at the site.

4.2 Direct Personnel Expense includes cost of salaries and of mandatory and customary benefits such as statutory employee benefits, insurance, sick leave, holidays and vacations, pensions and similar benefits.

ARTICLE 5

REIMBURSABLE EXPENSES

5.1 Reimbursable Expenses are in addition to the Fees for Basic and Additional Services and include actual expenditures made by the Architect, his employees, or his consultants in the interest of the Project for the following incidental expenses listed in the following Subparagraphs:

5.1.1 Expense of transportation and living when traveling in connection with the Project for other than regular trips from the office to the site, and for long distance calls and telegrams.

5.1.2 Expense of reproductions, postage and handling of Drawings and Specifications, excluding copies for Architect's office use and duplicate sets at each phase for the Owner's review and approval; and fees paid for securing approval of authorities having jurisdiction over the Project.

5.1.3 If authorized in advance by the Owner, the expense of overtime work requiring higher than regular rates; perspectives or models for the Owner's use; and fees of special consultants for other than the normal structural, mechanical and electrical engineering services.

ARTICLE 6

PAYMENTS TO THE ARCHITECT

6.1 Payments on account of the Architect's Basic Services shall be made as follows:

6.1.1 An initial payment of five per cent of the Basic Fee calculated upon an agreed estimated cost of the Project, payable upon execution of this Agreement, is the minimum payment under this Agreement.

6.1.2 Subsequent payments shall be made monthly in proportion to services performed to increase the compensation for Basic Services to the following percentages of the Basic Fee at the completion of each phase of the Work:

Schematic Design Phase	15%
Design Development Phase	35%
Construction Documents Phase	75%
Bidding or Negotiation Phase	80%
Construction Phase	100%

6.2 Payments for Additional Services of the Architect as defined in Paragraph 1.3, and for Reimbursable Expenses as defined in Article 5, shall be made monthly upon presentation of the Architect's statement of services rendered.

6.3 No deductions shall be made from the Architect's compensation on account of penalty, liquidated damages, or other sums withheld from payments to contractors.

6.4 If the Project is suspended for more than three months or abandoned in whole or in part, the Architect shall be paid his Fees for Services performed prior to receipt of written notice from the Owner of such suspension or abandonment, together with Reimbursable Expenses then due and all terminal expenses resulting from such suspension or abandonment.

ARTICLE 7

ARCHITECT'S ACCOUNTING RECORDS

Records of the Architect's Direct Personnel, Consultant and Reimbursable Expenses pertaining to the Project, and records of accounts between the Owner and the Contractor, shall be kept on a generally recognized accounting basis and shall be available to the Owner or his authorized representative at mutually convenient times.

ARTICLE 8

TERMINATION OF AGREEMENT

This Agreement may be terminated by either party upon seven days' written notice should the other party fail substantially to perform in accordance with its terms through no fault of the other. In the event of termination due to the fault of others than the Architect, the Architect shall be paid his Fees for Services performed to termination date, including Reimbursable Expenses then due and all terminal expenses.

ARTICLE 9

OWNERSHIP OF DOCUMENTS

Drawings and Specifications as instruments of service are and shall remain the property of the Architect whether the Project for which they are made is executed or not. They are not to be used by the Owner on other projects or extensions to this Project except by agreement in writing and with appropriate compensation to the Architect.

AIA DOCUMENT B131 • OWNER-ARCHITECT AGREEMENT • SEPTEMBER 1966 EDITION • AIA ®   **6**
© THE AMERICAN INSTITUTE OF ARCHITECTS, 1735 NEW YORK AVENUE, N.W., WASHINGTON, D.C. 20006

Figure 2: Owner, Architect Agreement Form (cont.)

ARTICLE 10

SUCCESSORS AND ASSIGNS

The Owner and the Architect each binds himself, his partners, successors, assigns and legal representatives to the other party to this Agreement and to the partners, successors, assigns and legal representatives of such other party with respect to all covenants of this Agreement. Neither the Owner nor the Architect shall assign, sublet or transfer his interest in this Agreement without the written consent of the other.

ARTICLE 11

ARBITRATION

11.1 All claims, disputes and other matters in question arising out of, or relating to, this Agreement or the breach thereof shall be decided by arbitration in accordance with the Construction Industry Arbitration Rules of the American Arbitration Association then obtaining. This agreement so to arbitrate shall be specifically enforceable under the prevailing arbitration law.

11.2 Notice of the demand for arbitration shall be filed in writing with the other party to this Agreement and with the American Arbitration Association. The demand shall be made within a reasonable time after the claim,

dispute or other matter in question has arisen. In no event shall the demand for arbitration be made after institution of legal or equitable proceedings based on such claim, dispute or other matter in question would be barred by the applicable statute of limitations.

11.3 The award rendered by the arbitrators shall be final, and judgment may be entered upon it in any court having jurisdiction thereof.

ARTICLE 12

EXTENT OF AGREEMENT

This Agreement represents the entire and integrated agreement between the Owner and the Architect and supersedes all prior negotiations, representations or agreements, either written or oral. This Agreement may be amended only by written instrument signed by both Owner and Architect.

ARTICLE 13

APPLICABLE LAW

Unless otherwise specified, this Agreement shall be governed by the law of the principal place of business of the Architect.

AIA DOCUMENT B131 • OWNER-ARCHITECT AGREEMENT • SEPTEMBER 1966 EDITION • AIA ®
© THE AMERICAN INSTITUTE OF ARCHITECTS, 1735 NEW YORK AVENUE, N.W., WASHINGTON, D.C. 20006   7

Figure 2:   Owner, Architect Agreement Form (cont.)

This Agreement executed the day and year first written above.

OWNER _____   ARCHITECT _____

                                         Architect's Registration No. _____

AIA DOCUMENT B131 • OWNER-ARCHITECT AGREEMENT • SEPTEMBER 1966 EDITION • AIA ®
© THE AMERICAN INSTITUTE OF ARCHITECTS, 1735 NEW YORK AVENUE, N.W., WASHINGTON, D.C. 20006   8

Figure 2: Owner, Architect Agreement Form (cont.)

posted to the individual Accounts Receivable sheets for each client. Any standard sheet or card system to record this information would be adequate.

Most small firms use ordinary checks, three to a page, providing space for description of the disbursements. They are posted to the customary Cash Disbursements journal.

Other than a General journal for a manual accounting system, there are no books or forms peculiar to this system which are not described or referred to in this chapter.

Contract forms (Figures 1 and 2) and cost-plus rates are set by the American Institute of Architects.

Peculiarities of Procedures

Cash Receipts and Disbursements. A petty cash imprest system is sometimes used, requiring the funding or setting aside of a fixed amount of cash for payment of petty expenditures. The employee responsible for the fund compiles each week, or each month, a report covering the amount disbursed; a check is issued for this sum to replenish the fund to the original amount. The report, of course, is accompanied by invoices receipted for each expenditure listed.

Many architects, however, feel it is simpler to reimburse the employee for out-of-pocket expenses.

Time and Payroll System

There is one out-of-the-ordinary procedure for payroll. Each employee's weekly hours should be categorized as "direct" or "indirect" time. Time for technical personnel is classed as direct, since it is charged to each individual job for cost accounting purposes. Clerical time, because it is an overhead expense, is indirect.

Use of the McBee "3 in 1" system is a real time-saver.

Reports to Management

The financial reports which are prepared quarterly consist of a profit and loss statement and the balance sheet. They require no comment.

Summary

In every business there are accounting requirements which are sufficiently similar to provide a basis for establishing uniform principles of construction.

All concerns receive and disburse cash, buy and sell goods, or dispense services, own properties, create liabilities, and earn profits or sustain losses. Since these factors are universally similar, they enable the principles to be universally applied. But to say that these principles are similar does not imply that the application in any two cases will be the same. Each concern has problems peculiar to itself which must be met by the systematizer.

Past experience has shown that in setting up a system for a professional who is not concerned with inventories or manufacturing, it is wiser to make the system as simple as possible as long as the overall results are achieved. The clients will then be happy and the accountant's welfare is promoted.

5

Associations and Clubs

BY DONNA H. SHARKEY
Public Accountant, Columbus, Ohio

Characteristics of the Business That Affect the Accounting System

Accounting in the field of associations and clubs presents a unique area of endeavor involving more in personal contacts than most types of business. Only during consultation for the purpose of preparation of individual, joint, or partnership tax returns does the accountant find the intimate confidences necessary for the initial and continued supervision of books of account for both associations and clubs. Policies not spelled out by the "rules" of the organization are changed from one "administration" to the next, and in this changeover there may be little continuity in thoroughness of record keeping, or business acumen.

Certainly this is an area in which an accountant may use his outgoing personality to the mutual advantage of his client and himself, by tactfully maneuvering an "invitation" to sit in on board meetings. He can encourage the financial officers to feel very welcome to counsel with him freely, and he can steer the governing board away from policies detrimental to proper accounting methods for handling funds received and disbursed, as will be demonstrated in this chapter.

The personnel of such organizations often forget the benefit (or ignore it) of obtaining a tax-exempt status for the association or club; not all such entities are entitled to exemption. These groups, particularly the associations, are voluntary or fellowship groups and often, though casually formed in the beginning, grow to surprising financial proportions, handling substantial amounts of money which must be accounted for properly—to the members, and to Uncle Sam. Then too, a nonprofit status can cease to be an allegation and become a reality only on installation of the proper accounting system.

FUNCTIONAL CHARACTERISTICS OF THE BUSINESS

For the purpose of these volumes, it is prudent to consider "associations" as a separate category from "clubs".

An association may consist of only a handful of loosely organized members, or it may have many members and affiliates working together under a substantial format.

A club, although having comparatively few members in some instances, ordinarily is still organized under a charter, with amendments thereto. It is controlled through bylaws, more or less formally adopted, to which (hopefully) the reigning officers adhere more strictly than in the case of the less formally organized "association" members.*

Associations. The fiscal period should be determined by the principal activities of the group. If a charitable organization, a fiscal period ending perhaps a month after the close of a specific drive to raise funds, or after the period of collecting the major portion of amounts pledged, should be considered.

As an example, a society formed for the purpose of preserving the historic aura of a particular section of a town, featuring modernization of existing homes for livability while still maintaining its period characteristics, might have as its prime annual project for raising funds a tour of the section promoted to the public, or a parade of homes and businesses to demonstrate yearly progress. Either project should necessarily occur, first, during the best predictable weather and, second, at a time when the largest number of persons might be available to patronize the project. This might be June in the

---

* Funk & Wagnalls College Dictionary defines association as ". . . a body of persons associated for some common purpose, society, league . . ."; a club as "a group of persons organized for some mutual aim or pursuit, *especially* a group that meets regularly."

North, Northeast, and Midwest; it might be February in the South and Southwest. Often the project may be planned with the idea of attracting future permanent residents to the area. Thus the fiscal periods could end, respectively, on August 31 and April 30.

Clubs. The fiscal period should be governed by the season or period of greatest activity, and should end as soon as practicable thereafter. As an example, a country club in the Northeastern or Central section of the country could adopt a fiscal year for the period beginning February 1, thereby including within that year all income from:

(a) Summer activities; golf, swimming pool, tennis, and riding
(b) Spring and summer weddings and receptions, along with graduation activities
(c) Fall activities of football luncheons, dinners and dances, golf-roundups, award dinners, etc.
(d) Holiday activities, and New Year's parties.

Also included would be resultant expenses of all these activities with invoices timely discounted and paid by the end of the fiscal year, January 31. The fiscal year could conceivably start as logically on March 1 or April 1, since ordinarily in these areas there is comparatively little activity during the early months of the year.

Conversely, in the Southern and Western resort areas fiscal years should end June 30, July 31, or August 31 for the same reasons. Choice of the most suitable suggested period should take into consideration due dates of local and state tax returns to cause as little overlapping as possible in record keeping.

PRINCIPAL ACCOUNTING PROBLEMS

Accounting problems with an association arise from two factors. The first is difficulty in ascertaining the persons having the current authority to supply information—officers are often unpaid, elected persons serving at irregularly scheduled meetings, and they are not always impressed with the importance of maintaining accurate records for the good of the association, as well as for their own protection.

Problems with club accounting arise from internal friction as to authority. The accountant must ascertain that his information is supplied by the officer commissioned to supply it accurately, be it the president, treasurer, secretary, chairman of the finance committee, or in the case of a country club, the executive manager.

Strict adherence to the association charter and amendments thereto must be followed in initiating and maintaining a bookkeeping system and instruction should be given by the accountant to the proper officer. Many times it is advisable to set up a much simplified format if members of the organization, elected from time to time, and changing often, are expected to keep such records current and accurate after the system is inaugurated.

Whether club or association, the personal contact in setting up and maintaining an effective accounting system is probably more essential than in any of the fields of accounting dealt with in these volumes. Upon successful personal relationships with the constituent members depends the accuracy of data supplied to the accountant—a persistent "drawing-out" of pertinent facts often otherwise thoughtlessly omitted by the contact officer.

In each type of organization, the officers and/or governing board are changed annually (sometimes more frequently) and often with little continuity of procedure in office; hence supervision to insure uniform financial methods is lacking, except for the accountant's influence.

Functional Organization

Associations ordinarily are formed for a specific purpose, or to attain a particular goal, and separation of activities is not usually necessary.

Clubs, as a general rule, embody many areas of operation, supervised by a manager, the president, or separate committees for each such activity. Each of the officers or committees is in turn responsible to the manager or president.

Principles and Objectives of the Accounting System

Since one activity may be intertwined, almost inextricably, with another, income should be shown from various classes of membership, i.e. from social, junior, full-voting, associate, nonresident, etc.; from initiation fees, restaurant and beverage sales, and from other activities—golf, tennis, billiards, swimming pool, locker rentals, etc.

For instance, the membership committee is responsible for screening applicants for membership and insuring the observance of rules by the members and guests; this committee also advises the board of trustees, or other governing body as to the advisability of the amount of dues to be paid, or other financial matters relating either to income or expenses arising from the membership.

Likewise the golf committee, or greens committee, is responsible for the policies invoked in operating the golf course, its maintenance, when it may be used and by whom. The committee sets the amounts of greens fees and selects the pro for the club. In turn, this committee is directly responsible to the president or manager.

Income and expenses must be segregated as to each separate department. Capital improvements play a vital role in the successful operation of a large club. A fine Olympic swimming pool, the best designed tennis courts, a top-flight golf course—all of these help to attract the most desirable prospective members who will be able to support these luxuries when they finally become members, and thereby perpetuate the high standards which are the aim of such an organization. Obviously such improvements as these are costly and often are funded by a special assessment against the members. The accounting system must provide for these reserve funds.

SPECIFIC OBJECTIVES OF THE SYSTEM

Accounting records acceptable to various government agencies as related to sales tax, observation of labor laws, preparation of other tax and information returns must be maintained.

Another necessary objective is proper allocation of expense items in relation to income, to spot inefficient operation effectively.

A fine club necessarily must attract businessmen who are highly successful. The correct accounting system can be helpful in obtaining such new members, where so desired, just as in a civic or political association, by providing the information necessary to a concise financial statement as a demonstration that the organization has a solid background. A statement of this kind may reflect the attainment of the goal of the organization through systematic management or club policy. In many cases, the statement may be less formal than that prepared for other types of businesses.

A practical, workable accounting system for a club or association takes the organization out of the haphazard, unregimented category and raises it to the level of a going business and a worthwhile undertaking deserving the respect of competitive clubs. Such a system will serve as a magnet to the right prospective members, whether the goal of that association or club is to make a profit, to aid charitable causes, or merely to see that the members enjoy belonging.

And finally, good accounting eliminates much friction often present in voluntary or fellowship groups by clearly showing just how much came in, where it went, what is left (assets) and what was accomplished in the whole process!

Classification of Accounts and Books of Accounts

Depending upon the size and policy of the association or club, either a simple bookkeeping system may be installed, with a minimum of account headings incorporated in a General ledger, or the more complex accounting system employed in larger organizations may be preferable. Where possible in these small groups about which these chapters are being written, the simpler the better, because of lack of experience, time, or inclination of the officers charged with maintenance of such records.

A larger, more formal club, with many activities, necessarily must have an accounting system adequate to reflect the many facets of its operation.

The chart of accounts below is adaptable to the latter type of organization and is flexible for the purpose intended, whether to show clearly to the constituent members which activities are making money (or losing it), or to draw attention to practices within the club which should be remedied.

Provision is made in the chart for real estate and other property either owned or leased, and for self-operated departments or concessions. Depending on club policy, therefore, it is obvious that all of the following accounts would not be used within one accounting system.

BALANCE SHEET ACCOUNTS.

ASSETS

Current assets

Cash operating funds

   1 Bank
   2 Cash Box Fund
   3 Office Petty Cash
   4 Postage Meter

Appropriated and reserve funds invested

   5 Special Funds Assessed for Capital Improvement
   6 Allowance for Annual Principal Payments
   7 Allowance for Taxes and Insurance

Accounts receivable

  11 Members' Dues
  12 House Accounts
  13 Special Assessments
  14 Outside Organizations
  15 Concessionaires

Inventories

  21 Bar
  22 Office
  23 Kitchen (includes swimming-pool and golf-course stands)
  24 Golf and Tennis Shops
  25 Tack Room
  26 Cigar Stand (includes cigarette machine)
  27 Janitor Supplies

Prepaid items

  31 Taxes
  32 Contracts (yearbook, etc.)

33 Insurance
34 Interest
35 Rentals

*Fixed assets—real estate,
improvements and equipment*

41 Land and Improvements
42 Buildings (includes garages,
shelter houses, swimming pools,
tennis courts, stables, boat
docks, golf-cart shed, etc.)
43 Clubhouse Furniture and
Equipment
44 Locker Rooms or Buildings
45 Kitchen Equipment (includes
glasses, china, and linens)
46 Bar Fixtures
47 Automotive Equipment
(includes trucks, tractors,
and automobiles)

LIABILITIES

Short-term payables

51 Accounts: Suppliers
52 Accounts: Concessionaires
53 Contracts
54 Notes
55 Principal Payments Due within
Year (fully funded)
56 Deposits on Special Parties
(outside guests)

Accruals

61 Salaries, Wages, and Commissions
62 Employees' Fund
63 Taxes and Assessments: Real
Estate
64 Excise Taxes Collected
65 Sales Tax

66 Interest Payable

Payroll Deductions

71 Social Security
72 Union Contributions
73 Income Tax Withheld: Federal
74 Income Tax Withheld: State
75 Income Tax Withheld: City

Employees' taxes payable

81 Workmen's Compensation
Liability
82 Social Security—Old Age
83 Social Security—Employment
(State)

Allowances

91 Bad Debts
92 Depreciation: Buildings (includes
garages, shelter houses, swimming
pools, tennis courts, stables)
93 Depreciation: Clubhouse Furniture and Equipment
94 Depreciation: Locker Room
Equipment
95 Depreciation: Kitchen Equipment
96 Depreciation: Bar Fixtures and
Equipment
97 Depreciation: Automotive
Equipment

Long-term payables

101 Mortgages
102 Contracts

NET WORTH

111 Members' Equity: Appropriated
112 Members' Equity:
Unappropriated

INCOME AND EXPENSE ACCOUNTS.

INCOME

Sales

121 Dining Room and Grill

122 Bar
123 Cigar Stand (includes
cigarette machine)

124 Golf and Tennis Shop
125 Tack Room

Cost of sales

131 Dining Room and Grill
132 Bar
133 Cigar Stand (includes cigarette
     machine)
134 Golf and Tennis Shop
135 Tack Room

Dues

141 Full-Voting Members
142 Social and Other

Fees

151 Initiation
152 Greens
153 Lockers
154 Fines

Concessions

161 Barber and Beauty Shop
162 Golf Shop
163 Tack Room

Activities

171 Swimming Pool
172 Tennis Courts
173 Riding Stable
174 Billiard Tables
175 Golf Cart Rentals (less
     maintenance)

Other income

181 Recovery of Bad Debts
182 Discounts Earned
183 Interest Earned
184 Cash Over

EXPENSES

Administrative

191 Salaries
192 Employees' Meals, Lodging,
     Transportation
193 Auditing and Legal
194 Publications (yearbook,
     announcements, etc.)
195 Postage, Freight, and Cartage
196 Stationery and Supplies
197 Telephone

Taxes

201 Payroll: Social Security
202 Payroll: Workmen's Compensa-
     tion Liability Insurance
203 Payroll: Unemployment
204 Real Estate
205 Income: City
206 Income: State
207 Income: Federal
208 Intangible (Personal Property)

Licenses

211 Miscellaneous

Services

221 Laundry
222 General Maintenance
223 Utilities
224 Janitor Labor (includes Supplies)

Insurance

231 General
232 Group Plans
233 Pension or Retirement Plans

Maintenance

241 Golf Course
242 Golf Shop

243 Stable and Tack Room
244 Clubhouse, Buildings, and
      Grounds
245 Tennis Courts
246 Swimming Pool
247 Locker Rooms

Depreciation

251 Buildings
252 Clubhouse Furniture and
      Equipment

253 Locker Room Equipment
254 Kitchen Equipment
255 Bar Fixtures and Equipment
256 Automotive Equipment

Other expense

261 Entertainment
262 Automotive Expense
263 Losses on Bad Debts
264 Interest Paid
265 Cash Short

ACCOUNTS PECULIAR TO THE BUSINESS

Cash Box Fund (No. 2). Money in this fund is for use in the dining room, for special parties, stands on grounds, etc.

Allowance for Taxes and Insurance (No. 7). This account includes real estate and intangible tax as well as Federal, state, and local income taxes.

Locker Rooms or Buildings (No. 44). This account is kept separately from Buildings (No. 42) because of fees charged for use.

Employees' Fund (No. 62). Sometimes a special percentage, such as 15 percent, is added to each food and beverage check, in lieu of the usual tip. The percentage system is used to provide a fund for distribution to employees of the lounge and restaurant; this special account is provided to show origin and distribution of this percentage collection.

Union Contributions (No. 72). Clubs in unionized areas are sometimes required to collect union dues from members by deductions from wages. In this case a separate account must be established to show deductions and subsequent disbursement to the union.

General Insurance (No. 231). In addition to the obvious and basic "fire and extended coverage" plus "general" liability, this account must encompass many loss possibilities. A great many clubs refuse to carry insurance to cover accidents on the golf course, tennis court, or swimming pool. Court decisions in the past have ruled that no club liability prevailed in situations where the injured individual caused his injury by his own choice and where no distinct negligence on the part of the club existed at the time of the accident. Individual liability policy protection is usually included in the insurance program of club members or their guests. Certainly few golfers—especially the high-handicap duffers—should be without coverage to afford protection of an unintended victim of an aimless shot. Similarly, careless diving in the pool and awkwardness on the tennis court should not result in expense to the host-club.

If club policy so indicates, life insurance may be carried on the manager of the club or other key personnel. The usual insurance must be included on trucks, automotive equipment and cars used to transport employees, etc., as well as liability insurance to protect users of golf carts.

Since country clubs are usually located in a rural area, premiums on fire and windstorm insurance are high. However, it is still necessary to cover items particularly related to the country-club business. For instance, a fire destroying records of accounts receivable might also cause the club to be inoperable for a period of time. Hence no dues might be payable until restoration of facilities; without collection of verified and insured accounts receivable, financial disaster might well occur. Business-interruption insurance can be invaluable. Income-loss insurance is also available, as well as a blanket crime policy to cover fidelity bond on employees, including forgery, safe breaking, drawer (cash) shortages, etc., and loss of cash in transportation to bank, or theft from premises.

In some organizations, consideration should be given to a bond to cover nonperformance of contract, as in the case of an agreement to cater and serve a large convention.

Clubhouse, Buildings, and Grounds (No. 244). Maintenance expenses for golf course and tennis courts are excluded from this account.

Locker Rooms (No. 247). Since fees are charged for the use of these rooms, maintenance expenses are kept separately from such expenses incurred in maintaining the golf course, tennis courts, etc.

Time and Payroll System

Usual procedures for time and payroll records should be followed, in addition to careful attention to the previously described collection and disbursements of percentage charges added to restaurant and beverage checks.

Time-Saving Ideas

To estimate probable tip income and thus aid employees of a club in the preparation of Form 4137, Schedule T(1040), a daily recording from food and beverage checks for each employee, as to dollar amount of service, is invaluable not only to the employee but to the employer. When an Internal Revenue Service audit of the employee's tax return reveals unreported tips, the employee's defense against such an audit will require verification through the employer, and the time-consuming detail involved can be minimized by anticipation of the situation.

Now that the Federal income-tax collection system is totally computerized and every tax return is audited, a record of each employee's probable tips (based on actual dollar amount of food and beverages served) is indeed a blessing.

Reports to Management

Associations. Reports to the management of associations should be general in nature. Members of these smaller groups are interested, primarily, in the honest handling of their funds, and in whether or not their particular goal has been, or is being, accomplished. The report, based on a simple financial statement consisting of income and expenses as well as a balance sheet, should show each member examining it whether or not the association goal has been reached, or the level of attainment, and how much further effort is required.

The report should be detailed in the area of disbursement of funds raised. Workers, usually unpaid volunteers in such an association, logically are most anxious to know that the fruits of their efforts have not been squandered by the treasurer (or anyone!).

Clubs. An annual report, in excellent form, should be presented to the voting members of a club at their annual meeting. The report should give a concise picture of the club's operation and fiscal history of its successes and failures over the past year and/or years. As a dependable guide for future planning of the club program, the report must be couched in lay terms for presentation to the members, translated from the technical phrases of the formal financial statement presented only to the board of directors or other governing body.

The actual financial statement to management should be composed of the standard schedules and exhibits: Statement of income and expense, balance sheet, statement of members' equity, both appropriated and unappropriated, and pertinent notes on each of these pages explaining any unusual affecting factors.

Summary

As the song eulogizes show business, "There's no business like . . .", a phrase most apt in describing operation, management, and results of associations and clubs. For the accountant, the association or club client provides a very pleasant relationship. The people involved in the operation, as well as the members, are in the organization because they want to be, and most of them are more than eager to cooperate with the accountant when they are shown the way.

6

Attorneys

BY JOSEPH G. ABOD

Accounting and Tax Practitioner,
Chicago, Illinois

Characteristics of the Profession That Affect the Accounting System

Admission to the Bar. Only attorneys who have been admitted to the bar may practice in courts and appear before certain commissions. Admission to the bar is conditioned upon obtaining a law degree from an accredited institution, and passing a state examination. Aside from the need of qualified academic and legal training, the attorney must acknowledge the belief in and profess loyalty to the United States Government.

Very often law firms engage associates with law degrees who have not yet passed the state bar examination. These associates, serving in positions comparable to that of interns, are exposed to the various rudiments of the practice of law by being permitted to file documents in court, do case research work, perform preliminary investigative work and other tasks for the principals of a law firm.

An attorney's practice is generally limited to the state in which he is a member of the bar. Some states have reciprocity agreements under which an out-of-state attorney may represent a client in a specific case, but prior court approval must be obtained. An attorney may practice before the U.S. Tax Court by filing a "Declaration" with the Internal Revenue Service. He avers, among other things, that he is an attorney and a member of the bar in good standing in his state, and that he is authorized to represent his client in all matters pending before the Internal Revenue Service. A lawyer may also be granted permission to practice before a United States District Court. To secure this permission he files a petition to practice in such court and submits with it a sponsor's affidavit attesting to the applicant's character, reputation, and experience at the bar.

Actual Practice. The practice of law by firms and individual attorneys may be with or without associates. When a firm is composed of two or more attorneys, it is usually organized as a partnership for the reason that personal service firms as a rule are prohibited by law from operating as corporations. A few states, however, do permit formation of professional corporations or associations. Corporations, per se, often employ attorneys on a full-time basis to represent them in court and to make appearances before state and Federal agencies.

A law firm may be required to handle a large variety of cases. Involved may be real estate transactions, the organization of corporations, preparation of applications for letters of patent, handling of personal injury claims and criminal cases, drafting of wills, and disposition of matters dealing with Federal income, estate, and gift taxes.

Most law firms follow such general practice, but some may specialize in a particular area such as criminal or patent law. In a larger firm it is usual for a number of the members to be specialists in one or more specific fields of the profession.

Very often members of a firm act as estate executors and are appointed as administrators of estates belonging to minors or to testators having no competent executors.

Aside from the practice of law, some firms or individuals engage in outside activities; real estate, for example, and the negotiation of financing requirements for clients.

FUNCTIONAL CHARACTERISTICS OF THE PROFESSION

A law firm naturally prepares a case in the best interests of the client. Therefore, no matter whom the firm may represent, be it plaintiff or defendant, sources of reference material are vital. A basic requirement for operation is the firm's or individual's own library consisting of State Appellate

Court Reports, Revised and Annotated Statutes, Shepard's Citations, Corpus Juris, Law Digests, American Law Reports, Fletcher's Cyclopedia Corporations, Corpus Juris Secundum System, form books, and other material germane to the firm's practice. The library should also include one of the prominent tax services with special emphasis on that portion of the tax laws dealing with Federal gift and estate taxes, as well as the Internal Revenue Code and the Income Tax Regulations.

An accounting system for attorneys usually bears hybrid characteristics because the cash method is used for income tax purposes, while the accrual method is used to establish internal controls. The calendar year is generally preferred to a particular fiscal period, from an accounting point of view.

PRINCIPAL ACCOUNTING PROBLEMS

Determination of fees is the principal problem. The handling of cash advanced for costs and other expenditures on behalf of clients is of paramount importance in the accounting procedure.

Functional Organization

In the case of partnerships, there may be a managing partner who supervises the function of the office; or the lead secretary may be delegated this responsibility. The number of employees will be governed by the size of the practice and the number of the partners. An average-sized firm would have personnel performing the functions of secretary, receptionist, stenographer, file clerk, bookkeeper, and librarian.

Principles and Objectives of the Accounting System

The essential features of an accounting system for attorneys provide for control of fees billed as well as for costs and expenses advanced for clients.

Fees and Basis of Remuneration. Time, of course, is the essence in establishing fees. For that reason an attorney should develop the habit of maintaining a meticulous diary from which he will be able to determine the exact time spent on any given case. The diary will also reveal time devoted to productive and nonproductive work.

Generally a law firm uses three basic types of fees. The annual retainer is a fixed fee for legal representation during a given period of time. Under a contingent retainer an attorney gets a fixed percentage of a settlement in a case. The third kind of fee is a single retainer whereby the attorney is engaged to render services in a specific matter.

A list of recommended fees for various services is published periodically by local and state bar associations. Such lists are available only to attorneys at law.

Classification of Accounts and Books of Accounts

The suggested chart of accounts below has been designed to simplify preparation of the financial and operating statements presented in Figures 11 and 12. Later suggestions in this chapter can easily be adapted to any classifications currently in use; however, the chart below is simple and helpful in organizing the General ledger to meet the needs of accountants in the field of law.

BALANCE SHEET ACCOUNTS.

ASSETS

Current assets

1	Regular Account
2	Trust Account
3	Cash on Hand
5	Petty Cash Fund
10	Accounts Receivable
15	Prepaid Expenses

Fixed assets

20	Office Equipment
20R	Accumulated Depreciation

LIABILITIES

Current liabilities

30	Clients' Funds in Trust Account
31	Tax Withheld
32	FICA Tax
33	U.C. Tax
34	FUTA Tax
35	Accounts Payable
40	Accrued Expenses

NET WORTH

50-C	A Capital Account
50-D	A Drawing Account
51-C	B Capital Account
51-D	B Drawing Account
60	Net Profit or Loss

INCOME AND EXPENSE ACCOUNTS.

INCOME

61	Fees Collected
65	Other Income

EXPENSES

71-S	Associates' Salaries
71-F	Associates' Fee Participations
75	Stenographers' and Office Salaries
80	Rent
81	Telephone
82	Books and Publications
83	Postage
84	Stationery and Supplies
85	Absorbed Costs
90	Other Expenses
100	Partners' Salaries

BOOKS AND FORMS PECULIAR TO THE PROFESSION

Client and Case Identification. Each case, rather than each client, is treated as a separate account. By using a prenumbered register (Figure 1) each case is assigned an identifying number which shows the year in which the case was initiated, the number of the firm to be credited with the case, and the case number.

For the year, the last two of the four numbers are used. To identify the firm member, each individual is assigned an identifying letter of the alphabet. Case numbers are cumulative each year; the most recent case number would indicate the total number of cases the firm has handled for the year to date.

Case and Client Register

Case Number			Date	Case
00	G	101	5-1 __	Armstrong & Co v Shore R.R.
				v
				v
				v
				v
				v
				v

Figure 1: Case and Client Register

Using 00 to indicate the year, and assuming that firm member Adam Brown was assigned the letter "G" and that the client in this case was Armstrong & Co., the case would be identified as 00-G-101.

```
                                        Armstrong & Co.
                                        846 River Road
                                        Batavia, Ill.

        Date                   Case                      Case Number
        5-1-00               v  Shore R.R.               00 G 101
```

Figure 2:   Quick Case Locator and Client Index File Card

The case number is cross indexed on a client's file card, called the "quick case locator" (Figure 2). All cases handled for a given client are permanently recorded on this index card.

Control of Cash Advances and Costs Chargeable to Cases. The books of original entry used to record cash advances and costs chargeable to cases are the Cash Disbursements journal, the Petty Cash journal, and the Office Charge to Clients journal.

Cash Disbursements Journal. Four columns are provided in the Cash Disbursements journal under an Accounts Receivable heading. Subheadings show the name of the client, case number, nature of the charge, and the amount thereof (Figure 3). Entries in the Accounts Receivable columns are posted to the client's ledger sheet and are entered in the Charges column for Costs, Advances, and Expenses. As a case progresses, it is imperative that all costs and charges are promptly charged to the client's account to expedite billing.

Section of Cash Disbursements Journal.

		Accounts Receivable			Fee Participations	
	Client	Case No.	Item	Amount	Name	Amount

Figure 3: Cash Disbursements Journal

Armstrong & Co.
846 River Road
Batavia, Illinois

Case No. 00 G 101

Fee Memo Account						Costs, Advances & Expenses		
Charges	Credits	Balance	Date	Explanation	Fol	Charges	Credits	Balance

Figure 4: Accounts Receivable Ledger Sheet

77

By using a combination Memo and Accounts Receivable ledger sheet (Figure 4); provision is made for a record of the memo charges for fees billed and collected as well as for the Accounts Receivable portion. The latter includes amounts due for charges for costs, direct expenses and cash advances, and a record of the collection of such charges.

Petty Cash Journal. This book is used to record, among other things, cash outlays related to cases and chargeable to clients. Such outlays are entered in a set of columns headed exactly like those shown in Figure 5. The charges are likewise posted to the client's ledger account, and are entered in the Charges column in the Costs, Advances, and Expenses section.

Office Charge to Clients Journal. Here are allocated charges to clients for toll telephone calls, postage, photocopy work, etc. In the case of toll telephone charges, a register is maintained at the switchboard where all toll charges are recorded. These charges are first checked against the telephone bill when it arrives, and charges to cases are then entered in the journal. The columnar headings in the journal are designed to handle the recording and distribution of such charges. (Figure 6)

Memo Record of Fees Billed and Control of Fee Participation. All fees, when billed, are entered in a Memo Billing Register (Figure 7). Postings are made from the register to the client's ledger sheet and are entered in

Petty Cash Journal

		Payee		Amount	Client	Case No.	Item	Amount	
						Accounts Receivable			

Figure 5: Petty Cash Journal

Office Charge To Clients Journal

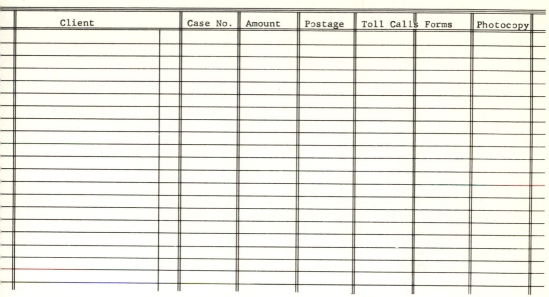

Client		Case No.	Amount	Postage	Toll Calls	Forms	Photocopy

Figure 6: Office Charge to Clients Journal

Memo Fee Register

Client		Inv.No.	Case No.	Amount	Distribution			
					A	B	C	D

Figure 7: Memo Fee Register

Cash Receipts Journal (left side of page)

| Date | Name | Bank Deposits | | Receipts | Accounts Receivable | | Total Fee | Office Fees |
		Regular	Special		Case No.	Amount		
					(right side of page)			
							Other	Receipts
			Fee Participations				Item	Amount
		A	B	C				

Figure 8:   Cash Receipts Journal

the Charges column in the Fee Memo Account section. The Billing Register could provide for a spread of the fees billed to indicate the production of each member of the firm.

An associate is often credited with a portion of a fee. In that event, a memo is placed on the office copy of the bill showing the name of the participant and portion of the fee to be paid to him.

Cash Receipts Journal. When a fee is collected, reference is made to the office copy of the bill from which fee participations, if any, are computed, and the amount is entered in the appropriate columns of the Cash Receipts journal. The entire fee is first entered in the Total Fee column. It is then broken down between office fees and fee participations. (Figure 8)

Collections of costs and advances are entered in the Accounts Receivable column, and these items are posted to the client's ledger sheet crediting costs and advances.

The fee participation, when paid, is charged to a column headed Fee Participations in the Cash Disbursements journal. On the theory that fee participations are paid in the same month in which collected, the columns so headed in the Cash Receipts and Cash Disbursements journals should be in agreement at the end of the month.

The size of the firm will govern the need of other books of original entry such as a Purchase journal, or one of the compact one-write payroll systems.

Accounts in the General ledger should be arranged to follow the format of the financial and operating statements shown in Figures 11 and 12.

Peculiarities of Procedures

Trust Funds (No. 2). A separate bank account should be maintained for funds received from closing real estate transactions, the settlement of law suits, and the like. Such funds should never be mixed with the firm's regular bank accounts. When a firm acts as executor of an estate or estates, separate checking accounts should be maintained for each estate to facilitate the preparation of the intermediate and final accounts required by the probate courts.

Clients' Funds in Trust Account (No. 30). This account shows amounts collected from closing real estate transactions, the settlement of law suits, and so on. The contra account to No. 30 is the Trust Account (No. 2).

Absorbed Costs (No. 85). Very often nominal costs are incurred in connection with cases that, for some reason or another, do not materialize. These costs are absorbed by the firm. It may also happen that at the conclusion of a case it may appear advisable to absorb the costs incurred therewith. The operating statement should show absorbed costs as a separate item. This item is detailed in the Analysis of Accounts Receivable (Figure 9).

Partner's Salary. Profit for the period is arrived at before consideration is given to partners' salaries as expenses. Partner's Salary accounts should be shown separately in the operating statement. (There may be variances in salaries between partners, according to time spent, the type of work involved, seniority, etc.)

Deduction of these salaries from the operating profit gives the amount of excess profit available for distribution among partners at predetermined, agreed-upon ratios.

Time and Payroll System

With only a few employees, the payroll can usually be handled through the regular checking account of the firm. The payroll section of the operating statement should show associates' salaries and fee participations as separate items and in total; stenographers' and other office salaries should also be shown separately.

Reports to Management

Operating Statement. The operating statement should show total fees collected as gross income, and this item should be supported by a separate

Date of Last Charge	Client				Case No.	Accounts Receivable	Absorbed Costs

Schedule "A-1"

A Law Firm
Analysis of Accounts Receivable
Covering Costs, Advances and Expenses
On Behalf of Clients
As Of

Figure 9: Analysis of Accounts Receivable

Statement of Fees Billed, Collections and Adjustments
And Remaining Fees Outstanding

As Of _____

	Total	Distribution				
		A	B	C	D	E
Fees Outstanding Beginning of Month	$	$	$	$	$	$
Add Fees Billed This Month	$	$	$	$	$	$
Total	$	$	$	$	$	$
Deduct Fees Collected This Month	$	$	$	$	$	
Balance	$	$	$	$	$	
Adjustments: (Explain in detail)						
Total Adjustments	$	$	$	$	$	$
Fees Outstanding At End of Month	$	$	$	$	$	$

Figure 10: Statement of Fees Billed, Collections and Adjustments and Remaining Fees Outstanding

schedule (Figure 10) showing fees billed, collections, adjustments (if any), and fees remaining outstanding.

Statement of Income and Expense. A statement of income and expense for a law firm is shown in Figure 11. Since attorneys generally operate on a cash basis, these statements should be marked to indicate this fact.

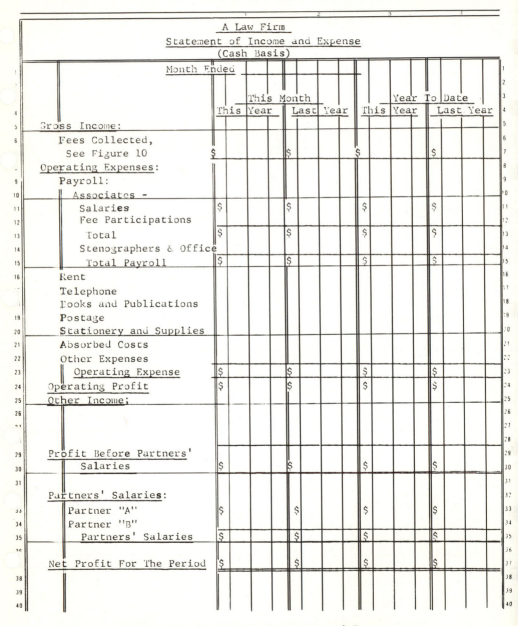

		This Month		Year To Date	
		This Year	Last Year	This Year	Last Year
Gross Income:					
Fees Collected, See Figure 10		$	$	$	$
Operating Expenses:					
Payroll:					
Associates –					
Salaries		$	$	$	$
Fee Participations					
Total		$	$	$	$
Stenographers & Office					
Total Payroll		$	$	$	$
Rent					
Telephone					
Books and Publications					
Postage					
Stationery and Supplies					
Absorbed Costs					
Other Expenses					
Operating Expense		$	$	$	$
Operating Profit		$	$	$	$
Other Income:					
Profit Before Partners' Salaries		$	$	$	$
Partners' Salaries:					
Partner "A"		$	$	$	$
Partner "B"					
Partners' Salaries		$	$	$	$
Net Profit For The Period		$	$	$	$

A Law Firm
Statement of Income and Expense
(Cash Basis)
Month Ended

Figure 11: Statement of Income and Expense

Reconciliation of Partners' Equity Accounts. The financial statement is designed to arrive at partners' equities, usually the excess of assets over deductions. In the illustration (Figure 12), the distribution of equity is shown for only two partners. If there are more than two, it might be necessary to prepare a separate schedule to show computation of each partner's equity, and then show the combined equity as a single item on the financial statement.

A   Law Firm
Reconciliation of Partners' Equity Accounts
As Of

Assets					
Cash:					
Regular Account			$		
Trust Account					
Cash On Hand					
Petty Cash Fund					
Total Cash				$	
Accounts Receivable;					
Due From Clients for Costs and Advances					
Per Schedule "A-1" (See Figure 9.)					
Prepaid Expenses					
Office Furniture and Equipment (Net)					
Total Assets				$	
Deductions:					
Clients' Funds in Trust Account			$		
Tax Withheld					
Payroll Taxes					
Total Deductions					
Partners' Equity					$

Individual Partners Share of Equity

	Partner "A"	Partner "B"	Together
Equity Beginning of Month	$	$	$
Share of This Months Profit			
Total	$	$	$
Drawings This Month			
Equity at End of Month	$	$	$

Figure 12:   Reconciliation of Partners' Equity Accounts

7

Auction Galleries

BY JOHN J. WELCH

**Accountant, Boca Raton, Florida;
Certified Public Accountant,
Massachusetts**

Characteristics of the Business That Affect the Accounting System

In many resort areas throughout the country, tourists may find varied and interesting entertainment in visits to auction galleries. During daytime or evening auctions, talented auctioneers charm their audiences with amusing spiels as they sell merchandise to the highest bidders. The items auctioned cover a vast range of prices and usage. For example, a typical auction may include the following: The latest inexpensive gadget, such as a can opener, auctioned off for $1.00 or less; an electric knife for under $10; an Oriental rug for $1,000; and a diamond ring for over $2,000.

Customers at these auction galleries also have the opportunity of buying, at retail, merchandise on display in the attractive showrooms. In addition galleries may stock, in inventory or on consignment, a fine assortment of jewelry, watches, silver, and other luxury items which may be examined by the customers and purchased at mutually agreeable prices.

FUNCTIONAL CHARACTERISTICS OF THE BUSINESS

The auction gallery business, because it is located in a southern or northern resort area, is usually a seasonal business open for sales only during the months when vacationers are present. The business may be conducted as a sole proprietorship, a partnership, or a corporation. It is often incorporated, with a fiscal year ending after the sales period ends. This provides opportunity for inventorying merchandise and closing the books of the corporation without interruption by sales or customers. Of even more significance, the seasonal nature of the business also provides time before sales begin during which perpetual inventory control records so essential to the business may be set up.

PRINCIPAL ACCOUNTING PROBLEMS

The principal accounting problems of auction galleries are created by the nature of the business: the rapidity of the auction sales; the variety and high value of inventory owned or consigned, being displayed and handled constantly by many employees and customers; and the ever-changing tourist-customer in and out of the resort area in perhaps a week or two. These unusual factors bring about the following specific accounting problems:

1. How can all sales be recorded quickly, accurately, and completely?

2. How can an effective perpetual inventory control be maintained on merchandise owned and consigned?

3. How can Receivables from Customers account cards be kept up to the minute at all times?

There is also one major overall accounting problem. The auction business is a fast-moving, varied, and involved operation. This raises the question: How can the office help keep everything up to date and yet find time to supply frequent informative operational reports to management?

Functional Organization

An auction gallery is often owned by two or more men who are also the principal auctioneers and salesmen. In addition, they handle the vital fuction of procuring inventory, either by outright purchase or by consignment arrangements with vendors. They usually plan advertising, special promotions, and unusual events such as the auction of an estate inventory. They require an alert, well-trained group to back them up:

1. One or more assistant auctioneers on the selling floor to display and deliver merchandise, collect cash, talk to customers, etc.

2. A cashier to receive and account for all cash and checks, to write up sales slips, and to make entries in a sales summary book as the auction progresses.

3. One or more receiving and shipping men to help display merchandise at auction and to handle incoming and outgoing goods.

4. A bookkeeper to maintain accounting records, possibly assisted by a typist-clerk who handles routine details.

Principles and Objectives of the Accounting System

Auction galleries are essentially retail sales organizations. Their income is derived from selling merchandise at prices high enough to cover costs of the items sold, plus a sufficient markup to leave a normal profit after expenses. Therefore, the accounting system should be aimed at informing management whether or not items are selling at prices which achieve a proper profit margin. With prices at auction varying so much, management needs to be supplied with operating results in statement form more frequently than in the usual retail business. As a result, a profit and loss statement, with costs of goods sold actually computed and with expenses deducted, should be given to management on a weekly basis.

SPECIFIC OBJECTIVES OF THE SYSTEM

The accounting system must be designed to control the problem areas of auction galleries discussed above. Specific objectives of the system described in this article include:

1. Every major cash sale (perhaps using $10.00 sales as the minimum measure of control) and every charge sale must be quickly, correctly, and completely recorded during the course of the auction.

2. A tight inventory control must be maintained, particularly on the frequently handled small but valuable jewelry items owned and consigned.

3. Receivables from Customers account cards must be posted up to date at all times. They must show clearly all transactions for ready reference: description of items bought at different times, disposition of merchandise (taken, held, to be shipped), exchanges, payments, terms, due dates of notes taken from customers, etc.

4. The bookkeeper and cashier must be provided with a simple but effective accounting system that can be kept up daily and proved quickly at least once a week.

5. Experience has demonstrated that management must consistently be able to ascertain that office help is maintaining daily and weekly control of the major accounts: cash, receivables, inventories, and payables.

6. Management, whose primary attention is always on the "sale", must be provided weekly information in condensed form to obtain quickly the facts needed to keep all phases of the business under its control.

Classification of Accounts and Books of Accounts

The following chart of accounts for an incorporated auction gallery is relatively simple compared, for example, with a retail store of the same volume. Expenses are listed alphabetically, without departmental grouping. Owner-managers are ordinarily in direct control of all expenses and usually authorize only those expenses essential to promoting, conducting, and accounting for sales.

BALANCE SHEET ACCOUNTS.

ASSETS

Current assets

101 Cash in Bank
102 Tax Bank Account
104 Petty Cash
108 Receivable from Customers
109 Refunds by Our Checks
110 Other Receivables
120 Inventory on Hand
130 Prepaid Expenses

Fixed assets

201 Fixtures and Equipment
202 Accumulated Depreciation

LIABILITIES

Current liabilities

401 Notes Payable
402 Accounts Payable
415 Accrued Expenses
420 State Sales Tax Payable
421 Payroll Taxes Payable
430 Accrued Federal Income Tax

NET WORTH

551 Capital Stock
555 Earned Surplus—(start year)
556 Net Income (this year to date)

INCOME AND EXPENSE ACCOUNTS.

INCOME

601 Net Sales
701 Cost Price (Goods Sold)

EXPENSES

801 Accounting
802 Advertising and Promotion

803 Bad Debts
804 Burglar Alarm Expense
805 Car Expenses
806 Commissions Paid
807 Customers' Refunds
808 Depreciation

809 Dues and Subscriptions
810 Donations
811 Electricity
812 Entertainment of Customers
813 Freight and Express
814 Giveaways
815 Gross Payroll—Officers
816 Gross Payroll—Others
817 Insurance
818 Interest
819 Legal
820 Licenses
821 Maintenance and Repairs

822 Merchandise Repairs
823 Miscellaneous Expenses
824 Office Supplies
825 Refreshments
826 Rent
827 Short or Over
828 Supplies
829 Taxes—Payroll
830 Taxes—Other
831 Telephone
832 Travel Expenses
833 Utilities
901 Federal Income Tax

BOOKS AND FORMS PECULIAR TO THE BUSINESS

The following books and forms peculiar to the business are listed in the time order of their setup and use by the bookkeeper and cashier.

In preparation for the opening of the doors to customers for auctions and sales, inventory is first received by the gallery. As invoices are received and merchandise is checked in, each different merchandise item is given a code number, which is tagged or written on the item and is also written on the invoice. This permits positive identification at the time each item is sold. A simple coding procedure may use the first one or two letters of the vendor's name, followed by a number for each type of item.

The invoices are then turned over to the office staff for entry. Invoices are entered in vendor control records of a standard type to show what is payable to each vendor.

Perpetual inventory records are then established. For items other than jewelry, such records can consist of a simple ledger sheet for each vendor, the left side used to list individually and identify each item; the right side is used, when any individual item is sold, to record sales slip number, date sold, and to whom sold. If a $10 selling price is used as the minimum control guide, no item costing under $6.00 will be listed for control. Jewelry items are usually set up, with detailed description, on small index cards, filed in item numerical order under each vendor's name. This permits easy use of the index card by auctioneer-salesmen to describe the item in detail at customer presentations.

It is particularly important in setting up these records that consigned merchandise items are separately accounted for. Not until a consigned item is sold does it become a purchase of inventory. It is therefore recommended that the Purchase journal and the Vendors' ledger be divided into two sections:

1. *"Accounts Payable."* This section is for vendors whose merchandise is purchased outright. However, it also includes vendor sheets for consignors, whose merchandise will become Purchases and Accounts Payable as soon as sold.

2. *"Consignments On Hand."* This is a subsidiary ledger, similar in content to the Accounts Payable section, except that it shows by vendor the invoices of consigned goods.

Inasmuch as the second section lists only invoices of consigned goods belonging to the vendor until sold by the gallery, with the total of this section representing "Consignments on Hand", these are not Inventory On Hand or Accounts Payable of the gallery. Therefore, it is not necessary to record the debits and credits to this section in the general books of the gallery. However, when a consigned item is sold, it is entered as a reduction of the particular vendor's account in the Consignments On Hand section. It is then recorded as a purchase and a payable in the regular Accounts Payable Purchase journal and its ledger. It should be obvious that the Consignments On Hand records represent the control for all consigned goods not yet sold.

With the foregoing inventory and payable records established, the auction gallery opens its doors and begins its sales period. When a particular sale is completed, the cashier makes out a sales slip (Figure 1) and posts it to the Receivable from Customers account card (Figure 2). The sales slip should be in triplicate, one for the customer, one to stay with the merchandise until delivered, and one for the permanent accounting record.

It is recommended that, for historical purposes, both cash and charge sales slips be posted to the customer's account card. Any cash sales slip posting would be marked "Paid" after the word "Total" of the sale on the card.

As an illustration, Figure 1 shows sales slip No. 3001 and its posting to the customer's card (Figure 2).

A new sales slip should thereafter be used to record any and all transactions with the customer and should be posted to his card. For example, if a note is taken from a customer in payment of his account, a sales slip should be made out and posted to the customer's card. The balance on the card, therefore, may represent either an open charge account or a note receivable from the customer.

The sales slip and the customer's card should also show, for ready reference later, the disposition of the merchandise and any special arrangements

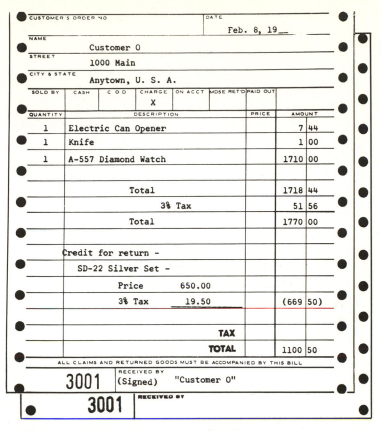

CUSTOMER'S ORDER NO				DATE			
				Feb. 8, 19__			
NAME	Customer O						
STREET	1000 Main						
CITY & STATE	Anytown, U. S. A.						

SOLD BY	CASH	C O D	CHARGE	ON ACCT	MDSE RET'D	PAID OUT	
			X				

QUANTITY	DESCRIPTION		PRICE	AMOUNT	
1	Electric Can Opener			7	44
1	Knife			1	00
1	A-557 Diamond Watch			1710	00
	Total			1718	44
	3% Tax			51	56
	Total			1770	00
	Credit for return -				
	SD-22 Silver Set -				
	Price	650.00			
	3% Tax	19.50		(669	50)
			TAX		
			TOTAL	1100	50

ALL CLAIMS AND RETURNED GOODS MUST BE ACCOMPANIED BY THIS BILL

3001

RECEIVED BY
(Signed)   "Customer O"

3001   RECEIVED BY

Figure 1: Sales Slip

NAME ____ Customer O

ADDRESS 1000 Main, Anytown, U. S. A.

19__ DATE	SALE- SLIP NO.	I T E M S	AMOUNT		DATE	SALE- SLIP NO.	I T E M S	AMOUNT	
2/6	2870	1 SD-22 Silver Set	650	00					
		3% Tax	19	50					
		Total Charged	669	50					
2/8	3001	1 Elec. Can Opener	7	44					
		1 Knife	1	00					
		1 A-557 Diam. Watch	1710	00					
		Total	1718	44					
		3% Tax	51	56					
		Total	1770	00					
		Credit for return -							
		1 SD-22 Silver Set	(650	00)					
		3% Tax	(19	50)					
		Total Charged	1100	50					
		Balance due	1770	00					

Figure 2: Customer's Account Card

SALESBOOK

Item No.		Total Cash Received	Charge Sales On (Deductions)	State Sales Tax
992	Antique Toy Box	14420		420
W-35	Glass Box	1648		48
S-71	Pair Figurines	1030		30
X-992	Ladies Ring		45320	1320
N-12	Ring - Returned for Refund	(41200)		(1200)
	Electric Can Opener			
	Knife			
A-557	Diamond Watch			5156
SD-22	Silver Set - Returned for credit		110050	(1950)
	Received on Account	205870	(205870)	
NSW	Luggage	18540		540
S 1900	Silver Figures	72100		2100
1879	Figures - Returned for Refund			—
99	Box		1980	60
	Miscellaneous Cash Sales	2744		74
	Total for evening	275152	(48520)	6598
	Less - Short	1000		
	Deposit	274152		
	Cost under $10 at 60%			

Sunday, February 8, 19__

Sales Under $10	Sales Over $10	Refunds By Our Checks	Sales Slip No.	Customer's Name	Cost Price
	14000		2996 Cust.	B	7000
	1600		2997	Z	1400
1000			2998	L	—
	44000		2999	M	27500
	(40000)		3000	N	(24000)
744			3001	O	—
100			"		—
	171000		"		106000
	(65000)		"		(39000)
			3002	A	
	18000		3003	N	10000
	70000		3004	R	41000
	(4500)	4500	3005	E	(3080)
	1920		3006	G	1160
2670					
4514	211020	4500			127980
					2708

Figure 3: Salesbook

NAME: ABC AUCTION GALLERY, INC.

WEEKLY OPERATING REPORT: AUCTION GALLERY

WEEK ENDED: February 14, 19 ___

SALESBOOK SUMMARY

	DEPOSIT	SHORT OR (OVER) ETC.	TOTAL CASH RECEIVED	CHARGE SALES OR (DEDUCTIONS)	STATE SALES TAX	SALES UNDER $10	SALES OVER $10	NET SALES	REFUNDS BY OUR CHECKS	COST PRICE OF COSTED ITEMS	COST PRICE OF OTHER ITEMS
SUNDAY	2 741	10	2 751	(485)	66	45	2 110	2 155	45	1 280	27
MONDAY	405	--	405	983	40	23	1 325	1 348	--	875	14
TUESDAY	504	(5)	499	1 191	49	252	1 389	1 641	--	930	151
WEDNESDAY	1 048	--	1 048	44	32	54	1 006	1 060	--	700	32
THURSDAY	2 083	--	2 083	9 980	247	172	11 644	11 816	--	7 450	103
FRIDAY	14 069	1	14 070	(8 250)	170	395	5 255	5 650	--	3 416	237
SATURDAY	1 701		1 701	1 928	106	425	3 098	3 523	--	2 010	255
TOTAL	22 551	6	22 557	5 391	710	1 366	25 827	27 193	45	16 661	819
										Total of both –	17 480
BEGINNING OF WEEK						7 894	45 899	53 793		30 595	4 737
END OF WEEK						9 260	71 726	80 986		47 256	5 556
										Total of both –	52 812

CONTROL SUMMARIES

	CASH IN BANK	TAX BANK ACCOUNT	RECEIVABLE FROM CUSTOMERS	ACCOUNTS PAYABLE	NOTES PAYABLE	INVENTORY ON HAND	CONSIGNMENTS ON HAND	DIAMOND INVENTORY IN UNITS			
								Rings	Bracelets	Watches	Other
BEGINNING OF WEEK	5 250	3 750	17 095	4 469	22 000	37 618	131 950	92	77	299	52
ADDITIONS FOR WEEK	22 551	710 / 218	5 391	7 800 / 3 294	5 000	7 800 / 3 294	10 900	20	11	41	9
TOTAL	27 801	4 678	22 486	15 563	27 000	44 712 / 306	142 850	112	88	340	61
DEDUCTIONS FOR WEEK	11 935	2 725	----	8 582	3 000		7 800	18	13	59	16
END OF WEEK	15 866	1 953	22 486	6 981	24 000	30 926	135 050	94	75	281	45

RECEIVABLE FROM CUSTOMERS

NAME	REMARKS	AMOUNT
Cust. A		50
B	(Note due 3/15)	6 280
C		480
D		1 000
G	(Past due)	550
M		983
N		79
O		1 770
P	(Due 3/10)	5 820
R		125
S		100
T		1 673
U		89
V		3 292
W		195
Total		22 486

ACCOUNTS PAYABLE

NAME	AMOUNT
Vendor A	1 028
" B	5 093
" C	622
" D	128
" E	99
" F	11
Total	6 981

NOTES PAYABLE

NAME	DUE	AMOUNT
Bank	May 15	5 000
Bank	June 15	5 000
Vendor G	Mar. 10	10 000
" H	Apr. 10	4 000
Total		24 000

INCOME STATEMENT

	START WEEK	THIS WEEK	END WEEK
NET SALES	53 793	27 193	80 986
COST PRICE	35 332	17 480	52 812
GROSS PROFIT	18 461	9 713	28 174
EXPENSES PAID	15 397	4 348	19 745
SHORT OR (OVER)	(90)	6	(84)
GIVEAWAYS	1 210	306	1 516
TOTAL EXPENSES	16 517	4 660	21 177
INCOME	1 944	5 053	6 997
GROSS PROFIT %:			
OF COSTED ITEMS	33	36	34
OF OTHER ITEMS	40	40	40
TOTAL	34	37	35

Figure 4: Weekly Operating Report

CHECKS PAID SUMMARY

NAME: ABC AUCTION GALLERY, INC.

Account 101 - Cash in Bank:

DATE	CHECK NUMBER	AMOUNT OF CHECK	ACCOUNTS PAYABLE	NOTES PAYABLE	REFUNDS BY OUR CHECKS	OTHER GENERAL LEDGER ACCTS ACCOUNT	AMOUNT	EXPENSE ACCOUNTS TOTAL EXPENSES	GROSS PAYROLL	FREIGHT AND EXPRESS	ADVERTISING AND PROMOTION	OTHER EXPENSES ACCOUNT	AMOUNT
2/8	892	10						10		10			
2/8	893	12 10	1 210										
2/8	894	3 120		300 0				120				818	120
2/8	895	45			45								
2/10	896	1 372	1 372										
2/10	897	1 000	1 000										
2/10	898	326						326		326			
2/10	899	559						559			559		
2/10	899	467						467			467		
2/10	900	100				130	100						
2/10	901	150				201	150						
2/10	902	879						879				826	879
2/10	903	552						552				832	552
2/14	904	75				421	(25)	100	100				
2/14	905	150				421	(50)	200	200				
2/14	906	180				421	(20)	200	200				
2/14	907	350				421	(50)	400	400				
2/14	908	350				421	(50)	400	400				
2/14	909	65				421	(20)	85	85				
2/14	909	47				421	(3)	50	50				
2/14	910	710				102	710						
2/14	911	218				102	218						

Total Acct. 101   11 935

Account 102 – Tax Bank Account:

| 2/14 | 107 | 1 525 | | 420 | 1 525 |
| 2/14 | 108 | 1 200 | | 421 | 1 200 |

Total Acct. 102   2 725

Weekly Journal Entries:

2/14	No. 1	----		(7800)	(7800)				7800		120
				(3294)	(3294)				(3294)		120
2/14	2	----			5000	(5000)			1480		120
2/14	3	----		(7800)	3000	(5000)		45	14480		701
				(3294)							

| Total for Week | 14 660 | | 8582 | | | 14779 | 4 348 | 1 435 | 336 | 1 026 | 1 551 |

Figure 5: Checks Paid Summary

99

for shipment, payment, etc. A new sales slip should be made out immediately upon any change of such arrangements being made with the customer.

In the front of the customer cards file, a control card, with daily totals posted, should be maintained.

The sales slips are posted in numerical order as soon as possible in the Salesbook (Figure 3). Note the posting of Sales Slip No. 3001 in this Salesbook, example of the page for February 8, 19—.

This page illustrates the posting of different types of transactions affecting sales and customers. Sales Slip No. 2996 is a cash sale, as are 2997, 2998, 3003, and 3004. No. 2999 and No. 3006 are charge sales, similar to No. 3001. No. 3000 is a customer's return of merchandise for cash refunded out of the day's cash receipts. No. 3005 is a customer's return of merchandise for which a check is issued. No. 3002 is a record of a payment received from a customer. Note that a sales slip is written out for every type of transaction affecting sales or the customer's account and is always entered in the Salesbook. The only minor exception may be for small cash sales accumulated during the sales period and entered in the Salesbook in one figure, such as is shown on the line "Miscellaneous cash sales—$27.44".

The last column of the Salesbook, "Cost Price", is entered as the perpetual inventory records are posted, usually on the day after the sale is made.

Figure 4 shows the Weekly Operating Report of the business. On the first line, in the Salesbook Summary section, is the posting from the Salesbook (Figure 3) of the total of transactions for Sunday, February 8, 19—. Cents have been omitted in this illustration and the subsequent report form for ease of reading. All forms, of course, should be designed for quick hand posting rather than for typing as shown in the illustrations.

The Salesbook Summary section of the Weekly Operating Report, as well as the Checks Paid Summary (Figure 5), is posted daily or at the end of the week. Both of these summaries are then totaled, proved to balance across, and their totals are then posted to various accounts shown on the Weekly Operating Report in the sections labeled "Control Summaries" or "Income Statement".

Using the Purchase journal and the Consignments on Hand journal for the week, totals are journalized for control summaries: Accounts Payable, Inventory on Hand, and Consignments on Hand. Journal entries for the week should be entered at the bottom of the Checks Paid Summary as illustrated (Figure 5).

Diamond Inventory in Units is posted from a separate daily running control record established for this purpose. Use of various categories as indicated is for ease of checking the items physically. This should be done immediately after each auction.

At the bottom of the Weekly Operating Report, detailed balances of Receivable from Customers, Accounts Payable, and Notes Payable are listed from supporting records. Finally, after the foregoing is completed, the income statement at the lower right-hand corner of the Weekly Operating Report is completed. The report is then ready to be presented to management for review.

The illustration given covers a typical week's operation. Various contra debits and credits to accounts may be readily traced from their sources on the Weekly Operating Report itself or on the Checks Paid Summary.

ACCOUNTS PECULIAR TO THE BUSINESS

Consignments on Hand. This major account peculiar to the business has been explained in foregoing comments.

Refunds by Our Checks. Account No. 109 is an exchange account which should zero out. The debit to this account comes from the Checks Paid Summary, and the credit comes from the Salesbook Summary on the Weekly Operating Report.

Cost Price (Goods Sold). No. 701 is a debit account which is the sum of the two columns, Cost Price of Costed Items and Cost Price of Other Items, on the Weekly Operating Report. The contra credit of this posting is to account No. 120, Inventory on Hand. This credit reduces the inventory by the cost price of all items sold. At the end of the season, after the perpetual inventory controls are checked out, an adjustment to this account is usually necessary for recording of the physical inventory.

Giveaways. Account No. 814 is the result of a compilation, daily and weekly, of inventory used as gifts, prizes, etc. The contra to this account is credited to No. 120, Inventory on Hand, as shown on the Weekly Operating Report (Figure 4).

Peculiarities of Procedures

The sales-receivable cycle and the purchases-payable cycle for auction galleries are usually under close control of management. Varied cycles are worked out in detail under the direct control of owner-managers, using their knowledge of arrangement and their best judgment. Also, cash receipts and disbursements procedures are ordinarily under their direct control. Owner-managers of galleries often give full instructions to the bookkeeper and cashier with respect to the flow of cash receipts and checks to be paid.

Time and Payroll System

There are no unusual factors affecting the time and payroll system, unless management furnishes any special arrangements to the office for detailed accounting thereof.

Cost Accounting and Departmental Accounting

In most auction galleries, because they are strictly sales organizations, no particular cost accounting is necessary except as previously noted.

Time-Saving Ideas

It should be particularly noted that the bookkeeping procedures described above are aimed at saving time and yet recording all transactions clearly and fully as soon as they are completed. Time is also saved at the end of the month or the season, if daily and weekly procedures are closely followed. The major accounts are tied out to controls and proved in detail at the end of each week, if the Weekly Operating Report is properly prepared. Of course, in addition, management must keep on top of unusual adjustments to accounts and must inform the office of them immediately for recording.

One minor but useful time-saving idea is to invest in an electric sales slip machine for the cashier's use.

Reports to Management

The Weekly Operating Report furnished to management should provide all the information necessary for operating the business on a week-to-week basis. In addition, this report and the Checks Paid Summary can be used to post to a complete General ledger set of accounts. A time-saving method of preparing the General ledger is to list all account names of balance sheet and income and expense accounts down the left margin of a wide columnar ledger sheet, and then post across the sheet, each week, debits and credits in two adjoining columns (from each Weekly Operating Report and Checks Paid Summary). These columns may then be totalled across monthly, or at the end of the season, in order to prepare a complete financial statement.

8

Auto Supply Stores

BY S. C. LEVIN

Accountant, S. C. Levin Accounting & Tax Service, Des Moines,
Iowa

Characteristics of the Business That Affect the Accounting System

With the millions of automobiles on the streets and highways today, the demand for parts replacement is enormous. Each auto manufacturer's representative stocks parts for his particular makes and models of cars. There are also thousands of automotive parts suppliers, independent of the auto manufacturers, who sell replacement parts and accessories for all makes of cars and trucks.

FUNCTIONAL CHARACTERISTICS OF THE BUSINESS

Usually these auto supply stores are both wholesale and retail establishments. Trade discounts are given to garages, body shops, and other repair establishments. Some auto parts stores also have machine shops where motors, transmissions, and differentials are repaired and rebuilt.

Except for slight fluctuations during the fall and spring seasons, the auto

103

parts business is fairly steady, and the accounting system can be set up on a calendar or fiscal year basis.

It is recommended that the system be fully accrued, and any unrecorded receipts, unpaid or prepaid expenses be set up in the proper prepaid, deferred, or accrual accounts, whichever apply.

Competition is rather keen in this line of business. Each firm usually has salesmen calling on oil stations, garages, body shops, etc., to supplement their over-the-counter business. Purchase discounts are generally based on volume and extra profits are often made in the Purchasing Department. Some firms maintain warehouses from which distributions are made to the stores; this usually warrants an extra "jobber's discount". The warehouse need not necessarily be the same company. It can be operated as a separate entity.

PRINCIPAL ACCOUNTING PROBLEMS

Principal accounting problems are the recording and identifying of receipts and disbursements on an individual store basis.

Records are maintained in one central office for all units including the central warehouse. Where a warehouse is not maintained, the main store records generally include the warehouse operations.

Perpetual inventories must be maintained for each store, and entries thereto made daily. An accounts receivable control is set up for each store also.

Where circumstances permit, all cash counted and reconciled should be witnessed by the store manager, who should also initial and verify all deposit slips, sales invoices, and cash and charge tickets which are sent from each store every day to the main office. It is recommended that the store manager open all the mail, pull out the checks, and run an adding machine tape on the checks. He should retain the tape and give the checks to an employee for making up the bank deposit. After the employee makes the deposit, he returns the validated duplicate deposit slip to his store manager for verification with the tape. Cash as well as checks would, of course, be handled in this same manner. The duplicate deposit tickets may then be submitted to the central store for accounting purposes, together with the other source documents necessary for original entry in the books of account.

In the operating section of the General ledger, each store is identified by a two-digit number added to the code number for each account. Account No. 301, representing Sales—Resale, would show 301-01 for store No. 1; account No. 301-02 would identify the item as Sales—Resale for store No. 2, etc.

Functional Organization

Orders for the replacement of stock are sent in daily to the office, usually along with the daily deposits. These orders are first checked against the store's perpetual inventory, and are then turned over to the stockroom or warehouse for filling and shipping.

Stores are usually located where a maximum of walk-in trade is available and also in areas where there are service facilities for automobiles and trucks. Where a great multiple of outlets exists, a separate department can be organized for the chain store operation with division into parts, accessories, machine shop, etc.

Principles and Objectives of the Accounting System

The primary objective, of course, is to furnish management with the necessary information regarding the operation of each individual unit. Only in this way can the profit or loss of each store be balanced against the total operation, and proper subsequent decisions made.

SPECIFIC OBJECTIVES OF THE SYSTEM

Data from the accounting system can be used to determine and to fulfill the needs and wants of the stores' present markets; as a basis to explore new markets to discover whether they can be served with present facilities at a profit; to eliminate waste in high inventory levels and increase inventory turnover; to strengthen internal control between the branch stores and the central office; to strengthen internal control within each store; to speed up collection of receivables.

Classification of Accounts and Books of Accounts

The chart of accounts for an automotive parts business contains the classifications most generally used in accounting systems with this exception: An identifying two-digit number is attached to each account or code number to designate the store to which the debit or credit applies.

As shown in the asset and liability section, each store has a separate code number, rather than the same number with an attached identifying number. Identifying numbers are used in the operating section only.

Usually one of the stores does the machine work for all, unless the stores are separated by great distances. Note the spacing of four numbers between each store's equipment account. For instance, Machine Shop Equipment for store No. 1 may be No. 163 and its accumulated depreciation allowance, No. 164. If store No. 2 has a machine shop, the equipment numbers would be 169 and 170, etc.

Code numbers may be used for titles for data processing purposes, such as No. 99 for assets, No. 100 for current assets, etc. The system is flexible enough to permit, for instance, the use of No. 121 for Accounts Receivable, No. 12101 for Allowance for Bad Debts when the last two digits are not used for area identification and/or any accounts subsidiary to this Accounts Receivable account. Late model computers, such as the 1401 or 1440, have no four-digit limit on the account numbers employed. Actually a five-digit numbering system is a requirement of the Interstate Commerce Commission for all Class 1, 2, and 3 carriers.

BALANCE SHEET ACCOUNTS.

ASSETS

Current assets

101 Cash Account Store No. 1
102 Cash Account Store No. 2
103 Cash Account Store No. 3
115 Cash Account—Change
116 Cash in Bank
119 Returned Checks
121 Accounts Receivable Store No. 1
122 Accounts Receivable Store No. 2
123 Accounts Receivable Store No. 3
135 Allowance for Bad Accounts
141 Inventory Store No. 1
142 Inventory Store No. 2
143 Inventory Store No. 3
155 Prepaid Insurance
156 Prepaid and Deferred Expenses
157 Investments—Short Term

Fixed assets

161 Store Equipment—Store No. 1
162 Accumulated Depreciation
163 Shop Equipment—Store No. 1
164 Accumulated Depreciation
167 Store Equipment—Store No. 2
168 Accumulated Depreciation
173 Store Equipment—Store No. 3
174 Accumulated Depreciation
179 Automotive Equipment
180 Accumulated Depreciation
185 Office Equipment
186 Accumulated Depreciation

Other assets

191 Organization Expense
192 Officers' Life Insurance
195 Investments—Long Term

LIABILITIES

Current liabilities

202 Accounts Payable
204 Accrued Local Taxes
205 Accrued FICA
206 Accrued Federal Withholding
207 Accrued State Withholding
208 Accrued Federal and State Employment Security Taxes
210 Accrued Sales Tax Payable
212 Accrued Corporation Income Taxes
214 Accrued Payroll
216 Accrued Employees' Bonuses
220 Notes Payable

Long-term or other liabilities

242 Notes Payable
243 Mortgage Payable

NET WORTH

Sole proprietorship

Owner's Equity

261 Investment Account
262 Drawing Account—General
263 Drawing Account—Medical

264 Drawing Account—Taxes
267 Profit or Loss to Date

Partnership

Partners' Equity

271 Partners' Investment Account
272 Partners' Drawing—General
273 Partners' Drawing—Medical

274 Partners' Drawing—Taxes
287 Profit or Loss to Date

Corporation

Stockholders' Equity

291 Capital Stock Issued—Common
295 Capital Surplus
296 Retained Earnings
297 Profit or Loss to Date

INCOME AND EXPENSE ACCOUNTS.

INCOME

301 Sales—Resale
302 Sales—Retail
303 Sales—Labor
304 Sales—Scrap
325 Other Income
380 Discounts, Refunds, and
     Allowances

Cost of sales

401 Cost of Parts Sales
403 Cost of Labor Sales
425 Other Cost of Sales
450 Machine Shop Supplies and
     Expense
499 Gross Profit

EXPENSES

Operating expenses

501 Payroll—Officers
502 Payroll—Office
508 Payroll—Sales
510 Payroll—Other
512 Advertising
514 Automotive Expense

515 Bad Debt Expense
516 Bank Charges
518 Cash Over—Short
520 Casual Labor
525 Depreciation Expense
527 Donations
528 Dues and Publications
537 Heat, Light, and Water
540 Insurance—General
541 Insurance—Employees
542 Interest Paid
545 Laundry and Uniform Expense
548 Legal and Accounting
550 Office and Store Supplies
552 Rent
556 Repairs
560 Salesmen's Car Expense
562 Taxes—FICA
563 Taxes—Federal and State
     Unemployment
564 Taxes and Licenses—Other
571 Telephone and Telegraph
573 Travel and Buying Expense
575 Unclassified Expense
599 Profit or Loss

ACCOUNTS PECULIAR TO THE BUSINESS

Cash Account Stores (No. 101, etc.). These accounts represent the day's cash receipts from sales, received on account, and other sources, if any. The amount represented here is the amount to be deposited the following day.

Cash Account—Change (No. 115). Here is represented the total of cash allotted each store for change. Unless increased or decreased by management, the amount remains the same at all times.

Returned Checks (No. 119) is a control for customers' checks returned by their banks. Some firms make a practice of charging returned checks back to their customers through Accounts Receivable. However, where a check has been accepted on a cash sale and returned, there may not be an Account Receivable account for this particular customer. The returned check should then be charged to account No. 119 and collection procedures started. It is recommended that account No. 119 be used as a clearing account for returned checks. Up-to-date bank balances require that returned checks be taken into consideration as soon as a notice of the returned item is received from the bank.

Accounts Receivable (No. 121 and up). The Accounts Receivable listing for each store is aged monthly. This is usually done when a trial balance

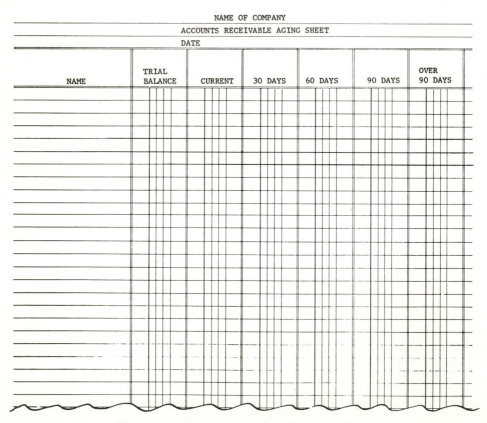

Figure 1: Accounts Receivable Aging Sheet

of the subsidiary ledger is taken. The aging may be accomplished with the use of a multicolumn sheet (Figure 1).

It is recommended that on the 15th of the month a survey of the Accounts Receivable balances be made to determine which accounts have not been paid. A second statement with a friendly reminder that the balance is still unpaid should be mailed at this time. This procedure will tend to prod some of the slow-paying accounts into action. Each store manager is advised of all delinquencies and must act on them. It is assumed that he is closer to the accounts than the central office and will get better results.

Allowance for Bad Accounts (No. 135). With a fully accrued system, it is recommended that a reserve for bad and doubtful accounts be maintained. Where there is a bad debt experience of at least five years, the percentum of bad debt losses to charge sales may be used as a basis for the setting aside of the monthly or annual reserve. However, with no past experience as a basis for decision, one-fourth or one-half of one percent of the charge sales for the period may be used. Some firms prefer to use a direct charge-off of bad debts. Such preference, of course, negates the use of a reserve for this purpose.

Inventories (No. 141 and up). Perpetual inventories must be maintained for each store daily. Perpetual inventory systems have many uses. They advise of the movement of the merchandise, whether certain items are understocked or overstocked, and facilitate removal of slow-selling items from one

INTERNATIONAL PARTS CORPORATION

INVENTORY CARD

MAX. ____________

STOCK No. ____________ DESCRIPTION ____________ MIN. ____________

PURCHASE RECORD			SALES MOVEMENT INFORMATION				SALES MOVEMENT INFORMATION			
DATE	QUANTITY ORDERED	√	DATE	RECEIVED	SOLD	BALANCE	DATE	RECEIVED	SOLD	BALANCE

PRINTED IN U. S. A.

* Courtesy of International Parts Corporation, Chicago, Illinois.

Figure 2: Perpetual Inventory Card (International Parts Corporation)

ARTICLE						SIZE / UNIT	MAX. / MIN			STOCK NO.		

RECEIVED			ISSUED			BALANCE	RECEIVED			ISSUED			BALANCE
DATE	ORDER	QUAN.	DATE	ORDER	QUAN.		DATE	ORDER	QUAN	DATE	ORDER	QUAN	

* Courtesy of Rissman Auto Parts, Des Moines, Iowa.

Figure 3: Perpetual Inventory Card (Rissman Auto Supply Company)

location to another, where sales of the items are better or where they are understocked. Recommended inventory cards are illustrated in Figures 2 and 3.

Physical inventories must be taken quarterly, semi-annually, or annually. The comparison of the physical to the perpetual inventories should be mandatory. Where the amount of any discrepancy warrants time and effort, it should be investigated.

If physical inventories are taken on an internal audit, they should be supervised, priced, and extended by the central office. However, when an external audit is being made, the independent accounting firm usually sets out the procedures to be followed with regard to the taking of the inventories as well as to accounting for cash, receivables, payables, and other balance sheet items.

Prepaid Insurance (No. 155). Insurance which generally is prepaid for a year or more has a rebatable value to the extent of the unexpired period. Therefore, it should be carried as a current asset and charged off periodically.

Equipment accounts (No. 161 and up). In order to allow differentiation in the system between the sales type of equipment (counters, shelving, display cases, etc.) and the operating type (grinders, milling and boring machines, drum turners, hydraulic presses, crankshaft balancers, etc.), different numbers are designated for each class. Account No. 161 should contain display and sales equipment; account No. 163 should contain shop equipment, etc.

110

Drawing Accounts—Medical, and *Drawing Accounts—Taxes (Nos. 263, 264, 273, 274).* In some small and medium-sized businesses, the proprietors or partners draw their living expenses from their businesses as needed. By classifying the tax deductible items as drawn, time spent in preparation of tax returns is minimized considerably.

Operating Accounts. The following operating section of the General ledger (Figure 4) now becomes a five-digit code numbering system by adding the store identification, two-digit numbers to each code, for data processing purposes.

SALES - RESALE

			Store No. 1	Store No. 2	Store No. 3	Store No. 4	Store No. 5	TOTAL	
1									1
2									2
3									3
4									4
5									5
6									6
7									7
8									8
9									9
10									10
11									11
12									12
13									13
14									14
15									15
16									16
17									17
18									18
19									19
20									20
21									21
22									22
23									23
24									24
25									25

* Courtesy of Rissman Auto Parts, Des Moines, Iowa.

Figure 4: Multicolumn General Ledger Sheet

For a manually operated system the use of multicolumned ledger sheets is recommended for the Sales, Cost of Sales, and Expense sections.

Sales and Income Accounts (No. 301 and up). In data processing use the unit to which the sale or income is applicable is identified by the last two numbers of the five-number code. No. 301 represents Sales—Resale or Wholesale. By using 30101, the account is identified as applicable to store No. 1; No. 30102, store No. 2; likewise, account No. 30203 would indicate retail sales for store No. 3. The separation of Sales—Resale and Sales—Retail is necessary for states having a retail or consumers' sales tax law.

Sales-Labor (No. 303). This account concerns the labor sales arising in the machine shop operation. Shop labor expense is charged to account No. 403.

Other Income and Expenses. Other income and expenses not pertinent to the business operation may be included in the chart as series 600 and 700 respectively.

BOOKS AND FORMS PECULIAR TO THE BUSINESS, WITH PROCEDURES

Sales-Receivable Cycle. All cash receipts, whether cash sales or receipts on Accounts Receivable, are recorded on numbered cash sales tickets (Figure

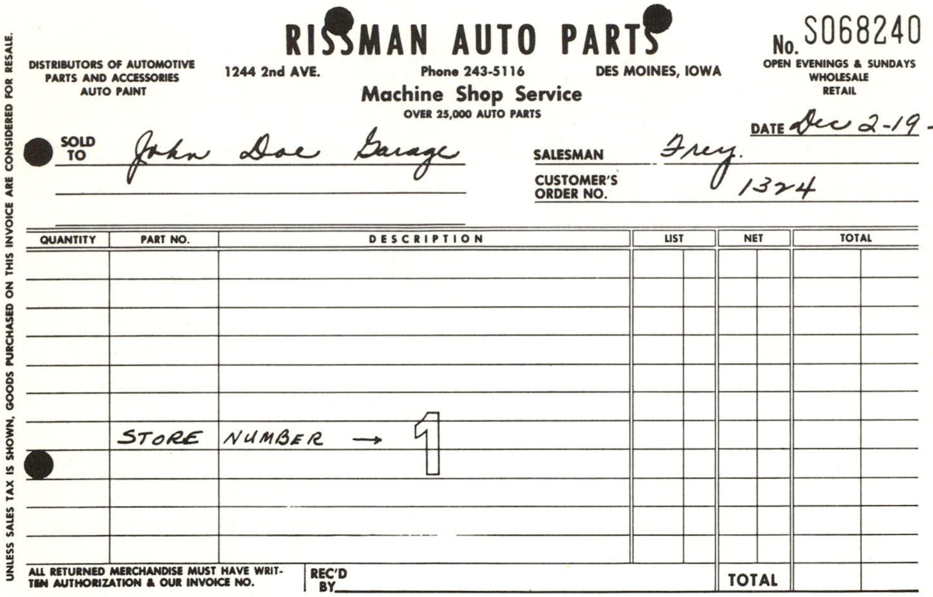

* COURTESY OF RISSMAN AUTO PARTS, DES MOINES, IOWA.

Figure 5: Cash Sales Ticket

5) in triplicate, thereby serving a dual purpose. Two copies are enclosed in the daily envelopes containing the day's deposit; the third is the customer's copy.

Charge tickets (Figure 6) are handled the same way. Charges to new customers should first be cleared with the central office. For easy identification, charge sales tickets should be of a color different from the cash sales tickets.

Since each store is assigned a separate series of ticket numbers, a control of the ticket numbers may be maintained by the use of a check sheet (Figure 7). Numbers 501 through 1000 are shown on the reverse side. Sepa-

RISSMAN AUTO PARTS

DISTRIBUTORS OF AUTOMOTIVE PARTS AND ACCESSORIES AUTO PAINT

1244 2nd AVE.   Phone 243-5116   DES MOINES, IOWA

Machine Shop Service

OVER 25,000 AUTO PARTS

No. S66097-1

OPEN EVENINGS & SUNDAYS
WHOLESALE
RETAIL

UNLESS SALES TAX IS SHOWN, GOODS PURCHASED ON THIS INVOICE ARE CONSIDERED FOR RESALE.

SOLD TO

SALESMAN

CUSTOMER'S ORDER NO.

DATE

QUANTITY	PART NO.	DESCRIPTION	LIST	NET	TOTAL

ALL RETURNED MERCHANDISE MUST HAVE WRITTEN AUTHORIZATION & OUR INVOICE NO.

REC'D BY

TOTAL

CHARGE SALE

* COURTESY OF RISSMAN AUTO PARTS, DES MOINES, IOWA.

Figure 6: Charge Sales Ticket

rate sheets are used for cash and charge tickets. Control is maintained by drawing a line through the number corresponding to the ticket number received at the central office. Unused numbers should be investigated immediately.

Shop tickets (Figure 8) are the responsibility of the shop foreman and are sent to the office each day where they are used as a basis for billing to customers.

A Cash Payment and Returns Ticket (Figure 9), numbered and controlled the same way as the Sales Tickets (Figures 5 and 6), is used for refunds and allowances. The cash payout heading on the ticket (Figure 9) is crossed out when an account is to be credited, and the "your account has been credited" is crossed out when a cash refund is made. Credits to customers' accounts and cash payouts for returned merchandise should be verified by someone other than the person allowing the credit or making the payout.

Cash Receipts and Disbursements. The branch stores will carry no cash on hand except the cash amount used for change. The entire amount of cash receipts for each day will be reduced to zero when deposits are made and will be credited daily.

Direct and Indirect Expenses. Where applicable, expenses should be charged directly to each store. Such expenses include items of rent, repairs, payroll, and others originating in and directly chargeable to each location.

113

CHECK SHEET FOR _____

SERIES:_____ 001 THROUGH_____ 500

1		51		101		151		201		251		301		351		401		451	
2		52		102		152		202		252		302		352		402		452	
3		53		103		153		203		253		303		353		403		453	
4		54		104		154		204		254		304		354		404		454	
5		55		105		155		205		255		305		355		405		455	
6		56		106		156		206		256		306		356		406		456	
7		57		107		157		207		257		307		357		407		457	
8		58		108		158		208		258		308		358		408		458	
9		59		109		159		209		259		309		359		409		459	
10		60		110		160		210		260		310		360		410		460	
11		61		111		161		211		261		311		361		411		461	
12		62		112		162		212		262		312		362		412		462	
13		63		113		163		213		263		313		363		413		463	
14		64		114		164		214		264		314		364		414		464	
15		65		115		165		215		265		315		365		415		465	
16		66		116		166		216		266		316		366		416		466	
17		67		117		167		217		267		317		367		417		467	
18		68		118		168		218		268		318		368		418		468	
19		69		119		169		219		269		319		369		419		469	
20		70		120		170		220		270		320		370		420		470	
21		71		121		171		221		271		321		371		421		471	
22		72		122		172		222		272		322		372		422		472	
23		73		123		173		223		273		323		373		423		473	
24		74		124		174		224		274		324		374		424		474	
25		75		125		175		225		275		325		375		425		475	
26		76		126		176		226		276		326		376		426		476	
27		77		127		177		227		277		327		377		427		477	
28		78		128		178		228		278		328		378		428		478	
29		79		129		179		229		279		329		379		429		479	
30		80		130		180		230		280		330		380		430		480	
31		81		131		181		231		281		331		381		431		481	
32		82		132		182		232		282		332		382		432		482	
33		83		133		183		233		283		333		383		433		483	
34		84		134		184		234		284		334		384		434		484	
35		85		135		185		235		285		335		385		435		485	
36		86		136		186		236		286		336		386		436		486	
37		87		137		187		237		287		337		387		437		487	
38		88		138		188		238		288		338		388		438		488	
39		89		139		189		239		289		339		389		439		489	
40		90		140		190		240		290		340		390		440		490	
41		91		141		191		241		291		341		391		441		491	
42		92		142		192		242		292		342		392		442		492	
43		93		143		193		243		293		343		393		443		493	
44		94		144		194		244		294		344		394		444		494	
45		95		145		195		245		295		345		395		445		495	
46		96		146		196		246		296		346		396		446		496	
47		97		147		197		247		297		347		397		447		497	
48		98		148		198		248		298		348		398		448		498	
49		99		149		199		249		299		349		399		449		499	
50		100		150		200		250		300		350		400		450		500	

THE REYNOLDS & REYNOLDS CO. DAYTON OHIO   LITHO IN U. S. A.

Figure 7: Ticket Number Control Sheet

114

Customer's Name _____ Address _____

Make _____ Model _____ Year _____ Engine _____

Work Received by _____ Work Done by _____

Date In _____
Date Out _____
Billed Invoice _____

N⁰ 8501-1

Ordered	Used		Price	Ordered	Done		Operation Number	List Price
		Pistons				Power Service		
		Piston Pins				Pin Fitting and Rod Aligning		
		Piston Pin Bushings				Piston Expanding		
		Piston Rings				Cut Top Grooves		
		Connecting Rod Bearings				Recondition Rods		
		Main Bearings				Cylinder Reboring		
		Cam Bearings				Install Cylinder Sleeves		
		Timing Chain				Valve Refacing		
		Timing Gears				Valve Seats Refinished		
		Valves—Intake				Valve Seat Rings Installed		
		Valves—Exhaust				Valve Guides Installed		
		Valve Guides—Intake				Crankshaft Grinding		
		Valve Guides—Exhaust				Aline Boring		
		Valve Springs				Install Cam Bearings		
		Gaskets				Cylinder Head Grinding		
		Timing Cover Oil Seal				Brake Shoes and Bands Relined		
		Rear Main Seal				Brake Drums Ground		
						Degreasing & Check For Cracks		
						Install Pin Bushings		
						Block Grinding		
						Disassemble & Assemble		

Figure 8: Machine Shop Work Ticket

115

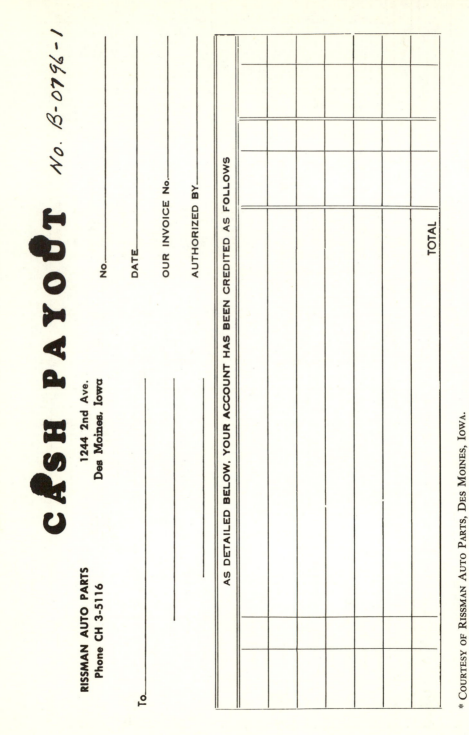

CASH PAYOUT   No. B-0796-1

RISSMAN AUTO PARTS
Phone CH 3-5116

1244 2nd Ave.
Des Moines, Iowa

To.

No.

DATE

OUR INVOICE No.

AUTHORIZED BY

AS DETAILED BELOW, YOUR ACCOUNT HAS BEEN CREDITED AS FOLLOWS

TOTAL

* COURTESY OF RISSMAN AUTO PARTS, DES MOINES, IOWA.

Figure 9: Cash Payment and Returns Ticket

PAYROLL - SALES

	Store No. 1	Store No. 2	Store No. 3	Store No. 4	Store No. 5	TOTAL	
1							1
2							2
3							3
4							4
5							5
6							6
7							7
8							8
9							9
10							10
11							11
12							12
13							13
14							14
15							15
16							16
17							17
18							18
19							19
20							20
21							21
22							22

'EYE EASE' HAMMERMILL LEDGER
18-406

Figure 10: Direct Expense, General Ledger Sheet

* COURTESY OF RISSMAN AUTO PARTS, DES MOINES, IOWA.

117

LEGAL AND ACCOUNTING

'EYE EASE HAMMERMILL LEDGER
18-406

	Store - 1 40%	Store-2 25%	Store - 3 15%	Store - 4 12%	Store - 5 8%	TOTAL
1						
2						
3						
4						
5						
6						
7						
8						
9						
10						
11						
12						
13						
14						
15						
16						
17						
18						
19						
20						
21						
22						

* COURTESY OF RISSMAN AUTO PARTS, DES MOINES, IOWA.

Figure 11: Variable Expense, General Ledger Sheet

118

Distribution of the expense should be made as shown on the Direct Expense, General Ledger Sheet (Figure 10).

There are other items such as advertising, bank charges, interest paid, legal and accounting expenses, etc., which cannot be attributed directly to each store but may be distributed on a percentage basis. The percentage may be determined by the relationship of each store's business to the total business for all stores. (See Figure 11.)

Warehouse Operation. It is sometimes desirable to maintain a warehouse separate and apart from the wholesale and retail outlets. This would require a separate company or corporation, even though both may be under the same ownership. If this is the case, the warehouse operation and accounting system, while somewhat the same as described for a multiple store system,

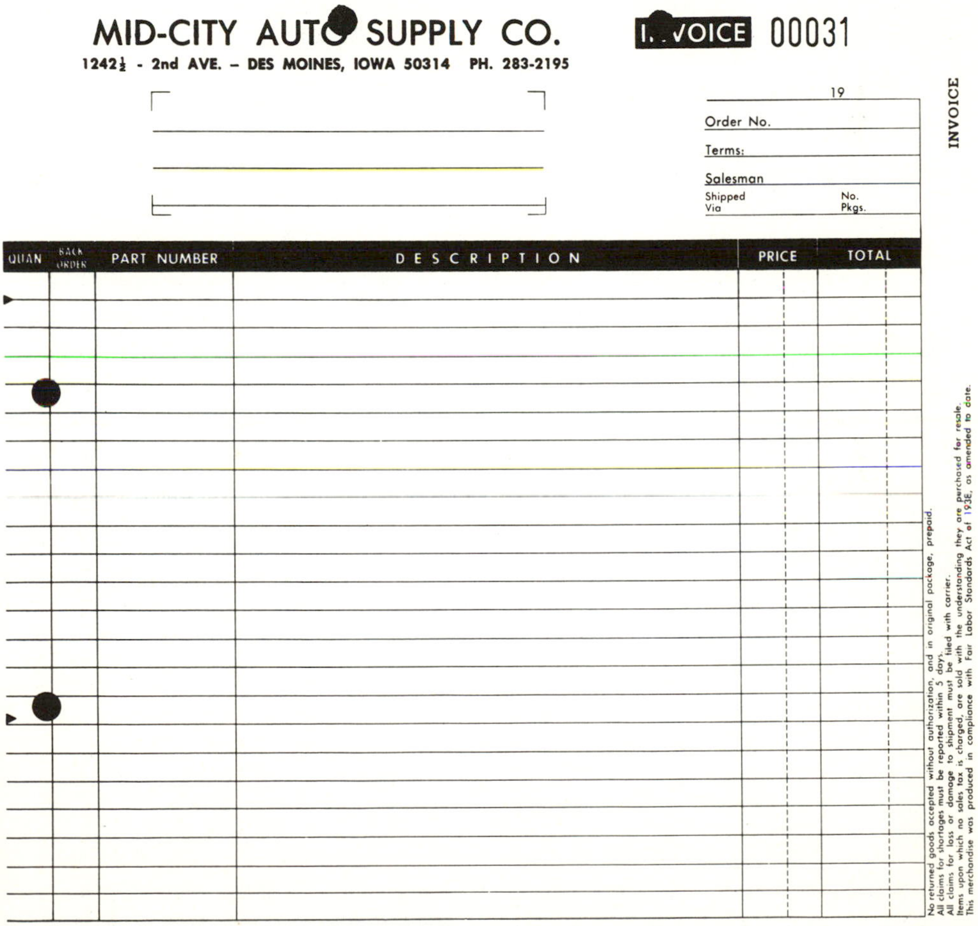

MID-CITY AUTO SUPPLY CO.

1242½ - 2nd AVE. – DES MOINES, IOWA 50314 PH. 283-2195

INVOICE 00031

19

Order No.

Terms:

Salesman

Shipped Via | No. Pkgs.

INVOICE

QUAN	BACK ORDER	PART NUMBER	DESCRIPTION	PRICE	TOTAL

No returned goods accepted without authorization, and in original package, prepaid.
All claims for shortages must be reported within 5 days.
All claims for loss or damage to shipment must be filed with carrier.
Items upon which no sales tax is charged, are sold with the understanding they are purchased for resale.
This merchandise was produced in compliance with Fair Labor Standards Act of 1938, as amended to date.

* COURTESY OF MID-CITY AUTO SUPPLY CO., DES MOINES, IOWA.

Figure 12: Warehouse Sales Invoice

should be conducted as a separate entity. Practically the same lineup of General ledger accounts may be used for the warehouse as for the auto parts store.

Charges would be made to each store on a quadruplicate form, one copy retained by the warehouse, one by the store, and two by the central office.

If a central office is used for both the warehouse and stores, one copy of the invoice (Figure 12) may serve as an Account Receivable item to the warehouse and an Account Payable item to the store concerned. Second copy would go to the Inventory Department.

With such an office arrangement, the warehouse should be billed monthly for its share of the cost of maintaining such an office.

Time and Payroll System

There are no peculiarities of procedures for payroll, other than those discussed under Time-Saving Ideas.

Time-Saving Ideas

Modern-day methods of accounting now include the data processing of financial statements and General and subsidiary ledgers. Data-processed or computerized accounting can produce almost automatically and at minimal cost information which heretofore had been prohibitive in cost and time, in a manually operated system.

If proper programming procedures have been followed, a complete profit and loss statement can be produced for *each* store showing the current month's operation and year-to-date figures. In the same operation a combined statement of profit and loss and a balance sheet can be produced.

Payroll computations, the payroll checks and quarterly reports, as well as W-2 forms, may be produced where there is a sufficient number of employees to warrant such production. Statistical information, such as gross and net profit percentages of each operation and overall percentages, are automatically produced. Inventory turnover, accounts receivable aging, and perpetual inventory records may also be produced on today's modern computers.

If a perpetual inventory is kept, slow-moving and obsolete stock can easily be recognized and corrected. Once documentation of the original source data is completed, a whole new world of information is opened up through automation.

Reports to Management

In operating a business of this type, management should require the following monthly reports: Operating statements for each store and a combined statement of all stores with percentages, a balance sheet, an accounts receivable analysis sheet for each store, a comparative sales and gross profit analysis, and a comparative inventory analysis. A cash flow or an application of funds statement should be provided at least annually.

In data processing, if so programmed, there can be a separate statement for each store and a statement of the combined operations on another sheet, all with individual percentages and month- and year-to-date figures.

In a manually operated system, a columnar work sheet of sufficient columns can show the month- and year-to-date operations of each store and a total combined operation indicating the month- and year-to-date for all stores.

One matter to which the accountant might profitably turn his attention in consultation with management is the subject of performance incentives. Store managers from whom production of sales and profits are expected must have some incentive for which to work. One possibility is a percentage based on a sales volume; another is on a gross profit basis; and a third method may be on net profit.

The net profit basis may be unfair in cases where one store may have extenuating circumstances whereby its cost of operations may be higher than another's. The manager of the one store might feel he has to work too hard to achieve the same results as a store in a more favorable position. Thus the percentage bonus on a gross profit basis may seem more fair. However, one store may have more wholesale sales, where discounts are given, than another. This would tend to decrease the percentage of gross profit.

The most simple method of incentive bonuses is based on net sales. This procedure can be set up on a volume basis, such as 1 percent on the first $3,000; 1½ percent on $4,000; 2 percent on $5,000, and so on.

Summary

Each individual is different, and his business methods are not the same as his competitor's. Therefore, the recommended system may not fit all of the auto supply stores, letter for letter; however, the system is flexible enough to be adaptable to any concern in this line of business.

With adequate controls, management will have sufficient information available to operate each store at a profit and thereby eliminate the possibility of a weak link in the chain of operation.

9

Automobile Dealers

BY FRITZ M. ANES

**Public Accountant; Consulting
Comptroller, Sunshine Motors,
Daytona Beach, Florida**

Characteristics of the Business That Affect the Accounting System

It is uniquely true that there are few lines of business in which the activities, methods of operation, and accounting procedures are so nearly standardized as in the automobile dealer industry.

This fact is due primarily to the control wielded by manufacturers of new automobiles who exercise discretion in the selection and retention of dealers who are to represent their brands. Consequently, the dealer's operational procedures are not only generally suggested or prescribed, but also constantly monitored by manufacturers' representatives in a sort of universal big brother movement to help facilitate success and to abort failure in the process of promoting the manufacturers' nationally advertised products.

On the other hand, there are some independent dealers, and many more dealing principally in used cars, who operate without any "parental" supervision or universally recommended system whatsoever. They seem to operate principally by instinct (which, if they are successful, happens to be keen).

This chapter is especially dedicated to the accountant who can benefit dealers in the first category by modifying, or those in the latter category by substantially compromising, their systems.

FUNCTIONAL CHARACTERISTICS OF THE BUSINESS

Almost every dealer in new automobiles also engages in the sale of used cars, the sale of parts at wholesale and retail, and in general auto repairs and services. Because of the amount of capital and/or financial liabilities involved in such a scope of operations, most dealers are incorporated.

Whether there is any advantage to operating on a calendar year or other fiscal period is a matter of conjecture. Even though new models of certain dealers' main lines may be introduced consistently at a certain time of the year, overall sales and service efforts are necessarily constant the year 'round.

Competition in the automotive field is so vast and keen as to warrant a chapter of itself on this subject. It is basic to say that public relations plays the most vital role in the degree of acceptance of a dealer's products. Many factors are involved, not the least of which are product appeal and availability, sales approach and trading acumen, range of prices, and terms and caliber of service rendered.

PRINCIPAL ACCOUNTING PROBLEMS

It is assumed that available financing, suitable facilities, qualified personnel, public acceptance, and volume of business are adequate for the purposes of the accounting objectives of this chapter. Thus the resourceful dealer is primarily concerned with profitability from the sales of his products, whether they be new cars, used cars, parts and service, or any combination thereof.

He need not be in doubt or resort to guessing about which price to charge for parts or service, because current parts price lists and proven labor-phase time margins are detailed in indexed guides published by all manufacturers for dealers. Only exceptional experiences to the contrary would qualify to amend these recommendations. New car prices are likewise prescribed but are variable.

Besides sales volume, the most important factor, therefore, in the profit ratio of this industry is costs. And this, as may be surmised by considering constant trade-in factors, advertising, inventory turnover, labor and administration, involves a multitude of potential "sins".

Inventory control can be a major problem, if there is either too much or too little emphasis placed on accurate cost control bookkeeping, which is ideal in principle but can border on the absurd in application. Only actual physical inventories, periodic or perpetual, are factual. Anything else is simply an estimate and should be regarded as such only.

Likewise, relation of overhead to sales can be monitored by analyzing comparable percentages and budgeting accordingly, but again with the reminder that this is dealing in estimates, which must be periodically reviewed and adjusted or allowances made for extenuating circumstances.

Functional Organization

Automobile dealerships are necessarily departmentalized. An accounting comptroller is required to supervise the maintenance of the General ledger, various journals, accounts receivable, payable and inventory controls, preparation of the firm's financial statements, and constant surveillance of the current condition and trend of dealer-financing and dealer-manufacturer relationships.

Immediately under the comptroller's supervision are as many employees as necessary to handle the typing and processing of automobile sales contracts and title transfers, the cashiering, processing of factory warranty and advertising claims, posting of Parts and Service Department sales tickets and repair orders issued, posting and billing of accounts receivable, and processing of accounts payable as well as general filing and secretarial activities.

The sales manager is responsible for a productive sales staff, effective advertising, sales promotion plans, attractive showrooms, and constant verification of values, proper operating condition, and eye appeal of all salable vehicles.

The service manager's job is probably the most demanding of all, in respect to resolving complaints and having the most frequent opportunities to promote long-range goodwill for the dealer. The service manager is responsible for the Parts Department (with a parts manager reporting to him), the mechanics, the miscellaneous servicemen, and all the shop equipment. These duties naturally embrace scheduling of all vehicle repairs, maintenance and services, plus adequate stocking and distribution of all parts and supplies.

Principles and Objectives of the Accounting System

Even a small, properly conducted dealership has several thousand dollars worth of inventory in its Parts Department, besides the equipment in its

Service Department, and easily another several thousand dollars represented in the inventory of its high variable stock of new and/or used cars. It is thus readily understandable how vital the operation of each department is to the efficiency of the dealership as a whole; and how important an adequate accounting system is to sustain a comprehensive control of activities of such an organization in its entirety.

In brief, the primary objective of a good accounting system in this type of business is to provide timely, comprehensive and departmentalized reports as nearly accurate or factually interpretive as possible. The reports must give the net result value or trend of current operations. Constant analysis and review of each department's operations are necessary to provide assurance of stability and progress, or warning of retrogression.

Classification of Accounts and Books of Accounts

Individual charts of account are available to franchised dealers from their mainline factory distributors. Deviations are usually employed only by relatively independent or more resourceful, longer established dealers who exercise the initiative to compromise or improvise to any proven, practical extent.

The chart of accounts is standard, yet somewhat modified for practical purposes of the small or medium-sized dealership. In preparation of this chapter, it is assumed that virtually all major vehicle sales contracts are financed by institutions other than the dealer, because the dealer who can finance both his dealership and his installment sales is the exception rather than the rule. The exception would warrant another chapter on the subject of dealer installment sales financing.

The account numbers in the chart correlate essentially with the recommended list of a leading national automobile manufacturer. They can be changed or expanded, depending on requirements of a particular franchiser or any data processing center.

BALANCE SHEET ACCOUNTS.

ASSETS

Current assets

100 Petty Cash
101 Cash on Hand—Clearing
102 Cash in Bank
103 Cash in Savings Accounts
106 Finance Contracts
110 Notes Receivable

111 Accounts Receivable—Parts
        and Service
112 Accounts Receivable—Vehicles
122 Factory Warranty Claims
        Receivable
123 Other Factory Receivables
125 Finance Reserve—Current
126 Marketable Securities

Inventory

130 New Cars (Make)
131 New Trucks (Make)
139 Demonstrators
140 Used Cars
141 Used Trucks
145 Other Vehicular Units
150 Parts
152 Major Accessories (Tires,
     Batteries, Radios, etc.)
154 Body and Paint Materials
156 Gas, Oil, Grease, and
     Compounds
158 Labor in Process
159 Sublet Inventory
160 Other Merchandise
171 Prepaid Insurance
175 Other Prepaids

Fixed assets

180 Land
181 Buildings and Improvements
182 Machinery and Shop
     Equipment
183 Furniture, Signs, and Office
     Equipment
188 Company and Service Vehicles
189 Leasehold and Improvements

Other assets

190 Finance Reserve—Deferred
191 Cash Value Life Insurance
193 Notes and Accounts—Officers
195 Other Assets
197 Recourse Contracts—Deferred

LIABILITIES

Current liabilities

200 Accounts Payable—Parts
201 Accounts Payable—Other
     Major
203 Prepaid Accounts Payable
     (Dr. Balance)

210 Federal Income Tax—Prior
     Years
211 State Income Tax—Prior
     Years
212 Estimated Federal Income Tax
     (Current)
213 Estimated States Income Tax
     (Current)
220 Notes Payable—New Vehicles
222 Notes Payable—Demonstrators
224 Notes Payable—Used Vehicles
227 Notes Payable—Other
230 Accommodation Exchange
232 Customer Car Deposits
235 Customer Insurance Premiums
240 Accrued and Withheld Federal
     Wage Tax
241 Accrued and Withheld State
     Wage Tax
243 Accrued Sales and Use Tax
     Payable
245 Accrued Real and Personal
     Property Taxes
250 Accrued Payroll and Com-
     missions
252 Accrued Insurance
254 Accrued Interest
256 Accrued Bonuses
259 Other Accruals

Long-term liabilities

260 Mortgages Payable
262 Notes Payable—Officers
264 Notes Payable—Other
270 Allowance for Doubtful Accounts
275 Allowance for Deferred Finance
     Reserve
277 Allowance for Deferred Recourse
     Contracts

Depreciation reserve

281 Buildings and Improvements
282 Machinery and Shop Equipment
283 Furniture, Signs, and Office
     Fixtures

288 Company and Service Vehicles
289 Amortization—Leasehold

NET WORTH

Corporate

290 Capital Stock
291 Retained Earnings
294 Dividends
299 Profit and Loss—Current

Proprietorship or partnership

290 Capital Investment
291 Partner A
292 Partner B
295 Drawing
296 Partner A
297 Partner B
299 Profit and Loss—Current

INCOME AND EXPENSE ACCOUNTS.

REVENUE

Vehicles

Sales Cost

300	400	New Car (Make)—Retail
301	401	New Car (Make)—Wholesale
302	402	New Car (Make)—Retail
303	403	New Car (Make)—Wholesale
304	404	New Car (Make)—Retail
305	405	New Car (Make)—Wholesale
310	410	New Truck (Make)—Retail
311	411	New Truck (Make)—Wholesale
312	412	New Truck (Make)—Retail
313	413	New Truck (Make)—Wholesale
315	415	Transportation and Predelivery
320	420	Used Cars—Retail
321	421	Used Cars—Wholesale
326	426	Used Trucks—Retail
327	427	Used Trucks—Wholesale

Parts and service

350	450	Parts—Wholesale
352	452	Body and Paint Materials
353	453	Parts—Counter Retail
355	455	Parts—Repair Order
356	456	Parts—Internal
357	457	Parts—Warranty Claim
358	458	Parts—Discount Earned and Allowed
359	459	Parts and Accessories Inventory Adjustment
360	460	Major Accessories
370	470	Labor—Customer
372	472	Labor—Body and Paint
374	474	Labor—Warranty Claim
376	476	Labor—Internal
378	478	Sublet Work
380	480	Lube, Gas, Oil, Compounds and Miscellaneous
390	490	Other Merchandise

Other income

500 Finance Reserve Income
505 Interest or Finance Charges
507 Insurance Commissions
512 Sale of Scrap
514 Gain or Loss on Sale of Assets
519 Other Income

EXPENSES

Variable sales expense

10 Sales Commissions and Incentives
15 Tags and Titles

16 New Car Policy Adjustments
18 Used Car Maintenance and
   Policy Adjustments

Semifixed sales expense

20 Salaries—Salesmen
23 Salaries—Sales Supervision
30 Vehicle Advertising
34 Demonstration Expense
37 Floor Plan Interest and Charges

Parts and service expense

40 Salaries—Parts
43 Salaries—Service
50 P&S Advertising, Promotion
52 Service Adjustments
54 Tools, Supplies, and Sanitation
55 Freight and Handling
   and Toll Communication
56 Company and Service Vehicle
   Expense
57 P&S Equipment Maintenance

Indirect expense

60 Salaries-Administrative
65 Employee Benefits
69 General Advertising, Promotion,
   and Travel
70 Rent or Lease

71 Depreciation—Buildings and
   Improvements
72 Insurance—Buildings
73 Taxes—Real Estate
74 Building Maintenance and
   Repairs
75 Interest—Mortgage
80 Utilities
82 Local Telephone
83 Wage Taxes
84 Personal Property Taxes
85 License Taxes and Fees
88 Insurance—General Operation
90 Office Expense including Postage
91 Legal, Audit, and Collection
92 Bad Debts (Cr. Recovered)
93 Dues and Subscriptions
94 Donations
95 Depreciation—Shop Equipment
96 Depreciation—Office and
   Showrooms
97 Maintenance—General
   Equipment
99 Salaries—Officers and Owners

Other deductions

550 Bonuses
560 Federal Income Tax
570 State Income Tax

ACCOUNTS PECULIAR TO THE BUSINESS

Finance Contracts (No. 106). A clearing account for amounts due from all financed vehicle sales contracts, its balance represents contracts on hand or in process. If all installment contracts were retained by the dealer, this account would serve as the Contracts Receivable ledger control.

Contracts sold with recourse (partially or totally guaranteed by dealer) are treated also as contingent liabilities by simultaneous, separate posting of such recourse amount in Accounts No. 197 (Deferred Recourse Contracts) and No. 277 (Allowance for Deferred Recourse Contracts). At the end of each month, the dealer must ascertain from the financial institutions carrying such contracts, how much principal of the dealer's liability has been paid. Nos. 197 and 277 would be adjusted accordingly to reflect only actual balances currently remaining on a contingent basis.

Factory Warranty Claims Receivable (No. 122). This formerly nonexistent account now has become one of the most active single accounts receivable in the average new car dealership. Recognition of the account has come about because repairs or corrections performed on new cars within a certain period of time after their sale, as covered by factory warranty policies, are compensated for by the factory.

New Cars Inventory (No. 130). This series allows for analysis into the various makes of new vehicles handled. When new vehicles are placed in demonstration service, they are retained in inventory but are transferred to No. 139 (Demonstrators). When sold, the demonstrators are credited to their respective make new vehicle sales accounts.

Sublet Inventory (No. 159). To maintain this account to proper advantage, it is necessary to keep an individual current schedule of sublet accounts payable as incurred, with the Service Department furnishing the necessary identifying references. From these references the Accounting Department can ascertain when each sublet charge has been allocated to a sales record for reconciliation purposes. To a dealer who has a considerable amount of sublet work done, this can be a major cost item and, therefore, a vital profit problem.

Finance Reserve—Current and Deferred (Nos. 125, 190, 275, 500). These accounts record the bonus rebates commonly granted by reciprocal financial institutions on contracts purchased from the dealer at what are considered favorable interest rates. The amounts are determined according to current negotiation status with the financial institutions involved. Nos. 190 and 275 represent the accumulated holdback not released by the finance companies until satisfaction of all such dealer's contracts held by them; whereas Nos. 125 and 500 are debited and credited, respectively, with that portion of the reserve earned in excess of the holdback and distributed to the dealer currently.

Accommodation Exchange (No. 230). This is a clearing account for recording balances due to be paid on cars taken in trade or repossessed, and for any other monetary obligations of a temporary suspense nature. Any balance outstanding in this account should be able to be readily reconciled.

Customer Insurance Premiums. No. 235 is credited with the portion of any insurance premiums due to the insurance underwriter and collected from customers who are sold auto or credit life insurance in connection with their purchase. Dealer's commissions on such premiums are credited to No. 507 (Insurance Commissions).

Sales Commission and Incentives. To No. 10 are allocated all the payments of compensation made to sales personnel over and above their individual, guaranteed, minimum base salaries, which are recorded in No. 20 (Salaries—Salesmen).

Tags and Titles (No. 15). In many states the dealer is required or permitted to collect from the purchaser, in addition to the sales price, the title transfer and license tag fees which are remitted to the state. This account is credited when posting the sale and debited when remittances are made. The reason is that most dealers incur the additional cost of purchasing dealer tags or title transfers as a customer accommodation, which inevitably results in an excess debit balance representing a net expense to the dealer.

New Car Policy Adjustments. No. 16 is charged with all repairs and services performed on a new car (after its sale) that are the assumed liability of the dealer, rather than of the customer, which would not be covered by the factory guarantee-warranty policy.

Used Car Policy Adjustments (No. 18). Charged here is that portion of all repairs and services performed on any used car after its sale and removal from inventory records. This is the portion that is the assumed liability of the dealer rather than the customer.

Service Adjustments. No. 52 is charged with all vehicle repair and service corrections that are caused solely by previous errors on the part of the Service or Parts Department. Unless the chief cause of such corrections is traced to defective parts, this expense item is virtually eliminated where service mechanics are employed on a flat rate job basis and not on hourly or weekly salary.

Freight and Handling (No. 55). This account is charged not only with transportation and special handling charges incurred on incoming parts orders but, for purposes of personal observation, also with phone tolls or special delivery charges incurred in processing any customer orders. The account would be credited with reimbursement of any such charges billed on dealer's sales records. (Note: Transportation charges on new vehicles are given special attention in revenue accounts Nos. 315 and 415).

Rent and Lease Expense. For financial statement and statistical comparison purposes, Nos. 70, 71, 72, 73, 74, and 75 may be grouped into a consolidated total under a general indirect expense classification titled Rent or Equivalent on summary reports.

Revenue. All operating income accounts are analyzed into Sales and Cost accounts by departments in order to project the perpetual inventory cost accounting principles that are universally acknowledged to be a requisite for self-preservation in this business.

The extent to which the dealer desires to exercise control of his inventory and costs is the determining factor in the detail of the cost accounting system. For the owners' best interests, any compromise should be limited.

BOOKS AND FORMS PECULIAR TO THE BUSINESS

Inasmuch as automotive dealerships represent a rather staunchly entrenched industry, long recognized as generally standardized, this chapter could easily be concluded simply by referring the reader at this point to any reputable printed forms and industry systems supplier such as The Reynolds and Reynolds Company, Dayton, Ohio, as a source of all the necessary reporting forms and books of account required to activate a dealership accounting system.

But if this "easy out" were chosen, you might derive no more information from this chapter than from any learned printed forms or computerized systems salesman, whose recommendations naturally would be influenced by the particular commodity he represents.

On the other hand, for purposes of comparison, it must be assumed that the reader has or will become exposed to such available standard forms and systems, in order that he may be conditioned to recognize the intent of the innovations to be discussed and thereby enabled to evaluate the extent of administering any or all of such applications.

In other words, if the following revelations do nothing but awaken the practitioner to the fact that there is still, as always, room for improvement in any existing practices, the purpose of the chapter will be fulfilled.

A chart outlining the progressive relationship of the various records necessarily employed by automotive dealerships is illustrated in Figure 1.

An examination of this chart readily discloses the required number of ledgers: (1) General, with six sections and (2) Accounts Receivable, with a control. As shown, journals required are (1) Car Sales, (2) Parts and Service Sales, (3) Receipts, and (4) Bank Deposits and Disbursements. The chart also identifies all the other principal forms and records utilized for the various phases of the dealership operation, lacking only descriptive details of their physical composition and application.

There is no problem whatsoever in securing all such descriptive details of the numerous *standard* forms currently available (including specimen copies) from any reputable printed forms publisher or systems supplier as previously mentioned. It is the prime concern of this presentation, therefore, to elaborate primarily on *modifications* of the usual standards referred to, based on actual experience of application.

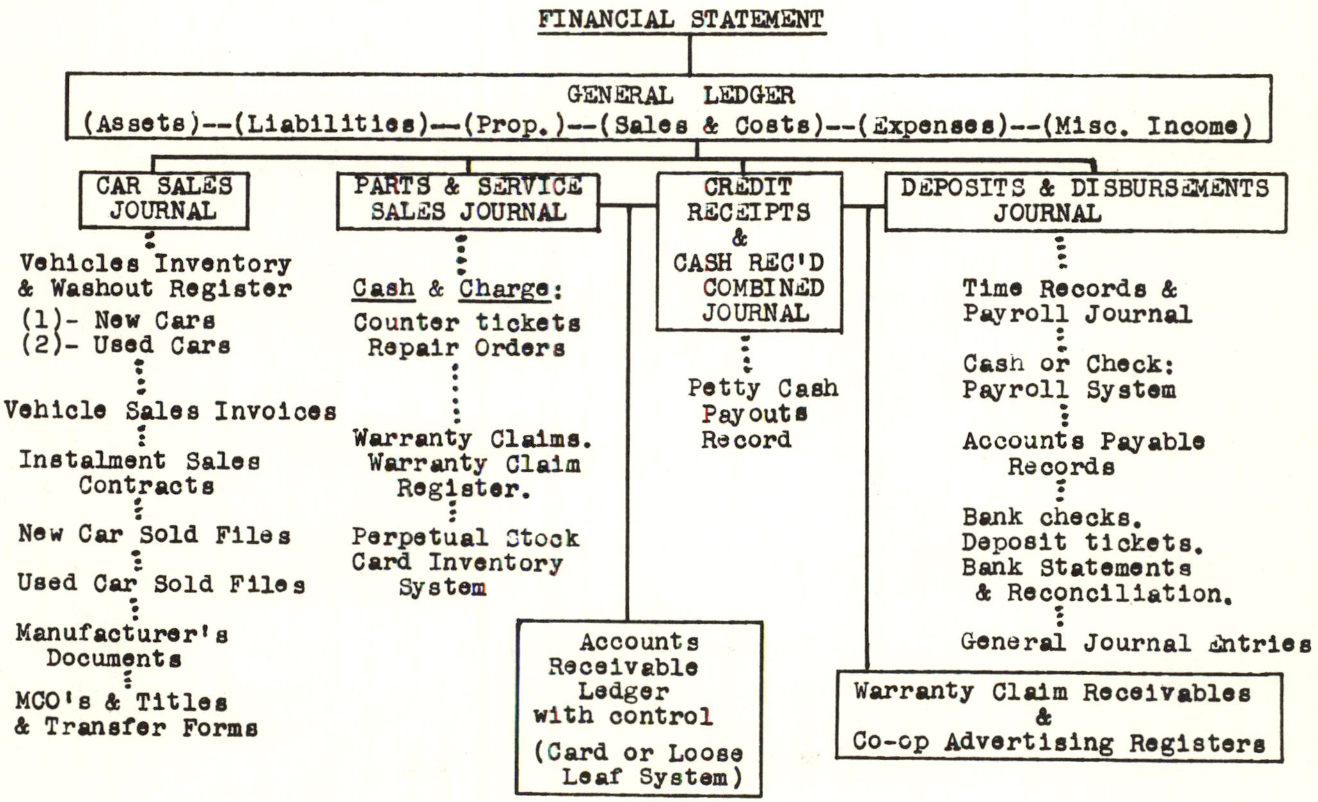

FINANCIAL STATEMENT

GENERAL LEDGER

(Assets)--(Liabilities)--(Prop.)--(Sales & Costs)--(Expenses)--(Misc. Income)

CAR SALES JOURNAL
- Vehicles Inventory & Washout Register
- (1)- New Cars
- (2)- Used Cars
- Vehicle Sales Invoices
- Instalment Sales Contracts
- New Car Sold Files
- Used Car Sold Files
- Manufacturer's Documents
- MCO's & Titles & Transfer Forms

PARTS & SERVICE SALES JOURNAL
- Cash & Charge:
- Counter tickets
- Repair Orders
- Warranty Claims. Warranty Claim Register.
- Perpetual Stock Card Inventory System

CREDIT RECEIPTS & CASH REC'D COMBINED JOURNAL
- Petty Cash Payouts Record

Accounts Receivable Ledger with control (Card or Loose Leaf System)

DEPOSITS & DISBURSEMENTS JOURNAL
- Time Records & Payroll Journal
- Cash or Check: Payroll System
- Accounts Payable Records
- Bank checks. Deposit tickets. Bank Statements & Reconciliation.
- General Journal Entries

Warranty Claim Receivables & Co-op Advertising Registers

Figure 1: Chart of Accounting System Records

It might also be pertinent to mention that the advantages of a full-line, pegboard type and/or computerized machine posting system installation for smaller dealerships is debatable. Factors to be considered in respect to their exclusive use are the initial and subsequent maintenance expense and how much of the time spent by the average manipulator of such systems is actually productive or repetitive or fumbling. In this respect, much depends on the working habits, inclinations, and disposition of the individuals responsible for the progressive accounting functions. As with all systems, some persons will be happy with those others deplore, whereas almost any intelligently designed system or combination of systems could suffice if properly applied.

VEHICLE SALES PROCESSING

One of the first subsidiary records to set up for any dealership the first of each month is a Vehicles Inventory and Washout register, preferably on letter or legal size columnar sheets in a loose-leaf binder. In the New Car register (Figure 2) and Used Car register (Figure 3) are recorded all vehicle trading activities as well as the dealer's cost of any improvements to such vehicles, as occurring and incurred during the month. At the end of each month the columns of each sheet are totaled for reconciliation with physical inventories and general books of account, and new like sheets are set up with a listing of those vehicles left on hand to start the new month.

The "washout" figure is the gross gain or loss realized as a result of any single or chain sequence transaction from the time any car is first acquired until the last car traded in on its sale is sold without another trade-in being involved. The final washout figures are then available for transfer to or comparison with any other records for reconciliation or statistical analysis. Until such washouts are finalized, they serve as a guide in the meantime for the dealer and sales personnel to tell at a glance how much effect any offer has had or will have on the profit margin of any single or combination chain of transactions.

On the completed Sales Invoice (Figure 4), the memorandum figures written in later (on the office copy only) represent the following references: 22.00 (at top right) is the salesman's commission; 96.39 is his total commission accumulated that week to date, inclusive; 2712.56 (at left) is the invoice basic cost of the new vehicle; 8-6449 (center) refers to the number of the new license tag secured for this purchaser; #5219 identifies the shop Repair Order (Figure 9) charging the $75 cost of the radar set; 2300 (center bottom) is the net amount receivable from finance institution; and #915 is the stock number assigned to the vehicle traded in.

NEW MAINLINE CARS   SEPT., (YEAR)

Date Rec'd Description	MCO in	Cost	Pd-Date Sale#-- Date	Add Chg Ref No.	Add Chgs $	Purchaser Surname	Gross Sales Price	WASHOUT & Trade-in No., if any
8/1 Helio 99H89361 2 Dr Blue		2712.56	#336-9/15 #500-9/14			White	3000.00	#905- 287.44
" Helio 99H43260 2Dr White		2712.56	265-9/7 495-9/6			Johnson	3000.00	#903- 287.44
8/15 Helio 99H9991 2 Dr red		2712.56	301-9/10 497-9/9	5219	R 75.00	Doe	3100.00	#904- 312.44
" Helio 99H9856 4 Dr red		2995.90	253-9/5 493-9/4			Smith	3333.33	#902- 337.43
" Helio 99H67321 4Dr white		2995.90	252-9/5 492-9/4	5157	R 75.00	Brown	3433.33	#901- 362.43
BEGIN SEP ON HAND		14129.48						
9/1 Helio 99H63467 2Dr red	9/10	2712.56						
" Helio 99H53892 2 Dr White	9/10	2712.56	370-9/26 507-9/25	5314	R 75.00	Grant	2900.00	/ 112.44
" Amphib 99A22678 2 Dr white	9/10	2250.90	340-9/17 502-9/16			Walker	2500.00	#906- 249.10
" Amphib 99A32613 3 Dr red	9/10	2395.50	363-9/21 505-9/20			McCormick	2750.00	#907- 354.50
" Amphib 99A33645 3 Dr blue	9/10	2395.50						
9/15 Helio 99H46732 4 Dr blue		2995.90						
" Helio 99H85762 4 Dr red		2995.90						
" Amphib 99A23111 2 Dr red		2250.90						
" Amphib 99A36789 3 Dr white		2395.50	376-9/30 509-9/29			Young	2550.00	/ 154.50
" Amphib 99A37654 3 Dr white		2395.50						
SEP PURCHASES--ADDS		25500.72			225.00			
TOTAL AVAILABLE		39630.20			225.00			
SEP SALES		23883.94	◄(Check CB)		225.00		26566.66	2457.72
END SEP & BEGIN OCT		15746.26	◄(Reconcile with inventory)				▲ (Reconcile with CS Journal plus transp. & access., less discounts)	

* COURTESY OF SUNSHINE MOTORS, DAYTONA BEACH, FLORIDA.

Figure 2: New Car Inventory and Washout Register

USED CARS   SEPT., (YEAR)

Stock No. (Circle when sold)	Description	Id. No.	Tag No.	From (Name & Inv.#)		Allowed, Plus any Prev. Add Chgs.	Prev. WASHOUT MARGIN Brt. Fwd.
(606)	Juggernaut 4 Dr	90J6541	8-1235	Jones	461	100.00	454.50
(610A)	Throwback 2 Dr	91T4567	8-3361	Archer	465	100.00	312.44
(701A)	Throwback Rdstr	89T3489	8-4512	Higby	470	100.00	216.12
703	Helio 2 Dr red	92H64591	8-9765	Watts	473	100.00	346.47
(705)	Amphib 2 Dr blue	95A43721	8-7659	Corby	475	500.00	255.44
801	Amphib 3 Dr Red	96A51117	8-5796	McDaniel	481	400.00	337.43
802	Helio 2 Dr white	97H24613	8-2228	Jordan	482	1000.00	354.50
(805)	Helio 4 Dr rd	95H74462	8-1199	Robbins	485	300.00	249.10
808	Helio 2 Dr white	96H34817	8-2178	Knowles	488	800.00	310.75
(809)	Helio 4 Dr red	97H57793	8-3561	Waters	490	1000.00	312.44
BEGIN SEPT. ON HAND						4400.00	3149.19
							362.43
901	Helio 2 Dr red	95H21159	8-5666	Brown	492	500.00	
(902)	Helio 2 Dr white	97H27543	8-5421	Smith	493	1000.00	337.43
903	Amphib 3 Dr red	95A34799	8-6769	Johnson	495	500.00	287.44
(904)	Amphib 2 Dr Blue	96A26544	8-1991	Doe	497	1000.00	312.44
(905)	Helio 4 Dr red	97H41179	8-2992	White	500	1000.00	287.44
610B	Throwback 2 Dr	90T8999	8-6556	Thackery	501	50.00	342.44
906	Amphib 2 Dr white	94A21761	8-7775	Walker	502	300.00	249.10
905A	Helio 2 Dr Blue	95H16333	8-1279	Small	504	100.00	287.44
(907)	Amphib 3 Dr Red	93A31199	8-5511	McCormick	505	100.00	354.50
				SEPT ONLY:		4550.00	2820.66
				TOTAL AVAILABLE		8950.00	5969.85
			LESS	SEPT SALES:		5200.00	3091.85
				BALANCE		3750.00	2878.00
	Plus recondition balance from opposite page					100.00	
				END SEPT & BEGIN OCT:		3850.00	2878.00

* Courtesy of Sunshine Motors, Daytona Beach, Florida.

Figure 3: Used Car Inventory and Washout Register

USED CARS - (Cont.)   SEPT., (YEAR)

Stock No.	This Mo.'s Reconditioning itemized by reference No.	Total Recon. this Mo.	Final UC Inventory Value	Sale Name &	Inv. No.	Sale Date & Price	WASHOUT (Carry fwd. if any trade-in)
606	313-100.00	100.00	200.00	Carter	498	9/10 100.00	354.50
610A	543-55.00, 566-15.00	70.00	170.00	Thackery	501	9/15 200.00	#610B- 342.44
701A	589-10.00, 592-12.00, 595-4.00	26.00	126.00	Mather	503	9/19 100.00	190.12
703		--	100.00				
705		--	500.00	Wright	506	9/24 300.00	55.44
801		--	400.00				
802		--	1000.00				
805	555-175.00	175.00	475.00	Watkins	494	9/5 400.00	174.10
808		--	800.00				
809	597-40.00	40.00	1040.00	Thorp	491	9/1 1000.00	272.44
901	572-45.00	45.00	545.00				
902		--	1000.00	Hollis	496	9/7 850.00	187.43
903	566-55.00	55.00	555.00				
904		--	1000.00	Simmons	499	9/12 800.00	112.44
905		--	1000.00	Small	504	9/20 1000.00	#905A- 287.44
610B		--	50.00				
906		--	300.00				
905A		--	100.00				
907	599-75.00	75.00	175.00	Sessions	508	9/25 100.00	279.50
SEPT TOTALS		536.00	9536.00				
SEPT SALES		486.00	5686.00			4850.00	2255.85
END SEPT & BEGIN OCT.		100.00	3850.00				

(Reconcile with Car Sales Journal)

Figure 3: Used Car Inventory and Washout Register (cont.)

In all cases of outside financing, the finance charge ($344.92 in Figure 4) may be completely ignored when posting the sales transaction in the Sales journal, because dealers do not participate in such finance charges except to the extent of any finance reserve allowance credit. Status of the latter is not computed until after the end of each month to compensate for the finance institution's credit reductions. These credit reductions are dependent upon the value of any interim prepaid or liquidated installment accounts and of which the dealer usually has no prior knowledge.

After the sale is consummated, the original invoice would pass to the

CAR INVOICE

TRIUMPH TR 4 · Jeep

SUNSHINE MOTORS
JERRY CLEM, IMPORTED CAR DEALER
112 S. Campbell St. Phone 252-3724
DAYTONA BEACH, FLORIDA 32014

Nº 993

SOLD TO: John Doe
5370 Certain Street
ADDRESS Anyplace, State

DATE 9/9/99
SALESMAN Ace
22.00 = 96.39

MAKE	YEAR	MODEL	BODY STYLE	COLOR	NEW OR USED	KEY NO.	SERIAL NUMBER	ENGINE NO.
Ford	99	Helio	2 Dr	White	New	2233	1234567	876543

2712.56 INSURANCE COVERAGE INCLUDES 8-6449
[X] FIRE AND THEFT [X] PUBLIC LIABILITY — AMT.
[X] COLLISION — AMT. DEDUCT. 100. [X] PROPERTY DAMAGE — AMT.

OPTIONAL EQUIPMENT AND ACCESSORIES

GROUP | DESCRIPTION | PRICE

Sunshine Motors A/R ---

#915

Payoff Fla. Bank -----

(99 Tag #8-1055)

2300

PRICE OF CAR	3000.00
FREIGHT AND HANDLING	
OPTIONAL EQUIP. & ACCESS.	
Radar #5219 = 75.00	100.00
SALES TAX	42.00
LICENSE AND TITLE	20.00
TOTAL CASH PRICE	3162.00
FINANCING	344.92
INSURANCE	100.00
TOTAL TIME PRICE	3606.92
SETTLEMENT:	
DEPOSIT	262.00
CASH ON DELIVERY 30 Days	100.00
USED CAR: YEAR 97 MAKE Ford	1000.00
MODEL Amphib BODY 3 Dr	(400.00)
SER. NO. 7654321	
MTR. NO. 887659	
PAYMENTS: 36 AT $ 73.47 Mo.	2644.92
AT $	
TOTAL	3606.92

NAME OF FINANCE COMPANY: Florida Natl. Bank, D.B.

FORM SA-131-C (6-63) THE REYNOLDS & REYNOLDS CO., CELINA, OHIO

* Courtesy of The Reynolds & Reynolds Company, Dayton, Ohio.

Figure 4: Vehicle Sales Invoice

purchaser, one copy serves as a permanent accounting record, and the third copy is kept with other data pertaining to the transaction in an individual file folder bearing the purchaser's name on the tab. The folders are filed alphabetically in the current year's section of a file drawer reserved for New Car Sales. A separate filing arrangement is likewise maintained for Used Car Sales transactions.

Installment sales contract forms (not illustrated) are customarily furnished by the lending institutions and will vary somewhat in text and composition according to state laws and the lender's individual policies. They will, however, bear relatively the same information as a sales invoice, plus the extra proverbial "fine print".

Processing of installment sales contracts, manufacturer's certificates or statements of origin (dealer's new car titles, commonly referred to as MCO's or MSO's), state titles, title applications, transfer forms, and supplemental manufacturers' documents requires the attention of a clerk well versed in the intricacies of the various localized technicalities involved.

JOURNALS

The most flexible area for general modification is in the composition of the four journals. The Cash Receipts Summary (Figure 5) is part of a compact, carbon-correlated, receipt-writing system that serves to provide both a receipt for the customer, with copy for departmental processing, and a journal page for the Accounting Department.

This form is used for recording all vehicle sale payments received from customers or finance institutions, and for all money received other than for cash sales of parts and service which are recorded in the Parts and Service Sales journal (Figure 6). At the end of each day's business, this Cash Receipts Summary is subtotaled. Any authorized petty cash payouts may then be listed in red as deductions in the Cash column, besides being properly extended as a debit or credit-deduction in an appropriate, corresponding account number Series column. The net result should coincide with a cash deposit in the bank.

Daily totals are carried forward from page to page until the end of the month for General ledger posting purposes.

The other three journal page headings shown in Figures 6, 7, and 8 illustrate to what extent the practitioner may deviate from the more common, available preprinted forms, most of which do not lend themselves to speed or simplicity of application, but may often sacrifice efficiency for superfluous volumes of paper space.

Each of these three key journal applications is incorporated in the simplest of available forms—loose-leaf or book-bound columnar pages (with or

DATE	RECEIPT NO.	RECEIVED FROM	Dr. #101 CASH	Cr. #111 ACCOUNTS RECEIVABLE	√	Cr. #112 Vehicle Accts. Rec.	Cr. #232 Car Deposit	Cr. #106 Finance Contrct	Dr. Under #100 Series	Dr. #100 & #200 Series	Dr. #300 #400 & #500 Series	Cr. Other Credts
1	2	3	4	5	6	7	8	9	10	11	12	13
9/9/99	900	JOHN DOE (#497)	262 00				262 00					

SUNSHINE MOTORS
IMPORTED CAR DEALER (JERRY CLEM)
112 S. Campbell Street
Telephone 252-3814   252-3724
DAYTONA BEACH, FLORIDA 32014

Nº   900

DATE	RECEIPT NO.	RECEIVED FROM	AMOUNT
9/9/99	900	JOHN DOE (#497)	$ 262 00

HOW PAID		PAID ON	
CASH	☐	ACCOUNT	☐
CHECK	☑	NOTE	☐

CAR DEPOSIT   BY _____ JC

Thank You!

FORM CDSA-508 (7-52)   THE REYNOLDS & REYNOLDS CO., CELINA, OHIO   LITHO IN U.S.A.

	TOTALS — THIS SUMMARY											
	BROUGHT FORWARD											
	FORWARD — NEW TOTALS											

FORM CDSA-1301(5-52)   THE REYNOLDS & REYNOLDS CO., CELINA, OHIO   LITHO IN U.S.

CASH RECEIPTS SUMMARY

SHEET No _____
DATE _____ 19 ___

ENTERED _____

* COURTESY OF THE REYNOLDS & REYNOLDS COMPANY, DAYTON, OHIO.

Figure 5: Cash Receipts Summary

without item spaces) that will, when opened flat, equal at least 24 columns across. Post binder sets are not recommended for use in any part of this system because of their awkwardness in handling.

The first step in setting up each of the journals is to insert the appropriate column title headings on the first and last page of any desired section or before and after any number of sheets, cutting only as much off the top of all the sheets in between the headed pages as will leave both the left and right top margin heading titles visible above all the sheets reposing in between. This will eliminate the necessity of constantly retitling column headings on individual pages.*

The headings of the various columns as shown should prove generally self-explanatory, but the cost accounting feature of the Parts and Service Sales system may warrant a little more detailed explanation.

It had long ago been deemed inadvisable from a practical standpoint to record both the selling price and cost price of each individual parts item in every transaction. Therefore, except for transactions involving vehicles and major accessories, the posting of actual cost prices is confined to purchases and inventory records; only quoted list prices and applicable discounts are used in recording sales. Experience determines the percentage of markup that should be used as a basis for constant, estimated cost accounting, subject to adjustment by periodic physical inventories. The extent of variances in the inventory adjustments will govern the extent of any further investigation into the activity of any department or operational phase.

It is assumed here that the percentages quoted have been authoritatively established as a dealership's average bases of its general parts list prices. In application, 60 percent of the total postings in column Acct. #350 (Wholesale Parts) is to be debited to account No. 450 (Cost of Wholesale Parts Sold) and credited to account No. 150 (Parts Inventory). Likewise, 60 percent of the total amounts in column Acct. #353 (Counter Parts) and #355 (Repair Order Parts) is debited to account Nos. 453 and 455 respectively, and credited to No. 150. Fifty percent of the total of column Acct. #380 is debited to account No. 480 and credited to No. 156. And if all parts used for internal (work on dealer-owned stock) are charged out at actual cost as they should be, an amount *equal* to the total of column Acct. #356 would be debited to account No. 456 and credited to No. 150. Any other material account columns' totals would be similarly handled with corresponding, summary debit and credit postings to the respective Cost of Sale and Inventory accounts.

---

* Loose-leaf binders and columnar sheets to serve this purpose are distributed by Data Management, Inc., Farmington, Connecticut.

PATENT PENDING

PARTS&SERVICE SALES		#101 Cash Clear.	#111 Accts. Rec.	Other Credits Dr.-red	(Memo) Taxable Sales	#243 Sales Tax Pay.	#458 Disc. Allowed	#350 Wholes. Parts	#353 Counter Ret.Pts.	#355 Repair Ord.Pts.	#380 Lube,Gas Oil Compounds,Misc.
Date Charge Ref. No.	Name	Dr	Dr	Cr		Cr	Dr	Cr	Cr	Cr	Cr
9/7 2501	J.Doe		32 14		31 20	94				12 00	6 70
543	UC#610A										
5219	NC-Doe										
07349	Doe-Gar.	2 28					40	2 68			
Sept. Totals		3 257 69	354 305	9 00 #519	6 409 71	1 92 53	42 70	2 29 50	8 39 85	1 946 75	2 129 5
					COSTS		{	60%= 137 70 (Dr.#450	60%= 503 91 Dr.#453	60%= 116805 Dr.#455	50%= 10648 Dr.#480) Cr.#156)

Line	Labor Cr	Labor Cr	Labor Cr	Mat'ls Cr	Parts Cr	Sublet Cr	Access. Cr	Addit. Dr	Service Dr	Policy Adjusts Dr	Invent. Addit. Dr	Policy Adjusts Dr
3	7 00					5 50						(#610A)
4		20 00			35 00						55 00	
5		15 00					60 00	75 00				
15	2519 50	750 00	324 00	157 80	251 18	277 45	360 00	225 00	215 00	100 70	586 00	100 37
18	50%=	50%=	50%=	70%=	Same:	Items:	Items:					
19	1259 75	375 00	162 00	110 46	251 18	210 15	280 00					
20	(Dr.#470	Dr.#476	Dr.#472	Dr.#452	Dr.#456	Dr.#478	Dr.#460)					
21				Cr.#154		Cr.#159	Cr.#152)					
22								RECAP	PARTS &	LABOR COSTS:		
24									137 70			
25									503 91	1259 75		
26									1168 05	375 00		
27									251 18	162 00		
28					from	Warranty	Claims	Page ---→	319 12 →	200 50		
29									2379 96	1997 25		
30									(Cr.#150)	↑		
31										(Deduct from		
32										D&D Journal		
33										Service Payroll		
34										Posting)		

 FORM G 606

* COURTESY OF DATA MANAGEMENT, INC., FARMINGTON, CONNECTICUT.

Figure 6: Parts and Service Sales Journal

PATENT PENDING

CAR SALES JOURNAL

Date	Ref. No.	Dr.#112 Acts. Rec.	Dr.#232 Car Deposits	Name	TRADE-IN Stk No.	Dr.#140 Amt.All.	Cr.#230 Payoff Exchang	Dr.#106 Finance Contr.	Cr.#243 Sales Tax Pay	Cr.#15 Tags,Titl Tags,Transf.	(Memo) Taxable Sales
9/9	993	100 00	262 00	John Doe	915	1000 00	400 00	2 300 00	FNB 42 00	20 00	2100 00
9/15	501	50 00	105 00	Wm.Thackray	610B	50 00			3 00	2 00	150.00
9/20	504		4 21 00	Robt.Small	905A	100 00		500 00	FNB 18 00	23 00	900.00
		--- SEPT. TOTALS ---	914 8 16			45 50 00	24 00 00	20,860 90	53 7 40	303 00	26,866 66
		598 00				(9 cars)					

(MEMO) Sales-man's Commiss.	USED CARS		New Mainline Cars (Disc. in red)			New Other Makes (Disc. in red)		ADDIT. OR ACCESS. Cr.#152	between Sales and cost Sales	Credit Misc. Extras	Other Credits (Dr.-red)	
	Sales	Cost	Allocat.	Sales	Cost	Sales	Cost	Cost				1
2 2 00			5000	2950 00	2 712 56			100 00	75.00	20.00	80.00 (235)	2
												3
												4
300	20000	17000										5
1800	100000	1000 00										
3151 17	4850 00	5686 00	4 5000	26216 66	23 883 94			30000	225 00	10000	40000	20
	(10 cars)			(9 cars)						(507)	(235)	21

Figure 7: Car Sales Journal

* COURTESY OF DATA MANAGEMENT, INC., FARMINGTON, CONNECTICUT.

PATENT PENDING

BANK DEPOSITS & DISBURSEMENTS	Cr.#102 Bank	Dr.#102 Bank	Cr.#101 Cash	Cr.#458 Discount Earned	DEBITS: #150 Parts	#152 152 Maj. Access.	#154 Bdy.Pnt. Mat'ls	#156 Gas,Oil Compounds	#159 Sublet
Date No. Identification									
1									
2									
3									
4									
5									
6									
7									
8									
9									
10									
11									
12									
13									
14									
15									
16									
17									
18									
19									
20									
21									
22									
23									
24									
25									
26									
27									
28									
29									
30									
31									
32									
33									
34									
35									
36									
37									
38									
39									
40									

Wage Taxes
W/H Fed.,St. #10,20,23 Compen.Tags,Titl. #15 Vehicle #80 Gen.Adv. #65 Suppl. #54 Frt & #55 300,500 Series 100,200 Series Und.100 Series All Other Credits
#99 Transf. Advert. Publ.Rel.sanlta. Handling Series
(Remittances in red)

| | 1 | 2 | 3 | 4 | 5 | 6 | 7 | 8 | 9 | 10 | 11 | 12 | 13 | 14 | 15 | 16 | 17 | 18 | 19 | 20 | 21 | 22 | 23 | 24 | 25 | 26 | 27 | 28 | 29 | 30 | 31 | 32 | 33 | 34 | 35 | 36 | 37 | 38 | 39 | 40 |

Figure 8: Deposits and Disbursements Journal

INVENTORY ACCOUNTS

Sublet Work, column account #378, and Major Acccessories entries, column account #360, should be individually identified to establish more nearly accurate cost figures to post, as they do not readily adapt to percentage application, unless the dealer has established a firm, consistent policy in all respects thereto.

Another point is deserving of mention. Depending upon the volume involved, the first page or two of each month's section in the Parts and Service Sales journal should be reserved solely for posting factory warranty claim work orders, in chronological order. They are also to be broken down into parts, labor and sublet credits, and to be charged to the respective Factory Claims Receivable accounts (Nos. 122, 122.1, 122.2, etc.).

A separate file folder and a Warranty Claim Memo register should also be maintained for each factory distributor's warranty claim copies in order to keep abreast of the status of claims pending settlement.

Totals of these warranty claim parts are also cost percentaged in the Parts and Service Sales journal recapitulation. If the factory allows as much as a 25 percent markup, 80 percent will be debited and credited respectively for cost accounting purposes.

Labor cost accounting application is no problem, especially when the mechanics are employed on a job flat-rate commission basis, as most of them are. The amount of their commission percentage is the percentage of each of the labor (including warranty labor) column totals that is debited to each column account's respective Cost account. The total of all labor costs thus debited is then subtracted from the Service Department's payroll allocation for that period, and then only the remainder of such payroll is debited to service salaries expense in the General ledger.

Even if the mechanics are not on a job flat-rate commission basis, if there is any consistency to the basis of establishing customer charges, there should be no difficulty in establishing an average labor cost percentage.

As a final commentary on the Parts and Service Sales journal, the daily total of amounts posted in its Cash Account No. 101 column (less any authorized cash payouts that may be recorded there in red and properly extended otherwise) should always equal the daily sum of cash available for deposit from that department. And it would also behoove the discriminating accountant to see that the totals of columns Acct. No. 130 (New Car Inventory additions), which usually represent major accessory installations, and Acct. No. 140 (Used Car Inventory additions), representing any repairs, added investments, or reconditioning of used cars in stock, reconcile with corresponding postings in the New and Used Car Inventory registers.

Because factory-distributor warranty claim forms vary considerably in

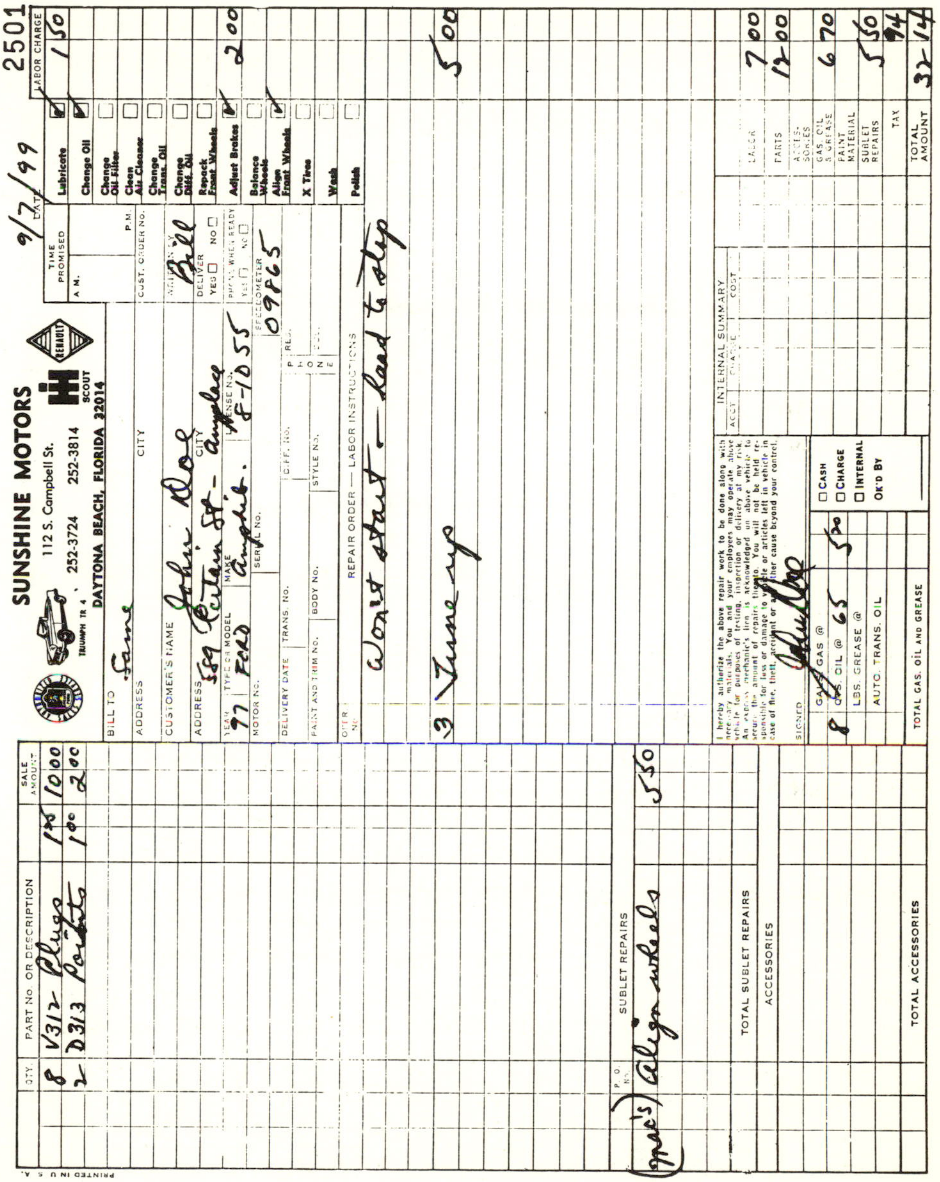

SUNSHINE MOTORS
112 S. Campbell St.
252-3724 252-3814
DAYTONA BEACH, FLORIDA 32014
TRIUMPH TR 4 SCOUT RENAULT

2501

TIME PROMISED A.M. P.M. DATE 9/7/99
CUST. ORDER NO.

BILL TO Same
ADDRESS CITY
CUSTOMER'S NAME John Doe
WRITTEN BY Bill
ADDRESS 589 Citrin St. CITY anyplace
DELIVER YES ☐ NO ☐
YEAR 77 TYPE OR MODEL Ford MAKE LICENSE NO. 8-1055
PHONE WHEN READY YES ☐ NO ☐
MOTOR NO. SERIAL NO. SPEEDOMETER 09865
DELIVERY DATE TRANS. NO. DIFF. NO. PHONE RES. BUS.
PAINT AND TRIM NO. BODY NO. STYLE NO.

OPER NO.	REPAIR ORDER — LABOR INSTRUCTIONS		LABOR CHARGE
		Lubricate ☑	1 50
		Change Oil ☑	
		Change Oil Filter ☐	
		Clean Air Cleaner ☐	
		Change Trans. Oil ☐	
		Change Diff. Oil ☐	
		Repack Front Wheels ☐	
		Adjust Brakes ☑	2 00
		Balance Wheels ☐	
		Align Front Wheels ☑	
		X Tires ☐	
		Wash ☐	
		Polish ☐	
	Won't start — hard to stop		
3	Tune up		5 00

QTY.	PART No. OR DESCRIPTION		SALE AMOUNT
8	V312 Plugs	1 25	10 00
2	D313 Points	1 00	2 00

P.O. No.	SUBLET REPAIRS	AMOUNT
(Mac's)	Align wheels	5 50
	TOTAL SUBLET REPAIRS	
	ACCESSORIES	
	TOTAL ACCESSORIES	

I hereby authorize the above repair work to be done along with necessary materials. You and your employees may operate above vehicle for purposes of testing, inspection or delivery at my risk. An express mechanic's lien is acknowledged on above vehicle to secure the amount of repairs thereto. You will not be held responsible for loss or damage to vehicle or articles left in vehicle in case of fire, theft, accident or any other cause beyond your control.

SIGNED John Doe

	GAL. GAS @	
8	QTS. OIL @ 65	5 20
	LBS. GREASE @	
	AUTO. TRANS. OIL	
	TOTAL GAS, OIL AND GREASE	

☐ CASH ☐ CHARGE ☐ INTERNAL
OK'D BY

INTERNAL SUMMARY: ACCT. CHARGE COST

LABOR	7 00
PARTS	12 00
ACCESSORIES	
GAS, OIL & GREASE	6 70
PAINT MATERIAL	
SUBLET REPAIRS	5 50
TAX	94
TOTAL AMOUNT	32 14

PRINTED IN U.S.A.

Figure 9: Repair Order

* COURTESY OF SUNSHINE MOTORS, DAYTONA BEACH, FLORIDA.

their composition and makeup according to the particular vehicle manufacturer issuing them, none is here illustrated; but the information required is basically the same as a typical Repair Order (Figure 9), plus additional details of each job's problems and solutions. Repair Orders usually consist of three copies, the third copy being constructed of a heavier manila stock (called the "hard copy"), so that it will withstand the treatment of accompanying the mechanic and vehicle being serviced until the job is completed.

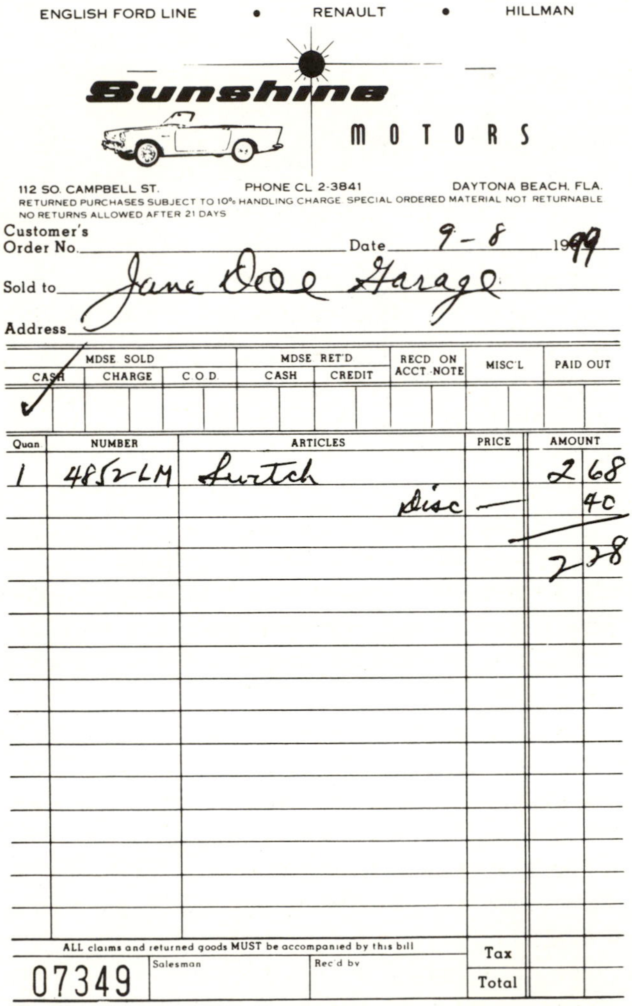
ENGLISH FORD LINE • RENAULT • HILLMAN

Sunshine MOTORS

112 SO. CAMPBELL ST. PHONE CL 2-3841 DAYTONA BEACH, FLA.
RETURNED PURCHASES SUBJECT TO 10% HANDLING CHARGE SPECIAL ORDERED MATERIAL NOT RETURNABLE
NO RETURNS ALLOWED AFTER 21 DAYS

Customer's Order No. ________ Date 9-8 19--

Sold to Jane Doe Garage

Address ________

MDSE SOLD			MDSE RET'D		RECD ON ACCT NOTE	MISC'L	PAID OUT
CASH	CHARGE	C O D	CASH	CREDIT			
✓							

Quan	NUMBER	ARTICLES	PRICE	AMOUNT
1	4852-LM	Switch		2 68
		Disc	—	40
				2 28

ALL claims and returned goods MUST be accompanied by this bill

07349 Salesman Rec'd by Tax Total

* Courtesy of Sunshine Motors, Daytona Beach, Florida.

Figure 10: Parts Counter Ticket

Besides the Repair Order, the other most common form used by the Parts and Service Department is a Parts Counter Ticket (Figure 10). These tickets are usually adequate in duplicate.

PURCHASES, PAYABLES, AND DISBURSEMENTS

Major payable accounts such as those for vehicles purchased, whether open account or floor planned, would rate individual pages in the General ledger. However, keeping detailed ledger payable pages on parts and supplies accounts is strictly optional, *provided* that an effective purchase order system is in operation and that all delivery tickets and invoices are thoroughly checked and counterchecked by responsible department personnel as received. The approved invoices may then be simply suspense-filed in segregated file folder compartments for later reconciliation with suppliers' monthly statements for payment and permanent filing.

Taped totals of the amounts represented by the reconciled Accounts Payable invoices and/or statements at the end of each month, subject to confirmation by taped totals of the respective checks issued in payment therefor, should suffice as the source by which to establish an adjusted parts and supplies inventory Accounts Payable figure each month for General ledger and financial statement purposes.

Too much emphasis may be placed on expecting a percentage or perpetual card inventory control system to be infallible, but too much emphasis can never be placed on a rigid control of inventory itself—by consistently checking all parts in and out via only certain limited-authority channels, the maintenance of a numerical control register of all (100 percent prenumbered) repair orders, counter tickets, and cash receipts, and by having serial or stock numbers physically assigned to individual major accessory items.

Three disbursement accounts warrant special attention. These are Sublet (No. 159), Vehicle Advertising (No. 30), and the varinumbered Payroll-Wages account.

Sublet charges incurred by a dealer could rapidly accumulate beyond expectations, and must therefore be closely watched to ascertain that all such liabilities are promptly and properly charged to their respective customer or internal billing accounts. Such information, whether instigated by a question or simply by spot checking, should be able to be readily verified by the purchase order system or by a separate Sublet register of charges incurred and billed by the Service Department.

As for Vehicle Advertising, a portion of certain local advertising incurred by new car dealers is often underwritten or contracted for by factory distributors, and is referred to as cooperative advertising. The extent of such reimbursed liability is determined in advance by agreement between the dealer and distributors. The various, prevalently involved formulas upon

UNISET—THE REYNOLDS & REYNOLDS CO., CELINA, OHIO—UNISET

FORM UAS 321 - WHITE
FORM UAS 321 - BUFF   PRINTED IN U.S.A.

DAILY TIME AND
JOB TICKET

EMPLOYEE'S NAME	(JOB TICKETS)	NO.		DATE

STRAIGHT TIME(HRS.)	FLAT RATE PRICE	R. O. No.	TIME	OFF	12
		EMP.NO. OPER. NO.		ON	
STRAIGHT TIME(HRS.)	FLAT RATE PRICE	R. O. No.	TIME	OFF	11
		EMP.NO. OPER. NO.		ON	
STRAIGHT TIME(HRS.)	FLAT RATE PRICE	R. O. No.	TIME	OFF	10
		EMP.NO. OPER. NO.		ON	
STRAIGHT TIME(HRS.)	FLAT RATE PRICE	R. O. No.	TIME	OFF	9
		EMP.NO. OPER. NO.		ON	
STRAIGHT TIME(HRS.)	FLAT RATE PRICE	R. O. No.	TIME	OFF	8
		EMP.NO. OPER. NO.		ON	
STRAIGHT TIME(HRS.)	FLAT RATE PRICE	R. O. No.	TIME	OFF	7
		EMP.NO. OPER. NO.		ON	
STRAIGHT TIME(HRS.)	FLAT RATE PRICE	R. O. No.	TIME	OFF	6
		EMP.NO. OPER. NO.		ON	
STRAIGHT TIME(HRS.)	FLAT RATE PRICE	R. O. No.	TIME	OFF	5
		EMP.NO. OPER. NO.		ON	
STRAIGHT TIME(HRS.)	FLAT RATE PRICE	R. O. No.	TIME	OFF	4
		EMP.NO. OPER. NO.		ON	
STRAIGHT TIME(HRS.)	FLAT RATE PRICE	R. O. No.	TIME	OFF	3
		EMP.NO. OPER. NO.		ON	
STRAIGHT TIME(HRS.)	FLAT RATE PRICE	R. O. No.	TIME	OFF	2
		EMP.NO. OPER. NO.		ON	
STRAIGHT TIME(HRS.)	FLAT RATE PRICE	R. O. No.	TIME	OFF	1
		EMP.NO. OPER. NO.		ON	

		HOUR		TIME
TOTAL	@ %	$		Flatwork or Piecework
		$		
BROUGHT FORWARD		$		
TOTAL PAY		$		

* COURTESY OF THE REYNOLDS & REYNOLDS COMPANY, DAYTON, OHIO.

Figure 11: Daily Time and Job Ticket

which such reimbursements are usually based could necessitate a special register for the purpose of keeping up with each distributor's account in this respect.

Time and Payroll System

Payroll procedure is relatively simple. Each mechanic is assigned an operator number and all repair order work is identified accordingly. Three-part, carbon-interleaved, time-and-job ticket sets (Figure 11) are provided for mechanics to complete in the process of reporting their earnings. A duplicate of each report is affixed by the gummed stub part of the time-and-job ticket to each repair order involved, for permanent record and verification by the payroll clerk.

When the payroll of all commission and salaried employees has been computed, each departmental classification is charged accordingly in the Disbursements journal, and any deductions credited at the same time. An important step to remember, though, when posting totals into the General ledger at the end of any period is that Service Salaries (No. 43) is to be debited only with that figure remaining after the cost of labor, as previously computed in the Parts and Service journal for the same period, has been deducted from the total Service Wages figure established in the Disbursements journal.

Peculiarities of Procedures

ACCOUNTS RECEIVABLE

Because of the many "one-shot" or "rare-visit" jobs that seem to prevail in any sales and service dealer's business, loose-leaf pages or file cards are recommended for use as Accounts Receivable records. Most of the problems in the Accounts Receivable field seem to stem from collections. This situation requires establishment of a firm payment terms policy as well as an individual placed in charge of administering this essential operation and capable of both vigorously and diplomatically enforcing it.

Although one function of the Deposit and Disbursements journal is to serve as a receptacle for most General journal entries, one will find it much easier to reconcile Accounts Receivable at any time if all Accounts Receivable entries have been confined to the Car Sales, Parts and Service Sales and Receipts journals. In exceptional cases, a clearing account such as Accommodation Exchange (No. 230) may be utilized to bypass a direct Accounts Receivable entry in the Disbursements journal.

It likewise will be found expedient to confine all New and Used Car

Service inventory-addition entries to the Parts and Service journal, and all whole vehicle transactions, including repossessions and dispositions to Scrap or Parts Inventory, to the Car Sales journal.

Time-Saving Ideas

There are a number of time-saving, single-writing payroll unit systems available on the market. If all payroll distributions are made by check, it is wise to contact the local bank for information on the latest combination check-journal-and-individual earnings record posting systems available. If payroll disbursements are by cash (regardless of the number of employees involved), one of the best no-carbon-required applications consists of a combination individual earnings record and double receipt for use in conjunction with the courtesy change envelopes commonly provided by banks free of charge.*

Also available are various, time-saving, combination quarterly and annual wage report forms ** which incorporate Federal and state reporting obligations into single-writing, carbon-interleaved operations.

Reports to Management

The standard financial reports which are prepared monthly are an aging schedule of outstanding Accounts Receivable such as is common to almost all businesses, and a special, combined balance sheet and departmentalized profit and loss statement.

Auto dealer financial statement forms are readily attainable from mainline factory distributors or commercial printed forms suppliers. A specimen of one of the most comprehensive and functional of these forms, as actually adapted to use by a successful, small-to-medium-sized, independent franchised dealer, is illustrated in Figure 12.

One facet of the operation represented by this particular statement deserves further discussion. It is the constant loss factor which is shown as incurred by the used car sales category. This loss application represents the more simple but perhaps least common of two lines of thought applicable to any dealership whose size or circumstances would not facilitate its Used Car Sales Department operation or management as a separate entity from its New Car Sales Department.

The "old school" method involves assessing a wholesale valuation to any used car taken in as a trade on any sale and designating as over-allowance

* Distributed by Auditmatic, Inc., P.O. Box 6034, Daytona Beach, Florida.
** Distributed by Municipal Forms & Systems Company, Inc., Durham, North Carolina.

(deductible from the gross profit otherwise realized on the sale of the original vehicle) whatever amount is allowed for the trade-in that is in excess of the assessed valuation. This method, however, requires juggling the figures on almost every sales transaction, and compounds the element of omission or errors in appraisals quoted by the Sales Department and in the computations required for posting by the Accounting Department. Yet, after all these manipulations, the final washout result or total auto sales gross profit margin figures will be the same as those arrived at by utilizing the actual figures originally recorded on the sales invoices without further ado.

The dealer who uses the actual quoted allowance method indicated by the used car loss constant principle also has discovered the psychological advantage that an inflated unit cost valuation has of implying a bargain in comparison to the asking sales price and, at the same time, of discouraging rash retail underpricing by an impetuous sales force. Such a loss treatment actually simplifies the used car sales accounting procedure, and requires inventory adjustment to an actual wholesale market basis only at the end of each fiscal year for tax purposes.

The used car inventory figure in the Assets column of the balance sheet section, however, should reflect the assessed market valuation after allowance for any adjustment. If there is any measurable fluctuation in the number of used cars remaining on hand from month's end to following month's end, it would be advisable to re-establish market valuations at the end of each month solely for inventory asset purposes.

The percentage and ratio-per-unit figures computed and shown besides sales and expense activity lines on the financial statement are the key guide lines for the analyst to observe in this business.

It will be noted that, for purposes of ready analysis and comparison, ratios-per-new-car-units-sold are utilized in lieu of percentages. This is to establish a consistent basis for interpretation, rather than to subscribe to an endlessly possible variety of hypothetical percentage theories.

Another subject of controversy is a factor commonly referred to as "service absorption". (See line 96, lower right section of Figure 12.) The formula used in determining what exact percentage of all overhead expenses is absorbed solely by the dealer's service operation varies according to various area opinions. The interpretation illustrated in this financial statement is based on Total Parts and Service Gross (line 42) vs. total overhead expense other than Vehicle Sales Expense (lines 53, 72, and 74).

The ideal percentage of "service absorption" to strive for in any respect is 100 percent, but several factors can easily prevent this. Among such factors are the extent that the Service Department marks up all charges for internal work on stock units, the amount of unrecorded time spent by service per-

REV. 67

DEALER FINANCIAL STATEMENT

FOR PERIOD OF **6** MONTHS ENDED **JUNE 30** 19____

DEALER
ADDRESS
CITY-ZONE-STATE

DEALER CODE NUMBER

Mo.____ Yr.____

BALANCE SHEET — ASSETS

			MONTH	YEAR-TO-DATE
1	CASH-PETTY-ON-HAND	100		
2	BANKS-IN TRUST	102	1218058	
3	FINANCE CONTRACTS	106	452737	
4	NOTES RECEIVABLE	110		
5	ACCOUNTS REC'BLE — VEHICLE	112	363153	
6	PARTS & SERVICE	114	769786	
7	ALLOWANCE FOR DOUBTFUL ACCTS.	270	66000( )	
8	JOBBING INCENTIVE	121		
9	MOTOR COMPANY — WARRANTY & POLICY CLAIMS	122	263677	
10	RECEIVABLES — VEHICLE HOLDBACK	123		
11	OTHER	124		
12	FINANCE CO. RECEIVABLES-CURRENT	125	52277	
13	MARKETABLE SECURITIES	126	1717728	
14	NEW VEHICLES — CAR	130	2006747	
15	TRK.	132	2673787	
16	DEMO	134		
17	USED VEHICLES — CAR	140	1004823	
18	TRK.	142		
19	PARTS	150	2666550	
20	ACCESSORIES	152	166200( )	
21	ALLOWANCE-P & A INVENTORY ADJUSTMENT	274		
22	OTHER SHOP	154		
23	MISCELLANEOUS MERCHANDISE	160	23505	
24	TOTAL PREPAIDS	170	20000	
25	TOTAL CURRENT ASSETS		1353031	
26	LAND	180	1455000	
27	BUILDINGS & — COST	181	5487888	
28	IMPROVEMENTS — DEPRECIATION	281	1938463( )	
29	EQUIPMENT — COST	186	1034559	
30	DEPRECIATION	286	449845( )	
31	LEASEHOLD & — COST	189	344603	
32	IMPROVEMENTS — AMORTIZATION	289	81006( )	
33	FINANCE CO. RECEIVABLES-DEFERRED	275	143670	
34	CASH VALUE OF LIFE INSURANCE	191		
35	NOTES & ACCTS.-OFFICERS & EMPLOYES	193		
36	OTHER ASSETS-NET	284		
37	LEASED VEHICLES-NET	195		
38	**TOTAL ASSETS**		**19531337**	

LIABILITIES

			MONTH	YEAR-TO-DATE
39	ACCOUNTS PAYABLE	200	584477	
40	CORPORATION INCOME TAX	210	300000	
41	Floor Plan — NEW VEHICLES AND DEMONSTRATORS	222	2983575	
42	USED VEHICLES	224		
43	NOTES PAYABLE — OTHER-SHORT TERM	226		
44	CURRENT PORTION-LONG TERM-OTHER	227		
45	DEPOSITS	230	40000	
46	CUSTOMER — ACCOMMODATION	232	23500	
47	SERVICE CONTRACTS	234		

NEW VEHICLES

			MONTH	YEAR-TO-DATE		PER NEW
MAIN LINE	SALES 300-1-2	01	2394800	14169405	A1	
	COST 400	02	1946064	11545138	13 RETAIL	76
	GROSS	03	448736	2624267		345,345.
SPORT	SALES300-1-2 X	04	2104900	6826434	A2	
	COST 400X		1680235	5532580	8 RETAIL	27
	GROSS	N	424665	1293854		531,479.
SPEC	SALES 300-1-2F		651480	3346330	A3	
	COST 400F	08	560180	2872647	3 RETAIL	14
	GROSS	P1	91300	474083		304,339.
	RETAIL	P2C			A4	RETAIL
	SALES300-1-2WT				D4	
	COST 400 WT				D5	RETAIL
	RETAIL				A5	RETAIL
	ALL FLEET				D6	
CAR INCENTIVES					A6	
TOTAL NEW CARS	SALES					PER NEW CAR SOLD
	PNCS 409				D7	
TOTAL NEW VEHICLES	SALES315-6-7L-M				A7	PER NEW CAR SOLD
	COST 415L-M					
Gross Pre-Dely. & Transportation:	SALES 315-6-7K		234338	1061738	A8	PER NEW
	COST 415 K		67767	437471		69 53.
	GROSS		166571	624267	A9	PER NEW
TOTAL NEW VEHICLES	SALES 315-6-75	COST	4254246	20387436	B1	PER NEW VEHICLE SOLD
	COST 3185	GROSS	313272	5016471		471,429.
USED VEHICLES	SALES 415S 418S	30:	1357300	6808525	B1	PER USED CAR RETAIL
	COST 415S 418S	24:	1578849	8126175		
TOTAL USED CARS	USED CARS RETAIL 325-327 428		(220549)	(1317650)		741(92
	USED CARS WHSL. 325-426 428	329			B2	PER USED CAR WHOLESALE
	COST 429,430				E4	
	SALES 343,345				B3	PER USED CAR SOLD
	COST 443-4-446				E3	

PARTS & SERVICE

			MONTH	YEAR-TO-DATE	B5
WHOLE-SALE	SALES 350		86120	736566	
	COST 450	GROSS	64590	552425	G2
			21530	184141	G3
JOBBING INCENTIVE	SALES 353 452		82200	500488	G6
COUNTER RETAIL	COST 453		49320	300294	
	GROSS		32880	200194	G4
SHOP	SALES 355 455		218111	1170593	B7
	COST		130867	702357	
	GROSS		87244	245089	G5
W&P CLAIMS	SALES 357 357		43636	196922	B8
	COST 462		35634	148167	G6
SHOP & COUNTER COST ACCESS.	SALES 360 460		8002	483067	B9
	GROSS		95920	348497	
			70576	134570	G7
			24444		
DISCOUNT EARNED	SALES GROSS		(1381)	(88256)	G8
TOTAL PARTS & ACCESS.	GROSS		(51706)	3047547	
CUST. REPAIR	SALES 370 470		161719	947052	67 81. C1
	COST		230064	1198764	C1
W&P CLAIMS	SALES 372		115032	599384	G9
	COST		115032	599380	
INT.	SALES 472		47835	501457	H1
	COST		23918	250729	
			23917	250728	
W&P CLAIMS	SALES 374 474		29960	181623	C3
	COST		23948	107101	H2
			5612	74522	
SUBLET REPAIRS	SALES 376 476		97420	336244	H3
	COST		94705	277309	
			2715	58935	
TOTAL LABOR	SALES GROSS		404879	2218008	C5
			147276	983565	61 84. C5
OTHER SHOP	SALES 380 481		41589	254185	H4
			19795	120594	
INT.	COST 390 396 495		21794	133591	
			35984	212856	
			35984	212856	

Total P&S Costs: 3,684,68

PARTS & SERVICE EXPENSE

			MONTH	YEAR-TO-DATE	
SALARIES — PARTS 40			85550	340600	36 29 H6
SERVICE 43			122614	685809	53 59 H7
POS ADVERTISING PROMOT.-TRAINING 50					H8
SERVICE ADJUSTMENTS					H9
TOOLS & SUPPLIES 54			17620	113764	7 3 9 7 H1

TOTAL PARTS-SERVICE-MISC.

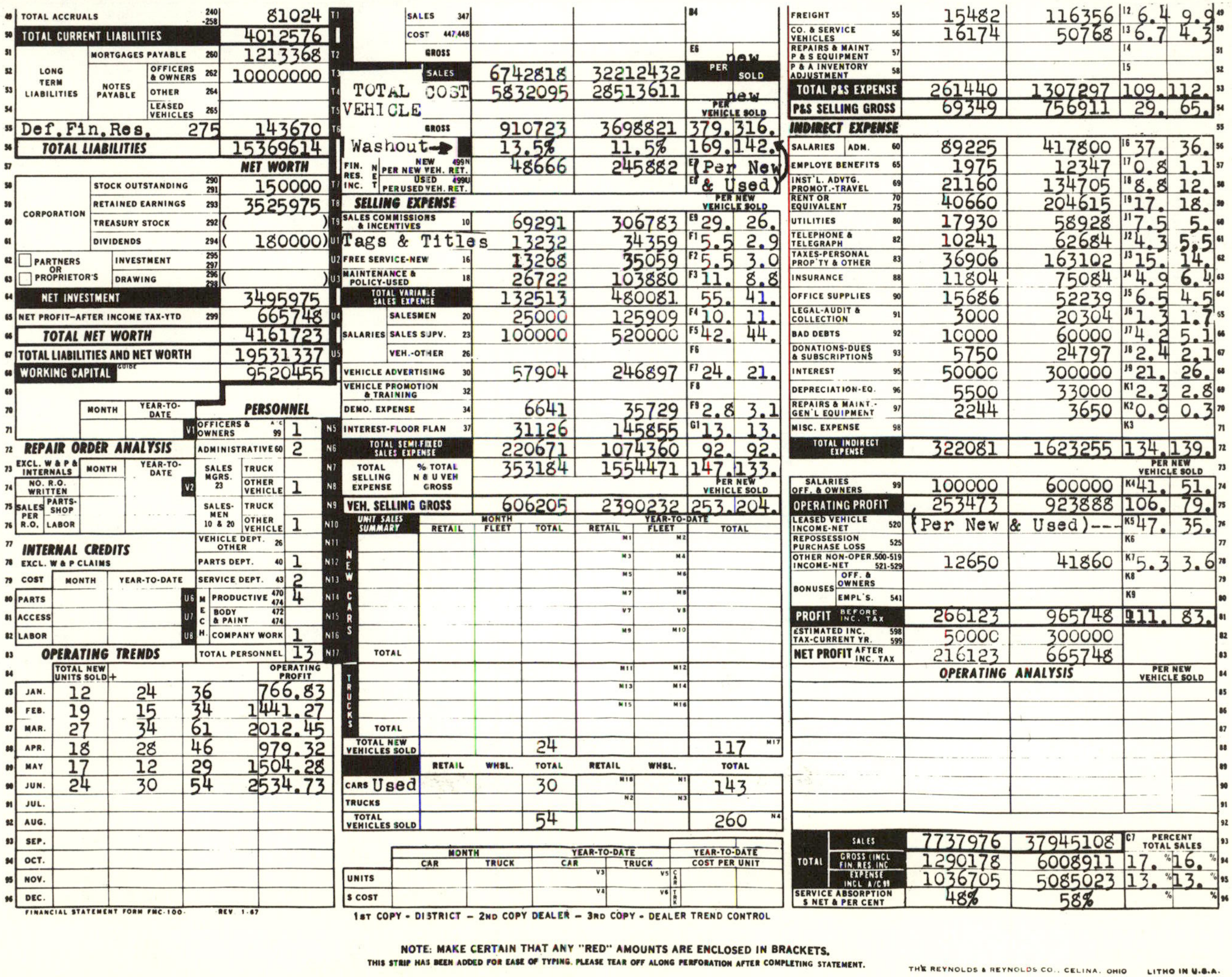

Figure 12: Dealer Financial Statement

* COURTESY OF THE REYNOLDS & REYNOLDS COMPANY, DAYTON, OHIO.

sonnel in behalf of Vehicle Sales activities, and the undetermined amount that overhead expenses would be decreased if there were *no* Vehicle Sales Department in operation. Therefore, if such deterrents are prevalent factors in a dealer's overall operation, as they commonly are, any "absorption" percentage from 50 percent up may be considered reasonable.

Summary

A review of this chapter should indicate that many facets of an automobile dealership require personal attention and constant analysis in an attempt to keep it functioning properly. An attempt has been made here to accent the highlights of such operation from an accounting standpoint, because therein lie the controls.

But just as a work of art is developed according to the talents and application of its artist, so is the effect of any function governed by the intent and ability of each individual involved.

10

Bakery Shops

BY MORRIS A. BLOOM

Certified Public Accountant and
Management Consultant,
Deal, New Jersey

Characteristics of the Business That Affect the Accounting System

Bakeries may be classified into three categories: (1) Units which bake and sell through their own distributing system, (2) Commission bakeries, which purchase from other bakeries and resell to the general public, and (3) Shops which are a combination of these two.

The ethnic composition of the neighborhood, a particular locale, and holidays and special days will act as determinants of the goods baked. Sour rye, twists, heavy pumpernickle, and hard ryes are baked only in certain areas to suit the tastes of individual religious groups. The appeals of Mother's and Father's Days, weddings, Valentine's Day, and birthdays elicit popular response and extra profit.

FUNCTIONAL CHARACTERISTICS OF THE BUSINESS

The bakery business is highly competitive, and its perishable products pose a special problem. Competition arises from other bakers, retail bakery outlets of chain stores, and "day-old, yesterday-baked" retail outlets of the chains. The owner would choose a calendar-year period if he desired industry comparisons. However, individual needs determine the fiscal period used.

The small bakery is subject to laws promulgated by boards of health and the U.S. Department of Agriculture. Milk licenses and food permits must be acquired; and mercantile and personal property taxes paid.

The trend of the future forecasts a reduction in the number of small shops which do their own baking. Increased wage rates and minimum wage scales will force many bakeries out of business. More items will be pre-packaged and ready for home freezers.

PRINCIPAL ACCOUNTING PROBLEMS

Other problems than a perishable inventory harass the proprietor of the small or medium-sized bakery. He needs adequate training in elemental business record keeping. He requires working capital to purchase on the most economical basis; often he cannot afford time-saving machinery.

He should exercise good cost control. Ingredients should not be mixed by

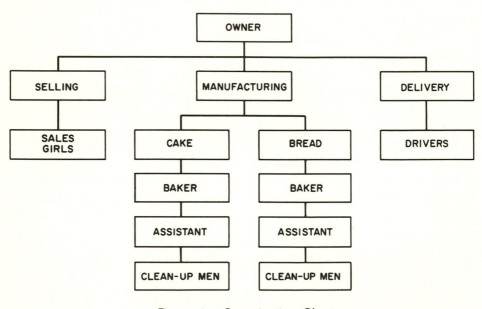

Figure 1: Organization Chart

his grandfather's rule of thumb but by a scientific method. In order to plan competently, the owner or manager should not be the principal laborer. Other problems confronting him include credit and collection policies involving wholesale customers, and improper control over plant temperature which causes a waste of power, fuel, and bakery products.

Principles and Objectives of the Accounting System

The ultimate objective of the system is to provide the owner with sufficient, easily understood, informational tools. With these tools he must be able to visualize each facet of his business, and to fuse them into an integrated whole.

Most bakeries, however, operate on a day-by-day basis. They are small and fail to take the long-range perspective. A structured, decision-making program which can be set up for them or which they can work out themselves would incorporate four plans:

1. Financial capitalization—explores sources of funds to maintain present sales level, sources of capital for new machinery or to alleviate major upheavals incidental to business cycles.

2. Production and marketing—discusses new products, new stores, or change of delivery routes and their feasibility.

3. Personnel—how changes in personnel can bring about effective and economical production.

4. Overview—a training plan to help the proprietor in learning to observe his business objectively from its past, through the present, to the predetermined future. This is the observative role; it is crucial. Has he planned to meet competition from mergers and from supermarkets?

In many cities universities are offering seminars, panel discussions, lectures, and short courses covering many phases helpful to the businessman. The Small Business Administration is doing the same. The Federal Government has a program whereby retired executives offer part-time management advisory services.

Classification of Accounts and Books of Accounts

Account titles must be brief and meaningfully arranged along the same general lines as financial statements. In this way the titles serve a cost control, informative purpose. The accounting system should be adapted to the owner's needs, with his complete acceptance of it. For medium-sized bakeries a simple cost control system is recommended. The categories used will determine the financial health of the business.

Individual accounts are similar to those found in the average cost control system. Exceptions would include such account titles as Inventory Consigned Out, Inventory Consigned In, Due to Proprietor, and Due from Proprietor.

To determine the managerial and operational ability of the owner, account numbers 101 through 120 are applied to groups of sales income accounts; 121 through 150 are assigned to production cost accounts. The latter would include Purchases, Direct Labor, Factory Utilities, Factory Supplies. Numbers 151 through 170 are relegated to a group of administrative expense accounts which serve data to management and test the efficacy of the owner's expense control ability. Numbers 171 through 200 are reserved for accounts which relate the expense experiences of the Sales Division.

BALANCE SHEET ACCOUNTS.

ASSETS

Current assets

1 Petty Cash—for cash registers
1a Petty Cash—for small expenses
2 Cash in Bank
3 Notes Receivable
4 Accounts Receivable
5 Inventory of Raw Material
6 Inventory of Work in Process
7 Inventory of Finished Goods
8 Inventory Consigned Out
9 Current Investments— Securities
10 Current Assets—Other
11 Organization Expenses
12 Prepaid Insurance
13 Prepaid Taxes
14 Prepaid Rent
15 Prepaid Assets—Other
16 Prepaid Assets—Other

Fixed assets

17 Land
18 Buildings
19 Fixtures—Store

20 Delivery Equipment
21 Factory Equipment
22 Fixed Assets—Other

LIABILITIES

Current liabilities

51 Accounts Payable
52 Notes Payable
53 Interest Payable
54 Payroll Payable
55 Taxes Payable
56 Exchanges
57 Due to Proprietor
58 Liabilities—Other
59 Accumulated Depreciation— Building
60 Accumulated Depreciation— Fixtures
61 Accumulated Depreciation— Delivery Equipment
62 Accumulated Depreciation— Factory Equipment
63 Accumulated Depreciation— Fixed Assets, Other

64 Accumulated Bad Debts
65 Accumulations—Other

Fixed Liabilities

66 Mortgage Payable

NET WORTH

67 Capital or Proprietorship
68 Drawing Account
69 Retained Earnings

INCOME AND EXPENSE ACCOUNTS.
SALES, COSTS, AND EXPENSES

101 Sales to Retail Customers
102 Sales to Wholesale Customers
103 Sales to Other Sources
104 Returns from Customers

COST OF PRODUCTION

121 Purchases of Raw Materials
122 Purchases of Finished Goods
123 Returns to Suppliers
124 Freight Inward
125 Factory Direct Labor
126 Factory Indirect Labor
127 Utilities—Fuel for Ovens
128 Utilities—Electricity
129 Utilities—Water, Heat, Sewer
130 Provision for Depreciation—
     Bakery Building
131 Provision for Depreciation—
     Bakery Equipment
132 Bakery Supplies—Ice,
     Containers, etc.
133 Bakery Repairs—Building
134 Other Bakery Expense

ADMINISTRATIVE EXPENSES

151 Compensation of Proprietor
152 Salaries and Wages—Other
     Administrators

153 General Repairs
154 Rent (where applicable)
155 Taxes
156 Interest
157 Contributions
158 Depreciation—Office Building
159 Telephone
160 Insurance
161 Utilities—Other than appor-
     tioned to Bakery
162 Legal and Audit
163 Other Administration Expense
165 Travel and Entertainment

SALES EXPENSES

171 Salaries of Salesmen
172 Salaries of Drivers
173 Rent (where applicable)
174 Taxes on Sales Salaries
175 Mercantile Licenses and Permits
176 Advertising and Promotion
177 Truck Repairs
178 Truck—Gas, Oil, etc.
179 Provision for Depreciation—
     Store Fixtures
180 Wrapping Materials
181 Office, Postage, Stationery
182 Other Selling Expense

BOOKS AND FORMS PECULIAR TO THE BAKERY SHOP

Frequently used are Petty Cash books (Figure 2) containing columns for yeast, eggs, and other bakery products purchases as well as ice and shop supplies.

A Voucher-Register/Purchase Record book (Figure 3) with headings for merchandise, shop supplies, and utilities is prevalently used.

PC-I			PETTY CASH BOOK			MONTH OF____ 19 ___		
DATE	TO WHOM PAID	AMOUNT PAID	BAKERY PRODUCTS	BAKERY SUPPLIES	CLEANING SUPPLIES	DELIVERY	OTHER ITEMS	AMOUNT
			YEAST EGGS	BAGS TWINE	MOPS PAILS	GAS OIL	CHARITY JOURNAL	

Figure 2: Petty Cash Book

PJ-I			PURCHASE BOOK			MONTH OF____ 19 ___		
DATE	FROM WHOM PURCHASED	ACCOUNTS PAYABLE CREDIT	MERCHDSE	BAKERY SUPPLIES	OTHER SUPPLIES	UTILIT	OTHER ITEMS	AMOUNT
			FOODS FLOUR EGGS SHORTNG	CONTAINER	WIPNG RAGS			

Figure 3: Voucher Register/Purchase Record

Recommended also are a Check Disbursement journal and a Cash Receivable/Sales journal resembling those used in other businesses, with inherent simple cost control mechanisms. The headings are quite the same, except that the books may be departmentalized for effective retail and wholesale data distribution.

It should be noted that often carload lots of sugar and flour are contracted for far in advance. The sight draft is frequently the instrument of financial settlement.

CR - I			CASH RECEIPTS BOOK					MONTH OF_____ 19 ___	
			RECEIPTS RETAIL		RECEIPTS WHOLESALE		DEPOSITS		
DATE	FROM WHOM REC'D	AMOUNT	STORES	ROUTE	STORES	OTHER	DATE	AMOUNT

Figure 4: Cash Receipts Book

CD - I				CASH DISBURSEMENTS BOOK			MONTH OF_____ 19 ___		GENERAL	
DATE	TO WHOM PAID	CHK #	AMOUNT	ACCOUNTS PAY DR.	GROSS PAYROLL	TAXES WITHHELD		OTHER	ITEM	AMOUNT

Figure 5: Cash Disbursements Book

ACCOUNTS PECULIAR TO THE BUSINESS

Inventory Consigned Out (No. 8) is an important component of the chart of accounts. It is also vital to the financial lifeline of the bakery business. A great portion of the office salary expenditure in many bakery entities is consumed in keeping subsidiary ledger accounts current for inventories consigned out. This is also true for inventories consigned in. The chain of retail outlets is pictured in the subsidiary ledger of consignments out. The control rests in the General ledger master account, Inventory Consigned Out. To the baker the figures in the control account determine, to a great degree, the trend of his business toward the profit he desires.

Two current asset accounts (Nos. 15 and 16) are designated as *Prepaid Assets—Other.* Such a double designation covers transactions peculiar to the bakery business. For example, when a baker seeks an off-season bargain, he may buy a large supply of paper bags at a tremendous saving. Either No. 15 or 16 would be employed in recording this transaction. Two accounts are used when a number of such transactions occur which are characteristic of the individual bakery.

Franchising has become a way of life in the U.S. economy, and its use has been rapidly increasing. Under fixed assets in the chart of accounts, an account labeled *Long-Term Asset Investment Franchise* could be placed to show that the bakery may have an investment in franchised baked goods outlets. There is no limit to the usage of the franchising idea in the bakery business.

Feeding information to a proprietor from an elaborate accounting system is, to say the least, mercurial. Very little will be meaningful or retained. It is wise to concentrate only on factual principles, such as the time-tested discovery that the greatest specific flow of dollars will be for merchandise purchases, labor, containers, and supplies in direct order. Utilities, taxes, rent, and/or depreciation will follow. Dollar containment within these areas spells healthy profits.

Peculiarities of Procedures

Bakeries which are commonly called commission bakeries should, in most instances, be termed combination commission bakeries. They often do not manufacture a full line of baked products from raw ingredients. These bakeries purchase much of the baked products in the finished state at wholesale prices for the purpose of reselling to the general public. They may have their own retail store outlets or be found in supermarkets as a counter concession. They may even have house-to-house retail routes.

Accounting methodology for these bakeries fits into a cost-of-sales format for a trading enterprise to the extent of their finished baked goods purchases. These are purchased per unit, dozen, gross, or pound. These finished goods purchases are integrated into their counterpart of goods actually baked by the owner. Separate sets of finished goods inventory book accounts often are kept for purchased goods apart from baked goods. Both accounts then are combined when total cost of goods sold is determined, and gross profit is reached.

Time and Payroll System

Time and payroll systems are similar to those used in other manufacturing firms. Straight-time rates, rather than price rates, are used. A good cake baker is a specialist. There is a great span of pay differential between his pay and that of a cake dough mixer. In many nonunion shops, employees are paid on a daily basis, which resembles more of a unit-of-work basis than an actual hourly pay system.

When a bread baker in a small bakery has produced the required number of breads for the day, his work is done and he is given the full day's pay. Wages, hours, and payroll book format are governed principally by state and Federal law. Governmental authorities are concerned with wages paid to and hours worked by women and minors.

Successful Cost Controls Must Provide Guidelines

A welter of questions bombards the baker from all sides. To shield himself from these slings and arrows of fortune and to help in eliminating them, the baker wants to know how much of each product must be produced each day to satisfy consumer demand with minimal waste, what by-products may be made and sold from leftovers, and so on. Inventory purchasing guide lines can be developed as a standard.

In cases where drivers deliver baked goods to stores and restaurants, the driver is charged for merchandise put onto his truck. He receives a duplicate delivery ticketbook. The ticket (Figure 6) shows new merchandise delivered and stale goods pick-up where permitted. When delivery is made, the restaurant owner keeps the original delivery ticket. He signs the duplicate ticket which is retained in the delivery book to be turned in to the Receiving Department at the end of the day. This department counts the returns and credits the driver for them.

The Bookkeeping Department charges and credits the individual driver for his full loads and returns. The duplicate delivery tickets become the basis for billing store and restaurant owners. A Weekly Sales Summary (Figure 7) is prepared for each customer to show deliveries and returns. (The item of Total Delivery Net is the difference between total deliveries and the total

```
┌─────────────────────────────────────────────────────┐
│                   GOOD MORNING !                      │
│                                                       │
│                 SWEET BUN BAKERY                      │
│                                                       │
│                   MAIN STREET                         │
│                                                       │
│                 YOUR TOWN, U.S.A.                     │
│   TO _____          19 __         │
│                                                       │
│   WE HAVE DELIVERED TO YOU LESS RETURNS              │
├─────────────────────────────────────────────────────┤
│              LARGE RYE                                 │
├─────────────────────────────────────────────────────┤
│              SMALL RYE                                 │
├─────────────────────────────────────────────────────┤
│              LARGE WHITE                               │
├─────────────────────────────────────────────────────┤
│              SMALL WHITE                               │
├─────────────────────────────────────────────────────┤
│              ROLLS                                     │
├─────────────────────────────────────────────────────┤
│              TWIST                                     │
├─────────────────────────────────────────────────────┤
│                                                       │
├─────────────────────────────────────────────────────┤
│                                                       │
├─────────────────────────────────────────────────────┤
│   #100              THANK YOU !                        │
└─────────────────────────────────────────────────────┘
```

Figure 6: Delivery Ticket

HONEY BUN BAKERY   WEEKLY SALES SUMMARY

CUSTOMER #   WEEK ENDING _____

	MON.		TUES.		WED.		THURS.		FRI.		SAT.		SUN.		TOTAL	UNIT	TOTAL
	DEL	RET	DEL	RET	DEL	RET	DEL	RET	DEL	RET	DEL	RET	DEL	RET	DELVD NET	PRICE	CHARGE
LG. RYE																	
SM. RYE																	
LG. WHITE																	
SM. WHITE																	
ROLLS																	
TWIST																	

FORM #   FOR INTERNAL CONTROL ONLY

Figure 7: Weekly Sales Summary

returns.) The Bookkeeping Department uses this summary to bill the customer.

An analysis of deliveries and returns for each customer is made on a control sheet, the Monthly Sales Analysis (Figure 8). By carefully observing sales to each customer and then summarizing sales to all customers by individual product, including the retail outlets owned by the proprietor, he will be able to predict his production needs for several months in advance. In time he will be able to predict quarterly, allowing for holiday fluctuations.

By converting his sales per product into the amounts of each ingredient needed to produce each and all products, purchasing needs can be determined. A proper analysis of sales, therefore, leads to proper analysis of inventory requirements. Since the inventory is perishable, items can be purchased for delivery on certain approximate dates. In this way, sufficient inventory is on hand for immediate production, but it is not large enough to cause spoilage.

Periodic physical inventories should be taken and compared with the Monthly Sales Analysis (Figure 8). Thus the proprietor may determine whether to reduce or accelerate his incoming receipts of merchandise for the next few months.

HONEY BUN BAKERY																				MONTHLY SALES ANALYSIS BY CUSTOMER AND PRODUCT CUSTOMER NUMBER		
	1	2	3	4	5	6	7	8	9	10	11	12	13	14	15	16	17	18	19	TOTAL UNITS SOLD	UNIT SALE PRICE	TOTAL DOLLAR SALES
LG. RYE																						
SM. RYE																						
LG. WHITE																						
SM. WHITE																						
ROLLS																						
TWIST																						
FORM #	FOR INTERNAL CONTROL ONLY																					

Figure 8: Monthly Sales Analysis

The best equipment to use for economy of operation and maximal utility of floor space, for best temperature control, the lowest cost per unit of production, the most rigid control over loss of weight, shrinkage, and moisture may be determined by inviting industrial equipment vendors to visit the bakery. In this way expert advice is obtained. Trade journals list each month the names and addresses of manufacturers of the finest and best bakery equipment. Moreover, there are many industrial and trade exhibits and shows in major cities. Local utility companies are helpful in giving advice on plant layout.

Inventory taking should be simplified. Flour by sacks, pastes by cans, oils by drums, yeast by poundage present few problems. Proper storage bins should be used to house nuts and chocolates. Pounds per cubic foot is a good yardstick of inventory measurement.

In the taking of inventory, experience has demonstrated that for each size container there is a certain weight of merchandise inside. For example, certain types of shortening may be purchased in a drum. If the drum measuring four feet high with a circumference of a certain number of inches contains 200 pounds of a certain ingredient, every foot of ingredient can be converted into weight. Therefore, each container can be inventoried by calculating weight per foot times unit cost per pound.

Time-Saving Ideas

In addition to the above guidelines, the ultimate in saving methods is achieved by the use of automatic equipment supervised by well-trained personnel. High-speed dough mixers feed the predetermined ingredients into molds, into ovens, and into containers. Skilled personnel are freed to supervise mixtures, assuring highest taste, color, size, and shape control. Unit cost of production is low. Greater quantities of basic ingredients per man hour of labor are produced. A good accounting system will present a graphic picture of phenomenal savings achieved. With these innovations the accountant will be able after a period of time to establish reasonably accurate standards of cost which may be used for budgetary purposes and product development.

Reports to Management

Monthly reports offered to management are centered about:
1. Balance sheets—the last two years through date.

2. Profit and loss statements—current month, year to date, and last year to date.

3. Lists of suggestions and basic reasons for ideas.

4. Budgets—where feasible.

5. Percentages of sales to specific items. Graphic illustrations of particular items are helpful.

HONEY BUN BAKERY				COMPARATIVE PROFITS BY MONTHS										
	JAN	FEB	MAR	TOTAL $	%	APR	MAY	JUNE	TOTAL $	%	HALF YEAR $	%	LAST YEAR SAME PERIOD $	%
SALES														
PURCHASES														
LABOR														
SUPPLIES														
UTILITIES														
OTHER														
TOT. FACTORY														
GROSS PROFIT														
ADMINISTRATIVE														
SELLING														
TOTAL EXPENSE														
NET PROFIT														
ADD OR SUBTR.														
EST. TAXES														
FORM #	FOR INTERNAL CONTROL ONLY												NEXT HALF YEAR ESTIMATE $	%

Figure 9: Sales and Profit Comparison Chart

Among reports to management, a tool which might be used is a Sales and Profit Comparison Chart. The purpose of using this chart is to present in dollars and percentages each main item which has a bearing on net profits. This is presented monthly and is kept on a cumulative basis. Often the proprietor has a wall chart with pins showing each additional sales outlet or an increase in dollar volume of sales. The comparison chart gives a concrete picture of the most important parts of the business. On one chart could be presented the sought-for goal in percentages. Another chart could present the actual figures. Often the accountant inserts the ideal percentages just over the actual.

The overall guidelines previously suggested will present management with goals and yardsticks to measure achievement and evaluate managerial thinking. When the accountant acts as consultant to the proprietor, consideration should be given to the following:

1. Identify the personal and business objective of the proprietor. Is he qualified?

2. Develop optimal patterns for overall business success. Can he perform?

3. Eliminate all past nonproductive lines. Are competitors doing the same?

4. Analyze successful areas periodically.

5. List sets of rules for all departments.

6. Secure benefits of trade associations and journals.

11

Beauty Shops

BY JEAN YOTT
Accountant, Detroit, Michigan

Characteristics of the Business That Affect the Accounting System

Human desire to appear at one's best is as old as time itself. There is an inherent desire within all of us to be well groomed, either for our own satisfaction or for others'. We even find this characteristic in the animal kingdom—witness Tabby hard at work with her tongue, Polly preening her wings, the pride of an American saddlebred horse, glossy mane and tail braided with colorful ribbons, as he enters the show ring.

Beauty shops or beauty treatments have always been a part of our culture; in fact, archeologists' findings reveal that precivilization men and women enjoyed the benefits of some form of beauty shop. Few businesses in the world can be assured of such perpetuity; beauty shops are omnipresent and as eternal as the human race. Beauticians have a heritage unique in history and not found in any other professions.

173

The impact of a "hair-do" administered by an expert beautician has a positive pyschological effect on milady, restoring or amplifying self-confidence. An incident witnessed by the author in a war plant a few years ago illustrates this statement. A competent woman engineer engaged in vital war work was harassed by government red tape, political job favoritism, and other war-produced irritations. She could not be dismissed but refused to work under existing conditions. Miss Engineer remained at home for a day and made a long-overdue visit to her beautician. The following day she discarded the drab uniform worn on the job, dressed in smart street clothes, presented herself in the superintendent's office, and calmly waited for his arrival. Her relaxed mind, neat apparel, and well-groomed appearance gave her the confidence needed to put across her opinions successfully. She won her point. This incident was impressive; the lesson learned has never been forgotten— not the winning of her point, but the lesson of the value of good grooming.

Among services offered by beauty salons to enhance personal grooming are shampooing and hair sets, permanents, hair straightening; hair frosting and tipping, and color rinses and dyeing; facials, manicures, pedicures, etc. Not only women, but men and children are recipients of these services. Sales of various items such as creams, hairnets, manicure supplies, and hair ornaments are merely a sideline and do not generally contribute materially to the profit picture.

Potential revenue from sale and servicing of wigs, wiglets, and hair pieces should not be overlooked. However, there are problems in this area to be explored. Wigs produce quite an obnoxious odor and cannot be manufactured or serviced in the same area with a beauty salon; these processes involve additional space, additional expense, additional employees. Shop owners should examine all available data on this odor problem when considering such an increase in services rendered to customers.

FUNCTIONAL CHARACTERISTICS OF THE BUSINESS

Many beauty shops make a point of catering to men customers, who prefer to make evening appointments. This source of revenue is often overlooked, especially by the smaller shops. The alert accountant will bring to the attention of his client this possible, profitable source of revenue.

Beauty shops usually operate on an appointment basis. Off-the-street business should be encouraged to fill in gaps caused by cancellations. With the proper attention, these walk-ins often become regular customers.

A beauty shop may be operated as a sole proprietorship, as a partnership, or as a corporation. In most states a cosmetologist license is required to be held by the owner or manager, and it is the responsibility of the accountant to see that there is compliance with the state law.

While there are many beauty shops in business, there is not as much competition as one would expect, a fact attributable to the very personal nature of the service supplied. Individual operators generally have their own customers who will follow their beautician should she (or he) make a change in location. A beauty shop can be likened to a joint venture.

Information obtained in the processing of Small Business Administration loans for beauty shops has disclosed, among others, the following facts: (a) Prestige shop customers object to a substitute operator when their favorite is not available. This objection may be confined to older customers. Walk-ins, of course, will not object but, if they like the operator to whom they are assigned, they will usually ask for the same one again and thus help to build a "clientele" for this particular operator. (b) In areas such as airline terminals, railroad terminals, and convention sites, there is definitely a competitive picture. Operators employed at these localities should be versatile, experienced, and as patient as Job. Transient customers patronizing these shops attempt to convey their wishes as to style, and the operator must be able to accommodate them. The selection of operators must, therefore, exclude all but the very experienced (and high priced). It has been the complaint of traveling women that the number of beauty shops in these areas does not begin to compare with the number of barbershops for men. A salon earning a reputation for satisfying customers who are transient can build a highly lucrative business. It is a field to consider.

Small Business Administration offices have data pertaining to these matters which are available upon request. The information varies with the geographical locations and has been compiled according to the needs of the communities.

Beauticians are both employees and independent operators. To illustrate: An operator is employed, usually on a percentage basis, and deductions are made from her pay for withholding tax, Social Security, etc. Quarterly reports are submitted to the Federal Government and to the state by her employer. The operator may bring her own special supplies and equipment if she wishes. If she supplies her own uniforms, special shoes, rollers, favorite tonics and dyes, these items, as well as attendance at seminars, conventions, and lectures, will be itemized on her personal income tax return. Tips, in excess of the amount reported to her employer, are included on her tax return as a self-employed person. The employer is responsible for Workmen's Compensation Unemployment insurance, malpractice insurance and, where a medical plan has been set up, the lump payment to the covering insurance company, regardless of whether deductions have been made from the operator's pay.

Many shops employ manicurists just for the convenience of their customers. The arrangement permits the manicurist to operate as an independent, keeping the full amount of the appointment and reimbursing management for materials used. Beauticians also enter into a booth arrangement similar to the manicurist agreement. However, the law varies in the different states as to the status of operators renting space in a shop, and thereby the relationship as outlined above between employee and employers would be waived. It is the responsibility of the accountant to check local statutes covering this situation before entering into a contract with an operator. Malpractice, public liability, and other local laws could very easily result in costly damage suits and cause failure of the business. The accountant must advise his client of these problems.

Beauty shop operation embodies characteristics not found in any other business. It is controlled by both management and operators and calls for maximum diplomacy and tact on the part of the owners and the investors.

PRINCIPAL ACCOUNTING PROBLEMS

The principal problem is control of the cash account. There are very few receivables because patrons customarily pay cash at the time of service. In addition supplies are usually purchased by cash taken from daily receipts. The cash account can become cumbersome so that frequently inaccurate data are given to the accountant.

Beauty shop inventories should be kept to a minimum because of the possibility of spoilage, the ever-changing trends in cosmetics, hair dyes, and so on. Equipment inventories often present a problem for the same reason. New types of dryers, chairs, and the changing of government safety requirements on equipment make necessary frequent turnover of equipment, with the inevitable paper work involved. The recently enacted law requiring reporting of tips to the employer has added to accounting problems and should not be overlooked by the accountant when setting a fee.

Another problem concerns the fact that rental leases often combine rent and power charges. The accountant should request that rent and power be separated so that electricity expense can be controlled. In this way a piece of faulty equipment can be spotted more readily.

Functional Organization

In many shops the owner or manager is himself an operator. With no specialized departments, all operators are presumed capable of performing the variety of services offered to customers. The only exceptions would be the manicurist arrangement previously mentioned; the receptionist or desk girl; or someone to do light cleaning (such as sweeping up hair after a haircut), washing of towels and robes, sterilizing brushes and combs (state law), serving coffee, obtaining sandwiches or other food for customers or staff. In the smaller shops, the operators and manager may double as receptionist or desk clerk. When this situation exists, friction can be avoided and a healthy communications atmosphere established, by clearly defining the following:

(a) Exact duties of the cleaning woman, or if none is employed, to what extent the operator will keep her own area clean.

(b) Whether operators with open time should sterilize brushes in order to avoid a pile-up of this work and a shortage of clean brushes.

(c) Delegation of answering the telephone in the absence of the desk girl or owner.

(d) Delegation of cashiering in absence of desk girl or owner.

(e) Policy in setting up appointments. The operator should be consulted before telephoned appointments are made for her. This is not only a courtesy but eliminates trouble stemming from an appointment which may be in conflict with previous plans of the operator.

A cosmetologist license is not easy to obtain. To date, no national cosmetology board has been formed; therefore, requirements vary from state to state. Average hours required of class work and practical application range from 1200 to 1500 in an accredited school. The course may be taken in night classes or full time during the day, as long as the required hours are credited. Cost runs from $1,000 up.

After graduation the student must take both a written and a performance examination, usually held at the state capital. These take about six hours, the written examination in the morning, practical work in the afternoon. The written test is in the nature of a true or false questionnaire and covers questions on bone structure, muscles, nerve centers, use of electricity, chemistry, workings and functions of the Board of Cosmetology, etc. The practical work requires demonstration of contour curls, pin curls, fingerwaving, rolling, permanent waving, hair styling, tinting and frosting, etc. Should the student fail the examination, she may take it again—the number of repeats varies in the different states. Once a license has been issued, it must be renewed annually. Failing this, another examination will be required. Licenses are renewed on a given date each year. Even though the first license may be issued a short time before the official expiration date, on that date it must be renewed. In addition an operator wishing to open up her own shop must prove employment as a beautician for one year prior to becoming a shop owner.

Principles and Objectives of the Accounting System

The objective of beauty shop accounting is to present a factual picture of the financial condition of the business. Reports should be prepared frequently and in more detail than usual. Operators receive a percentage of their individual gross income from appointments. Therefore, if business is slow, management will not be able to meet overhead with its percentage. It is imperative that the accountant's reports accurately reflect the profit trend before the business becomes mired in financial troubles.

Classification of Accounts and Books of Accounts

A standard chart of accounts can easily be adapted to the needs of the business. It is helpful to classify the sales record by categories of items subject to sales tax and to excise tax; by services rendered, such as hair styling, shampoos and sets, manicures, arches, facials, etc.; by products sold, e.g., wigs, hair pieces, accessories, etc. Such breakdowns will provide management with a useful analysis of the trend of operations and will also be a time saver for the accountant when preparing government reports.

BOOKS AND FORMS PECULIAR TO THE BUSINESS

There are no special forms needed for this type of business other than those discussed later. Daily appointment sheets to be used at the desk, individual charge slips used by the operators, and Check registers are all standard and can be obtained either from beauty supply houses or from stationery stores.

Journals and ledgers recommended include the Cash book, General journal, Check register, Sales journal, Payroll journal, and Accounts Payable journal. If the bookkeeper or accountant is not utilizing one of the many data processing centers, a hand-posted General ledger should be included. Data processing of the various journals automatically provides management with a printed general ledger, profit or loss statement, and balance sheet, thus eliminating the old-style General ledger.

Peculiarities of Procedures

DEPRECIATION

The usual procedures employed by an experienced accountant would be adequate for the business, with perhaps the exception of the depreciation schedules. Because of the low trade-in allowed by beauty supply houses, it is advisable to set up a high salvage value on new equipment. This procedure will protect management at the time of replacement and also in the event of dissolution of the business.

CASH BOOK

All cash received at the desk should be entered in an informal Cash book. Total of these entries at the close of the day should agree with the total of operators' sales slips and the accessory sales slips. Often the desk girl will leave before some customers are "finished". There are two ways of handling this situation. The customer can be informed that the cashier is closing out for the day and would she mind paying her bill now, or the operator may inform the cashier of the amount of the charge. A cash memo is then substituted for the cash and verified the next day.

Importance of the Cash book cannot be too strongly emphasized. Management has gratefully referred to the daily Cash book as a "scratch book" where cross-outs and erasures, informal entries, and casual notes are not out of place. The Cash book can be one of the most important and useful journals in the shop.

FRANCHISE ASSOCIATIONS

Owners of small and medium-sized shops should investigate the services offered by franchise associations. These services are a fairly recent development, born of the necessity to combat ever-rising overhead costs for individual shops—a sort of supermarket approach to the cost problem. There are several associations offering such help in the United States; they can be contacted through beautician suppliers and beauty schools. A brief outline of the mechanics of the franchise arrangement follows:

1. A shop contracting a franchise must change its business name to include the name of the association. Examples:

    (a) Shop name: "Anne's Beauty Shop"
         Association name: "Parlor of Beauty"
         change shop name to: "Anne's Parlor of Beauty"
    (b) Shop name: "Lou and Betty's"
         change shop name to: "Lou and Betty's Parlor of Beauty."

The reason for the fusion of names is that "Parlor of Beauty" is the heading under which both local and national advertising appears, with the participating shops listed as affiliates.

2. The association has the advantage of bulk purchasing of supplies, and the saving is passed onto the participating shops.

3. The association furnishes expert instructors to coach newly graduated operators, and to provide refresher courses and teach new techniques to experienced operators employed by participating shops.

4. The association publishes the latest information on new developments in the field of cosmetology and beauty shop equipment.

5. Assistance is given in obtaining operators and other personnel.

6. The association reserves the right to conduct a periodical, certified audit of affiliated shops' records.

Whether a beauty shop decides to join a franchise association depends entirely upon the individual situation. Association fees are based upon a percentage of gross income.

Among advantages of membership are that participating shops retain their independent status; are relieved of the search for competent operators; will be guaranteed delivery of supplies at a lower cost and in greater variety; in addition, advertising should bring in business, particularly customers from other localities who have become familiar with association ads; shops can keep abreast of new developments in the field; and accuracy of shop records may improve when it becomes known that an auditor will be making periodical examinations.

Time and Payroll System

Official forms for reporting tips (Figures 1 and 2), obtained from the Internal Revenue Service, should be used. They must be signed by the employee.

Standard payroll journals and individual compensation sheets practicable for beauty shops can be obtained from beauty shop supply houses. However, the Payroll journal (Figure 3) should have enough space to record tips reported to management and the amount deducted for tips. These extra columns are needed in addition to the regular deduction for Social Security and withholding taxes.

If a standard payroll check is used, there is adequate space for this information on the stub given to the employee. If payroll checks are not used, standard payroll deduction slips can be purchased in pads at any business forms store. Do not fail to provide employees with a record of their earnings

Detach along perforation and give to your employer

Form **4070** (Jan. 1966) U.S. Treasury Department Internal Revenue Service	**EMPLOYEE'S REPORT ON TIPS**	Social Security Number
Employee's name and address		
Employer's name and address		
Month or shorter period in which tips were received from ...., 19......, to ...., 19......		Amount $..............
Signature		Date

Figure 1: Employee's Report on Tips

DAILY RECORD OF TIPS

EMPLOYER'S NAME

MONTH	YEAR

Date	Tips	Date	Tips
1	$	17	$
2		18	
3		19	
4		20	
5		21	
6		22	
7		23	
8		24	
9		25	
10		26	
11		27	
12		28	
13		29	
14		30	
15		31	
16		Total $	

Form **4070A** (1–66)

Figure 2: Daily Record of Tips

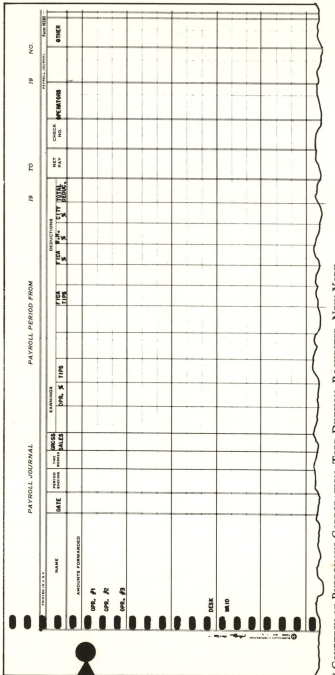

Figure 3:   Payroll Journal

and deductions. It can be a costly omission in the event of a dispute, a payroll audit, or a wage and hour investigation.

Time-Saving Ideas

A time-saving device for the accountant or the receptionist—whoever makes up the payroll—is to add a column headed "Gross Sales" (Figure 3) and enter in this column the gross amount of the appointments for each operator. Her percentage of the gross would appear in the next column as the gross pay, and deductions would be computed from that figure. Thus the Payroll journal doubles as a Sales journal, with the exception of incidental miscellaneous sales made in the shop.

Reports to Management

Beauty shop accounting is not complicated but does require more personal attention and more frequent financial reports than the average business.

In addition to balance sheet and profit and loss statement, management should receive a detailed cash flow statement and a confirmation on the accuracy of the bank statement. All cash received and cash paid out should be substantiated by petty cash slips (signed), invoices, or sales slips. A recent embezzlement case divulged how very easy it can be for dishonest persons to divert cash amounts systematically unless there is a tight control. The cash flow report should reconcile the total cash paid out plus bank deposits and any charges, with the gross income.

Another important personal report is a comparison statement of operators' earnings. This report can be compiled from the daily appointment slips (Figure 4) turned in by the operators.

The breakdown in the comparison statement should include: (a) Operators giving permanents; (b) operators giving shampoo and wave; (c) operators giving haircuts or styling; (d) those performing tinting, etc. An analysis of such a report will guide management in the consideration of hiring new employees. To illustrate: The report indicates several operators exceedingly proficient in permanent waving and who evidently prefer this type of customer. However, the report may also indicate that only one or two of the operators are servicing tinting and frosting customers, and that nearly all of them are expert stylists. A record kept to show appointments turned down because no one was available for the service requested will inform management of an uneven distribution of "talent". This information can be invaluable in hiring practices—in avoiding a "top-heavy" shop; that is, a shop with too many operators expert in just a few lines. New employees can then

Boulevard Coiffures

Name_____

Address_____

Date_____ Phone No. _____

Op.	Item	Amount	
	Hair Cut		
	Arch		
	Hair Set		
	Rinses		
	Permanent Wave		
	Manicure		
	Hair Coloring		
	Hair Treatments		

* COURTESY OF BURROUGHS CORPORATION, TODD DIVISION, ROCHESTER, NEW YORK.

Figure 4: Daily Appointment Slip

be screened to fill in the gaps. Experienced operators can be hired according to their specialty and the need of the shop. Requests for graduates from the schools can also specify any particular type of student needed most.

Conclusion

Management of a beauty shop can be challenging. Sound business practices are essential for survival; "kid glove" handling is required of operators who are not just employees but artists who can become at times temperamental and quite difficult.

There is always the possibility of an operator's "pulling out" on her own and taking her clientele with her. Management must do all possible to make the shop a pleasant and profitable place to work. Policy in this regard can mean the difference between a successful business venture and failure.

The accountant can play an essential role in assisting management to success. He must be the watchdog over government reports, renewal of licenses, factual and up-to-date financial reports, and constructive counseling. Beauty shop owners are not always the best business people in the world and usually need a little prodding to watch the recording of daily transactions so that correct reports can be prepared. There is a wide gap between the atmosphere of a beauty salon and that of the accountant's desk. It is the task of the accountant to bridge that chasm with practicality and thus offset the often happy-go-lucky or careless environment of this personal service organization.

12

Builders and Developers (Residential)

BY JAMES TEN HOEVE

Manager, Real Estate Development Division, Stephen P. Radics & Company, Certified Public Accountants, Paterson, New Jersey

Characteristics of the Business That Affect the Accounting System

Before undertaking the installation of a system or performing an audit of a builder or developer, the accountant should become acquainted with the terminology, functions, and problems of this particular business. To this end he would be wise to learn from the builder just what functions exist. These would include purchase of land, site preparation, hiring of labor and tradesmen, engaging subcontractors for specialized lines, organizing administrative and supervisory personnel, methods of buying materials, compliance with union and governmental requirements and, finally, the sales organization.

The local building supply house can be a good source of information regarding types of materials, method of billing, discounts available, and terms of payment. Furthermore, the supply house manager can also describe the types of homes popular in the area, such as one story, one and one-half story, two story, split level, and the types classified as colonial, ranch, etc., as well as the approximate cost of each.

The banker can inform the accountant of interest rates, terms of payment on percent of completion, amounts usually withheld from subcontractors, requirements to qualify for loans under the Federal Housing Administration or the Veterans Administration, and the methods they use to appraise property.

Another vital source of information is the "Residential Cost Handbook," a loose-leaf compilation of various costs classified for fair quality, average quality, and good quality. Kept up to date quarterly, the book * also provides a means of replacement cost for residential building. It explains and illustrates the square foot method and the segregated cost method as well as furnishes data of physical depreciation or functional obsolescence and many other useful suggestions. Perhaps the most important factor is the "local multiplier" that is applied on the basic costs to adjust them in relation to locality by region, state, and municipality.

The "Marshall Valuation Service" *, similar to the "Residential Cost Handbook", contains cost figures for occupancies other than residential. Of special interest to accountants are historic cost trend indexes for buildings and a number of categories of the installed equipment.

"The Accounting System for All Builders" ** was prepared by the NAHB Business Management Committee and offers a complete chart of accounts, organization chart, and many schedules for job costs, overhead expenses; land, land improvements, and indirect costs; balance sheet, profit and loss statement, and numerous basic concepts.

Another fine source is "Encyclopedia of Accounting Systems" *** which devotes 34 pages to a chapter on large-sized building contracting businesses. It offers some of the functional and asset peculiarities, principles and objectives of the system, account classification, payroll system, cost system, plant and equipment, reports to management, and other related subjects. In addition many ruled forms are illustrated such as Job Cost Ledger Sheet, Equipment Register, Cost of Construction in Progress, and others.

If the accountant reads the following system description, reviews the references above, and consults people associated with the industry, he will then be ready to approach his client and carry on intelligently a discussion of any phase of the industry.

---

* Written and published by Marshall and Stevens Publication Company, 1617 Beverly Boulevard, Los Angeles, California.
** Prepared as an industry service by the National Association of Home Builders, Washington, D.C., in cooperation with the United Gypsum Company. First printed, August 1965, in the *Journal of Homebuilding*.
*** Prentice-Hall, Inc., Englewood Cliffs, New Jersey, 1956, Vol. 1.

Building Site. In choosing a site, it is important to become familiar with local taxes, town ordinances, water and sewage regulations, road and sidewalk requirements, size of building lots, condition of land, and engineering costs.

Mass-Produced vs. Custom-Built Homes. When homes are mass produced, the developer may buy in carloads and save money. He also may have the mill precut the studs, jack studs, headers, etc., to fit the limited number of styles of homes he will build. Disadvantages of carload buying are the cost of freight, sorting, delays, misappropriation of material, necessity of carrying large inventories which may on occasion exceed the savings enjoyed by carload buying. It is possible the material may not be pre-inspected or the quality may be inferior.

For custom-built homes, the materials and workmanship must be scrutinized daily by the builder. The profit made on either type of house varies. For a custom-built house many changes and extras are requested, and on these items the contractor usually makes an additional profit.

This chapter will limit discussion to a residential builder and developer whose organization would build 25 to 50 homes a year. He will buy or accumulate raw land which will be developed into lots and upon which he will erect homes for sale. While the same accounting principles would apply to a larger organization, the procedures would be somewhat different because of the larger volume.

Because a smaller builder is often without a full office staff which would include accountants, cost estimators, and special clerical help, the accounting system must function with a minimum office complement.

FUNCTIONAL CHARACTERISTICS OF THE BUSINESS

For a builder in the northeastern, midwestern, and northwestern states, where snow and cold are factors, the normal business year from April 1 to March 31 would be ideal. Building operations usually taper off during December and practically come to a standstill between January 1 and February 15. As the weather opens up, limited operations such as excavations may begin during the latter part of February and early March. Ignoring these considerations, some builders carry on their work on a calendar-year basis.

In southern, southwestern, and southeastern states where temperate climate prevails, local conditions should be considered by the builders and developers in deciding whether a calendar year or a fiscal year should be used. Conditions other than weather may be more important in reaching such a decision.

Residential building and developing is a highly competitive industry. Accurate costs, good quality homes, and an alert sales force are mandatory for progress in this field of building.

PRINCIPAL ACCOUNTING PROBLEMS

One of these problems is inadequacy of cost records. The type of accounting system used must furnish the builder with accurate cost figures. If he builds houses on contract, his cost estimates must be conclusive before he bids. A builder on speculation develops his own tract of land and builds upon the land acquired. He will adjust his costs to accurate figures before placing the final selling price on his homes.

No builder today wants to sell homes based on a square foot or cubic foot cost. This method of estimating cost lost its popularity as homes became more sophisticated and included such things as central air conditioning, built-in vacuum cleaners, complete public address systems, and other luxury items. There are several ways of accounting for costs, but each requires a degree of responsibility by both job foremen and material suppliers. The control of materials on the job and to the job is a problem and is often supervised by the proprietor or corporate principal. These problems will be dealt with later in detail.

Functional Organization

A residential home builder's functional organization must include several departments. These need not be elaborately set up but must be comprehensive enough to include Estimating, Construction, Accounting and Clerical, Sales, and Planning. The first four are self-evident as to function. The Planning Department must schedule the accumulation of land parcels, to obtain a contiguous whole parcel. The department must also clear all legal roadblocks up to the point of getting final clearance from the local governing body for approval of the subdivision. There is nothing which prevents a smaller builder from establishing all of the above functions even though he has a small staff.

Supervision by the owner is the most economical way to operate the business. The owner will see that the materials, labor, and subcontractors will be available as needed and thus waste of time will be eliminated. Time is a major cost. Supervision is the most important element. If the owner is not familiar with construction, he should delegate supervision of the development to a construction superintendent.

It would be the construction superintendent's responsibility to make the on-the-job decisions from day to day and to maintain liaison with the owner on other matters such as materials, labor, and subcontractors.

The following phases of operation would be the Construction Division's responsibility:

1. Land preparation, test borings, leveling, and filling when necessary.

2. Excavation.

3. Foundation and concrete work.

4. Frame—deck, shell, outside trim, roof, and siding.

5. Inside—walls and ceiling (dry wall or plaster), floors, tiles, trim, doors, casings, cabinets, baseboard, closets, etc.

6. Specialties, usually subcontractors—plumbing, heating, electrical work, painting, insulation, bathroom fixtures and tile, and rug laying.

Principles and Objectives of the Accounting System

There are two primary methods of handling income and expenses, and unit costs: The cash basis and the accrual basis. A hybrid system is often used in which all receipts and disbursements are recorded as made or received (Figures 1 and 2).

In using the hybrid system a separate sheet is maintained for each job to accumulate job costs (Figure 3).

If the principal or principals feel that accumulation of costs by categories is not important to their method of operation, the cash basis of accounting may be used. Principal variation of the Cash Disbursement book (Figure 4) is that job costs will be accumulated in the records by use of the book. Additional columns may be added, depending on the number of jobs being constructed simultaneously. When this Cash Disbursement book is used, the Job Cost Sheet (Figure 3) is not necessary.

If the accrual method is preferred, an Accounts Payable book (Figure 5) will be the principal record for accumulating job costs. Distribution is made to each job by columnar distribution. If the volume of vendors' invoices is very great, the accrual method would be desirable. When this type of Accounts Payable register is used, the Cash Disbursements book (Figure 6) would be employed.

The builder should be consulted to determine whether job costs are desired in total or by categories. This will be a factor in determining which method of accounting to use. In each case, however, at the end of each fiscal period great care should be exercised to assure that all unpaid invoices are reflected on the records either by journal entry at year end or by direct entry in the Accounts Payable register.

SPECIFIC OBJECTIVES OF THE SYSTEM

The system must provide for management the costs on each job as they are being completed and must also provide the necessary data to determine if the business was run profitably during the year. The required detail to

A CORPORATION
CASH RECEIPTS

Date	Name	Amount	Customers Deposits	Notes Receivable	Contracts Receivable	Mortgage Receivable	Construction Mortgage Payable	Interest Income	Rental Income	Installment Sales Payments	Other Receipts Amount	Account
6/1	John & Mary Smith (Dep. on M.67)	$ 5,000.00	$ 5,000.00									
6/2	Ezra Brown	1,200.00		$ 1,200.00								
6/3	John Green	5,500.00			$ 5,500.00							
6/8	James White	140.50								$ 140.50		
6/9	Brown Bros (Rental of Equipment)	150.00							$ 150.00			
6/15	City National Bank	10,500.00					$10,500.00					
6/25	John & Mary Smith (Additional Dep. on M-67)	3,000.00	3,000.00									

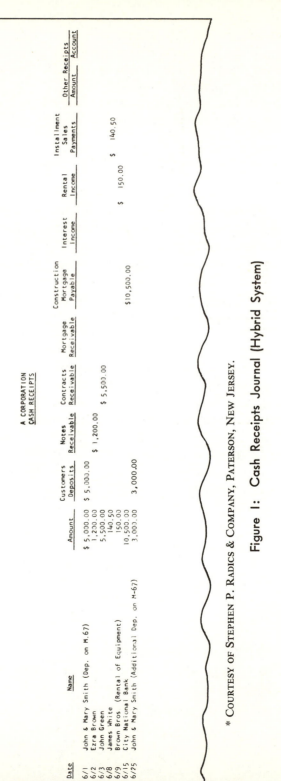

* COURTESY OF STEPHEN P. RADICS & COMPANY, PATERSON, NEW JERSEY.

Figure 1: Cash Receipts Journal (Hybrid System)

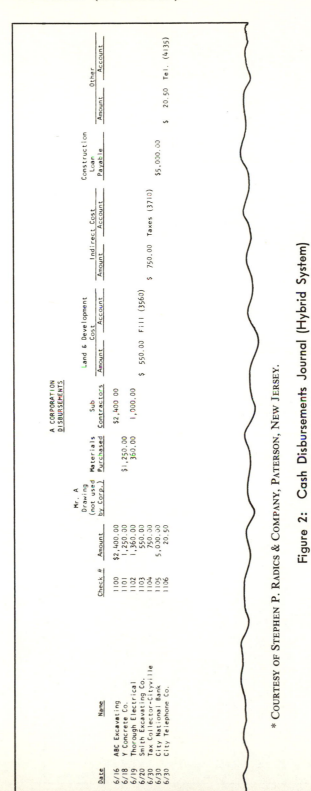

A CORPORATION
DISBURSEMENTS

Date	Name	Check #	Amount	Mr. A Drawing (not used by Corp.)	Materials Purchased	Sub Contractors	Land & Development Cost Amount	Account	Indirect Cost Amount	Account	Construction Loan Payable	Other Amount	Account
6/16	ABC Excavating	1100	$2,400.00			$2,400.00							
6/18	Y Concrete Co.	1101	1,250.00		$1,250.00								
6/19	Thorough Electrical	1102	1,360.00		360.00	1,000.00							
6/20	Smith Excavating Co.	1103	550.00				$ 550.00	Fill (3560)					
6/30	Tax Collector-Cityville	1104	750.00						$ 750.00	Taxes (3710)			
6/30	City National Bank	1105	5,000.00								$5,000.00		
6/30	City Telephone Co.	1106	20.50									$ 20.50	Tel. (4135)

* COURTESY OF STEPHEN P. RADICS & COMPANY, PATERSON, NEW JERSEY.

Figure 2: Cash Disbursements Journal (Hybrid System)

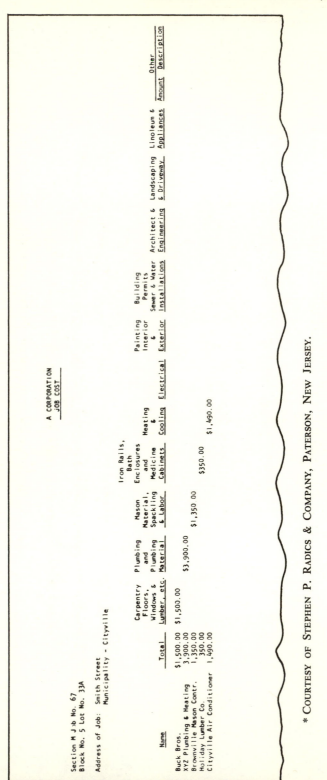

A CORPORATION
JOB COST

Section M Job No. 67
Block No. 5 Lot No. 33A

Address of Job: Smith Street
                 Municipality - Cityville

Name	Total	Carpentry Floors, Windows & Lumber, etc.	Plumbing and Plumbing Material	Mason Material, Spackling & Labor	Iron Rails, Bath Enclosures and Medicine Cabinets	Heating & Cooling	Electrical	Painting Interior & Exterior	Building Permits Sewer & Water Installations	Architect & Engineering	Landscaping & Driveway	Linoleum & Appliances	Other Amount Description
Buck Bros.	$1,500.00	$1,500.00											
XYZ Plumbing & Heating	3,900.00		$3,900.00										
Brownville Mason Contr.	1,350.00			$1,350.00									
Holiday Lumber Co.	350.00				$350.00								
Cityville Air Conditioner	1,490.00					$1,490.00							

Figure 3:   Job Costs Sheet (Hybrid System)

*COURTESY OF STEPHEN P. RADICS & COMPANY, PATERSON, NEW JERSEY.

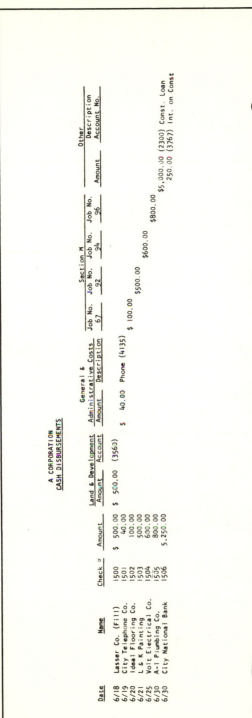

* COURTESY OF STEPHEN P. RADICS & COMPANY, PATERSON, NEW JERSEY.

Figure 4: Cash Disbursements Journal (Cash System)

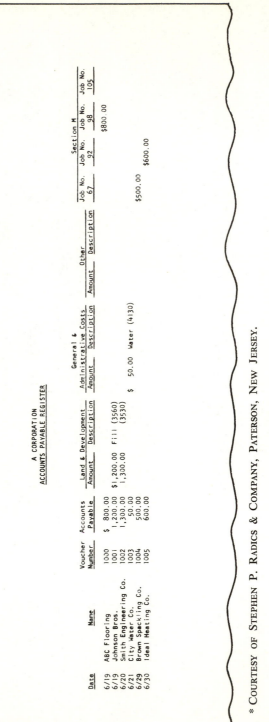

A CORPORATION
ACCOUNTS PAYABLE REGISTER

Date	Name	Voucher Number	Accounts Payable	Land & Development Amount	Description	General & Administrative Costs Amount	Description	Other Amount	Description	Section M Job No. 67	Job No. 92	Job No. 98	Job No. 105
6/19	ABC Flooring	1000	$ 800.00									$800.00	
6/19	Johnson Bros.	1001	1,200.00	$1,200.00	Fill (3560)								
6/20	Smith Engineering Co.	1002	1,300.00	1,300.00	(3530)								
6/21	City Water Co.	1003	50.00			$ 50.00	Water (4130)						
6/29	Brown Spackling Co.	1004	500.00							$500.00			
6/30	Ideal Heating Co.	1005	600.00								$600.00		

Figure 5: Accounts Payable Register (Accrual System)

* COURTESY OF STEPHEN P. RADICS & COMPANY, PATERSON, NEW JERSEY.

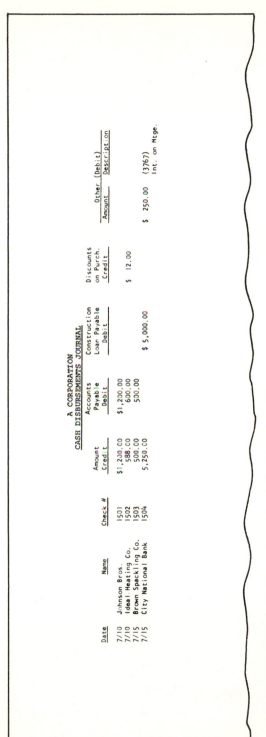

A CORPORATION
CASH DISBURSEMENTS JOURNAL

Date	Name	Check #	Amount Credit	Accounts Payable Debit	Construction Loan Payable Debit	Discounts on Purch. Credit	Other (Debit) Amount	Description
7/10	Johnson Bros.	1501	$1,200.00	$1,200.00				
7/10	Ideal Heating Co.	1502	588.00	600.00		$ 12.00		
7/15	Brown Spackling Co.	1503	500.00	500.00				
7/15	City National Bank	1504	5,250.00		$ 5,000.00		$ 250.00	(3767) Int. on Mtge.

Figure 6: Cash Disbursements Journal (Accrual System)

* COURTESY OF STEPHEN P. RADICS & COMPANY, PATERSON, NEW JERSEY.

prepare income tax returns, whether Schedule C or a corporate return, must also be forthcoming from the accounting records.

Control and detail of man hours utilized on each job must be provided by the foreman. He should record any transfer of material from one job to another after its initial delivery so the proper cost is allocated to each job.

As in all accounting systems, great emphasis must be placed on accuracy of information given to the Accounting Department or public accountant.

Classification of Accounts and Books of Accounts

The chart of accounts for the residential builder and developer may of course be modified to fit each client's particular situation. In addition, if a system is so extensive that the client cannot understand it easily, then the accountant must consolidate the accounts under fewer classifications. For small developers and in areas where good bookkeepers are scarce, the following four classifications have been used successfully: Cost of material, cost of labor, other related costs and expenses, and overhead. This is simple, understandable, and yet sufficient and to the purpose. When the accountant performs his audit and prepares the financial statements, he may at that time further analyze some of the important expenditures and present them under special schedules or exhibits.

BALANCE SHEET ACCOUNTS.

ASSETS

Current assets

1000 Cash—Checking Account
1010 Cash—Trustee Account
1015 Petty Cash
1100 Investments—Bank Certificates of Deposit
1110 Stocks

Receivables

1210 Mortgages Receivable
1220 Contracts Receivable
1230 Notes Receivable
1250 Accrued Interest Receivable

Inventories

1260 Land—Improved Subdivisions or Lots
1265 Construction in Progress
1270 Material—Unused and Unassigned
1275 Unimproved Land (Raw Acreage or nonsubdivided)

Prepaid assets

1350 Prepaid Insurance
1360 Prepaid Taxes
1370 Prepaid Interest

Fixed assets

1410 Trucks and Autos
1419 Accumulated Depreciation
1420 Construction Machinery
1429 Accumulated Depreciation
1430 Shop—Land and Buildings
1439 Accumulated Depreciation
1440 Furniture—Model Dwellings

1449 Accumulated Depreciation
1450 Office Furniture and Equipment
1459 Accumulated Depreciation

Other assets

1610 Utility Deposits
1620 Escrow Deposits
1660 Municipal Tax Liens and Deposits

LIABILITIES

Current liabilities

2000 Accounts Payable
2100 Notes Payable (Bank Loans, etc.)
2300 Construction Mortgages Payable
2310 Loans Payable
2320 Commissions Payable (on Houses Sold)
2330 Customers' Deposits
2335 Escrow Deposits

Payroll deductions

2351 FICA Payable

2352 Federal Withholding Tax
2353 State Unemployment and Disability Tax Payable

Other current liabilities

2360 Accrued Salaries and Wages
2370 Accrued Real Estate Taxes
2380 Accrued Interest Payable

Long-term liabilities

2390 Mortgages Payable
2399 Deferred Profit on Installment Sales

NET WORTH

Corporation

2501 Capital Stock
2502 Surplus
2503 Retained Earnings
2599 Profit and Loss

Proprietorship

2501 Mr. A—Capital Equity
2550 Mr. A—Drawing
2599 Profit and Loss

INCOME AND EXPENSE ACCOUNTS.

INCOME

3010 Sales—Residential
3020 Sales—Extras
3025 Sales—Land
3030 Income on Installment Sales
3040 Interest Income
3050 Rental Income
3060 Commissions Earned
3090 Discount on Purchases

EXPENSES

Job costs

3290 Cost of Construction Sold

Land and development

3510 Roads and Curbs

3520 Water Mains
3530 Engineering
3540 Surveys
3550 Legal, Subdivision, and Municipal Costs
3560 Fill (Dirt, Gravel, etc.)

Direct costs

3601 Salary—Foremen
3605 Wages—Construction
3610 Masonry
3620 Carpentry
3630 Plumbing
3640 Heating and Air Conditioning
3650 Sheet Metal
3660 Electrical
3670 Appliances

3675 Flooring
3676 Tiling (Ceramic-Bath, etc.)
3677 Asphalt Floor Tiling
3685 Rough Lumber
3686 Trim Lumber and Costs
3690 Electrical Fixtures
3691 Iron Railings
3695 Other Material
3698 Excavating
3699 Other Subcontractors

Indirect costs

3710 Real Estate Taxes
3715 Heat, Light, Water
3720 Permits
3725 Occupancy Costs
3726 Cleaning
3728 Landscaping

Depreciation

3729 Construction Machinery
3739 Shop Buildings
3749 Model Homes Furniture
3760 Union Dues Paid
3762 Union Welfare Expense
3764 Closing Fees
3765 Equipment Rentals
3766 Customers' Complaints
3767 Interest on Construction Loans
         and Mortgages

General and administrative

4106 Wages—Administrative and
         Planning

4107 Wages—Estimating and Clerical
4109 Commissions Paid
4110 Office Expense
4115 Postage
4116 Interest on Other Mortgages and
         Loans
4120 Stationery and Printing
4125 Advertising
4129 Office Rent
4130 Heat, Light, and Water
4135 Telephone
4139 Uniforms
4140 Machinery Fuel and Supplies
4142 Automotive—Gas, Oil, and
         Maintenance
4143 Repairs—Vehicles and
         Machinery
4145 Repairs—Other
4146 Real Estate Taxes—Other
4147 Payroll Taxes
4148 State Franchise Taxes
4150 Insurance (Fire and extended
         coverage on Construction in
         Progress)
4151 Casualty and Liability Insurance
4152 Workmen's Compensation
         Insurance
4290 Uncollectible Accounts

Depreciation

4419 Automotive Equipment
4459 Office Furniture and Fixtures
4500 Legal and Accounting
4550 Travel and Entertainment
4555 Rental—Equipment

ACCOUNTS PECULIAR TO THE BUSINESS

Cash—Trustee Account (No. 1010). This account is used to segregate customers' deposits.

Contracts Receivable (No. 1220). With reference to houses constructed on the owner's land, this account would record unpaid portions of contracts.

Notes Receivable (No. 1230). Recorded here would be secured balances on either contracts or outright sales of houses.

Construction in Progress (No. 1265). Here are reflected year-end inventories of both finished and incomplete houses.

Accounts Payable (No. 2000). This account is used to accumulate unpaid invoices and vouchers at year end.

Escrow Deposits (No. 2335) records deposits held out at closings or due to municipalities' requirements.

Mortgages Payable (No. 2390). Included here are mortgages which are due in more than one year, for houses sold on contract.

Deferred Profit on Installment Sales (No. 2399) is used when a house is sold on an extended contract.

Land and Development Expenses Control (Series 3500). A builder who develops his own tract of land usually is required to install roads and curbs, water mains, and sewer lines; sometimes he must plant trees as required by the municipality. As a condition of the subdivision approval obtained from the city, all of the above stipulations are met. The accounts in the 3500 group record these expenses.

Direct Costs Control (Series 3600). These expense accounts may be broken down into construction categories. Another system often preferred is to use two accounts to accumulate these costs from the Cash Disbursement book, namely: Materials Used (No. 3650) and Subcontractors (No. 3660). The need of management will dictate which group of accounts is to be utilized. If the hybrid system is employed, however, these costs should be posted to the job cost sheets by category. The purpose is to match actual costs with original estimates.

Indirect Costs Control (Series 3700). Most of these accounts are self-explanatory; however, Occupancy Costs (No. 3725) might be elaborated upon. It is used to accumulate any costs incidental to preparing the house for final occupancy by the owner. Included would be special preparation of floors, municipal certificates of occupancy and related costs. Union Dues Paid (No. 3760) and Union Welfare Expense (No. 3762) are assessments to the builder by construction unions.

Construction Mortgages Payable (No. 2300). As advances are made by the mortgagee they are recorded here.

Income on Installment Sales (No. 3030) would be used where a contingent sale is made and the buyer pays on a monthly basis. When the payments have reduced the principal balance sufficiently to permit the buyer to secure a conventional mortgage, a normal closing takes place, and the Installment Sales Contract is terminated.

BOOKS AND FORMS PECULIAR TO THE BUSINESS

The records necessary are essentially the same as any other business. Each

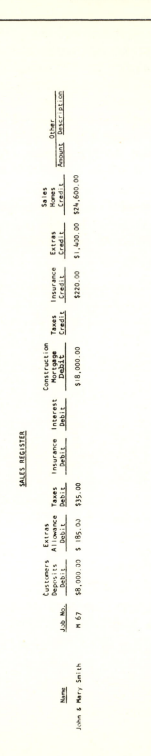

Figure 7: Sales Register

* Courtesy of Stephen P. Radics & Company, Paterson, New Jersey.

house built must have its own file to reflect the actual cost of labor, materials, other costs, and overhead. To do this, a job number must be assigned for each building and when materials are purchased, or acquired from the warehouse, the invoice or requisition order must be identified by the job number.

Sales are not reflected on the books until a sales closing takes place. Customers' deposits received on contemplated sales are the initial point at which a sales contract is drawn. When the home is completed the buyer is informed, and a closing date is set. At the closing, adjustments are made between buyer and seller for construction extras, taxes on real estate, utility adjustments, and insurance. The data from the closing statement in turn is entered in the Sales register (Figure 7).

An example of the closing statement is shown in Figure 8.

Peculiarities of Procedures

PURCHASES-PAYABLE CYCLE

When an accrual method of accounting is used, an Accounts Payable register is required. Here two alternatives are present. If totals are required by management by categories (as represented by the 3600 direct cost control account series), a multicolumn book of perhaps 24 columns should be used. If costs will be accumulated in the Accounts Payable book by job number, the number of columns will merely depend on how many jobs are being run simultaneously. Under the hybrid system, of course, the Job Sheet (Figure 3) is used to maintain costs on each job.

At the end of the year all costs for the houses sold are transferred to Cost of Construction Sold (No. 3290). This may be done by the following representative entries. Assume that Job 94 and Job 96 have been sold, and that costs have been accumulated through Accounts Payable by job numbers. The entry would be:

(Dr)	Cost of Construction Sold	#3290	40,000	
(Cr)	Costs Job 94			20,000
(Cr)	Costs Job 96			20,000

To reflect costs of houses sold during the year.

If the 3600 accounts (direct costs) are used, the following entries would be representative of those to be used:

(Dr)	Cost of Construction Sold	#3290	50,000	
(Cr)	Direct Costs	#3600		50,000

To close individual accounts representing costs of material and subcontractors used.

(Dr)   Construction in Progress   #1265   10,000
(Cr)   Cost of Construction Sold #3290   10,000
       To reflect house in various stages
       of construction remaining in
       inventory at year end.

GREEN & BLACK, ATTORNEYS
CLOSING STATEMENT
6/28/

Seller: A Corporation
Purchasers: John & Mary Smith

Credits to Seller:
    Selling Price $24,600.00
    Extras - Finished Room in Basement
            Electric Eye on Garage Doors   1,400.00
    Insurance Policy Transferred to Purchaser   220.00

Total Due to Seller   26,220.00

Credits to Purchaser:
    Initial Deposit $ 5,000.00
    Tax Adjustment-Taxes paid to
      June 15, 19__ (13 days)   35.00
    Extras Allowance on Electrical
      Fixtures and Medicine Cabinet   185.00

Total Credits to Purchaser   5,220.00

Due to Seller   21,000.00

Disbursed as follows:
    Payment of Construction Mortgage to
      City National Bank   18,000.00
      Interest due on above   -0-
                                                                18,000.00

Additional Amount due to Seller: 3,000.00

    Certified Check from John & Mary Smith
    drawn on First Cityville National Bank   3,000.00

Purchasers: Seller:

Signed _____   Signed _____
        John Smith   Abel Brown
                                          President-A Corporation
Signed _____
        Mary Smith

* COURTESY OF STEPHEN P. RADICS & COMPANY, PATERSON, NEW JERSEY.

Figure 8: Closing Statement

Under either system the cost of land development and the indirect costs would likewise be transferred to Cost of Construction Sold by appropriate entries at year end.

Other than the General ledger no other books or records should be required, except for those already discussed or mentioned later.

ESTIMATING AND SELLING

Estimating costs is important. When a developer plans a 50-houses area, by building a model home for each style of house he will be able to compare the estimate with the actual costs and either adjust the selling price to yield the desired profit, or else he will cut costs by eliminating some nonessentials.

The pro rata share of costs of roads, curbs, water mains, and similar items must be included in the land costs for each building plot in the entire development. These are often municipal requirements and may not be completed for several months after some homes have been finished and sold. The accountant should be sure that provision is made in the cost structure for these items.

Time and Payroll System

The payroll books may be standard. However, most construction businesses make provision for checking off union dues. Direct payment by the employer to the union is usually done on behalf of the owner's employees. Allocation of labor costs in total must agree with the totals posted to the job costs weekly, under whichever system of accounting for these costs is used, as previously discussed. As used here, the Payroll book becomes a book of original entry; a write-once system of handling payroll is assumed.

In addition to allocating materials to the proper account, labor should be watched very closely, especially when a number of jobs are done during the same day. A good payroll record is only as good as the cooperation from the foreman in making the proper entry on the time sheet, or card. A good supervisor is essential to enforce this requirement.

Time-Saving Ideas

All invoices should be checked for three purposes: (1) To ascertain if all the material shown in the original lumber lists has been received. These lists are essentially the specifications of the material to be used on each job, based on plans and specifications. (2) To determine if all the prices and extensions are correct. (3) For subsequent posting to Job Cost Sheets (Figure 3).

Vendors should be advised to place job numbers on all invoices and that all material should be delivered to the specific job locations. Some material

A CORPORATION
STATEMENT OF INCOME
For The Year Ended _____

Sales Income:
   Sale of Houses and Land $
   Income from Extras   _____

Less: Cost of Sales:
   Construction Costs - Schedule 1. $
   Sub-Contracts and Labor
   Material Costs
   Land and Improvements
   Indirect Building Costs   _____

Add: Construction Costs in Process March 1, 19__   _____

Less: Construction Costs in Process February __, 19__   _____
                                                                              _____

Gross Profit on Sales

Add: Current Profit on Houses Sold on
       Installment Contracts   _____

Other Income:
   Miscellaneous Income
   Rent Income
   Interest Income
   Profit on Current Installments
    of Equipment -Contract   _____

Less: Operating Expenses - Schedule 2.   _____

Less: Other Deductions   _____

Net Income Before Provision for Federal Income Taxes

Less: Provision for Federal Income Taxes   _____

NET INCOME FOR PERIOD $_____

* Courtesy of Stephen P. Radics & Company, Paterson, New Jersey.

Figure 9: Profit and Loss Statement

such as medicine cabinets may be kept in central stores and allocated to jobs as drawn. Control of material by construction foremen is vital, to ensure proper allocation to jobs under construction.

Reports to Management

FINANCIAL REPORTS

The financial reports are prepared annually. Interim statements may be made at management's request. Inventories can be determined by the accurate job cost sheets maintained and by bringing Accounts Payable to a current status. The financial reports consist of a balance sheet, a profit and loss statement, and a statement of stockholder's equity or proprietor's equity.

Profit and Loss Statement (Figure 9). In building operations such as have been discussed, the accuracy of the costs accumulated on various jobs will provide the basis for determining what the closing inventory is. Land costs are likewise important to the accuracy of the profit and loss statement. Unless all the added costs of developing the land are included, the profit and loss statement will not give an accurate portrayal of the operations of the business.

Usually schedules are provided as part of the statement to enable management to visualize the breakdown in costs between various categories. Schedules are shown for construction costs (Figure 10) and operating expenses (Figure 11).

Conclusion

The accounting system suggested here is not presented as the sole solution to a particular builder's problem. The public accountant who familiarizes himself with the basic information and the references presented can use this system and make whatever improvisations are needed to meet his client's requirements.

The developer devotes most of the day under pressure, consults with his office manager, his job foreman, his suppliers, numerous subcontractors, inspectors, and city officials as well as his banker. The developer may perform manual tasks to show how certain jobs should be done. At the end of the day he may look over plans and blueprints, check estimates, consider pending weather reports, negotiate with subcontractors, or contact prospective customers. The accountant should, therefore, encourage the builder to delegate authority. Most residential developers and builders have found a capable construction superintendent a necessity in their operations.

The public accountant is a vital part of the builder's activity as he seeks to guide his client into sound business practices.

A CORPORATION
CONSTRUCTION COSTS
For The Year Ended _____

Sub-Contracts and Labor:

Masonry
Carpentry
Painting and Decorating
Plumbing
Tiling
Drywall
Insulation
Flooring
Glass and Glazing
Electrical
Linoleum
Heating
Driveways
Landscaping
General Contracting
Excavating and Back Fill   _____

                                                              $ _____

Material Costs:

Lumber and Trim
Electrical Fixtures
Kitchen Cabinets and Vanitories
Garage Doors
Appliances
Hardware and Siding
Septic Tanks
Medicine Cabinets, Mirrors and Tub Enclosurers
Other Material Costs   _____

                                                              $ _____

Land and Improvements:

Inventory of Improved Lots - March 1, 19__ $
Purchase of Additional Land

Less: Inventory at February __, 19__   _____

Total Land and Improvement Costs Applicable to Current Period $ _____

* COURTESY OF STEPHEN P. RADICS & COMPANY, NEW JERSEY.

Figure 10:   Construction Costs Schedule

Indirect Building Costs:

Building Permits	$
Real Estate Taxes	
Engineering	
Architect Fees	
Insurance	
Supplies	
Sales Commissions	
Interest on Construction Loans	
Cleaning Model	
Utilities	
Repairs and Maintenance	
Closing Fees	
Equipment Rentals	
Customer Complaints	
Payroll Taxes	
Depreciation on Machinery and Equipment	
Miscellaneous	
Payroll	
	$

Figure 10:   Construction Costs Schedule (cont.)

A CORPORATION
OPERATING EXPENSES
For The Year Ended-

Telephone	$
Repairs and Maintenance - Other	
Light, Heat and Water	
Auto Expenses	
Travel and Entertainment	
Advertising	
Postage, Printing and Office Supplies	
N J. Corporation Business Tax	
Interest on Mortgages	
Real Estate Taxes - Investment Property	
Other Taxes	
Legal and Accounting	
Depreciation - Investment Property	
Depreciation - Furniture and Fixtures	
Miscellaneous	
	$

* COURTESY OF STEPHEN P. RADICS & COMPANY, NEW JERSEY.

Figure 11:   Operating Expenses Schedule

13

Building Material Suppliers

BY A. WHITMER WEIGEL

Public Accountant; Administrator of Accounting Systems and Procedures, Corning Glass Works, Corning, New York

Characteristics of the Business That Affect the Accounting System

The wide line of products available in a hardware store and in a lumberyard is the fascination of this kind of endeavor. Few men—young, old, or in between—are not awestruck by the variety of tools, paints, electrical supplies, wallboard, windows, storm doors, roofing, plumbing items, and the myriad of other supplies which are available from building material vendors.

The very fact that there is such a wide selection provides the opportunities for the accountant to produce information on sales along some sort of "family" or product lines. As is true in most businesses, certain types of products will tend to run in a gross margin pattern, as 33-1/3 percent, 40 percent, etc. This same family arrangement normally is a good basis for selection of locations within the store. This grouping has the natural organization of departments (and subdepartments) as an inherent characteristic.

With definition of the categories of products and services to be sold, it

211

follows that sales and cost of sales information is accumulated along the same pattern. Typical examples are these categories: Lumber and building materials; hardware (includes rentals); electrical and plumbing supplies. The frequently found pattern of a cash register throw-out slip for items picked up in the store and carried out, and a handwritten sales slip carried from the store to the warehouse for items to be picked up at the warehouse, is discussed along with other aspects of the accounting system, including inventory records and the use of 13 accounting periods per year.

FUNCTIONAL CHARACTERISTICS OF THE BUSINESS

Volume variations, which are natural to a building materials dealer, stem primarily from the seasons and, frequently, from abnormalities of the weather. The seasonal changes will move the emphasis from air conditioners and screening materials to storm doors and snow shovels. The result of wind and rain storms coming in any of the seasons, however, may present a sudden call for significant quantities of glass, roofing material, and related products.

That seasonal changes cause modifications of volume for building materials dealers is true in well over half of the United States. Also it is accepted that the business year should not end in the busy season. Thus general usage follows the calendar year, unless the dealer has a slower time other than the period when imitation fireplaces, wreaths, and candles are being returned to storage.

The high investment in inventory, store, and warehouse buildings and in land eliminates fly-by-night operators and causes the serious investor to consider carefully all aspects before entering the building materials field. Admittedly, the offsetting influence in selected areas is recent (or increasing) investment in new homes and business buildings.

It is common to find sales on both a cash and a credit basis. The cash basis is used for the over-the-counter sales to the public, whereas credit sales are restricted to major sales as to contractors for framing, sash doors, kitchen cabinets, etc., for a new home or for reconstruction. When major reconstruction is by the property owner, normally the local banking facilities provide the capital and the transaction is in cash with the building material suppliers.

Opportunities to take advantage of the 13-period year rather than the 12-month year appear especially desirable for the building materials dealer. Advantages include equal four-week periods for each accounting report, no complications of extra weekends because of the day of the week on which the first day of the month falls and, in general, an overall continuity which permits management to make more realistic comparisons of one accounting period with another.

PRINCIPAL ACCOUNTING PROBLEMS

The wide variety of products, which makes a building material supplier's store such an interesting place, is the cornerstone of the unique accounting problems which create the "accountant's nightmare". This nightmare stems from the markup on the many items, the potential of hundreds of stock ledger cards, and the related inventory problems.

The extremely large volume (up to 1500 items) requires a determination of whether to use the routine of cost and quantity records for each item, with the resulting high requirement of clerks' time, or the retail inventory method. The latter has much less requirement for the time of clerks with only slightly lessened information, which does not necessarily mean substantially reduced control. Offsetting the inability of stock ledger records of each item to show when the reorder point is reached is the practical technique of packaging or marking those items which represent the minimum ordering point. This is effectively accomplished when adequate attention is given to it by the warehouseman.

Advantages of the retail method of pricing appearing in *The Accountant's Handbook* * are the following:

1. Taking of inventories is facilitated as well as the adjusting of records departmentally at various dates other than the close of fiscal period.

2. Taking of inventories at retail figures is simpler than taking them at cost prices.

3. Decline of inventory values because of falling prices is obtained automatically as soon as retail prices are reduced.

4. Effect of markdowns on profits is apparent.

5. Intelligent preparation of merchandise budgets is facilitated.

6. A basis is afforded for insurance settlements.

Functional Organization

Responsibilities of the company president are many, of course, but the greatest load he must carry is his function as general sales manager in a business which exists on selling. An organization recognizing the benefits of assigning responsibility and authority along the natural lines and functions of the business suggests vice-president titles for departments of Finance, Lumber & Building Materials, Hardware, Electricity & Plumbing, and Purchasing & Advertising.

The organizational chart (Figure 1) demonstrates this type of organization.

---

* Paton, W. A. (Ed.), *The Accountant's Handbook*. New York: Ronald Press, 1957, ch. 12, p. 50.

The chart makes evident the decision to centralize warehousing and delivery responsibility under Lumber and Building Materials. This is particularly appropriate because of the warehousing volume required for that segment of the business.

At such time as electrical supplies and fixtures are established as a department with adequate volume, or it is concluded that this field of endeavor should stand alone, a new department will be born. Similarly the setting up of a Millwork Department would call for enlarging the organization. The chart illustrated is considered as the simplest and most practical for a true building material supplier who would serve construction personnel and the burgeoning do-it-yourself trade.

As established earlier, sales are of two major types: Over-the-counter sales to walk-in customers and the supplying of contractors' needs from a bill of materials for new construction or repair construction. Walk-in customers respond to such enticing lures as demonstrations on painting, furniture refinishing, home remodeling, etc. The respective department heads are responsible for planning such demonstrations (normally utilizing manufacturers' personnel) and planning for timely advertising of selected products and opportune specials to clear the shelves or otherwise provide props for a slipping volume.

Customers served by the bill of materials are sources of major sales volume and, therefore, the president carries the responsibilities of soliciting their trade. He must select additional contractors to solicit, and he must be available to those who are already regular customers.

Purchasing and Advertising, as one responsibility, works well in centralizing expenditures of funds and in assuring "company consideration" rather than "department considerations" in these matters. With frequent full-page advertisements this department head resolves the apportioning to lumber, hardware, and other areas of the amount of space, location, use of cuts, etc., within the ad. If the Purchasing and Advertising manager can effectively solicit manufacturers' assistance on ads, benefits therefrom help greatly to offset the desire of each department head to seek the full page. The apportioning of advertising cost to the corporation and each department helps also to curb excessive demands for advertising. The advertising program embraces newspaper, radio, and television with the usual minor amounts of institutional advertising in school and convention publications.

An additional responsibility of the Purchasing and Advertising manager may be chairmanship of the Advertising Budget Committee.

Functions of the financial vice president are carried out by the controller and the treasurer who report to this vice president. The treasurer is responsible for extending credit to customers, collecting open accounts, and the

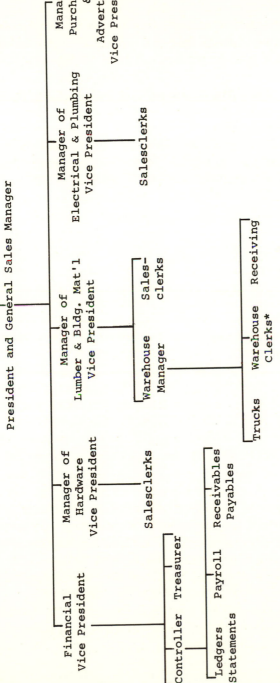
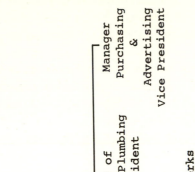

Figure I: Organizational Chart

* Also load products into customers' trucks, station wagons, and personal cars.

normal corollary of maintaining on hand an adequate supply of cash. He is in charge of personnel records, and these duties would include applications for employment, completed authorizations for payroll deductions, and related items. The controller is responsible for the smooth running of income and expense reporting and for improvements in the system. The fruits of his labor and the means to attain them are discussed in the balance of the chapter.

Principles and Objectives of the Accounting System

Principles followed in the accounting system here described are the adoption of 13 periods per year for reporting retail inventory method (tied to a first in—first out system) for establishing inventory values, the accumulation of cost and sales data by major merchandising departments, and a single administrative cost department for other costs.

SPECIFIC OBJECTIVES OF THE SYSTEM

These aims are to provide income and cost summaries quickly and economically. The system can be handled within the offices of the store and without investment in a computer or the use of a service bureau for it. Recognition is given, however, to the fact that volume transactions invite computer feasibility studies; with adequate volume, computer applications would appear.

Classification of Accounts and Books of Accounts

BALANCE SHEET ACCOUNTS.

ASSETS

Current assets

Cash and bank

101 Petty Cash
102 Cash Register Fund
103 Bank (Commercial)

Receivables

104 Accounts Receivable
104A Provision for Uncollectible
        Accounts
105 Contracts Receivable
106 Notes Receivable
107 Accrued Interest Receivable

Inventories

200-298 (Detailed below)
299 Inventory Valuation Reserve

Other current assets

131 Prepaid Rent
132 Prepaid Insurance
133 Prepaid Taxes
134 Office Supplies
135 Wrapping Supplies

Investments

151 Securities of Affiliated
        Companies

152-159 Other Long-Term Investments

Property, plant, and equipment

161 Land
162 Buildings
162R Accumulated Depreciation
163-169 Other Plant and Equipment Accounts
163R-169R Accumulated Depreciation Accounts

LIABILITIES

Current liabilities

Notes and Accounts Payable

301 Accounts Payable
305 Contracts Payable (less than one year)
306 Notes Payable
311 Sales Tax Payable
321 Employee Payroll Deductions
321A FICA Withheld
321B State Disability Insurance
321C Income Tax Withheld (Federal)
321D Income Tax Withheld (State)
321E Income Tax Withheld (City)

322 Employer Payroll Taxes Payable
322A FICA
322B Unemployment Insurance—Federal
322C Unemployment Insurance—State
325 Accrued Payroll
326 Accrued General Taxes
327 Accrued Interest Payable
329 Other Accrued Liabilities

Long-term debts

341 Contracts Payable (longer than one year)
342 Mortgages Payable
343-349 Other Long-Term Debts

NET WORTH

Corporate accounts

391 Capital Stock
391A Capital Stock—Authorized
391B Capital Stock—Unissued
391C Subscriptions to Capital Stock
398 Earned Surplus
  3981-3985 Earned Surplus Reserves
399 Profit and Loss—Current

INCOME AND EXPENSE ACCOUNTS.
REVENUES

Sales

400-499 (As detailed below)

Cost of sales

500-599 (As detailed below)

OPERATING EXPENSES

601 Supervision
602 Sales Salaries
603 Warehouse Salaries
604 Clerical
606 Overtime
608 Vacations
611 Operating Supplies
612 Small Tools
614 Cash Over and Short
615 Postage, Unallocated Freight
616 Gasoline and Oil
617 Repairs to Delivery Equipment
618 Licenses
619 Insurance—Auto
621 Telephone
622 Electricity

623 Gas
631 Insurance (other than Auto)
632 Property Taxes
633 Payroll Taxes
634 Other Taxes
641 Advertising
642 Provision for Uncollectible
Accounts
651 Cost of Replacements and
Repairs (Customers)
655 Travel and Entertainment
656 Memberships, Dues, and
Subscriptions
661 Repairs to Building
662 Repairs to Warehouse—Interior
663 Repairs to Displays
664 Repairs to Equipment (except
Delivery)
665 Repairs to Tools
671 Depreciation—Buildings
672 Depreciation—Warehouse,
Interior
673 Depreciation—Displays

674 Depreciation—Equipment
(except Delivery)
675 Depreciation—Tools
679 Depreciation—Delivery
Equipment

OTHER INCOME

701 Cash Discounts Taken
702 Interest Earned
708 Miscellaneous Income

OTHER DEDUCTIONS

751 Cash Discounts Allowed
752 Interest Expense
758 Miscellaneous Expense

DEPARTMENTS

11 Administration
12 Controller
21 Lumber and Building Materials
22 Electrical and Plumbing
23 Hardware
24 Warehouse

In the preceding chart, the significant difference from any other mercantile business appears in the recognition of 21 classes of inventory, sales, and cost of goods sold. These classes are indicated in detail in the following chart.

Condensation of all activities into four departments for reporting purposes demonstrates the possibility of controlling operations in a limited number of cost centers.

It is recognized that greater volume in any of the combined areas or the introduction of new ones may cause the company to add other cost centers.

Records and forms used are discussed in the section, Peculiarities of Procedures.

CLASSIFICATION OF MATERIALS

Inventory	Sales	Cost of Sales	Materials
211	411	511	Lumber—framing, siding, flooring, wood fencing
215	415	515	Plywood—unfinished
216	416	516	Prefinished Plywoods
221	421	521	Windows and doors
225	425	525	Mouldings—sills, frames and trends, etc.

Inventory	Sales	Cost of Sales	
231	431	531	Masonite Products, Insulite siding, insulation, homosote, etc. Sheetrock, rock lathe
232	432	532	Masonry Products, land tile, sewer tile and fittings, etc.
233	433	533	Metal Products, metal roofing, metal louvres, vents, etc.
235	435	535	Roofing and roof products, asphalt shingles
237	437	537	Nails
241	441	541	Paints and paint sundries
244	444	544	Housewares, waxes, polishes, clocks, gum and candy and small appliances
245	445	545	Sport goods
247	447	547	Hardware items
251	451	551	Plumbing, heating, supplies and fixtures
256	456	556	Floor tile and cements
261	461	561	Electrical supplies, wire, etc.
263	463	563	Lighting fixtures
264	464	564	Frigidaire sales
265	465	565	Kitchen cabinets
266	466	566	Nutone, hoods, fans, etc.
268	468	568	Service sales and parts and labor
269	469	569	Cutler-Hammer sales
271	471	571	Horticulture, lawn and garden supplies, seed, bulbs, fertilizer, etc.
274	474	574	Unpainted furniture
276	476	576	Christmas merchandise
—	497	597	Rentals
—	498	—	Markdowns
299	—	—	Inventory Valuation Reserve

Peculiarities of Procedures

Under direction of the financial vice president and the controller the techniques described in the remaining paragraphs tell the store of the company's efforts—and whether or not the projected profit goal has been met. In order that the various forms may be complete, the fictional name, Ace Building Material Supplies, is used in Figures 3, 4, 7, and 8.

CASH REGISTER

Inasmuch as making a profit is a fact of life, full recognition is given to attaining economical accounting routines. Sales are recorded through cash register rings and the resulting accumulations available from them. Daily

CASH REGISTER SLIPS

For cash sales carried from store	For charged items picked up at warehouse or delivered	For cash received on accounts
245 6.32	265 219.00	000 320.30
241 5.10	264 37.51	
241 .15 tx	263 81.10	
	221 120.07	
11/11 11.57 CA		11/11 320.30
	11/11 457.68 CR	

Figure 2: Cash Register Throw-Out Slips

reports are available with sales breakdown by the 27 established categories and designations of these amounts by CA (Cash Sales) or CR (Sales on Account). The register will also record cash offsetting Accounts Receivable (AC); that is, sales previously recorded. Examples of various cash register slips (throw-out slips) and their use are shown in Figure 2.

Merchandise picked up from the warehouse by the customer or delivered by the building material supplier's truck is recorded by hand-written detail as shown in Figures 3 and 4. In either case, the information will have been recorded on the cash register and the throw-out slip is stapled to the larger warehouse slip by the cashier. The throw-out slip shown in the middle Figure 2 would be attached to the warehouse slip illustrated in Figure 3.

The cash register is the central mechanism as it is used also to ring cash refunds (as for merchandise sold for cash and returned) and recording payments on account (for merchandise delivered on open account).

Accumulation of the sales data in the controller's office each morning makes it possible to proceed immediately to apply cost percentages to the sales and produce the value for cost of goods sold. Expenses are recorded through Cash Disbursements and General journal entries.

RETAIL INVENTORY METHOD

Use of the retail inventory method is fast and practicable. It is the key to maintaining a minimum of priced inventory records and, therefore, produces the opportunity to save the expense in terms of payroll dollars and related fringe benefits for two to three clerks.

Routine for the retail inventory method begins with receipt of invoices from vendors. The invoices are stamped and coded as shown in Figure 5.

ACE BUILDING MATERIALS

SOLD TO   _J WALTERS_

ADDRESS   _RIVER ROAD SUBURBIA, N.Y._

DELIVER TO   _PICK UP_

_11/11_

CLASS	QUAN	DESCRIPTION		PRICE
265	4	CABINETS #3618	LOT	219.00
264	1	COOK TOP #7291		37.51
263		FIXTURES	LOT	81.10
221	4	SASH	LOT	120.07
				457.68
			TAX	——
			TOTAL	457.68

TERMS   _ON ACCT_

Figure 3: Warehouse Slip

(for Credit Sale from Warehouse)

Ace Building Materials

SOLD TO __Cash__   DATE __11 / 11 /__

ADDRESS_____   DELIVERY ADDRESS_____

CITY_____   CITY_____

CUSTOMER ORDER NO.		SOLD BY _34_					
QUANTITY	CODE	DESCRIPTION			LIN. FT	UNIT PRICE	AMOUNT
2	247	100# Salt – Water Softener			2	1 90	3 80

TERMS: _Cash_

__20708__

Thank You For This Order
WE LOOK FORWARD TO SERVING YOU AGAIN
MERCHANDISE NOT RETURNABLE WITHOUT THIS SLIP.
N R L A INC -ROCHESTER N Y

TOTAL OF MERCHANDISE	3 80
SALES TAX	15
TOTAL INVOICE ▶	3 95

Figure 4: Warehouse Slip
(for Cash Sale at Warehouse)

Purchases are then recorded as:

Dr	Inventory (237)	832.00	
Cr	Accounts Payable (301)		640.00
	Inventory Valuation Reserve (299)		192.00

MATERIAL RECEIVED _10/2_
PRICE CHECKED __CL__

CLASS	COST	SELLING PRICE
237	640.00	832.00
TOTAL	640.00	832.00
INVENT. VAL. RESERVE	192.00	O.K. TO PAY
TOTAL	832.00	JB

Figure 5: Stamped and Coded Invoice (Retail Inventory Method)

Adjustments in prices from the originally recorded amount are critical to the system and are, therefore, subjected to a numerical control (as to the

PRICE CHANGE AUTHORIZATION					
DATE 4/2				NO. 0620	
CLASS	DESCRIPTION	PRICE		QTY	VALUE
		OLD	NEW		
247	GRASS SEED SPREADER	8.40	11.20	30	84.00
247	SNOW SHOVELS	3.20	2.10	18	19.80
					64.20

PROPOSED BY: C Redin

APPROVED BY: J Black

Figure 6: Price Change Authorization

transaction) to be sure each one is given the same treatment. The form shown in Figure 6 is used.

The Price Change Authorization (Figure 6), along with all others processed in that period, is summarized in a journal entry which uses the net value for all of the authorizations. To reflect authorization No. 620 (Figure 6), the entry is:

Dr   Inventory Valuation Reserve (299)   64.20
     Cr   Inventory (247)   64.20

Supplementing the discussion of the accounting routines, it is desirable to see how the individual invoices are posted. The Inventory Ledger Record (Figure 7) is maintained by a posting machine. On this record, by accounting period, each purchase for resale is shown at its cost and selling price. In this method the gross margin percent for all items of a class is developed. The sample Inventory Ledger Record shows purchases in an accounting period costing $5810, with a sales value of $7593.20. The average markup for the period was 30.69 percent, which resulted in an average cost of sales of 76.51 percent.

The markup percentage by class is remarkably stable each period. Even so, to assure continuity and avoid fluctuation because of isolated examples of

Ace Building Materials

Nails   CODE # 237

OLD BALANCE		DESCRIPTION	DATE	ACCOUNT NO.	DEBIT		BALANCE	
COST	RETAIL				COST	RETAIL	COST	RETAIL
		American Wire	10/2		640.00	832.00	640.00	832.00
640.00	832.00	General Steel	10/2		880.00	1135.20	1520.00	1967.20
1520.00	1697.20	American Wire	10/9		1200.00	1584.00	2720.00	3551.20
2720.00	3551.20	Smith, Roberts & Loll	10/10		380.00	486.40	3100.00	4037.60
3100.00	4037.60	Sarnoff, Inc.	10/12		1350.00	1782.00	4450.00	5819.60
4450.00	5819.60	American Aluminum	10/14		410.00	557.60	4860.00	6377.20
4860.00	6377.20	Johnson & Stover	10/20		950.00	1216.00	5810.00	7593.20

This Period

Average mark up 30.69%

Cost of sales 76.51%

Figure 7: Inventory Ledger Record

either fortunate or "forced" buying, the reports (income statement and balance sheet) for each period are based on the percentages developed for the current period plus those developed for the five previous periods. Where buying is extremely seasonal, a longer period of time is sometimes used to assure reasonable percentages. Use of the six-period average permits scanning of the period percentages for the trend of change, if any exists.

Time and Payroll System

No special problems in payroll accounting exist in this system. The usual routine of timekeeping and establishing of gross and net earnings apply. Commissions are not normally a part of paying employees in this industry.

The problem of controlling total payroll cost in each department is a function of the department head who also approves all of the variations from a standard work week, irregularities in clock rings, vacation payments, etc. The measurements of his department's activity in payroll matters are assurance of his continued interest in these matters.

Consistency of payroll practices is assured through: (1) payroll policies issued by the controller, and (2) checking of payroll computations as an internal audit function.

Reports to Management

Reports to management include the profit and loss statement and the balance sheet. In preparing the profit and loss statement the sales are recorded as follows:

> Lumber and building materials: Nos. 411 through 435, and 465.
> Hardware: Nos. 437 through 447, 464, 466, 468, 471, 474, 476, and 497.
> Electricity and plumbing: Nos. 451 through 463.

The basic profit and loss statement (Figure 8) tells the story for the current period. It is supplemented for meetings of the board with the addition of similarly composed statements showing:

1. Year to date
2. Comparisons to budget for:
   a. The period with variances
   b. Year to date with variances
3. Comparisons to prior year for:
   a. The period
   b. Year to date.

Ace Building Material Supplies
Suburbia, New York

Period _____, 19

	Lumber and Building Materials	Hardware	Electrical and Plumbing	Total
Sales				
Store	$ xx	$ xxx	$ xxx	$ xxx
Contractor	xx	xxx	xxx	xxx
Total	$ xx	$ xxx	$ xxx	$ xxx
Cost of Goods Sold	xx	xxx	xxx	xxx
Gross Margin	$ xx	$ xxx	$ xxx	$ xxx
Departmental Expense				
Payroll	$ xx	$ xx	$ xx	$ xx
Advertising	xx	xx	xx	xx
Replacement Parts	xx	xx	xx	xx
Miscellaneous	xx	xx	xx	xx
Total Departmental Expense	$ xx	$ xx	$ xx	$ xx
Operating Margin	$ x	$ x	$ x	$ xx
Administrative Department and Non-operating items				xx
Net Profit				$ xx

Figure 8: Statement of Profit and Loss

These additional comparisons are not illustrated since they are of the same format and would not add to explanation of the system.

In Figure 8 other income and deductions are included in nonoperating items.

A balance sheet of the standard variety is also prepared for board members at the end of each period.

14

Catering (Industrial)

BY WILLIAM L. LAUGHLIN

Chief Accountant, Oakdale Cotton
Mills, Jamestown, North Carolina

Characteristics of the Business That Affect the Accounting System

Since man first found it necessary to feed himself at his job, because distance or time limitations made it impractical for him to return home to eat, numerous methods have been employed to satisfy this requirement. There are those of us who can recall the familiar lunch box invariably carried by most workers in industry not too long ago. The sight of a small child taking sustenance to an industrial plant for a family member can still be seen at some of our modern industrial locations.

Thus it was that a large segment of the working population had no choice of eating facilities, because of the very nature of the work or location of the plant. Affected were persons in the construction field, companies situated in suburban areas, and industries that did not see fit to invest in any form of food facilities for their employees. This situation made clear a need that is now being met in two ways.

One is the company-owned or -leased employee cafeteria. It can be elaborate or not, depending on the company's requirements, but the function remains the same as the private lunch box: To feed the worker in a specified period of time without his leaving the job site.

The second method which fulfills food requirements of the employee is a new business known as industrial food catering. This business incorporates most of the better features of the company-owned cafeteria, the privately owned vending machine, and of course the once indispensable, but often inadequate, lunch box.

Characteristics of the many industrial catering operations are varied in some respects but uniformly similar in others. Typical of the business is that distributing units, which are entirely mobile, operate from a centrally located company headquarters. Each unit must adhere to a strict schedule of service stops that in most cases are permanent. Each unit is completely equipped to serve hot and cold food and sundry items as well as tobacco products. Cleanliness and advantageous display of all items must be paramount features of each unit, and each must be operated by a clean, courteous, salesman-type operator.

Successful industrial catering businesses are almost invariably multiple-unit operation as distinguished from a one-truck, owner-operated business, which in almost every instance proves to be a failure. One characteristic has been found to be a distinctive element in financial success. The successful business will manufacture one of the most profitable selling items carried by the operating unit, i.e., sweet goods: doughnuts, cinnamon rolls, cakes, pies, and other pastries, etc. A successful company primarily engaged as a bakery will find the operating of an industrial food catering service, if run on a proper scale, a most profitable subsidiary. A wholesale manufacturer of sandwiches can also increase his chances of success by the operation of an industrial food catering service. These two types of company have an excellent opportunity of placing before the public through the subsidiaries the merchandise of the parent company. There is a far better chance for the catering service to operate at a profit when two such major items are provided by the parent company.

FUNCTIONAL CHARACTERISTICS OF THE BUSINESS

The natural business year, or calendar year, is usually used in the industrial catering business. Although seasonal changes may affect the sales of some products carried by the industrial catering units, overall the sales are subject to very little fluctuation. For example, coffee sales may drop in the summer months, but sales volume is recovered through cold drinks of various kinds. When a route is well established, sales volume will not suffer by seasonal changes even though inclement weather precludes outside work, because construction proceeds inside dwellings and buildings being erected. It is a peculiarity of the business that cold weather seems to promote larger sales even from a smaller group of people at work.

The industrial suburban growth and the healthy economic conditions prevailing today have created keen competition in the industrial catering field, and have been responsible for the steady growth of a properly operated business of this type.

PRINCIPAL ACCOUNTING PROBLEMS

The accounting requirements of an industrial catering business call for unique deviations from any other accounting system.

Control forms and charts for both the business and for personnel constitute the major differences in accounting for an industrial catering system. Since the products are perishable and of various profit levels, control forms such as the ones shown in this chapter are necessary, perhaps to a greater extent than in businesses that do not incorporate operating units. In addition, each of the operating units could almost be considered a separate business entity.

To summarize, the company accountant must control as many as ten individual operating units, and maintain individual records for each. At the same time he must consolidate this information into a clear, lucid picture for management.

Functional Organization

The food catering business requires knowledgeable managers and route supervisors, persons preferably with pleasant personalities who can meet the public and who possess all the attributes of first-class salesmen. It is the duty of the managers and supervisors to establish routes, to maintain a congenial relationship between managers and supervisors of the businesses that their company serves, and to assure a prompt, efficient, courteous relationship between customers and route salesmen. Probably the most important function of management, however, is strict control.

Personnel of an industrial catering organization usually is comprised of a sales manager, assistant sales manager, office manager and accountant, route supervisors, and various clerical employees. It has been my experience that the accountant for this type of business will perform more duties that are considered management services than in most fields of accounting. The nature of the business, and the fact that it is a new one, places unusual but challenging responsibilities on the accountant. His interpretation of the control systems is relied upon in most cases.

Principles and Objectives of the Accounting System

It is the intention of this chapter to point out some of the accounting variations required by this business and thus provide the accountant with proven control systems. Catering services which operate with very strict control, especially if the distributing units exceed two in number, will be those surviving in this growing, competitive field. While admittedly not the only ones that could be employed, these control systems have been of valuable assistance in operation of industrial catering services consisting of as many as 20 completely equipped operating units.

Classification of Accounts and Books of Accounts

A chart of accounts for this industry will bear little difference from any number of other organizations allied to the field, so that no detailed discussion is necessary.

BOOKS AND FORMS PECULIAR TO THE BUSINESS

Control. Control as it applies to this system would be defined as follows:

1. Control of purchased merchandise into the company's stockroom, and control of the issuance of merchandise to the individual unit operating.

2. Careful inventories of stockroom and trucks at regular intervals not to exceed one week in duration. Truck inventories should be taken by two persons, the driver-salesman and a management representative. Stockroom inventories should be taken with a person responsible for the stockroom, and the issuing of merchandise to the drivers and a management representative.

The first form distinctive to this business is known as the Route Salesman Checkout Sheet (Figure 1).

The checkout sheet serves a dual purpose. Although it is called the Salesman's Weekly Inventory, it is also used as a daily report from the driver, who marks the appropriate information on the left side and fills in the day's date. On the Saturday report, the right side is compiled from the week's reports to provide a summary control of the operation.

The form lists the items that the mobile unit sells; they are charged out to the unit at retail value. After he has taken inventory of his truck each day, the driver-operator replenishes his stock by filling in this form and turning it in to the stockroom supervisor. This sheet will show the merchandise checked out, the quantity of each item, and the retail price. It is important that the

RT. NO._____   **SALESMAN'S**   DATE_____
                                    WEEKLY INVENTORY

SALESMAN_____

STOCK ON TRUCK -

CASH BOX   -_____

       TOTAL   -

ITEMS CHECKED OUT

LAST INVENTORY -

WEEKS CHARGES -_____

     TOTAL OUT -

WASTE IN   -_____

       TOTAL   -

STOCK RETURN -_____

SALES   -

TAX   -_____

MONEY DUE   -

MONEY IN   -_____

SHORT   -_____

OVER   -_____

GROSS PAY   -_____

SIGNED SALESMAN

_____

Figure 1: Route Salesman Checkout Sheet

No._____   Daily
                          Stockroom Control   SALESMAN
DATE_____

ITEMS	QUANTITY	TOTAL	ITEMS	QUANTITY	TOTAL
Cake - 5¢					
Cake - 10¢					
Candy - 5¢					
Candy - 10¢					
Gum - 5¢					
Sweets - 15¢					
Coffee Cups-10¢					
Coffee Cups-15¢					
Cups - 1¢					
Drinks 3.12					
Potatoe Chip - 10¢					
Juice - 15¢					
Juice - 25¢					
Nabs - 5¢					
Nuts - 5¢			DAILY TOTAL _____		
Nuts - 10¢					
Dope - 5¢			WASTE IN _____		
Dope - 10¢					
Dope - 15¢					
Tob.-25¢					
Tob.-30¢					
Cigars - 5¢					
Cigars - 8¢					
Cigars - 10¢					
Cigarettes - 30¢					
Donuts - 10¢					
Milk					
Sand.					

Figure 2:   Daily Stockroom Control Form

form be correctly dated and the driver's signature placed in its proper place. The driver's inventory is checked by management at the end of each week, and with the daily addition to the driver's account of his checkout records, proper control of the unit's sales will be reflected. It will be noted that provision is made on this record to show sales for each day's operation.

For stockroom control a record such as Figure 2 should be maintained.

The Daily Stockroom Control Form is kept by the person responsible for stockroom merchandise. It is his responsibility to sign receipts from wholesalers, ascertain correctness of the quantity of the delivered merchandise, and to sign it into the stockroom as an addition to his present stock. This form should show daily withdrawals against each item of merchandise cumulatively against all operating units. Receipts, and withdrawals from stockroom, plus beginning and ending inventories checked by management at the end of each week, should provide proper stockroom control. Any discrepancies in any item of merchandise between the beginning inventory, the receipts, the withdrawals, and the ending inventory, if significant at all, should be carefully investigated by management.

Because some items carried by operating units are highly perishable, a report known as the Stales Sheet (Figure 3) is called for in this type of business.

This report will show the name of the turned-in item, its retail cost, and the quantity received by the stockroom supervisor. It is then reduced from the operator's checkout sheet to give him full credit for the merchandise. This report should be conscientiously maintained on each operating unit, as it gives to management a clear picture of the perishable items that are not selling well, and thus can be effective in the purchasing policy of the company.

The accountant for an industrial catering service will soon note that some items will be what is known as high-profit merchandise. Others will show moderate overall profit, and some items will be almost break-even merchandise.

In considering the various levels of profit return, perhaps the most profitable of all items has been found to be coffee. After a little experience the accountant may watch the sale of coffee on an industrial catering unit, and from that sales figure determine the success or failure of that particular unit. This is not an overstatement; most catering concerns will eventually find themselves using to advantage a form known as the Coffee Checkout Sheet (Figure 4).

Because coffee is the most profitable of merchandise, it is also the most difficult item to control. The writer has found that the company can do little more than to charge out the cups, at retail price, to the driver-salesman.

Usually made of plastic or styrofoam and of 6-ounce capacity, the cups should be printed with the catering company's name shown conspicuously (to facilitate correct inventory). A plain cup can be purchased cheaply at numerous places and can be substituted for the company's own, unless the extra expense of the printed cup is resorted to.

The Coffee Checkout Sheet (Figure 4) is somewhat comparable to the Route Salesman Checkout Sheet (Figure 1). After checking in his receipts each day and filling out the next day's checkout sheet, the driver will also complete the Coffee Checkout Sheet, date, and sign it. By comparing the number of gallons of coffee checked out by each operating unit, and allowing for coffee return at the end of the day, and by noting the number of cups checked out by the driver, management can in some degree control the sales, or reflect the true sales, of this most profitable item. These records, of course, are not infallible, but they will offer the accountant some degree of control that perhaps is not even discernable by other members of the company.

Two other forms are applicable to the control of fresh food issued daily to the individual unit. Figure 5 is the Sandwich Checkout Sheet, and Figure 6 the Milk and Doughnut Sheet. These forms are made out by the driver at the close of each day and are turned in to the route supervisor.

Up to this point, the records discussed are those kept in the office of the route supervisor and those considered as particularly concerned with operation of an industrial food catering service. Each of these records is regularly turned in to the company Accounting Department. Importance of these records should never be minimized, since they provide the initial control for the entire operation. The successful company must maintain an adequate Bookkeeping or Accounting Department in charge of an accountant-office manager. It is at this juncture that the company's records will begin to coincide with other known and accepted accounting practices.

There are several important records peculiar to the industrial food catering business, to any business that is primarily mobile, and to management. The Truck Record Form (Figure 7) will bear a date, the truck or route number, and the driver-salesman's name. It will show the operating expense of the truck, such as tires, gasoline, repairs, etc., which have no direct bearing on the purchased merchandise carried by the particular unit. This form should be filled out each week by the Accounting Department, and naturally it is of no concern to anyone but management personnel.

Speedometer readings at the beginning and ending of each week should be included on this form to provide management with the amount of distance covered by each unit during its operating week. Mileage is an important factor in cost control, and should be considered in the allocation of service stops to each operating unit in order to provide maximum service to a

STALES SHEET

Week of	Sunday		Monday		Tuesday		Wednesday		Thursday		Friday	
	Price	Quantity	Price	Quantity	Price	Quantity	Price	Quantity	Price	Quantity	Price	Quantity
Bread												
Hamburger												
Wienie Rolls												
Ft. Long												
Barbecue												
L. Club												
Totals												
Salesman												

Figure 3: Stales Sheet

COFFEE CHART

	#1		#2		#3		#4		#5		#6		#7		#8		#9	
	OUT	IN	OUT	IN	OUT	IN	OUT	IN	OUT	IN	OUT	IN	OUT	IN	OUT	IN	OUT	IN
MONDAY																		
TUESDAY																		
WEDNESDAY																		
THURSDAY																		
FRIDAY																		
SATURDAY																		
Total OUT / Total IN																		
Sold			Sold		Sold		Sold		Sold		Sold		Sold		Sold		Sold	

COFFEE CHART

	#1		#2		#3		#4		#5		#6		#7		#8		#9	
	OUT	IN	OUT	IN	OUT	IN	OUT	IN	OUT	IN	OUT	IN	OUT	IN	OUT	IN	OUT	IN
MONDAY																		
TUESDAY																		
WEDNESDAY																		
THURSDAY																		
FRIDAY																		
SATURDAY																		
Total OUT / Total IN																		
Sold			Sold		Sold		Sold		Sold		Sold		Sold		Sold		Sold	

Figure 4: Coffee Checkout Sheet

ROUTE #_____ NAME_____ DATE_____

| | HOT SANDWICHES | | | | COLD SANDWICHES | | |

HOT SANDWICHES					COLD SANDWICHES		
		ORDER	FILLED			ORDER	FILLED
	50¢				**40¢**		
Country Ham		_____	_____	Corned Beef and Cheese		_____	_____
				Baked Ham		_____	_____
	40¢				**35¢**		
Sausage and Egg		_____	_____	Ham, Lettuce, and Tomato		_____	_____
Ham and Egg		_____	_____				
Pork Chop		_____	_____		**30¢**		
Steak (Gravy)		_____	_____	Chopped Ham and Cheese		_____	_____
Liver		_____	_____	Ham and Potato Salad		_____	_____
Chicken		_____	_____				
Roast Beef		_____	_____				
Fish		_____	_____		**25¢**		
Roast Turkey		_____	_____	Corned Beef		_____	_____
Meat Loaf		_____	_____	Pimento Cheese		_____	_____
				Chicken Salad		_____	_____
	35¢			Ham Salad		_____	_____
Cheeseburger		_____	_____	Bologna and Cheese		_____	_____
Foot Long		_____	_____	Tomato		_____	_____
Barbeque		_____	_____	Egg Salad		_____	_____
Barbeque Chicken		_____	_____	Spiced Ham and Cheese		_____	_____
Big Boy		_____	_____	Spiced Ham		_____	_____
				Bologna		_____	_____
	30¢			Chopped Ham		_____	_____
Smoked Sausage		_____	_____				
Hamburger (Onion)		_____	_____		**35¢**		
Hamburger (Slaw)		_____	_____	Potato Salad		_____	_____
	25¢						
Ham Biscuit		_____	_____		**10¢**		
Sausage Biscuit		_____	_____	Boiled Egg		_____	_____
	35¢				**10¢**		
Soups		_____	_____	Pickles		_____	_____
	35¢				**15¢**		
Beans		_____	_____	Pastries		_____	_____
Cream Potato		_____	_____				
Hush Puppies		_____	_____				
Plate Lunch		_____	_____		**20¢**		
	20¢			Banana Pudding		_____	_____
Cheese Dog		_____	_____				
Hot Dog (Onion)		_____	_____				
Hot Dog (Slaw)		_____	_____	Signed_____			

Figure 5: Sandwich Checkout Sheet

MILK   ORDER   **DOUGHNUTS**

#1		#6		#1		
____	Pt. Sw.	____	Pt. Sw.	G -	____	Doz. Pks.
____	Pt. Cho.	____	Pt. Cho.	C -	____	Doz. Pks.
____	Pt. But.	____	Pt. But.	J -	____	Doz. Pks.
____	Pt. Or.	____	Pt. Or.	B -	____	Doz. Pks.
____	Pt. Gra.	____	Pt. Gra.			
____	1/2 Pt. Sw.	____	1/2 Pt. Sw.	#2		
____	1/2 Pt. Cho.	____	1/2 Pt. Cho.	G -	____	Doz. Pks.
____	Milkshake	____	Milkshake	C -	____	Doz. Pks.
____	Qt. Half & Half	____	Qt. Half & Half	J -	____	Doz. Pks.
				B -	____	Doz. Pks.
#2		#7				
____	Pt. Sw.	____	Pt. Sw.	#3		
____	Pt. Cho.	____	Pt. Cho.	G -	____	Doz. Pks.
____	Pt. But.	____	Pt. But.	C -	____	Doz. Pks.
____	Pt. Or.	____	Pt. Or.	J -	____	Doz. Pks.
____	Pt. Gra.	____	Pt. Gra.	B -	____	Doz. Pks.
____	1/2 Pt. Sw.	____	1/2 Pt. Sw.			
____	1/2 Pt. Cho.	____	1/2 Pt. Cho.	#4		
____	Milkshake	____	Milkshake	G -	____	Doz. Pks.
____	Qt. Half & Half	____	Qt. Half & Half	C -	____	Doz. Pks.
				J -	____	Doz. Pks.
#3		#8		B -	____	Doz. Pks.
____	Pt. Sw.	____	Pt. Sw.			
____	Pt. Cho.	____	Pt. Cho.	#5		
____	Pt. But.	____	Pt. But.	G -	____	Doz. Pks.
____	Pt. Or.	____	Pt. Or.	C -	____	Doz. Pks.
____	Pt. Gra.	____	Pt. Gra.	J -	____	Doz. Pks.
____	1/2 Pt. Sw.	____	1/2 Pt. Sw.	B -	____	Doz. Pks.
____	1/2 Pt. Cho.	____	1/2 Pt. Cho.			
____	Milkshake	____	Milkshake	#6		
____	Qt. Half & Half	____	Qt. Half & Half	G -	____	Doz. Pks.
				C -	____	Doz. Pks.
#4		#9		J -	____	Doz. Pks.
____	Pt. Sw.	____	Pt. Sw.	B -	____	Doz. Pks.
____	Pt. Cho.	____	Pt. Cho.			
____	Pt. But.	____	Pt. But.	#7		
____	Pt. Or.	____	Pt. Or.	G -	____	Doz. Pks.
____	Pt. Gra.	____	Pt. Gra.	C -	____	Doz. Pks.
____	1/2 Pt. Sw.	____	1/2 Pt. Sw.	J -	____	Doz. Pks.
____	1/2 Pt. Cho.	____	1/2 Pt. Cho.	B -	____	Doz. Pks.
____	Milkshake	____	Milkshake			
____	Qt. Half & Half	____	Qt. Half & Half	#8		
				G -	____	Doz. Pks.
#5		#10		C -	____	Doz. Pks.
____	Pt. Sw.	____	Pt. Sw.	J -	____	Doz. Pks.
____	Pt. Cho.	____	Pt. Cho.	B -	____	Doz. Pks.
____	Pt. But.	____	Pt. But.			
____	Pt. Or.	____	Pt. Or.	#9		
____	Pt. Gra.	____	Pt. Gra.	G -	____	Doz. Pks.
____	1/2 Pt. Sw.	____	1/2 Pt. Sw.	C -	____	Doz. Pks.
____	1/2 Pt. Cho.	____	1/2 Pt. Cho.	J -	____	Doz. Pks.
____	Milkshake	____	Milkshake	B -	____	Doz. Pks.
____	Qt. Half & Half	____	Qt. Half & Half			

Figure 6:   Milk and Doughnut Sheet

DAILY MOTOR TRUCK OPERATING COST RECORD

Truck No. _____

For Month of _____ 19___

Route No. _____

Driver _____

Date	OPERATING DATA						DAILY EXPENSE														Remarks
	Miles	Speed-ometer Reading	1,000 Mi. Check-Up	6,000 Mi. Check-Up	Tune-Up	Brakes Relined	Gasoline		Oil-Grease		Misc. Tire Expense	Repairs						Accident		Misc. Expense	
							Gals.	Cost	Qts.	Cost		Chassis		Body				Parts	Labor		
												Parts	Labor	Parts	Labor	Parts	Labor				
1																					
2																					
3																					
4																					
5																					
6																					
7																					
8																					
9																					
10																					
11																					
12																					
13																					
14																					
15																					
16																					
17																					
18																					
19																					
20																					
21																					
22																					
23																					
24																					
25																					
26																					
27																					
28																					
29																					
30																					
31																					
Total																					
Average																					

THE OFFICE SERVICE COMPANY

Figure 7: Truck Record Form

maximum number of stops, with the coverage of a minimum number of miles. The company's route supervisor should be familiar with this form, because part of his job is to maintain truck operating expenses within a reasonable percentage of the unit's total operating cost. Each item on Figure 7 can be a revelation to the company's accountant. It will tell him how the operator is handling his equipment and will show him how the company is maintaining in good order a valuable asset. Oil changes, safety inspection, and proper maintenance of the vehicle will be reflected here as well as any negligence on the part of responsible personnel.

The next accounting procedure performed by the bookkeeping section should be considered one of the most important controls which provide management with the complete picture of each mobile operating unit. This is the Route Control Sheet.

Figure 8 is simply a 16-column worksheet form familiar to all accountants. It consists of 44 vertical lines that can be adapted to show pertinent factors concerning the operating unit. One such form for each unit can illustrate one month's total operation.

Headings listed across the top of the form should follow a pattern similar to the one listed here in numerical order. The first columnar heading is the date. In the upper left-hand corner are the route number and the salesman's name. The upper right-hand corner should show the accounting period the form covers, usually one month. The form itself is divided vertically into four-week periods subtotaled at the end of each week. An aggregate total footing the page gives the monthly operation.

Listed horizontally across the page should be the following headings: Beginning Inventory; Charge-Outs; Stales; Sales; Salesman's Salary; Truck Expense; Operating Expense; Cost of Sales; Sales Tax; Total; Ending Inventory; Receipts Turned In; Receipts Due; Overage or Shortage; and Profit or Loss.

It can readily be seen that this form is in a large part a record composed of figures extracted from the records and reports previously discussed in this chapter, i.e., Route Salesman's Checkout Form (Figure 1) reflecting daily sales, charge-outs, and receipts; some of the headings such as truck expense, repairs, gasoline, etc., will be taken from the Truck Route Sheets (Figure 7). Other headings such as operating expense must include the expense attributed to the company not reflected in purchased merchandise, salesman's salaries, etc. This will include management salaries, office salaries, rent, and all other operating expenses connected with the business divided percentage-wise among the operating units, the same percentage applying to each unit.

After familiarizing himself with this form the accountant can watch the progress of each operating unit and carefully note serious deviations from

The table itself is a blank Route Control Sheet form with the following column headings (reading across): Date, Beginning Inventory, Week's Charges, Total, Ending Inventory, Waste In, Sales, Cost Sales, Estimated Overhead, Estimated Truck Exp., Sales Tax, Salesman's Expense, Money Due, Money In, Over Shortage, Profit Loss.

ROUTE # 1

Figure 8: Route Control Sheet

the norm. It will enable him to call management's attention to such things as shortages in receipt turn-ins, the excess of stales return, and other pertinent factors. This form should be posted daily and subtotaled weekly. It will reflect in the profit and loss column the condition of each route, and the totals of each route sheet will give easy access to the condition of the company itself. This form graphically tells the story of the entire company's operation as it pertains to the operating units. Stress should be laid on proper control of such headings as operating expense; excessive or exorbitant figures listed under these headings will cause a well-controlled route with good sales to suffer. It is important that company operating expenses be kept in line to insure a profitable enterprise. The total receipts of the company are the combined receipts of the routes. Total expense of the company is divided proportionately among the routes. The surplus, or lack of it, will be the profit or loss; it can be readily determined by correct posting and studying of this form. One prime advantage of Figure 8 is that it provides management with information needed to make adjustments quickly.

The Route Control Sheet and the form next to be described are perhaps the two most important control reports available to management.

Breakdown of Sales (Figure 9) is again a 16-column worksheet form. The purpose is to provide management with information concerning the type of merchandise being sold and the quantity that is distributed from each operating unit. This form should list vertically the route numbers of each operating unit. Horizontally across the top of the page should be listed the types of merchandise normally distributed by the company. Headings may be grouped to contain several items of the same type. The form will show the sales figure for each item by each operating unit.

It is desirable to post to this form after each week's operation. Figure 9 can even be used indirectly to ascertain the correctness of inventories and the distribution of merchandise. Just as is done for Figure 8, the Breakdown of Sales should be subtotaled each week and totaled, footed, each month. It will reveal to the accountant the sales strengths and sales weaknesses of each unit. It will delineate the units selling the high-profit items, and those whose average sales are not up to par with other operating units. It is a truism that high sales can lead to bankruptcy if they are not of the right type, that is, revealing an appropriate percentage of profit. The Breakdown of Sales furnishes management with an overall picture of the sales development of each unit and has proved to be a valuable accounting asset to management.

Peculiarities of Procedures

Other than the special forms that have been listed in this chapter there are no peculiar procedures, or procedures not found in any other type of busi-

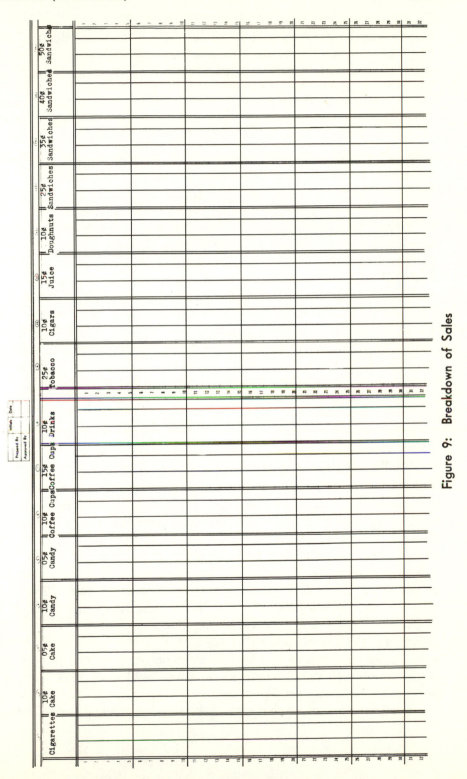

Figure 9: Breakdown of Sales

ness. The forms listed here are considered subsidiary forms that are important to the regular set of books. In this type of operation the books should consist of a General ledger, Accounts Payable ledger, and a General journal. The one notable peculiarity has been stated elsewhere that there are no Accounts Receivable sanctioned by the company.

Time and Payroll System

The normal procedure in the industrial catering business is to pay driver-salesmen a reasonable base salary plus commission. The commission will provide incentive and create a healthy spirit of competition among the route salesmen. If a route salesman does not report for work, and his route must be operated by a route supervisor, it is customary to deduct the percentage commission from the regular salesman's weekly earnings; however, the base pay is not affected if absence is not habitual. It might be pointed out here that route salesmen for an industrial catering service usually enjoy the same fringe benefits that are available in any progressive organization, such as paid vacations, paid holidays, and year-end bonuses based on sales for that year. The employees of a well-run industrial catering service will earn above average wages for similar work in other fields. The payroll can be made up from the Route Control Sheet as it shows the driver's gross sale and his percentage; in most cases the base pay is the same for all salesmen.

Reports to Management

This chapter has dealt primarily with accounting controls which have proved successful in the operation of a mobile industrial catering service. They have been utilized to advantage by the writer and were in some part initially introduced by me for application to this business. Since nothing could be found in accounting literature to use as a guide line, these reports were prepared as aids to the normal accounting cycle; they are offered here as examples that certainly could be improved upon and enlarged.

Management should be aware, in this business, of an element that distinguishes the mobile catering service from most other businesses. The route salesman, after several years of service to the same customers, will begin to assume that his operation belongs to him. The customers he serves are his friends; and this fact generates a problem. A suggested procedure is to find among route salesmen those who indicate supervisory or management potential. These men should be trained and developed along these lines and promoted as conditions permit.

The human element of this type of business is probably the one most difficult to control. There should be no credit extended to customers on the service routes. This should be company policy; but usually it will be found that the driver-salesman will assume this responsibility himself. If this is the case, he should be held strictly accountable at the close of each sales day for the collection of his receipts. The collection of sales taxes, a vital function of the driver-salesman, is also an integral part of this work. He should be held accountable for this tax collection.

There should always be among the company's route supervisors men who can operate all routes of the business, and they should be available to fill in for an absent driver-salesman without any interruption of the route's normal function.

This chapter has mentioned controls sufficient for the operating units; it is hoped that these guide lines and suggestions will be useful to the accountant who acquires among his clients an industrial catering service.

15

Cemeteries

BY FREDERICK F. CUE

**Public Accountant, East Green-
bush, New York; Secretary-Treasurer, East Greenbush Cemetery
Association, Inc.**

Characteristics of the Business That Affect the Accounting System

The primary purpose of a cemetery is to provide sequestered burial places and to maintain the grounds in an attractive manner. Graves are dug, foundations for monuments are installed, bronze markers and other bronze items are sold, and in some instances a shop is maintained to sell grave-decorating supplies to visitors. Crematories and related facilities for preserving ashes are sometimes operated by a cemetery. In many states there are state and local laws, ordinances and regulations governing many of the elements of operation. These should be ascertained by the accountant as soon as possible.

FUNCTIONAL CHARACTERISTICS OF THE BUSINESS

Thirty-three states now have laws regulating the operation of cemeteries. Many of these states require the submission of annual reports to cemetery

249

boards or other official governmental bodies having legal responsibility for enforcement of cemetery statutes and regulations. In New York State, all cemeteries (other than those operated by religious organizations and governmental units) must send an annual financial report to the State Cemetery Board on a calendar-year basis.

Governmental reporting requirements are an important factor in establishing a fiscal year. Weather is another important influence. In climates where the ground freezes and a heavy snow cover exists, most outdoor activities in cemeteries are suspended or drastically reduced from December through March. The calendar year is a good choice wherever this situation exists, since this type of fiscal period does not break up the eight-month term of maximum outdoor activities. In areas like lower California where freezing and snow are not problems, the fiscal period would not be affected by the weather and could be based on other factors such as lot sale cycles, local death cycles, and reporting requirements.

Some cemeteries are commercial enterprises and are interested in making a profit. Most are nonprofit, however, operated by cemetery associations, fraternal or benevolent societies, religious bodies, or governmental units.

PRINCIPAL ACCOUNTING PROBLEMS

In its initial development, and in subsequent expansions, a cemetery operation has the same cost allocation problems as a real estate development. The property must be surveyed and burial plots laid out. Roads and surface drains must be installed. Lawns must be planted and the property landscaped. The original land and development costs should be apportioned to each lot. This facilitates the setting of adequate selling prices and assures a proper return of capital investment. For commercial enterprises this also establishes the profit realized on each lot sale.

The selling price of a burial lot (or right) should include an amount which will yield an annual investment income sufficient to provide for its permanent maintenance. Many state laws require the establishment of permanent care funds. New York State law requires that a minimum portion of the selling price be preserved in a Permanent Maintenance Fund. The principal of this fund may not be expended except for certain purposes specified in the State Cemetery Law; and then only with the permission of a Supreme Court judge. This accounting problem is of a fiduciary nature.

Burial lots or rights are sometimes sold on an installment plan. No special accounting problems are involved when the purchase is financed through an outside financial organization. If the cemetery carries the accounts, installment accounting principles and problems exist.

Cemeteries are the recipients of gifts and bequests. Unrestricted gifts and bequests do not present any problems, as the disposition of these is subject to the decision of the policy-setting body of the cemetery. Restricted gifts and bequests present the trust accounting problem of assuring that each is used as specified by the donor. Under New York State law, gifts and bequests for care of graves must be placed in a Perpetual Care Fund. The principal of this fund may not be used under any circumstances.

The dependence of a cemetery on income from investments to finance part or all of its maintenance work means accounting for these numerous investments and the collection of interest and dividends. In many states it is required that funds dedicated to permanent maintenance, whether these be by gift, bequest or the setting aside of a portion of the selling price, be maintained in a separate, irrevocable trust. Usually strict regulations are imposed on the types of investments, the amount, the methods of transfer to the cemetery, and the use of the funds by the cemetery. For example, New York State law limits the amount of principal which can be invested in common stock.

Funds invested in amortizing first mortgages often involve the collection of payments in escrow for the subsequent liquidation of real estate taxes and insurance premiums on the mortgaged property. This presents the necessity to account for the receipts and disbursements of each escrow agreement.

A cost accounting problem of considerable magnitude exists. It is essential to know how much it costs to dig and fill a grave, clean up debris, repair the roads, paint the fences, etc. The fees charged for interments, monument foundations (the two major sources of current revenue), and other services, should cover the direct and indirect costs of providing these services. In New York State, these fees are subject to approval of the State Cemetery Board. Requests to increase fees must be supported by data from good cost accounting records. Alert business administration would make similar demands even where not required by law. The cost of maintaining graves is necessary for determining the proper fees for annual care and indicating when the portion of the lot's selling price for permanent maintenance should be raised.

Functional Organization

The operation of a cemetery involves the following functions:

(1) Administration, (2) investment of funds, (3) office work, (4) sales, (5) interments, disinterments, and inurnments; (6) monument foundations, stone work, bronze markers, and other bronze items; (7) maintenance of grounds, mausoleums, and columbariums; (8) maintenance and repair of equipment and buildings. In some cases the cemetery may also operate a crematory.

In a large cemetery, these functions would be segregated into the following organizational units:

1. General Administration (Administration, Investments, and Office)
2. Land, Crypt, and Niche Sales
3. General Maintenance (Grounds, Public Mausoleums, and Columbariums)
4. Interments, Disinterments, and Inurnments
5. Foundations and Stone Work
6. Bronze Markers and Other Bronze Items
7. Perpetual Care
8. Annual Care and Gardening
9. Crematory

As the size of the cemetery decreases, these basic functional units are combined until in a small rural cemetery, the first two are performed by the secretary-treasurer under the direction of the board of trustees. The remaining functions (excluding the crematory) are performed by a part-time superintendent with the occasional employment of special help or services.

Principles and Objectives of the Accounting System

Where an accounting system for cemeteries must provide the data required in the annual report to the State Cemetery Board, the system must assist management to fulfill the fiduciary responsibilities established by law and to support the validity of fees being charged. The probable existence of laws regulating the operation of cemeteries in the client's state, as well as ordinances in localities, should be determined.

For small cemeteries, records maintained on a cash basis will be satisfactory. A file of unpaid bills receivable, and unpaid bills payable, will suffice for control of these items. A schedule of equipment, with depreciation computations, provides depreciation data for periodic costing purposes and reviews. Amortization tables can be used for keeping account of mortgage payments received and escrow deposits. Other investments can be scheduled. Large cemeteries should maintain double-entry accrual accounting records with an integrated cost accounting system.

A budget is advisable because of the limited income and the legal prohibition against impairing trust funds and maintenance fund principal. The accounting system should provide the data necessary to show how the budget is being executed.

Classification of Accounts and Books of Accounts

The following chart of accounts can be adapted to the needs of any size or type of cemetery. In states where separate trust funds are required, or where it is believed desirable that they be maintained, the Perpetual Care Fund and the Permanent Maintenance Fund would be in a separate set of records. By prefixing each account with a Fund designation, the various fund accounts can be identified and grouped. Prefixes can also be used to analyze income and expenses by departments (cost centers) when such are warranted by the size of the cemetery operation.

BALANCE SHEET ACCOUNTS.

Fund Codes: 1000 General Fund
2000 Perpetual Care Fund
3000 Permanent Maintenance Fund

ASSETS

Current assets

Cash and bank

101 Petty Cash
102 Cash on Hand
103 Cash in Checking Accounts
104 Cash in Savings Accounts

Marketable securities

111 Stocks
112 Other Readily Marketable Securities

Receivables

122 Installment Accounts Receivable
123 Accounts Receivable
129 Accrued Assets (Interest, Dividends, etc.)

Inventories

131 Materials and Supplies
134 Finished Goods
137 Cemetery Lots for Sale

Other current assets

141 Prepaid Expenses and Deferred Charges
142 Advances to Salesmen
143 Due from Perpetual Care Fund
144 Due from Permanent Maintenance Fund

Investments

152 First Mortgages Owned
153 Investments Not Readily Marketable

Property, plant, and equipment

161 Undeveloped Land
162 Uncompleted Land Development Costs
164 Buildings
165 Cemetery Equipment
166 Motor Vehicles
167 Office Furniture and Fixtures
164R-167R Accumulated Depreciation Accounts

Other assets

192 Deposits of Payroll and Income Taxes withheld from Employees

LIABILITIES

Current liabilities

Notes and Accounts Payable

201 Notes Payable
205 Contracts Payable (less than one year)
206 Accounts Payable (Trade)
207 Accounts Payable for Lots Repurchased
211 Sales Tax Payable
221 Employee Payroll Deductions
    2211 Social Security Taxes (Old Age)
    2213 State Disability Insurance
    2214 Income Tax Withheld (Federal)
    2215 Income Tax Withheld (State)
    2216 Income Tax Withheld (City)
222 Employer Payroll Taxes Payable
    2221 Social Security Taxes (Old Age)
    2222 Federal Unemployment Tax
    2223 State Unemployment Tax

225 Accrued Payroll
226 Accrued Income Taxes Payable
227 Accrued Interest Payable
229 Other Accrued Liabilities

Other current liabilities

232 Portion of Collections Due Permanent Maintenance Fund
233 Portion of Collections Due Perpetual Care Fund
236 Deposits Received from Prospective Purchasers
237 Escrow Accounts
238 Dividends Payable

Long-term debts

241 Contracts Payable (longer than one year)
242 Mortgages Payable

Contingencies

260 Commissions Payable on Installment Sales Collections
261 Unrealized Profit on Installment Sales

NET WORTH

291 Capital Stock
297 Capital Surplus
298 Earned Surplus
299 Profit and Loss—Current

INCOME AND EXPENSE ACCOUNTS.

REVENUE

Sales

301 Graves and Plots—Cash or Open Account
302 Mausoleum Crypts—Cash or Open Account
303 Columbarium Niches—Cash or Open Account

305 Graves and Plots—Installment Basis
306 Mausoleum Crypts—Installment Basis
307 Columbarium Niches—Installment Basis
311 Interments
312 Disinterments

313 Inurnments
314 Foundations and Stone Work
315 Bronze Markers and Other
      Bronze Items
321 Annual Care and Gardening
331 Cremations

Cost of goods sold

401 Graves and Plots—Cash or
      Open Account
402 Mausoleum Crypts—Cash or
      Open Account
403 Columbarium Niches—Cash
      or Open Account
405 Graves and Plots—Intallment
      Basis
406 Mausoleum Crypts—Install-
      ment Basis
407 Columbarium Niches—Install-
      ment Basis
411 Interments
412 Disinterments
413 Inurnments
414 Foundations and Stone Work
415 Bronze Markers and Other
      Bronze Items
421 Annual Care and Gardening
431 Cremations

EXPENSES

*Single-department expense
  classification*

500 Expenses—Control

Multidepartment classification

501 General Administration
502 Land, Crypt, and Niche Sales
503 General Maintenance
504 Interments, Disinterments,
      and Inurnments
505 Foundations and Stone Work
506 Bronze Markers and Other
      Bronze Items
507 Perpetual Care

508 Annual Care and Gardening
509 Crematory

Salaries and wages

11 Administration
12 Supervision
13 Clerical
14 Wages
15 Vacations
16 Commissions
17 Watchmen

Supplies

21 Stationery
22 Operating Supplies
23 Gasoline and Oil
24 Automotive Supplies
25 Perishable Tools
26 Postage

Utilities and services

31 Heat, Light, Water, and Power
32 Telephone and Telegraph

Taxes

41 General
42 Payroll

Insurance

51 General
52 Workmen's Compensation
53 Employee Benefits

Depreciation

64 Buildings
65 Cemetery Equipment
66 Motor Vehicles
67 Office Furniture and Fixtures

Repair and maintenance

74 Building
75 Cemetery Equipment
76 Motor Vehicles
77 Office Furniture and Fixtures
78 Roads, Walks, and Paths

Other expense

81 Advertising
82 Losses on Bad Accounts
83 Donations
84 Dues and Subscriptions
85 Professional Services
86 Travel
87 Rentals

OTHER INCOME

602 Interest Earned

603 Dividends Received
604 Capital Gains
605 Deposits Forfeited
606 Gifts and Bequests
607 Filing Fees
609 Miscellaneous Income

DEDUCTIONS FROM INCOME

652 Interest Expense
654 Capital Losses
659 Miscellaneous Income

Obtain full expense subaccount numbers by adding the department number to the basic expense account number, i.e., 505-14 Wages—Foundations and Stone Work Department.

BOOKS AND FORMS PECULIAR TO THE BUSINESS

The journals and ledgers ordinarily used in a medium-sized business are applicable to a cemetery accounting system. Provision must be made for distributing labor costs by functions such as interments, foundations, general maintenance, annual maintenance, perpetual care, etc. Where volume justifies, various mechanical and electronic systems are available to expedite the record-keeping functions. A small cemetery will find the following combined Cash Receipts and Payments Record (Figure 1) adequate to its needs.

The following is an outline and description of some special records which, while not of an accounting nature, are essential to the proper management of a cemetery.

Record of Burials. This should be maintained in a permanently bound record book. The essential data to be recorded are: Name, age, date of burial, lot, plot or part thereof in which burial was made. Other information which may be recorded are the burial permit number, place of birth, last residence, occupation, sex, date and cause of death, lot-book page number, name of undertaker, physician, and owner of lot.

Lot Record. This is a permanent record of each lot sold or unsold. It shows the lot numbers, the number of graves in each lot, the area in square feet, the allocated cost, the list selling price, and the amounts to be allocated to the Current Maintenance Fund and the Permanent Maintenance Fund. When a sale is completed, the date, reference number, purchase price, number of graves sold, and the sales price are recorded. A notation is made when the deed is issued. If deeds are numbered, the deed number is recorded. Subsequent repurchases or transfers are also recorded in this record.

Burial Request, Order, and Report. This form is used to record the essen-

CASH RECEIPTS

DATE	DESCRIPTION	TOTAL RECEIVED	LOT SALES	PER. MAINT. FUND		INTER- MENTS	PER. CARE FUND		INTEREST & DIVIDENDS	ANNUAL CARE	OTHER	
				PRINCIPAL	INCOME		PRINCIPAL	INCOME			ACCOUNT	AMOUNT

CASH PAYMENTS

DATE	DESCRIPTION	TOTAL PAID	CHECK NO.	DEDUCTIONS FROM WAGES				GROSS SAL. & WAGES	SUPPLIES & EXPENSES	FOR ACCOUNT OF		OTHER	
				FED	FICA	STATE	OTHER			P. MAINT FD.	P. CARE FD.	ACCOUNT	AMOUNT

Figure 1: Cash Receipts and Payments Journal for a Small Cemetery

tial data regarding a proposed burial. This is checked against the lot record and if found proper, burial is authorized in a particular lot and grave, and the form is sent to the superintendent who orders the grave dug and the requested inurnments provided. A copy of the form is returned to the office by the superintendent when the services have been completed.

Other Communication Between Office and Superintendent. There must be a formal system of notifying the superintendent of lot sales, foundation and stone work to be done, annual care to be provided, special services paid for, complaints, etc. There must also be a reverse flow of purchase requests, receiving reports, notices of work performed, time cards, reports of hiring and layoff, and other personnel transactions.

Time and Payroll System

There are no peculiarities involved in this business. Wages may be on an hourly, unit, or weekly basis. Withholding taxes must be withheld and accounted for. Union dues and other deductions may be involved. Incentive payments may be found. The cost accounting system will determine to what extent time will have to be identified with specific functions or locations.

Cost Accounting and Departmental Accounting

The elements involved in determining the solvency (the term, profitability, would be used in a profit-seeking organization) of each department in a cemetery operation are well illustrated and summarized in a sample operating statement recommended by the New York State Cemetery Board (Figure 2). This statement incorporates the accounting requirements and standards of the New York State Cemetery Law. It can be modified to meet the legal requirements of other states when necessary. It can also be modified to meet the varying needs of different-size cemeteries. Emphasis is placed on the necessity of separating the funds to provide for ready analysis and reporting of each department and interdepartment transaction.

Principal departments are listed across the top of the statement and lettered "A" through "I". Departments "E", "F", "G", or "H" may be eliminated to the extent one or more are not applicable to a particular cemetery.

The income, expenses, and deductions enumerated on the left side of the sample may be modified to reflect particular needs. The statement (Figure 2) calls for detailed schedules to support or explain each item of expenses and deductions reported. The scope of these supporting schedules depends on the size and management needs of each operation.

Name of Cemetery..........

NUMBER OF ACRES (Total) _____
SOLD _____
UNSOLD _____

DEPARTMENTAL ANALYSIS OF INCOME AND EXPENSE

For Year Ending..........

	Total	A Land, Crypt and Niche Sales	B Current Maintenance	C Interments, Disinterments, and Increments	D Foundations and Stone Work	E Bronze Markers and Other Bronze Items	F Perpetual Care	G Annual Care and Gardening	H Cemetery	I General Administrative Overhead
INCOME										
1. Sale of Graves and Plots	$	$ (85%)	$ (15%)	$	$	$	$	$	$	$
2. Sale of Mausoleum and Niche Spaces		(85%)	(15%)							
3. Interments and Disinterments										
4. Device, Greens, Tent and Grave Liners										
5. Foundations, Curbing, Walks, etc.										
6. Bronze Memorials										
7. All Other Bronze Items										
8. Annual or Seasonal Care										
9. Planting, Decorations and Other Gardening										
10. Cremations										
11. Filing and Recording Fees										
12. Miscellaneous Income										
13. Investment Income:										
14. General Funds										
15. Permanent Maintenance										
16. Perpetual Care										
17. TOTAL INCOME	$	$	$	$	$	$	$	$	$	$
EXPENSES AND DEDUCTIONS										
18. Wages, Salaries and Commissions (a)	$	$	$	$	$	$	$	$	$	$
19. Payroll Taxes and Related Costs (b)										
20. Other Direct Costs and Materials (c)										
21. Indirect Materials and Maintenance Costs (d)										
22. Depreciation and Amortization Costs (e)										
23. General and Administrative Expenses (f)										
24. Allocation to Permanent Maintenance (g)										
25. Due to Shareholders or Certificates										
26. TOTAL EXPENSES AND DEDUCTIONS	$	$	$	$	$	$	$	$	$	$
27. Surplus (or Deficit) before Overhead Allocation	$	$	$	$	$	$	$	$	$	$
28. Allocation of Overhead (h)	-0-									$
29. Surplus (or Deficit) from Operations	-0-	$	$	$	$	$	$	$	$	-0-

(a) Attach detailed schedule indicating method of determining costs and allocations of same.
(b) Attach detailed schedule similar to (a) above.
(c) Attach detailed schedule itemizing costs and to what department charged.
(d) Attach detailed schedule itemizing costs and indicate method of allocation of same.
(e) Attach detailed schedule itemizing costs and indicate method of allocation of same.
(f) Attach schedule itemizing such costs.
(g) This amount will be based upon the obligation to allocate to the trust fund from Land, Crypt and Niche sales, in any event not less than 10% of gross sales. (A New York State requirement.)
(h) Allocation of excess overhead is based upon the percentage that the income of each department bears to total income, exclusive of the General and Administrative Overhead Department.

Figure 2: Illustration of a Departmental Cost Statement

Reports to Management

For small cemeteries (50 or fewer interments a year) a simple statement twice a year of receipts and disbursements on a cash basis for each fund will suffice (Figure 3).

A cost analysis, once a year, should provide sufficient warning as to fees which are becoming inadequate. Most small cemeteries were established many years ago. The land was either donated or the cost so low that it was recovered a long time ago. Improvements, buildings, and equipment were not capitalized, and as the equipment was replaced, the replacement cost was charged off. The chief fiscal concerns of the management of a small cemetery are (1) to make certain that the Permanent Maintenance Fund principal increases so that income will also increase to the extent necessary to pay for the increasing cost of maintenance, (2) preserve the fund balances, (3) keep expenditures within income, and (4) increase income to the extent needed. A suggested formula for determining the necessary level of the Permanent Maintenance Fund principal and the portion of lot sales prices which should be set aside is presented in Figure 4.

As the size of the operation increases, the need for more frequent issuance of financial reports increases until monthly reports are necessary. When the operation is large enough to warrant the talent needed to maintain an accrual accounting system and account for capital assets (see chart of accounts), a regular balance sheet, following generally acceptable accounting theory and format, should be prepared monthly. The need to test the adequacy of Permanent Maintenance Fund accretions is even more important to a larger cemetery.

A monthly profit and loss statement should be presented. In order to judge results, the items of income and expenses should be shown in comparison with a budget (see previous reference to the need for a budget under Principles and Objectives). If a budget has not been prepared, then a comparison with the previous years' results will provide some idea of the direction in which the fiscal affairs are moving.

Summary

The operation of a cemetery in some states is not unlike that of a public utility. Rates must be approved by a state regulating agency and a cemetery, once started, must continue to operate. While cemeteries operated by religious and governmental units are usually exempt from state regulations, it would be prudent to apply the same financial criteria to them and assure the

SMALL CEMETERY ASSOCIATION, INC.
FUND REPORTS AS OF DECEMBER 31, 19__

GENERAL FUND

FUND BALANCE BEGINNING OF PERIOD $15,100.00

INCOME:
Lot and Grave Sales - Gen'l Fund Portion $1,000.00
 "   "   "   "   - Permanent Maint. Portion 1,000.00
Interest Earned   900.00
Interment Fees   1,500.00
Foundations   500.00
Annual Care   300.00
Other   100.00   5,300.00
TOTAL TO BE ACCOUNTED FOR $20,400.00

EXPENSES:
Salaries and Wages   4,000.00
Payroll Taxes   300.00
Supplies and Materials   800.00
Repairs   300.00
Insurance   300.00
Professional Fees   400.00
Other   200.00   6,300.00
FUND BALANCE BEFORE INTER-FUND TRANSACTIONS $14,100.00

DUE FROM (PERMANENT) MAINTENANCE FUND   2,300.00

DUE FROM PERPETUAL CARE FUND   1,000.00

DUE FROM TRUST FUNDS   200.00   3,500.00
                                                              $17,600.00

DUE TO PERMANENT MAINTENANCE FUND   1,000.00

FUND BALANCE END OF PERIOD (See attached Schedule for Assets) $16,600.00

PERMANENT MAINTENANCE FUND

FUND BALANCE BEGINNING OF PERIOD $50,000.00

INCOME:
Interest $2,000.00
Dividends   500.00   2,500.00
TOTAL TO BE ACCOUNTED FOR $52,500.00

Due from General Fund - Lot and Grave Sales   1,000.00
Due to   "   "   - Maintenance Costs   -2,300.00   (1,300.00)
FUND BALANCE END OF PERIOD (See attached Schedule for Assets) $51,200.00

(Similar data would be presented for the
Perpetual Care Fund and any other trust funds.)

Figure 3: Simple Fund Report for Small Cemetery

ANY CEMETERY
STATEMENT OF PROJECTED FUNDING REQUIREMENTS AND ANNUAL
CURRENT REVENUE NEEDS FOR MAINTAINING GROUNDS AND GRAVES

Area to be Maintained	In Acres	IN GRAVE SPACES Per Acre	Total	INTERMENTS Per Grave Space	Total
Total area of Cemetery	50	(a)950	47,500	1	47,500
Already Sold	25	950	23,750	1	23,750
Available for Sale	25	950	23,750	(b)1	23,750
Developed	10	950	9,500	(b)1	9,500
Undeveloped	15	950	14,250	(b)1	14,250

(a) Based on 4' x 10' graves with a 2' wide access path every 2
     rows of graves.
(b) This could be increased to 2, and possibly 3, but the latter
     presents serious excavation problems because of the necessary
     depth of the lowest grave.

Funding Needs	For Acreage Sold	For Developed Acreage Not Sold	For Undeveloped Acres	For Total Cemetery
Number of Graves	23,750	9,500	14,250	47,500
Operating Income needed per Grave	(c) $2.00	$2.00	$2.00	$2.00
Total Income Needed	$47,500	$19,000	$28,500	$95,000
Current Rate of Investment Return	5%	5%	5%	5%
Principal Fund Needed	$950,000	$380,000	$570,000	$1,900,000
Less Present Principal on Hand	$200,000	--	--	$200,000
Deficiency or Need	$750,000	$380,000	$570,000	$1,700,000
Allocate to unsold Graves	-$750,000	+$300,000	+$450,000	--
To be Raised from Sales	--	$680,000	$1,020,000	$1,700,000
Amount needed per grave sold	--	$71.50	$71.50	$71.50

CURRENT MAINTENANCE   37,500
 ($47,500 - $10,000)

Est. Annual Grave Sales   ←—500 graves

Current Maintenance Allocation
 from each Grave Sold   ←—(d) 75.00

(c) This should be determined each year, using Figure 2 Costs.
(d) May also be expressed as a percentage of selling price of Graves.
(e) This is the current annual investment income from the $200,000
     Principal Fund Balance in the Permanent Maintenance Fund.

Figure 4:   Annual Projection of Amount Needed (in addition to recovery of
            capital investment) to Cover Current Maintenance Deficiency and
            to Yield a Principal Fund Adequate to Future Need

same financially sound, continuing operation as for supervised cemeteries. State regulating agencies are usually an excellent source of advice on particular problems and so are the various associations of personnel and business organizations interested in cemetery operations. The accounting system should yield the information necessary for management to control expenditures and accumulate the funds necessary to operate the cemetery in perpetuity.

16

Chemical Manufacturing

BY MARC A. FREDERICK, SR.

Partner and Founder, Marc A. Frederick Sr. & Company, Long Beach, California; Chairman of the Board, MAF Development Corporation, Long Beach; President, Commercial Industrial Management Services Company, Long Beach; President, Cimsco Data Processing Company, Long Beach; Director, Aerlab, Inc., Norwalk, California; Director, Elliff Engineering and Manufacturing Company, Inc., Paramount, California

Purpose of the Chapter

This system is written for the process manufacturer such as the chemical products manufacturer, manufacturer of greases/lubricants, and thread dope, and manufacturers of other items adaptable to the processing system.

Because the accountant so often is looking for ideas in systems, perhaps for an industry which is foreign to him, this chapter will be broad rather than specific. For instance, when ingredients of a formula are discussed, the ingredients may be limited to two or three. A formula may have more or fewer ingredients in it, but the accountant would use the same principles, expanding or contracting, accordingly, his inventories and the number of ingredients going into the processing.

Characteristics of the Business That Affect the Accounting System

This industry, as a whole, is one whose products are manufactured (processed) in accordance with a formula (recipe). The ingredients are mixed in certain quantities, and often in a certain sequence. They then may be subjected to heat, cold, or a combination of both. They may be subjected to pressures in one form or another. These sequences of happenings must be analyzed and broken down by the accountant to enable him to establish certain key points wherein costs of manufacturing can be accumulated.

Key points may vary from one product to another. In large plants, there will be a department for the manufacture of each product, and so process cost accounting may be the method to use. However, in a small to medium-sized business, where capital will usually limit the amount of equipment available as well as space, the producer must limit production to one or two items at a time, clean his equipment, and start on the next product line. The accountant may wish to use job cost methods here, rather than process cost.

FUNCTIONAL CHARACTERISTICS OF THE INDUSTRY

In either case—job cost or process cost—the industry requires good cost figures. In the manufacturing of soaps, cleaning detergents, and greases, competition is extremely high. Unless the businessman has accurate and fine cost figures on which he can rely, competition will soon have him out of business.

Albeit competition is characteristic of any business, it is not quite as forceful in some as in others. The industries mentioned above are in the latter category.

In a small to medium-sized plant there is usually a basic product that the manufacturer depends on to enable him to meet his everyday costs. The other products will give his profits *if* he is operating on a profitable basis. Depending on the capital and available space for production (and sales), the basic product will be in continuous production, while the rest of the production equipment will be used alternately between the other items he produces.

Too often this businessman does not know what his cost is . . . what his breakeven point is. He might be better off to drop one of his lines, or perhaps to add more equipment. None of these questions can be answered properly unless the costs are known.

Certain manufacturing firms may have products that are seasonal in nature. These may cause peak production periods. Care must be taken, whenever possible and not contrary to IRS ruling, to establish the firm's fiscal period so it will end at a time when inventories would be at the lowest point and work schedules at a minimal. This will ease the accountant's burden and reduce the client's year-end cost, such as inventory taking, and it will not interfere with his busy season. Better cooperation is the important by-product here.

PRINCIPAL ACCOUNTING PROBLEMS

The main problem which confronts the accountant, especially where cost systems are in effect, is the accuracy and consistency in filling out the necessary documents inherent to any cost system. The larger the firm, the more cooperation can be expected; the smaller the firm, the more reluctance on the part of the owner as well as the employees to filling out and maintaining the forms necessary to a cost system.

A certain manufacturer will have a basic product which is manufactured day in and day out in Department A. He will also have several other products which are handled in Department B. Here, there is justification in using the process cost for Department A, and job cost method for Department B.

Should some accountants not wish to use the process cost, then the job cost method can still be used successfully by the assignment of a job cost number to coincide with the batch number. This is a natural way of assigning both batch process and job cost numbers, and they are tied into production runs automatically. Department A would have an "A" or "1" prefix; Department B, a "B" or "2" prefix. The numerals are preferable in the event electronic equipment might be used in the future.

It is important, therefore, for the accountant to formulate the plan of operation of the system from the very first. He should evaluate the functions of the various departments, available help, how he expects to accumulate the material costs, labor costs, other direct, and indirect production costs. This must all be done with the minimum of change from existing methods. The client's confidence must be acquired from the beginning and reluctances coped with tactfully. A good cost system means use of material control and use of requisitions.

In a small plant and even in some larger ones, little or no control exists. Employees simply draw the required materials and go about their business. Waste, spillage, breakage, and thefts are easily accomplished. No records are generally kept or if they are, the employees "estimate" the amount of each item going into a job. If any attempts are made at cost control, they are usually on a system which is separate from the books of accounts. There is seldom any effort to try to reconcile these costs with the books of accounts; for the most part costs are so incomplete as to generally render them entirely or at least almost entirely useless.

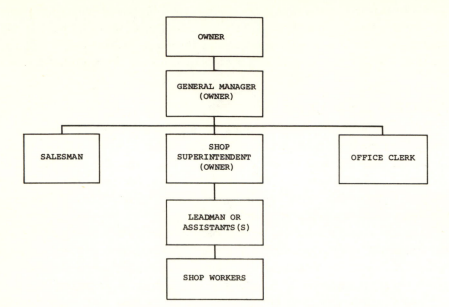

Figure I: Simple Organizational Chart

The accountant may find that in order to establish a worthwhile set of books with an integrated cost system, he may first have to render some management advisory services.

Functional Organization

Delegation of responsibility and complexity of records will depend upon the size of the firm, i.e., number of personnel, number of departments, and number of product or line items. Figure 1 shows the organization chart for a comparatively small and simple manufacturer, while Figure 2 pertains to a larger and more complex firm.

Classification of Accounts and Books of Accounts

Following is a General ledger chart of accounts. This chart may be expanded or contracted to meet the specific circumstances of each client. Only the controlling accounts of the manufacturing or burden accounts are in the main body of the chart.

The Manufacturing Expense ledger chart of accounts follows the General ledger chart. This is done so as not to confuse the reader when reference to an account is made.

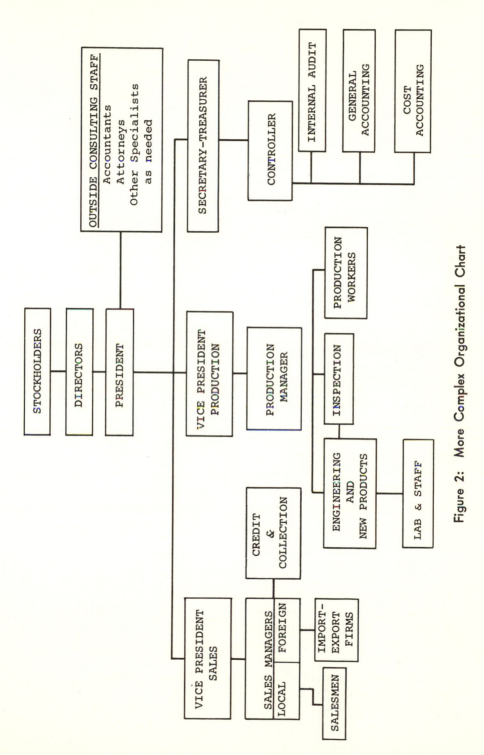

Figure 2:   More Complex Organizational Chart

BALANCE SHEET ACCOUNTS.

ASSETS

Current assets

1010 Cash on Hand
1020 Petty Cash
1030 Cash in Bank—General
1040 Cash in Bank—Payroll
1070 Accounts Receivable—Trade
1092 Accounts Receivable—Officers
1111 Inventory—Raw Material
1112 Inventory—In Process
1113 Inventory—Finished Goods
1120 Prepaid Expenses

Fixed assets

1200 Land
1210 Buildings
1211 Depreciation, Buildings
1230 Equipment
1231 Depreciation, Equipment

Other assets

1430 Deposits Refundable
1440 Organization Expense

LIABILITIES

Current liabilities

1510 Accounts Payable
1520 Accrued Salaries
1530 State Disability Insurance
1550 FICA and Withholding Tax Payable
1570 Sales Tax Payable

Long-term debt

1810 Notes Payable
1811 Notes Payable—Officers
1830 Contracts Payable
1850 Mortgages Payable

Deferred credits

2170 Security Deposit on Sales Orders
2180 Deferred Income

NET WORTH

2221 Capital Stock Issued
2222 Paid-In Capital
2250 Treasury Stock
2324 Retained Earnings
2325 Dividends Paid

INCOME AND EXPENSE ACCOUNTS.

INCOME

2360 Sales—Nontaxable
2470 Sales—Taxable
2480 Discount on Sales—Nontaxable
2481 Discount on Sales—Taxable
2490 Returned Sales—Nontaxable
2491 Returned Sales—Taxable

Cost of sales

2530 Material Purchases
2585 Manufacturing Overhead
2589 Variance Account

EXPENSES

Sales expense

2610 Advertising
2620 Commissions
2640 Auto Expense
2641 Delivery Expense
2660 Dues and Subscriptions

General and administrative

2705 Officers' Salaries
2710 Wages
2730 Payroll Taxes

2731 Directors' Fees
2750 Auto Expenses
2760 Depreciation
2790 Utilities
2800 Insurance
2810 Licenses and Taxes
2811 Real Estate Tax—County
2812 Real Estate Tax—City
2830 Legal and Accounting
2831 Auditing Fees
2840 Repairs and Maintenance
2850 Rent

2880 Phone
2890 Office Supplies
2940 Organization Expense

OTHER INCOME

3050 Interest Earned
3060 Discounts Taken

OTHER EXPENSE

3120 Interest Paid
3130 Factoring Fees and Cost

As mentioned before, provision for numbers for each of the account titles should be made to allow for possible future processing on electronic card or computers. This provision is wise, regardless of whether processing would be done through the client's own equipment or through a data processing center.

Manufacturing Expense ledger accounts are given below.

1112. *Inventory in Process*
  .02 Labor
  .06 Materials
  .10 Operating Supplies
  .14 Repairs
  .15 Maintenance and Janitorial
  .17 Depreciation
  .20 Payroll Taxes

  .24 Freight In
  .28 Rent
  .30 Utilities
  .32 Equipment Rental
  .35 Personal Property Tax
  .37 Insurance
  .39 Workmen's Compensation
  .40 Supervisory Salaries

Once the chart of accounts is completed, the General ledger is fairly well organized. When using a numerical system such as the one above, it will behoove the accountant to allow for sufficient numbers between each account used to enable him to add future accounts if need be.

ACCOUNTS PECULIAR TO THE BUSINESS

When the cost system is integrated into the general books of accounts, there will be certain accounts found to be peculiar to a cost system. These have been taken from the chart of accounts and a brief description of each follows:

Inventory—Raw Materials (No. 1111) is the controlling account. The detail of this account may be a cardex system, or any other suitable record to keep a chronological record of the number of units and the amount or value on hand of each item. The total amounts or value of all the detail cards or sheets of paper on which each item is recorded, must agree with the control in the General ledger—No. 1111. This account is charged with all materials purchased rather than charging them to a purchase account. No. 1111 is credited with amounts consumed, or taken out and placed into production.

Inventory—In Process (No. 1112). This account is charged (debited) with the total direct labor payroll and with the total materials taken out of Inventory—Raw Materials. It is also charged with the amount of overhead costs. These costs are listed in the chart above as Manufacturing Expense ledger accounts. Account No. 1112 is credited with the totals of each job card when the job is finally completed.

Inventory—Finished Products (No. 1113). The account is charged with the total of each job completed. Inventory—In Process (No. 1112) would be credited as above indicated. No. 1113 is credited with amount sold.

Factoring Fees and Cost (No. 3130). These costs should not be buried in other accounts but should be separate from other costs, for management's inspection and analysis.

Peculiarities of Procedures

RELIEVING THE VARIOUS INVENTORY ACCOUNTS

All incoming materials are charged to the Inventory—Raw Materials account (No. 1111) and labor and indirect costs to Inventory—In Process (No. 1112). These accounts are relieved at the end of the month as follows:

1. All completed job cost cards are added, and the total of all cards charged to Inventory—Finished Products (No. 1113).

2. Total of the Material column from all cards is credited to Inventory—Raw Material (No. 1111).

3. Totals of the Labor and Overhead columns from all cards are credited to Inventory—In Process (No. 1112).

Next, all cards for work in process, i.e., work begun during the month and not completed at close of business on the last work day of the month, are added, and:

1. Total of the Material column is charged to Inventory—in Process (No. 1112) and credited to Inventory—Raw Material (No. 1111).

2. Total of the material for the previous month is reversed by debiting Raw Material (No. 1111) and crediting In Process (No. 1112).

3. Labor and overhead (or indirect costs) are already charged to the In Process account (see above) and, therefore, no adjustments or journal entry is required.

This latter method is simpler and much faster but only as accurate as the standard rates established.

When using standard cost, the variance, that is the difference (more or less) between actual cost and standard cost, is charged or credited to the Variance Account (No. 2589). If the Variance Account balance is small and remains so, the standard costs are probably within close proximity of actual costs; but if they vary widely, a second look and recomputation of the rates used may be in order.

Standard rates should be changed whenever cost changes and should be reviewed at least once a year.

ELEMENTS OF COST FLOW

The three Inventory accounts described above (Nos. 1111, 1112, and 1113) are peculiar to the manufacturing industry as a whole and are allied to a cost system. They are the General ledger's controlling accounts of the Manufacturing ledger.

Figure 3 illustrates the flow of elements of cost in chart form. The Inventory—Raw Materials account (No. 1111) is charged with all direct materials and packaging materials; boxes, plastic containers, cartons. Larger types of packaging for shipping are not considered a direct charge and, therefore, are charged to Operating Supplies (No. 1112.10), an indirect manufacturing expense.

Indirect manufacturing costs, oftentimes referred to as overhead costs, are those costs which cannot readily be charged to a specific job lot or are too insignificant to cost out on a unit basis and charged directly to the job.

Such costs would be rent, depreciation on plant and plant equipment, supervisory labor, repairs and maintenance on equipment, taxes on equipment, operating supplies, insurance, etc. Although a part of manufacturing, they are indirect costs.

To break them down per job may involve accounting costs that would not be justified; hence the accumulation of such manufacturing costs in the "Plant ledger" or "Manufacturing Cost" section of the General ledger.

There are several ways to allocate this burden to the various jobs. The most popular method is based on direct labor hours. Other methods are: direct labor dollar costs, direct machine hours, square footage basis (for rental cost allocation); however, the direct labor hours system is used in the examples that follow because it is a timesaver and more accurate.

An account must be maintained for direct labor hours on each cost ledger card by month so that each job may be allocated its proper share of burden or overhead.

HOW TO MAKE THE SURVEY FOR THE COST SYSTEM

Before designing any cost system, much time and many false starts will be saved by the survey.

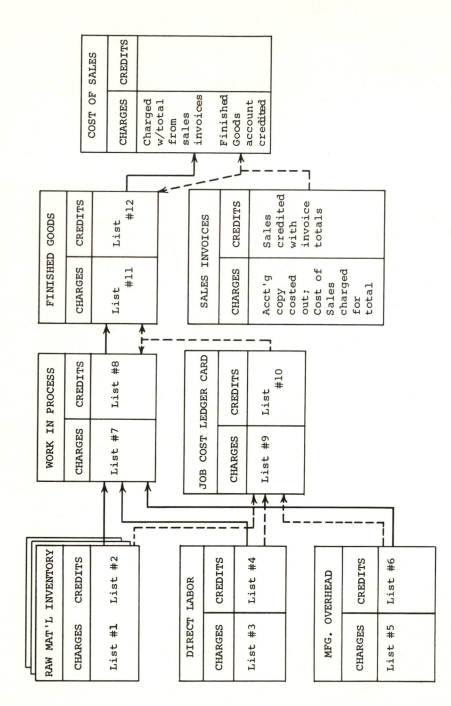

Figure 3: Flow of Elements of Costs at Each "Station" from Raw Materials to Total Cost of Sales

Footnotes to Figure 3.

List #1.   Raw materials coming in are charged, and Accounts Payable is credited.

List #2.   This account is credited with raw materials withdrawn, and the Work is Process account is charged.

List #3.   Charged with the total of the Direct Labor column of the Payroll journal; Cash in Bank -- Payroll is credited.

List #4.   Total of this account is transferred to In Process at end of the month.

List #5.   This account is charged with manufacturing rent, utilities, depreciation, supervision salaries, repairs and maintenance, payroll taxes, insurance, etc.

List #6.   Total of this account charged to In Process at month end.

List #7.   Charges from raw material, direct labor, and overhead accounts.

List #8.   This account is credited with the total of each completed job at end of month.

List #9.   Totals of labor, subcontracts, materials, share of overhead, etc., for each job completed during month are added, and this total is credited to Work in Process and debited to Finished Goods account.

List #10. Credited with the total cost of the job.

List #11. Total of completed jobs is charged to Finished Goods account (from Work in Process).

List #12. Finished Goods account credited at end of month with total of goods sold.

The survey is twofold: The plant survey (processing) and the physical layout of the plant. To make the plant survey the accountant goes through the plant with his client, who explains each process, beginning with receipt of raw materials and packaging supplies and their storage location, all the way through to storage of the completed product ready for shipment. Assessment of the physical layout of the plant would include equipment, materials, processing stations, mode of moving ingredients from one point to another and to completion. The two surveys should parallel each other.

From notes taken, a chart (Figure 3) should be drawn to depict the entire process of each product to determine the cost accumulating centers or accounts to be used.

In Figure 4 the flow of raw materials, packaging and operating supplies, direct labor, and overhead expenses starts at left (1), moves to inventory (2), then to the product being mixed (3). At this point raw materials, supplies, direct labor, and overhead are charged to Inventory—In Process. In the next step in processing (3) a catalyst from the operating supplies account is charged to Inventory—In Process. In step (4) the product, now completed, is being packaged and is finally stored (5), ready for shipment when sold.

In this way the accountant becomes familiar with the client's plant and methods of operation. With the procedure reduced to a flow chart, the accounts in which costs are accumulated up to predetermined points of processing are made clearer and easier to follow. Unnecessary work is eliminated and a better cost picture is obtained.

The detail, i.e., the number of accounts that will be used to accumulate the direct costs and the manufacturing costs, will be controlled by the size of the firm. The principle, however, remains the same.

COSTING METHODS

Before going into the descriptions of subsidiary records to the controlling accounts for goods in process and finished goods, a brief look should be cast at several available types of costing methods. They are:

1. Job Cost System
2. Process Cost System
3. Hybrid Cost System
4. Operational Cost System
5. Class Cost System
6. Lot or Release Cost System
7. Standard Cost System
8. Historical Cost System
9. Predetermined Cost System

*Job Cost System.** Cost is gathered or compiled for a specific job order, the quantity of which has been predetermined and a number assigned. The

* Eric L. Kohler, *A Dictionary for Accountants,* Englewood Cliffs, N.J.: Prentice-Hall, Inc., 1952.

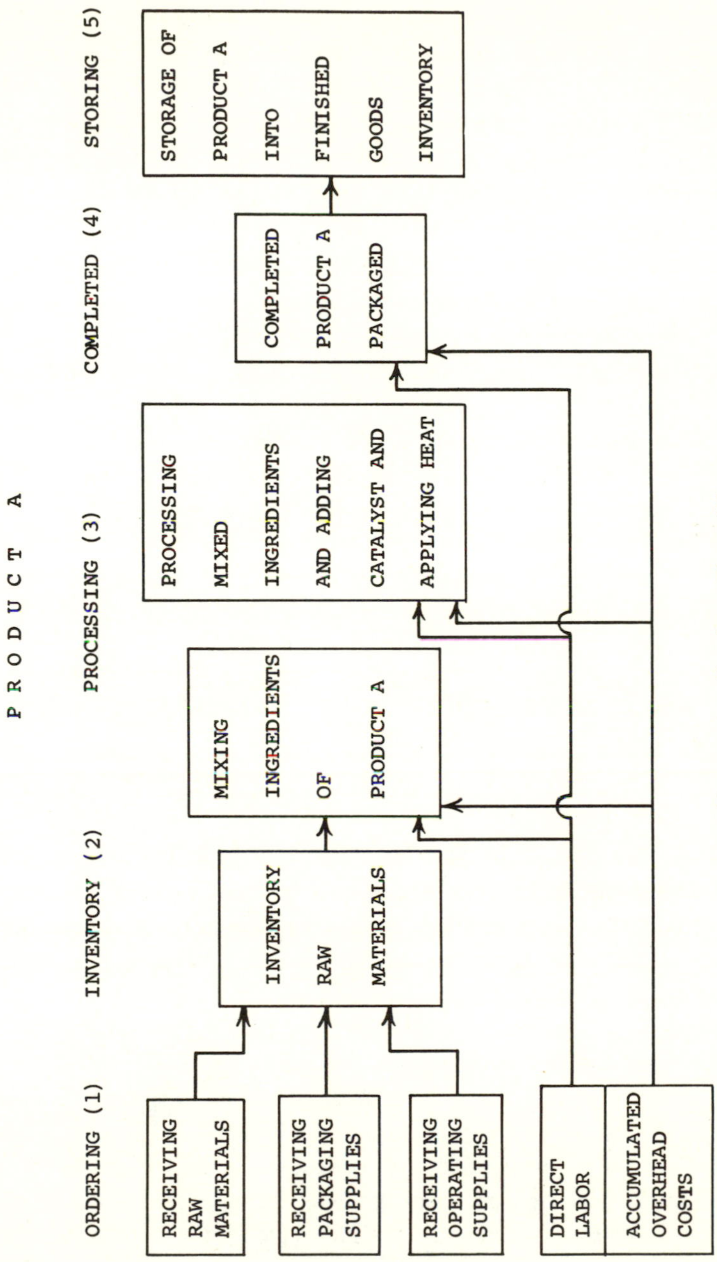

PRODUCT A

ORDERING (1)   INVENTORY (2)   PROCESSING (3)   COMPLETED (4)   STORING (5)

Figure 4: Product Flow Chart

materials, direct labor, direct expenses, and a portion of the overhead are charged to this identifiable job order.

*Process Cost System.** In this system costs are charged to processes rather than to specific units. Process cost is good where the units cannot be identified or separated as in a job order cost system.

Hybrid Cost System. This system is so named because it is a combination of two or more of the systems described here. That is, a Process and a Job Cost combination, for example, using a Historical as well as Predetermined or Standard Cost methods.

Operational Cost System. This method is a refinement of the Process Cost. Costs are accumulated by operation rather than a process as a whole. Thus the unit cost is determined by adding the costs of all operations. A more detailed accounting is required and a sounder base for standard costs is established.

Class Cost System. Recommended as particularly suitable for foundries and paper mills. Basically, similar "classes" of products are grouped together by batches and a job number is assigned to each batch. The costs of manufacturing are thus obtained and divided by the total units to obtain the per unit costs. The system provides savings of time and money and is basically comprised of the Job Cost and Process Cost methods of accounting. Obviously this system can only be used where the various products are similar enough to warrant combining production of them.

Lot or Release Cost System. That type of production subject to engineering changes would be applicable to this system. Here an order of 100 may be broken into lots of 10, 15, 15, 25, and 35. An aircraft manufacturing firm would fit this category.

Standard Cost System. A Standard Cost system is one wherein the component costs—parts, labor, overhead, etc.—are costed out at a standard cost. Arrived at scientifically, this cost is assigned to the parts, components, operations, and/or processes. It can be used in the Job Cost as well as the Process Cost system.

Historical Cost System. In a Historical or actual cost system the records summarize costs as they occur. Costs are determined only after the manufacturing operations or services have been rendered. Principal advantage of the Historical Cost system is that costs actually incurred are recorded for a specific job or for a given period. This system is indispensable for governmental contracts based on cost-plus-fixed-fee agreement.

Historical costs are regarded as of little value in the control of operations due to lack of comparability between periods and the absence of standard

---

* Eric L. Kohler, *A Dictionary for Accountants,* Englewood Cliffs, N.J.: Prentice-Hall, Inc., 1952.

units of measurement. Also by the time statements are out, it is too late to correct costs that are excessive inasmuch as the job is completed.

Predetermined Cost System. As the word implies, predetermined costs are those established before production. This system is used when management is primarily interested in what costs should be rather than in what they are. Predetermined costs may be "educated" estimates or standard costs acquired scientifically.

For more detailed information on the various cost methods, reference is made to Section 6, pages 8 through 22, *Acountants Handbook, 4th edition,* edited by Rufus Wixon and Walter G. Kell, copyright (c) 1956, The Ronald Press Company, New York.

DEVELOPING THE SYSTEM

After decision is made of the appropriate cost method to use (the one best suited to the client and one in which he will cooperate in obtaining necessary accounting data), the system must be developed and put into practice. The following formula for oil and grease cleaner, shown below, will serve as a basis for the Job Cost system as explained. The formula is broken down into ingredients and unit cost at standard prices.

OIL AND GREASE CLEANER ID #101

	Unit	Total
32½ lbs. Sodium sulphate	$ .0113	$ .367
10 lbs. Trend neutral beads	.1083	1.083
10 lbs. Soda ash	.0436	.436
10 lbs. Borax	.0475	.475
10 lbs. Calcium oxide (miracle lime)	.0540	.540
5 lbs. 666 (metze)	.1333	.667
10 lbs. TSP (tri-sodium phosphate)	.0700	.700
10 lbs. Kence (calcium carbonate)	.0129	.129
3 cans (32½ lb. each)	.9400	2.820
TOTAL DIRECT MATERIAL COST		$7.217

Note that standard material costs have been used to price out the several ingredients in this formula. The mixer used is a small one and will handle up to 350 pounds at a time. The container is a 32½-pound size; each batch will fill 10 containers.

BOOKS AND FORMS

Before proceeding further, familiarity with the forms used in the system will help to clarify and pave the way to understanding of the applications discussed.

Five forms constitute the basis of the system. They are a journal sheet, the Record of Invoices and Work in Progress; another journal sheet called the Record of Checks Drawn; a subsidiary ledger card from the Job Cost ledger; a second subsidiary ledger card from the Accounts Payable ledger; and a deck of Accounts Payable checks.

The Record of Invoices and Work in Progress (Figure 5) is used to record *all* invoices regardless of whether they are charged directly or indirectly to a job order. This will include accrued payroll—direct and indirect.

The Accounts Payable ledger card (Figure 6) is made up for each vendor and is used (with carbon) to enter invoices on the Invoice journal (Figure 5) on the Accounts Payable Pegboard System (Figure 8), and also when paying (Figure 10).

The Job Cost ledger card (Figure 7) is prepared to show the following information:

1. Job number (same as batch number)
2. Job name (Oil and Grease Cleaner, as shown in the preceding formula)
3. In lieu of "address", insert the total number of pounds produced for this batch, and number and size of containers.

The system being adapted to manufacturing job cost was actually designed for contractors. However, with some slight modifications, it can be converted to manufacturing use, thus saving much time for the write-up work. It will also reduce the number of potential errors in duplicating the entries into subsidiary records.

When an invoice is received, the Record of Invoices (Figure 5) is placed on the pegboard to be held in place as shown in Figure 8. The carbon papers are then placed on the left side over the Record of Invoices and the other appropriate carbons at the right side.

The Accounts Payable ledger card is pulled from the file and is placed on the left side of the pegboard, directly on top of the carbons and the journal as shown in Figure 8. If the invoice is for a general expense, the entry may now be made.

The purchase may be for an item to be charged directly to a job; for instance, materials bought from the ABC Company for use on job No. 123. After the ABC Company's Accounts Payable ledger card is placed at the left over the Record of Invoices, the job order card No. 123 (Figure 7) is also placed over the Record of Invoices, on the right-hand side. When used with carbon, this Job Cost ledger card makes it possible to enter and distribute simultaneously the expenditures to the job order card, whether direct materials or outside work. The latter would be entered in the column labeled Subcontracts.

Information on the invoice would be entered at left on the Accounts Payable ledger card (Figure 6), i.e., date, invoice number, the amount of the

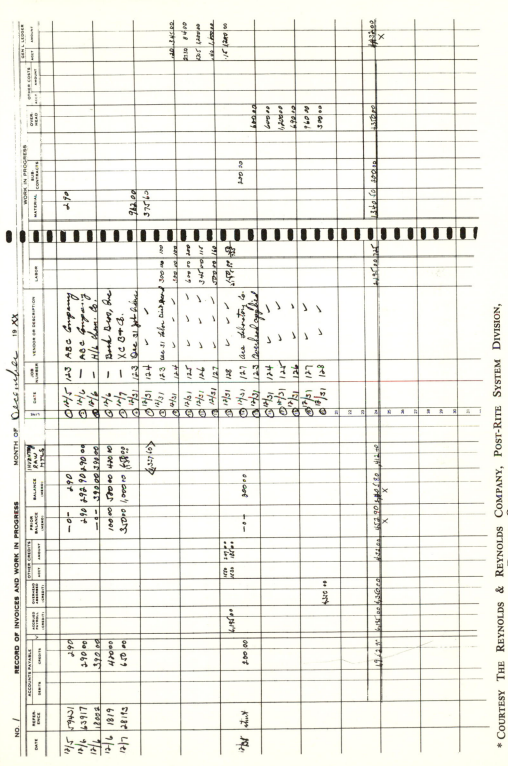

* COURTESY THE REYNOLDS & REYNOLDS COMPANY, POST-RITE SYSTEM DIVISION,
DAYTON, OHIO.

Figure 5: Invoice Register

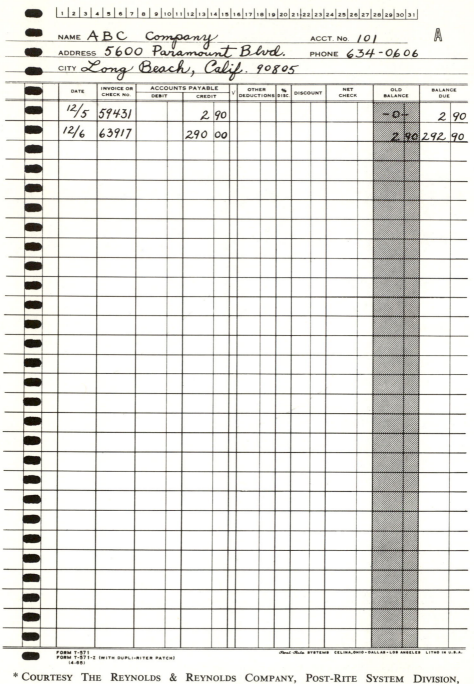

| | | | | | | | | | | | | | | | | | | | | | | | | | | | | | | |
|1|2|3|4|5|6|7|8|9|10|11|12|13|14|15|16|17|18|19|20|21|22|23|24|25|26|27|28|29|30|31|

NAME A B C Company   ACCT. No. 101   A

ADDRESS 5600 Paramount Blvd.   PHONE 634-0606

CITY Long Beach, Calif. 90805

DATE	INVOICE OR CHECK NO.	ACCOUNTS PAYABLE		V	OTHER DEDUCTIONS	% DISC.	DISCOUNT	NET CHECK	OLD BALANCE	BALANCE DUE
		DEBIT	CREDIT							
12/5	59431		2 90						-0-	2 90
12/6	63917		290 00						2 90	292 90

FORM T-571
FORM T-571-Z (WITH DUPLI-RITER PATCH)
(4-65)   Post-Rite SYSTEMS CELINA, OHIO · DALLAS · LOS ANGELES LITHO IN U.S.A.

Figure 6: Accounts Payable Ledger Card

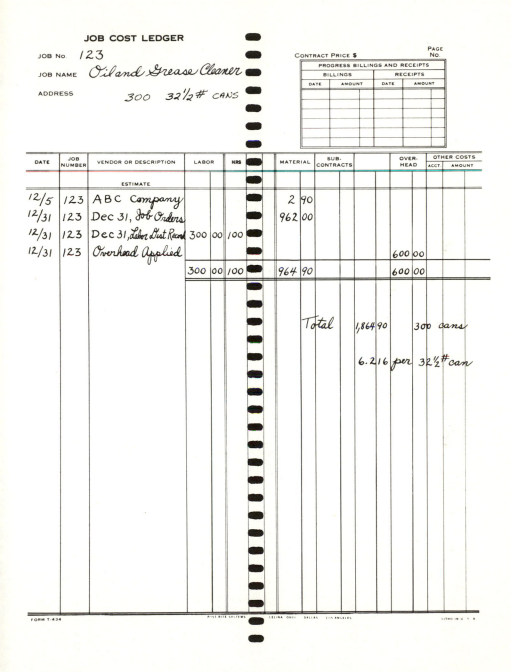

JOB COST LEDGER

JOB No. *123*

JOB NAME *Oil and Grease Cleaner*

ADDRESS *300 32½# cans*

CONTRACT PRICE $ _____   PAGE No. _____

PROGRESS BILLINGS AND RECEIPTS			
BILLINGS		RECEIPTS	
DATE	AMOUNT	DATE	AMOUNT

DATE	JOB NUMBER	VENDOR OR DESCRIPTION	LABOR	HRS	MATERIAL	SUB-CONTRACTS	OVER-HEAD	OTHER COSTS ACCT.	AMOUNT
		ESTIMATE							
12/5	123	ABC Company			2 90				
12/31	123	Dec 31, Job Orders			962 00				
12/31	123	Dec 31, Labor Dist Record	300 00	100					
12/31	123	Overhead Applied					600 00		
			300 00	100	964 90		600 00		
					Total	1,864 90		300 cans	
						6.216 per 32½# can			

FORM T-434   POST-RITE SYSTEMS   CELINA OHIO   DALLAS   LOS ANGELES   LITHO IN U S A

* COURTESY THE REYNOLDS & REYNOLDS COMPANY, POST-RITE SYSTEM DIVISION, DAYTON, OHIO.

Figure 7: Job Cost Ledger Card

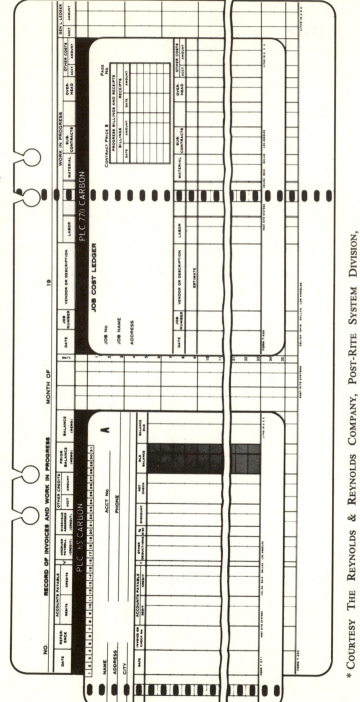

Figure 8:   Accounts Payable

*Courtesy The Reynolds & Reynolds Company, Post-Rite System Division, Dayton, Ohio.

bill credited in the Accounts Payable section; in the shaded area, the old balance owed ABC Company, if any. Then add the amount of the current invoice (amount in Credit column) to the old balance and enter the new amount owed in the Balance Due column.

Moving to the right of the pegboard, on the Job Cost ledger card (Figure 7) enter on the same line the date of entry, the job number, vendor's name (ABC Company), and the amount of the invoice in the Material column. If the material is for more than one job, take out the other Job Cost ledger cards and enter date, job number, and amount chargeable to each job separately. However, in this case, blank lines will remain on the left side of the journal, inasmuch as the total material bill was charged to one Accounts Payable card. To keep from lining up the next entry on a line already used on the right, simply circle each line number located in the center of the journal as it is used. This is done whether the line is used on the right side only, left side only, or both.

Inasmuch as the total of this particular invoice is for a specific job, the entire amount of the invoice is entered on the Job Cost ledger card under Materials column (assuming the invoice is for materials). With the entries completed as explained, the journal (Figure 5), the subsidiary Accounts Payable card (Figure 6), and the Job Cost ledger card (Figure 7) are all complete. With the use of carbons, the journal was automatically created and is a true and exact copy of the subsidiary records, thus assuring us of the accuracy of the entry.

Rent, the portion allocated to factory overhead, is entered in the General Ledger column and charged to account No. 1112.28 (Inventory—In Process), while the balance is charged to account No. 2850 (Rent, the general and administrative expense), and entered on the same line (off the Job Cost ledger card) in the General Ledger column at the far right of the journal (Figure 8).

After all invoices are thus entered, and usually at the end of the month, bills for invoices will be paid. This is easily accomplished by placing the white journal of Record of Checks Drawn (Form T-431*) on the pegboard (Figure 10), the same as was done with the Invoice journal form. Once more the carbons are set in place, and now a "bank" of checks (Figure 9) is set on the left side of the pegboard.

The appropriate Accounts Payable ledger card is removed from the file and slipped under the checks, so that the first available blank line is aligned *under* the strip of carbon on top of the check. The date, check number, gross amount of last balance (if this creditor is being paid in full) and the discount, if any, and the net check amount are entered. The previous balance would be followed by a "0" if paid in full; the name of the creditor is then entered. With this one simple entry the Check Record journal is completed, the Accounts

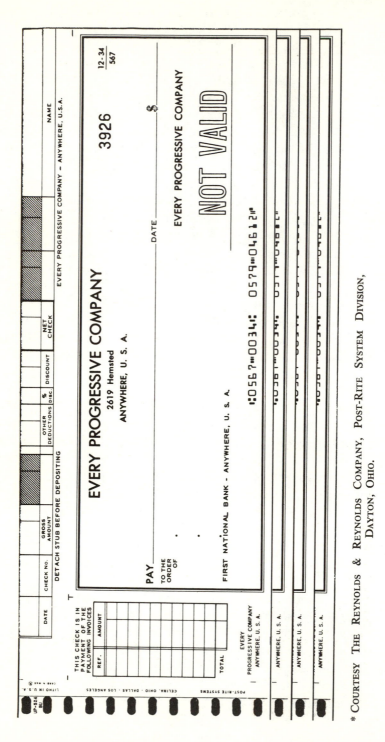

Figure 9: Check for Accounts Payable

* Courtesy The Reynolds & Reynolds Company, Post-Rite System Division, Dayton, Ohio.

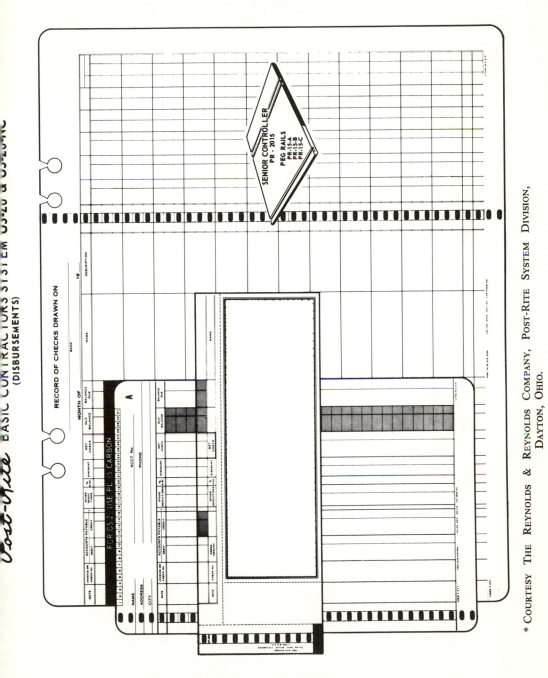

Figure 10:   Check Writing

* COURTESY THE REYNOLDS & REYNOLDS COMPANY, POST-RITE SYSTEM DIVISION, DAYTON, OHIO.

Payable ledger card is updated (subsidiary posting completed), and the check is all that need be made. Note that the carbon strip remains on the check and acts as a voucher; however, a voucher for additional detail is provided at the left.

On the check record, the right-hand side is used with the Job Cost ledger card only when a purchase is being made and paid for at time of purchase. In such an event no Accounts Payable card is used; hence the invoice record will not be used. Only the net check column is used with the date on the left side and the job card is used on the right.

In order to be consistent, however, it may be preferable to open an Accounts Payable card for miscellaneous one-time purchases, where it would not be practical to set up a payable card with a vendor's name for only one purchase. This card would be called "Accounts Payable Clearing". In that event the invoice would be posted in the Invoice Record as indicated, then placed on the check record and zeroed immediately by check payment. In any event, the accountant should choose either of the above methods, and once having made up his mind, follow through consistently.

For accounts using the cash basis, the Accounts Payable card would not be used nor Form T-433, the Invoice Record (Figure 5). In such cases the Job Cost ledger card would be used with the checks on Form T-431, the Record of Checks Drawn, exclusively.

Referring back to Figure 8, when the one entry is complete, distribution is also complete. There remains only to post to the Manufacturing Expense ledger those entries distributed to the General Ledger column at right. This can be done monthly at the time of posting to the ledger accounts. In practice it would not be practical to order 20 pounds of material—enough for just a small batch—so the journal is modified to make large purchases of materials possible and to bring them into the Inventory—Raw Materials (No. 1111). This is done simply by heading the blank column of the journal, next to Balance (memo) column, as follows: Inventory—Raw Materials. Now, larger, more convenient purchases may be made, and entry is accomplished as outlined above, but the account—the debit portion of the entry—is made in the newly headed column, and the Job Cost ledger card is not used. Compare line 1 with line 2 of the journal in Figure 5.

It can readily be seen by this comparison that the number of entries as in line 1 would render the system too cumbersome; hence the method in line 2 is adopted. However, there must be a means of distributing the material to each job. Figure 11 will do this nicely.

The Job Order Schedule (Figure 11) is a simple form which accomplishes several purposes. First, job orders are assigned and controlled. Second, the materials used are controlled through predetermined standard costs as indi-

JOB ORDER SCHEDULE

Month of _____ 19 ____

DATE	JOB NO.	DESCRIPTION	ID #	MAT'L ST. COST	NO. OF UNITS	TOTAL COST MAT'L	DATE STARTED	DATE COMPLETE	POSTED TO CARD
12/5	123	Oil and grease cleaner	101	9.62	100	962.00	✓ 12/5	12/5	12/6
12/5	124	Rug cleaner	119	12.52	30	375.60	✓ 12/5	12/5	12/6
		TOTAL				1,337.60 ✓			

Figure 11: Job Order Schedule and Direct Materials Applied

cated by the formula ID number, as in ID #101. Third, the scheduled starting date and the completion date. Fourth, the date the materials were posted
to Job Cost ledger card.

Figure 5, lines 6 and 7, indicates the fashion in which the monthly Job
Order Schedule is posted to each Job Cost card and journal, thus relieving
the Inventory—Raw Materials by a red or bracketed entry in the Inventory
—Raw Materials column and posting to the Job Cost card overlaid on the
journal, charging work in process.

THE PAYROLL DISTRIBUTION RECORD

The Payroll Distribution Record (Figure 12) is a simple and convenient
method of handling the payroll information for small shops. If a separate
bank account is used, or if separate checks (such as write-it-once payroll
checks) are used for recording payroll, the right side of the journal will have
columns for analytical purposes. These may be headed as in Figure 12 and
posted to the journal at month's end.

Although it is admittedly not mandatory to post all information to this
journal (Figure 5, Record of Invoices), it is advisable to journal through this
form at least all items that are distributed to Job Cost ledger cards. Note that
direct hours are posted to the card and through the carbon onto the journal.
A separate Job Cost ledger card for lines 8 through 13 has, of course, been
used. Particular attention is drawn to lines 1, 6, and 8 where Job Cost ledger
card for Job No. 123 has been employed. Likewise, lines 7 and 9, both items
being charged to Job No. 124, would be entered on Job No. 124 Job Cost
ledger card.

The other columns will be explained as they are recapped at month's end.

So far, invoices for materials, direct and indirect labor, and general and
administrative labor with overhead payroll taxes and general and administrative payroll tax distribution have been explained and demonstrated in Figure
7, Job Cost ledger card. There remains the manner of allocating to each Job
Cost ledger card the balance of burden or overhead costs. However, a way
must be found to gather these costs and allocate them properly to the job in
an equitable manner. The direct labor hours will be used for this purpose.

OVERHEAD DISTRIBUTION

Before going through an example of overhead distribution, it is necessary
to know what this amount is. The Manufacturing Expense ledger accounts,
shown in the chart of accounts, give a breakdown of the overhead accounts
used. This section of the chart, as is the case with the General ledger chart,
may be expanded or contracted to suit each individual client. It is well to
remember that the fewer the accounts, the better. Use only accounts that will
be pertinent and informative to the client. If there is no useful purpose in

LABOR DISTRIBUTION RECORD

MONTH _____ 19___

DATE	TOTAL PAYROLL	PAYROLL TAXES	GEN. & ADMIN.	SUPV. & INDIRECT	JOB NO. 123 HRS.	AMT.	JOB NO. 124 HRS.	AMT.	JOB NO. 125 HRS.	AMT.	JOB NO. 126 HRS.	AMT.	JOB NO. 127 HRS.	AMT.	JOB NO. 128 HRS.	AMT.	JOB NO. 129 HRS.	AMT.
12/7	1,585.00	110.00	300.00	700.00	100	300.00	50	150.00	20	60.00	15	45.00	10	30.00		—		—
12/14	1,390.00	97.00	300.00	700.00		—	50	150.00	80	240.00		—		—		—		—
12/21	1,600.00	112.00	300.00	700.00		—		—	100	300.00	100	300.00		—		—		—
12/28	1,620.00	113.00	300.00	700.00		300.00	100	300.00					150	470.00	50	150.00		—
	6,195.00	432.00	1,200.00	2,800.00	100	300.00	100	300.00	200	600.00	115	345.00	160	500.00	50	150.00		—

Figure 12: Payroll Distribution Record

having a certain account, then it is most likely not needed and this category of expense can be combined with another account.

Two principal sources of original entry will probably be used to accumulate overhead expenses. The first is the journal (Figure 5) for all purchases on account, thus using the Accounts Payable card (Figure 6); and, second, the Check Disbursement register. For the purpose of illustration, there will be disregarded the possibility of a third source, that of cash paid out which would be taken from the petty cash.

In smaller firms several items are handled on a cash disbursement basis; that is, they are accounted for at time of payment. Such items are rent, utilities, and phone, to name a few of the more common. Other items, especially where the frequency of purchase is numerous during the month's cycle, would be entered on the Accounts Payable card and journal and charged directly to specific overhead expense accounts in the General Ledger column.

The Check register generally will have sufficient columns to enable the accountant to set up his manufacturing expense distribution and the general and administrative expense distribution as well. At month's end the posting to the General ledger accounts will be made as well as those to the manufacturing accounts.

Before summarizing the month's end posting procedure, one more item must be discussed. It is the farming out of certain functions or subcontracting part of the process. This may become necessary where specialized facilities are lacking and their use would not be sufficient to warrant the client to process in his own plant. Line 14 of Figure 5 gives an illustration of this type of transaction where both the Accounts Payable card (Figure 6) and the Job Cost ledger card (Figure 7) are used to make this entry.

In summarizing the above procedure, it is noted that direct materials and overhead expense are charged directly to the Inventory—Raw Material account (No. 1111), or to Raw Materials Purchase account, if desired; and the Overhead Expense account (No. 2585), respectively, and are not charged out to Job Cost ledger card at time of recording the incoming materials; likewise, the labor is first distributed to the job cost numbers and summarized at month's end as shown in Figure 12.

The manufacturing expenses are recapped from the check record and the Invoice journal (Figure 5) and are likewise not posted to the Job Cost Record card immediately.

Note that direct labor and manufacturing overhead are distributed at actual cost, whereas direct materials is at standard cost.

The Job Order Schedule (Figure 11) is recapped at month's end and distributed to each Job Cost ledger card as indicated by entries on lines 6 and 7 of the journal (Figure 5), with the labor and labor hours as indicated on lines

8 through 13 of the same journal. If any subcontract work is ordered, it would be for a particular job and would be entered directly to the Job Cost card at time of entry on the journal—see line 14. Should this cost be for more than one job, as for example, special mixes of ingredients requiring specialized equipment, the jobs would be farmed out, mixed per specifications, and brought back into inventory. The standard cost of these ingredients is adjusted upwards to reflect this special handling. There would be no separate subcontract costs showing under such a procedure since they would be absorbed in the adjusted price of the materials.

APPLYING OVERHEAD RATE

At the end of the month the manufacturing expense accounts, with the exception of direct labor and direct materials (already distributed), are totaled. The direct labor hours for the month are also added and divided into the total manufacturing expenses, thus establishing the overhead rate per direct labor hour, sometimes called the burden rate.

For example, it is assumed that the total manufacturing expenses for December were $4,350, and that total direct labor hours were 725. Burden

$$\text{rate} = \frac{\text{manufacturing expenses}}{\text{direct labor hours}} = \frac{\$4,350}{725} = \$6.00 \text{ per direct labor hour.}$$

Referring back to Figure 5, lines 15 through 20, note that the overhead applied for each Job Cost ledger card was compiled, each line using the proper Job Cost card as indicated by the job number.

The overhead rate will vary from month to month depending on the total direct hours' work for each month, and the variable elements of cost.

POSTING THE INVOICE JOURNAL

When all the entries as indicated above have been completed for the month and entered on this journal, the journal is then footed, and cross footed, to insure its balance, and totals are posted to the various General ledger accounts.

The Job Cost ledger cards (Figure 7) are then totaled and cross added. The Job Order Schedule (Figure 11) indicates that 100 units were placed into production. The ID #101 formula (shown under the subheading, Developing the System) shows that one unit of the formula will produce three 32½-pound cans; therefore, 100 units will produce 300 32½-pound cans. Dividing this 300 into the total cost of $1,864.90 equals $6.22 per 32½-pound can.

GENERAL COMMENTS

It is difficult to state that a standard overhead rate should or should not be used. Generally speaking, with the small client it is better not to use standards unless there is no other way out. As indicated by most cost books on accounting, unless a thorough study of costs were made to arrive at a true and meaningful standard cost figure, it would be useless to use standard costs.

The accountant must bear in mind, however, the size of the client's business, the amount of detail work involved, and the time needed to operate the system he has installed or plans to install. If good standard cost figures can be obtained, they should be used. Modifications may have to be made in the system outlined above to simplify the work and reduce write-up time either for the accountant or his client's staff; a simpler system may be preferable.

One method to simplify and eliminate excessive detail work, especially with the smaller client, is the use of standard cost. The accountant must be aware of the necessity to formulate *accurate* standard rates, or the system could be useless.

Once the cost of manufacturing an item has been established, the accountant must yet be aware that selling expenses and general and administrative cost must be taken into consideration along with taxes and finally an allowance for a profit substantial enough to enable the company to pay a fair dividend and have some funds left over for future growth.

BREAKEVEN CHART (FIGURE 13)

To enable the accountant to guide his client, the accountant must be ready to supply him with proper information, so the client may sell competitively and still achieve the standards described above. In order to accomplish these aims, the cost of manufacturing must be identified so that it can be split into variable costs and fixed costs.

Variable costs	*Fixed costs*
Materials	Depreciation
Labor	Janitorial
Operating supplies	Rent
Repairs and maintenance	Equipment rental
Payroll taxes	Insurance
Freight in	Supervisory salary
Utilities	
Personal property tax	
Workmen's compensation	

The accountant will find the Breakeven chart useful to clarify to the client the amount of sales needed to accomplish any given objective. This type of chart can be further categorized by department as shown by lines A and B on the chart (Figure 13).

Line A breaks down the total variable of manufacturing costs, and sales

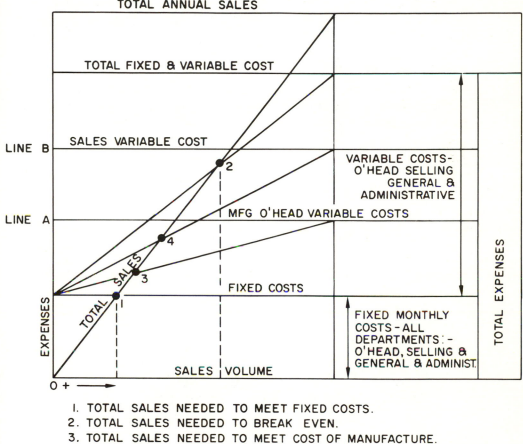

1. TOTAL SALES NEEDED TO MEET FIXED COSTS.
2. TOTAL SALES NEEDED TO BREAK EVEN.
3. TOTAL SALES NEEDED TO MEET COST OF MANUFACTURE.
4. TOTAL SALES NEEDED TO MEET COST OF MFG. & SELLING COST.

* THE BREAKEVEN SYSTEM, SPENCER A. TUCKER, PRENTICE-HALL, INC., 1963.

Figure 13: Breakeven Chart

efforts are identified by line B. The same could be done for other cost factors such as income tax.

The formula to compute this mathematically is as follows:

$$\text{Breakeven Point} = \text{Fixed expenses} \div \left[100\% - \left(\frac{\text{Variable expenses}}{\text{Sales}}\right)\right]$$

1. Divide Variable expenses, $1200, by Sales, $3000 = 40%.
2. Subtract 40% from 100% = 60%.
3. Divide Fixed expenses, $800, by 60% = $1,333. This is the break-even point.

Sales below $1,333 will produce a loss for the company, whereas sales above $1,333 will produce a profit.

The formula can be used to determine the amount of sales needed to justify the purchase of new equipment, plant, and the like.

17

Churches

BY OLIVER Q. FOUST

Oliver Q. Foust & Company, Public Accountant; President, O. Quay Financial Management Corporation; President, Quay Charitable Foundation, Inc.; Secretary, Small Business Financing, Inc., all of Sacramento, California; President, Vienna Convalescent Hospital, Inc., Lodi, California

Characteristics of the Church That Affect the Accounting System

The differentiating characteristic of a church as opposed to a business is perhaps the absence of the profit motive. Even though the profit motive does not pertain, there are ways and sources from which the church obtains its receipts.

The principal source of revenue is from church membership. The benevolent desire to belong to a church and, thereby, to help support it, is obvious. The church perpetuates its existence by increasing membership, preparing budgets, and making these budget costs familiar to the membership. Income from pledges is desirable, since weekly donations are not sufficient to sustain the church budget. Raffles, church-sponsored programs, and many sundry money-raising drives are apparent throughout the whole country. The central organization of some churches appropriate funds which are channeled to the local churches. Thus it would seem that this class of income should be recognized and provided for in the church budget.

The word "churches" embraces a multitude of "faiths" that have governed the soul, mind, and character of mankind since the dawn of civilization. Whether man's faith has concerned the pagan gods, Buddha, Confucius, Moses, Jesus Christ, or Mohammed, the common factor is the need of an organization with preachers, priests, rabbis, brothers, elders, or other titled members and their followers, parishioners, or congregations. The organization is in operation to offer a service that requires funds to defray operating expenses of the various programs. An accounting system is essential to account for receipts and expenditures of the various funds.

To simplify matters, this chapter will confine discussion to four of the major faiths—the Roman Catholic, the Protestant, the Jewish, and the Greek or Eastern Orthodox. Each has a different terminology, organization, and authority. All differ to some extent in their activities, programs, and sources of income. For example, the Synagogue and the Greek Orthodox Church use their school facilities for language schools in addition to religious Sunday schools.

The accountant should make himself aware of the policies of the church board or council and devise a system of accounting and a chart of accounts based on these policies.

FUNCTIONAL CHARACTERISTICS

Even though the church is not taxed on its income * because it has an exemption status, the United States Government requires each entity of each central organization to file information returns. These information returns are similar to conventional income statements generally prepared on a cash basis. It would seem that the accountant in dealing with accounting systems for churches would address himself to the cash received and disbursements system of accounting, or cash basis fund accounting. However, if the accountant receives the engagement of a large institution, he would recommend that the church put the accounting system on an accrual basis to provide for encumbrances on the current funds. In large institutions, current liabilities owed should be reflected in the financial statement.

PRINCIPAL ACCOUNTING PROBLEMS

The public accountant should consider carefully the concept of fund accounting. He is familiar with cash receipts and cash disbursements as a method of general accounting, and it is assumed that most of his work will be setting up a system that will control the proper classes of income and the proper classes of expenditures. In most cases it is recommended that the

---

* IRS 501(3)(c).

public accountant adopt a system that the lay people, who run the church, can live with. After reviewing the items of church receipts and expenditures, the public accountant will know whether to operate in one general fund or set up a fund for each church project on a departmental basis. (See discussion under Books and forms peculiar to the business.)

The second accounting problem the public accountant will encounter is to determine whether the lay people are doing a good job of policing the pledge system and how the activity is maintained. A simple pegboard arrangement charging the member with the amount of money that he has pledged would seem to function well as a control over receivables due from pledges. However, when the items are totaled and deposited in the general fund bank account, a receipt journal should be used, debiting the cash account and crediting membership income, pledge income, or some connotation to clarify what character of income is being receipted.

A third accounting problem is the method of handling and allocating proper payroll costs. The public accountant should review the work of staff members paid by the church and ascertain how much of these services should be charged to the various departments or whether the item should be handled as administrative costs in the general fund. Different church boards review these items differently; therefore, the accountant would be wise to adopt and organize a system that is flexible.

One problem which seems to appear consistently in accounting for churches can only be resolved by a generous application of tact when the accountant wishes to recommend changes or improvements. Human nature plays a vital part here, and there is a peculiar upsurge of sensitiveness to criticism. The feelings of people performing free services must be treated delicately, they should be complimented, criticism of the individual or the committee should be bypassed, and only constructive criticism for the good of the establishment should be offered. The accountant cannot be too careful in this regard.

Functional Organization

Some churches conduct their business as associations. This practice should be discouraged; the accountant should suggest to the church board that an attorney be consulted so that the many advantages that accrue in doing business as a corporation be realized. It is recommended that any church body should address itself to doing business as a corporation. It is a healthy business environment of business relationships that provides benefits to the members and to the community which the church serves. Fees for incorporating a nonprofit church are very small.

Typical organization of a small church is shown in Figure 1.

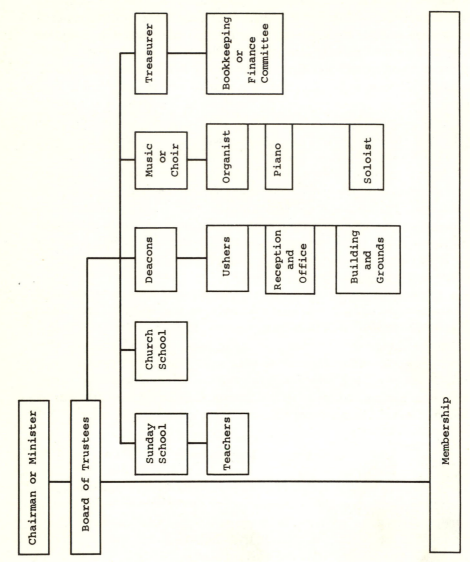

Figure 1: Organizational Chart

Principles and Objectives of the Accounting System

Segregation of the classes of income and expenses is vital as a basis for reports to local church management, to a higher echelon of the church government, and to regulatory bodies such as the United States Government. The entire income must be shown, even in the cases where particular collections are earmarked for forwarding elsewhere, to church headquarters, for example. In addition, because of the nature of the organization, church members are entitled to know about current financial affairs in specific detail.

SPECIFIC OBJECTIVES OF THE SYSTEM

The principal objective is to provide a simple set of cost controls. By this means the finances of the church may be handled in a more accurate and businesslike way, so that the church affairs may rest on a solid financial structure.

Classification of Accounts and Books of Accounts

Because of the variety of church endeavors and the classes of income, it is difficult to supply a chart of accounts that is ample; however, the following chart is offered as a starter, and enlargements are to be made as needed.

The chart can include expenditures in all or the general fund as the church board desires.

BALANCE SHEET ACCOUNTS.

ASSETS

Current assets

110 Cash in Bank
120 Petty Cash Fund
140 Pledges Receivable
150 Investments
151 Bonds
152 Stocks
153 Other
160 Due from Other Funds

Fixed assets

171 Land
172 Buildings
173 Furniture and Fixtures
174 Other (including Reading
       Room Library)

175 Construction in Progress

LIABILITIES

Current Liabilities

210 Notes Payable
220 Accounts Payable
       221 Withholding Taxes Payable
       222 Federal Old-Age Taxes
              Payable
       229 Collections due Church
              Headquarters

Other Liabilities

230 Mortgages Payable
270 Due to Other Funds

NET WORTH

280 Surplus Invested in Fixed Assets

INCOME AND EXPENSE ACCOUNTS.

INCOME	EXPENSES
301 Church Operating Income	501 Wages
302 Church School Operating Income	502 Subcontract
303 Home Mission Operating Income	503 Rent
	503A Parsonage Allowance
304 Poor Operating Fund	504 Telephone
305 Youth Operating Fund	505 Insurance
306 Foreign Mission Operating Fund	506 Building
307 Building Operating Fund	507 Office Supplies and Postage
308 Senior Fellowship Operating Fund	508 Dues
	509 Auditing
309 Youth Fellowship Operating Fund	510 Maintenance and Repairs
	511 Auto
310 Radio Operating Fund	512 Church Envelopes
311 Subsidies	513 Depreciation Sinking Fund
	515 Miscellaneous

ACCOUNTS PECULIAR TO THE CHURCHES

Income (Nos. 301-311). No. 301, Church Operating Income, is the general fund account. All items included to maintain the church are credited to this fund, and all items of upkeep to the church are charged to that fund. Nos. 302-309 are the specific fund accounts, each with its own set of expenses (Nos. 501 to 515).

Radio Operating Fund (No. 310). Those church members who believe in the broadcast of Sunday sermons, youth advisory programs, etc., are willing to donate large amounts to this fund. Expenses naturally would be charged to the fund.

Subsidies (No. 311). Subsidiary income usually comes from the higher echelons of the church organization. This income may be received from a local, a regional, or a national constituency, or from an international constituency. A footnote as to the source can be detailed in any presentation to the church board. Usually there are no restrictions to these subsidiary funds, and the board allocates from this fund to other funds. If restrictions do exist, then the expenditures must be made exactly in accordance with the higher echelon direction or other foundation requirement.

Subcontract (No. 502). This expense account often comprises a conglomeration of items. In the Building Fund, No. 502 would refer to the general contractor. For the annual financial campaign, it would concern the hiring of a professional to plan and administer the campaign. This account is used particularly for outside services and if expansion is needed, then the treasurer would explain the outside services in each fund.

Parsonage Allowance (No. 503A). This account pays the minister for the rent of his home or pays him directly in cash in lieu of rent. This account should be separate, not included in the Wages account. This allowance is given to the pastor as a nontaxable item of his income.

Office Supplies and Postage (No. 507). Included here would be cost of church envelopes, with a credit to No. 301; or the accountant might prefer to set up a separate account and assign another number, such as 512. Expenses related to the annual financial campaign would also be charged to No. 507 and credited to No. 301.

Depreciation Sinking Fund (No. 513). Depreciation expense is not recognized in fund accounting unless the church board wants to set up a charge known as Depreciation Sinking Fund.

BOOKS AND FORMS PECULIAR TO THE CHURCHES

To provide a more comprehensive understanding of the four great denominations earlier mentioned, the following illustrations exhibit certain peculiarities of each.

The Greek Orthodox priest receives all his religious instructions from the bishop, while the board of directors establishes the operating policy and handles all the income and expenses. Members are called to an annual meeting and are given a financial statement (Figure 2). Their income is from dues, collections, sale of candles, and holiday special collections.

The Catholic church is operated by a local priest in accordance with a system prescribed by his area bishop. The priest receives all the money from every source, counts it at his leisure, pays all the expenses, keeps his own books, and prepares a financial statement (Figure 3) for the bishop, but not necessarily for his parishioners. Records are kept on a fund basis, and each fund shows its income and expenditures.

The Jewish synagogue has a board which decides on the assessment of each member's dues and handles all the money and expenditures. There is also a special "seats" payment for the high holidays.

Protestants receive their principal income from pledges that are usually paid by envelope at the weekly collection. The best and completely detailed reports are made to the members and cite accomplishments and efforts of each committee.

As a general rule, all churches are similar to each other insofar as receipts, expenses, and community functions are concerned.

SAINT GEORGE GREEK ORTHODOX CHURCH
Year 19__

INCOME

Candles and Collections		$7690.07
Envelopes (incl. Easter and Christmas)		1560.30
Membership Contributions		9937.00
Memorial Contributions (Bldg. Fund)		761.00
Building Fund Tray		675.40
Language School Revenues		270.15
Special Donations (Bldg. Fund)		1935.53
Flower Collections	390.60	
Paid out	234.50	
Net		156.10
Dividends (Investment Income)		116.60
Archdiocese Obligations (Collected)		2873.00
19__ Dance and Raffle (Bldg. Fund)		2529.05
Interest on Savings Accounts		1406.99
Total Income		29911.19

EXPENDITURES

Salaries			
Clergy (incl. S.S. taxes)			6500.00
Choir Director			900.00
Organist			480.00
Sexton			385.00
Chanter			725.00
Teacher			2960.00
Payroll Taxes (Teacher)			167.80
Automobile Expenses			1200.00
Office Supplies			353.54
Gas and Electricity			678.02
Fuel			2245.61
Maintenance and Repairs			3303.01
Archdiocese Obligations Paid			2873.00
Language and Sunday School Expenses			581.54
Telephone			282.29
Candles			801.50
Postage			210.61
Choir Expenses			181.10
Basketball Uniforms	Col.	110.00	
	Pd.	111.48 Net Pd.	1.48
Church Supplies			134.43
Travel Expenses			180.00
Donations and Gifts			255.20
Insurance			1341.50
Water			134.20
Conferences and Conventions			318.19

Figure 2: Greek Orthodox Financial Statement

EXPENDITURES (cont.)

```
Mexico Mission              Pd.     350.00
                            Col.    255.00              95.00
                     Total Expenditures      $27288.02
```

CASH RECONCILIATION

```
January 1, 19__ Balances
     Bank No. 1                              $5865.63
     Bank No. 2                               4178.86
     Bank No. 3                              10066.51
     Bank No. 4                              13276.43
     Bank No. 5                              10000.00
               Total Cash in Bank 1/1/__                  $43387.43
Year 19__ Income                                          29911.19
               Total 19__ Income                         $73298.62

Total 19__ Expenditures   27288.02 plus 27.08 adjust.     27315.10
               Net Cash Value for Year 19__              $45983.52


December 31, 19__ Cash on Hand
     Bank No. 1                              $3233.59
     Bank No. 3                              10480.69
     Bank No. 4                              13812.77
     Bank No. 5                              10371.47
     Bank No. 6                               8085.00
               Total Cash 12/31/19__                     $45983.52
```

INVESTMENTS

```
50 shares of _____      3027.08           2484.00
435 shares of _____      3000.00           4398.00
525 shares of _____      5000.00           8451.00
                             11027.08          15333.00
                          (orig. cost)     (market value)

          Total Liquid Assets              $61316.52
```

Figure 2: Greek Orthodox Financial Statement (cont.)

FINANCIAL STATEMENT OF ST. BRIDGET CHURCH FOR THE YEAR 19__

RECEIPTS		EXPENDITURES	
Seat Money (Door)............ $	7,059.82	Priests' Salaries, Extra Priests, Sexton	
Offertory....................	39,283.78	Domestic & Other Labor, Organist....$12,569.07	
Special Parish Collections,		Social Security, Taxes, Blue Cross....1,551.87	
Monthly, Annual, Fuel etc......	11,271.66	Fuel...................................1,624.61	
Votive Lights...............	1,388.09	Gas & Electricity..................... 829.30	
Christman Fair..............	2,305.00	House Allowance...................... 2,306.68	
Interest....................	101.94	Infirm Priests...................... 100.00	
Contributions - Flowers,		Missions & Retreats.................. 445.00	
Church donations, etc........	1,026.12	Altar Supplies...................... 1,467.69	
Books, coke, etc.............	232.56		
Stole Fees..................	375.00	CHURCH SUPPLIES & EXPENSES........... 1,634.90	
Catholic Transcript..........	322.00		
		RECTORY EXPENSES - (Station-Wagon)...	231.98
TOTAL ORDINARY REVENUE	$63,365.97	Telephone...........................	510.18
Real Estate.................	1,000.00	Transportation......................	1,534.00
		CHURCH FURNISHINGS...................	351.56
Catholic Relief, Holy Land,		RECTORY "	177.21
Easter Charities, Peter's Pence,			
Mission Sunday, Mission Co-op,		CHURCH REPAIRS	2,321.70
Catholic University........	3,747.60	RECTORY "	96.04
Development Fund...........	1,490.00	TOTAL CHURCH & RECTORY	$27,751.79
Regional High School Fund...	114.00	Catholic Transcript.................	279.00
		Diocesan Collections................	3,747.60
TOTAL SPECIAL RECEIPTS	$ 6,351.60	Development Fund....................	1,490.00
		Regional High School Allocation......	5,711.60
TOTAL RECEIPTS FOR THE YEAR	$69,717.57	Cathedraticum......................	3,121.82
BALANCE ON HAND - Jan. 1, 19	$12,242.22		
		TOTAL SPECIAL EXPENDITURES	$14,350.02
TOTAL..........	81,959.79	Text Books, Coke, Supplies..........	417.78
		Teaching Sisters....................	500.00
		Insurance...........................	2,892.99
		Payment on Debt.....................	20,500.00
		Interest on Debt....................	2,663.45
		Appraisal...........................	31.68
		Donation Millennium Fund...........	100.00
		OTHER EXPENSES	$ 27,105.90
		TOTAL EXPENSES FOR 19__	$ 69,207.71
		BALANCE ON HAND - DEC. 31, 19__	$ 12,752.08
		TOTAL............	$ 81,959.79

REMAINING DEBT ON THE CHURCH, PARISH HALL & RECTORY
        DECEMBER 31, 19· $35,000.00

Figure 3: Catholic Financial Statement

CONGREGATION ISRAEL

STATEMENT OF CURRENT POSITION
as of December 31, 19___

CASH IN BANK			$ 6,756.60
RECEIVABLES			
Dues - Current Year	$ 3,355.00		
Dues - Previous Year (past due)	373.75		
Other, past due	65.00	$ 3,793.75	
Seats		865.00	
Hebrew School - not included		----	
Cemetery Upkeep		30.00	
		$ 4,688.75	
Less: Estimated Uncollectible		300.00	4,388.75
TOTAL CURRENT ASSETS			$11,145.35
CURRENT LIABILITIES - Accounts Payable			1,439.32
EXCESS OF CURRENT ASSETS OVER CURRENT LIABILITIES			$ 9,706.03

Figure 4: Hebrew Statement of Current Position

CONGREGATION ISRAEL

COMPARATIVE SCHEDULE OF RECEIPTS

Calendar Years 19___ and 19___

	Previous Year	Current Year
Dues and Donations	$ 28,661.16	$ 29,169.32
Sisterhood	2,300.00	2,300.00
United Jewish Appeal	2,000.00	2,000.00
High Holiday Seats	2,145.00	4,420.00
Chevra Kadisha	1,537.50	2,330.00
Religious School Fees	4,640.00	5,887.00
Rentals	2,500.00	2,335.00
TOTALS	$ 43,783.66	$ 48,441.32

Figure 5: Hebrew Comparative Schedule of Receipts

CONGREGATION ISRAEL

COMPARATIVE SCHEDULE OF EXPENDITURES
Calendar Years 19__ and 19__

HOUSE COMMITTEE ITEMS	19	Current Year
Shamis	$ 5,775.80	$ 6,739.30
Helper	2,286.05	3,120.00
Repairs and Improvements (Fig. 7)	972.16	1,032.30
Heat	1,604.86	1,728.12
Electricity and Gas	1,188.56	1,009.54
Water	66.84	66.84
Maintenance Supplies	275.00	343.65
Insurance	1,262.62	2,617.20
Laundry	148.61	144.58
TOTAL HOUSE COMMITTEE ITEMS	$13,580.50	$16,801.53
OTHER COSTS		
Salary - Rabbi	$ 9,000.00	$ 9,916.65
Salaries - Teachers	8,900.00	12,012.29
Salaries - Teachers (Sunday School)	2,601.00	2,268.00
Office Salaries	2,226.75	2,907.87
Financial Secretary	100.00	100.00
Pension and Rent	736.65	105.00
Postage	404.27	475.26
Stationery and Printing	781.75	979.50
Supplies	204.32	314.62
Religious School Supplies (Net)	703.54	746.99
Telephone (Net)	208.58	224.57
Refreshments	28.53	16.02
FICA (Payroll) Tax	481.65	816.53
Cantor's Services	800.00	800.00
Gifts	------	51.08
Adult Education	------	102.89
Chevra Kadisha	670.15	869.11
Dues	400.00	400.00
Convention Expense	186.00	115.00
Legal and Accounting	100.00	100.00
Miscellaneous	99.59	96.75
	$42,213.28	$50,219.66

Figure 6: Hebrew Comparative Schedule of Expenditures

CONGREGATION ISRAEL

ANALYSIS OF REPAIRS AND IMPROVEMENTS

Year ended December 31, 19__

REPAIRS

Painting	$ 150.87	
Plumbing and Heating	151.24	
Stairs	85.36	
Miscellaneous	59.83	$ 447.30

IMPROVEMENTS

Folding Doors	$ 485.00	
Architect's Fees	100.00	585.00

TOTAL REPAIRS AND IMPROVEMENTS $ 1,032.30

Figure 7: Hebrew Analysis of Repairs and Improvements

Peculiarities of Procedures

CASH RECEIPTS AND DISBURSEMENTS

Most churches use the envelope as the means to bring pledged income into church coffers. The envelopes are numbered, and a file is kept of the number assigned to each member. Other envelopes may be placed along the back of the pews for use by visitors or transient attenders, and for special collections. Each envelope bears a space for name, address, and telephone number.

Members may pay their pledges by check at any time interval desired; or they may place their offerings in the envelopes and deposit them in the collection plate on Sundays. Picked up by the ushers, the collections are turned over to the deacons or to the minister who counts receipts and delivers them to the treasurer. The latter records payments made by the members and totals the loose collection of currency and offerings from visitors.

By a separate pegboard system the treasurer then receipts to the various funds and disburses by check (Figure 14) for commitments which are due. He also computes all totals and reports transactions by the month and to date.

REPORT OF THE TREASURER
For the year 19___

INCOME:

Current Pledges 19___	$31,348.45
Recovery – Previous Year	2,924.87
Plate	1,165.23
TIDINGS	37.15
First Offering	58.40
Church School	490.82
Parish House Rent	45.00
Lease	1,500.00
Advance Pledges	3,558.10
Investment Income	13,007.26
Less Bank Charges	1,009.34 → 11,997.92

TOTAL INCOME	$53,125.94
(19___ Est. $52,325)	

EXPENSE:

	Actual	Budget
Religious Education	$1,763.78	$2,250
Salaries	24,890.99	24,494
Transportation	1,225.07	1,150
Personnel Contingency	68.00	100
Social Security	788.97	807
Office & Christian Enlistment	2,548.02	2,600
Contingencies	----	100
Sinking Fund	----	150
Utilities	4,312.74	3,500
Music (Worship Service)	731.35	660
Per Capita	305.20	380
Annuity	1,709.40	1,710
Pastor's Health Insurance	252.00	252
Insurance	2,459.25	2,200

Benevolences (World Service):

Interfaith Committee	35.00
Ministry to Students (Wesleyan)	850.00
Silver Lake	200.00
U.C. of Christ	1,500.00
World Council	25.00
National Council	25.00
Local Council	17.54
Congregat. Library	25.00
Pastors' Christmas Fund	50.00
World Services Tapes	25.00
Day Care Center	55.00
Miscellaneous	20.00

Funds for Use by Trustees:

	Actual	Budget
Repairs	2,827.54	5,475
Interest	7,097.12	
	869.01	
Principal	1,800.00	10,500

	Actual	Budget
TOTAL EXPENDITURES	$53,648.44	$56,328

ASSET ACCOUNTS	Bank Balance
Pastor's Fund	328.70
Choir Fund	400.96
Flower Fund	349.20
Checking Account	374.59
Special Savings Account	2,598.77
Church Renovation Fund (incl. $3,000 held by Trustees)	14,971.04

LIABILITY ACCOUNTS	Ledger Balance
Pastor's Fund	504.59
Choir Fund	455.60
Flower Fund	507.71
In Memoriam	21.70
Conference Fund (School)	438.98
Missions and Benevolences (School)	----
Note Payable	13,700.00
Balance	$16,184.48

CHURCH RENOVATION FUNDS	Budget
Organ Replacement Fund	$50,000.00

Income	Expense
$21,658.98 *	$5,474.50

Special Collections:

India Famine Relief	$164.51
One Hour of Sharing	307.59
Neighbors in Need	191.20
	$663.30

* Memorials	$2,216.00
Bequests	18,277.81
Miscellaneous	1,175.17

Figure 8: Protestant (Congregational) Report of Treasurer

STATEMENT OF CONDITION
January 1, 19___

	ASSETS	LIABILITIES
A) Buildings - 325 Market St.	$329,000.00	
A) Land - 325 Market St.	26,000.00	
A) Parsonage - 15 Southmoreland Drive	35,000.00	
A) Organ	50,000.00	
A) Furniture, Fixtures & Equipment	20,000.00	
A) Antique Communion Set	6,325.00	
A) Hubbard Fund	10,228.24	
A) Hazelton Fund	10,799.84	
B & C) Combined Trust Funds (Market Value $307,070)	179,021.80	
B) Reverend James Trust Fund (Market Value $51,784)	32,539.00	
Cash on Hand and in Banks	2,923.36	
FUND ACCTS: Renovation, Pastor, Flowers, Choir	13,049.90	
D) Pledges for 19___, Actual & Anticipated	38,288.00	
Unpaid Balance of 19___ Pledges	3,337.55	
Notes Payable		$ 13,700.00
Pledges Paid in Advance		3,578.10
Reserve for Withholding Tax		370.44
FUND ACCTS: Pastor, Choir, In Memoriam, Confer.		1,928.58
Renovation Funds - Organ		43,870.50
- Architect		2,700.00
Net Worth		690,365.07
	$756,512.69	$756,512.69

(A) Based on appraisal in 19___.
(B) March 10, 19___ market value.
(c) To be transferred to Organ Fund in May 19___.
(D) Adjusted to reflect increase from second fund appeal, as of April 1, 19___.

Figure 9: Protestant (Congregational) Statement of Condition

REPORT OF THE CHURCH SCHOOL TREASURER
_ _ _ _ _ December 31, 19_ _ _ _ _ _ _

Balance forward as of January 1, 19__:
    Special Gift - Cornelius Fund $ 15.00
    Missions and Benevolences   33.04
    Conference Fund   298.23 $ 346.27

Receipts:
    Conference Fund   Donations   452.50
                        Conference 251.75   704.25
    Church Commitment   1708.47
    Sunday Offering:
       Current Expenses   424.26
       Missions & Benevolences   215.55   639.81
    Special Offering, One Great Hour of Sharing   32.89
    Library - Willing Workers   31.96   3117.38

        TOTAL RECEIPTS $3463.65

Expenditures:
    Missions and Benevolences   248.59
    Special Offering - One Great Hour of Sharing   32.89
    Conference Fund   567.50
    Special Gift - Cornelius Fund   15.00
    Equipment   481.50
    Library   133.00
    Youth   59.51
    Bibles   198.69
    Juice and Crackers   33.34
    Church School:
       Curriculum   786.40
       Supplies   41.55
       Teaching Aids   92.45
       Staff Training   113.15
       Offering Envelopes   50.92
       Special Projects & Programs 34.47
       Vacation Bible School   73.71
       Miscellaneous   66.00   1258.65

        TOTAL EXPENDITURES   3028.67

        BALANCE FORWARD:
           Conference Fund   434.98

                                $3463.65

Figure 10: Protestant (Congregational) Report of Church School Treasurer

CHURCH OF THE HOLY TRINITY

Budget 19__

ESTIMATED OPERATING INCOME:

Pledge Income	$54,500.00	
Easter Offering	1,500.00	
Christmas Offering	1,000.00	
Plate Offering	1,500.00	
Church School	750.00	
Other Income	2,250.00	$61,500.00

ESTIMATED OPERATING EXPENDITURES:

Rector's Services	$ 9,000.00	
Assistant Rector's Services	5,250.00	
Other Clergy Services	1,400.00	
Director of Education	2,500.00	
Secretarial Services	3,900.00	
Organist Services	3,200.00	
Sexton Services	4,200.00	
Social Security, Blue Cross and State Medical Service	1,300.00	
Transportation	2,500.00	
Support of the Episcopate and Diocesan Administration	2,000.00	
Music	500.00	
Pension Contribution - Clergy	2,850.00	
Office Expenses and Church Supplies	3,200.00	
Telephone	900.00	
Proportionate Share for Missions	11,000.00	
Christian Education	1,300.00	
Interest on Indebtedness	4,000.00	
Amortization of Debt	3,000.00	
Contingency and Miscellaneous	1,000.00	
Inter-Church Ministry to Students at Wesleyan University	1,000.00	
Youth Work	250.00	
Theological Education	200.00	$64,450.00

Excess of operating expenditures over operating income	$2,950.00

ESTIMATED INVESTMENT INCOME:	$17,000.00

ESTIMATED HOUSING EXPENDITURES:

Heat	$ 4,250.00	
Insurance	2,300.00	
Repairs and Maintenance	4,000.00	
Administration of Trust Funds	1,600.00	
Power and Water	1,900.00	$14,050.00

Excess of Investment Income over Housing Expenditures	$2,950.00

Figure 11: Protestant (Episcopalian) Estimated Budget

CHURCH OF THE HOLY TRINITY

Budget Statement for 19__

INCOME:	Budget (This Year)	Actual (This Year)	Proposed 19__
Christmas Offering	$ 1,000.00	$ 967.75	$ 1,000.00
Easter Offering	1,500.00	1,451.50	1,500.00
Initial Offering	----	62.40	----
Plate Collections	1,500.00	1,691.85	1,500.00
Investment Income	14,500.00	17,267.24	17,000.00
Income from Pledges	51,000.00	51,146.91	54,500.00
Church School Income	750.00	600.00	750.00
Income from Other Sources	3,150.00	2,248.79	2,250.00
TOTAL INCOME	$73,400.00	$75,436.44	$78,500.00

EXPENSES:			
Rector's Services	8,500.00	8,500.00	9,000.00
Assistant Rector's Services			5,250.00
Other Clergy Services	5,950.00	5,850.00	1,400.00
Director of Education			2,500.00
Transportation	2,500.00	2,642.94	2,500.00
Parish Secretarial Services	3,600.00	3,600.00	3,900.00
Organist Services	2,500.00	2,500.00	3,200.00
Sexton Services	3,900.00	3,965.64	4,200.00
Clergy Supply	200.00	----	----
Social Security, Blue Cross	1,300.00	1,150.76	1,300.00
Support of Episcopate and Diocesan Adm.	1,900.00	1,861.00	2,000.00
Music	500.00	758.95	500.00
Heat - Parish and Clergy Houses	4,000.00	4,774.63	4,250.00
Pension Contribution, Clergy	2,650.00	2,673.00	2,850.00
Office Expense and Church Supplies	3,200.00	3,642.83	3,200.00
Insurance	2,300.00	2,219.55	2,300.00
Telephone	800.00	956.07	900.00
Power and Water	1,800.00	1,969.56	1,900.00
Repairs, Maintenance, and Supplies	5,000.00	5,763.29	4,000.00
Administration of Trust Funds	1,400.00	1,398.83	1,600.00
Proportionate Share, Missions	10,000.00	10,190.00	11,000.00
Christian Education	2,400.00	2,504.42	1,300.00
Interest and Amortization of Debt:			
Interest	3,500.00	3,475.95	4,000.00
Amortization	3,000.00	3,000.00	3,000.00
Contingency and Miscellaneous	800.00	1,260.35	1,000.00
Inter-Church Ministry to Students	1,000.00	1,000.00	1,000.00
Theological Education Sunday Off.	200.00	200.00	200.00
Youth Program	500.00	555.10	250.00
TOTAL EXPENSES	$73,400.00	$76,412.87	$78,500.00

Figure 12: Protestant (Episcopalian) Budget Statement

Monthly Statement

INCOME:	Current Month Jan. 1, 19__	Year to Date 19__	Budget 19__
Christmas Offering	$	$	$ 1,000.00
Easter Offering			1,500.00
Initial Offering			
Plate Collections			1,500.00
Income from Investments			20,500.00
Income from Pledges			56,000.00
Income from Church School			750.00
Income from Other Sources			3,000.00
TOTAL INCOME	$	$	$84,250.00
EXPENSES:			
Rector's Services	$	$	$10,000.00
Assistant Rector's Services			6,000.00
Other Clergy Services			1,400.00
Director of Education			1,250.00
Transportation			2,500.00
Parish Secretarial Services			3,900.00
Assistant Secretarial Services			1,500.00
Organist Services			3,500.00
Sexton Services			5,000.00
Social Security, Blue Cross, C.M.S.			1,600.00
Support of Episcopate and Dioc. Adm.			2,000.00
Music			600.00
Heat - Parish and Clergy Houses			4,250.00
Pension Contribution - Clergy			3,250.00
Office Expense and Church Supplies			3,200.00
Insurance			3,150.00
Telephone			900.00
Power and Water			2,100.00
Repairs - Maintenance and Supplies			4,000.00
Administration of Trust Funds			1,500.00
Proportionate Share - Missions			11,500.00
Christian Education			1,300.00
Interest on Debt			4,000.00
Amortization of Debt			3,000.00
Contingency and Miscellaneous			1,000.00
Inter-Church Ministry to Students			1,000.00
Theological Education Sunday Off.			200.00
Youth Program			350.00
M.R.I. Program			300.00
TOTAL EXPENSES	$	$	$84,250.00
Excess of Expense over Income	$	$	$
Excess of Income over Expense	$	$	$
Cash on Hand	$	$	$

Figure 13:   Protestant (Episcopalian) Monthly Statement

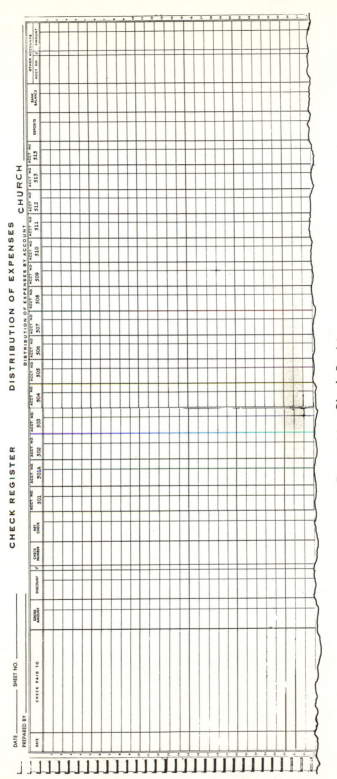

Figure 14: Check Register

Amount Received	Received From	Receipt Number	301	302	303	304	305	306	307	308	309	310	311

Receipt No. 11111

Date _____

301 - Operating Income
302 - Church School Operating Income
303 - Home Mission Operating Income
304 - Poor Operating Fund
305 - Youth Operating Fund
306 - Foreign Mission Operating Fund
307 - Building Operating Fund
308 - Senior Fellowship Operating Fund
309 - Youth Fellowship Operating Fund
310 - Radio Operating Fund
311 - Subsidies

Church Treasurer
_____ Church Name

Figure 15: Pegboard Receipt

DATE _____	CASH RECEIPT JOURNAL													
AMOUNT RECEIVED	RECEIVED FROM	RECEIPT NUMBER	301	302	303	304	305	306	307	308	309	310	311	

Figure 16: Cash Receipt Journal

RECEIVABLES

The accountant should design a pegboard system for pledges receivable and collections (Figure 15). He should also design a Funds Receivable journal (Figure 16) and a Funds Disbursement journal, both of which may follow a pegboard setup.

As funds are received from the various church operations, their receipt is acknowledged by use of the form shown in Figure 15. At the top of the reverse side is a one-time carbon, and underneath is placed the Accounts Receivable (Cash Receipt) journal (Figure 16). Thus in one operation the receipt is issued and a carbon record made for accounting purposes.

COST CONTROLS

The pastor will probably appoint a chairman to head each committee that is in charge of the church school, home missions, poor fund, youth advisory, foreign mission, building, senior and youth fellowship funds, etc. Each month the treasurer will compile the Fund Transactions of Revenue and Expenditures (Figure 17), which is actually a General ledger to control cash accounting by funds.

Each chairman receives a copy of the report pertaining to his committee.

FUND TRANSACTIONS OF REVENUE AND EXPENDITURES
FOR THE MONTH OF _____

	301 Church Operating	302 School Operating	303 Home Mission	304 Poor Operating	305 Youth Operating	306 Foreign Mission	307 Building Operating	308 Senior Fellowship	309 Youth Fellowship	310 Radio Operating	311 Subsidies
Fund Balance from Previous Report											
Received This Month											
* Disbursements This Month											
501 Wages											
501A Parsonage Allowance											
502 Subcontract											
503 Rent											
504 Telephone											
505 Insurance											
506 Building											
507 Office Supplies and Postage											
508 Dues											
509 Auditing											
510 Maintenance and Repair											
511 Automobile											
512 Church Envelopes											
513 Depreciation											
Sinking Fund											
515 Miscellaneous											
Fund Balance to Date											

* Any detail analysis in Exp. Accts. 501 to 515

Figure 17. Fund Transactions of Revenue and Expenditures

The reports seem to be more effective when they are submitted during the second week following the month of the businss transaction.

The chairman of each committee prepares the budget from known income in the past and known expenses reviewing historical costs. The committee chairman presents his budget to the board for approval, naming the specific income items which he proposes during the year and how he intends to spend the money. Once the budget is approved and adopted, then it is the treasurer's responsibility to see that the chairmen of these specific funds do not overspend themselves at any time.

Time and Payroll System

There are no peculiarities regarding payroll. A one-write system would be adequate.

Reports to Management

On an annual basis the church treasurer would prepare a balance sheet by physical inspection and would total the pledges receivable, investments, etc., and would note all liabilities. Figure illustrations under the section, Books and Forms Peculiar to Churches, show statements prepared on an annual basis.

Duties of the accountant are to design the system and to audit the work of the treasurer. Of help to the accountant in setting up a church system are the following references: *"Nonprofit Corporations and Associations"* *; *"Accountants' Encyclopedia"* **; and *"CPA Handbook"* ***.

Recommendations to the Accountant

In setting up the accounting system and especially in recommending changes or improvements, the public accountant cannot place too much emphasis on the need for dealing with the church body with all the tact he possesses. These individuals devote many hours of time and effort on a gratis basis; hence criticism is especially hard to accept. Sometimes it is best to discuss the recommendations with the person who is primarily responsible and let him take it from there.

It is ironic that an accountant wishes to perform work of this nature so

* Oleck, Howard O. Englewood Cliffs, N.J.; Prentice-Hall, Inc., 1956.
** Englewood Cliffs, N.J.: Prentice-Hall, Inc., 1962, Vol. I, Ch. 20, Forms Control, Design and Management; Ch. 21, How to Set Up Internal Reports for Managerial Purposes; Ch. 32, Fund Accounting for Institutions.
*** New York City: American Institute of Accountants, 1953, Ch. 16, Reliance upon Internal Control; Ch. 18, Financial Statement Presentation; Ch. 22, Development of Accounting Systems.

that he may serve the community and his profession, but is hampered by the various temperaments of people involved. For example, the accountant may wish to recommend that the cash should be counted immediately after collection rather than at a subsequent time several days later when one or more deacons may find it convenient to be present. He may feel it incumbent upon himself to propose that the cash should always be counted by a minimum of two persons and that it should on no account be left in a place easily accessible to church employees or visitors. Such changes in church procedure, of course, follow obvious accounting principles of control; yet in making these suggestions, the accountant cannot plan on being asked to do this work again.

In business based on the profit motive, where duties are paid for, it is expected that the auditor make recommendations for the protection of company assets. The auditor should exercise the same care in examining church records as he does for a business, but the diplomacy required in presentation of recommendations must be markedly superior.

18

Computer Service Bureaus

BY GIL JOHNSON

Public Accountant, White Bear
Lake, Minnesota

Characteristics of the Business That Affect the Accounting System

Service bureaus are, as the name implies, primarily service organizations. They engage in one or more of a variety of services including research and development, a large area of general statistical processing, accounting, test scoring, and programming for other installations. In addition to these activities, the bureaus provide professional services in engineering, accounting, and management consulting.

FUNCTIONAL CHARACTERISTICS

On the whole, service bureaus do not seem to consider themselves plagued by any peak season in their business year, an indication that other factors would dictate use of a natural business year. Accounting firms, for instance, with their large year-end tax loads, would be interested in a June 30 closing. In other fields a calendar year may be desirable.

Competition in the business is from other service bureaus in the same field or, in the case of accounting, companies which have installed their own service centers and find they have time to sell. Since companies with time to sell are only interested in spreading costs, there is a tendency toward price cutting. Price reductions can be somewhat overcome by offering professional services, but such an addition brings with it greater need for cost control.

PRINCIPAL ACCOUNTING PROBLEMS

Cost must receive emphasis in the service bureaus. Since other professional services are also provided, ability to distribute administrative expenses between the service center and the professional consulting department is essential. The nature or type of business does not indicate that formal job costing is necessary or even desirable. If a job or a contract is performed, production is recorded on a unit basis. A cost distribution and billing can be made on the basis of machine time or work unit, such as punch cards which are produced or handled. Cost distribution is discussed in a later section.

The ever-present problem of receivables and collections is a part of data processing, as it is in other businesses. The accounting system, therefore, must be designed to control this problem. Facilities must be set up for aging accounts. If the accounting is done by data processing, the standard processing of receivables is adequate. If data processing is not used, a duplicate carbon of the bill may be filed alphabetically and when a rebilling of the same accounts is made it may be attached to previous billings. This provides a good aging control.

Functional Organization

The small and medium-sized service bureau requires up to four departments: Administrative, Data Processing, Professional, and Research. When a center is first organized, these functions will be combined. A service bureau may need just two of the four departments; for instance, the Administrative Department may absorb the Professional and Research responsibilities. As the center grows, Professional and Research activities may be separated from the Administrative Department into a combined department. With further growth, a Research Department may be taken from the Professional Staff.

Administrative functions include general supervision. In addition, the functions would embrace responsibility for correspondence, billing, preparation of checks, deposits of money, and the preliminary work necessary for records to be prepared for data processing. If the records are kept on the service bureau's own equipment, a unit charge should be made to the Administrative Department, the same as if the work were done for a client. This charge should not include profit, however. Costs of the Administrative Department are then charged back to the productive departments, based upon percentage of income contribution by each department.

For example, a service bureau is engaged in accounting. It has three departments: Administrative, Data Processing, and a Professional Tax and Audit Staff. The Audit Staff does audit work for those clients not using the monthly write-ups. Monthly write-ups may be defined as the preparation of journals, ledgers, and monthly reports that are normally prepared for clients by public practitioners. The Professional Department also contributes time to the Data Processing Department in connection with the monthly write-ups. The Professional Department will bill the audit client and the Data Processing Department for its time. The total of these two billings represents production of the Professional Department. Fees billed from the Data Processing Center and the Accounting Department form the basis for distribution of administrative costs.

The Data Processing Department has the responsibility of operating data processing equipment as instructed by the Administrative Department. If work of a professional nature is necessary, it should be done by a professional staff. An example would be coding checks and handling nonrecurring items in an accounting processing center.

The Professional Staff has the responsibility of providing services such as auditing, engineering, management consulting, analyzing statistical data for either the Data Processing Department or as an additional service. Most service bureaus have some type of professional staff, depending on their interest, to provide other services beside processing.

A research group, the last addition to the organization chart, could very well become one of the most important departments. Responsibility of the Research Department is to develop new work for the service bureau and to update old routines. Its personnel would also test the various routines for efficiency and relevance and would study the reports to find ways of making them more meaningful. The latter is often done by the Professional Staff until this task becomes too time consuming for them; it is then properly placed under the jurisdiction of the new Research Department. Because of the nonproductive nature of the Research Department, its expenses are borne by the other departments of the bureau. An hourly rate is charged to each to cover Research Department costs, including labor.

Principles and Objectives of the Accounting System

Income. The high cost involved in operation of a service bureau calls for an eagle eye on expenses. Thus it is advantageous to divide income between the service center and any other professional or consulting services which may be rendered. With the processing of statistical information, provision for interpretive service is quite understandable. Two natural divisions of income, therefore, are created.

Expenses. Expenses should be divided along organizational lines to provide for budgeting and budgetary controls. Detail accounts may be established within each division and apportioning made from nonproductive areas or divisions to the productive group. Apportionment of administrative expense is best divided on the basis of income from other departments. A Professional Department can base apportionment on time spent and include a rate for principals if no salary is paid them.

Apportionment of expense can be accomplished in one of two ways. It may be by a formal entry on the accounts, or it may simply be made on the reports on a monthly basis. If formal entries are made, contra accounts should be used in the departments originating the apportionment. If the apportionment is handled on a report, no additional accounting is necessary; however, accumulation of such charges is not as well recorded. If the accounts are themselves kept by data processing, formal entries would be desirable.

Example 1—The following journal entries reflect formal basis of recording apportionment:

Professional Department Expense	XXXXX	
Research Department	XXXXX	
Data Processing Department	XXXXX	
Administrative Department Contra Accounts		XXXXX

Example 2—If expenses are apportioned on the basis of monthly reports, the following could be used:

Data Processing Department direct costs	XXXXX
Administrative Department cost @ X per unit	XXXXX
Total Department expense	XXXXX
General Administrative expense, actual cost	XXXXX
Less apportioned to Processing Department	XXXXX
Variance favorable (unfavorable)	XXXXX

Costs and expenses should be collected in a general departmental account much the same as overhead for the productive departments. The account should assume its share of service from other departments. The total costs may be developed monthly and apportioned over the work on a unit basis.

In the development of unit costs, each piece of equipment should be considered. Four factors affecting the value of the unit are the monthly rental of equipment, the portion of time an operator must be present, the percentage of time the machine will be in operation, and the rate at which the equipment will produce. Secondary consideration should be given to the type of work.

Example: Installation has been made at the Business Service Center of a key punch, a sorter, an output printer, and a calculator. The key punch rents for $70 per month, has a capacity of from 300 to 550 cards per hour, requires an operator constantly, and will be in operation most of the time. The sorter has capacity of 450 cards per minute per pass, rents for $40 per month, operates 20 percent of the time, and requires an operator constantly. The output printer and the calculator each rent for about $200 per month, each has a capacity of 150 cards per minute, will operate 35 percent of the time, and will require an operator only 10 percent of the time.

These facts make it evident that the key punch should have a much greater cost per unit than the sorter. If the key punch is assigned a factor of 5 for payroll work and 3.5 for other work, the sorter a factor of .1 and the output printer and calculator each a value of 1.5, these factors would be applied to the monthly output of each machine to arrive at total units produced (number of cards times factor = units produced). Total production department cost divided by total units will equal the unit cost. The unit cost is now applied back to the equipment factor to arrive at a card cost. This procedure should be continued long enough to develop a trend; once a trend has been established, a standard card cost should be used. After that variance accounts should be set up and become the control point for cost control.

If work is done on a job basis or on a contract, all that is required is to record card production for each machine. When the job is complete, the card costs are applied to the record of cards produced, profit is figured, and billing is accomplished. The problem of billing is discussed in the section titled "Time-saving ideas".

SPECIFIC OBJECTIVES OF THE SYSTEM

Any accounting system must encompass three objectives:

1. The system must be simple.
2. It must be adequate.
3. It must be expandable.

Simplicity. The profession of accounting is baffling enough without the burden of ambiguous titles or obscure accounts within the General ledger. It sometimes seems that an accounting system is created principally to make an impression. Actually the only ones impressed by a complicated system are the uninformed, because an overly complex system is more time consuming and more apt to cause errors. If an accountant really desires to show his mettle, he probably will find a simple system much more difficult to develop.

Adequacy. Simplicity does not imply inadequacy. Much study is required to discover what the accounting system is to accomplish. If information is not relevant, there is no reason to provide special treatment. Neither should information be duplicated. This does not mean that some type of subsidiary to a General ledger is not required for its greater detail. The test of relevance is the biggest single test of adequacy. For instance, suppose it was decided to divide sales into six categories. If the statistics so compiled are never used, the categories are futile and therefore should be combined.

Expandability. Most accounting systems are set up when a business is new or small in size. What is simple and sufficient then may later prove to be highly inadequate for a growing firm. It is equally an example of poor management to set up a million-dollar system for a ten-thousand-dollar business. If a system becomes obsolete and must be discarded, much valuable information will be discarded with it. Since most accounting information is compared with historical statistics, a major change in system may make such comparisons difficult or impossible. On the other hand, if a system is expandable, comparisons may be retained.

Classification of Accounts and Books of Accounts

The chart of accounts for a service bureau should include the following:

BALANCE SHEET ACCOUNTS.

ASSETS

Current assets

1102 Cash on Hand
1105 Cash in Bank (Name of Bank)
1120 Accounts Receivable
1710 Prepaid Interest
1730 Rental Deposits
1780 Work in Progress

Fixed assets

1210 Furniture and Fixtures
1211 Allowances for Depreciation
1212 Additional First-Year Depreciation
1240 Buildings
1241 Allowance for Depreciation
1250 Land
1250 Rights to Leasehold
1271 Amortization of Leasehold

LIABILITIES

Current liabilities

2101 Accounts Payable
2112 Payroll Taxes Payable
2135 Notes Payable
2141 Equipment Contracts Payable
2170 Provision for Federal and State Income Taxes
2180 Equipment Leases

Fixed liabilities

2210 Mortgages Payable

NET WORTH

3150 Capital Stock Outstanding
              or
3101 Proprietorship

3102 Personal Drawing
3152 Profit and Loss
3154 Retained Earnings (if corporation)

INCOME AND EXPENSE ACCOUNTS.

INCOME

4001 Data Processing Fees
4101 Fees from Professional Services

EXPENSES

6100 Administrative Expense

6198 Administrative Apportionment
6200 Data Processing Expense
6300 Professional Department Expense
6398 Professional Apportionment
6400 Research Expense
6498 Research Apportionment

ACCOUNTS PECULIAR TO THE BUSINESS

Apportionment Accounts. These are contra accounts which serve as variance accounts. The department accounts are to be subdivided by using a standard expense code. By employing a two-digit number, 99 detail accounts can be coded. Of the expense code, one detail should be an apportionment account to collect apportionment from other departments.

Apportionment contra accounts need no detailed subdivision. For tax purposes, simply apply the apportionment contra accounts to the departmental apportionment. By combining detail from the departments, expenses for the tax return can be prepared. The detail of each department can be used for expense control or budgeting.

An example of the journal entries for apportionment follows:

To apply apportionment of administrative expense:

Professional Department Expense-apportionment	XXXX	
Data Processing-apportionment	XXXX	
Administrative Apportionment Contra		XXXX

To reverse apportionment for tax preparation:

Research Apportionment Contra	XXXX	
Professional Department Contra	XXXX	
Administrative Contra	XXXX	
Data Processing-Apportionment		XXXX
Professional Department Expense Apportionment	XXXX	

An example of the expense code might be:

01 Supplies	52 FICA Expenses
02 Advertising	61 Interest
05 Utilities	62 Insurance
41 Wages and Salaries	99 Apportionment

Peculiarities of Procedures

Work in Progress. The use of the system described precludes the necessity of a job order or work-in-progress account, with the jobs in progress set up as a subsidiary. All direct costs are collected in the operating "overhead" or more properly, these two accounts are in a sense combined. If there is any work in progress at the end of the year, its value will be the work completed and transferred to the Work-in-Progress account at the end of the year. The account can be handled much the same as Accounts Receivable or Accounts Payable by charging or crediting when the books are closed; the closing entries can be reversed at the beginning of the new year. Books of account can vary widely. This is somewhat due to modern techniques in accounting. Basically, the books of account stem from the use of ledger and journal. Of course, a double entry is a prerequisite. If the book of original entry is started from a combination journal, an efficient system may be devised even if punch card method is used.

Expenses. Major division of expenses, set up by organizational lines, must be subdivided by expense items. This is done by setting up an expense code. The code should include all of the detail classifications for all accounts. By adding code numbering, a code number will be the same item of expense regardless of the division. For example, General and Administrative Expense may be account No. 6100; Data Processing Operating Expense, No. 6300; Wages and Salaries, No. 41. Administrative Salaries would, therefore, be Account No. 6141; Data Processing Salaries would be No. 6341.

Leasehold. Since equipment leasing is such an important part of data processing, special treatment is required as well as application of good judgment. If a long-term lease has been arranged to cover essentially the life of the equipment, the lease should be discounted as though it were a loan and amortized over the term of the lease; the discount would represent interest. If the lease allows the equipment to be moved on a 90-day notice, the only liability which exists is 90 days' rent, and virtually no rights to leasehold would exist. The only applicable accounting would be the showing of the 90-day rent accrual.

Time and Payroll System

The direct labor force should be paid on an hourly basis. This can be done by employees keeping their own time or by the use of a time clock. The Professional and Research Departments, however, should allocate their time to the work they do whether it is for another department in the bureau or consists of outside services. Such allocation makes distribution costs possible. If an hourly base is used by the Data Processing Department, it should be figured by machine hours rather than by personnel hours. In this way there is no need to apply direct labor hours to the job. Personnel hours will be prorated by machine hours.

Time-Saving Ideas

Work Units. Emphasis has been placed upon the use of work units, which must have the same basis. This means that if machine hours are used, then machine hours are the unit of measure on all equipment in a department. However, another department may prefer to use a different base. It is important to keep daily records on all units produced, both internally and productively. The use of work units as a measure greatly simplifies daily record keeping.

Billing. Standard costs have been developed as a method to arrive at billing by adding profit. If, for instance, 20 percent is the margin within the particular branch of data processing, the 20 percent is added to the standard costs to provide the profit. If standard costs are used, a record of the total units produced must be kept. The total units produced multiplied by the standard will equal total standard cost. Comparison of the total standard cost with the total charged to the production department will show the variance.

To determine activity of the client, time or unit cost records should be kept on each client. Such records provide a history of the client's growth as well as information as to future requirements on the part of the service center. This will also serve as a means to record the center's billable time.

Reports to Management

Profit and Loss Statement. The monthly profit and loss statement (Figure 1) should make use of the variance information which has been provided. Variances are good indicators of the fees charged and the level of activity. If the data on the current month and year to date are provided, management has both the short- and long-term view of variances and income.

Additional exhibits of departmental expenses can be attached to the statement shown in Figure 1. The report is designed, first, to give management an overview; and second, to provide more detailed study of areas which seem to require special study.

Management statements should be simplified as much as possible for the convenience of the busy executive. Information should be contained in a few meaningful totals which can be evaluated easily. If other information then appears to be necessary, it can be supplied through supplementary reports.

MANAGEMENT REPORT

For month ending ————————————, 19————

	Month	YTD
Data processing		
1 Income	$ =====	$ =====
2 Data processing expense	——	——
3 Less cost of unbilled service-units of unbilled production @ standard cost	——	——
4 Cost of data processing income	——	——
5 Gross profit from data processing (line 1 less line 4)	$ =====	$ =====
Professional service		
6 Income	$ ——	$ ——
7 Professional department expense	——	——
8 Less apportionment to other departments	——	——
9 Cost of professional services	——	——
10 Gross profit from professional services (line 6 less line 9)	——	——
11 Total gross income (line 5 and line 10)	$ =====	$ =====
Expense		
12 Administrative expense	$ ——	$ ——
13 Less apportionment	——	——
14 Line 12 less line 13	——	——
15 Research expense	——	——
16 Less apportionment	——	——
17 Line 15 less line 16	——	——
18 Net income (line 11 less line 17)	$ =====	$ =====

Fig. I. Management Statement

19

Dance Instruction Studios

BY PAUL L. WILLIAMS

Public Accountant, Fort Smith, Arkansas

Characteristics of the Business That Affect the Accounting System

Dance instruction is given for a number of reasons. In the case of children, to acquaint them with one of the social graces, to develop poise and charm, and/or to start them on the road to professional dancing. Adults take dancing lessons to add new steps or techniques to those they already know, or to acquire the art of dancing in the first place; to develop social graces; to obtain physical exercise; to meet new people and find new friends. Dancing is a recommended means of mental and physical therapy as well as an outlet for individual expression and a profound sense of rhythm and appreciation of music. It is also a way to promote relaxation and social awareness, contacts, and compatability for the elderly.

Studios providing instruction vary according to clientele, and the type of lessons given is dependent upon the desires of the individual. The two principal categories of studios cater to children, and to adults.

Children's studios usually offer tap, ballet, "modern jazz," and interpretive dancing. In the spring, annual dance recitals are presented so that children may display their skills. Classes are composed of students approximately the same age; and, hopefully, each class contains 15 or more students. The child may start lessons as young as three or four years old and continue for a decade or more. The grace and social poise acquired are of benefit in maturity, and sometimes after years of instruction and practice, a child emerges as a dancer of ability and promise, with motivation and persistence to become a star or starlet.

The adult dance studio is a more sophisticated and involved type of organization. Ballroom dancing is principally offered, although jazz, tap, ballet, and theatre arts (theatrical dancing) may be available according to demand. Classes in square dancing, because of space requirements, are most often held in an armory or hall, are paid for by cash in advance, taught by visiting teachers or callers, and cover only a few weeks or months.

In the studios, however, students may take one or more medal courses in ballroom dancing. Courses range from beginning steps to highly advanced patterns; each leads to presentation of a medal or trophy for successful completion of all requirements including examinations and exhibitions. Courses embody such dances as bossa nova, cha-cha, foxtrot, mambo, merengue, paso doble, pechanga, rhumba, samba, swing (single, double, triple, and D.C. or Western), tango, waltz, Viennese waltz. On the other hand, students may prefer to sign up for just a few lessons in one or two types of dance. An adult studio is the more versatile, both in its presentation of dance and because it serves men and women of all ages beyond 18.

The two standards of ballroom dancing in America are the American Standard and the International or Continental Standard. The latter is promoted in the United States by traveling representatives of the United Kingdom Alliance of Professional Teachers of Dance and by the Imperial Society of Teachers of Dance, Inc., also of England. Both of these organizations, operating under financial arrangements with the studio, train and certify American instructors in International as well as students, under the aegis of their teachers who have previously earned such certification. The steps required and the seven grades of achievement are rigidly controlled and standardized.

The American Standard of Dance, however, deviates according to studio inclination, since no single organization has yet achieved sufficient status to act as a central certifying authority. There is, however, loose agreement between chains and independents, so that while the different steps and stylings taught may vary, the five grades in the American Standard are fairly comparable in ascending complexity.

In contrast to class lessons characteristic of children's studios, adults may take either private or class lessons, or both.

FUNCTIONAL CHARACTERISTICS OF THE BUSINESS

The teaching of children usually starts in early fall and ends with the spring recital; generally the studio closes during the summer. For personal convenience the fiscal year is preferred, and the closing would be in June, July, or August; however, because of income tax requirements, a calendar-year closing poses fewer problems and therefore is more feasible. The adult studio continues instruction year 'round especially since the advent of air conditioning; hence the closing date can be set at any time convenient for management. A calendar year is the normal choice.

A cash basis system would be applicable for a children's studio. The more complex adult studio would be apt to follow an accrual basis of reporting, as will be discussed later.

Competition plays a minuscule role in the life history of children's studios. However, the adult studios find it a large factor affecting their operation. The latter type of studio may be what is known as an independent; that is, one managed by the owner; or the organization may be one of a chain. In this case the studio is generally franchised by a nationally known personality. It is characterized by instruction controlled by the franchiser, a competent and successful method of training new teachers, an aggressive sales organization, and cross-country dance competitions as one of its sales "gimmicks". Competition thus exists between franchised studios of opposing chains, while the independent and smaller studios must buck their comparable neighbors as well as the franchised organizations.

Generally speaking, the adult dance studio operation requires a heavy outlay of cash. A children's dance studio can, and often is, started and maintained with comparatively little cash outlay.

PRINCIPAL ACCOUNTING PROBLEMS

Many adult students are unable to pay cash for a course of lessons and must sign a note at the time the contract is entered into. The note is discounted, and the finance company or bank holds out a certain percentage of the total note until it is paid off. This type of transaction is handled through the Finance Company (Bank) Trust Fund. In the event a note is uncollectible, the bank or finance company charges the depositor or studio with the amount not received. This amount, of course, would be taken from the reserve funds held in the trust fund.

The Grantor's Trust Fund is a sum, usually based on a percentage of lesson income, which is paid by the licensee to the grantor of the franchise. Held in escrow or trust, the fund ordinarily is required by the grantor to cover the cost of teaching out lesson contracts in the event the franchise holder cannot meet such obligations. The fund is, in effect, the licensee's money and can earn him interest.

The nature of the dance instruction operation often requires a larger than usual amount of repair and improvements to a rental unit before it can fulfill requirements as a studio. Such expense should be set up as a leasehold improvement.

Franchises are a special problem to the accountant. Normally the franchise fee is paid in advance by the licensee regardless of the number of lessons sold. The cost represents the right to do business under the established name of the instruction system. If the rights are for a definite period of time, these rights should be amortized over that period of time; if the rights are perpetual, then the entire cost of the franchise would be an intangible asset and would not be chargeable over any particular period but would remain on the books.

There are cases where a licensee is charged the regular fee for the privilege but is required to pay an additional fee for a certain number of units or lessons sold. The latter fee would then be a direct expense and would be charged off annually.

The cost of starting a children's studio can be nominal, because often the owner-manager's home will suffice as the studio; or an old store building may be cleaned and converted into a studio. Equipment is limited to a piano, a record player, and a few pieces of office furniture.

In the sophisticated adult studio the initial cost and maintenance are appreciably higher. Staff salaries come to a considerable amount; and in franchised studios, the cost of the franchise is an additional expense. A large ballroom and several smaller individual instruction rooms are required. There must be office and multiple restroom facilities and a reception area. Each instruction room must have a record player or a tape machine; a loudspeaker or an intercom system is invaluable. Other equipment, such as extra chairs, glassware, and dishes for parties, is necessary.

Since the children's studio usually operates on a cash basis, there are few accounting problems involved. However, if the owner-manager has converted part of his residence to a studio, a certain percentage of all residence expense should be charged into operating expenses. These would include such items as real estate tax, fire insurance, interest on mortgage, general repairs, maintenance of grounds, etc. Special repairs to the studio area should be charged in full to the operating statement of the studio; however, if they have a life of over one year, they could be considered improvements by IRS and would then require amortization over the life of the lease or the life of the improvements, rather than being a direct charge to operating expenses.

Functional Organization

A studio for children is generally operated by the owner, who also does the selling and the instruction. He (she) may hire one or more assistants for teaching. In many cases, the business is run as a sole proprietorship, but if two or more individuals are involved in the studio ownership, the business could be operated as a partnership. The owner-manager must be able to sell himself to the children as a mentor and as a friend and to instill the desire to be taught. He must also have a character and a responsibility which the parents themselves will honor and admit by allowing their children to attend his classes.

The adult dance studio, usually a corporation, is operated by a manager, or in the case of a small independent studio, by the principal officer. This person is in charge of creating a sales force, maintaining a suitable staff of dance instructors, and supervising the two departments so they function at their maximum. The manager may never see students during the time they take instruction. This manager does not have to sell himself; he must sell the studio name, or the dance(s).

In a larger studio there may be an assistant manager, a supervisor of teachers who is himself an instructor, and a director of dance who plans the classes for the various grades within the standards of dance.

Instruction is sometimes given in private homes for private groups, but in the main teaching is done at the studio. Class lessons are provided in foot patterns, styling, posture, etc., with one instructor for five to fifteen students; and there is consistent and popular demand for private lessons, i.e., one instructor for each student. New students are often taught in a small private room away from other dancers until their self-confidence enables them to join the others.

Principles and Objectives of the Accounting System

A cash receipts and disbursement system is adequate for the average children's studio, but an accrual system is definitely suggested for the adult dance studio.

SPECIFIC OBJECTIVES OF THE SYSTEM

No accounting system can be adequate unless it furnishes management with facts essential to operation. Complexity of the reports would depend upon management understanding, which is as varied as the many fields which management controls.

Classification of Accounts and Books of Accounts

The following chart of accounts is recommended:

BALANCE SHEET ACCOUNTS.

ASSETS

Current assets

101 Petty Cash Fund
102 Cash on Hand
105 Cash in Bank
108 Notes Receivable—Students
110 Customer Account
112 Advances to Employees
130 Investments
140 Grantor's Trust Fund
145 Finance Company (Bank) Trust Fund

Fixed assets

151 Land
152 Building
153 Less: Accumulated Depreciation
157 Studio Equipment
158 Less: Accumulated Depreciation
163 Office Equipment
164 Less: Accumulated Depreciation
167 Automobile
168 Less: Accumulated Depreciation
177 Leasehold Improvements
178 Less: Accumulated Amortization

Other assets

180 Franchise

181 Less: Accumulated Amortization
190 Prepaid Insurance
195 Utility Deposits
196 Deposits for Workmen's Compensation

LIABILITIES

Current liabilities

202 Accounts Payable
205 Students' Loans Payable
215 Installment Loans
230 Payroll Deductions
    231 Federal Withholding Tax
    232 State Withholding Tax
    233 City Withholding Tax
    234 FICA
240 Employer Payroll Taxes Payable
    241 State Unemployment Insurance
    242 Federal Unemployment Insurance
245 Accrued Taxes Payable
250 Due on Untaught Lessons

NET WORTH

Corporation

290 Capital Stock Issued
295 Retained Earnings
298 Current Profits

Proprietorship

290 Invested Capital
295 Drawing Account

Partnership

290 Invested Capital—Partner A   294 Drawing Account—Partner A
291 Invested Capital—Partner B   295 Drawing Account—Partner B

INCOME AND EXPENSE ACCOUNTS.

REVENUE

302 Dance Instruction
312 Instructor Income
323 Commissions Income

EXPENSES

Salaries

402 Instructors' Salaries
405 Manager's Salary
410 Maintenance Salaries
415 Clerical Salaries
420 Salesmen's Salaries or
     Commissions

Selling expense

502 Franchise Fee (where needed)
510 Records, Tapes, etc.
515 Advertising
520 Other Business Promotion

General and administrative

602 Leasehold Improvements
603 Rent
605 Electricity, Water, and Gas
610 Telephone
615 Maintenance and Repair
620 Building Depreciation
625 Studio Equipment Depreciation

626 Office Equipment Depreciation
630 Automobile Depreciation
635 Maintenance Supplies
636 Office Supplies
637 Other Supplies
640 Office Life Insurance
645 Group Insurance
646 Workmen's Compensation
     Insurance
650 Retirement Plan
655 Other Insurance
660 Payroll Taxes
665 Property Taxes
670 Other Taxes
675 Automobile Expense
676 Entertainment
678 Travel
679 Dues and Subscriptions
685 Donations
690 Miscellaneous

OTHER INCOME

710 Discounts Earned
715 Interest Earned

DEDUCTIONS FROM INCOME

750 Allowances Given
765 Interest Expense

BOOKS AND FORMS PECULIAR TO THE BUSINESS

It is vital to maintain accurate records of the students' instructional hours and the payments on their contracts. The Teachers' Weekly Report (Figure 1) not only provides information on the students' lessons but also on the pupils' status, i.e., whether they are active or inactive (inactive is no appointment in the last two weeks, and NFA means no future appointment); whether they have standing appointments at the same time each week with the teacher; data about examinations taken, medal course, party attendance, etc. As indicated in the upper left corner, a junior student is one who has signed for a small program of lessons as compared with a medal-course student. An exchange student is one, coming in from another studio, whose lessons are already paid for elsewhere.

In an independent studio the Daily Report of New Business (Figure 2) is filled out by the receptionist as students come in for appointments or make payments. In case the student signs a note in payment for classes or private lessons, the proceeds from discounting of this note would appear on this report. The initial deposit, of course, would be shown at the time the contract is signed. The reverse side of the Daily Report concerns phone calls made by the Advertising Department, source of prospect's name, whether contacted, appointment made and verified, whether prospect appears for the lesson, and any rebookings.

The receptionist's Daily Report for a franchised studio (Figure 3) is designed for use by all member studios for weekly submission to the central office of the franchiser. Names of students are, therefore, omitted, and only figures are entered. In the upper left box, B.P. refers to a budget plan. In the middle box at right, T.O. concerns turnovers or students transferring from beginning lessons to an extension, or from an extension to a renewal. R.L. is return losses—students returning for lessons after an absence. P.F. means paid and finished with lessons. The next T.O. is transfers out, or those students moving to a studio elsewhere. Losses cover pupils who drop out for one reason or another. In the box at the foot of the illustration, C.V. Total refers to the cumulative value total; S.F. is classes in basic steps; Styl., those in styling; and Cuts (at left) has to do with students' programs which are cut back or dropped.

The Activity (Cash) Sheet is compiled each day by the bookkeeper and records details of all sales and cash received. It is the source of all bookkeeping entries. Forming a simple one-write system, the sheet is made in duplicate; a carbon is placed over the first sheet, and the bottom half of the Student Control Card (Payments), shown on the front of Figure 5, is placed on top. The Course column is the number of hours signed for. The Miscellaneous Payment column would include the amount of interest if the student is on a budget plan; money paid for special offers, etc. Sold By column gives the name of the teacher(s) involved.

The total amount of the deposit is circled at the end of the day, and the date of deposit written on a separate line. Thus several days' entries may be made on a single sheet.

The Student Control Card, often called the pupil's ledger card or student course card, is a permanent record of payments made (Figure 5) and hours taken (Figure 6). Some studios prefer to combine this information on a

DATE _____   **TEACHER WEEKLY REPORT**   TEACHER _____

No. of Pupils and are they Reg. Jr. or Exch?	Name of Pupil (1st, 2nd initial and last name)	Hours out of Total Hours Enrolled	TRANSFERS		Hours this Week (3 or more for)	+ or –	Active or Inactive or N.F.A.	+ or –	Is Pupil on Standing?	+ or –	Type and date of Next Exam	+ or –	Did Pupil attend Party this week?	+ or –	Is Pupil on Medal Course? If so, which one?	+ or –	No. of Guests Sold	+ or –	TOTAL + s after subtracting –1
			IN or OUT	FROM or TO															

	PREVIOUS TOTAL			THIS WEEK			TOTAL					
	Tried	Sold	HOURS	Tried	Sold	HOURS	Tried	Sold	HOURS	Pupils to start week _____	Hours Taught _____
ORG.										Transfer In _____	Standing Hours _____
EXT.										Transfer Out _____	Pre-books _____
REN.										Pupils to End Week _____	Actives _____
TOTAL										Guests Sold _____	Inactives _____
										No. of Pupils at Party _____	N.F.A. _____

* COURTESY OF KURT SCHOEN'S CO-OP DANCE HOBBY CLUB, WASHINGTON, D.C.

Figure I: Teacher's Weekly Report

RECEPTIONIST DAILY REPORT

Earned Total _____

Date_____
Income Recd._____
Cash over Desk_____
Fin. Co._____
Other_____
Other_____
Other_____
Other_____
Other_____
Other_____
Total_____

Source	Name of Pupil	Time	Hours	Amount	Teacher	Interviewer

NO. SALES   SALES GROSS   APPOINTMENTS   OTHER INFO

TOTAL WEEKLY:

* COURTESY OF KURT SCHOEN'S CO-OP DANCE HOBBY CLUB, WASHINGTON, D.C.

Figure 2: Daily Report of New Business (Independent)

Receptionist Daily Report
New Business

| | | ADVERTISING DEPT. | | | | | | |
Source	Caller	Hrs.	Calls	Contacts	Appts.	Ver.	Showed Up	Rebook

for Payroll

Figure 2: Daily Report of New Business (Independent) (cont.)

single card. Where the two cards are used, they are clipped together and filed alphabetically. At top left of each figure the Course column is special courses, such as a guest special; Orig. refers to original sale; Ext. means extension or added lessons purchased; R#1, etc., is contract renewals. Listing of payments continues onto the reverse of the card (Figure 5) where at the foot is space for notations on the budget plan if it is used. Information for the card may be obtained from the Teachers' Weekly Report (Figure 1) and/or the Daily Report of New Business (Figures 2 and 3).

The Student Control Card for hours taken (Figure 6) details the type and number of lessons taken and the balance on hand. Notations are continued on the reverse side. The top half of the card may be written simultaneously with the top half of the pupil's payment card (Figure 5). S.P.S. (center section of Figure 6, at right) is parties attended.

The control cards in Figures 5 and 6 are more valuable when color coded. Blue cards may be compiled for students taking International; white denotes the American Standard; green, classes in exercise, posture, and figure control; yellow for jazz, tap, ballet, and theatre arts classes. Another method of color coding has been utilized for payments. Green, for example, for students paying cash; pink for those on the installment plan; blue, students who have signed with one studio but are taking with another; yellow, transient or beginner students.

Studio_____Date_____

GROSS	
D CASH	
A	
Y B.P.	
W CASH	
E	
E B.P.	
K	
TOTAL	

	DAY		WEEK	
	TRIES	SALES	TRIES	SALES
INTERVIEW				
EXTENSIONS				
RENEWALS				
GUESTS				

HRS. TAUGHT	
D REG.	
A	
Y JR.	
CLASS	
W REG.	
E	
E JR.	
K CLASS	

ACTIVE	REG.	JR.
TOTAL		
NEW		
T.O.		
R.L.		
TOTAL		
P.F.		
T.O.		
LOSSES		
TOTAL		

SALES			DAY		C.V.			WEEK		C.V.
	#	PRI	CLASSES	STYL.	TOTAL	#	PRI	S.F.	STYL.	TOTAL
INT										
EXT										
REN										
TOTAL										
CUTS										
TOTAL										

* COURTESY OF THE FRED ASTAIRE WORLD OF DANCE, WASHINGTON, D.C.

Figure 3: Daily Report (Franchised Studio)

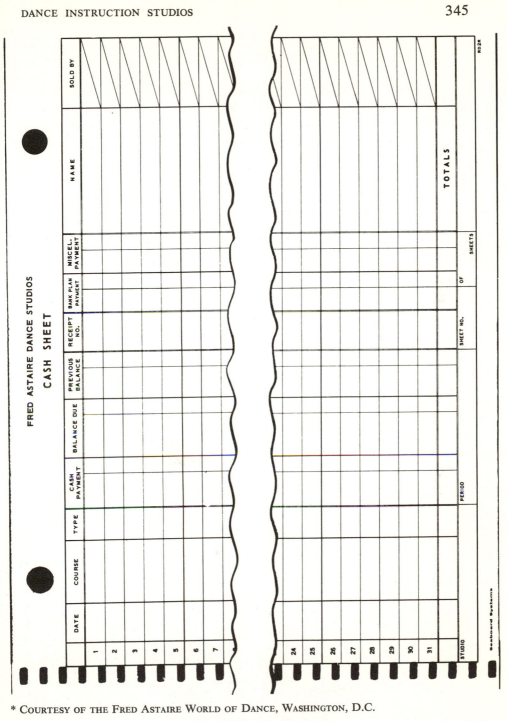

Figure 4:   Activity (Cash) Sheet

MR.
MRS. _____   HOME   BUSINESS
MISS   PHONE _____   PHONE _____

STREET _____ CITY _____

	Date	Course	Amount	Teacher	Commission Paid	Terms
Course						
Orig.						
Ext.						
Ext.						
R # 1						
R # 2						
R # 3						

	DATE	COURSE	TYPE	CASH PAYMENT	BALANCE DUE	PREVIOUS BALANCE	RECEIPT NO.	BANK PLAN PAYMENT	MISCEL. PAYMENT
1									
2									
3									
4									
5									
6									
7									
8									
9									
10									
11									
12									
13									
14									
15									
16									
17									

STUDENT CONTROL CARD   Fred Astaire Dance Studios

* COURTESY OF THE FRED ASTAIRE WORLD OF DANCE, WASHINGTON, D.C.

Figure 5: Student Control Card (Payments)

NAME _____

	DATE	COURSE	TYPE	CASH PAYMENT	BALANCE DUE	PREVIOUS BALANCE	RECEIPT NO.	BANK PLAN PAYMENT	MISCEL. PAYMENT
1									
2									
3									
4									
5									
6									
7									
8									
9									
10									
11									
12									
13									
14									
15									
16									
17									
18									
19									
20									
21									
22									

BUDGET (Payment received)			BUDGET (Payment received)			BUDGET (Payment received)		
Date	Amount	Balance	Date	Amount	Balance	Date	Amount	Balance

STUDENT CONTROL CARD   Fred Astaire Dance Studios

Figure 5: Student Control Card (Payments) (cont.)

MR.
MRS. _____   HOME   BUSINESS
MISS   PHONE _____   PHONE _____

STREET _____   CITY _____

	Date	Course	Amount	Teacher	Commission Paid	Terms
Course						
Orig.						
Ext.						
Ext.						
R # 1						
R # 2						
R # 3						

TEACHERS & SALES	Date	Free Style		Choreography		Lead & Follow		S. P. S.		Amount	
		Taken	Left	Taken	Left	Taken	Left	Taken	Left	Used	BALANCE

STUDENT CONTROL CARD   Fred Astaire Dance Studios

* COURTESY OF THE FRED ASTAIRE WORLD OF DANCE, WASHINGTON, D.C.

Figure 6:   Student Control Card (Hours)

Other than the Payroll journal, three basic journals are recommended, to be kept on standard 30-column sheets as the record of daily transactions. Cash receipts and disbursements might be recorded in a combination journal. The Check register and the General journal would record payment of bills and miscellaneous General journal types of entry. Totals of these journals would be posted monthly into the General ledger. The General ledger, because it reveals the life history of the organization, must be current at all times. An additional book, the Notes journal, may be helpful as a record of those students who pay by installment.

ACCOUNTS PECULIAR TO THE BUSINESS

Advances to Employees (No. 112). Because of the nature of the business and the extra expense required for competitions, trips, costumes, corsages for students, etc., this account is often needed in studio accounting, even though its use is not recommended.

Investments (No. 130). When a new class begins, or a number of students start lessons, there may be a certain amount of surplus funds. Rather than to leave this money in the cash account in the bank, it is advisable to convert it into short-term investments which will create additional income.

Grantor's Trust Fund (No. 140). Explanation of this account has been given under the section, Principal Accounting Problems. The money could well be placed in a savings account to draw interest.

Finance Company (Bank) Trust Fund (No. 145). Since this is a trust fund, the finance company or bank controls the fund until the installment note has been paid in full. At that time the cash (a percentage of the total on the student contract) is transferred to the funds of the studio. In other types of business this account is often referred to as the Dealers' Loss Reserve.

Leasehold Improvements (No. 177). This type of improvement should be amortized over the lifetime of the lease or the lifetime of the improvement, whichever is less. The reserve account, of course, is Accumulated Amortization (No. 178).

Franchise (No. 180). As discussed earlier, if the franchise is perpetual, the entire cost of the franchise rights is shown as a permanent, intangible asset and remains on the books for the entire period the studio operates. In the event it goes out of business, then of course the franchise cost would be considered part of the cost of sale.

If the rights are for a specified period of time, cost must be amortized over that period. In this event an account would be set up under the title of Accumulated Amortization—Franchise (No. 181) and would contain the balance of the yearly amortization charges made in the past. Under some circumstances, however, it may be advisable to charge off the cost of the franchise either to Retained Earnings, if a corporation, or to Investment, if an individual proprietorship or partnership. This would be an unusual treatment and is not the normal method employed to handle such a transaction.

Students' Loans Payable (No. 205). Most adult students work during the day and take their dancing lessons at night. Thus it is a convenience for them if the studio acts as a collecting agent for the finance company. The transaction would be recorded as follows:

> (Dr)   Cash $xxxx
>   (Cr)   Students' Loans Payable $xxxx

The Students' Loans Payable is a clearing account; as soon as possible a check would be written to satisfy the note due.

Most studios prefer to have the student make his payments directly to the bank or finance company, inasmuch as the studio incurs costs if payments are made there as an accommodation. While many retail stores use such transactions as a means of attracting customers into the stores, in hope of another sale, it is doubtful if this effect would apply in the dance instruction business.

Installment Loans (No. 215). In the event the studio purchases equipment on an installment loan, the amount should be entered in the proper fixed asset account at its cost. Any prepaid interest should be entered in its proper account and the entire installment liability would be entered in No. 215. If there is more than one installment loan, proper designation may be made by setting up separate accounts for each of the loans, or by using a subsidiary ledger with No. 215 as a controlling account.

Due on Untaught Lessons (No. 250). When the student signs the contract, the total amount is credited to this account. A ledger card for the student (Figure 5) would be set up to show this amount of credit due him in lessons. As he takes his lessons the ledger card, as well as the account, would be debited and the revenue account, Dance Instruction (No. 302), would be credited. The total balance of all student ledger cards should at all times equal the account balance. This reconciliation should be done no less than once a month, perhaps oftener.

Instructor Income (No. 312). The need for competent instructors in the dance business is eternal. Classes and lessons for instructors are vital to the life of the studio, since the teachers' reputations are often drawing cards which attract new students. Fees received from instructors would be entered in account No. 312. This type of income is kept separately, since many times management has an agreement with an instructor that the fee will be returned if the teacher remains with the studio a specified length of time (usually one year) after instruction is completed. In cases of such agreements, a reserve fund could be set up to cover such rebates to the instructors, and the net fee would comprise income to the studio.

Peculiarities of Procedures

SALES-RECEIVABLE CYCLE

Dancing lessons are sold as a unit of so many lessons for X number of dollars. At the time the student agrees to this arrangement, he signs a contract and either pays in cash or signs a note which the studio converts into cash via a financing organization. This latter transaction is recorded as follows:

a. (Dr)   Notes Receivable—Students $xxxx
              (Cr)   Prepaid Dance Instructions $xxxx
b. (Dr)   Cash in Bank (deposit) $xxxx
   (Dr)   Finance Company (Bank) Trust Fund $xxxx
   (Dr)   Grantor's Trust Fund $xxxx
              (Cr)   Notes Receivable—Students $xxxx

When a student signs up for lessons with a chain, he may pay for his lessons at the home studio but take the lessons at another location with a "visiting" studio of the same franchising agency. The charges are made at the visiting studio in a Visiting Students' Book and are a chargeback to the home studio. In this case the franchiser acts as a clearing agent; after all charges and credits are in, the franchiser advises each studio of the amount of its current receivables and payables. The amount the home studio receives would be recorded thus:

(Dr)   Customer's Accounts $xxxx
           (Cr)   Dance Instruction $xxxx

PURCHASES-PAYABLES CYCLE

When a student has used another studio to receive his actual instruction, the home studio will set up a payable to the visiting studio:

(Dr)   Due on Untaught Lessons $xxxx
           (Cr)   Accounts Payable $xxxx

CASH RECEIPTS AND DISBURSEMENTS

Most dance studios are small enough so that one person may act as bookkeeper, accounts receivable clerk, and cashier. A need for internal audit and control is obvious, as it would be in any other business in these circumstances.

Two recommendations for control are these: (1) Invoices and statements should be presented at the time checks are signed by the owner-manager or licensee, for comparison purposes and for proper notation. (2) The manager or owner should open the mail so that he is aware of complaints as well as exercising control over cash received and turned over to the cashier-bookkeeper. A post office box might be advantageous to make certain that all mail is first available to the manager or owner.

Time and Payroll System

INSTRUCTION SALARIES

The adult studio is an educational institution and must compensate instructors according to their achievement in dance. Each has the opportunity to improve his ability and performance by taking additional "hours" and advancing to the next higher grade in either or both of the two standards. Moving upward in the hierarchy of dance standards is comparable to earning various college degrees, including rigid examinations before each standard is completed and exhibitions as demonstrations of proficiency. As the instructor advances, his pay scale (the amount he receives per lesson taught) also advances. Special accounting, therefore, is required to insure that instructors are properly paid.

Each teacher may receive a Teachers' Appointment Book at the time he is accepted as a member of the staff. A separate page is used for each day; each page records the following data: (1) student name, (2) time of lesson, (3) type of lesson, and (4) student signature to show he received the instruction.

Other studios issue an Appointment Book to the teacher for each student, who initials the square containing notes and date of his lesson. After each lesson the book is turned over to the bookkeeper, who credits the teacher with the required number of hours and marks the student's hours on his ledger card (Figure 6). The book is then returned to the teacher's file ready for the next lesson.

Typical of records indicating data in detail for payment of teachers is the Teacher's Payslip. Figure 7 shows a payslip filled out by a teacher for an independent studio. It is checked against the student's signature as he signs for his lesson, so that any discrepancy can be eliminated at once. The number of hours taught, both private and class, are added each day, and the week's totals are posted to the right side of the report for payroll and tax purposes.

An example of the payslip as applied to chain studio operation (Figure 8) includes spaces for payments made for working on holidays, for trips made to dance competitions, etc.

A sales approach common to most studios is to offer one or more free lessons to a prospective student. If one teacher is assigned to prospective

TEACHER'S PAYSLIP

| Name: | | LAST | | FIRST | | Dependents | | Week Ending |

PUPILS

DAILY TIME	Monday	Tuesday	Wednesday	Thursday	Friday	DAILY TIME	Saturday	Sat'day TIME
1						1		10
30						30		30
2						2		11
30						30		30
3						3		12
30						30		30
4 3						4		1
30						30		30
5						5		2
30						30		30
6						6		3
30						30		30
7						7		4
30						30		
8						8		
30						30		
9						9		
30						30		
10						10		
30						30		
11						11		
PRIVATE								
CLASS								TOTALS
TRNG								
OFF/DESK,								

	COMMISSIONS					TYPE	TOT. HRS.	PER HR.	AMOUNT
DATE SOLD	PUPIL	TYPE	COURSE	%	AMOUNT	PRIVATE PARTY			
						TRAINING			
						SALARY			
						COMM. DRAW			
						OFFICE DESK			
						PHONE RM. BONUS			
						CLASS			
						TYPE			AMOUNT
						GROSS PAY			
						FICA			
						D.C. TAX			
						U.S. TAX			
						ADVANCES			
						INSURANCE			
REMARKS:			TOTAL COMM.			TOTAL DEDUCTIONS NET PAY			

* COURTESY OF KURT SCHOEN'S CO-OP DANCE HOBBY CLUB, WASHINGTON, D.C.

Figure 7: Teacher's Payslip (Independent)

Name _____ Studio _____ W.E. _____

Exemptions _____ Super. _____ Position _____

HOURS/TYPE	MON	TUES	WED	THURS	FRI	SAT	Total	Rate	Earnings
Private								Hrs @	$
Jr. Hour								Hrs.@	$
CLASS								People @	$
								Hours @	$
Misc.								Hrs.@	$
							Total Hours:		Total:
Staff Trg.								Hrs @	$ ST
Desk/Office								Hrs.@	$ D/O

COMMISSIONS	Amt	%	Comm.		
			Total Comm.		
			Salary		Gross Salary
			Special Party		FICA
			Bonus		FWT SWT
			Holiday		INS.
			Trip		SAV. ADV.
			Misc.		Total Deductions
					Net Salary

MONDAY		TUESDAY		WEDNESDAY	

THURSDAY		FRIDAY		SATURDAY	

* COURTESY OF THE FRED ASTAIRE WORLD OF DANCE, WASHINGTON, D.C.

Figure 8: Teacher's Payslip (Franchised Studio)

students, his salary could be handled as a selling expense, and it could be recorded as commissions on the Teacher's Payslip. A fair system often used is an hourly rate plus a commission if the course is sold.

Basically the appointment books are an accumulation of hours. Therefore, the accumulation of the teacher's time might be handled by a one-write system or a payroll journal in a manner essentially the same as any payroll procedure.

OTHER SALARIES

Studio personnel other than teachers, such as the receptionist, bookkeeper, janitor, etc., are normally paid a straight salary per week which creates no problem. Part-time help who make phone calls to prospective customers (Figure 2, reverse) are usually paid by the hour and receive a percentage of the amount when a prospect signs up, or a commission for a prospect who appears for an initial free lesson.

Further Suggestions

Purchase of Franchise. An accountant is advised to review the franchise rights at the time a franchise purchase is contemplated. For instance, a small independent studio may consider joining a chain, and the accountant's opinion would be a vital part in making the decision.

Student Report to Management. A help to management in evaluating the worth of instruction would be students' grading of their teachers. A simple system of excellent, very good, good, fair, and poor might be used in such classifications as ability to teach, knowledge of step patterns, knowledge of technique, ability to get along with others, etc., with a space for additional comment. It is axiomatic that personality is highly significant in teacher-student relationships, and allowance should be made for personality clashes.

Management would, however, find such student grading helpful in determining pay raises and in straightening out those instructors, particularly beginning teachers, who need help in performance, teaching technique, or human relations. This suggestion of a student report is not strictly within the purview of accounting but does fall within the realm of management consulting as an effort to improve the service provided and thus, indirectly, to increase income as well as customer satisfaction.

Instructors as Salesmen. Teachers have an excellent chance to sell additional dance lessons or courses while instructing their students. To encourage selling, management should pay commissions to teachers who are responsible for bringing in "new" business. Another way in which instructors act as salesmen is by personal appearances. Often they may be required by management to visit well-known, popular hotels and restaurant dining rooms. Here their dancing is an attempt to attract favorable comment for the particular dance studio. Again, studios often arrange dancing parties for students at the popular hotels. Favorable comment not only comes from outsiders who watch the performances, but from the students themselves who enjoy the plaudits of the audience and decide to take more lessons, or to sign up for the next advanced course.

Special Tax Consideration. The Internal Revenue Service generally looks upon the total cash receipts as income for that tax year. It has not recognized as a deduction from income the account, "Due on Untaught Lessons", particularly if this account represents a cash reserve. It is recommended that the accountant investigate this area of the income tax law before proceeding.

Reports to Management

A statement of earnings—profit and loss statement—should be presented at least once a month. It should show the current month's earnings and accumulative earnings for the current fiscal period, as well as comparatives of previous month and year. The statement of financial condition—balance sheet—should be compiled for management at least each three months. The franchiser of a chain may require this statement more often, probably each month.

20

Dentists

BY RICHARD V. BIBBERO

President, Medical Management Control, San Francisco, California; author of "The Bibbero System of Dent-A-Counting," "The Bibbero System of Personal Financial Control," and "The Doctor's Hiring Manual"; consulting editor, "Dental Management"; Member, California Health Review and Program Council

Characteristics of the Profession That Affect the Accounting System

Dentistry is a personal service profession. Its history is closely intertwined with medicine, and in many countries the dentist is known as a doctor of medicine specializing in dentistry. Most of dentistry is practiced by individual practitioners; the trend toward partnerships or organizations is very slow. Most dentists enter private practice shortly after receiving their D.D.S. or D.M.D. degrees. A few work for a short time for other dentists on a percentage basis in order to acquire the starting capital for private practice.

The great majority of all the dentists practice general dentistry although there are certain recognized specialties requiring postdoctoral training within the practice. These specialties are oral surgery, which has to do with extractions and fractures; periodontics, which concerns diseases of the gum; endodontics, regarding diseases and repair of the root canal; orthodontics, which refers to alignment of the teeth and jawbone; pediodontics, which has to do with care of children's teeth. There is also some degree of specialization among men doing crowns, bridges, and dental plate work although most general dentists are trained to handle these problems.

Significant changes have occurred in the profession due to vast improvements in the equipment available to the dentist and to the improvements in anesthesia which have allowed him to materially expand his working time per patient.

In the past the dentist has had only minor contact with the problems of prepaid dental insurance or with the various government agencies. This isolation is rapidly disappearing, and the future will see dentists as involved with the government and insurance problems as other parts of the healing arts professions currently are.

FUNCTIONAL CHARACTERISTICS OF THE PROFESSION

Most dentists report both income and expenses on the basis of cash receipts and disbursements and use the calendar year as the taxable year. Profit margins in dentistry are good and, with wider public acceptance of oral health needs, have been steadily increasing; however, the dentist's ability to earn, as contrasted with most of the other learned professions, is singularly limited to his physical ability. Bodily injury or disease tends to disrupt the dentist's earning pattern to a far greater degree than other professions. Dentistry is one of the high-cost, capital equipment professions. While the financing terms from banks, equipment houses, and finance companies are reasonably liberal, it takes the dentist a number of years to pay off his initial capital investment.

PRINCIPAL ACCOUNTING PROBLEMS

The major accounting problem areas of the dentist are: (1) control of cash, (2) control of accounts receivable, (3) control of costs and fees, (4) personal financial control and net worth growth, and (5) income and property taxes.

Functional Organization

The general divisions of work fall within the following broad ranges: (1) the dentist, (2) dental chair-side assistants, (3) dental hygienists, (4) dental laboratory technicians, (5) office help including bookkeeping, typing, reception, clerical, and secretarial. Generally, all of the help are under the personal control and guidance of the dentist so that the organizational structure is one of extreme simplicity. Many dental hygienists are compensated on a percentage basis and in such cases cost accounting of their functions is essential.

Principles and Objectives of the Accounting System

The prime objective of most dentists' offices is to maintain an accounting system that will provide operating control and tax return data. Income is based on cash receipts, and expenses are based on cash disbursements. All receipts and disbursements are cleared through bank accounts. Because of the similarity in most dental practices, the income and expense statement should contain a percentage breakdown for management control and comparison with published operating ratios.

From a tax return point of view, the Accounts Receivable for the cash basis dentist are considered as memo accounts; however, from an internal control point of view, a hybrid system providing 100 percent control by reflecting all charges, payments, and adjustments through the General ledger is desirable. This control plus the monthly balancing of detailed patient ledgers to the General ledger control will help eliminate errors and reduce the chances of employee theft.

Because of the elective nature of most large cases, the dentist usually establishes his fee for the case before he starts his work. His case costs are also affected by the various types of material he can use, i.e., gold, amalgam, porcelain. Having set his overall fee for the case at the start, he should maintain, as a part of his clinical record system, his actual costs of time, materials, and lab fees so that on completion of the case he can compare his actual performance with his estimates. The prepaid insurance plans require this procedure.

SPECIFIC OBJECTIVES OF THE SYSTEM

The objectives of the accounting system are primarily tax-return, tax-audit, and tax-planning oriented. From a point of view of the tax return the dentist must be able to prove all of his income and expense items.

The major method in accomplishing this objective is through having all receipts and disbursements flow through bank accounts. In the situation where the dentist owns outside income property or securities, it is usually desirable to establish separate bank accounts for recording these transactions.

Classification of Accounts and Books of Accounts

A cash-basis General ledger with the traditional business sections and an Accounts Receivable control account with offsetting contra account of

Unearned Income satisfy the typical dental need. The usual dental balance sheet accounts are:

ASSETS	LIABILITIES
Cash Clearing	Current Payables (including taxes)
Petty Cash	Contracts Payable
Tax Savings Accounts	Notes Payable
Accounts Receivable	
Less Contra Account—	**NET WORTH**
Unearned Income	Capital
Fixed Assets	Withdrawal
Allowances for Depreciation	

The fixed asset accounts usually follow the group asset accounting principles, classifying the assets according to their type, life, and method of depreciation. There are two major classifications of assets: (1) Office furniture and equipment and (2) dental, technical, scientific, and X-ray equipment. The usually acceptable life span on both of these asset classes is ten years. Some of the items have durability beyond the ten years, but the technical obsolescence involved in the profession mitigates against a life much in excess of a decade. Depreciation records are maintained in simple tax return order.

It is recommended that the accountant establish his own chart numbers, since the numbers would differ depending upon whether the accounting is done by computer, on a posting machine, or by hand.

A satisfactory chart of accounts for the income and expense accounts follows the business and professional tax return schedules.

Taxes	*Misc. Expenses*	
Rent	Automobile (where	Misc. Professional
Repairs	used in business)	Expense
Salaries	Drugs and Supplies	Office Expense
Insurance	Laboratory Expense	Professional Promotion
Professional Fees	Laundry	Telephone, including
Retirement Plan—	Maintenance	Answering Service
Employees' Share	Meetings, Dues, and	Utilities
	Subscriptions	

As most of the dentists are individual entrepreneurs with the problems of personal financial control and net worth growth, it is useful to have a chart of accounts for the withdrawal section so that the accountant may aid in the planning of personal uses of funds as well as those used in the practice. A satisfactory chart of accounts for the personal financial control section would be as follows.

Auto Expense (Personal)

Cash—Personal

Children—Allowance

Clothing, etc.

Clubs

Contributions

Drugs and Sundries (Nontax-
    deductible)

Entertainment, Educ., Rec., etc.

Food

Health (Tax-deductible Drugs,
    MDs, etc.)

Home Improvements

Household Help

Insurance—Life

Insurance—H&A

Insurance—General

Interest

Investments

Laundry and Cleaning

Linens, etc.

Miscellaneous Casualties

Mortgage Payments

New Furniture, Appliances, etc.

Note Payments

Political

Presents and Gifts

Reading Matter

Rent

Repairs and Upkeep

Savings

Support of Dependents

Taxes—Household Employees

Taxes—Federal

Taxes—State

Taxes—Real Property

Taxes—Personal Property

Telephone

Utilities

Vacation Expenses

BOOKS AND FORMS PECULIAR TO THE PROFESSION

Accounts Receivable accounting and control plus the clinical record cost control and insurance problems give rise to a specialized set of books and forms which are peculiar to dentistry.

Dental Patient Registration Form (Figure 1). Each new patient must provide the dentist's office with the essential clinical, credit, and insurance billing information which will allow the dentist's office functions to be performed. This permanent financial information is usually taken on a form filled out by the patient at the time of his first visit. The data can be passed through credit bureaus for an adequate check on the patient. This is particularly necessary where extensive full-mouth restorations will be undertaken. At this same time the dentist's office should inform the patient of its various policies regarding appointments, broken appointments, credit extension arrangements, and emergency procedures.

The Patient's Clinical Record. The clinical record in addition to containing the diagnostic and treatment data is also a vital record in the insurance billing cycle and in the job costing and fee evaluating procedure.

Figure 2 shows a multifunction dental-clinical record designed to be photocopied for insurance billing as well as showing the following essential identifying information on both the patient and the dentist: the diagnosis, insurance coverage, the procedures performed, the current standing of the patient's fi-

PATIENT INFORMATION FOR MEDICAL RECORDS　　　　　　　DATE _____

| LAST NAME | FIRST | MIDDLE | SOCIAL SECURITY NO. | DATE OF BIRTH |

| HOME ADDRESS | STREET | CITY | STATE | HOME PHONE |

| OCCUPATION | EMPLOYED BY |

| EMPLOYER'S ADDRESS | STREET | CITY | STATE | PHONE NO. |

| SPOUSE'S NAME | REFERRED BY |

OTHER IMMEDIATE FAMILY MEMBERS WHO WILL BE PATIENTS

IN CASE OF EMERGENCY CONTACT - NAME, ADDRESS AND PHONE NUMBER OF RELATIVE OR FRIEND

▶ MEDICAL INSURANCE INFORMATION

COMPANY	POLICY NUMBER
COMPANY	POLICY NUMBER
COMPANY	POLICY NUMBER

▶ IF SOMEONE OTHER THAN PATIENT IS RESPONSIBLE FOR PAYMENT PLEASE COMPLETE THIS SECTION

| NAME OF RESPONSIBLE PARTY | HOME ADDRESS | PHONE NO |

| OCCUPATION | EMPLOYED BY |

| EMPLOYER'S ADDRESS | PHONE NO. |

FORM NO. MDP. 8410　　© 1965　MED-DENT PUBLISHING CO.　SAN FRANCISCO

* COURTESY OF MED-DENT PUBLISHING COMPANY, SAN FRANCISCO, CALIFORNIA.

Figure 1: Dental Patient Registration Form

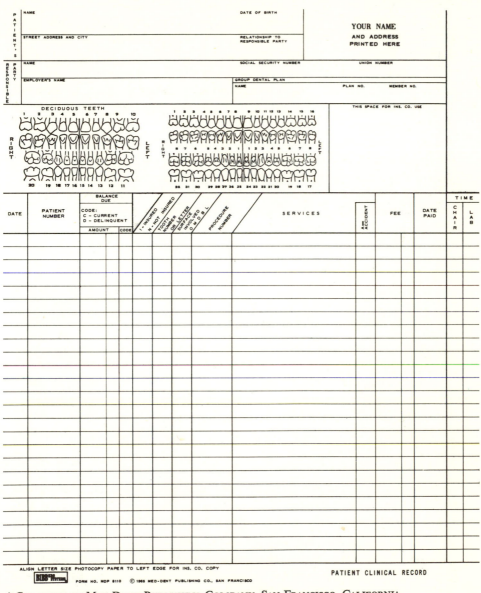

Figure 2:   Patient Clinical Record

nancial account, the date the bill was paid, and the chair time and laboratory cost involved.

Dental-Clinical Record Jackets. The dental-clinical record forms along with any other diagnostic material such as X rays, are housed in color-coded, dental-clinical, record jackets. These jackets (Figure 3) are set up at the time the new patient enters the office. Space is provided on the outside of the jacket to boldly record clinical data, such as patient's allergies, sensitivities, illnesses, and deformities as well as the patient's physician, for constant reminder purposes.

These jackets are all color coded for either library type or file cabinet filing. The color coding of the clinical record jackets for easy alphabetic filing and pulling of the records is a tremendous time saver in the dentist's office.

Service Codes for Ledger Cards, Statements, Visit Slips, Clinical Records and Insurance Billing. The dental service organizations affiliated with the various state dental societies have devised a series of Procedure Codes covering all of the various procedures performed in dentistry. They have classified these codes as follows:

Classification of Service	*Procedure #*
1. Visit and Examination	010-099
2. Roentgenology and Pathology	100-199
3. Oral Surgery	200-299
4. Drugs	300-399
5. Anesthesia	400-449
6. Periodontics	450-499
7. Endodontics	500-599
8. Restorative Dentistry (fillings, inlays, crowns, bridges)	600-699
9. Prosthetics	700-799
10. Space Maintainers	800-899
11. Fractures and Dislocations	900-999

These procedure numbers perform the same functions in dentistry as the relative value service code numbers perform in medicine. The detailed procedure numbers under the various classifications outlined above may be obtained from any of the state or local dental societies.

Patient Visit Data. There are two acceptable methods of organizing the flow of clinical information for Accounts Receivable posting between the dentist in his dental treatment room where the services are performed and his office aide who must maintain his financial records. Postings can be made either from (1) the clinical record or (2) a specially designed patient visit slip.

If the clinical record method is used, the dentist's office aide should numerically stamp with a numbering machine each patient's chart in sequential

Patients Last Name (2nd Letter in Last Name E-H)   First   Middle   Residence Phone Number   Business Phone Number

Patients Last Name
(2nd Letter in Last Name E-H)

First   Middle

Patients Physician Name, Address, Phone,

Allergies:

Sensitivities — Medication, Anasthesia

Impairments or Diseases

Presentation Due

X-rays

Models

Chart

Work Schedule

Estimates

Contract

√ Check each step when completed

Notes:

Presentation Due

X-rays

Models

Chart

Work Schedule

Estimates

Contract

Form No. M.D.P. 8160 © 1966 Med-Dent Publishing Co., San Francisco

* COURTESY OF MED-DENT PUBLISHING COMPANY, SAN FRANCISCO, CALIFORNIA.

Figure 3: Dental-Clinical Record Jacket

order of appointment in the patient number column on the clinical record (Figure 2). This same number is entered on the Daily journal sheet and acts as a control to be sure that all fees for services rendered are correctly recorded in the Daily journal and on the patient's ledger card. When posting the fee, the procedure number should also be recorded in the correct space.

If a specially designed patient visit slip system is preferred by the dentist, such slips should be supplied with preprinted control numbers which are listed on the Daily journal to assure accurate posting of all visits. Figure 4 shows a sample of a special preprinted visit slip which is also used for reappointments and cash receipting.

Cash Receipting System. A duplicate, serial-numbered, cash receipt form is essential in the operating of the dentist's office. One copy of the receipt must be given to the patient and the other copy should act as the posting medium to record the receipt of cash on the patient's permanent financial ledger card record.

This receipting function can be performed with a normal prenumbered duplicate receipt book or with a special print of the multipurpose patient visit slip.

For those dentists who use the clinical record as the means of transmitting the professional service data from the operatories to the business office, the use of a receipt book is recommended. Where the dentist prefers to use the patient visit slip for getting service information to his business office, it would be preferable to use the same form as a patient cash receipt.

Patient's Financial History—The Ledger Card (Figures 5 and 6). The importance of the financial history of the patient is increasing; need for a good financial record complete with insurance data is obvious; and this record should be maintained in the dental office for ready reference at all times. The ledger card may be produced by a handwritten control (peg) board system or by an accounting machine system, depending on the size of the practice. In order to maintain control of Accounts Receivable, the ledger card should be posted simultaneously with the journal, regardless of the system used. Photocopying the ledger card to produce the patient's monthly statement is highly efficient. Good ledger cards, for either a hand- or machine-prepared system, should contain the patient's essential, permanent, financial data at the top, the body set as a financial statement, and at the bottom of the statement the professional services grouped and coded in accordance with the previously mentioned procedure code classifications. Ledgers are of a size to be photocopied, using a half sheet (5½ x 8½) of photocopy paper, for billing purposes.

Computer services also maintain Accounts Receivables and prepare monthly statements for dentists' offices. Those services which remove the pa-

ACCOUNTING COPY

Nº 16

J. P. JONES, D.D.S.   S. C. SMITH, D.D.S.
STATE LIC. NO. A14013   STATE LIC. NO. B302
GENERAL DENTISTRY
100 MAIN STREET, ANY TOWN, ANY STATE 73012
PHONE: (207) 387-4791

DATE

NAME

| PROFESSIONAL SERVICE | PROFESSIONAL SERVICE | PROFESSIONAL SERVICE |

1. VISIT AND EXAM. 010-099
2. X-RAY AND PATH. 100-199
3. ORAL SURGERY 200-299
4. DRUGS 300-399
5. ANESTHESIA 400-449
6. PERIODONTICS 450-499
7. ENDODONTICS 500-599

8. RESTORATIONS 600-699
9. PROSTHETICS 700-799
10. SPACE MAINTAIN. 800-899
11. FRACTURES & DISLOC. 900-999
12. OTHER PROC.

☐ PRIVATE   ☐ BLUE CROSS   ☐ BLUE SHIELD   ☐ IND.   ☐ WELFARE   ☐ GOV'T   ☐ OTHER

REMARKS:

OLD BALANCE $
TODAY'S FEE $
NEW BALANCE $

AMOUNT RECEIVED TODAY
$ _____ BY _____
              ☐ CASH
              ☐ CHECK

10 MIN.   15 MIN.   20 MIN.   30 MIN.   45 MIN.   60 MIN.
M T W T F S   WKS   MOS   DAYS   PRN

NEXT APPOINTMENT
DAY   DATE   TIME

FORM MDP 8130 © 1965   MED-DENT PUBLISHING CO., SAN FRANCISCO

PLEASE RETURN THIS SLIP TO RECEPTIONIST

Figure 4: Patient Visit Slip

* COURTESY OF MED-DENT PUBLISHING COMPANY, SAN FRANCISCO, CALIFORNIA.

BILLING NAME					NAMES OF OTHER FAMILY MEMBERS		

PATIENT'S NAME

RES. PHONE		BUS. PHONE					

FINANCIAL RATING			TOTAL ESTIMATE	DOWN PAYMENT	BAL. DUE WHEN FINISHED	MONTHLY PAYMENTS	WEEKLY PAYMENTS	OTHER PLANS
PROMPT	SLOW	NO REC.						

THE BIBBERO SYSTEM FORM NO. MDP. 8500   © 1965 MED-DENT PUBLISHING CO. - SAN FRANCISCO

ALEXANDER O. MILTON, D.D.S.

680 BANCROFT AVENUE
SAN LEANDRO, CALIFORNIA 94577
TELEPHONE: 569-0218

STATEMENT TO:

- - - - - - - - - - - - - - - - TEAR OFF AND RETURN UPPER PORTION WITH PAYMENT - - - - - - - - - -

DATE	PAYMENTS			PROFESSIONAL SERVICE	FEE	LAST AMOUNT IN THIS COLUMN IS BALANCE DUE
	BANK NUMBER	BY CHECK OR P.M.O.	BY COIN OR CURRENCY			

PROFESSIONAL SERVICE CODE:

A -AMALGAM RESTORATIONS	G -GOLD RESTORATIONS	FMXR-FULL MOUTH X-RAY
P -PORCELAIN RESTORATIONS	D -DENTURE	XR -X-RAYS
PL-PLASTIC RESTORATIONS	PD -PARTIAL DENTURE	XE -EXTRACTION
C -CROWN	PRO-ORAL PROPHYLAXIS	MA -MISSED APPOINTMENT
J -JACKET	DS -DEEP SCALING	T -TREATMENT
EX-EXAMINATION	CON-CONSULTATION	RC -ROOT CANAL
FB-FIXED BRIDGE	SFT-STANNOUS FLUORIDE TREATMENT	TC -TOTAL CARE

ALEXANDER O. MILTON, D.D.S.
680 BANCROFT AVENUE, SAN LEANDRO, CALIFORNIA 94577 TEL. 569-0218

* COURTESY OF MED-DENT PUBLISHING COMPANY, SAN FRANCISCO, CALIFORNIA.

Figure 5: Ledger Card—Hand Posted

BILLING NAME			NAMES OF OTHER FAMILY MEMBERS				
PATIENT'S NAME							
RES. PHONE		BUS. PHONE					
FINANCIAL RATING			TOTAL ESTIMATE	DOWN PAYMENT	BAL. DUE WHEN FINISHED	MONTHLY PAYMENTS	WEEKLY PAYMENTS	OTHER PLANS
PROMPT	SLOW	NO REC.					

THE BIBBERO SYSTEM FORM NO. MDP. 8500   © 1965 MED-DENT PUBLISHING CO. - SAN FRANCISCO

J. P. JONES, D.D.S.   S. C. SMITH, D.D.S.
STATE LIC. NO. A14013   STATE LIC. NO. B302
GENERAL DENTISTRY
100 MAIN STREET, ANY TOWN, ANY STATE 73012
PHONE: (207) 387-4791

STATEMENT TO:

- - - - - - - - - - - - - - TEAR OFF AND RETURN UPPER PORTION WITH PAYMENT - - - - - - - - - - - - -

DATE	PROF. SERVICE	CODES RELATIVE VALUE	DOC-TOR	FEES	PAYMENTS	LAST AMOUNT IN THIS COLUMN IS BALANCE DUE
					BALANCE FORWARD ➤	

PROFESSIONAL SERVICE CODE:

1. VISIT AND EXAM.	010-099	5. ANESTHESIA	400-449	9. PROSTHETICS	700-799
2. X-RAY AND PATH.	100-199	6. PERIODONTICS	450-499	10. SPACE MAINTAIN.	800-899
3. ORAL SURGERY	200-299	7. ENDODONTICS	500-599	11. FRACTURES & DISLOC.	900-999
4. DRUGS	300-399	8. RESTORATIONS	600-699	12. OTHER PROC.	

J. P. JONES, D.D.S.   STATE LIC. NO. A14013   S. C. SMITH, D.D.S.   STATE LIC. NO. B302
100 MAIN STREET - ANY TOWN, ANY STATE 73012 - PHONE: (207) 387-4791

* COURTESY OF MED-DENT PUBLISHING COMPANY, SAN FRANCISCO, CALIFORNIA.

Figure 6: Machine Ledger Card

JOURNAL OF DAILY CHARGES, PAYMENTS & DEPOSITS

DEPOSIT SLIP DETAIL
(Attach to Bank Deposit Slip)

BANK NUMBER	BY CHECK OR PMO	BY COIN OR CURRENCY	ADJ.	PROFESSIONAL SERVICE	FEE	NEW BALANCE	OLD BALANCE	PATIENT'S NAME		VISIT SLIP NUMBER	DISTRIBUTION
									1		
									2		
									3		
									4		
									5		
									6		
									7		
									8		
									9		
									10		
									11		
									12		
									13		
									14		
									15		
									16		
									17		
									18		
									19		
									20		

DEPOSIT SLIP DETAIL
(Attach to Bank Deposit Slip)

BANK NUMBER	BY CHECK OR PMO	BY COIN OR CURRENCY

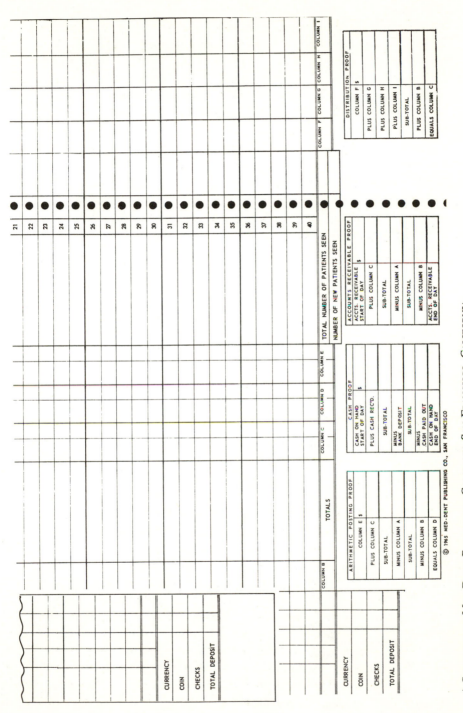

* COURTESY OF MED-DENT PUBLISHING COMPANY, SAN FRANCISCO, CALIFORNIA.

Figure 7: Journal of Daily Charges

tient ledger card from the dentist's office have proven difficult to operate where there is much of an insurance, Medicare, or welfare volume of practice.

Journal of Daily Charges, Payments, and Deposits (Figure 7). Most dental practices do not have a large enough volume of daily posting to warrant an accounting machine. A control (peg) board system achieves high speed-record production at low cost. The aide can produce in mere seconds three key financial records based on the Patient Visit Slip (the Clinical Record) or a patient's payment check. The three are: the day sheet, the bank deposit slip, and the ledger card. The control board helps align the forms so that the forms and the underlying carbons line up atop each other. Information written on the uppermost form (ledger card), therefore, appears in the proper place on the forms below. Since the aide can fill out the day sheet, the bank deposit slip, and the ledger card in one writing rather than three, complicated posting procedures are eliminated and so are most posting or transcribing errors. The information recorded in this single posting is:

1. Full banking and receipts data plus an edge-gummed slip for attaching receipts detail to a bank deposit slip. Restrictively endorsed checks can be posted directly to the daily journals and ledger cards.
2. Adjustments.
3. Services performed, coded as per the legend at the bottom of the card.
4. Fees charged.
5. New and old balances.
6. The patient's name.
7. The patient visit slip or control number.
8. Distribution of the fees charged—either by doctor in a multiman office or by functions in a single-man office. (Professional-Hygienist-X-ray-Lab.)

Proof of Daily Work. The daily journals should be proved out to check (1) that the arithmetic is correct, (2) that the money received and money banked have been correctly handled, (3) that the Accounts Receivable for the day have been balanced, and (4) that the distribution of work among the dentists or by function has been correctly made. Proof totals should be posted to the monthly recap form to establish cumulative totals for the month.

Billing the Private Patient. Most dentists bill their patients monthly. To prepare statements most efficiently, an aide should photocopy the ledger card. Whether the ledger card has been produced on a hand-posting control board or in an accounting machine is immaterial. Up to 500 monthly statements can be produced in less than half a day by photocopying. Photocopy paper used for the statement should have a perforation across the top, so that it can be used as a Remittance Advice form by the patient. Through the use of a photocopy method of reproducing ledger cards as statements, an external audit of the internal system is achieved. The patient gets a copy of the ledger card which was produced simultaneously with the Daily journal.

Many offices have achieved reductions in peak load labor requirements for billing by using the cycle billing method. Some offices mail out one quarter of the Accounts Receivable ledger every week; others mail out a single letter of the alphabet every day. Either method of dividing the billing load reduces end-of-month pressure in the office.

Mailing Private Patient Monthly Statements. Efficient processing of the private patient statements from the photocopy machine to the patient and back to the dentist with the payment is accomplished by a special-purpose, prestamped, outbound window envelope with a tear-off, unstamped, reply envelope. The outbound envelope is designed so the statement is folded as the envelope is closed and sealed. Prefolding and stamping time is eliminated. The collection cycle is shortened by using a pre-addressed reply envelope.

The Recall System. Most dental offices accept the responsibility of attempting to maintain good patient oral health. The primary method by which this is accomplished is through the periodic visit of the patient to the dental office. In most instances the patients request that the dentist notify them when it is time for the next appointment. This is called the "recall system". The dentist's office usually files a card with the patient's name under the correct date for the recall and notifies the patient either by mail or by phone prior to time for his next appointment. If the patient so desires it, an appointment is made. A sound recall system is not only the best guarantee of good patient care but also provides the dentist's office, over a period of years, with a predictable volume of routine professional work which can be scheduled to the mutual advantage of both the dentist and his patients.

The patient signs the front side of the Patient Demand Recall Card (Figure 8) in the dentist's office; the card is filed until time for the next appointment to be made. It is then sent to the patient in an envelope; the card is so inserted that the patient reads the reverse side first.

The forms and systems outlined here provide for intensive control of the financial aspects of the dentist's practice. Where his practice is significantly smaller than the average, the forms and systems can be modified to fit individual needs of the practice. In this respect the dentist's accountant can use his own initiative in solving the problems. He must be sure he does not overlook any of the necessary functions of good record control in trying to achieve simplification.

INSTRUCTIONS TO PATIENT:

SIGN YOUR NAME AND ADDRESS BELOW IF YOU WANT US TO SEND YOU A REMINDER NOTICE
OF THE TIME FOR YOUR NEXT APPOINTMENT.

_____   _____
TODAYS DATE   DATE OF NEXT APPOINTMENT

_____
NAME

_____
ADDRESS

_____
CITY   STATE   ZIP

(front)

(reverse)

APPOINTMENT REMINDER

IN ACCORDANCE WITH YOUR REQUEST, THIS CARD IS TO REMIND YOU THAT NOW IS

THE TIME TO CALL THE OFFICE FOR YOUR NEXT REGULAR APPOINTMENT.

DOCTORS NAME

DOCTORS ADDRESS

CITY AND STATE

DOCTORS TELEPHONE NUMBER

* COURTESY OF MED-DENT PUBLISHING COMPANY, SAN FRANCISCO, CALIFORNIA.

Figure 8:   Patient Demand Recall Card

As in other professions and businesses, the fundamental part of the office procedures is the General ledger. It would contain entries from the Cash Receipts journal, the Disbursement journal, General journal, Payroll ledgers and journals, the asset ledger accounts, the liability ledger accounts, and the capital ledger accounts. The Receivables journal and ledger are subsidiary to the General ledger.

ACCOUNTS PECULIAR TO THE PRACTICE OF DENTISTRY

Total Care (T.C.). As the ability of the dentist to maintain the lifelong, dental good health of his patients has materially increased, it has been possible for the dentist to schedule an entire course in oral therapy for the patient and to predict its total cost in advance. When the patient has agreed to cost and terms, the dentist usually bills the entire estimated cost and shows each of the future visits as a T.C. item on his ledger card and journals. Payment schedules are also set up at this time to complete payment at the approximate completion of the case.

Petty Cash. Most dental offices require minor amounts of cash on hand to be maintained for payment of minor office expenses and to make change for patients. A practical method for controlling this petty cash is to establish an imprest Petty Cash account. The dentist issues a check to establish this account initially. After the account has been set up, disbursements are made from the account and are recorded either in a notebook or on a voucher slip. When the account gets low, the dentist reimburses the account by check to the previously established level and distributes the check according to classification of the expenditures. The dentist's accountant can periodically verify the Petty Cash account.

Patient Refunds and Fee Adjustments. The increasing amount of dental insurance has given rise to the problem of the dentist's receiving duplicate payment for his work. He usually looks to the patient to pay his bill and when an insurance company also pays the dentist directly, he will credit the patient's account with the amount and make a refund, by check, to the patient. When the check is issued, the dentist makes a fee adjustment to remove the credit balance from Accounts Receivable. In other cases patients may move or terminate a case before the entire service contemplated in the total care charge has been rendered. In this case the doctor must issue a credit, either on a visit slip or on the clinical record, to authorize his aide to reduce the charge shown on the ledger card. Should the reduced charge be lower than the payments received, the dentist will issue his check and make the adjustment entry to have the ledger cards reflect the true facts.

Peculiarities of Procedures

CASH RECEIPTS CYCLE

Many dental offices will have either large credit balances or large payments against the account before the work is done. This is because of the large amount that the dentist must lay out for laboratory work and materials such as gold, silver, and platinum in advance of his completing the restoration for the patient. In most cases the dentist gets an advance payment from the patient to cover these items. In addition, there is a rising percent of the total money received by the dentist from insurance companies and government agencies. At billing time the dentist must determine who will bear the responsibility for the bill and whether there is any joint responsibility between the patient and the insurance company.

PURCHASES-PAYABLES CYCLE

Most dental offices are on a 30-day, purchases-payables basis. Purchases are charged directly to a drugs and supplies expense account. In cases where the purchases and use of gold are very large, the charging of gold purchases through a gold inventory account and the use of the cost of goods sold accounting technique should be set up to maintain an inventory balance of this precious metal.

EXPENSE-SHARING ARRANGEMENTS

Many dentists practice in expense-sharing arrangements. They are not partnerships but arrangements where certain of the office expenses are shared. The devising of a simple yet effective system to meet this need should include a bank account for disbursement of the authorized expenses as the primary record-keeping source. The individual dentists usually keep their own Accounts Receivable and reimburse the joint account in accordance with their agreed expense-sharing ratio.

Time and Payroll System

Dental offices have a very low ratio of personnel to doctor. Therefore, a very simple payroll system, all that most offices require, would include the check with the stub advising the employee of his gross payroll, his deductions, and the net payroll; a ledger card for each employee to correctly compute his tax returns; and a journal of payroll checks drawn so the employer will have a fundamental cost record.

The normal pay periods are semimonthly on a flat salary basis. However, some chair assistants work on an hourly basis and some hygienists work on a percentage of the billed fee basis. Where the special compensation bases are set up, it is necessary to maintain the subsidiary records to provide the necessary payroll data.

Cost Accounting and Departmental Accounting

Cost accounting in a dental office is done on a clinical record. The dental chair time and the laboratory appliance costs should be figured at the end of each particular case to be sure that the treatment estimated cost and the actual cost are correct and that the dentist's profit per case is in line with his plan.

The departmental accounting that is done can be accomplished by breaking down the fees at the time they are charged on the Daily journal. Most dentists departmentalize their revenue accounts into professional, X-ray, hygienists, and other sources.

Time-Saving Ideas

Photocopying Equipment. Significant economies in operation of the dentist's office can be effected through the use of appropriate photocopying equipment. The principal functions where time and cost can be saved are in getting out the monthly billing statements, processing insurance claims, producing Medicare bills, and copying clinical records for consultation reports.

Appointment System. Time control of the dentist and his aides is accomplished by the appointment system. A well-designed system allows the dentist to indicate to his aide the time needed on a reappointment and allows the office aide to appoint new patients on a basis of the average time needed. A system should be used with the correct headway based on the dentist's type of practice. Appointment pages are designed with headways of 5, 10, 15, or 20 minutes; thus, the dentist and his assistants discover at a glance what their daily work schedules will be. Good appointment records are loose leaf for ease in photocopying and are prepared in pencil on ledger stock to facilitate changes and erasures.

Reports to Management

FINANCIAL REPORTS

The principal financial reports are (1) the income, expense, and budget statement, (2) the cash flow statement, (3) the money received and banked,

INCOME, EXPENSE AND BUDGET
CASH FLOW STATEMENT

19	A/C NO.	ACCOUNT DESCRIPTION	%	INCOME & EXPENSE YEAR TO DATE	BUDGET YEAR TO DATE
	1				
	2				
	3				
	4	TOTAL NET CHARGES FROM PRACTICE			
	5				
	6				
	7				
	8	TOTAL NET RECEIPTS FROM PRACTICE			
	9	EXPENSES			
	10	12a TAXES: PAYROLL			
	11	b TAXES: PROFESSIONAL PROPERTY			
	12	13a RENT ON PROFESSIONAL PROPERTY			
	13	b RENT ON PROFESSIONAL PROPERTY—OTHER			
	14	14 REPAIRS			
	15	15a SALARIES & WAGES (NET)			
	16	b EMPLOYEE BENEFITS			
	17	16 INSURANCE: PROFESSIONAL & BUSINESS			
	18	17 PROFESSIONAL FEES			
	19	20 RETIREMENT PLAN—EMPLOYEE SHARE			
	20	21 INTEREST—PROFESSIONAL/INDEBTEDNESS			
	21	25a AUTOMOBILE EXPENSE			
	22	b DRUGS & SUPPLIES			
	23	c LABORATORY EXPENSE			
	24	d LAUNDRY EXPENSE			
	25	e MAINTENANCE			
	26	f MEETINGS, DUES & SUBSCRIPTIONS			
	27	g MISC. PROFESSIONAL EXPENSE			
	28	h OFFICE EXPENSE			
	29	i PROFESSIONAL PROMOTION			
	30	j TELEPHONE			
	31	k UTILITIES			
	32	l			
	33	m			
	34				
	35	TOTAL EXPENSES FROM PRACTICE			
	38	NET INCOME FROM PRACTICE (BEFORE DEP.)			
	39	DEPRECIATION (ANNUAL ENTRY ONLY)			
	40	RECEIPTS (OTHER SOURCES)			
	41				
	42				
	43				
	44	TOTAL NET INCOME			

RECEIPTS & ALLOCATIONS SUMMARY CONTROL		19
RECEIPTS ON HAND START OF MONTH		
ADD:		
PROFESSIONAL RECEIPTS		
MISCELLANEOUS RECEIPTS		
REDEPOSITS—RC		
+ TOTAL MONTHLY RECEIPTS		
LESS:		
TOTAL DEPOSITS		
CASH PAID OUT		
WITHDRAWN BY DOCTOR		
— TOTAL CASH ALLOCATIONS		
RECEIPTS ON HAND END OF MONTH		

© Ⓜ Medical Management Control
FORM 654-1C

* COURTESY OF MEDICAL MANAGEMENT CONTROL, SAN FRANCISCO, CALIFORNIA.

Figure 9: Income, Expense, and Budget Statement

(4) the Accounts Receivable control, (5) the balance sheet, (6) the Accounts Receivable age analysis.

1. *Income, Expense, and Budget Statement (Figure 9).* The statement is prepared each month to reflect results of the practice for the current month (in column at left), for the year to date, and for the budget or planned year to date. Shown are the practice charges, practice receipts, practice expenses, and other receipts to provide a total net income. A depreciation figure is entered annually in the closing of the books and preparing of the tax return.

Separate journals reflecting income and expense, and ledgers showing asset cost and liabilities, should be kept on all investments. Figures 10 and 11 show the forms used for marketable securities information. Figure 12 shows the form used for real estate investments, and Figure 13 shows the form used for notes payable, including mortgages and contracts. Establishment of separate bank accounts for nonpractice investment areas will facilitate the current record keeping problem. The results of outside investment activities are summarized after arriving at practice net income to determine total net income.

2. *Cash Flow Statement (Figure 14).* The monthly cash profit is picked up from the income, expense, and budget statement and carried forward to the cash flow statement. To this cash profit are added cash on hand and in the bank at the first of the year plus additional borrowings in cash, capital contributions, and receipts from dividends, outside business ventures, and other sources. Deductions are made for payments for assets, contracts, and other loans. The resultant figure is the cash available for personal use or withdrawal. It is essential to figure this amount in order to plan for savings, investment, and net worth growth and to allow the dentist to keep his personal spending within his ability to earn. For the individual dentist, a record is kept of withdrawals for personal use, broken down between tax deductible and nondeductible uses. Any money not withdrawn is reflected in the final balances on hand and balances in the bank. Cash flow information is recorded for the month, for the year to date, and in relation to the plan for the year to date.

3. *Money Received and Banked.* The monthly receipts and allocations summary control shows receipts on hand in the office at the start of the month; money received during the month; money deposited, money paid from cash receipts or withdrawn by the dentist during the month. The resulting figure should be the receipts on hand in the office at the end of the month. Maintenance of this information should enable the auditor to check the flow of money through the office.

4. *Accounts Receivable Control.* A good control device shows Accounts Receivable at the start of each month plus additions to and subtractions from

FORM 9910   **STOCKS — ACQUISITION AND DISPOSITION**   Pg_____

COMPANY NAME			COMPANY ADDRESS		

☐ COMMON
☐ PREFERRED | NAME OF PREFERRED ISSUE | PAR VALUE | EXCHANGE | INDUSTRY

LOCATION OF SECURITIES | TRANSFER AGENT | DIVIDEND RATES

CONVERSION | CALLABLE | PARTICIPATING

ADDITIONAL INFORMATION | ☐ COMMUNITY PROPERTY ☐ SEPARATE PROPERTY | OWNER

PURCHASES AND OTHER ACQUISITIONS

DATE ACQUIRED	No. OF SHARES	PRICE PER SHARE	CERTIFICATE NUMBER AND SOURCE OF ACQUISITION	TOTAL COST OR OTHER BASIS	CUMULATIVE INVESTMENT

SALES OR GIFTS OF STOCK, RIGHTS, ETC.

DATE DISPOSED	No. OF SHARES	PRICE PER SHARE	CERTIFICATE NUMBER (S) SOLD (G) GIFT OTHER DISPOSITION INFORMATION	NET SALE OR DISPOSITION PRICE	TOTAL COST OR OTHER BASIS	PROFIT OR (LOSS) ST-Shrt Term LT-Lng Term

(left margin, vertical text) THE BIBBERO SYSTEM OF PERSONAL FINANCIAL CONTROL   TM REG.   © BY MMC PUBLISHING CO., SAN FRANCISCO, CALIF. — 1963

* COURTESY OF MED-DENT PUBLISHING COMPANY, SAN FRANCISCO, CALIFORNIA.

Figure 10: Stocks—Acquisition and Disposition

FORM 9910A   **STOCKS — DIVIDEND AND VALUATION DATA**

| NAME COMPANY | | | | | | | | TYPE OF STOCK AND DIVIDEND CREDIT DATA ☐ COMMON ☐ QUALIFYING ☐ PREFERRED ☐ NON-QUALIFYING | | | OWNER: ☐ HUSBAND (H) ☐ WIFE (W) ☐ JOINT (J) | | |

DIVIDEND RECORD								VALUATION RECORD			
DATE RECEIVED	RATE	No. OF SHARES	AMOUNT OF DIVIDEND*	DATE RECEIVED	RATE	No. OF SHARES	AMOUNT OF DIVIDEND*	DATE	MARKET PRICE PER SHARE	TOTAL MARKET VALUE OF HOLDINGS	MARKET OVER COST — GAIN OR (LOSS)

*DESIGNATE WITH LETTERS
OI — ORDINARY INCOME
CG — CAPITAL GAIN
RC — RETURN OF CAPITAL

* COURTESY OF MED-DENT PUBLISHING COMPANY, SAN FRANCISCO, CALIFORNIA.

Figure 11: Stocks—Dividend and Valuation Data

FORM 9935   **REAL ESTATE — ACQUISITION, IMPROVEMENTS AND TYPE OF PROPERTY**   Pg.

LOCATION OF PROPERTY	TYPE OF PROPERTY

NAME OF LEGAL TITLE HOLDER	☐ JOINT TENANTS ☐ TENANTS IN COMMON

LOT No.	BLOCK No.	OTHER INDENTIFICATION	COUNTY WHERE RECORDED	TAX STAMPS	DATE RECORDED	BOOK No. PAGE No.

TOTAL ASSESSED VALUE	ASSESSED VALUE OF LAND	ASSESSED VALUE OF IMPROVEMENTS	DATE OF ASSESSMENT

ACQUIRED FROM	TITLE INSURANCE INFORMATION

TOTAL COST PRICE	CASH PAID	VALUE OF PROPERTY TRADED	MORTGAGES

DEPRECIATION ALLOCATION	VALUE OF LAND	VALUE OF IMPROVEMENTS	SALVAGE VALUE	LIFE OF IMPROVEMENTS	DEPRECIATION METHOD

PROPERTY TAX RATE:			FIRE INSURANCE:	
CITY	COUNTY	OTHER	RATE	COVERAGE

OTHER DATA

ADDITIONAL IMPROVEMENTS

DATE	DESCRIPTION OF ITEM	DEPRECIATION		SALVAGE VALUE OF IMPROVEMENT	ITEM COST	CUMULATIVE COST OF IMPROVEMENTS
		LIFE	METHOD			

DEPRECIABLE VALUES

YEAR	DEPRECIATED VALUE START OF YEAR	IMPROVEMENTS OR ADDITIONS THIS YEAR	TAXABLE DEPRECIATION CLAIMED THIS YEAR	DEPRECIATED VALUE END OF YEAR	YEAR	DEPRECIATED VALUE START OF YEAR	IMPROVEMENTS OR ADDITIONS THIS YEAR	TAXABLE DEPRECIATION CLAIMED THIS YEAR	DEPRECIATED VALUE END OF YEAR

MEDICAL MANAGEMENT CONTROL • SAN FRANCISCO, CALIFORNIA

TRADE MARK REGISTERED

COPYRIGHT 1962

* COURTESY OF MED-DENT PUBLISHING COMPANY, SAN FRANCISCO, CALIFORNIA.

Figure 12:   Real Estate Record

FORM 9950   **NOTES PAYABLE** (INCLUDING MORTGAGES AND CONTRACTS)   Pg____

PAYABLE TO		ADDRESS	
DATE MADE	LOAN No.	DATE MATURES	AMOUNT OF PRINCIPLE
PRINCIPAL PAYABLE		PREPAYMENT PROVISIONS	
INTEREST PAYABLE	%	INSURANCE	LIFE	OTHER
ENDORSEMENT COLLATERAL GUARANTEE			DATE RECORDED
REAL PROPERTY LOANS	LOCATION AND DESCRIPTION	LOT No.	BLOCK No.

DATE	TOTAL AMOUNT PAID	INTEREST		TAXES — INSURANCE — MISC.		PAID ON PRINCIPAL	PRINCIPAL BALANCE
		AMOUNT	PAID TO	DESCRIPTION	AMOUNT		

* COURTESY OF MED-DENT PUBLISHING COMPANY, SAN FRANCISCO, CALIFORNIA.

Figure 13: Notes Payable Record

the Accounts Receivable during the month. It provides for balancing the Accounts Receivable at the end of each month.

The advent of dental insurance and dental financing plans has materially increased the collection ratio in most dentists' offices. On the other hand the problem of the delinquent account has not been eliminated. Collection follow-up in the form of either letters or stickers usually starts after two months following the initial billing for the service. Letters or stickers of increasing severity are used until such time as the dentist determines that the account should be turned over to an outside collection agency for appropriate action. Normally when the dentist turns the account over to a collection agency, he will personally sign the authorization for it to be written off, as a measure of protection against theft. When the account is written off and turned over to an outside collection agency, the account is removed from the active Accounts Receivable. If the volume of accounts written off to collection is significant, then the Accounts Receivable should be broken down into two major controls. The major controls would be current accounts and delinquent accounts in the hands of collectors.

In most instances where the volume of write-offs to collectors is not great, payments received from the collection agency are recorded as a new charge and a simultaneous payment in the record-keeping system. Most collection agencies deduct their collection fees before remitting to the dentist. In the cases where a special control has been established for the delinquent accounts, a write-off must be put through the records to adjust for the collection agency fees.

5. *Balance Sheets.* The periodic balance sheet is a two-section statement. Section One covers the practice assets and liabilities; Section Two, the Personal Financial Control section, contains the cost and current valuation on all the personal asset, nonpractice obligations, and insurance data. Both sections should be maintained on a current basis. The statement resembles the type of financial statement filed with a bank.

6. *Accounts Receivable Age Analysis (Figure 15).* This statement should be prepared periodically for all accounts. It provides the dentist with a detailed list by name and total amount due on all the accounts that make up his Accounts Receivable total. In addition, each individual account is analyzed as to how long it has been unpaid.

The unpaid accounts are grouped according to the date of the last unpaid charge. The charges from zero to three months are normally considered current because of the time involved in processing insurance claims. Accounts from three to six months should be subject to significant collection follow-up. Accounts from six to twelve months usually represent hardship cases which the dentist does not want turned over for outside collection action. Accounts

CASH FLOW STATEMENT

Page 2

19	AC NO.	ACCOUNT DESCRIPTION	%	YEAR TO DATE	BUDGET YEAR TO DATE
	44	TOTAL NET PROFESSIONAL INCOME			
		ADD:			
		RECEIPTS ON HAND — B.O.P.			
		CASH IN BANK — B.O.P.			
		OTHER SOURCES			
	60	BORROWINGS			
	70	ADDTL. CAPITAL CONTRIBUTIONS			
		DIVIDENDS, INTEREST, ETC.			
		TOTAL CASH AVAILABLE FOR EXPENDITURES:			
		LESS — EXPENDED AS FOLLOWS:			
	50	CASH PAYMENTS FOR ASSETS			
	60	CONTRACT PAYMENTS			
	60	LOAN PAYMENTS			
	70	CAPITAL CONTROL			
	77	SUSPENSE			
		TOTAL EXPENDITURES			
		CASH AVAILABLE FOR PERSONAL USE			
		WITHDRAWALS — NON-TAX DEDUCTIBLE			
	80	SELF & HOME			
	81	FEDERAL INCOME TAX — CURRENT YEAR			
	82	FEDERAL INCOME TAX — PREVIOUS YEAR			
	83	SAVINGS			
	84	INVESTMENT			
	85	LIFE INSURANCE			
		WITHDRAWALS — TAX DEDUCTIBLE			
	90	CONTRIBUTIONS			
	91	INTEREST			
	92	TAXES			
	93	MEDICAL & DENTAL			
	94	HEALTH & DISABILITY INSURANCE			
		TOTAL WITHDRAWALS			
		CASH POSITION — E.O.P.			
		LESS - RECEIPTS ON HAND — E.O.P.			
		BANK BALANCE — END OF MONTH			

ACCOUNTS RECEIVABLE SUMMARY

_____ 19 _____

			MONTH		YEAR TO DATE	
TOTAL ACCTS. RECV. BALANCE START OF MONTH — PER BOOKS						
PROFESSIONAL CHARGES — GROSS						
- WRITE-OFFS TO COLLECTOR						
- CREDIT ADJUSTMENTS						
+ DEBIT ADJUSTMENTS						
TOTAL NET CHARGES — LINE 4						
PROFESSIONAL RECEIPTS — GROSS						
- REFUNDS						
- RETURNED CHECKS						
TOTAL NET RECEIPTS — LINE 8						
TOTAL ACCOUNTS BALANCE END OF MONTH — PER BOOKS						
TOTAL ACCOUNTS BALANCE END OF MONTH — PER ANALYSIS						
DIFFERENCE BOOKS OVER ANALYSIS BOOKS UNDER ANALYSIS						
COLLECTION RATIO (GROSS RECEIPTS - YTD ÷ GROSS CHARGES - YTD)						%
NUMBER OF MONTHS OF RECEIVABLES OUTSTANDING						

○ Ⓜ Medical Management Control

FORM 654-2C

* COURTESY OF MEDICAL MANAGEMENT CONTROL, SAN FRANCISCO, CALIFORNIA

Figure 14: Cash Flow Statement

ACCOUNTS RECEIVABLE AGE ANALYSIS

Dr. _____

Address _____   Date _____

PATIENT'S NAME	TOTAL ACCOUNT RECEIVABLE	DISTRIBUTION OF ACCOUNTS RECEIVABLE BY AGE				REMARKS
		0 - 3 MONTHS	3 - 6 MONTHS	6 - 12 MONTHS	OVER 1 YEAR	

BIBBERO SYSTEMS   FORM NO MDP 5810   © 1965 MED-DENT PUBLISHING CO., SAN FRANCISCO

* COURTESY OF MED-DENT PUBLISHING COMPANY, SAN FRANCISCO, CALIFORNIA.

Figure 15: Accounts Receivable Age Analysis

over one year usually represent long-term, litigation cases or other unusual circumstances. If the collection ratios are low or if the total amount in the Accounts Receivable significantly exceeds three months of charges, then breakdowns of the Accounts Receivable on a month-by-month basis may assist in rectifying the Accounts Receivable situation.

21

Drugstores

BY E. W. MOORE

Public Accountant, Alva, Oklahoma

Characteristics of the Business That Affect the Accounting System

In merchandising circles, evolution of the apothecary shop to the drugstore of today has become legendary. At the turn of the century the shop had little impact on the economy of its neighborhood. A drugstore was essentially what the name implies—a store chiefly for compounding doctors' prescriptions by a pharmacist from drugs and chemicals (mixed by mortar and pestle) and for dispensing of these prescriptions to the sick and ailing.

The store usually occupied a corner site. Colored, ornamental cut-glass vases of a unique design prominently displayed in the show windows, advertised the type of business within. The door boasted the name of the proprietor, followed by a capital R with a small x on the tail. This same designation of Rx is still used on drugstore stationery and doctors' prescriptions. Eventually a candy counter was installed, and about the same time the old-fashioned soda fountain with its ornate marble decorations and baroque glass mirror heralded the beginning of the merchandising activities so indispensable to the modern drugstore.

Today numerous lines of cutlery, dishes, clothing, books, and magazines range side by side with drug sundries, cosmetics, and specialty merchandise of every kind and description. There is no question that in the mid-Twentieth Century the drugstore is a vital part of the economy where it is located.

Regardless of the diversification so common to the modern drugstore, sometimes called a pharmacy, the prescription counter is the heart of the business. Even though most drugs and medicines are prepared by pharmaceutical manufacturers, the pharmacist is still licensed by the state. It is he who has the responsibility of double checking contents of prescriptions, dosages prescribed by the physician, and accuracy of labels. In this capacity he is an indispensable link between the doctor and his patient. He is an asset to the community he serves.

FUNCTIONAL CHARACTERISTICS OF THE BUSINESS

Inventories are vital to drugstore life. As in any merchandising function, they must be carefully taken, priced, extended, and totaled. To conserve time, inventories may be taken by a team from a pharmaceutical house for what is usually a nominal fee. This practice means the proprietor does not have to close the store during inventory. Valuable time is saved, sales are not lost, and earlier preparation of the profit and loss statement is achieved.

December sales are usually the largest of the year but drop off sharply after Christmas, at which time some store owners begin the year-end inventory. If inventories are taken quarterly, semiannually, or at year end, the profit and loss statements may be prepared for these periods. For periods when actual inventories are not taken, hypothecated inventories may be used for the preparation of approximate profit and loss statements.

As in any other business, profits vary. Determining factors include management policy, organization, type and size of store, locality, the site, and competition from discount stores and military dispensaries. Record keeping in the average-sized store is often done by the store manager's wife, a part-time bookkeeper, and a public accountant. The preparation of sales tax reports, quarterly payroll reports, and annual W-2's for employers may or may not be done by the public accountant, depending on the size of the store, local employment conditions, and other circumstances. This would also be true of the posting of the various journals to the General ledger on a monthly, quarterly, or other basis for preparation of the trial balance. Other reports such as the profit and loss statement or balance sheet may or may not be requested each time a trial balance is taken. The taking of the monthly Accounts Receivable ledger trial balance and sending of monthly statements to customers in most cases is done by the bookkeeper or clerical assistant. A trial balance of the Accounts Payable ledger would also be taken if a Purchase journal is in use. Larger stores and chain stores employ a full-time office manager and one or more bookkeepers and clerks, depending on the volume of business. In this instance, the function of the public accountant may be limited to a periodic examination of the books and records and preparation of income tax returns.

PRINCIPAL ACCOUNTING PROBLEMS

The prime requisite of any drugstore accounting system is the safeguarding of cash from the time it is received from the customer to the time of the bank deposit. Because stores operate on a long work day and some are open seven days a week, two or more shifts of clerks are employed. In addition, the shelves and counters are loaded with innumerable small articles. Petty theft and the careless handling of cash, with resultant unnecessary losses, are constant threats: only a proper and rigid accounting of cash can eliminate them.

After cash has been checked, accounted for, and banked, it is equally important to see that it is properly disbursed. As purchase invoices are numerous, they should first be OK'd as to quantity by the person who checks incoming shipments. They should also be initialed by those responsible for checking the purchase price, and proving of extensions and total amounts of the invoices. Checks can then be issued for payments, at which time the invoices or statements to which invoices are attached should show the date paid and check number before filing in a paid-file cabinet. Items of expense and payments of any nature should all be authorized before checks are issued to payees. In this connection it is preferable that all checks issued be countersigned by one authorized to do so, in addition to the individual authorized to sign. This is for the mutual protection of all concerned.

Functional Organization

There are three general classifications in business and industry: manufacturing, service, and trading. The drugstore falls into the latter classification as it caters to the retail trade. Buying is done in quantities at wholesale prices and sold for retail. From these trading transactions the owner or owners anticipate a gross profit from sales sufficient to absorb all operating and overhead costs and yield a fair net profit.

Departments. The pharmacy and merchandise sales are the principal departments of a drugstore. The Merchandise Sales Department may be separated into sections as shown in the chart of accounts, revenue section under sales. Lunch counters, fountains, and sometimes gift shops are operated as separate departments, but more often are leased to independent operators. Lease agreements are usually made on a flat rental basis, percentage of sales, or a combination of both.

Some store managers or owners claim that fountains are not suitable or profitable. Others feel that though the fountain operation is not profitable it attracts trade and thus increases customer store traffic. Both of these conditions are due, to a large degree, to the store location and the class of trade peculiar to the locality.

Personnel. Personnel division follows the same general departmental classification with the exception of the manager, buyer, Stock Department manager, and office personnel whose duties are interrelated with all departments (Figure 1). Pharmacists are the only employees of the pharmacy. The Merchandise Sales Department employees are the floor manager, salesclerks, cashiers, and stock clerk. All accounting and clerical duties are assigned to the office employees.

Principles and Objectives of the Accounting System

Sales, Purchase, and Expense journals must be designed to reflect properly the gain and loss for any given period. They must also reflect any changes in asset and liability accounts. Most stores operating as individual proprietorships or partnerships operate on a calendar-year basis. Some corporations also operate on a calendar-year basis, but the majority use different quarter-year endings for fiscal-year periods.

The majority of retail stores operate on the accrual basis of accounting, particularly where daily sales are charge and cash; both are considered income for sales and income tax purposes on the day of sale.

When stores sell for cash only, they operate on a cash basis. Stores selling for both cash and charge may also operate on a cash basis for income and sales tax purposes; total reportable daily income would be cash sales and daily cash collections of charge accounts.

The first year's income tax reporting for either the cash or accrual basis is an automatic election and cannot later be changed except by permission of the Commissioner of the Internal Revenue.

SPECIFIC OBJECTIVES OF THE SYSTEM

The accounting system must provide for the accurate and prompt recording of all transactions of the business. All accounts must reflect transactions relating to the business. Accounts appearing in the balance sheet must show

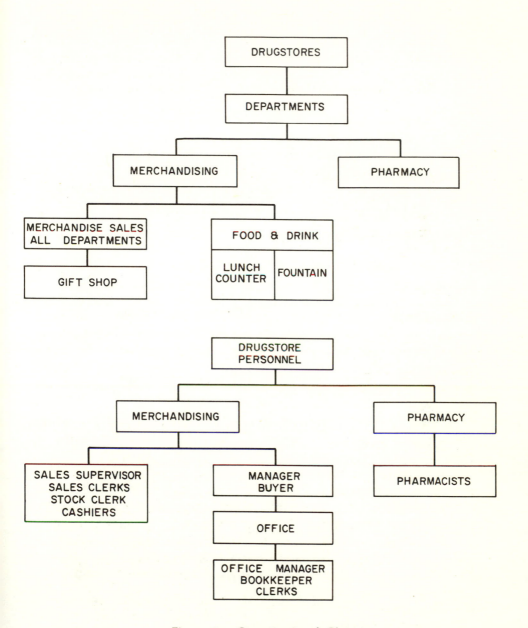

Figure I: Organizational Chart

their true value to indicate properly the financial position at the end of any given period. All items of revenue, purchase cost, and expense charges must be reflected in the accounts applicable to them, in addition to accurately stated inventories, to determine the operating profit or loss for any given period.

Classification of Accounts and Books of Accounts

The grouping of accounts into the four general categories of assets, liabilities, income, and expense separates balance sheet accounts from those used in the profit and loss statements, and the numbering of accounts more readily identifies them. The grouping and numbering are essential in the data processing system of accounting. The chart is also helpful and desirable for the pen and ink method of record keeping. A typical chart follows:

BALANCE SHEET ACCOUNTS.

ASSETS

Current assets

Cash and bank

101 Cash on Hand
102 Cash in Bank
103 Petty Cash Fund
104 Drawer Cash-Registers

Receivables

122 Accounts Receivable
122R Estimated Uncollectible
        Accounts
127 Due from Officers and
        Directors
128 Employees, Owners, and
        Partners

Inventories

131 Drugs (Prescription
        Department)
132 Package Medicines
133 Fountain Supplies
134 Tobacco, Confectionery, and
        Periodicals

135 Toiletries
136 Liquors
137 Sundries
138 Operating Supplies
139 Pharmaceutical Supplies

Other current assets

141 Prepaid Insurance

Fixed assets

161 Land
162 Buildings
162R Accumulated Depreciation
163 Fountain Fixtures and
        Equipment
163R Accumulated Depreciation
164 Store Fixtures and Equipment
164R Accumulated Depreciation
165 Office Furniture
165R Accumulated Depreciation

If leased premises are occupied, substitute the following accounts:

162 Leasehold Improvements
162R Accumulated Amortization
166 Lease Account—Rental

Other assets

191 Deposits, Rent, Utilities, etc.
192 Goodwill

LIABILITIES

Current liabilities

Notes and Accounts Payable

201 Notes Payable, Banks
202 Notes Payable, Other
205 Contracts Payable
206 Accounts Payable
211 Sales Tax Payable
221 Employee Payroll Deductions
    221-1 Social Security Taxes
    221-2 State Disability Insurance
    221-3 Income Tax Withheld
          (Federal)
    221-4 Income Tax Withheld
          (State)
    221-5 Income Tax Withheld
          (City)
222 Employer Payroll Taxes Payable
    222-1 Social Security Taxes
    222-2 Federal Social Security
          Taxes (Unemployment)
    222-3 State Social Security
          Taxes (Unemployment)
225 Accrued Payroll
226 Accrued General Taxes
227 Accrued Interest Payable

229 Other Accrued Liabilities
230 Due to Officers and Directors
231 Allocated Lease Reserve
232 Allowance for Bad Debts
233 Allowance for Taxes

Long-term debts

241 Contracts Payable (longer than
    1 year)
242 Mortgages Payable
243-249 Other Long-Term Debts

NET WORTH

Corporate accounts

291 Capital Stock
    291-1 Capital Stock Authorized
    291-2 Capital Stock Unissued
297 Capital Surplus
298 Retained Earnings
299 Profit and Loss—Current

*Sole proprietorship or partnership
    accounts*

291 Capital
    291-1 Partner A
    291-2 Partner B
292 Drawing
    292-1 Partner A
    292-2 Partner B
299 Profit and Loss—Current

INCOME AND EXPENSE ACCOUNTS.
REVENUE

Sales

301 Prescriptions
302 Packaged Medicines
303 Fountain
304 Tobacco, Confectionery, and
    Periodicals
305 Toiletries
306 Liquor
307 Sundries

Purchases

401 Prescriptions
402 Packaged Medicines
403 Fountain
404 Tobacco, Confectionery, and
    Periodicals
405 Toiletries
406 Liquor
407 Sundries
408 Freight Paid In
409 Returns and Allowances

EXPENSES

500 Expenses (control)

Salaries and wages

501 Managers
502 Owner's Salary
503 Partner's Salary
503-1 Partner's Salary
512 Clerical and Office
513 Sales
514 Pharmacists

Supplies

521 Stationery and Office Supplies
522 Operating Supplies
523 Fountain Supplies
524 Pharmaceutical Supplies
526 Postage

Utilities and services

531 Heat, Light, and Water
533 Telephone and Telegraph
534 Laundry

Taxes

541 General
543 Payroll—Social Security
544 Payroll—Unemployment

Insurance

551 General
552 Retirement Plan
553 Compensation
554 Group Insurance

Depreciation

562 Buildings
563 Fountain Fixtures and Equipment
564 Store Fixtures and Equipment
565 Office Furniture and Fixtures

Repair and maintenance

572 Buildings

573 Fountain Fixtures and Equipment
574 Store Fixtures and Equipment
575 Office Furniture and Fixtures

Other expense

579 Accounting and Legal
580 Advertising
581 Bank Charges
582 Business Promotion
583 Delivery Charges
584 Contributions
585 Dues and Subscriptions
586 Inventory Expense
587 Lease Amortization
588 Lease Rental
589 Licenses and Tags
590 Merchant Police
591 Parking Fees
592 Postage and Express
593 Rent Paid—Building
594 Rent Paid—Equipment
595 Temporary Labor
596 Trash Hauling
597 Unclassified

Other

598 Losses on Bad Accounts
599 Losses on Bad Checks

OTHER INCOME

601 Cash Discounts Taken
602 Interest Earned
603 Gain and Loss
604 Sale of Capital Assets
605 Charged-Off Accounts Collected
608 Cash Over
609 Miscellaneous Income

DEDUCTIONS FROM INCOME

651 Discounts Allowed
652 Interest Expense
658 Cash Short
659 Miscellaneous Losses

BOOKS AND FORMS PECULIAR TO THE BUSINESS

Journals of original entry should be kept simple in design so that they give only the basic requirements for information used in sales tax and payroll tax reports, income tax reports, and data helpful to management. Other journals required are the Payroll journal, a Monthly Accrual and a General journal, and a Purchase journal, if desired.

Ledgers required are the General and the Accounts Receivable ledgers, and an Accounts Payable ledger when a Purchase journal is used.

Reports needed are discussed elsewhere in the chapter. They are the Daily Cash Report—Sales and Receipts (Figure 2), the Daily Cash Report—Cash Disbursements (Figure 2), and the General Ledger Trial Balance (Figure 16). The Yearly Bank Reconciliation Form is shown in Figure 10.

ACCOUNTS PECULIAR TO THE BUSINESS

Normally, drugstore accounts are basically the same as those used for other retail establishments with one possible exception, the Lease Rental account (No. 588). Stores renting or leasing buildings they occupy may be billed on a flat monthly basis plus a percentage of gross sales. Some stores, when remodeling or acquiring new equipment, tend toward leasing rather than purchasing equipment, with the privilege of ownership at the termination of the lease contract.

Expense Accounts. Provision has not been made in the chart for segregation of expenses. The small drugstore which does not operate a fountain or maintain a large stock of merchandise would not necessarily need such a segregation. Other pharmacies might wish to group expenses as General and Administrative, Soda Fountain, Liquor Department, etc., or they might prefer to break down group expenses into the categories of Direct Store Expenses and Indirect Store Expenses.

Whenever desired, Salaries and Wages (Nos. 501, 502, 503, etc.) may be included for those major expense group accounts. Other additional accounts such as Inventory, Sales, and Cost of Sales may be inserted in the chart without disturbing the original numbering system. The account numbering plan follows a definite pattern which permits the addition of accounts for unusual circumstances. Similarly, accounts that are not needed can be omitted without affecting the numerical arrangement of those retained.

If expenses are not analyzed by departments, the complete expense account number is determined by using the expense control No. 500. Thus the number for Sales Salaries is 513. When departmental analysis is required, the applicable expense item number is appended to the departmental number. Therefore, Sales Salaries accounts would be numbered 513-1, 513-2, 513-3, etc.

When salaries are paid to an individual proprietor or partners, these items are not allowable business expenses for income tax reporting. They may be included as salaries in the operating expense schedule of the profit and loss statement. For income tax purposes, salary accounts must be eliminated from the operating expense schedule and shown as personal withdrawals from the business. When salary checks are issued, the charge to owners' or partners' salaries should be charged directly in the expense column of the Check register. They should not appear in the regular Payroll record.

For individuals and partners, contributions are not allowable as business expense deductions. They should be charged to the individual's drawing account when paid by a business check. For corporations, contributions are limited to 5 percent of taxable income for Federal operating expense deductions.

Since account titles indicate their purpose, further explanation is not necessary.

Peculiarities of Procedures

The retail drugstore of today has been accepted as a more or less general merchandise store. However, one feature distinguishing it from every other type of retail establishment is the kind of professional service it is equipped and licensed to supply. To be licensed as a drugstore, the concern must maintain a prescription laboratory with one or more registered pharmacists in charge at all times. Actually, accounting for a retail drugstore does not necessarily differ materially from that of any other retail merchandising business.

Drugstore operations are not always the same. Much depends on the policies and procedures of individual owners and managers. Changes in ownership and management will often necessitate changes in the manner of handling cash receipts and disbursements. The accounting system in use must be flexible enough to adapt to any changes management may require. This may result only in columnar changes in certain forms in use and in some cases the redesigning of new ones.

Accounting has been called the language of business. With this phrase in mind, journals and forms illustrated in this chapter have been designed specifically for drugstore accounting.

CASH RECEIPTS AND DISBURSEMENTS

The Daily Cash Report—Sales and Receipts (Figure 2) is found in the upper half of the illustration. Source of entries for this report is readings from the cash register. The report need not be elaborate but should account

PREPARED BY   DATE

DAILY CASH REPORT - SALES AND RECEIPTS

#	A/C#	Cash Register Readings-Sales and Receipts	Month	Year	#
		Store _____ Day _____			
1	300	Gross Sales - Cash		xxx	1
2	300	Gross Sales-Charge(Do not use for cash basis)		xxx	2
3	300	Cash Collections-A/C rec. (Cash basis only)		xxx	3
4		Total Taxable Sales	xxx		4
5	122	Cash Collections-A/C Rec.(Do not use for cash basis)		xxx	5
6	211	Sales Tax Collected		xxx	6
7	___	Taxable Receipts _____		xxx	7
8	___	Non Taxable Receipts		xxx	8
9		Total Cash Receipts	xxx		9
10		Total - Taxable Sales and Cash Receipts	xxx		10
11	122	Deductions-A/C Rec. Charges (Sales)		xxx	11
12		Refunds and Allowances		xxx	12
13		Total Deductions	xxx		13
14		Net Cash to Account for	xxx		14
15	101	A. M. Balance - Cash on Hand	xxx		15
16	608	Total Cash to Account for	xxx		16
17	658	Cash Overage or Shortage	Over	Short	17
18		Actual Cash Count	xxx		18
19	102	Cash Banked (Deposit)	xxx		19
20	101	P. M. Balance - Cash on Hand	xxx		20
21	*	CONTINUATION-CASH DISBURSEMENTS	xxx	xxx	21
22	*	Not required when petty cash system is used.	xxx	xxx	22
23		Payments made from cash register drawer	xxx	xxx	23
24		Amount available for bank deposit (Line 19)	xxx		24
25		Less cash payments listed below	xxx	xxx	25
26	400	Merchandise Payments		xxx	26
27		Expense Charges	xxx	xxx	27
28		Accounts	xxx	xxx	28
29			xxx	xxx	29
30			xxx	xxx	30
31		Total Expense Charges xxx		xxx	31
32		Other Payments	xxx	xxx	32
33		Accounts	xxx	xxx	33
34		Total Other Payments xxx		xxx	34
35		Total Cash Payments	xxx		35
36		Line 24 minus Line 35- Cash Banked	xxx		36
37		Checked by _____ Entered by _____	Sales Tax Memo		37
38		Remarks _____	Wholesale		38
39			Exempt Sales		39
40			Total		40
41					41
42					42
43					43

NesMbill   6002 IVORY; 6202 GREEN; 6402 WHITE; 7202 TRANSLUCENT; 7402 CANARY   PRINTED IN U.S.A.

Figure 2: Daily Cash Report—Sales and Receipts—Cash Disbursements

PREPARED BY   DATE

S A L E S   and   R E C E I P T S   J O U R N A L

Accounts Year ..... Month Day	122 Accounts Receivable	409 D E B I T S Returns Allowances	101 Cash Received	658 Cash Shortage	301-307 Sales Credits	211 Sales Tax State-City
1						
2						
3						
4						
5						
6						
7						
8						
9						
10						
11						
12						
13						
14						
15						
16						
17						
18						
19						
20						
21						
22						
23						
24						
25						
26						
27						
28						
29						
30						
31						
32 Totals						
33						
34						
35						
36						
37						
38						
39						
40						
41						
42						
43						

6005 IVORY; 6205 GREEN; 6405 WHITE; 7205 TRANSLUCENT; 7405 CANARY   PRINTED IN U.S.A.   6 GREEN; 6405 WHITE;

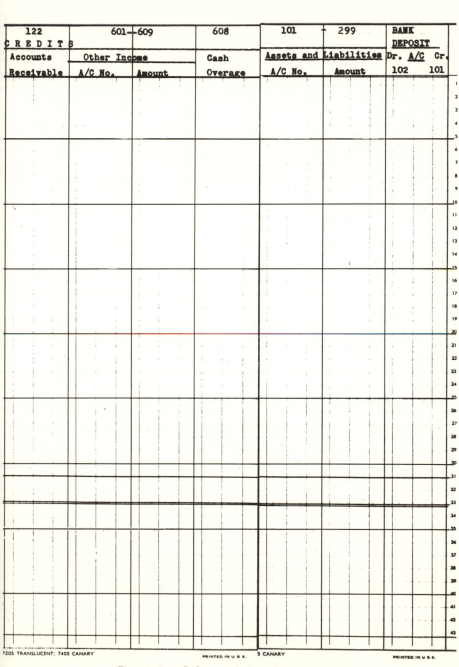

PREPARED BY   DATE   PREPARED BY   DATE

122 CREDITS	601—609		608	101 — 299		BANK DEPOSIT	
Accounts Receivable	Other Income		Cash Overage	Assets and Liabilities		Dr. A/C Cr.	
	A/C No.	Amount		A/C No.	Amount	102	101

7205 TRANSLUCENT; 7405 CANARY   PRINTED IN U S A.   5 CANARY   PRINTED IN U.S.A.

Figure 3: Sales and Receipts Journal

PREPARED BY   DATE

. . . . Y E A R L Y   S U M M A R Y . . . .
S A L E S   and   R E C E I P T S   J O U R N A L

Accounts Year .... Month	122 Accounts Receivable	409 Returns Allowances	101 Cash Received	301-307 Sales Credits	658 Cash Shortage	211 Sales Tax State-City
			D E B I T S			
January						
February						
March						
April						
May						
June						
July						
August						
September						
October						
November						
December						
Yearly Totals						

ALLOCATION of SALES

A/C Account No.	January	February	March	April	May	June
301 Prescriptions						
302 Packaged Med.						
303 Fountain						
304 Tob-Cfty-Pds.						
305 Toiletries						
306 Liquor						
307 Sundries						
Totals						

PREPARED BY   DATE   PREPARED BY   DATE

122 CREDITS	601--609		608	101	299	BANK DEPOSIT
Accounts Receivable	Other Income		Cash Overage	Assets and Liabilities		Dr. A/C Cr.
	A/C No.	Amount		A/C No.	Amount	102 101
July	August	September	October	November	December	Yearly Totals

7265 TRANSLUCENT ()405 CANARY   PRINTED IN U S A   5 CANARY   PRINTED N _ S A

Figure 4: Sales and Receipts—Yearly Summary

CASH PAID OUT JOURNAL   This form not required if petty cash system is used.

Account Nos Year ..... Month Day	101 CREDIT Cash Account		DEBITS						DEBITS
1									
2									
3									
4									
5									
6									
7									
8									
9									
10									
11									
12									
13									
14									
15									
16									
17									
18									
19									
20									
21									
22									
23									
24									
25									
26									
27									
28									
29									
30									
31									
32 Totals									
33									
34									
35									
36									
37									
38									
39									
40									
41									
42									
43									

6005 IVORY; 6205 GREEN; 6405 WHITE; 7205 TRANSLUCENT; 7405 CANARY   PRINTED IN U S A.   5 GREEN; 6405 WHITE; 7205 TRANSLUCENT;

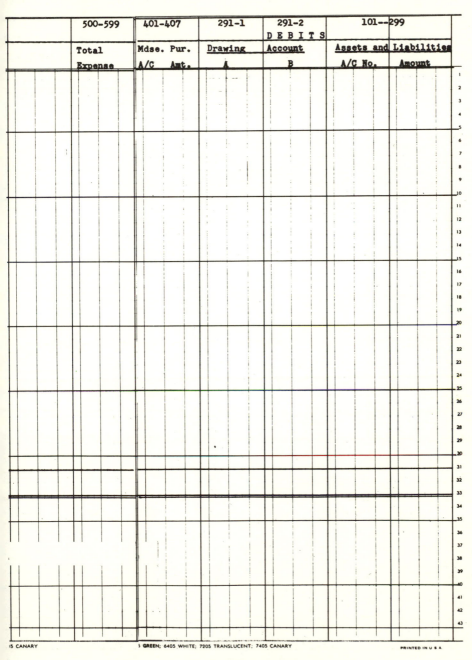

Figure 5: Cash Disbursements Journal

PREPARED BY   DATE

.... Y E A R L Y   S U M M A R Y ....
C A S H   P A I D   O U T   J O U R N A L   This form not required if petty cash
                                                     system is used.

	Account Nos. Year ..... Month	101 CREDIT Cash Account			D E B I T S						D E B I T
1											
2	January										
3											
4	February										
5											
6	March										
7											
8	April										
9											
10	May										
11											
12	June										
13											
14	July										
15											
16	August										
17											
18	September										
19											
20	October										
21											
22	November										
23											
24	December										
25											
26	Yearly										
27	Totals										
28											
29											
30											

ALLOCATION OF PURCHASES

	A/C No. Account	January	February	March	April	May	June	July
34	401 Prescriptions							
35	402 Packaged Med.							
36	403 Fountain							
37	404 Tob-Cfty-Pds.							
38	405 Toiletries							
39	406 Liquor							
40	407 Sundries							
41								
42	Totals							
43								

6005 IVORY; 6205 GREEN; 6405 WHITE; 7205 TRANSLUCENT; 7405 CANARY

PREPARED BY   DATE

	500-599	401-407		291-1	291-2	101--299		
	Total Expense	Mdse. Pur. A/C	Amt.	Drawing A	DEBITS Account B	Assets and Liabilities A/C No.	Amount	

| August | September | October | November | December | | Yearly Totals |

5 GREEN; 6405 WHITE; 7205 TRANSLUCENT; 7405 CANARY

PRINTED IN U S A

Figure 6: Cash Disbursements—Yearly Summary

for all cash received from sales, customer collections, and all other sources. Since cash has no identity, the bookkeeper must give careful attention to preparation of the Daily Cash Reports; they are the recorded source of cash received from all sources. It is helpful if these reports are mimeographed or printed and the reports numbered serially.

Source of entry for the Sales and Receipts Journal (Figure 3) is figures shown in the Daily Cash Report—Sales and Receipts (top half of Figure 2); 31 lines are provided, one for each day's totals.

The use of a work sheet as a supplement to the Daily Cash Report—Sales and Receipts (Figure 2) providing columns for accounts 301 to 307 will give a daily breakdown of sales by departments. Monthly totals can be recorded on Allocation of Sales section (bottom half of Figure 4), Yearly Summary—Sales and Receipts journal. Detailed discussion of the Yearly Summary journals will be found later in this section under subheadings, OTHER PROCEDURES and *Yearly Summary Journals*.

Source of entry for the Cash Paid Out Journal (Figure 5) is figures shown in the Daily Cash Report—Sales and Receipts (lower half of Figure 2); 31 lines are provided, one for each day's total. The use of a work sheet as a supplement to the Daily Cash Report—Sales and Receipts (Figure 2) providing columns for accounts 401 to 407 will give a daily breakdown of purchases by departments.

Monthly totals can be recorded on Allocation of Purchase section (bottom half of Figure 6), Yearly Summary—Cash Paid Out Journal (Figure 6). When a petty cash system is used for cash pay-outs, the bottom half of the Daily Cash Report—Sales and Receipts (Figure 2) and the use of this journal will not be required.

In reference to the receiving and paying out of cash, internal control is essential. The accumulation of the various totals for the records is best obtained by the use of a cash register. Each employee if possible should be assigned a separate drawer in the cash register. A stated amount of cash for change should be placed in the drawer each morning, and the employee should be held responsible for cash shortages. If exceptions are made, shortage should be charged to account 658 in the Yearly Summary—Sales and Receipts journal (Figure 4) or the Cash Paid Out journal (Figure 5). Overages are to be credited to account No. 608.

At check-out time the manager or owner should check the register and the register tape ring-out total should be compared with the cash on hand. Nominal shortages and overages are normal. The cash register should provide a receipt for each customer and a separate key should be employed for cash sales, cash collections on open accounts (charge sales) and miscellaneous receipts. Keys for cash pay-outs should be employed for merchandise purchases, expense account charges, and miscellaneous payments. Keys may also be employed to record sales of merchandise by departments.

Preliminary Proof Sheet. Most bookkeepers, or those assigned to check the daily cash, prefer to prepare a preliminary Daily Cash Report of the sales and receipts and of the cash disbursements as a proof sheet. Cash register tapes received from store cashiers are, of course, the principal source of money coming in. When cash is counted and balanced, shortages, overages, or any apparent discrepancies can be traced before totals are transferred to the permanent Daily Cash Reports (Figure 2). A bound columnar book or columnar pad may be used for the preliminary proof sheet.

If at all possible, all cash receipts shown on the Daily Cash Reports should be banked intact. This method provides better accountability of cash at all times.

Check Register-Disbursement Journal. The Check Register-Disbursement journal (Figure 7) is designed to meet the usual requirements for the recording of checks issued. Any check register in use with additions or changes to conform to the chart of accounts is acceptable. A supplementary work sheet for recapping the expense charges for the month will give the monthly totals for the classification of expense accounts.

These totals can then be entered in the Check Register-Disbursement journal—Analysis of Expense (Figure 8). A supplementary work sheet for recapping the merchandise purchases charges for the month will give the monthly totals for the merchandise purchases by departments.

These totals can then be entered in the Yearly Summary—Check Register-Disbursement journal.

A Yearly Bank Reconciliation form (Figure 10) is provided for those who prefer this type of bank reconciliation.

PURCHASE-PAYABLES CYCLE

Purchase Journal (Figure 11). The source of entry is all invoices received from wholesalers, suppliers, and others. When a Purchase journal is used, care should be taken at the year end to see that all invoices are entered in this journal for merchandise bought, and that they are included in the ending inventory. When checks are issued for payment of invoices, they are entered in the Accounts Payable column of the Check Register-Disbursement journal (Figure 7).

A Purchase journal is effected by paying each purchase invoice due for each current month by using a month-end dated check. This procedure brings all purchases into the books in the same month in which purchases are received and merchandise put into stock. The amount of purchases for the month is that shown in the Merchandise Purchase column of the Check

PREPARED BY   DATE

CHECK REGISTER - DISBURSEMENT JOURNAL

Year	Account Nos		102 CREDITS				401--407 D
Month Day	Payable To	Check No.	Amount of Check	Other Credits A/C No.	Amount	Merchandise A/C No.	Purchase Amount
1							
2							
3							
4							
5							
6							
7							
8							
9							
10							
11							
12							
13							
14							
15							
16							
17							
18							
19							
20							
21							
22							
23							
24							
25							
26							
27							
28							
29							
30							
31							
32							
33							
34							
35							
36							
37	Totals						
38							
39							
40							
41							
42							
43							

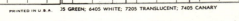

PREPARED BY   DATE   PREPARED BY   DATE

206 ITS ccounts ayable	500--599		225 Accrued Payroll	291-1 Drawing A	291-2 Accounts B	101--299	
	Expense A/C No.	Accounts Amount				Assets and Liabilities A/C No.	Amount

DEBITS

CANARY   PRINTED IN U.S.A. 05 GREEN; 6405 WHITE; 7205 TRANSLUCENT; 7405 CANARY   PRINTED IN U.S.A.

Figure 7: Check Register—Disbursement Journal

PREPARED BY   DATE

. . . . Y E A R L Y   S U M M A R Y . . . .
C H E C K   R E G I S T E R – D I S B U R S E M E N T   J O U R N A L

A/C No.	ACCOUNT	January	February S.T.	March S.T.	April S.T.	May S.T.
502	Owner's Salary					
503	Partner's Salary					
503 -1	Partner's Salary					
521	Stationery & Office Sup.					
522	Operating Supplies					
523	Fountain Supplies					
524	Pharmaceutical Supplies					
526	Postage					
531	Heat–Light–Water					
533	Telephone and Telegraph					
534	Laundry					
541	Advalorem Taxes					
551	Insurance-General					
552	Insurance-Retirement					
553	Insurance-Compensation					
554	Insurance-Group					
572	Repairs & Maint-Building					
573	Repairs & Maint-Foun. Fix.					
574	Repairs & Maint-Store Fix.					
575	Repairs & Maint-Office Fix.					
579	Accounting – Legal					
580	Advertising					
581	Bank Charges					
582	Business Promotion					
583	Delivery Expense					
584	Contributions					
585	Bus. Dues-Subscriptions					
586	Inventory Expense					
588	Lease Rental					
589	Licenses and Tags					
590	Merchant Police					
591	Parking Fees					
592	Freight-Express					
593	Rent Paid-Building					
594	Rent Paid-Equipment					
595	Temporary Labor					
596	Trash Hauling					
597	Unclassified					
x	Monthly Totals					
*	S.T. – subtotal if used					

E   PREPARED BY   DATE

A N A L Y S I S   O F   E X P E N S E

June	July	August	September	October	November	December	YEARLY TOTALS
S.T.	S.T.	S.T.	S.T.	S.T.	S.T.	S.T.	

PRINTED IN U S A   PRINTED IN U S A

Figure 8: Analysis of Expense—Check Register Disbursement Journal

PREPARED BY   DATE

. . . . Y E A R L Y   S U M M A R Y . . . .
C H E C K   R E G I S T E R - D I S B U R S E M E N T   J O U R N A L

| Year ..... | 102 | | | 401-407 | * 206 | 225 |
| | CREDITS | | | DEBITS | | |
Month	Amount of Check	Other Credits A/C No.	Amount	Mdse. Purchases	Accounts Payable	Accrued Payroll
January						
February						
March						
April						
May						
June						
July						
August						
September						
October						
November						
December						
Yearly Totals						

* A/C 206 - Use only when Purchase journal is used.

A/C No.	Account	ALLOCATION of PURCHASES January	February	March	April	May	June
401	Prescriptions						
402	Packaged Med.						
403	Fountain						
404	Tob-Cfty-Pds.						
405	Toiletries						
406	Liquor						
407	Sundries						
	Totals						

500--599		291-1	291-2	101--299			
Expense A/C No.	Accounts Amount	Drawing A	Accounts B	Assets and A/C No.	Liabilities Amount		
							1
							2
							3
							4
							5
							6
							7
							8
							9
							10
							11
							12
							13
							14
							15
							16
							17
							18
							19
							20
							21
							22
							23
							24
							25
							26
							27
							28
							29
							30
							31
							32
July	August	September	October	November	December	Yearly Totals	33
							34
							35
							36
							37
							38
							39
							40
							41
							42
							43

PRINTED IN U.S.A.

Figure 9: Yearly Summary—Check Register Disbursements Journal

Register-Disbursement journal account (Nos. 401-407) (Figure 7). More outstanding checks result, but purchase charges are current.

The breakdown of purchases by departments is shown in the Yearly Summary—Purchase journal. A work sheet as a supplement to the journal should be provided for the breakdown of expense charges.

Because of the amount of work and extra expense involved, most small stores do not make use of a Purchase journal.

OTHER PROCEDURES

General Journal. The General journal (Figure 13) is used for the recording of transactions which can not readily be recorded in the other books of original entry, and for adjusting entries. The General journal is also used for closing into the profit and loss account at the year end, preparatory to closing into Net Worth when an individual proprietorship or partnership, or the Retained Earnings account when a corporation. Any standard General journal form is acceptable for use.

Accrual Journal. This journal (Figure 14) is used for month and accrual entries for stores which accrue prepaid expenses and other charges each month. It is essential for drugstores preparing current profit and loss statements via either the pen-and-ink method of recording or a data processing system. The Accrual journal is basically an expense journal and is in itself a yearly summary from which postings are made to the General ledger every month. For other periods, totals of various months are figured and entered in the blank lines between months.

When a Depreciation Schedule similar to that shown in Figure 15 is attached to a tax return, allowance for depreciation (to-date reserve) and original cost (ledger amount) should reconcile with accounts shown in the General ledger.

Yearly Summary Journals. When books are posted monthly and a trial balance is taken, entries can be made to the General ledger directly from the various journals of original entry. Yearly Summary journals (Figures 4, 6, 8, 9, 12, 14, and 18) are provided for quarterly, semiannual, and other periods. Summary journals are used in connection with the following journals: Sales and Receipts, Cash Paid Out, Check Register-Disbursement journal, Purchase journal, and Payroll journal. The Yearly Summary for the Check Register-Disbursement journal—Analysis of Expense (Figure 8) and the Accrual journal (Figure 14) have been discussed; these summary journals should be posted monthly to the General ledger prior to preparation of the trial balance. The various accounts in the breakdown of sales by departments, the Yearly Summary—Sales and Receipts journal (Figure 4); the breakdown of merchandise purchases, Cash Paid Out journal (Figure 5);

Client _____ Address _____

Bank _____ Period _____ 195___

E. W. Moore. Public Accountant, Alva, Okla.

BANK RECONCILIATION

Particulars	Month Jan. July		Month Feb. Aug.		Month Mar. Sep.		Month Apr. Oct.		Month May Nov.		Month June Dec.	
	x	x	x	x	x	x	x	x	x	x	x	x
Beginning Balance												
Deposits												
Total												
Checks Issued												
Ending Balance												
Outstanding Checks												
Balance per												
Bank Statement	x		x		x		x		x		x	
Deposits in Transit												
Adjusted Balance												
Bank Statement												
	No.	Amount	No.	Amount	No.	Amount	No.	Amount	No.	Amount	No.	Amount
Outstanding Checks												
Per Detail To Right												

Figure 10: Yearly Bank Reconciliation

PREPARED BY

PURCHASE JOURNAL

Year Day Month	Account Nos. Purchased From	Their Date	Their Invoice No.	206 CREDITS Amount of Invoice	Other A/C No.
1					
2					
3					
4					
5					
6					
7					
8					
9					
10					
11					
12					
13					
14					
15					
16					
17					
18					
19					
20					
21					
22					
23					
24					
25					
26					
27					
28					
29					
30					
31					
32					
33					
34					
35					
36					
37	Totals				
38					
39					
40					
41					
42					
43					

PREPARED BY   PREPARED BY   DATE

This form not required when merchandise purchases are charged direct from Check Register

Credits Amount	Merchandise A/C No.	Purchases Amount	501--597		101--299	
			Expense A/C No.	Accounts Amount	Assets and A/C No.	Liabilities Amount

Figure 11: Purchase Journal

205 TRANSLUCENT; 7405 CANARY   205 TRANSLUCENT 7405 CANARY   PRINTED IN U S A

PREPARED BY

.... Y E A R L Y   S U M M A R Y ....
P U R C H A S E   J O U R N A L

Year	206			401-407	501-- 597	
	CREDITS					
Month	A/C Payable	Other	Credits	Merchandise	Expense	Accounts
	Invoice Amt.	A/C No.	Amount	Purchases	A/C No.	Amount
January						
February						
March						
April						
May						
June						
July						
August						
September						
October						
November						
December						
Yearly Totals						

ALLOCATION of PURCHASES

A/C Account No.	January	February	March	April	May	June
401 Prescriptions						
402 Packaged Med.						
403 Fountain						
404 Tob-Cfty-Pds.						
405 Toiletries						
406 Liquor						
407 Sundries						
Totals						

Kraftbilt 6005 IVORY; 6205 GREEN; 6405 WHITE; 7205 TRANSLUCENT; 7405 CANARY

PREPARED BY   DATE   PREPARED BY   DATE

This form not required when merchandise purchases are
charged direct from Check Register-Disbursement journal.

101--299 Assets and Liabilities							
A/C No.	Amount						
							1
							2
							3
							4
							5
							6
							7
							8
							9
							10
							11
							12
							13
							14
							15
							16
							17
							18
							19
							20
							21
							22
							23
							24
							25
							26
							27
							28
							29
							30
							31
							32
July	August	September	October	November	December	Yearly Totals	
							34
							35
							36
							37
							38
							39
							40
							41
							42
							43

PRINTED IN U S A.

Figure 12:   Yearly Summary—Purchase Journal

and the Yearly Summary—Purchase journal (Figure 12) should also be posted directly to the General ledger if it is desired that these accounts appear individually in the monthly trial balance. Otherwise the control accounts, Merchandise Sales (300) and Merchandise Purchases (400) will be sufficient.

When Yearly Summary journals are not used (all postings being made to the General ledger from the journals of original entry), then the Check Register-Disbursement journal—Analysis of Expense (Figure 8) and the Yearly Summary Accrual journal (Figure 14) are used as journals of original entry and postings are made direct to the General ledger.

The only printed forms shown are the Yearly Bank Reconciliation (Figure 10) and the Payroll journal (Figure 17). The Daily Cash Report—Sales and Receipts (Figure 2), the General Ledger Trial Balance (Figure 16), and the Depreciation Schedule (Figure 15) may be printed, typed, or mimeographed. Headings for all other forms may be inked in on 11x17 columnar sheets. There is no preference for General ledger sheets.

Subsidiary Ledgers. These are the Accounts Receivable and Accounts Payable ledgers. Whether to use the conventional type of ledger, envelope ledger types, or the open, unpaid individual files depends somewhat on the type of store, the volume of business done, and clerical help available. When monthly postings are completed in the ledgers, a monthly trial balance should be taken regardless of the kind of ledgers used. Routine procedure of posting employee charges and charges to owners and partners in the Accounts Receivable ledger, and in the manner they are to be paid or credited, should be decided by management. No Accounts Payable ledger will be necessary if the Accounts Payable journal is not used.

General Ledger. Accounts in this ledger should be numbered, grouped, and indexed, the same as shown in the chart of accounts. When monthly balance sheet and profit and loss statements are requested, totals in the various journals of original entry and the General journal are made directly to the General ledger. When postings are completed, a trial balance is taken as shown in Figure 16. When this procedure is followed, the yearly summary of the various journals is not required.

General Ledger Trial Balance (Figure 16). This is a combination trial balance, balance sheet, and profit and loss statement.

The use of an expense control account No. 500 in the General ledger posting expense accounts in total from the various journals will eliminate the various expense accounts in the General ledger. Monthly totals of the expense accounts can then be entered in the Analysis of Expense (Figure 8), including the addition of a supplementary sheet which should include expense charge accounts originating from the Payroll, Accrual, and General journals,

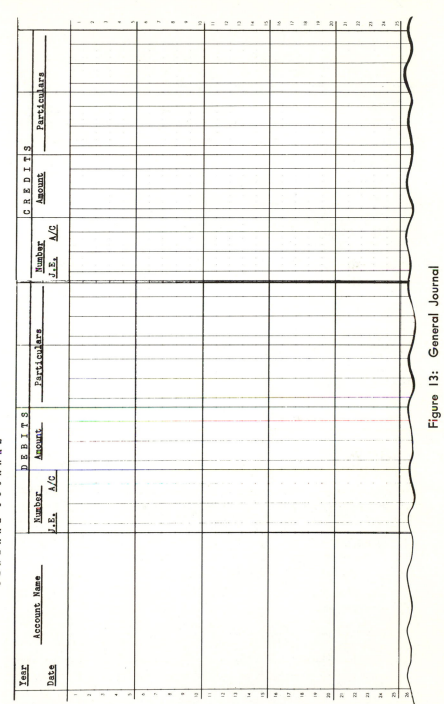

Figure 13: General Journal

PREPARED BY

. . . . Y E A R L Y S U M M A R Y . . . .
M O N T H L Y A C C R U A L J O U R N A L

Account Nos. Year . . . Month	551 DR. Insurance General	141 CR. Prepaid Insurance	598 DR. Losses on Bad Accounts	232 CR. Allowance Bad Debts	541 DR. Advalorem Taxes	233 CR. Allowance for Taxes
January						
February						
March						
April						
May						
June						
July						
August						
September						
October						
November						
December						
Yearly Totals						

MONTHLY ALLOCATION of DEPRECIATION CHARGES

A/C No.	Account	Jan.	Feb.	March	April	May	June
562	Buildings						
563	Furniture F&E						
564	Store Fix & E.						
565	Office Fix &E.						
	Total Charges To Depreciation Column						

PREPARED BY   DATE   PREPARED BY

587 DR. Lease Amortization	231 CR. Allocated Lease-Res.	562-565 DR. Depreciation Total Chgs.	ACCUMULATED DEPRECIATION CREDITS			
			162R Buildings All Locations	163R Fountain Fix-Equip	164R Store Fix.-Equip.	165R Office Furniture

July	August	September	October	November	December	Yearly Totals

PRINTED IN U.S.A.   5 GREEN; 6405 WHITE; 7205 TRANSLUCENT; 7405 CANARY

Figure 14: Accrual Journal

Client _____ Address _____ Year ____ or ____ Months ending ____ 19 ____

Date Acq'd	DEPRECIATION SCHEDULE / DESCRIPTION OF ARTICLE / SUPPORTING (S) SOLD OR SALVAGED (T) TRADED IN SCHEDULE	S OR T	ORIGINAL COST / LEDGER AMOUNT	VALUES — LESS SALVAGE	VALUES — DEPRECIABLE BASIS	LIFE YEARS	RATE %	DEPRECIATION — CURRENT YEAR	DEPRECIATION — PRIOR YEARS	TO DATE RESERVE	PRESENT BOOK VALUE / DEPRECIABLE BASIS	INVESTMENT CREDIT — AMOUNT	YEAR ACQ'D	RECAPTURE — YRS AMOUNT
1														
2														
3														
4														
5														
6														
7														
8														
9														
10														
11														
12														
13														
14														
15														
16														
17														
18														
19														
20														
21														
22														
23														
24														
25														
26														

Designed by E.W. Moore Public Accountant   ALVA, OKLA 9-64

Figure 15:   Depreciation Schedule

and the Purchase journal (if used), reconciling at each month end with the Expense (control) account, No. 500. This practice saves considerable time in posting and trial balance take-off. A majority of accountants, however, prefer to post all accounts to the General ledger.

Year-End Closings. Adjustments are made and the closing inventories brought into the books before the final General ledger trial balance is taken. Profit and loss accounts are then closed into the Profit and Loss account, which then is closed into Net Worth or Retained Earnings. Final balances in the asset and liability accounts are forwarded as beginning balances in the General ledger for the new accounting year.

Time and Payroll System

Time Records. If the time books used and work sheets employed for preparation of payroll reports and yearly W-2 forms, reconcile with quarterly and yearly totals, their use should be continued. In Figure 17 are shown time payroll records. One is a regular form, the other includes daily time records.

Payroll Journals. A Payroll journal (Figure 17) should be used which will record all payroll checks in the order in which they are issued as well as provide columns for the gross amount earned and for all Federal, state, and city tax deductions and other deductions authorized by the employee. The amount earned column is a charge to Salaries and Wages (No. 500), or the charges may be departmentalized. The last column to the right should show the net amount earned including a memo column for the check number. Additional columns should be provided for the accrual of Social Security and unemployment tax charges.

When the Payroll journal is used, only the monthly total of the net amount earned needs to be transferred to the Disbursements journal (account No. 225).

Monthly totals should be transferred to the Yearly Summary—Payroll journal (Figure 18).

When the bank statement is reconciled, cancelled payroll checks can be checked off the memo check number column to determine those outstanding. Quite often separate checks are used for payment of salaries; a regular store check is deposited in a separate payroll account for the net amount of the payroll for the period paid. This procedure lessens the number of checks issued from the regular store account and allows for a separate reconciliation of the payroll account. If possible, the bookkeeper should make up the payroll; it should be approved and initialed by the person who authorizes salaries to be paid.

		PREPARED BY			DATE	

STORE _____

General Ledger Trial Balance   Sheet 1

Period _____

A/C No.	ASSETS	Previous Balance		xxx	Current Balance			
101	Cash on Hand							1
102	Cash in Bank							2
103	Petty Cash Fund							3
104	Drawer Cash - Registers							4
122	Accounts Receivable							5
130	Inventories							6
141	Prepaid Insurance							7
161	Land							8
162	Buildings							9
								10
	Totals			xxx				11
								12
								13
	LIABILITIES			xxx				14
200	Notes Payable							15
206	Accounts Payable							16
211	Sales Tax Payable							17
221-1	Soc. Sec. Taxes							18
221-2	State Disability Ins.							19
221-3	Inc. Tax W. H. (Fed.)							20
221-4	Inc. Tax W. H. (State)							21
221-5	Inc. Tax W. H. (City)							22
222-1	Soc. Sec. Taxes							23
222-2	Fed. Soc. Sec. (Employ.)							24
222-3	State Soc. Sec. (Emp.)							25
225	Accrued Payroll							26
232	Allowance for Bad Debts							27
233	Reserve for Taxes							28
241	Contracts Payable							29
	(Longer than one year)							30
291-1	Capital Stock Authorized							31
291-2	Capital Stock Unissued							32
297	Capital Surplus							33
298	Earned Surplus							34
299	Profit & Loss-Current							35
								36
								37
	Totals			xxx				38
	Net Profit or Loss							39
	before Inventories	xxx			xxx			40
	To Agree With Assets			xxx				41
								42
								43

6004 IVORY, 6204 GREEN, 6404 WHITE, 7204 TRANSLUCENT, 7404 CANARY   PRINTED IN U S A.

Figure 16:   General Ledger Trial Balance

PREPARED BY   DATE

STORE _____

General Ledger Trial Balance   Sheet 2

Period

A/C No.	REVENUES	Previous Balance	Period Totals	Current Balance		
1	301-7 Sales-Mdse. & Pharmacy					1
2						2
3						3
4	Totals					4
5						5
6	PURCHASES					6
7	401-8 Purc.-Mdse. & Pharmacy					7
8	408 Freight Paid In					8
9	409 Returns and Allowances					9
10	Totals					10
11						11
12	OTHER INCOME					12
13	601 Cash Discounts Taken					13
14	605 Charged off accounts					14
15	collected					15
16	608 Cash Over					16
17	609 Miscellaneous Income					17
18						18
19	Totals					19
20						20
21	DEDUCTIONS FROM INCOME					21
22	652 Interest Expense					22
23	658 Cash Short					23
24						24
25	Totals					25
26						26
27	TRIAL BALANCE					27
28		Dr.		Cr.		28
29	Assets			xxx		29
30	Liabilities	xxx				30
31	Sales	xxx				31
32	Purchases-Cost of Sales			xxx		32
33	Expense			xxx		33
34	Other Income	xxx				34
35	Deductions from Income			xxx		35
36	Totals					36
37						37
38						38
39						39
40						40
41						41
42						42
43						43

6004 IVORY; 6204 GREEN; 6404 WHITE; 7204 TRANSLUCENT; 7404 CANARY   PRINTED IN U.S.A.

Figure 16: General Ledger Trial Balance (cont.)

| | | PREPARED BY | DATE |

STORE _____

General Ledger Trial Balance   Sheet 3
Period

A/C No.	EXPENSES	Previous Balance	Period Totals	Current Balance		
1	500	Salaries and Wages				
2	520	Supplies				
3	531	Heat, Light, & Water				
4	533	Telephone and Telegraph				
5	534	Laundry				
6	541	General Taxes				
7	543	Payroll-Soc. Sec. Taxes				
8	544	Payroll-Unempl. Taxes				
9	551	General Insurance				
10	554	Group Insurance				
11	560	Depreciation				
12	572	Building Repair & Maint.				
13	574	Rep.-Store Fix. & Equip.				
14	579	Accounting and Legal				
15	580	Advertising				
16	581	Bank Charges				
17	582	Business Promotion				
18	583	Delivery Charges				
19	584	Contributions				
20	585	Dues and Subscriptions				
21	586	Inventory Expense				
22	587	Lease Amortization				
23	588	Lease Rental				
24	589	Licenses and Tags				
25	590	Merchant Police				
26	591	Parking Fees				
27	592	Postage and Express				
28	593	Rent Paid-Building				
29	594	Rent Paid-Equipment				
30	595	Temporary Labor				
31	596	Trash Hauling				
32	597	Unclassified				
33						
34						
35		Totals				
36						
37						
38						
39						
40						
41						
42						
43						

6004 IVORY; 6204 GREEN; 6404 WHITE; 7204 TRANSLUCENT; 7404 CANARY   PRINTED IN U.S.A.

Figure 16:   General Ledger Trial Balance (cont.)

	PREPARED BY		DATE	

STORE _____

General Ledger Trial Balance   Sheet 4 _____

Period _____

		1	2	3	4	
		PROFIT AND LOSS - Inventory Basis				
			Period	Yr. to Date		
1	Gross Sales					1
2	Purchases					2
3	Gross Profit before Inventories					3
4	Operating Expense					4
5	Profit or Loss before Inventories					5
6	Other Income					6
7	Deductions from Income					7
8	Net P&L before Inventories					8
9	Ending Inventory - Add					9
10	Beginning Inventory - Subtract					10
11	Net P&L after Inventories					11
12						12
13						13
14						14
15						15
16		PROFIT AND LOSS - Cost of Sales Basis				16
17			Period	Yr. to Date		17
18	Gross Sales					18
19	Cost of Sales					19
20	Gross Profit - Sales					20
21	Operating Expense					21
22	Operating Profit					22
23	Other Income					23
24	Deductions from Income					24
25	Net Profit or Loss					25
26						26
27						27
28						28
29						29
30						30
31						31
32						32
33						33
34		N O T E				34
35						35
36	All accounts shown in chart of accounts not listed in this General					36
37	Ledger Trial Balance.					37
38						38
39						39
40						40
41						41
42						42
43						43

6004 IVORY, 6204 GREEN; 6404 WHITE; 7204 TRANSLUCENT; 7404 CANARY   PRINTED IN U.S.A.

Figure 16: General Ledger Trial Balance (cont.)

Pay Roll No.————— Sheet No.————— _Journal_

NAME	Employed As A/c No	DAILY TIME "A" Absent—"H" Holiday														
		1	2	3	4	5	6	7	8	9	10	11	12	13	14	15
		16	17	18	19	20	21	22	23	24	25	26	27	28	29	30	31
TOTALS																

Prepared by......................................

Checked by......................................

Posted by......................................

Approved ....

*KEY TO SYMBOLS—"Hours" R indicates Regular. O indicates Overtime.
Basis "H" Hour "W" Week
SM Semi-Monthly M Monthly.

Designed by E. W. Moore, Accountant and Auditor, Alva, Okla.

LABOR CHARGES

Deduction Credits

OTHER CHARGES | A/c

A/c No	Account	Amount	5c
			5.
			5.
			5.
X	Totals		

Pay Roll period ending _____ 196___

COMPUTATION						Labor Charges Amount Earned *No Post*	DEDUCTIONS								PAYMENT		
REGULAR TIME			OVERTIME				*221-1* FEDERAL Soc. Sec.	*221- 3-4-5* *Withholding* *Fed*	*9-C*	*Other Charges* *Ak No*	*Amount*	*Msc*	*(N.P.)* Total	*225* Amount	Ck. No.
Hrs.	Rate	Amt. Earned	Hrs.	Rate	Amt. Earned										

(al Amount Earned)

Account	Amount
Managers	
Clerical Office	
Sales	
Pharmacists	
AL LABOR CHARGE	

TAX ENTRIES

Posted	Charge—Soc. Sec. Tax Account *543* % Amt. Earned)		
	Credit—Dir. Int. Rev.—Soc. Sec. Div. *221-1*		
Entered	Charge—Unemp. Tax Account *544* % Amt. Earned)		
	Credit—Unemp. Tax Dep't. *222-3*		
Date	Charge—P. R. Excise Tax A/c *544* % Amt. Earned)		
	Credit—Excise Tax Dep't.—Int. Rev. Div *222-2*		

Figure 17:   Payroll Journal

PREPARED BY   DATE

. . . . Y E A R L Y   S U M M A R Y . . . .
P A Y R O L L   J O U R N A L

Account Nos. Year ..... Month	501 Managers Salary	512 Clerical Salaries	513 Sales Dep. Salaries	514 Pharmacists Salaries	543 Fed Tax Soc. Sec.	544 Fed. Tax Unemployment	221-1 Taxes Pay. Soc. Sec
			D E B I T S				
January							
February							
March							
Total							
1st Quarter							
April							
May							
June							
Total							
2nd Quarter							
July							
August							
September							
Total							
3rd Quarter							
October							
November							
December							
Total							
4th Quarter							
Yearly							
Totals							

6005 IVORY; 6205 GREEN; 6405 WHITE; 7205 TRANSLUCENT; 7405 CANARY   PRINTED IN U.S.A.   5 GREEN; 6405 WHITE; 7205 TRANSLUCEN

PREPARED BY   DATE   PREPARED BY   DATE

221-3	221-4	221-5	222-3-4	CREDITS			225
CREDITS				Other Credits-Misc. Deductions			Accrued
Taxes Pay. d. W.H.	Taxes Pay. State W.H.	Taxes Pay. City-W. H.	Taxes Pay. Unemployment				Payroll

Figure 18:   Yearly Summary—Payroll Journal

Family employees in drugstores are often the wives, sons, daughters, and other relatives of individual proprietors or partners. For the method of handling this situation, refer to the Treasury Department, Circular E, Employer's Tax Guide, No. 15, p. 16, under listing of Family Employees.

Cost Accounting and Cost of Sales

The accounting system discussed here makes no provision for cost accounting or cost of sales method of costing as all merchandise offered for sale is purchased with the cost predetermined. All individual items are considered a part of the whole and are not costed separately with one exception. Some accountants who use data processing convert to the cost of sales method. The factor often employed is an anticipated fixed percent margin of profit. As sale prices change and volume of sales varies, margins of profit change accordingly. When factors are changed during the year to meet this condition, better costing will result, and the monthly statements will reflect a truer condition.

Time-Saving Ideas

Yearly Summaries. The adoption of the yearly summary system of the various journals is advised in several respects for small and medium-sized stores. The yearly summaries are so designed that only one journal page is required for the year's entries, one line for each month of the year. Little time is required for each month's entries. Double spacing allows blank lines for cumulative totals covering as many periods as desired during the year for posting to the General ledger. Trial balances are taken for the period posting. Some stores may require only one posting for the full year's total. If totals are cumulative, pertinent information for sales, purchases, and expense totals are readily available for the yearly summary journals any month during the year. When the accountant has posted all totals to the various journals, the public accountant can at this point call for the journals for posting to the summary journals. For different periods they may be mailed to him. The public accountant can then make all postings to the General ledger, prepare the General ledger trial balance, and compile balance sheets and profit and loss statements. This method saves a considerable number of accounting hours of preparation with the resultant savings of accountant fees.

Yearly summaries lend themselves to quicker and easier preparation, and the totals of these summaries of the various journals can give sufficient information for the year's business. For a small store operating as a sole proprietorship, this procedure can be the basis of balance sheets and profit and loss statements without resorting to the use of the General ledger.

Accounts Receivable Ledger. Some stores have dispensed with the Accounts Receivable ledger. The recording of customer charges and payments is being done by a computer service company. Their service also includes mailing monthly statements to customers in window envelopes. The list of unpaid accounts furnished by computer at the month end should be in agreement with the Accounts Receivable control account in the General ledger. Charges to owners, partners, and employees should possibly be excluded and charged direct to receivables, under the Employees, Owners, and Partners account (No. 128).

Printers of bank checks are now offering both regular and payroll checks printed in original and duplicate and in loose-leaf or book form. On duplicate copies a coding box is imprinted as a means of simplifying data processing.

When the conventional handwritten Check register is used the account numbers shown in the coding box of the duplicate copy can be posted direct to the appropriate columns in the Check register. This will dispense with all other columns, saving recording time. However the use of this method should have the sanction of management.

Dispensing with the Accounts Receivable ledger, the Accounts Payable journal, and the combination General ledger trial balance will shorten the number of accounting hours required.

Reports to Management

There is always a continuous volume of detailed work to be done in the Accounting Department of a drugstore. This is particularly true at quarterly and year-end periods. At such times the public accountant can render valuable service to the Accounting Department. By closing the books when necessary, preparing balance sheets and profit and loss statements as well as Federal income tax returns, he frees the Accounting Department for routine work including computation of period and year-end inventories.

Paying to owners and partners salaries comparable to those of store managers or other employees for similar services is desired. More realistic operating cost and net operating profit result when this practice is followed. In the year-end balance sheet, salaries so paid will be shown as withdrawals from the business. This does not apply to a corporation which has no owners or partners; corporation employees are considered subject to Social Security and withholding deductions.

Operating statements and other reports that management may require can be compiled from the daily summary journals and from the combination General ledger trial balance.

Stores with a large volume of sales may contemplate switching to data processing accounting. Before coming to any definite decision, a complete analysis of the accounting system for the last few years should be made. The principal factor to be determined is the approximate number of hours involved for a month or any period as a base for comparison. An estimated cost for similar periods should be requested from the processing firm. Regardless of the status quo on future potential, before a change of operation is made, a careful appraisal should take into consideration the cost of the equipment if purchased, operating cost, and results expected.

Pen and ink recording may still be more desirable for small and medium-sized drugstores. It is also less costly from the standpoint of installation and operation and should continue to furnish information helpful to management.

A system tailored to the needs of the business, faithfully followed and adhered to, is the essential requirement. To provide more effective management tools, balance sheet data and financial ratios in these journals have been expanded. Increased interest in the return-on-investment concept has prompted expansion of this area.

Trade journals, to name a few, Drug News Weekly, Drug Topics, American Druggist, and American Professional Pharmacist, are published as a service to the drug profession and are intended to provide an authoritative review of community pharmacy operations. Their objective is to aid the pharmacist-manager in his decision-making function.

The Eli-Lilly Company of Indianapolis provides an annual statistical service dealing with management operations. This service is available to the retail drug trade, and interested members of management will experience little difficulty in selecting a similar-type operation for comparison with their actual data.

Conclusion

Any system in use must be designed to furnish all necessary data for the preparation of Federal and state income, payroll, and sales tax reports.

All transactions in journals and forms in use should be promptly and logically recorded. Then the individual balances in the income, operating, and asset and liability accounts, at the closing of any one period, will insure the correct status of the business at a period closing.

In this respect accounting, management, and government are interrelated and interdependent.

22

Dry Cleaning and Pressing

BY W. K. McCRANEY
Public Accountant, Tyler, Texas

Characteristics of the Business That Affect the Accounting System

A small or medium-sized dry cleaning and pressing business is most often operated or owned individually and is generally run on a cash-and-carry basis. The proprietor does the lion's share of the work with assistance of from one to ten persons.

Services offered to customers restore and renew articles of clothing to usefulness and wearability and thus insure the industry an integral place in textile maintenance.

Among these services are cleaning, pressing, and storage of garments. A dyeing service may be included. Repair, such as sewing on buttons, taking up hems of dresses, etc., may be offered. Delivery to pick up and return clothing to the homes of customers is sometimes employed. Some concerns add a laundry service. Laundering and cleaning may be performed at the business site, or they may be handled on a commission basis for another company.

Pickup stations, sometimes used throughout a city, are placed at convenient locations for the patronage. At least once each day the garments are transported to the main plant for service. Clothing is then returned to the pickup station for delivery to the customer. The stations may be considered as branches of the main plant; thus records must be installed to reflect the accounting controls to the main office.

Storage is usually concerned with garments not needed during a particular season and may include the storage of furs. The small storage fee covers bailee insurance in case of fire, theft, or damage to articles, and miscellaneous perils covered by the policy.

FUNCTIONAL CHARACTERISTICS OF THE BUSINESS

The seasonal nature of the industry has a heavy impact. Spring and fall cleaning creates peak volumes, and the advent of holidays imposes an extra work load upon employees. Easter and Christmas are the two peak holidays. While volume is low in many cities during the summer vacation period, plants receiving resort trade have a corresponding rise in sales volume during those months.

A great many customers ask for "hurry-up" service for special occasions or for holidays. From this customer habit has evolved the "hour service" offered by some cleaners and the popular one-day service.

Competition within the industry is keen with prices fluctuating greatly between quality cleaners and those whose interest is more in quick profit than good service. Special "sales" are sometimes offered as an inducement to attract new customers. However, patronage seems most often to be a matter of habit and convenient location of the dry cleaning site.

Another source of competition is the customer who may perform the services at home, hire a service worker to do it, eliminate the service altogether, or purchase materials that make such service unnecessary. The spectacular betterment of home pressing equipment, the spate of new cleaning fluids and their improved quality, the advent of air conditioning and television which make ironing less onerous, and the rise in the cost of living all tend to encourage the housewife to perform dry cleaning and pressing services herself.

The average establishment operates on the calendar year. Many companies, however, prefer a fiscal year which is more convenient since it can be set arbitrarily not to follow the two frenetic holiday seasons.

PRINCIPAL ACCOUNTING PROBLEMS

One of the major problems of the business is the control of costs. Since payroll comprises over half of each dollar of gross profit, the normal op-portunities to cut costs are lessened. Control of materials and supplies assumes greater importance, particularly waste in their use. Waste should be controlled by keeping supplies in a locked room and issuing them periodi-cally, such as once or twice a week, via a requisition form. Unused supplies should be returned periodically and a credit memorandum issued for them.

A small cleaning and pressing concern does not need a large inventory of supplies. Since purchasing of these materials is limited, the manager usually performs this function. An inventory should be taken at least every six months by actual count. For an expanded business, however, a perpetual inventory system is a good answer to the inventory control question.

The annual depreciation rate is high because of frequent improvements in the equipment; obsolescence is thus more of a factor than replacement of worn-out machines.

The average sale in dry cleaning operations is small, since it ranges from 60¢ to $5.00. Thus the owner-manager is interested in keeping the cost of accounting down to a rock-bottom minimum. A common difficulty exists in finding a unit of physical measurement of production or sale. There is no effective way to compare various pieces, shapes, sizes, or bundles of clothing that come in, either in one concern or between different plants. Therefore, the most satisfactory method is to transform items of cost into percentages of sales. Such a method, however, must be affected by variations in price and the changing value of the dollar itself.

The goodwill of the business is always at stake. Many different methods of cleaning and a variety of materials are used in the process. All garments cannot be cleaned in the same manner or with the same kind of cleaning fluid. Some garments contain caution labels stating the kind of treatment the material needs; others do not have these labels and pose a problem to the cleaner. He must exercise care in achieving results satisfactory to the client, and his personnel must be knowledgeable about the types of fabrics that are to be cleaned. Every garment which goes through the cleaning process in the establishment is a measure of the goodwill the owner or manager strives to build.

Functional Organization

The four definite functions the business must perform are the selling of services, execution of these services, financial management, and reporting and bookkeeping.

In smaller companies these functions are primarily exercised by the owner, who also supervises his employees. Delegation of duties depends largely on growth of the concern and secondarily on the ability of the manager to delegate.

Since this is a service business with no product to sell, the cycle of operations is interesting because production, sales, and accounting take place concurrently, as shown in Figure 1.

Principles and Objectives of the Accounting System

As is true of most businesses, the principal purposes of an accounting system for dry cleaners and pressers is to provide management with accurate, up-to-date, financial records, and reports which help to safeguard the owner's investment in the business. The system should be practical of execution, and the simpler the better. A diversity of books of accounts and numerous detailing are often unnecessary for this particular business.

SPECIFIC OBJECTIVES OF THE SYSTEM

It is desirable that specific information regarding sales, receivables, and collections be reported each week. This is especially important in the case of deliverymen who make daily collections. Each routeman should be required to turn in his cash every day; and at the end of the week he must make

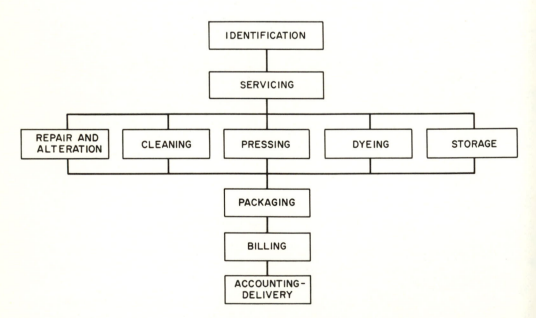

Figure I: Flow Chart

a report of the names of his customers, amount paid, amount due, and cash reported.

Equally as vital are data on total sales. It is desirable to make comparison at any time with the previous week's sales, or with sales of the comparable week for the previous month or year.

Where a concern has charge sales, the method may be used of charging Accounts Receivable with all sales and then crediting the account with the total received. The balance after the cash received has been applied should equal at all times the total of the unpaid customers' tickets on hand. Although the customers may pay cash upon receiving the serviced garments, it is not an immediate cash sale as considered in the purchase of over-the-counter merchandise. The finished work may be called for at the end of the day, after a week, or at some indefinite time.

If a business uses both cash and charge sales, five methods may be employed to control the abstraction of receipts:

(1) Use prenumbered sale slips, central cashier, cash register, daily reconciliation of sales tickets, register tapes, and cash receipts.
(2) Separate the duties of cashier and bookkeeper. Mail receipts should be handled by a special employee and cashier. Reports should be checked against the list of daily cash receipts.
(3) All credit memos and bad debt charge, if required, should have independent approval of management.
(4) Provide accounting control for accounts previously charged off.
(5) Separate bookkeeping and cash handled through the services of a third employee to prepare bank deposits. Receipts would be deposited in full, with a petty cash fund used for paying small items, refunds and general office expenses supported by vouchers.

Classification of Accounts and Books of Accounts

The typical chart of accounts for a cleaning and pressing business would employ the numerical system of classification shown below:

BALANCE SHEET ACCOUNTS.

ASSETS

Current assets

101 Petty Cash
102 Cash Undeposited
103 Cash on Deposit
104 Other Cash
105 Accounts Receivable—Customers
106 Accounts Receivable—Employees
107 Notes Receivables—Short Term
108 Inventories—Supplies

Fixed assets

131 Furniture & Fixtures
    131A Accumulated
         Depreciation
132 Plant Machinery
    132A Accumulated
         Depreciation
133 Autos & Trucks
    133A Accumulated
         Depreciation
134 Buildings
    134A Accumulated
         Depreciation
135 Other Fixed Assets
    135A Accumulated
         Depreciation
136 Land

Investments

141 Stocks & Bonds

Other Assets

151 Deposits
152 Prepaid Expenses

LIABILITIES

Current liabilities

161 Accounts Payables

162 Social Security Taxes
163 Employees Income Taxes
164 State Employment Taxes
165 State Sales Taxes
166 Real & Personal Taxes
167 Other Payables

Long-term Liabilities

181 Notes Payables
182 Mortgages Payables

NET WORTH

Corporate accounts

201 Capital Stock
208 Retained Earnings
215 Profit & Loss—Current

*Sole proprietorship or
   partnership accounts*

201 Capital
    201A Partner A
    201B Partner B
203 Drawing
    203A Partner A
    203B Partner B
215 Profit & Loss—Current

INCOME AND EXPENSE ACCOUNTS.

REVENUE

Service Income

220 Call & Delivery
221 Commissions
222 Other Income

EXPENSES

301 Advertising
302 Auto & Trucks
303 Bad Debt
304 Commissions
305 Donations

306 Dues & Subscriptions
307 Depreciation Expenses
308 Insurance—General
309 Insurance—Compensation
310 Inspections—Boiler
311 Legal & Auditing
312 License & Permits
313 Payroll Taxes
    313A Social Security
    313B Employment Taxes
    313C Real & Personal Taxes
    313D Sales Taxes
    313E Other Taxes

314 Salaries
    314A Clerical Salaries
    314B Plant Labor
    314C Deliveryman Salaries
    314D Other Salaries
315 Telephone & Telegraph
316 Travel

318 Utilities
320 Interest
321 Office Supplies
322 Rent
323 Bank Charges
324 Repairs & Maintenances

BOOKS AND FORMS PECULIAR TO THE BUSINESS

A double-entry system is the best method for accounting because of the self-balancing feature. For most small and medium-sized establishments a combined Cash book and General journal will be sufficient as a book of original entry. This book can be designed with the various columns to meet needs of the particular client. If the business is on the cash basis only, there would be no need for an Accounts Receivable ledger; but if there are charge sales, then this subsidiary ledger is important.

An Accounts Payable ledger should be installed if the invoices are not paid immediately upon receipt of the goods or services and the business operates on the accrual basis. The business should have a Payroll register showing the various wage data needed to prepare the payroll tax forms and year-end summary of wages paid and deductions.

Supporting documents for the entries in the above records would be the daily service ticket (Figure 2), charge sales, and invoices from vendors.

Peculiarities of Procedures

CASH RECEIPTS AND DISBURSEMENTS

Where a cash-and-carry system is followed, the amount of the transaction in the cash account is greater than that of any other account. Thus particular attention is required to cash internal control. Cash is received through the mail, directly over the counter, and from outside salesmen and collectors, and therefore readily lends itself to possible manipulation. Collections by mail should be itemized on a Daily Cash Tally Sheet which will show date, source, and amount:

Daily Mail Collections   Date————————

Customer	Description	Amount

Daily Cash Tally Sheet

Cash received over the counter may be listed on the cash register tape and checked against the sales slip or daily service ticket (Figure 2).

Sales or service slips should be prenumbered and the numbers strictly accounted for.

The Daily Cash Report required at the end of the day is shown in Figure 3.

ACCOUNTS RECEIVABLE

If the business operates extensively on a charge account basis, Accounts Receivable are of prime importance. As the services are rendered, the daily service ticket (Figure 2) should be entered into the Accounts Receivable ledger, manually or by machine. This is to be used for all services. Total balance of this account should agree at the close of the month with the balance of the Accounts Receivable control.

Too much emphasis cannot be placed on constant review of the accounts for delinquencies, and initiation of collection efforts.

Credit is usually limited by time, which in turn will limit the amount of credit extended. Experience with an account also has a bearing on the amount. Unless the establishment has a delivery system, the COD customer

---

BOW STREET CLEANERS

NAME _____

ADDRESS _____

ITEMS	AMOUNT	ITEMS	AMOUNT
COATS	_____	DRESSES	_____
PANTS	_____	SKIRTS	_____
VESTS	_____	WAISTS	_____
OVERCOATS	_____	COATS	_____
JACKETS	_____	SLACKS	_____
SHIRTS	_____	TIES	_____
SWEATERS	_____	HATS & CAPS	_____
RAINCOATS	_____	STORAGE	_____
TICKETS NO I ___		TOTAL CHARGE	$_____

Figure 2. Daily Service Ticket

```
┌────────────────────────────────────────────────────────────┐
│            BOW STREET CLEANERS & DYERS                       │
│        720 WEST BOW STREET-TYLER, TEXAS                      │
│            DAILY CASH REPORT        DATE _____            │
├──────────────────────────────┬───────────────────────────────┤
│        CASH RECEIPTS          │      CASH DISBURSED           │
├──────────────────────────────┼───────────────────────────────┤
│ CASH BROUGHT FORWARD $____    │ BANK DEPOSIT        $____      │
│ TODAY'S CASH RECEIPTS:        │ CASH PAID OUT EXPENSES:        │
│ SERVICE INCOME        ____    │ _____ ____      │
│ OTHER INCOME          ____    │ _____ ____      │
│ OTHER RECEIPTS:               │ _____ ____      │
│ _____     ____    │ _____ ____      │
│ _____     ____    │ _____ ____      │
│ _____     ____    │ _____ ____      │
│ _____     ____    │ _____ ____      │
│ CASH OVER             ____    │ CASH SHORT           ____      │
│                               │ WITHDRAWALS          ____      │
│ TODAY'S CASH TOTAL    ____    │ TOTAL CASH PAID OUT  ____      │
│                               │ CASH ON HAND         ____      │
├──────────────────────────────┼───────────────────────────────┤
│ TOTAL CASH DEBITS  $ ____     │ TOTAL CASH CREDITS $ ____      │
└──────────────────────────────┴───────────────────────────────┘
```

Figure 3: Daily Cash Report

would be eliminated and also the problem of a deliveryman's extending credit without authority. If the customer desires credit, arrangement should be made with management before goods are delivered to the customer. The amount of cash collections should agree with the total amounts of the tickets out for collection.

EXPENSES

If bills are paid promptly, then the cash book and voucher record can be combined into one volume. A summary of the outstanding invoices would be charged to Accounts Payable when paid in a later period. If the accounts are not paid promptly or systematically, then an Accounts Payable entry should be made for invoices when received and another one would be made when they are paid during the same accounting period.

SALES

The proof of sales or service rendered is the daily service ticket (Figure 2). The actual sequence of a service charge begins with the customer or deliveryman bringing in the garments for processing. At this time they are examined for any items left in the pockets, such as pens, pencils, and even money. Identification tickets in pliofilm are attached to the garments; in some instances the name of the owner may be written on the inside of the garment with a special crayon used for that purpose. The identification is really a multiple ticket. One remains with the garment and the other is sent to the Accounting Department. The stub from the ticket, which is prenumbered, should be given to the owner when the garments are received.

A daily or weekly summary of sales is recommended for charging Accounts Receivable with the transactions involved. When the number of transactions is of great volume, it is to the owner's interest to consider buying an accounting machine to control Accounts Receivable. Such a decision would be determined by the owner or manager upon the basis of his experience.

Time and Payroll System

Individual payroll records for each employee should show the usual data. Control over wages paid in cash can be exercised by having the employee sign a payroll receipt which shows gross pay, deductions, and net wages.

Weekly payroll totals should be summarized for posting. The totals may be compiled with the weekly sales data into a combination sales and payroll report which demonstrates at once to management the correlation between the two. A summary of payroll and sales report is illustrated in Figure 4.

SUMMARY OF PAYROLL & SALES   WEEK OF _____

Employee	No. Hours Regular/ Overtime	Hourly Rate	Gross Earned	Deductions S.S. & W.H.	Other	Net

Totals

TOTAL SALES   _____

RATIO   _____

Sales-Year   _____

Payroll-Yr.   _____

RATIO   _____

Figure 4: Summary of Payroll and Sales

STATEMENT OF PROFIT AND LOSS

for period ended May 31, 19___

	Month of May (This Year)	(Last)	Year to Date May 31, 19
RECEIPTS:	$_____	$_____	$_____
Cleaning & Pressing services	_____	_____	_____
Repair	_____	_____	_____
Dyeing	_____	_____	_____
Storage	_____	_____	_____
Other Receipts	_____	_____	_____
TOTAL RECEIPTS	$_____	$_____	$_____
Deduct Expenses:			
Code 300 - 400	_____	_____	_____
Total Operating Expense	$_____	$_____	$_____
ADD NONOPERATING INCOME	_____	_____	_____
Less Nonoperating Expense	_____	_____	_____
NET PROFIT	$_____	$_____	$_____

Figure 5: Statement of Profit and Loss

BALANCE SHEET
ENDED DECEMBER 31, 19__

ASSETS		LIABILITIES AND CAPITAL	
Current Assets:		Current Liabilities:	
Cash on Hand & Deposit	$_____	Accounts Payables	$_____
Accounts Receivable	_____	Notes Payable	_____
Inventories	_____	Payroll Taxes Pay.	_____
Other Assets	_____	Other Payables	_____
Total Current Assets	_____	Total Current Liab.	_____
Fixed Assets		Long Term Liabilities	
Depreciable Assets	_____	Mortgages	_____
Less Depreciation	_____	Notes	_____
Land	_____	Total Long Term Lia.	_____
Total Fixed Assets	_____		
Investments:			
Stocks and Bonds	_____		
Other	_____		
Total Investments	_____		
Other Assets		Net Worth	
Deposits	_____	Capital	_____
Prepaid Expense	_____		
Total Other Assets	_____		
Total Assets	$_____	Total Liabilities	$_____

Figure 6: Balance Sheet

Time-Saving Ideas

The prenumbered sales and storage ticket (Figure 2) covers both regular service and storage, so that an extra form is thus eliminated.

Reports to Management

The major function of internal control is to furnish management with essential reports on which sound business judgment can be made. In addition to reports previously discussed, a monthly profit and loss statement (Figure 5) is necessary as well as the annual statement.

A balance sheet should be furnished as often as desired and always at the close of the calendar or fiscal year (Figure 6). Expenses may be shown in detail.

23

Employment Agencies

BY EZRA E. STEVENS

Public Accountant, San Mateo,
California; State Treasurer, Cali-
fornia Employment Agencies
Association

Characteristics of the Business That Affect the Accounting System

Employment agencies are service organizations furnishing personnel placement services to business on two bases: employer-paid fee (EPF) and appli-
cant-paid fee (APF). Personnel of employment agencies act as consultants
on employment problems, both to large and small businesses. When the
agency works on a specific contract basis, it is known as an executive search
firm. The discussion in this chapter refers to permanent placement services
as opposed to services providing temporary help.

FUNCTIONAL CHARACTERISTICS OF THE BUSINESS

Ordinarily an employment agency operates on a calendar-year basis, since
November and December are generally the slow months. Some summer
months are also somewhat slow. This fact may move an agency to adopt a
fiscal year ending on June 30.

Competition among agencies is acute. In addition, private employment agencies must compete with the United States Employment Service and with state-subsidized Departments of Employment which may perform functions other than personnel consulting.

PRINCIPAL ACCOUNTING PROBLEMS

The accounting organization should provide for analysis of EPF/APF, male/female, and permanent/temporary placements. Agencies which have more than one consultant must break down receipts by each consultant to satisfy commission payment requirements and to ascertain results obtained by each person.

Functional Organization

A large agency may be organized in the manner illustrated by Figure 1. Where the agency is corporate in structure the chart should reflect the operations executive, either the president or vice president, with the other officers holding staff positions along with the board of directors.

Smaller agencies may use one person to direct the Female and Male Departments. There are many owner-operated (one-desk) agencies which handle all categories of placements. Necessarily the accounting for each type would be adjusted, in detail only to personal requirements.

Principles and Objectives of the Accounting System

The accounting system should reflect income by placement categories. In many states quarterly reports (Figure 2) must be submitted to the Labor Department regarding number and amount of placements as well as dollar amount by types of business, male/female, and permanent/temporary.

EMPLOYMENT AGENCY QUARTERLY REPORT

INSTRUCTIONS

Every employment agency must file with the Labor Commissioner a quarterly report of placements made and fees collected, using the form on the reverse side.

The report must be filed on or before the 10th day of the month following the end of the quarter for which the report is made.

A report must be filed for each quarter. If no placements have been made or fees collected, submit a report stating "No placements" or "No fees collected," or both.

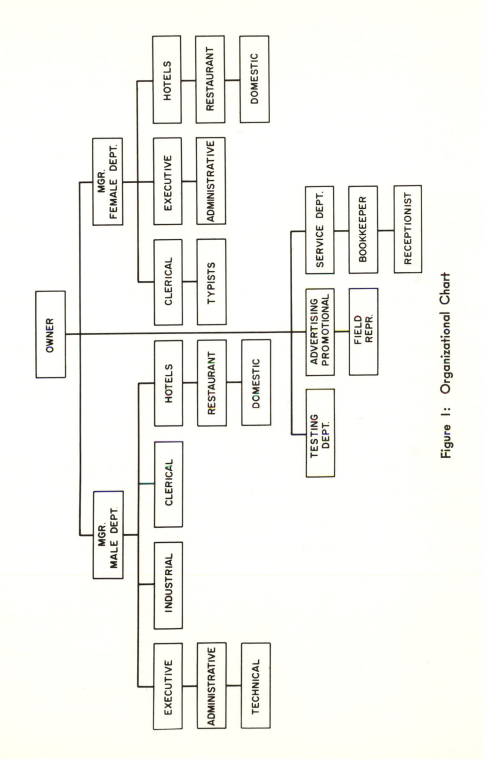

Figure I: Organizational Chart

SIGMUND ARYWITZ
State Labor Commissioner

State of California
Department of Industrial Relations
DIVISION OF LABOR LAW ENFORCEMENT
455 Golden Gate Ave., San Francisco

Mailing Address:
P.O. Box 603
San Francisco, Calif. 94101

EMPLOYMENT AGENCY QUARTERLY REPORT

(*Check appropriate date*)   For the 19____   Quarter ended March 31 □   June 30 □   September 30 □   December 31 □

Agency..   City............................   License No............................

Street............................   Contract Receipts used: No............ through............

(*See Reverse Side for Instructions*)

FEES PAID BY APPLICANT

FIELD OF EMPLOYMENT	Temporary (jobs lasting 90 days or less)				Permanent (jobs lasting more than 90 days)			
	MEN		WOMEN		MEN		WOMEN	
	PLACEMENTS MADE	FEES COLLECTED (*Omit cents*)	PLACEMENTS MADE	FEES COLLECTED (*Omit cents*)	PLACEMENTS MADE	FEES COLLECTED (*Omit cents*)	PLACEMENTS MADE	FEES COLLECTED (*Omit cents*)
1. Commercial		$		$		$		$
2. Baby sitters								
3. Domestic								
4. Hotel and restaurant								
5. Nurses and medical (Other than private duty)								
6. Teachers								
7. Technical								
8. Miscellaneous								
TOTAL								

FEES PAID BY EMPLOYER

	$	$	$	$
1. Commercial				
2. Baby sitters				
3. Domestic				
4. Hotel and restaurant				
5. Nurses and medical. (Other than private duty)				
6. Teachers				
7. Technical				
8. Miscellaneous				
TOTAL				

I hereby certify the above to be a correct statement of the business of this agency for

the quarter ended .... *19*.....   Dated .... 19.....   [SIGNED] ....

Figure 2. State Quarterly Report

Please note that the report has two sections, one for placements on which the fee is paid or to be paid by the applicant, and one for those on which the fee is paid or to be paid by the employer. It is important that the placements made and fees collected be reported in the proper section, according to the source of the fee.

Entries should be made in the various columns as follows:

FIELD OF EMPLOYMENT: Classify placements made and fees collected by field of employment, according to the following definitions:

1. **Commercial**—includes office, sales, advertising employees and kindred workers.
2. **Baby sitting**—includes and is limited to care of children in private homes, without accompanying domestic duties.
3. **Domestic**—includes domestic and personal servants and day workers in homes, except "baby sitters."
4. **Hotel and restaurant**—includes workers in hotels, bars, restaurants, bakeries, and lunch counters, and kindred workers, not including office employees.
5. **Nursing and medical**—includes practical, vocational and graduate nurses, office nurses, doctors, and other medically trained persons, including laboratory technicians. (Does NOT include private duty nurses.)
6. **Teaching**—includes public and private school teachers in all grades.
7. **Technical**—includes laboratory technicians (other than medically trained) engineers, lawyers, architects, and professional workers generally other than medical.
8. **Miscellaneous**—includes factory workers, laundry workers, garage and service station workers, beauty operators, models, and all others not included in any of the above classifications.

PLACEMENTS MADE: Include only placements made during the quarter for which you are reporting, and for which fees were collected or are to be collected. Do NOT include placements for which fees were refunded.

FEES COLLECTED: Include all fees collected during the quarter for which you are reporting, regardless of when the placements were made. Do NOT include fees which were refunded.

Generally it is best to have direct costs and expenses accounted for in total by departments (men and women). An overhead factor can be allocated to the Men's and Women's Departments on an average basis for analysis purposes.

SPECIFIC OBJECTIVES OF THE SYSTEM

Specifically the accounting system should be designed to produce practical statements that management can use as tools in making decisions in such varied areas as advertising promotion, the number of personnel to be in the work force, material, telephone effects, job solicitation, and field contact work by outside personnel. Ideally it should be on an accrual basis to reflect profit more correctly.

Classification of Accounts and Books of Accounts

The breakdowns here should be meaningful for management purposes as well as for preparation of tax returns. The chart of accounts shown below reflects a medium-size operation.

BALANCE SHEET ACCOUNTS.

ASSETS

Current assets

101 Cash in the Banks—
    General Funds
102 Cash in the Banks—
    Trust Accounts or Savings
104 Cash in the Banks—
    Petty Cash
105 Accounts Receivable—
    Trade, etc.
107 Accounts Receivable—
    Returned Checks
108 Accounts Receivable—Others
110 Loans Receivable
112 Loans Receivable—Officers
113 Loans Receivable—Employees
115 Notes Receivable

Properties and fixed assets

135 Office Furniture and Fixtures
    99-135 Accumulated
           Depreciation
140 Auto Equipment
    99-140 Accumulated
           Depreciation
143 Leasehold Improvements

Other assets

170 Investments—Goodwill
180 Security Deposits—Rent
181 Security Deposits—Utilities
185 Security Deposits—
    Miscellaneous

Prepaid and deferred expenses

190 Prepaid Interest
191 Prepaid Insurance
    1-191 General
    2-191 Employees' Groups
192 Prepaid Taxes—Property
193 Prepaid License
195 Prepaid Miscellaneous
196 Prepaid Organizational
    Expenses
197 Clearing Account

LIABILITIES

Current liabilities

202 Accounts Payable—Trade
205 Contracts Payable
    1-205 Office Equipment
    2-205 Auto
206 Loans Payable—Officer
207 Loans Payable—Open
210 Notes Payable
    1-210 Banks
    4-210 Officers
    5-210 Others
211 Payroll Taxes Withheld—
    Federal Income
212 Payroll Taxes Withheld—FICA
213 Payroll Taxes Withheld State D/I
215 Accrued Payroll Taxes—FICA
    (Employers Share)
216 Accrued Payroll Taxes—
    State D/I

217 Accrued Payroll Taxes—
 Federal U/E
224 Accrued Miscellaneous Taxes
230 Accrued Payroll
 1-230 Wages
 2-230 Bonus—Commissions

231 Accrued Compensation Insurance

STOCKHOLDERS' EQUITY

251 Capital Stock Issued—Common
255 Treasury Stock
280 Retained Earnings—
 Current Operating

INCOME AND EXPENSE ACCOUNTS.

INCOME

301 Placement Fees
 1-301 Men's—Permanent
 2-301 Women's—Permanent
 3-301 Men's—Temporary
 4-301 Women's—Temporary
302 Labor Contracts
315 Commissions
317 Gain or Loss on Disposal of
 Capital Assets
318 Gain or Loss on Sale of
 Equipment
319 Miscellaneous Other Income

EXPENSES

Direct expenses

351 Commissions
352 Payroll Taxes
353 Employees' Benefits
355 Telephone
356 Advertising

Indirect and overhead expenses

402 Wages

1-402 Agency
2-402 Labor Contract
403 Payroll Taxes
404 Employees Benefits
408 Office Supplies—Postage,
 Stationery, Printing, etc.
409 Dues and Publications
410 Utilities
412 Rent
413 Repairs and Maintenance
420 Business Promotion
421 Auto Expense
422 Travel Expense
430 Professional Fees
432 Collection Expenses
435 License
441 Property Taxes
442 Interest Costs
444 Insurance Costs
445 State Franchise Tax
447 Loss on Bad Debts
448 Depreciation and Amortization
449 Miscellaneous

BOOKS AND FORMS PECULIAR TO THE BUSINESS

The books of account include the normal Cash Receipts (Figure 3), Cash Disbursements (Figure 4), and Placement Sales (Figure 5) records plus the General ledger. If books are kept on an accrual basis, a Voucher Register (Figure 6) chould be maintained.

Special quarterly and yearly reports are required by some state Labor Departments. Figure 2 provides data required by the State of California and could be altered easily to conform to requirements in other states.

RECORD OF CASH RECEIVED MONTH OF 19 NO.

WILMER * SERVICE LINE STANDARD CASH RECEIVED FORM 182A

Deposit	Net Amount Received	Day	Received From	Accts Receiv'le	√		√		√	General Ledger-Cr. Acct.	General Ledger-Cr. Amount	√
			AMOUNTS FORWARDED									

* Courtesy of the Wilmer Service Line, North Hollywood, California.

Figure 3: Cash Receipts Journal Page

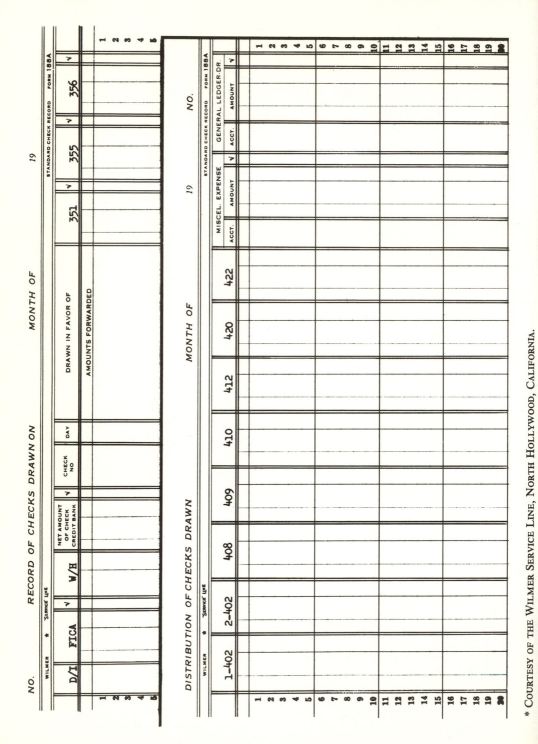

PLACEMENT SALES JOURNAL

Date	Applicant Placed	Contr. No.	Coun-selor No.	Temp. Perm.	Amount of Fee			
					A.P.F.		E.P.F.	
					Male	Female	Male	Female
1/2	Ted Smith	106	1	P	165.00			
1/2	James Herb	108	1	P			185.00	
1/2	Theda King	109	2	T				32.60

* COURTESY OF THE WILMER SERVICE LINE, NORTH HOLLYWOOD, CALIFORNIA.

Figure 5: Placement Sales Journal

NO.   RECORD OF Vouchers Payable   MONTH OF   19

STANDARD CHECK RECORD   FORM 188A

WILMER * SERVICE LINE

			CHECK NO	DAY	DRAWN IN FAVOR OF	355	356	408

AMOUNTS FORWARDED

DISTRIBUTION OF Vouchers   MONTH OF   19   NO.

STANDARD CHECK RECORD   FORM 188A

WILMER * SERVICE LINE

409	410	413	420	421	422	430	432	MISCEL. EXPENSE		GENERAL LEDGER-DR		
								ACCT	AMOUNT	ACCT	AMOUNT	

* COURTESY OF THE WILMER SERVICE LINE, NORTH HOLLYWOOD, CALIFORNIA.

Peculiarities of Procedures

Computation of fees of applicants placed is usually based on a fee schedule approved by the state Labor Department. Figure 7 shows a sample fee schedule with its explanations and restrictions. Fees, as noted, may be computed on a monthly or annual basis. Temporary fees are also computed on a separate basis.

Time and Payroll System

Ordinarily the work force may include both standard-salaried and commission employees. Records must, therefore, include information that enables the owner to compute commissions periodically. A Payroll Journal Form is shown as Figure 8.

Cost and Departmental Accounting

Departmental accounting may be desired to differentiate between the Men's and Women's Departments. Placements would then be allocated between these departments. Other such direct cost allocations would include Wages, Commissions, Payroll Taxes, and other employment costs; Telephone, Advertising, and any other expenses subject to direct allocation. Indirect and overhead expenses generally should be apportioned on a space-occupied basis.

Reports to Management

FINANCIAL REPORTS

Prepared periodically, the financial reports needed are a profit and loss statement, a statement of assets and liabilities, and a statement of source of funds and their application.

Profit and Loss Statement. The profit and loss statement may be computed by month or by quarter as desired by management. Ordinarily a monthly submission of this report is preferable and on an accrual basis for correct reflection of profits or losses for proper guidance of management. Results of operation for the current period and year to date, compared with the previous year's results for the same period, are shown in Figure 9. The statement is arranged to reflect direct and indirect expenses peculiar to the employment agency industry. It may be management's choice to have the statement detailed by departments (Men's & Women's) with a summary profit and loss statement attached.

JOHN DOE PLACEMENT AGENCY INC.

PERMANENT PLACEMENT FEES

SALARIES UNDER $600.00 PER MONTH

35% OF 1ST MONTH'S SALARY – PAYABLE IN 30 DAYS
        5% DISCOUNT IF PAID WITHIN 5 DAYS
40% OF 1ST MONTH'S SALARY – IF PAID AFTER 30 DAYS

SALARIES $7,200.00 TO $9,999.00 PER ANNUM

5% OF ANNUAL SALARY – PAYABLE IN 30 DAYS
        10% DISCOUNT IF PAID WITHIN 5 DAYS
7% OF ANNUAL SALARY – IF PAID AFTER 30 DAYS

SALARIES $10,000.00 AND OVER PER ANNUM

10% OF ANNUAL SALARY – PAYABLE IN 30 DAYS
        10% DISCOUNT IF PAID WITHIN 5 DAYS

TEMPORARY PLACEMENT FEES
(LASTING 90 DAYS OR LESS)

10% OF TOTAL GROSS EARNINGS RECEIVED IN PERIOD NOT TO EXCEED
        90 DAYS, TO BE PAID AS WAGES ARE RECEIVED. TOTAL TEMPORARY
        FEE SHALL NOT EXCEED CORRESPONDING PERMANENT FEE.

"IF THE APPLICANT PAYING A CASH FEE FAILS TO OBTAIN EMPLOYMENT
THE EMPLOYMENT AGENCY SHALL, UPON DEMAND THEREFOR, REPAY THE
AMOUNT OF THE FEE TO THE APPLICANT. UNLESS THE FEE IS RETURNED
WITHIN 48 HOURS AFTER DEMAND, THE EMPLOYMENT AGENCY SHALL PAY
TO THE APPLICANT AN ADDITIONAL SUM EQUAL TO THE AMOUNT OF THE FEE".

(SECTION 1643, CALIFORNIA LABOR CODE.)

Figure 7: Fee Schedule

PAYROLL JOURNAL

Date	Total Placement Fees	Basic Amount	Bonus Amt.	Total Commission	D/I	FICA	W/H	Net Pay	Check No.
1/15	1,800.00	1,500.00	300.00	750.00	7.50				

Figure 8: Payroll Journal

JOHN DOE PLACEMENT AGENCY, INC.
COMPARATIVE STATEMENT OF INCOME AND EXPENSE
For March and the 3 Months Ended Mar. 31, 19 & 19

	March 19	3 Months to March 31, 19	19
Income			
Placement Fees – Permanent	8,206.10	22,004.25	19,985.15
– Temporary	560.70	1,210.16	951.62
Total Income	8,766.80	23,214.41	20,936.77
Direct Costs			
Commissions	3,252.65	10,684.24	9,560.82
Payroll Taxes	65.62	254.06	225.62
Employees Benefits	162.50	474.51	435.69
Telephone	286.77	665.78	670.81
Advertising	968.66	2,244.23	2,168.19
Total Direct Costs	4,736.20	14,322.82	13,061.13
Gross Margin	4,030.60	8,891.59	7,875.64
Indirect & Overhead Costs			
Wages	650.00	1,950.00	1,650.00
Payroll Taxes	-	58.50	47.60
Stationery, Printing Office Supplies	365.81	804.42	782.10
Dues and Subscriptions	100.00	343.00	343.00
Rent	400.00	1,200.00	1,200.00
Entertainment & Business Promotion	95.60	304.92	284.60
Auto Expense	-	20.00	121.58
Travel & Meeting Expense	180.06	250.39	225.80
Professional Fees	25.00	75.00	75.00
License	-	175.00	175.00
Insurance	-	25.00	25.00
Corporation Franchise Tax	100.00	100.00	100.00
Miscellaneous	1.07	2.52	4.49
Total Indirect & Overhead Costs	1,917.54	5,308.75	5,034.17
Net Profit Before Depreciation	2,113.06	3,582.84	2,841.47

Figure 9: Comparative Statement of Income and Expenses

JOHN DOE PLACEMENT AGENCY, INC.
STATEMENT OF ASSETS AND LIABILITIES
As of December 31, 19___ & 19___

	19	19	Increase (Decrease)
ASSETS			
Current Assets			
Cash on Hand & In Banks	3,698.52	2,567.14	1,131.38
Accounts Receivable	12,260.69	10,130.82	2,129.87
Loans Receivable - Employees	750.00	1,050.00	(300.00)
Prepaid Expenses	269.28	212.67	56.61
Total Current Assets	16,978.49	13,960.63	3,017.86
Property and Fixed Assets			
Furniture and Fixtures	8,265.43	8,265.43	
Auto Equipment	8,750.00	8,750.00	
Leasehold Improvements	1,865.70	1,865.70	
	18,881.13	18,881.13	-
Less: Accumulated Depreciation & Amortization	1,162.65	132.80	1,029.85
Total Fixed Assets	17,718.48	18,748.33	(1,029.85)
Other Assets			
Good Will	10,000.00	10,000.00	-
Security Deposits	350.00	350.00	-
Total Assets	45,046.97	43,058.96	1,988.01
LIABILITIES			
Current Liabilities			
Accounts Payable	1,216.74	911.47	305.27
Loans Payable - Officers	2,500.00	5,000.00	(2,500.00)
Payroll Taxes Withheld	314.16	284.15	30.01
Accrued Taxes	165.18	131.72	33.46
Accrued Wages & Commissions	714.28	562.90	151.38
Total Current Liabilities	4,910.36	6,890.24	(1,979.88)
STOCKHOLDERS EQUITY			
Authorized Capital Stock - 25,000 Shares $1.00 Par Value, all issued	25,000.00	25,000.00	-
Accumulated Earnings	15,136.61	11,168.72	3,967.89
Total Stockholders Equity	40,136.61	36,168.72	3,967.89
Total Liabilities & Stockholders Equity	45,046.97	43,058.96	1,988.01

Figure 10: Statement of Assets and Liabilities

PLACEMENTS BY COUNSELORS
For the Month of _____

Applicant Placed	M or F	Amt. of Fee	Refund (if any)	Remarks
John Jones				
(1)(counselor)				
Ted Smith	M	185.00		
James Herb	M		—	
(1)(counselor)				
Ray Cormick	M			
(1) List counselors alphabetically				
Total no. of applicants placed and total fees by each counselor				

Figure 11: Placements by Counselors

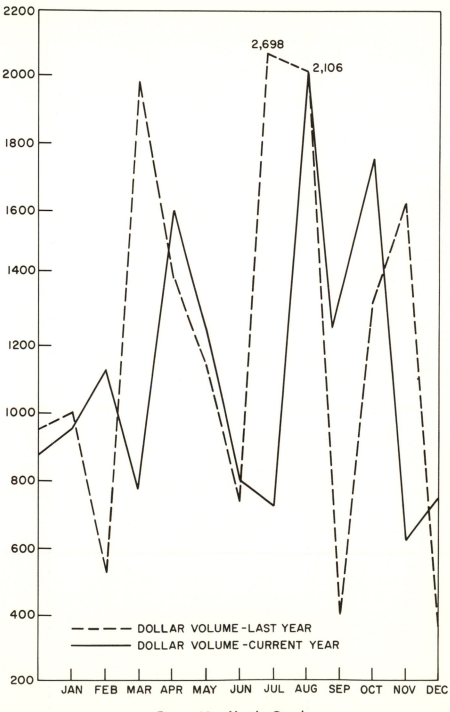

Figure 12: Yearly Graph

Statement of Assets and Liabilities. Figure 10 reflects the assets and liabilities in comparison form between the current year and the previous year. An additional breakdown to show the increase and decrease of each item is often helpful.

STATISTICAL REPORTS

Placement by Counselors. The form shown in Figure 11 is prepared to reflect placements by counselor, by men and women, and by fees billed, plus refunds required and a column for remarks. The Refund column is indicative of client satisfaction with services received.

Summary Placement Report. This report is prepared on a quarterly basis to indicate the placements made and the fees collected by men and women, and by category (commercial, industrial, hotels, restaurants, domestic, etc.). Data in this report are the basis for compilation of summary reports for governmental bodies (Figure 2).

Monthly and Annual Graph Charts. Another helpful reporting tool is a monthly graph chart showing the number of applicants compared with the number of placements actually made. To a limited extent the chart indicates a counselor's ability to place applicants as well as the effectiveness of advertising in bringing in applicants. A yearly graph (Figure 12) is a dramatic illustration of seasonal trends of the agency industry and indicates to management the degree of effort expended over a year's activities.

24

Engineers

BY GEORGE KERASIDIS

Controller, Transportation Consultants, Inc., Washington, D.C.

Characteristics of the Profession That Affect the Accounting System

Engineering is the applied science which is concerned for the benefit of mankind with the economical utilization of matter, sources of power in nature, and physical forces. Persons who have gained knowledge of this science through study and practice build bridges, roads, skyscrapers, ships, planes, dams, and a myriad of structures necessary to our technology.

Many engineers, especially beginners, do not give enough time or attention to financial matters. Rather they concentrate on their professional problems, which they understand better and can cope with more easily. The accountant must assist management in formulating policies and in making plans for carrying them out. He must help management in planning control and coordination of operation, and it goes without saying that he installs and main-

473

tains all accounting records and procedures necessary for conduct and protection of the business.

The important role that financial matters play in engineering firms is being recognized by educational institutions, and courses such as accounting and economics are being added to the curriculum of the engineering student.

All this underlines the need for a qualified accountant and the application of a sound system for an engineering firm.

FUNCTIONAL CHARACTERISTICS OF THE PROFESSION

The profession of engineering, as is true with other professions, has been practiced under personal responsibility. Further, laws in some of the states prohibit the business operation of engineering in a corporate form.

Modern technological requirements and general business evolution demand that the engineer no longer be limited to a restricted field but utilize a multitude of skills and specialized talents with the necessary supporting personnel to meet successfully the needs of multimillion-dollar projects. The corporation offers an engineering firm almost unlimited possibilities for growth.

Advantage of the perpetual succession or continuous life in corporate form accrues to the engineering firm as well as to any other business. However, before the young engineer decides to practice his profession under corporate procedure, he should make certain that this practice is allowed by the laws of the state in which he intends to establish his office.

Decision as to whether the accounting system will be cash or accrual depends primarily on two factors. A cash basis will be sufficient for the one-man office or in general for the small operation. It may, however, tend to distort the real financial position of the enterprise, since income is recognized only after it is received and expense only after it is paid out. The accrual basis accounting system will offer a more accurate picture of the firm's finances, but it may not be as flexible.

The second factor to consider is the advantages and disadvantages of each system in reference to income taxes. The cash basis offers the possibility of accelerating expenses and delaying receipts by holding onto invoices to clients. In a small organization where the owner may also have outside income, this may at times be highly desirable. Under the cash basis, worksheet adjustments—made on financial statements to reflect the Accounts Receivable and the Accounts Payable—will offer a statement that will reflect the financial position more correctly.

Engineering practice does not face a cyclical peak as such, though adverse winter weather may somewhat slow business activities. The calendar year, therefore, is most adaptable for accounting purposes and is most widely in use by engineers.

Functional Organization

In the small organization there usually are no departments. The firm may be so specialized that it acts as one department; or it may be so small that the same engineers will be used in more than one field.

Departments will be found in larger operations where the company offers services in more than one area. Each supervised by a director, such departments would include the following: Architecture, Civil and Sanitary Engineering, Mechanical Engineering and Power, Electrical Engineering, Planning, Administration, and Finance. The latter two might be combined in one section under direction of the treasurer.

Depending on the organizational form of the company, department heads may be the partners-owners of the business; or in the smaller corporation they may be members of the board of directors. The latter is not necessarily the rule. Corporations may operate under the aegis of a very small board of directors.

It is a good practice that all directors are engineers with the possible exception of the treasurer. It is equally good and wise for the treasurer to have formal education and experience in finance. If there is no engineer-director available with these qualifications, then a non-engineer but qualified finance man would be installed as treasurer, regardless of whether he is a member of the board.

Principles and Objectives of the Accounting System

The objective of the system is to record adequately all costs and income to assist management in negotiating a contract, in controlling costs during the project time, in billing the client, and in collecting the fees. It is evident that a detailed cost system is necessary.

Classification of Accounts and Books of Accounts

In setting up the chart an attempt was made to arrange the accounts to allow for flexibility and change or expansion as individual needs would require. The accounts are grouped in the usual manner. Data and figures to be recorded in the ledger accounts come from payroll records, Cash Receipts and Cash Disbursements journals, as later discussed.

BALANCE SHEET ACCOUNTS.

ASSETS

Current assets

Cash accounts

110 01 Cash—Bank No. 1
110 02 Cash—Bank No. 2
110 03 Cash—Bank No. 3
110 04 Cash—Bank No. 4
111 01 Petty Cash—Home Office

Accounts receivable

121 01 Accounts Receivable—
        Employees
122 99 Accounts Receivable—
        Others
211 01 Notes Receivable

Investments

291 01 U.S. Government
        Securities
291 02 Other Bonds and Securities

Fixed assets

311 01 Real Estate Property—
        Office Building
311 11 Furniture and Equipment
311 12 Allowance for Depreciation
        of Furniture and Equipment
311 13 Vehicles
311 14 Allowance for Depreciation
        of Vehicles

Other assets

411 01 Deposits—Airline Credit
        Account

411 02 Deposits—Utilities
419 98 Payroll Clearing
419 99 Suspense

LIABILITIES

Current liabilities

511 01 Taxes Payable—Federal
        Withholding
511 02 Taxes Payable—FICA
511 03 Taxes Payable—State
        Withholding
511 11 Federal Income Tax Payable
512 01 Notes Payable

Long-term liabilities

531 01 Mortgage Payable—Office
        Building

NET WORTH

Partnership

611 01 Capital, Partner A
611 02 Capital, Partner B
611 03 Capital, Partner C
621 01 Drawings, Partner A
621 02 Drawings, Partner B
621 03 Drawings, Partner C

Individual proprietorship

611 01 Capital
611 02 Drawings

Corporation

611 01 Capital Stock—Common
611 02 Capital Stock—Preferred
611 03 Retained Earnings

INCOME AND EXPENSE ACCOUNTS.

INCOME

711 01 Operating Income

719 01 Nonoperating Income

EXPENSES

Indirect

811 01 Administrative Home
        Office Salaries

811 02 Administrative Overtime Salaries
811 03 Administrative Field Salaries
811 04 Administrative Vacation Salaries
811 05 Administrative Sick Leave Salaries
811 08 Contractual Labor
812 01 Taxes—Automobile Tags
812 02 Taxes—State Filing Fee and License
812 03 Taxes—Personal Property
812 04 Taxes—Federal Unemployment
812 05 Taxes—State Unemployment
812 07 Taxes—FICA
812 08 Provision for U.S. Corporation Income Tax
812 09 State Corporation Income Tax
812 10 Real Estate Taxes
812 99 Taxes—Miscellaneous
813 01 Rent
813 02 Communications
813 03 Postage and Expenses
813 04 Office Supplies and Expenses
813 05 Proposal Costs
813 06 Insurance
813 07 Dues, Publications, and Subscriptions
813 08 Interest
813 09 Repairs and Maintenance
813 10 Printing and Reproduction Costs
813 11 Depreciation
813 12 Contributions
813 13 Penalties and Fines
813 14 Vehicle Operation
813 15 Bank Charges
813 16 Job Development
813 17 Contributions to Employees' Profit Sharing Plan
813 18 Bonus
813 19 Travel Expenses
813 20 Equipment Rental
813 21 Consultants' Fees
813 22 Accounting and Legal Fees
813 50 Loss on Sale and Abandonment of Equipment
813 90 Applied Overhead
813 99 Miscellaneous

Direct costs

911 00 Project ABC
911 01 Salaries—Field
911 02 Salaries—Travel
911 03 Salaries—Vacation
911 04 Salaries—Home Office
911 05 Overseas Differential
911 06 Transportation—Personnel
911 07 Transportation—Air Freight —Personal Effects
911 08 Transportation—Surface Shipments—Personal Effects
911 09 Transportation—Household Effects
911 10 Subsistence—Travel per Diem
911 11 Equipment, Materials, and Supplies
911 12 Miscellaneous Expense
911 13 Insurance Premiums
911 14 Other Direct Costs
911 50 Overhead

BOOKS AND FORMS PECULIAR TO THE PROFESSION

Cash Disbursements Journal. As outlined in the chart of accounts, the journal is set up to give adequate information on the direct accounts as well as the indirect accounts, by project and category of expense.

Cash Receipts Journal. This journal, too, is set up to provide information on the source and nature of income.

The Cash Receipts and General journals do not differ from those of any other business. Other books required include the Payroll journal and the General ledger, plus a record of precontract costs. In this journal would be set down the date of the invitation for a proposal, the name of the subject work, plus actual out-of-pocket expenses and payroll expense incurred in preparation of the proposal.

The Precontract Costs journal is kept independently of the accounting books. The purpose it serves is to offer means for measurement of these costs and, where feasible, the journal provides an easy way to transfer these costs to the direct costs and receive reimbursement from the client should the latter agree to it.

Peculiarities of Procedures

The ensuing procedure followed in a general form should be helpful and will offer data that management needs to arrive at intelligent decisions.

A contract is awarded after a proposal is submitted to the client. The proposal has been prepared on the basis of an estimate which includes all direct costs such as labor, transportation, supplies, communications, etc., as well as a portion of the indirect accounts (overhead) and the fee. The overhead and the fee will be discussed later.

The proposal's estimate of cost becomes a budget for the contract; close control of project expenses, as compared with the budget, is required for profitable completion of the work. Of course, accuracy in estimating is of prime importance.

At the end of the month the direct costs of each contract are transferred to a Job Cost Control Report (Figure 1).

Columns 1, 2, and 3 indicate the date, the description, and the check number issued for the disbursement or the number of the journal entry if a charge originates from the General journal. Column 4 is used for the amount of the disbursements for the charge. The total of disbursements for the account is extended to column 5.

Column 6 is the total of all charges to the account to date, that is, including charges for the current month. Column 7 is used for the budget figure. The difference between what was expended to date and what was budgeted (column 7 minus column 6) is inserted in column 8 and indicates if funds are still available for the account.

In the case of two or more subaccounts, this procedure is repeated, and then the totals of the subaccounts of columns 5, 6, 7, and 8 are extended to columns 9 through 12.

An example of control accounts and subaccounts is salaries and wages broken down to subaccounts such as Field, Travel, or Home Office Salaries. Where there are no subaccounts, for instance, Insurance Premiums, the totals of columns 5 through 8 are repeated in columns 9 through 12.

Grand totals are obtained for the last four columns, and these totals indicate expenditures during the current month, the total of indirect costs of the contract to date and in comparison with the budget, the amount of funds still available for completion of the project.

This Job Cost Control Report (Figure 1) gives to management the direct costs of each project as well as the basis for invoices to the client in the case of cost-plus-fixed-fee contracts.

The importance of the budget cannot be overemphasized. However, the budget, and in general the Job Cost Control Report, are not sufficient. The latter indicates what has been expended and the unexpended balance, but it does not show whether direct costs follow the same trend as the progress of work.

The engineer in charge of the project prepares a Progress of Completion Report at the end of each month to indicate the percentage of completion of the project. This percentage then is compared with the percentage of the Expended To Date amount. This is the ratio of the Expended To Date figure to the budget figure.

Another method of presenting this information is by the use of graphs (Figure 2).

The engineer in charge prepares the budget for the project. Then he compiles a graph for each account and a graph for the overall budget of the entire project. The budget is indicated on the graph as he expects it to be used. At the end of each month the amount that appears under the heading, Expended To Date, on the Job Cost Control Report is also plotted on this graph. The graph then illustrates in dollar amounts the relationship of the progress of completion to the expended funds.

Another method, very satisfactory to engineers, is the graph that shows a curve for the budget and a curve for the work to be completed. The abscissa (Y axis) is calibrated for 100 percent and the ordinate (X axis) for time, in months (Figure 3).

At the end of each month the percentage of completion is plotted as is the percentage of Expended To Date of the Job Cost Control Report. Thus in one glance the progress of the job can be seen both in terms of completion and costs. This graph is to be used only for the overall project and not for each individual account.

JOB COST CONTROL REPORT

PROJECT_____ROUTE 2 (OVERPASS)_____

CONTRACT NO.____BPR 29-45-367_____

CONTRACT DATE____7 SEPTEMBER 19__

DATE	DESCRIPTION	CHECK NO.	DAILY EXPENDITURES	DETAIL TOTAL FOR MONTH	EXPENDED TO DATE	BUDGET	
(1)	(2)	(3)	(4)	(5)	(6)	(7)	
FIELD SALARIES							
31 MARCH	JOE DOE	3,101	500.00				
31 MARCH	JOHN BROWN	3,102	750.00	1,250.00	3,250.00	12,000.00	
TRAVEL SALARIES					100.00	200.00	
HOME OFFICE SALARIES							
31 MARCH	JOE DOE	3,101	250.00	250.00	1,250.00	2,000.00	
TOTALS							
TRANSPORTATION – PERSONNEL							
24 MARCH	DIPLOMAT TRAVEL SERVICE	4,653	89.75	89.75	230.75	450.00	
TRANSPORTATION – AIR FREIGHT & EXCESS BAGGAGE				.00	.00		
TOTALS							
INSURANCE PREMIUMS					248.50	250.00	
TOTALS							
SUPPLIES, MATERIALS & EQUIPMENT							
14 MARCH	BURROUGHS BUSINESS MACHINES	4,331	15.00				
15 MARCH	ABC SUPPLIES CO.	4,536	24.50				
15 MARCH	G & K STATIONERY CO.	4,537	37.00	76.50	376.50	500.00	
TOTALS							
MISCELLANEOUS							
28 MARCH	BELL TEL. CO.	4,733	129.00				
29 MARCH	PETTY CASH (POSTAGE)	4,784	15.45	144.45	739.45	1,000.00	
TOTALS							
GRAND TOTALS							

DATE _31 MARCH___ 19_____

UNEXPENDED BALANCE	TOTAL FOR MONTH	EXPENDED TO DATE	BUDGET	UNEXPENDED BALANCE	
(8)	(9)	(10)	(11)	(12)	
8,750.00 *					
100.00 *					
750.00 *					
	1,500.00	4,600.00	14,200.00	9,600.00 *	
219.25 *					
.00 *					
	89.75	230.75	450.00	219.25 *	
1.50 *					
	.00	248.50	250.00	1.50 *	
123.50 *					
	76.50	376.50	500.00	123.50 *	
260.55 *					
	144.45	739.45	1,000.00	260.55 *	
	1,810.70	6,195.20	16,400.00	10,204.80 *	

PAGE NO.   1 OF 1

Figure 1: Job Cost Control Report

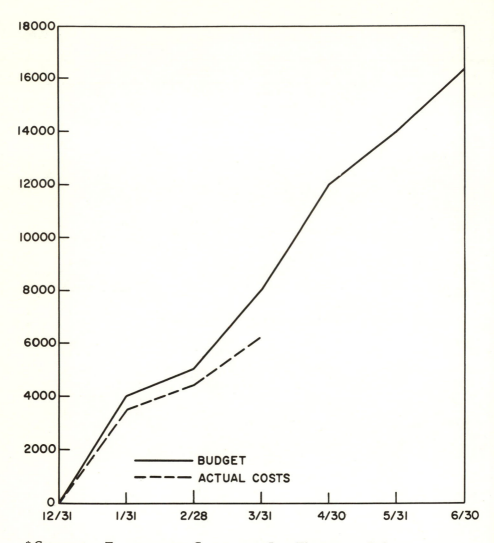

* COURTESY OF TRANSPORTATION CONSULTANTS, INC., WASHINGTON, D.C.

Figure 2:   Dollar Amount of Completion

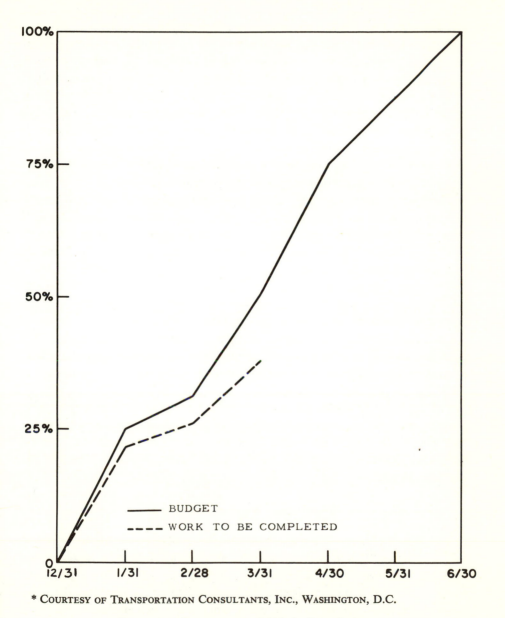

* COURTESY OF TRANSPORTATION CONSULTANTS, INC., WASHINGTON, D.C.

Figure 3:   Percentage of Work Completion

OVERHEAD AND FEES

So far only direct costs have been dealt with, the method of recording, and the way these reports are presented to management.

It is obvious that there should be a way for each project to carry part of the indirect costs. The indirect costs are charged to the various projects based on the overhead rate. This is done through a General journal entry.

At the end of each month a Schedule of Indirect Costs and a Schedule of Direct Labor are prepared. The ratio of the total indirect costs to total direct labor is the overhead rate in the form of a percentage. The latter is used in allocating the indirect costs to the various projects. This is done by applying as a factor the overhead rate to the direct labor of each project. The result is the dollar amount to be charged to the particular project.

The journal entry will debit to the overhead account of each project the amount applicable to it and credit the total of debits to the account, Applied Overhead (No. 813 90). At the end of the year the balance of this account equals the total of indirect costs. This account is then closed to the Retained Earnings account.

There are engineering firms which prefer to use a fixed factor for the operating costs. This may vary from 1.00 to 2.5 or more. To have any meaning it must be based on some consistent method of computation.

On a cost-plus-fixed-fee type of contract the fee is the firm's profit. This must be adequate to offer a fair return on the funds invested in the business, to compensate for the risk of being in business, and to be a source of capital necessary for growth and expansion.

The importance of control over operating costs is evident in any type of contract. It is to the engineer's interest to offer professional quality at the least possible cost. It is of double importance to control operating costs on lump-sum contracts, where any trimming of indirect costs will benefit the engineer directly.

Time and Payroll System

Time sheets (Figure 4) are completed semimonthly or monthly by technical staff employees. These are the people in the engineering, administrative, planning, and professional fields who are paid on a salary basis regardless of hours worked. For cost purposes, the monthly salary is distributed to the various jobs based on the ratio of hours worked on each project to the total hours worked during the period.

The technical staff time record is the same as shown in Figure 4 except that the last line (compensable overtime hours) is not filled out by these employees.

SEMI-MONTHLY TIME REPORT

EMPLOYEE TITLE	PERIOD ENDING	EMPLOYEE NAME	APPROVED BY:
	MONTH DAY YEAR		

1/16	2/17	3/18	4/19	5/20	6/21	7/22	8/23	9/24	10/25	11/26	12/27	13/28	14/29	15/30	/31	TOTAL	JOB NUMBER	JOB NAME	STATE	CONSTR SITE	DO NOT BILL

COMPENSABLE OVERTIME HOURS																TOTAL	AUTH. BY	
																		EMPLOYEE SIGNATURE

Figure 4: Time Sheet

Cash Flow Statement

	January	February	March	April	May	June
Bank Balance	57163	86783	58283	4783	783	32283
Collections on A/c Receivable	84245	42500	22500	17500	29000	24000
Expected Collections — W.I.P.	23750	18000	12000	21000	31000	28000
Expected Collections—New Work	—	—	9500	32000	41000	62000
Cash Available for Operations	165158	147283	102283	75283	101783	146283
Direct Salaries	35500	39000	42500	33000	24000	26000
Other Direct Costs	18250	23500	26200	16000	14000	8000
Management + Admin. Salaries	16200	17000	17300	16500	16500	16500
Other Ovhd. Costs	8425	9500	11500	9000	9000	9000
Total Operating Costs	78375	89000	97500	74500	63500	59500
Cash balance—End Month	86783	58283	4783	783	38283	86783

Figure 5: Projection of Cash Flow

Time sheets for hourly employees are prepared on a biweekly basis since they are paid every two weeks at a rate which amounts to an hourly rate based on a 40-hour week.

Reports to Management

The budgetary control is of much value, though operation may vary greatly. In fact, it varies so greatly that in most cases it is difficult even to forecast the volume of sales for the following year. Based on the experience of prior years, a budget is set up for all indirect costs. Interim operating statements are used for comparing performance against budget.

Budgetary control will be helpful but, alone, it will not be enough to eliminate or even control waste and inefficiency. Budgetary control will not uncover mismanagement of tools and supplies and it will not eliminate inefficient and wasted time and effort. An internal check should be part of management's effort in reducing overhead costs.

In addition to the usual financial statements, one report greatly appreciated by engineers is the projection of cash flow (Figure 5). It is preferable that this report be prepared for a period of 12 months. At times the length of this period may be impracticable, especially when it is impossible to forecast the volume of business. In such instances a six-month projection may serve the purpose.

Summary

This chapter is not addressed to an engineer, nor is it written to transform an engineer into an accountant. The chapter is intended to be of some help to the qualified accountant in setting up the system that will be more than just bookkeeping. It is hoped that this chapter will assist in furnishing the engineer with a tool for successful management of his business.

25

Entertainers and Athletes

BY S. ARTHUR SEIDMAN

Principal, Seidman and Associates, Baltimore, Pikesville, and Stevenson, Maryland; for 19 years Consultant to business, industry, and individuals in accounting, management, and personnel

Characteristics of the Business That Affect the Accounting System

The history of business has always included and was made originally by the individual. This chapter will present suggestions for an accounting system for the nonmercantile person in a personal service endeavor. It will explore and recommend the application for individuals of an appropriate accounting system.

Professionals in the entertainment world are often members of unions, teams, performing companies, or other associations or groups. Their assignments and engagements are frequently transient and temporary. Emoluments that derive from these services might be considered special in comparison with those of other businesses because of the size of the fees which pay the individual, in addition to time, for use of his name, for a copyright, patent, franchise, endorsement, or the like.

A definition of "entertainers" would include, but not be limited to, the actor, musician, dancer, singer, artist, composer, performer, producer, director, coach, athlete, author, radio and TV announcer or master of ceremonies, speaker or comedian, and other individuals whose services result in parallel accounting problems.

FUNCTIONAL CHARACTERISTICS OF THE BUSINESS

Most individuals observe a calendar-year fiscal period; however, professional athletes and other persons might find preferable, even though they are unincorporated, a different fiscal year based on their appropriate seasonal needs.

Here, again, most individuals will account on the cash basis; in some cases accrual basis accounting might benefit the entertainer or athlete even though he is not utilizing inventory, for he may be on a regular billing period. The most portentous aspect of these lines of endeavor is the fluctuations of periods of employment which will be discussed later with appropriate suggestions. For example, an assignment could range from a temporary five-minute "appearance" up to a two-year contract with the Baltimore Oriole baseball team, or a lifetime TV contract.

Competition is so prevalent in the entertainment field that a bare mention should suffice. In perhaps no other line of endeavor does competition so quickly weed out the unproficient. While Lady Luck is often responsible for an entertainer's first "big break," no individual can maintain any degree of success in the field without talent, practice, experience, application, and often that indefinable, overall trait summed up as "personality".

PRINCIPAL ACCOUNTING PROBLEMS

The principal problem related to the individual's record keeping might be the frequency or looseness in justifying and evidencing his unique transactions. These might include costume or equipment that would usually be personal but which is often apportioned to a business purpose for these people. Classification and definition of these items as to whether they are a depreciable expenditure or current expense prove interesting to the accountant.

"Bunching" is a financial phenomenon characteristic of those earning their living by entertaining others. It refers to both the type and nature of entertainers' income and presents an owner's tax and accounting problem.

Meticulous documentation over an extended period can be advantageous for the application of income averaging. Careful notes should be kept because of the gross fluctuations of operating expenses and investments and in holding periods while the individual is creating a "style", object of art, or his professional proficiency.

Other problems might pertain to application of the entertainer's time and expenses on a voluntary or personal basis rather than on the profit-making assignment.

Functional Organization

Although the general approach may seem at times oblique, the generally accepted accounting principles still, of course, apply.

The principal function of the entertainer is determined by (1) contract, organization, or union; (2) group, i.e., a company, team, or the like; (3) agent or representative; or (4) independent or free-lance status.

As to time and space, the entertainer offers his efforts in the form of franchise, copyright, endorsement, royalty, and other agreements often written, sometimes oral or otherwise, and with or without other individuals or corporations. Many ramifications present themselves in dealing with the public at large.

Principles and Objectives of the Accounting System

The system should be set up to cope intelligently with the exigencies necessitated by the invariable periods of financial feast or famine. A thorough control of cash and expenditures is paramount.

SPECIFIC OBJECTIVES OF THE SYSTEM

Here the systems man might attempt to promote a realistic, regular drawing account for his client and to set up a budget review at least quarterly to tie in with estimated tax installments.

Classification of Accounts and Books of Accounts

BALANCE SHEET ACCOUNTS.

ASSETS

Current assets

1010 Cash on Hand
1050 Cash in Bank
1100 Accounts Receivable
1150 Notes Receivable
1200 Investments

Fixed assets

1210 Real Estate

1260 Accumulated Depreciation
1310 Professional Equipment
1360 Accumulated Depreciation
1510 Vehicles
1560 Accumulated Depreciation
1610 Goodwill

LIABILITIES

Current liabilities

2010 Accounts Payable

2020 Notes Payable   2250 Loans Payable
2100 Provision for Income Taxes

Long-term liabilities
                                           NET WORTH

2210 Mortgage Payable   2810 Entertainer's Account Name
                                     2850 Withdrawals

INCOME AND EXPENSE ACCOUNTS.

INCOME

3100 Regular and Current Revenues
3150 Contractual and Special
      Appearance Fees and
      Revenues
3200 Endorsements and Residuals
3250 Other Fees and Revenues

EXPENSES

5050 Advertising
5100 Auto Gas and Oil
5150 Auto Repair
5170 Bank and Financial Charges
5250 Casual Labor

5270 Depreciation
5300 Entertainment and Gifts
5350 Equipment Repair and Rental
5400 General
5430 Heat, Power, and Light
5450 Insurance
5550 Postage and Stationery
5570 Professional Dues
5600 Professional Fees
5650 Salary and Wages
5700 Taxes
5800 Telephone and Answering
      Service
5860 Travel and Transportation
5880 Uniforms and Costumes

ACCOUNTS PECULIAR TO THE BUSINESS

This chart of accounts would only be representative of a few individuals. Many unique aspects of the method of dealing of the individual must be accounted for to seek his particular needs. An exemplification might be the costumes or uniforms set up in accounts for rapid write-offs.

BOOKS AND FORMS PECULIAR TO THE BUSINESS

Any highly systematized or elaborate accounting system would not be suggested because of the complexities in separating and gathering data on expenditures made by the entertainer during his daily routine. Since the accountant is not with his client regularly, and an entertainer cannot be expected to carry around his own set of books, the client must assist the accountant in compiling information about income and expenses.

A small record or memo book would serve well for the entertainer, such as Beach's "Common Sense" Traveler's Expense Book, available at any stationer's. This is a simple little diary with each day of the month on a separate page and expense items listed down the page next to the amount column. The back of the booklet lists summaries by days, for cash, for automobile expenses, and collections.

From this personal memorandum booklet the accountant can pick up all

THE IDEAL SYSTEM, REG. U. S. PAT. OFFICE. MADE IN U.S.A.

IDEAL SYSTEM · FORM 421

	DATE 19__	MEMORANDA	1 SERVICES PAID IN CASH	2 SERVICES CHARGED ON ACCOUNT	3 TOTAL SERVICES RENDERED (COLS. 1+2)	4 CASH RECEIVED ON ACCOUNT	5 OTHER CASH RECEIVED	6 TOTAL CASH RECEIVED (1+4+5)	7	8	9	10	11	12	
1															1
2															2
3															3
4															4
5															5
6															6
7															7
8															8
9															9
10															10
11															11
12															12
13															13
14															14
15															15
16															16
17															17
18															18
19															19
20															20
21															21
22															22
23															23
24															24
25															25
26															26
27															27
28															28
29															29
30															30
31															31
32															32
33		TOTALS													33

THE IDEAL SYSTEM

REG. U. S. PAT. OFFICE PUBLISHED BY THE IDEAL SYSTEM CO., LOS ANGELES

* BY PERMISSION OF THE COPYRIGHT OWNERS, THE IDEAL SYSTEM COMPANY, LOS ANGELES, CALIFORNIA

Figure 1: Income from Professional Services

MONTHLY SUMMARY -- STATEMENT OF INCOME

THE IDEAL SYSTEM. REG. U. S. PAT. OFFICE. MADE IN U.S.A.   IDEAL SYSTEM. FORM 424-B

STATEMENT OF INCOME - YEAR 19___	JULY	AUGUST	SEPTEMBER	OCTOBER	NOVEMBER	DECEMBER	TOTAL FOR YEAR
TOTAL CASH RECEIPTS from Services Rendered or							
TOTAL SERVICES Rendered							
TOTAL PURCHASES and Other Costs Paid or							
TOTAL NET COST of Services Rendered (Subtract)							
GROSS PROFIT FROM PROFESSION							
EXPENSES:							
Payroll, Employees Total Earnings							
Interest							
Taxes and License							
Rent and Repairs							
Professional Dues and Subscriptions, Advertising							
Telephone, Light, Power, Heat and Water							
Office Supplies, Postage, Printing							
Advertising							
Insurance							
Car Expenses							
Other Expenses							
TOTAL EXPENSES:							
DEDUCTIONS:							
Bad Debts							
Depreciation							
Contributions							
Other Deduction							
TOTAL DEDUCTIONS							
TOTAL EXPENSES AND DEDUCTIONS (Subtract from Gross Profit from Business)							
NET PROFIT FROM BUSINESS							
Plus All Other Income Not Included Above							
Total							
Less All Other Deductions Not Included Above							
TOTAL NET INCOME FOR YEAR							

THE IDEAL SYSTEM CO., LOS ANGELES
PUBLISHED BY
REG. U. S. PAT. OFFICE
THE IDEAL SYSTEM

* By permission of the copyright owners, The Ideal System Company, Los Angeles, California

THE IDEAL SYSTEM, REG. U. S. PAT. OFFICE. MADE IN U. S. A.

IDEAL SYSTEM · FORM 425

YEAR 19____

	JANUARY	FEBRUARY	MARCH	APRIL	MAY	JUNE	
PURCHASES—CASH AND CREDIT: Amount Owing for Material & Supplies, Fees & Other Costs at End of Period							1
Total Purchases, Fees & Other Costs Paid during Period (From Summary, Line 12)							2
Total (Line 1 Plus Line 2)							3
Amount Owing for Material & Supplies, Fees & other Costs at Beginning of Period							4
TOTAL CASH AND CREDIT PURCHASES, FEES AND OTHER COSTS FOR PERIOD (Line 3 Minus Line 4)							5
Enter Total Cash and Credit Purchases, Fees & Other Costs from Line 5 above on Line 8 below.							6
							7
NET COST OF PURCHASES, FEES & OTHER COSTS: Total Cash & Credit Purch., Fees, & Other Costs for Period (From Line 5 above)							8
Inventory of Material & Supplies on hand at Beginning of Period							9
Total (Line 8 Plus Line 9)							10
Inventory of Material & Supplies on hand at End of Period							11
TOTAL NET COST OF SALES OR SERVICES RENDERED (Line 10 Minus Line 11)							12
							13
							14
Enter "Total Net Cost of Sales or Services Rendered" from Line 12 above on Line 31 of "Monthly Statement of Income," Form 424-A or 424-B.							15
							16
							17
The word "Period" in this form means the "Month" for the monthly columns and the "Year" for the yearly column.							18
							19
							20
Lines 13 to 33 of this page remain blank.							21
							22
							23
							24
							25
							26
							27
							28
							29
							30
							31
							32
							33

THE IDEAL SYSTEM CO., LOS ANGELES
PUBLISHED BY
REG. U. S. PAT. OFFICE
THE IDEAL SYSTEM

* BY PERMISSION OF THE COPYRIGHT OWNERS, THE IDEAL SYSTEM COMPANY, LOS ANGELES, CALIFORNIA

Figure 3: Accrual Basis Schedule

ACCRUAL BASIS SCHEDULE

USE THIS SCHEDULE WHEN PREPARING "STATEMENT OF INCOME" AND INCOME TAX REPORT ON ACCRUAL BASIS
(SEE "SUMMARY" INSTRUCTIONS PAGE)

THE IDEAL SYSTEM, REG. U. S. PAT. OFFICE. MADE IN U. S. A.

THE IDEAL SYSTEM
REG. U. S. PAT. OFFICE
PUBLISHED BY
THE IDEAL SYSTEM CO., LOS ANGELES

IDEAL SYSTEM - FORM 425

Line	YEAR 19___	JULY	AUGUST	SEPTEMBER	OCTOBER	NOVEMBER	DECEMBER	YEAR
	PURCHASES—CASH AND CREDIT:							
1	Amount Owing for Material & Supplies, Fees & Other Costs at End of Period							
2	Total Purchases, Fees & Other Costs Paid during Period (From Summary, Line 12)							
3	Total (Line 1 Plus Line 2)							
4	Amount Owing for Material & Supplies, Fees & other Costs at Beginning of Period							
5	TOTAL CASH AND CREDIT PURCHASES, FEES AND OTHER COSTS FOR PERIOD (Line 3 Minus Line 4)							
6	Enter Total Cash and Credit Purchases, Fees & Other Costs from Line 5 above on Line 8 below.							
7								
8	**NET COST OF PURCHASES, FEES & OTHER COSTS:** Total Cash & Credit Purch., Fees, & Other Costs for Period (From Line 5 above)							
9	Inventory of Material & Supplies on hand at Beginning of Period							
10	Total (Line 8 Plus Line 9)							
11	Inventory of Material & Supplies on hand at End of Period							
12	TOTAL NET COST OF SALES OR SERVICES RENDERED (Line 10 Minus Line 11)							
13								
14								
15	Enter "Total Net Cost of Sales or Services Rendered" from Line 12 above on Line 31 of "Monthly Statement of Income," Form 424-A or 424-B.							
16								
17								
18	The word "Period" in this form means the "Month" for the monthly columns and the "Year" for the yearly column.							
19								
20								
21	Lines 13 to 33 of this page remain blank.							
22								
23								
24								
25								
26								
27								
28								
29								
30								
31								
32								
33								

Figure 3: Accrual Basis Schedule (cont.)

THE IDEAL SYSTEM, REG. U. S. PAT. OFFICE. MADE IN U. S. A.

PAYMENTS – ALL CASH AND CHECKS PAID OUT

IDEAL SYSTEM - FORM 423

THE IDEAL SYSTEM

REG. U. S. PAT. OFFICE
PUBLISHED BY
THE IDEAL SYSTEM CO., LOS ANGELES

	1	2					3	4	4A	4B	4C	5	6	
	BANK DEPOSITS	BANK BALANCE (2+1−3)	DATE 19__	CHECK NUMBER	TO WHOM PAID	MEMORANDA	PAID OUT BY CHECK	PAID OUT BY CASH	DEDUCTIONS FROM EMPLOYEE'S EARNINGS: F. O. A. B. & UNEMP. INS.	WITHHOLDING TAX	OTHER DEDUCTIONS	MATERIAL AND SUPPLIES	FEES PAID OTHERS	
1														1
2														2
3														3
4														4
5														5
6														6
7														7
8														8
9														9
10														10
11														11
12														12
13														13
14														14
15														15
16														16
17														17
18														18
19														19
20														20
21														21
22														22
23														23
24														24
25														25
26														26
27														27
28														28
29														29
30														30
31														31
32														32
33						TOTALS								33

Figure 4: Distribution of Expenses (cont.)

DISTRIBUTION OF EXPENSES

IDEAL SYSTEM - FORM 423

THE IDEAL SYSTEM, REG. U. S. PAT. OFFICE. MADE IN U. S. A.

	7 OTHER COSTS	8 PAYMENTS TO OR FOR CLIENTS	9 PAYROLL, EMPLOYEE'S TOTAL EARNINGS	10 CAR EXPENSES	11 RENT AND REPAIRS	12 OFFICE SUPPLIES, POSTAGE, PRINTING	13 TAXES AND LICENSES	14 INTEREST AND INSURANCE	15 TELEPHONE, LIGHT, POWER, HEAT, WATER	16 PROFESSIONAL DUES AND SUBSCRIPTIONS ADVERTISING	17 OTHER EXPENSE NAME OF ACCOUNT	18 OTHER EXPENSE AMOUNT PAID	19 OTHER PAYMENTS NAME OF ACCOUNT	20 OTHER PAYMENTS AMOUNT PAID	
1															1
2															2
3															3
4															4
5															5
6															6
7															7
8															8
9															9
10															10
11															11
12															12
13															13
14															14
15															15
16															16
17															17
18															18
19															19
20															20
21															21
22															22
23															23
24															24
25															25
26															26
27															27
28															28
29															29
30															30
31															31
32															32
33															33

THE IDEAL SYSTEM
REG. U. S. PAT. OFFICE
PUBLISHED BY
THE IDEAL SYSTEM CO., LOS ANGELES

Figure 4: Distribution of Expenses

* BY PERMISSION OF THE COPYRIGHT OWNERS, THE IDEAL SYSTEM COMPANY, LOS ANGELES, CALIFORNIA

expenses paid out of cash as well as other miscellaneous information. A gift from an association or an agent, for example, in the form of personal property, would be noted. Other expenses could come from the individual's checkbook.

Another simple routine is use of file folders for all information relating to income (contract, royalties, dividends, rents, interest), expenses (costumes, travel, entertainment, auto, health club) and general items (copyrights, investments, special costumes, and equipment). These different sources provide data for the books kept by the accountant.

Many simple single-entry, commercial systems are available. One of these is the "Ideal" loose-leaf accounting book (Figures 1, 2, 3, 4).

Another is the "Johnson", bound, individual accounting journal (Figure 5).

These may often suffice as the accountant's records for the average performer or athlete. Either would be appropriate for the situation.

For individuals whose affairs are more complex and who might engage a regular private secretary, attention should be given to the highly efficient, write-it-once, carbonized-type systems, such as published by Remington Rand or Shaw-Walker (Figures 6 and 7).

The illustrations in Figure 6 represent somewhat of an ultimate approach to bookkeeping for the individual; although not as comprehensive or polished as the data processing system described in the chapter on Taverns in this "Portfolio". Frequently one writing will produce four or five accounting transactions simultaneously without need for recopying or posting. This sort of system prevents errors that often occur in normal, individual record keeping. One writing could produce the envelope (by use of see-through windows), the check, the check stub, the original entry; and, in some cases, the posting to ledger or subsidiary ledgers or even billing statements.

Time and Payroll System

No usual system is applicable because of the peculiar nature of remuneration in the entertainment field. However, depending upon the mode of pay, the entertainer or athlete might look with favor upon an analysis by his accountant of his time allocated to his various points of activity. With the cooperation of the client, such an analysis would be well worth the time and effort expended.

The accountant could set up code letters to differentiate types of income. For example, code A might apply to regular appearances; code B to contractual and special appearances; C would cover endorsements and residuals; D, charitable appearances; E, goodwill and public relations appearances; F, other unassigned time.

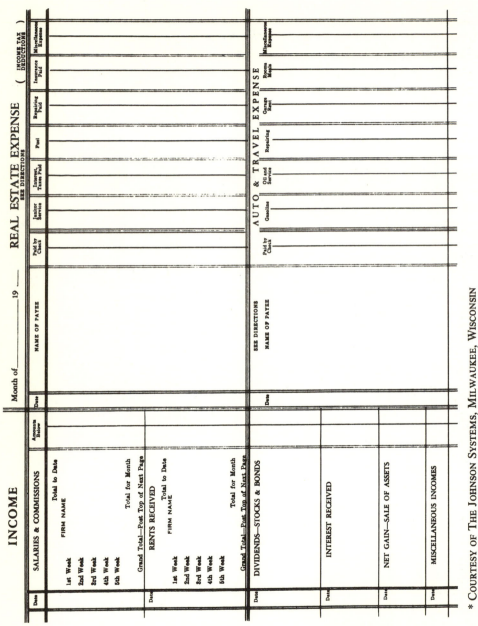

Figure 5: Individual Accounting Journal

* COURTESY OF THE JOHNSON SYSTEMS, MILWAUKEE, WISCONSIN

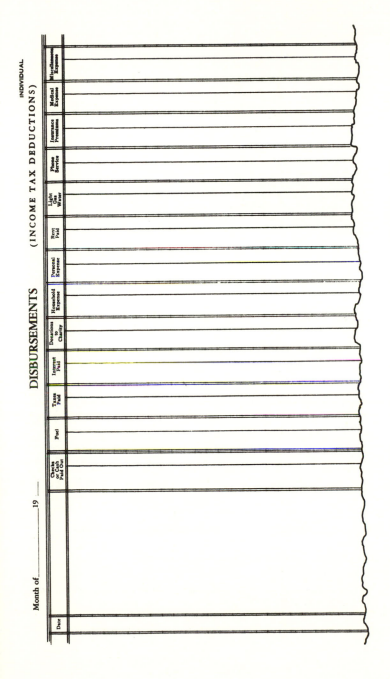

Figure 5: Individual Accounting Journal (cont.)

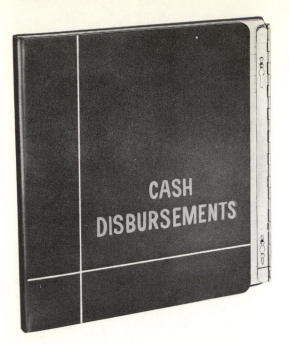

Figure 6:   Disbursements Journal

* COURTESY OF SHAW-WALKER COMPANY, MUSKEGON, MICHIGAN.

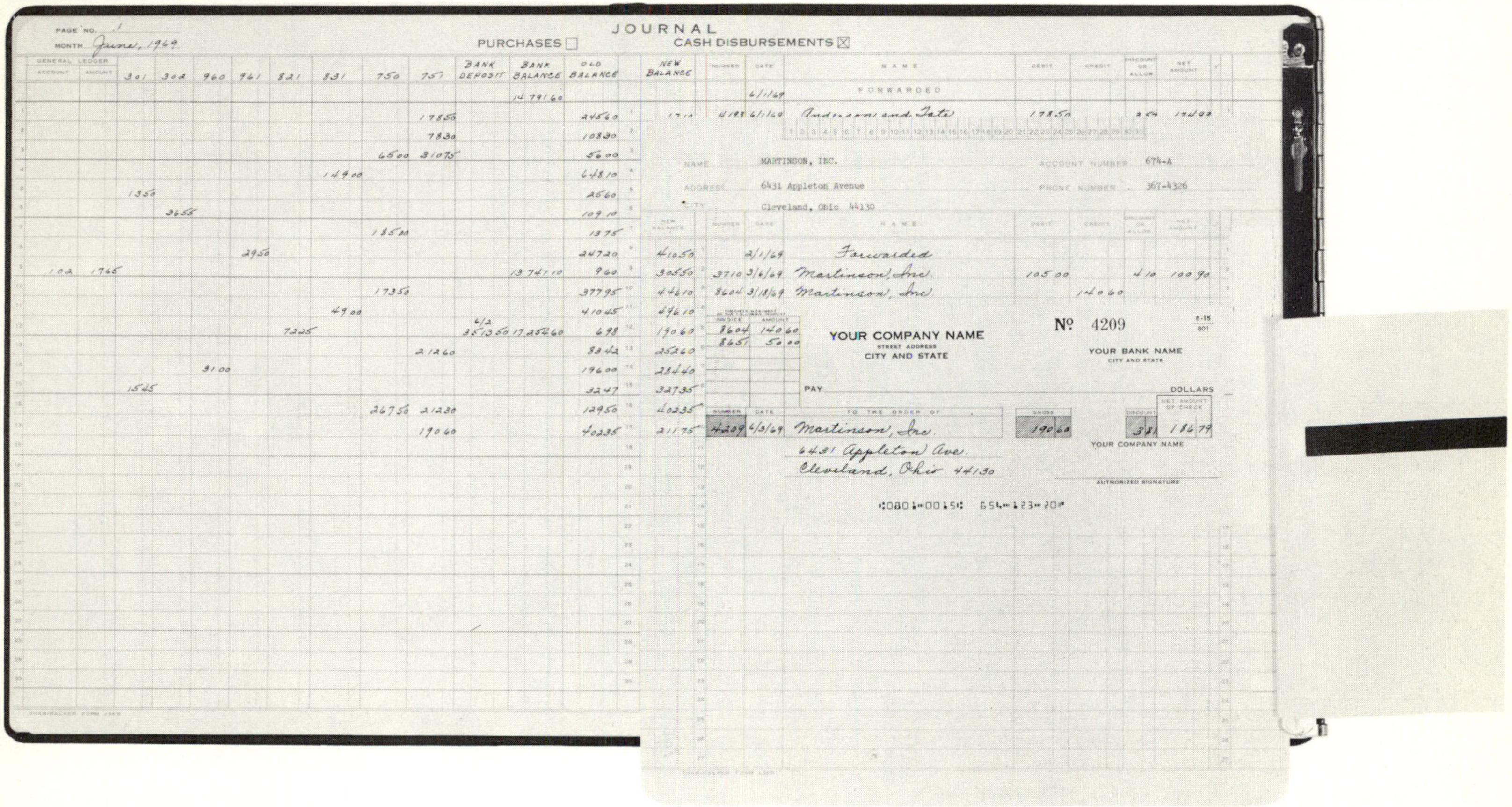

* Courtesy of Shaw-Walker Company, Muskegon, Michigan.

Figure 7: Accounts Payable and Vendor Ledger

Reports to Clients

The usual reports to management would not be applicable to the individual. One suggested report to the client, however, might well be a "management" report submitted annually. This report would begin with specifically enumerated recommendations advising the client of the frequency and control of his drawing account and personal expenditures, or increasing his efforts in more lucrative types of activities. The report would then go on to discuss these recommendations and outline them in priority of time and/or money.

Among these recommendations would be definite suggestions for a realistic, regular drawing account. Another would be a budget review with advice that excess funds especially be earmarked for savings accounts, so that expenses could be budgeted for a future period when the client would not have adequate cash flow-in. Prepayment of certain fixed costs would be recommended, for such items as insurance, auto loan installments, taxes via estimated quarterly payments for Federal, Social Security, and state taxes as well as any applicable city or local assessments.

This chapter is an attempt to offer practical routines of a businesslike nature to a field not conducive to the usual accounting methods. More thorough control of cash and expenditures is valuable and essential for entertainers. The accountant can provide a real service to these individuals by fostering a long-range attitude acceptable to suggested common sense and accounting procedures and forms. Such a management advisory service would be a real benefit to these clients in terms of their future security and estate problems.

26

Farmers

BY TOM A. BRIGHAM

Certified Public Accountant, Normal, Illinois

Characteristics of the Business That Affect the Accounting System

Agriculture is generally considered to provide food and clothing or the raw materials for these items. It does, however, include such diverse industries and activities as timber and fish hatcheries.

Geographical location has a great deal to do with the products raised on any given farm. Some common types of enterprise which are based on geographical location are cornbelt, wheatbelt or wheatland, cotton belt, and dairy belt farms. The major cash crop raised in each of these locations is reflected in the name.

In almost all instances, however, there is a combination of crops raised on any farm. It is not uncommon to have more than one grain raised, or a combination of grain and livestock. In certain Midwestern farms, for example, the major grain raised is corn. It, in turn, is used in the feeding operation, so that the major crop that actually is sold from the farm is beef and/or hogs.

Over recent years the tendency has been for farms to become fewer in number and larger in size. This trend was brought about both by expansion of urban areas and the need for farms to be larger to insure their economical operation. This increase in size of the average farm has brought about a great expansion in the amount of capital necessary. Land costs per acre and the number of acres needed to make a farm a profitable "unit"—as well as the capital investment in high-priced machinery—have virtually removed the farm from the classification of small business.

Throughout this recent increase in size of unit, the farms have still remained basically owner operated. This characteristic is typically referred to as a family-type farm, as opposed to corporate ownership. One noticeable difference between the family-type farm of today and that of several decades ago is the more businesslike manner in which it is managed. The efficient operator today can discuss cost per unit of production, depreciation, cost of capital, etc., in such a manner that a casual observer might feel he were listening to a conversation between two manufacturing plant managers.

Even with the expansion of capital investment, both to start and to maintain farming operations, it appears that the single-entry bookkeeping system still serves the need of the farmer. Frequently the actual record keeping is done on forms provided by management services through universities, banks, or farm organizations. This type of form allows the operator a better basis of comparison between his operation and that of other farmers.

FUNCTIONAL CHARACTERISTICS OF THE BUSINESS

Most farm operations have a fiscal year which coincides with the calendar year. This is a direct result of the need for specific information which will satisfy requirements of the Federal income tax return. Since the majority of farm operations are reported on a cash basis, the records are also maintained in this manner. This means that inventories are not usually maintained on harvested, unsold crops or on raised livestock except as it would be used as an alternate method of filing for tax purposes.

Geographical variations in farming, and the resultant differences in crops, would dictate some slight variance in farm records. In almost all instances, the records maintained by farmers are designed to keep track of the cost of production of each unit separately and also to provide total cost of the finished products. The accounts are frequently named or designed to synchronize with Schedule F of the Federal income tax return.

Another circumstance which requires specialized record keeping is the type of operation based on ownership. Frequently a farm is owned by one person and operated by another. This necessitates record keeping by landlord and tenant. The exact pro rata of expenses and division of crop profit are a direct function of the lease arrangement. In some instances the lease follows a strictly cash rent basis in which the rent is treated as an expense by the tenant. It is more common, however, to have a share basis where certain types of expenses are borne by each of the two parties and other expenses are shared on some formula between them. Thus a more precise record-keeping system would be required here than in the case of an owner-operated farm.

Because of the climatic conditions necessary for farming, in most instances the records are kept in a manner to reflect the production or crop year.

PRINCIPAL ACCOUNTING PROBLEMS

One of the accounting problems in an agricultural type of business is the difficulty of prorating costs among various crops or other production units. In order to analyze effectively the efficiency of the various production units, it is necessary for the farmer to prorate these costs.

As an example, various fertilizers applied to one field have residual benefits for crops over a period of time. In addition a by-product of one crop may be of benefit to another crop or production unit. An instance of the latter benefit is the common practice of grazing a cornfield after the crop has been harvested. Fallen corn or ears left on the stalks provide food for beef cattle or other livestock. It is difficult to prorate the cost of this feed, either to the livestock or as a reduction of the cost of the corn crop by this amount.

One way of resolving this problem is to estimate the value of corn left in the field by marking off a section of the field and counting the unpicked or fallen ears. Using this as a basis, the dollar value of the entire field could be estimated and shown as an increase in income for the grain enterprise and as an expense for the cattle enterprise.

Fieldmen or personnel from extension units of universities have often indicated guide lines which may be followed in such situations. The majority of farmers have arrived at a satisfactory manner of prorating these expenses.

Functional Organization

The farm accounting system is divided in most cases into sections based on production units, such as various crops, livestock that is produced, and expense categories based on location. An example of the various classifications that might be used is shown on the code sheet (Figure 1), which is used by one farm organization as a suggestion to member farmers.

ENTERPRISE IDENTIFICATION CODE

Item	Code	No.	Item	Code	No.
Beef Cattle		1 5	Crops		0 2
Dairy		1 0	Corn, Grain		4 2
Hogs		0 4	Seed Corn		4 4
Sheep		2 1	Sweet Corn		4 7
Other Livestock		3 4	Oats		4 9
Chickens		2 5	Wheat		5 1
Broilers		3 0	Soybeans		5 3
Turkeys		3 2	Other Seed		5 9
Other Poultry		3 1	Hay		6 1
			Forage		6 4
			Fruits		6 5
			Tomatoes		6 6
			Other Vegetables		6 7
			Other Crops		6 8

* COURTESY OF THE AGRICULTURAL BUSINESS SERVICE COMPANY, BLOOMINGTON, ILLINOIS.

Figure 1: Code Sheet

Principles and Objectives of the Accounting System

Since most farms are still basically family owned, with bookkeeping done by a member of the family, the specific records are normally those which will provide with a minimum of effort all of the information the farmer must have. These informational needs are generally only twofold:

1. To satisfy outsiders. These are various governmental agencies such as the Internal Revenue Service, and lending agencies such as banks, mortgage grantors, or landlords.

2. To provide data for management decisions. This classification implies that the records must be kept on a production basis.

In almost all instances these records are maintained on a single-entry cash basis.

SPECIFIC OBJECTIVES OF THE SYSTEM

Foremost among the objectives is the acquisition of data to satisfy mandatory requirements of the Federal income tax return. This objective probably overshadows all others as a motivating factor in record keeping.

Another factor would be to provide information on the various strengths and weaknesses of individual production units. These data help to determine which operations should be emphasized in order to produce the optimum income from the capital invested.

Record keeping must also provide information to satisfy credit granting agencies, and to allow for proper division of income and expense between landlord and tenant. The family nature of many farms makes it essential that a businesslike record be kept so that equitable distribution of income and expense can be made. Such a record should establish a basis for distribution of property in the event death or some other reason causes redistribution of the assets among the various family members.

Increasing emphasis in recent years has been placed upon the managerial usage of records. Farm organizations, as well as universities, have compiled information collected from a sampling of farmers in order to better advise them in management of their operations. One such organization is the Farm Bureau Farm Management group, which keeps standard account books and

CODE INDEX
FARM RECORD and BUSINESS ANALYSIS SERVICE

AGRICULTURAL BUSINESS SERVICE COMPANY
1701 TOWANDA AVENUE
BLOOMINGTON, ILLINOIS 61702

A FARM BUREAU SERVICE

TRANSACTION IDENTIFICATION CODE

EXPLANATION	Code	No.					EXPLANATION	Code	No.				
Sale or Purchase for CASH	1						Payment on ACCOUNT	3					
Sale or Purchase on CREDIT	2						Payment by TRADE	4					

ITEM IDENTIFICATION CODE

Item	Code		No.				Item	Code		No.			
CROPS							**LIVESTOCK**						
Corn, Grain	4	2					Beef Cattle	1	5				
Seed Corn	4	4					Beef Calves	1	6				
Sweet Corn	4	7					Beef Heifers	1	7				
Oats	4	9					Beef Cows	1	8				
Seed Oats	5	0					Beef Bulls	1	9				
Wheat	5	1					Beef Feeders	2	0				
Seed Wheat	5	2					Dairy Cattle	1	0				
Soybeans	5	3					Dairy Calves	1	1				
Soybeans, Seed	5	4					Dairy Heifers	1	2				
Sorghum	5	5					Dairy Cows	1	3				
C.C.C. Corn	4	3					Dairy Bulls	1	4				
Other Grains	5	6					Hogs	0	4				
Other Seeds	5	9					Feeder Pigs	0	5				
Hay	6	1					Market Hogs	0	6				
Forage	6	4					Breeding Gilts	0	7				
Fruits	6	5					Sows	0	8				
Tomatoes	6	6					Boars	0	9				
Other Vegetables	6	7					Sheep	2	1				
Pasture	7	2					Lambs	2	2				
Woodlot	7	3					Ewes	2	3				
Idle Cropland	7	1					Other Livestock	3	4				
Silage	4	8					**POULTRY**						
Other Crops (straw, etc.)	6	8					Chickens	2	5				
							Layers	2	8				
							Chicks	2	6				
							Pullets	2	7				

FORM NO. 20 *REVISED 8-66*

* COURTESY OF THE AGRICULTURAL BUSINESS SERVICE COMPANY,
BLOOMINGTON, ILLINOIS.

Figure 2: Code Index

Item	Code			No.			Item	Code			No.		
Hens	2	8					PROPERTY ITEMS						
Roosters	2	9					Land	0	1	0	0		
Broilers	3	0					Buildings & Improvements	0	2	0	0		
Turkeys	3	2					Tiling	0	2	1	3		
Poults, Turkeys	3	3					Machinery & Equipment (Purch. or Sale)	0	3	0	0		
Other Poultry	3	1					Automobile	0	3	0	1		
PRODUCTS							Combine	0	3	0	9		
Milk	3	5	0	1			Corn Picker	0	3	1	1		
Cream	3	5	0	2			Corn Planter	0	3	1	2		
Other Dairy Products	3	5	0	0			Corn Combine	0	3	1	3		
Eggs	3	6	0	0			Cultivators	0	3	1	5		
Wool	3	7	0	0			Discs	0	3	1	7		
Other Livestock Products	4	1	0	0			Feed Grinder	0	3	2	3		
							Hay Baler	0	3	3	0		
CROP RELATED ITEMS							Hog House, Portable	0	3	3	4		
Chemicals	7	6	0	3			Hog Fountains & Feeders	0	3	3	5		
Fertilizer	7	4	0	0			Milking Machine	0	3	3	9		
Lime & Rock Phosphate	7	5	0	0			Mowers	0	3	4	0		
Marketing (Except trucking)	7	6	0	4			Rotary Hoe	0	3	4	2		
Seed Certification	7	6	0	1			Shop Tools	0	3	4	7		
Other Crop Items	7	6	0	0			Small Tools	0	3	4	8		
LIVESTOCK RELATED ITEMS							Tractors	0	3	5	0		
Breeding Fees	3	8	0	0			Trailers	0	3	5	1		
Commercial Feed	4	0	0	0			Trucks	0	3	5	2		
Supplements	4	0	0	1			Wagons	0	3	5	3		
Complete Feeds	4	0	0	2			Other Equipment	0	3	5	7		
Minerals & Vitamins	4	0	0	3									
Antibiotics	4	0	0	4			GENERAL ITEMS						
Grinding & Mixing	4	0	0	5			Auto Operating Expense (Farm)	8	3	0	0		
Dairy Cleaners	4	1	0	3			Cash Rent	7	8	0	0		
Egg Cleaners	4	1	0	4			Custom Work	7	7	0	0		
Marketing (Except Trucking)	4	1	0	6			Electricity (Farm)	8	5	0	0		
Registration Fees	4	1	0	2			Farm Organization Dues	9	0	0	1		
Shearing	4	1	0	5			Fuel, Oil & Grease	8	2	0	0		
Testing Fees	4	1	0	1			Motor Fuels	8	2	0	1		
Veterinary & Medicine	3	9	0	0			Motor Oils	8	2	0	2		
Other Livestock Items	4	1	0	0			Grease	8	2	0	3		
							Heating Fuels	8	2	0	4		
							Gasoline Tax Refund	8	2	0	6		

Figure 2:   Code Index (cont.)

Item	Code			No.		Item	Code			No.	
Government Payments	8	9	0	0		Other Labor Expense	7	9	1	1	
Feed Grain Program	8	9	0	1		Patronage Refunds	9	0	0	6	
Wheat Program	8	9	0	2		Repairs: Buildings	8	0	0	1	
ASC Program	9	0	0	4		Fence	8	0	0	2	
Insurance (Farm)	8	7	0	0		Machinery	8	1	0	1	
On Crops	8	7	0	1		Equipment	8	1	0	2	
On Livestock	8	7	0	2		Other Repairs	8	1	0	3	
On Machinery	8	7	0	3		Subscriptions	9	0	0	2	
On Buildings	8	7	0	4		Taxes: Real Estate	8	6	0	1	
Interest (Farm)	8	8	0	0		Personal Property	8	6	0	2	
Labor	7	9	0	0		Income, Federal	8	6	0	3	
Operator's Own	7	9	0	1		License Plates	8	6	0	5	
Landlord's Own	7	9	0	2		Telephone	8	4	0	0	
Operator's Family	7	9	0	3		Trucking	7	7	0	0	
Landlord's Family	7	9	0	4		Water	9	0	0	3	
Hired—Full-time	7	9	0	6		Misc. (postage. etc.)	9	0	0	5	
Hired—Part-time	7	9	0	7							
Meals	7	9	0	9							
Social Security	7	9	1	0							

See Reverse Side for Instruction

Figure 2: Code Index (cont.)

compares production unit costs such as a bushel of corn. Cooperating farmers are volunteers from the membership of the Farm Bureau and continue in the group year after year.

Classification of Accounts and Books of Accounts

Most farm accounts are kept on the cash basis. It is not uncommon to have one account which serves for both business and personal expenditures. For this reason, a complete set of books is not usually maintained. Accounts most frequently used are reflected in Figure 2. Ordinarily any one farmer would use only a small portion of these accounts.

ACCOUNTS PECULIAR TO THE BUSINESS

Inventories. These may be classified as (1) permanent or fixed assets and (2) production inventories. In the first category would be placed such items as buildings, equipment, and breeding livestock. The second would contain inventories of products held on hand which will be sold within a year or two. These would include crops (corn, soybeans, etc.) as well as livestock (feeder cattle, feeder hogs, etc.). In the case of livestock held for long terms, such as breeding stock or milk cows, a much more detailed record is kept. For example, there would be shown on the inventory sheet—for each individual cow producing milk—the gallonage per month, the animal's weight, initial cost, feed cost, veterinarian expenses, and so on. If purebred cattle are part of the farm operation, the record would be expanded to include sire and other genealogical and detailed information necessary for registry.

Payment in Kind. Frequently there are arrangements with tenants or hired men which necessitate that part of their payment is in the form of food, lodging, etc. Special accounts must then be set up for this situation. As an example, if a house is provided for the tenant or hired man, depreciation on this item would be kept separately from depreciation of machinery. Frequently certain amounts of food are supplied to the employee as part of his wages.

BOOKS AND FORMS PECULIAR TO THE BUSINESS

Records most usually maintained by farmers are inventories, production and performance records, depreciation schedules, record of assets, and the usual income and expense details. These records do not differ materially from records kept by other cash basis businesses except as mentioned elsewhere in the chapter.

Peculiarities of Procedures

INCOME AND EXPENSES

Sales and receipts, and/or other receipts and expenses, normally must be classified by industry or department. In Figure 3, for the period of April through June, hogs produced a total return of $782.32 which was allocated as follows: The landlord's share was $111.50, while the operator's was $670.82.

Further breakdown is provided in the Detailed Listing of Current Transactions (Figure 4), which indicates that $559.32 was procured from the sale of hogs on May 10 and a boar on April 18. Source of these entries is usually directly from the checkbook of the farmer in the case of expenses and from the bank deposit slip in the case of income.

One recent innovation which makes the farmer's accounting more simple is utilization of a space on the check (Figure 5) for a coding of the reason for the purchase. This practice has proved valuable in the preliminary collection of data. In the case of a multi-item purchase, there is also room to enumerate what the expenses are.

Each individual classification of income is shown on the deposit slip

AGRICULTURAL BUSINESS SERVICE COMPANY

An Affiliate of the Illinois Agricultural Association

1701 Towanda Avenue
Post Office Box 325
Bloomington, Illinois 61701
Telephone 309 828 0021

(12345) Sample
→ *Farm No.*
Report is confidential.

PROCESSED 07/16/   FOR   3   MONTHS ENDING   JUNE, 19

RETURNS AND EXPENSES (IN DOLLARS)

NOTE: This page shows the summary of return and expense items. The detail listing is shown on following pages

→ Amount still owed on respective items

	CURRENT		YEAR TO DATE		NET CREDIT BALANCE	
	LANDLORD	OPERATOR	LANDLORD	OPERATOR	LANDLORD	OPERATOR
	• • • RETURNS • • •					
HOGS	111.50	670.82	111.50	2061.32	0.	0.
BEEF CATTLE	400.00	400.00	400.00	3378.40	0.	0.
FEEDER CATTLE	6622.21	6622.19	6622.21	6622.19		
TOT.CAPITAL INC.	7133.71	7693.01	7133.71	12061.91		
CORN,GRAIN	600.00	600.00	2517.77	600.00	0.	0.
SOYBEANS	810.00	810.00	2098.16	2098.16	0.	0.
HAY	60.00	60.00	60.00	60.00	0.	0.
OTHER	37.50	111.15	37.50	111.15	0.	0.
TOT.OPERATG.INC.	1507.50	1581.15	4713.43	2869.31		
TOTAL RETURNS	8641.21	9274.16	11847.14	14931.22	0.	0.
NON-FARM 1			0.	134.28		
	• • • EXPENSES • • •					
MACH..EQUIPT.	100.00	100.00	100.00	550.00	0.	0.
HOGS	75.00	375.00	75.00	2125.00	0.	0.
FEEDER CATTLE	2625.00	2625.00	2625.00	2625.00		
TOT.CAPITAL EXP.	2800.00	3100.00	2800.00	5300.00		
VET.,MEDICINE	14.00	50.50	14.00	75.50	0.	419.36
COMM. FEEDS	168.00	168.00	168.00	803.36	84.00	419.36
CORN,FEED	0.	0.	0.	130.00	0.	0.
SEEDS	0.	75.00	0.	75.00	0.	200.00
FERTILIZER	500.00	500.00	750.00	750.00	500.00	200.00
OTH.CROP EXP.	163.00	163.00	163.00	239.50	0.	163.00
CUSTOM WORK	0.	60.00	0.	60.00	0.	0.
LABOR	0.	285.00	0.	410.00	0.	0.
REP.,MACH-EQP.	0.	81.10	0.	181.96	0.	-51.53
FUEL,OIL,GREASE	0.	6.73	0.	62.48	-0.	0.
TELEPH..ELEC.	0.	19.23	0.	58.00	0.	0.
TAXES	0.	170.00	0.	170.00	0.	0.
INSURANCE	0.	163.00	0.	163.00	0.	0.
INTEREST	0.	70.00	0.	140.00	0.	0.
OTHER	0.	0.	0.	130.00		
TOT.OPERATG.EXP.	845.00	1811.56	1095.00	3448.80		
TOTAL(EXCL.INT)	3645.00	4941.56	3895.00	8608.80	0.	0.
TOTAL(INCL.INT)	3645.00	4911.56	3895.00	8745.80	584.00	730.83

(NON-FARM 1) → *Not included in above tobl.* 0.   1218.00

NET CASH(EXCL.INT)   4996.21   4432.60   7952.14   6322.42

* COURTESY OF THE AGRICULTURAL BUSINESS SERVICE COMPANY,

An Affiliate of the *Illinois Agricultural Association*

Post Office Box 325
Bloomington, Illinois 61701
Telephone 309 828 0021

12345   PROCESSED 07/16/   FOR   9 MONTHS ENDING   JUNE, 19

DETAILED LISTING OF CURRENT TRANSACTIONS

DATE	DESCRIPTION	NUMBER	QUANTITY	TEST/GRADE	OPER.-SHARE	LANDL.-SHARE
			• • • INCOME ITEMS • • •			
	MARKET HOGS					
5/ 10	HOGS - $23.50	10	23.65		559.32	
		10	23.65		559.32	-0-
	BOARS					
4/ 18	BOAR, DUROC	1	5.25		31.50	31.50
6/ 7	BOAR, DUROC	1	3.50	140.00	31.50	31.50
					80.00	80.00
	BEEF BULLS					
5/ 7	BULL	1	12.00	620.00	400.00	400.00
		1	12.00		400.00	400.00
	BEEF FEEDERS					
5/ 12	STEERS /27.00	20	200.00		2650.07	2650.08
		20	200.00		2650.07	2650.08
4/ 20	STEERS	15	175.60		-0-	
5/ 16	STEERS /27.00	30	300.00	4658.00	3972.12	3972.13
		45	475.60		3972.12	3972.13
	CORN,GRAIN					
4/ 2	SM CORN /$1.20	-0-	1000.00		600.00	600.00
		-0-	1000.00		600.00	600.00
	SOYBEANS					
6/ 8	SOYBEANS /$3.00	-0-	540.00		810.00	810.00
		-0-	540.00		810.00	810.00
	OTHER HAY					
6/ 12	ALFALFA HAY	-0-	3.00		60.00	60.00
		-0-	3.00		60.00	60.00
	OTHER					
4/ 4	SERVICE CO REF	0			73.65	
6/ 14	ELEV PAT REF	0	-0-		37.50	37.50
					111.15	37.50
	NON FARM					
4/ 3	AT+T STOCK DIV				37.18	
5/ 15	STOCK DIVIDEND				17.10	
6/ 30	CASH RENTAL-CITY	0	-0-		75.00	
					129.28	-0-
			• • • EXPENSE ITEMS • • •			
	MACH.-EQUIPT.					
4/ 21	2-SOW HOUSE	0	-0-		100.00	100.00
		0	-0-		100.00	100.00
	FEEDER PIGS					
5/ 10	FEEDER PIGS	10	5.00		300.00	
		10	5.00		300.00	-0-

* Courtesy of the Agricultural Business Service Company,
Bloomington, Illinois.

Figure 4: Detailed Listing of Current Transactions

Figure 5:   Farm-Coded Check

(Figure 6). Use of this slip simplifies the record keeping a farmer must do and provides a neater, more efficient summary of information for the tax accountant or consultant who ultimately prepares the tax return for the farmer. In addition, more information for managerial use is available for the farmer periodically through the year.

DEPRECIATION

Regulations established by the Internal Revenue Service require that certain information be maintained on assets which are depreciated or may later be depreciated. This category would include, but not be limited to: Buildings (including the house and additions to it), tractors and other equipment, breeding livestock, etc. A separate card (Figure 7) should be set up for each asset purchased. When additions (not repairs) are made, they also should be recorded. Because the IRS Code changes frequently, it is important that the above information be maintained on any asset which is or might be used on the farm. For example, the house might be converted to rental property at the time the farmer retires or constructs a new house. Unless the cost of the original dwelling and additions or remodeling have been maintained, the correct basis could not be determined.

A schedule of depreciation (Figure 8) can be used to supply information

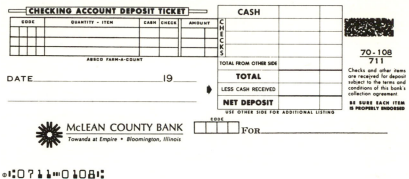

Figure 6:   Farm-Coded Bank Deposit Slip

for Schedule F. This schedule of depreciation has the advantage of being usable for a number of years so that laborious recopying is not required.

The information provided by Figures 7 and 8 is necessary to determine whether a given asset should be classified as long term, short term, section 1250, 1245, etc.

Time and Payroll System

Most farmers find it necessary to employ hired men. Current Federal income tax rulings should be checked to determine whether or not payments in the form of housing, meals, etc., are taxable to the recipient or not. Most smaller farm operations do not have employees; hence the payroll problem is not major.

Reports for Management

Because of the relatively long production schedule in farming operations, reports for management purposes are not as frequent as they are in other forms of business. A period shorter than one month is rarely used, and it is not uncommon to have reports come in only at the end of a crop year or other period of production.

| DESCRIPTION | _FARMALL TRACTOR_ | | ITEM NO. _1_ |
| LIFE _5_ METHOD _SL_ COST _6028.00_ | | | PURCHASED FROM _JONES CO._ |

ADDITIONS		REVISED		
DATE	AMOUNT	BASIS	COST	6028.00
			ADDITIONS	
			REVISED BASIS	
			DEPRECIATION TAKEN	
			SELLING PRICE	
			GAIN OR LOSS	
			DATE OF SALE	
			SOLD TO	

Figure 7: Depreciation Card

For more efficient management, frequent reports are recommended; under an automated system it is possible to get periodic reports showing income and expenditures.

This enterprise information provides cost of a given production unit for the period as well as to date. It allows certain decisions to be reached relative to cutting back. Due to the relatively long period of time required to raise a crop or to finish livestock, it is difficult for management to make major decisions during the period, but these reports do provide a good basis for decision for the next period of time.

The balance sheet is usually prepared only at the end of the year and/or when it is necessary for outsiders such as a banker.

Many farmers keep their own records which precludes the previously mentioned examples. They can prepare a summary such as the one shown in Figure 10. This report is set up for the owner to group his expenditures and income into broad categories so that the overall income of the farm can be examined at a glance. If more detailed information is desired, the same format as Figure 9 might be used by the operator.

Although these monthly reports are quite simplified, their advantage is that the farmer can assess the progress of his business rather than to wait until the end of the year.

RECORD OF DEPRECIABLE ASSETS

DATE OF PURCHASE	ITEM	COST	SALVAGE VALUE	LIFE	METHOD OF DEP.	DEPRECIATION					
						19___	19___	19___	19___	19___	19___
JANUARY 1, 19	TRACTOR	6028.00	1028.00	5	SL	1000.00					

Figure 8: Schedule of Depreciation

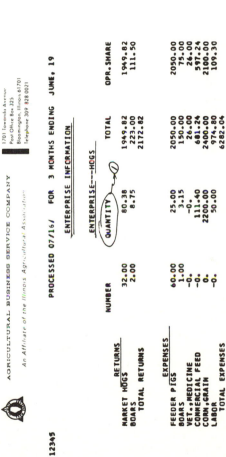

AGRICULTURAL BUSINESS SERVICE COMPANY

An Affiliate of the Illinois Agricultural Association

1701 Towanda Avenue
Post Office Box 325
Bloomington, Illinois 61701
Telephone 309 828 0021

PAGE 7

12345   PROCESSED 07/16/   FOR   3 MONTHS ENDING   JUNE, 19

ENTERPRISE INFORMATION

ENTERPRISE---HOGS

	NUMBER	QUANTITY	TOTAL	OPR.SHARE
RETURNS				
MARKET HOGS	32.00	80.38	1949.82	1949.82
BOARS	2.00	8.75	223.00	111.50
TOTAL RETURNS			2172.82	
EXPENSES				
FEEDER PIGS	60.00	25.00	2050.00	2050.00
BOARS	1.00	3.15	150.00	75.00
VET.,MEDICINE	-0-	-0-	26.00	26.00
COMMERCIAL FEED	-0-	111.40	681.24	597.24
CORN,GRAIN	-0-	2200.00	2400.00	2100.00
LABOR	-0-	50.00	974.80	109.30
TOTAL EXPENSES			6282.04	

NET RETURNS   -4109.22

① Qut. for livestock, Bu. for grain, etc.

* COURTESY OF THE AGRICULTURAL BUSINESS SERVICE COMPANY,
BLOOMINGTON, ILLINOIS.

Figure 9:   Report of Periodic Expenditures

MONTHLY INCOME AND EXPENSE STATEMENT (Cash Basis)

For Month of_____

INCOME:

Grain   _____

Livestock   _____

Feed/Seed   _____

Milk   _____

Wool   _____

Other   _____

    TOTAL   _____

EXPENSES:

Labor   _____

Fuel   _____

Seed   _____

Feed   _____

Fertilizer   _____

Vet   _____

Depreciation (Estimate) _____

Dues/Subscription   _____

Supplies   _____

Other   _____

    TOTAL   _____

      NET INCOME OR LOSS   _____

Figure 10: Monthly Report of Expenditures

27

Florists (Retail)

BY THEODORE PANAGIOTIS

Administrative Officer, Army
Map Service, Corps of Engi-
neers, U.S. Army; formerly
Chief, Accounting, Clerical, and
Training Division, Small Busi-
ness Administration, Providence,
Rhode Island

Characteristics of the Business That Affect the Accounting System

"Say it with flowers" is a slogan commonplace in our lives. That special birthday, that extraordinary occasion, and those time-honored holidays, weddings, and funerals call for flowers in one form or another.

Retail florist shops are principally located in metropolitan business districts, neighborhood residential areas, or in small towns. The florist in the downtown shop caters to transients and telephone callers in most cases, has both cash and charge sales, makes deliveries, and carries sidelines such as art novelties and pottery. The neighborhood store is a shop of goodwill, personal and friendly service, and convenience to the area. A small-town florist usually has a greenhouse, makes roadside sales, and has agents in nearby towns who telephone orders.

It is up to the retail florist, through an outside public accountant, to install an accounting system that will provide the information needed for efficient management of the business. Profitable operation of the florist shop also requires that the retailer be of artistic temperament, have considerable physical stamina, and be knowledgeable about the care and handling of a broad variety of plants and flowers.

FUNCTIONAL CHARACTERISTICS OF THE BUSINESS

A retail florist business can be operated as a single proprietorship, the most common form (and in many cases a family affair), as a partnership, or as a corporation. Records are usually kept on a calendar basis.

Statistics for the past few years indicate that the number of retailers has increased proportionately faster than the population, so that many shops are doing a rather small volume of business. There is competition in the field since the general public prefers the automobile that can travel miles, to the ordinary feet that used to stay in the neighborhood.

Retail florist shops are especially busy at Easter and Christmas time and prior to Mother's Day and Memorial Day. Business is fair in the fall and usually slow in the summer except for June weddings.

PRINCIPAL ACCOUNTING PROBLEMS

The principal accounting problem is that of maintaining an adequate and balanced inventory since seasonal variations in the demand for and supply of flowers are marked. In this respect, does the florist buy intelligently?

These working functions of buying and selling must be carefully controlled. Transactions should be regularly recorded in expense ledgers which can be scrutinized periodically for sales and profit changes. It is a well-known fact that the less skillful handlers sustain financial losses in the summer with their above average surpluses of flowers.

Also highly important among buying and selling techniques, and often neglected by the owner, is a friendly working relationship with his supplier as well as keeping abreast of special events that lead to sales of the supplier's stock.

Another accounting problem concerns transactions through the FTD (Florists' Transworld Delivery Association) and with fellow operators in other localities.

Functional Organization

The typical retail flower shop is divided into three activities: (1) Sales or showroom with its attractive shop front, display tables, stands and shelves, and walk-in refrigerator with flowers; (2) Workroom area with its tables and counters, with drawers for such supplies as wrapping paper, ribbons, pins, etc., plus the delivery truck; and (3) Office area with its desk and filing cabinets.

Service in all its aspects is the most essential ingredient of a successful retail florist business. Orders are taken in the first activity, processed and delivered by the second, and records of the transactions are maintained in the third. The size of the business and clientele determines whether one, two, or more persons can handle the three activities.

Principles and Objectives of the Accounting System

The purpose of this chapter is to explain how to set up an accounting system for retail florists. Basically the ordinary retailing system covers income, costs, and expenses; but an important consideration that reflects the entire operation is extraordinary service to the customer. Not shown in the records are these human emotions that go into the business. Costs thus reflect the community spirit of the retail florist, since he usually is one of the leading businessmen in the area.

The chief aim of an effective accounting system is to make the operation of the business more efficient and to help in planning, forecasting, and control. Reports compiled through the record-keeping system help in the maintenance of proper sales, price and inventory ratios in relation to prevailing economic conditions.

The retailer may ask himself, "Can I increase sales by more advertising? Can I meet competition by offering better service, or even cutting prices?" The retailer must also answer this poser: "Could I outlast a period of recession, or a difficult price adjustment period?"

These are some of the questions that can be answered by studying regular reports obtained from accounting records. Trends may also be spotted while they are still developing, such as an abnormal increase in charge sales, over-buying, lagging collections on receivables, or an alarming decrease in working capital.

Classification of Accounts and Books of Accounts

The chart of accounts for a retail florist business, shown below, is typical. A system should be started with at least these accounts. Other names and accounts can be added as they are needed in growth of the operation. It is understood that account numbers could be changed to suit any record-keeping situation.

BALANCE SHEET ACCOUNTS.

ASSETS

Current assets

101 Cash in Bank
102 Petty Cash
122 Accounts Receivable
122R Estimated Uncollectible
         Accounts
123 Commissions Receivable—
         FTD "Outgoing"
124 Agent Commissions
         Receivable
131 Merchandise Stock
132 Operating Supplies
141 Prepaid Insurance
142 Prepaid Taxes
143 Other Deferred Charges

Fixed assets

161 Land (omit if premises are
         rented)
162 Buildings (substitute Leasehold
         Improvements if rented)
162R Accumulated Depreciation
         (Amortization if rented)
163 Furniture and Fixtures
163R Accumulated Depreciation
164 Delivery Equipment
         (including Automotive)
164R Accumulated Depreciation

LIABILITIES

Current liabilities

201 Notes Payable
202 Accounts Payable
         2021 Clearing House Charges
                  Payable
211 Sales Tax Payable

221 Employee Payroll Deductions
         2211 Social Security Taxes
         2212 State Disability Insurance
         2213 Income Tax Withheld
                  (Federal)
         2214 Income Tax Withheld
                  (State)
222 Employer Payroll Taxes Payable
         2221 Social Security Taxes
         2222 Federal Social Security
                  Taxes (Employment)
         2223 State Social Security Taxes
                  (Employment)
223 Accrued Payroll
         2231 Accrued Commissions to
                  Agents
         2232 Accrued Commissions—
                  FTD "Incoming"
224 Accrued General Taxes
225 Other Accrued Liabilities

Long-term debts

231 Mortgages Payable

NET WORTH

Corporate accounts

291 Capital
292 Retained Earnings
293 Profit and Loss—Current

*Sole proprietorship or
partnership accounts*

291 Captial
         2911 Partner A
         2912 Partner B
292 Drawing
         2921 Partner A
         2922 Partner B
293 Profit and Loss—Current

INCOME AND EXPENSE ACCOUNTS.

REVENUES

Sales

301 Merchandise Sales
    3011 Class 1
    3012 Class 2
    3013 FTD
    3014 Other

Cost of sales

401 Cost of Merchandise Sold
    4011 Class 1
    4012 Class 2
    4013 FTD
    4014 Other

EXPENSES

500 Expenses—Control
503 General and Administrative

Salaries and Wages

511 Supervision
512 Employees

Selling

521 Advertising and Promotion
522 Travel and Entertainment
523 Commissions to Agents
524 Commissions—FTD "Incoming"
525 Clearing House Charges

Delivery

531 Delivery, excluding Wages
532 Supplies—Wrapping, Boxes, etc.
533 Express—Cartage, In

Occupancy

541 Rent
542 Utilities—Heat, Light and Power, Water
543 Repairs and Maintenance

Depreciation

552 Buildings
553 Furniture and Fixtures
554 Delivery Equipment (including Automotive)

Overhead

581 Donations
582 Insurance
583 Interest
584 Losses on Bad Accounts
585 Memberships, Dues, Publications
586 Miscellaneous
587 Office Supplies, Stationery, Postage
588 Other Taxes and Licenses
589 Payroll Taxes
590 Professional Services
591 Telephone and Telegraph

OTHER INCOME AND DEDUCTIONS

Other Income

601 Cash Discounts Taken
602 Cash Over
603 Miscellaneous Income

Deductions from Income

651 Cash Discounts Allowed
652 Cash Short
653 Miscellaneous Losses

ACCOUNTS PECULIAR TO THE BUSINESS

Commissions Receivable—FTD "Outgoing" (No. 123) and *Agent Commissions Receivable (No. 124).* These two current asset accounts concern revenue that is due the retail florist for filling orders through the FTD or by private means.

Merchandise Stock (No. 131). This account can be broken down into two or more categories. For example, Fresh Flowers, Plants, etc. (No. 1311) and Artificial Flowers and Gifts (No. 1312).

Operating Supplies (No. 132). This is an inventory account and should be handled on a monthly basis with a beginning and ending amount and an estimate of the quantity of wrapping paper, wire, cartons, boxes, labels, ribbons, and other supplies used during the month to charge to the expense account.

Clearing House Charges Payable (No. 2021). These are charges due orders cleared through the FTD.

Accrued Commissions to Agents (No. 2231) and *Accrued Commissions FTD "Incoming" (No. 2232).* These accounts cover commissions due to others on orders made through the FTD or by private means.

Clearing House charges (outgoing orders) and credits (incoming orders) are accounts that are peculiar to the florist operating on a retail basis. Such charges and credits are taken care of periodically through the central clearing house and are reflected in the following accounts: Commissions Receivable—FTD "Outgoing" (No. 123), an asset account; Clearing House Charges Payable (No. 2021) and Accrued Commissions—FTD "Incoming" (No. 2232), liability accounts; FTD (No. 3013) and FTD (No. 4013), revenue accounts; Commissions—FTD "Incoming" (No. 524), Clearing House Charges (No. 525), and Memberships, Dues, Publications (No. 585), expense accounts.

Fresh Flowers, Plants, etc., Class 1 (No. 3011), Artificial Flowers and Gifts, Class 2 (No. 3012), and FTD Sales (No. 3013) are breakdown accounts under Merchandise Sales. No. 3013 is chiefly commissions for outside orders made through the Association. If the amounts here are substantial, a No. 3014 account could be established for commissions on outside orders made through private means.

The Class 1 and 2 titles shown above (Nos. 4011 and 4012) are part of the Cost of Merchandise Sold series, as well as the FTD Costs (No. 4013). The latter chronicles costs in connection with filling outside orders through the Association. Account No. 4014 could also be set up, if necessary, to deal with costs contracted on outside orders made through private means.

Greenhouse. If the florist has a greenhouse, the accounts to be set up would include Greenhouse Stock (No. 1313) under the current asset, Merchandise Stock (No. 131); Greenhouse Flowers, Plants, etc. (No. 3015) under the sales account, Merchandise Sales (No. 301); and Greenhouse Flowers,

FLOWERS AND GIFTS

by

WOODLAWN FLOWER SHOP

725-7079   478 West Avenue
              Pawtucket, Rhode Island

No. 978654   Date_____

Deliver to:_____

           _____

           _____

                    Date wanted_____

AMOUNT	DESCRIPTION	COST

CARD_____

    _____

    _____

    _____

Charge to:_____

          _____

          _____

          _____

     PAID   CHARGE   C.O.D.   TEL. DEL.

     ____   _____   _____   _____

_____

_____

Figure 1: Sales Invoice

Plants, etc. (No. 4015) under cost of sales account, Cost of Merchandise Sold (No. 401).

BOOKS AND FORMS PECULIAR TO THE BUSINESS

Business is conducted in triplicate; an original and two copies of each sales invoice, dated, are made in numerical order (Figure 1). The original is kept by the florist for filing and referral, one copy is kept for use as a work slip, and the third is for the customer.

Filing and referral originals are put away on a monthly basis, after posting from sales invoices to the Sales journal and then to individual Accounts Receivable ledger. Cash referrals should give names and addresses whenever possible and should be marked by the florist with special notations such as color choice, whether for male or female, the type of floral arrangement—in case of repeat orders. In addition to the usual credit sales, cash sales made to regular customers can also be recorded in the individual ledger.

Names and addresses from both sales invoices and/or ledgers are used in sending circulars, advertising cards, and other materials. (Sending Christmas cards, for example, is definitely good business.) Transients who pay cash are left on referrals only.

Cash sales are grouped and one entry made in the Sales journal. At the end of each month total sales, both credit and cash, from this journal should

WEEKLY REPORT OF ORDERS FILLED

Sent to _____

Code No. _____
Report No. _____

Date _____

Sending member Code No.	Del.date	Recipient	Gross Amt.

Figure 2: FTD Report

equal the sum of charges added to monthly statements and cash sales total.

The workshop sales invoice is thrown away when an order is filled, but not before the initials of the worker are checked, to be sure the order has gone out, and transferred to the file copy.

Sales of flowers or other merchandise to be delivered in other localities are recorded on a special form (Figure 2) that is periodically sent to the FTD Clearing House.

Other than the Sales journal and the Accounts Receivable ledger, already mentioned, books which are recommended for the business include a Cash Receipts journal, a Cash Disbursements journal, General and Purchase journals, and General and Accounts Payable ledgers.

Peculiarities of Procedures

There are no out-of-the-ordinary procedures for the sales-receivables and purchases-payables cycles, nor for cash receipts and disbursements.

Time and Payroll System

Cost Accounting

No peculiarities are associated with the time and payroll system or with cost accounting.

Reports to Management

Such reports as a profit and loss statement (Figure 3), a balance sheet, an inventory control report (all of these internal reports are compiled by the accountant for his florist client), and an outside FTD report are prepared periodically, preferably monthly.

Only the inventory report and the outside FTD report require comment.

Inventory Control Report. This periodic report offers data on the types of flowers and other merchandise that sell at certain times of the year. The report is an invaluable tool for management, barring unforeseen shortages or other unnatural influences.

FTD Report. Prepared by the Clearing House Department of the Florists' Transworld Delivery Association, the report lists the number of outgoing and incoming orders by months and years and allows for comparisons and percentage changes. This report is a service to member florists.

PROFIT AND LOSS STATEMENT
for the year ending_____

SALES
    Class 1_____ $_____

    Class 2_____ $_____
    Total_____ $_____

COST OF MERCHANDISE SOLD
    Class 1_____ $_____

    Class 2_____ $_____
    Total_____ $_____

GROSS PROFIT $_____ $_____ $_____

FIXED EXPENSES
    Depreciation(breakdown)___$_____

    Insurance_____ _____

    Interest_____ _____

    Rent_____ _____

    Taxes and licenses_____ _____

    Utilities(breakdown)_____ _____
    Total fixed expenses_____ $_____
BALANCE $_____

VARIABLE EXPENSES
    Delivery(breakdown)_____ $_____

    Losses on bad accounts____   _____

    Professional services_____   _____

    Repairs & maintenance_____   _____

    Salaries and wages_____   _____

    Selling(breakdown)_____   _____

    Telephone & telegraph_____   _____

    Other(breakdown)_____   _____
    Total variable expenses___ $_____
    Total all expenses_____ $_____

NET PROFIT $_____

Figure 3: Profit and Loss Statement

28

Fuel Oil (Retail Dealers)

BY CHARLES S. M. CAMERON

Public Accountant; Vice President-Manager, Glendale Coal & Oil Company, Charlestown, Massachusetts; Manager-Comptroller, Glen Coal & Oil Company, New Bedford, Massachusetts

Characteristics of the Business That Affect the Accounting System

The retail fuel oil business involves truck delivery of oil to household and commercial consumers. Available to them are six basic grades of oil: Kerosene #1 and water white; furnace oil #2; diesel #50, and three heavy oils, #4, 5, and 6.

Kerosene is not in demand today as it once was when the kitchen range was a prime user of this product. The basic grade oil for household use is now furnace oil. Burners are adapted and designed to handle a certain grade of oil, which may be light or heavy. Heavy oil burners can, however, burn furnace oil with proper burner adjustments. Large commercial buildings use any one of the varied grades of heavy oil, although on occasion light oil may be purchased for them.

Sales of fuel oil are highly seasonal. Oil burner cleanings and overhauls start in the spring and continue through fall, although domestic hot water customers continue to receive oil during the off season. It is not uncommon for a fuel company to sell appliances, air conditioners, boats, and other merchandise during the slow season.

Very few oil companies who have handled coal in the past will handle it today. The reason is that the coal business is on the same path of decline already followed by the kerosene industry. Fuel oil companies who have customers desiring to buy coal contract with coal dealers to deliver this product for them. The fuel oil companies can retain Receivables on their books and thus open the way for future conversions to oil. Contracts with coal dealers permit oil companies to sell off their own coal trucks, loaders, and other equipment. New capital is, therefore, channeled into the business; and other cash is freed for improved maintenance of oil trucks and purchases of new equipment.

Fiscal year of the fuel oil business varies. Closings usually occur between March and August, depending upon the desires of management.

FUNCTIONAL CHARACTERISTICS OF THE BUSINESS

There are nine basic departments upon which a fuel business may be built, as shown in Figure 1.

Billing is often done by several departments to ease the burden. The

X Y Z FUEL COMPANY

ORGANIZATIONAL CHART

President

Vice President-Manager   Treasurer   Vice President- Sales & Operations

Accounting & Billing   Service

Payroll   Sales

Credit Department   Trucks

Machine Operators   Oil Shipper (Degree Day)

Switchboard & Billing

Figure 1: Organizational Chart

Credit Department handles delinquent accounts, ages the accounts each month, and processes all new credit applications as submitted by the Sales Department. The term "Operations" as used in the title of Vice President— Sales & Operations includes supervision of truck repairs, mechanics' duties, and garage upkeep, all of them specifically a part of the Truck Department. Other duties that department performs are oil delivery, truck servicing, inventory of tires, batteries, etc. The Degree Day System described in a later paragraph is under jurisdiction of the Oil Shipping Department.

Principles and Objectives of the Accounting System

The accounting requirements for a retail fuel business do not present any special problems. There are, however, certain areas in the system which merit individual mention:

Points. The use of the point system comes into play where price adjustments are to be made in order to meet competitive prices. The point system is applied both to heavy oil and to light oil customers. When city, state, and Federal governments and large commercial businesses ask for quotations on oil deliveries covering a period of time, the quotations must include the price, allowances (if any), the number of gallons to be delivered, and the storage capacity. Such bids are usually based on tank car price, plus whole cents or points. Or the allowances may be figured by deducting the points from the retail price. The gallonage volume is the usual basis in determining the total number of points to be allowed.

The points refer to or represent portions of one cent broken down into tenths. For example, 50 points = 1/2 cent; 80 points = 8/10 of one cent. Mathematically these would appear as $.005 and $.008. Five points would be written as $.0005; eight points as $.0008, etc. This is not to say that allowances of whole cents are not given. They are, and quite frequently. These allowances are charged directly to sales or sales allowances. Care must be taken that the distinction between allowances and discounts is clear. Discounts are charged directly to the expense account.

Inventories. Inventories are priced on a First-In-First-Out (FIFO) basis, which is particularly advantageous during the "summer-fill" months. This period usually runs from May through September. A product purchased during this time from the major supplier by the retail owner is not paid for until October. Prices are lower, and usually the low-priced inventory carries right into the higher price season.

Oil that lies close to the bottom of the storage tank is usually unobtainable because of the placement of pipe outlets and because of the sediment that settles in the bottom of the tank. An estimate valued in dollars should be established regarding this "unobtainable" oil and should be taken into consideration in computing the ending inventory. This is done by deducting the estimated value from the gross inventory and thus netting out the inventory. Trucking is applied to the cost according to the rate charge per gallon.

Degree Day System. Automatic fuel oil delivery is the nerve center of the retail fuel oil business. Such delivery for household consumption is best accomplished by using what is called the Degree Day System. Based on temperature fluctuations, the degree days are figured from 65° Fahrenheit. The highest and lowest temperatures for a certain day are added and then divided by 2. The result is subtracted from the standard 65°; the minus degrees thus obtained are called degree days for that particular day. Automatic oil deliveries are set up on a "K" factor, which is computed as follows:

1. The previous degree day total (last delivery) is subtracted from the current degree day total after current delivery.
2. The net difference is divided by the number of gallons delivered. The result is the "K" factor.
3. This "K" factor is multiplied by the tank size (usually 200 gallons), and the result is the degree day number when the next delivery is due.

Degree days and "K" factors are figured for each customer and are recorded on a card, as shown in Figure 2.

Customer
Address

DATE	GALS. DELVD	K	D. D. TO-DATE			NEXT
11-26	145	3.1	1130			1750
12-14	162	2.8	1589			2169
12-29	147	3.1	2056			2676
1-13	155	2.8	2501			3061
1-27	171	3.0	3018			3618
2-9	175	2.9	3528			4108

Figure 2: Degree-Day Record Card

If, for example, a customer received 175 gallons of oil on February 9, a check of his card shows 510 degree days between the last delivery on January 27 and the current delivery on February 9 (3528 minus 3018). The 175 gallons delivered is divided into the sum of 510, resulting in the new "K" factor for the next delivery (2.9). The customer's standard tank holds 275 gallons. From this amount is deducted the reserve of 75 gallons; a net of 200 gallons remains. The net of 200 is multiplied by the "K" factor of 2.9 with a result of 580 degree days, or the time necessary to elapse before the next delivery. Next step is to add the accumulated degree days to date (3528) to the 580 degree days just figured. The result is the degree day figure of 4108 for the next delivery.

During the warm or off season it is necessary to compensate for the use of fuel oil consumed in hot water units. To do this, six degree days are added when the mean temperature is 62° and higher.

Interestingly enough, the Credit Department is tied closely to the Degree Day System. Fluctuations in degree days are a forecast to the Credit Department of the trend of the charges going against Receivables. Thus the Degree Day System is in close relationship to company financing.

It is not practical to place heavy oil (black oil) on a Degree Day System because of the volume that is delivered at one time (usually 4500 gallons). If a whole load cannot be taken at one time by a customer, the remaining load must be returned to the plant or point of pickup. Such a procedure entails time and money. Heavy oil accounts, therefore, keep track of their own oil needs and call when they can take a full load. The Degree Day System, then, is primarily for the delivery of #2 furnace oil (household).

Degree days for each day are furnished by the weather bureau and are also listed each day in the newspaper. The degree day count usually begins September 1 of each year.

Classification of Accounts and Books of Accounts

GENERAL LEDGER

The General ledger can be as long or short as necessary. The separate departments as depicted in the organization chart (Figure 1) are charged for all expenses incurred. Books are kept on the accrual basis. The following chart of accounts lists 137 possible accounts that carry from the balance sheet right through the profit and loss section.

BALANCE SHEET ACCOUNTS.

ASSETS

Current Assets

1-1   Cash

1-2   Petty Cash
1-3   Deposit on Bids
1-4   Exchange Account
1-5   Investments

1-6 Accounts Receivable—
     Light Oil
1-7 Accounts Receivable—
     Heavy Oil
1-8 Miscellaneous Accounts
     Receivable
1-9 Inventory—Light Oil
1-10 Inventory—Heavy Oil
1-11 Inventory—Service Parts
     and Equipment
1-12 Notes Receivable

Other Current Assets

1-13 Cash Surrender Value
     Insurance
1-14 Prepaid Insurance
1-15 Prepaid Registrations
1-16 Prepaid Real Estate Taxes
1-17 Prepaid Life Insurance
     Premiums
1-18 Goodwill

Fixed Assets

1-19 Land
1-20 Buildings
1-21 Allowance for Depreciation—
     Buildings
1-22 Automobiles
1-23 Allowance for Depreciation—
     Automobiles
1-24 Trucks
1-25 Allowance for Depreciation—
     Trucks
1-26 Furniture and Fixtures
1-27 Allowance for Depreciation—
     Furniture and Fixtures

1-28 Garage Equipment

LIABILITIES

Current Liabilities

2-1 Accounts Payable—Merchandise
2-2 Accounts Payable—Expenses
     (optional)
2-3 Accounts Payable—
     Miscellaneous
2-4 Notes Payable
2-5 Notes Receivable Discounted
2-6 Accrued Payroll
2-7 Accrued Expenses
2-8 Prepaid Customers' Receivables
2-9 State Unemployment Tax
     Payable
2-10 Federal Unemployment Tax
     Payable
2-11 Federal Old Age Pension
     Payable
2-12 Employees' Income Tax
     Payable—Federal
2-13 Employees' Income Tax
     Payable—State
2-14 Real Estate Taxes Payable
2-15 Employees' Bonds—Savings

Long-Term Liabilities

2-16 Mortgage Payable

NET WORTH

3-1 Preferred Stock—Issued
3-2 Preferred Stock—Treasury
3-3 Common Stock—Issued
3-4 Common Stock—Treasury
3-5 Retained Earnings

INCOME AND EXPENSE ACCOUNTS.
INCOME

4-1 Sales—Light Oil
4-2 Allowances—Light Oil
4-3 Sales—Heavy Oil
4-4 Allowances—Heavy Oil
4-5 Sales—Oil Burners & Service

4-6 Allowances—Oil Burners &
     Service
4-7 Sales—Discounts—Heavy Oil
4-8 Sales—Discounts—Light Oil

Cost of Sales

5-1 Purchases—Light Oil

5-2 Discounts Received
5-3 Purchases—Heavy Oil
5-4 Purchases—Heavy Oil Solvents
5-5 Purchases—Oil Burners & Service
5-6 Cost of Sales (Inventory Clearing)

EXPENSES

Expenses—Sales

6-1 Sales Salaries
6-2 Sales Expense—Miscellaneous
6-3 Car Expense
6-4 Gasoline & Oil
6-5 Telephone
6-6 Christmas Expense
6-7 Donations
6-8 Advertising
6-9 Telephone Campaign
6-10 Credit Reports
6-11 Commissions

General and Administrative

7-1 Salaries
7-2 Officers' Salaries
7-3 Credit Department Salaries
7-4 Heat and Light
7-5 Telephone
7-6 Postage
7-7 Printing and Stationery
7-8 Interest
7-9 Professional Fees
7-10 Legal and Auditing
7-11 Capital Stock Expense
7-12 Cleaning Office
7-13 Miscellaneous
7-14 Car Expense
7-15 Gasoline and Oil
7-16 Group Insurance
7-17 Depreciation—Automobiles
7-18 Director's Fees
7-19 Insurance
7-20 Over and Short
7-21 Membership and Dues
7-22 Depreciation—Furniture and Fixtures

7-23 Taxes
7-24 State and Federal Unemployment Taxes
7-25 Federal and State Income Taxes
7-26 Federal Old Age Benefit Taxes
7-27 Life Insurance Premiums

Oil Department

8-1 Delivery Labor
8-2 Vacation Labor
8-3 Garage Labor
8-4 Welfare Fund—Mechanics
8-5 Pension Fund—Mechanics
8-6 Welfare Fund—Other
8-7 Pension Fund—Other
8-8 Uniforms
8-9 Hired Trucking
8-10 Shipping Office Salaries
8-11 Office Salaries
8-12 Garage Expenses
8-13 Gasoline & Oil
8-14 Truck Parts
8-15 Oil Truck Equipment
8-16 Registrations
8-17 Truck Insurance
8-18 Truck Taxes
8-19 Depreciation—Oil Trucks
8-20 Truck Tires
8-21 Telephone
8-22 Printing and Stationery
8-23 Advertising

Oil Burner Expenses

9-1 Gasoline and Oil
9-2 Automobile Expense
9-3 Telephone
9-4 Printing and Stationery
9-5 Commissions
9-6 Labor
9-7 Postage
9-8 Depreciation—Service Trucks
9-9 Truck Tires
9-10 Truck Parts
9-11 Truck Registrations
9-12 Truck Insurance

The current asset labeled Prepaid Registrations (No. 1-15) refers to the cost of registering the trucks with the Registry of Motor Vehicles for the calendar year. The cost is allocated over 12 months.

Peculiarities of Procedures

CASH RECEIPTS

The cash receipts for each day are recorded on a Master Cash Sheet (Figure 3). Such recording enables the deposit to be made immediately after all cash and checks received have been entered. The cash sheet is then forwarded to the Accounts Receivable posting clerk (machine), and the cash item is posted to the proper customer's ledger card. Without the use of the cash sheet, the posting clerk would have to stop all other posting work each morning and post all checks and cash at once in order to expedite and insure daily deposits. The cash sheet method permits posting of daily cash as the clerk can get to it.

CASH DISBURSEMENTS

The disbursement book picks up everything that is paid out via checkbook. The Accounts Payable are cleared, Miscellaneous Expenses are paid, Petty Cash is replenished, and expenses charged. The Cash Disbursements book presents no special problems. It is routine.

SALES

The sales for each day are priced, extended, and totaled. Delivery tickets are tallied for total gallons for the day. This total is checked against the truck inventories at the close of business each day. All trucks have meters and the opening reading is subtracted from the closing reading; the result should be the same as the total of the tickets that were metered by that truck. Each truck is numbered, and a driver is assigned to that particular truck. Each delivery ticket (Figure 4) carries the name of the driver, truck number, customer's name, and meter reading. Made out in triplicate, the original white copy is for the office, the yellow second copy for the customer, and the third (cardboard) copy is the salesman's commission record.

The customer's name is printed on each ticket by an addressograph plate, an operation done at the office by the Oil Shipping Department. Sales for each department are then recorded on a Master Sales Sheet (Figure 5). Thus the daily sales are centralized and then recorded in the Sales book.

The item called Kil-Sludg,* shown on line 6 of Figure 5, is a heavy oil solvent. Its prime purpose is to dissolve sediment that settles on the bottom

* Trademark patented by Standard Chemicals, Inc., Natick, Massachusetts

X Y Z COMPANY

CASH RECEIPTS

Date	Received from	Net Cash Deposited (Dr.)	Discounts (Dr.)	Allowances (Dr.)	Other Adjustments (Dr.)	Accounts Receivable		Cash Sales (Cr.)	Deposits
						H.O. (Cr.)	L.O. (Cr.)		

Figure 3: Master Cash Sheet

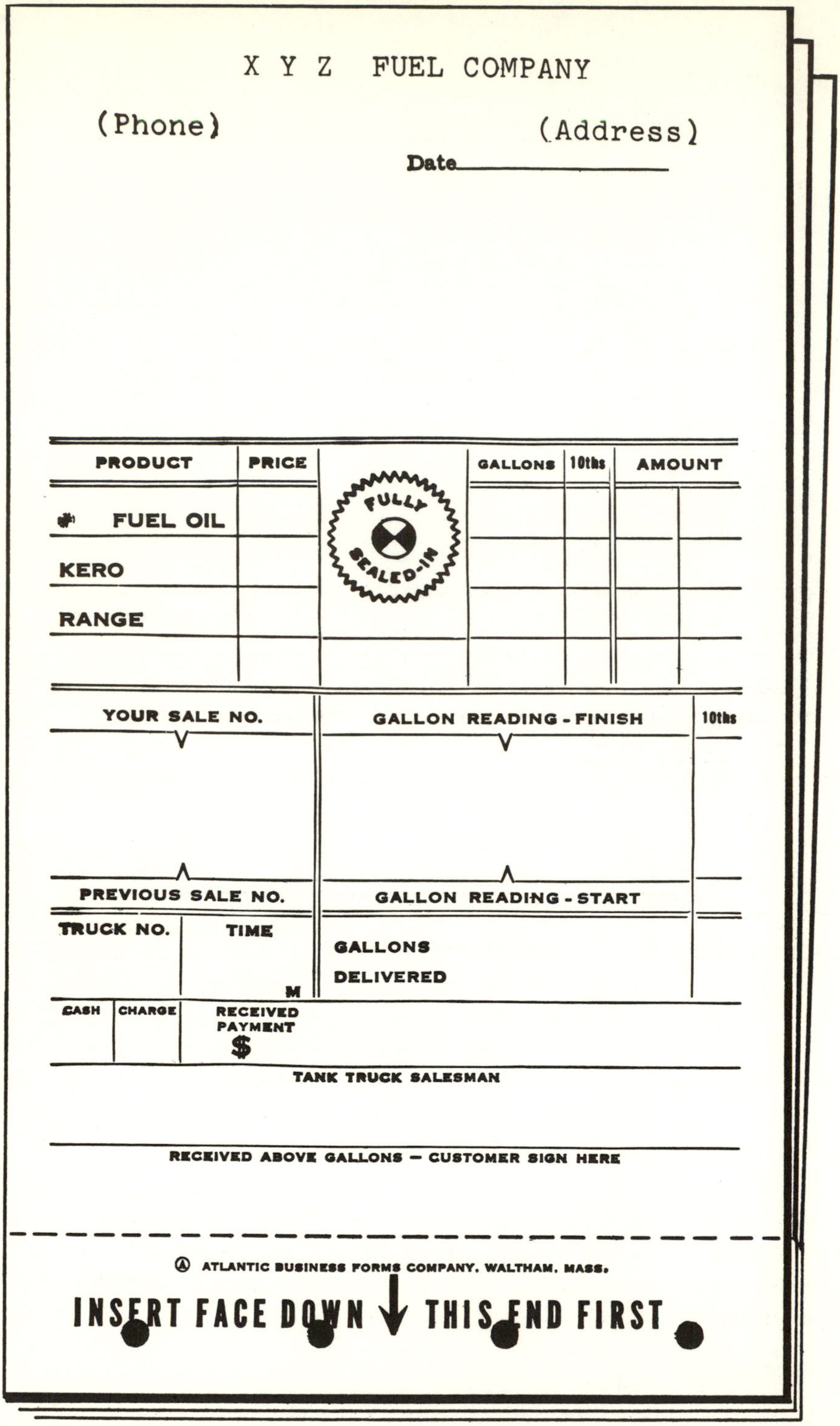

X Y Z FUEL COMPANY

(Phone)   (Address)

Date_____

PRODUCT	PRICE			GALLONS	10ths	AMOUNT
❀ FUEL OIL		FULLY SEALED-IN ⊗				
KERO						
RANGE						

YOUR SALE NO.	GALLON READING - FINISH	10ths
∨	∨	

∧	∧	
PREVIOUS SALE NO.	GALLON READING - START	

TRUCK NO.	TIME	GALLONS DELIVERED
	M	

CASH	CHARGE	RECEIVED PAYMENT $	

TANK TRUCK SALESMAN

RECEIVED ABOVE GALLONS — CUSTOMER SIGN HERE

- -

Ⓐ ATLANTIC BUSINESS FORMS COMPANY, WALTHAM, MASS.

INSERT FACE DOWN ↓ THIS END FIRST

* COURTESY OF ATLANTIC BUSINESS FORMS COMPANY, WALTHAM, MASSACHUSETTS

Figure 4: Oil Delivery Ticket

540

X Y Z FUEL COMPANY DATE _____			
#1 (RANGE) OIL RETAIL	GALLONS	CHARGE SALES	CASH SALES
#2 FUEL OIL			
#4 HEAVY OIL			
#5 HEAVY OIL			
#6 HEAVY OIL			
KIL-SLUDG			
BURNER SERVICE			
STOKER SERVICE (HARD & SOFT)			
BURNERS			
SALES TAX (PARTS NO CHARGE TO CUSTOMER)			
SALES TAX BURNERS AND PARTS CHARGED			
MISCELLANEOUS ITEMS			

Figure 5:   Master Sales Sheet

of the storage tanks. The Kil-Sludg is liquid and usually two gallons is added to 3000 gallons of oil, either at the pick-up rack or at the delivery location prior to unloading; the Kil-Sludg is poured into the storage tank before the oil hose is connected.

Accounts Receivable are broken down into two categories, Light Oil and Heavy Oil. The breakdown by type of oil is shown in the Sales book, the Cash Receipts book, the interoffice journals, etc., and is therefore carried into the General ledger and, of course, into the Machine Posting Department.

PURCHASES

Purchase invoices, the bills received from suppliers, include not only products but telephone, light, uniforms, restroom supplies, etc. The bills are approved and initialed by the department heads to which they pertain and are forwarded to the bookkeeper for entering. The invoices are then approved for payment by the treasurer or the vice president-manager.

Purchases are allocated between two separate books, the merchandise book and the expense book. The distinction lies in the fact that the purchases of product, burner parts and equipment, and any other major purchases, such as insurance, are recorded in the merchandise book. An Accounts Payable subsidiary is provided. Each expense purchase that is paid is checked off in the expense book. At the end of the month any open items are picked up on an adding machine tape. Thus there are two Accounts Payable: A Merchandise Accounts Payable and an Expense Accounts Payable.

JOURNALS

Adjustments made on the Accounts Receivable ledger accounts are handled by interoffice journal vouchers (Figure 6). The type of adjustments would include price corrections, posting to wrong accounts, allowing discounts and allowances, picking up Notes Receivable against Accounts Receivable, etc. These vouchers are recorded on journal summary sheets at the end of the month and are entered in the General journal.

SERVICE

The Service Department inventory is allocated between the trucks and the stockroom. Inventory cards (Figure 7) are kept for this purpose. The daily work slips are costed each day and recorded on a master sheet. Thus instant cost of sales information is provided at month's end, and the master sheet also accounts for free parts out of inventory under the free parts service contracts.

In order to speed delivery and to improve service to customers, the delivery vans are equipped with two-way radios. A service dispatcher handles all the customer service calls, records them on a call sheet, and relays these calls by radio to the servicemen on the road.

COAL

When coal is handled by fuel oil companies, the hard coal (anthracite) and the soft coal (bituminous) are set up as separate accounts in the General ledger, the Purchase book, and the Sales book. The interoffice journals would also specify both hard and soft coal. The Credit Department handles slow-paying accounts in the same manner as oil accounts. The most frequent COD payments (credited to the Cash Sales column in Figure 3) are received from hard coal customers. This does not imply less favorable credit among those customers but merely a preference on their part to pay cash.

Time and Payroll System

The payroll system involves individual employee Payroll ledgers, checks, and weekly payroll summary sheets. The ledger is one in common usage. Name of employee, address, Social Security number, number of dependents, and hourly rate or flat salary are typed at the top. The gross salary, overtime included, if any; all tax deductions; and special deductions such as insurance, payment for oil, union dues, etc., are spread across the line under the proper column headings. This same information is transferred to the employee's payroll check on a perforated strip provided for this use. Before the employee cashes the check, he separates the strip from the check along the perforation and keeps the strip as part of his own records. Checks are totaled, and the amount tallied is recorded on the checkbook stub and charged to the net payroll account in the Cash Disbursements book.

A weekly payroll summary sheet reflects the same information as is on the Payroll ledger and check number of each employee. At the end of the month the weekly payroll summary sheets are consolidated on a master sheet and the totals of Federal taxes, state taxes, FICA taxes, and all other deductions are posted to the General ledger. The salaries and wages are

X Y Z FUEL COMPANY

JOURNAL ENTRY #..............................

DATE ....

DEBIT .... $..............

ADDRESS ....

CREDIT .... $..............

ADDRESS ....

REASON ....

.... MADE OUT ....

APPROVED

_____ _____
Credit Manager General Manager

Figure 6: Interoffice Journal Voucher

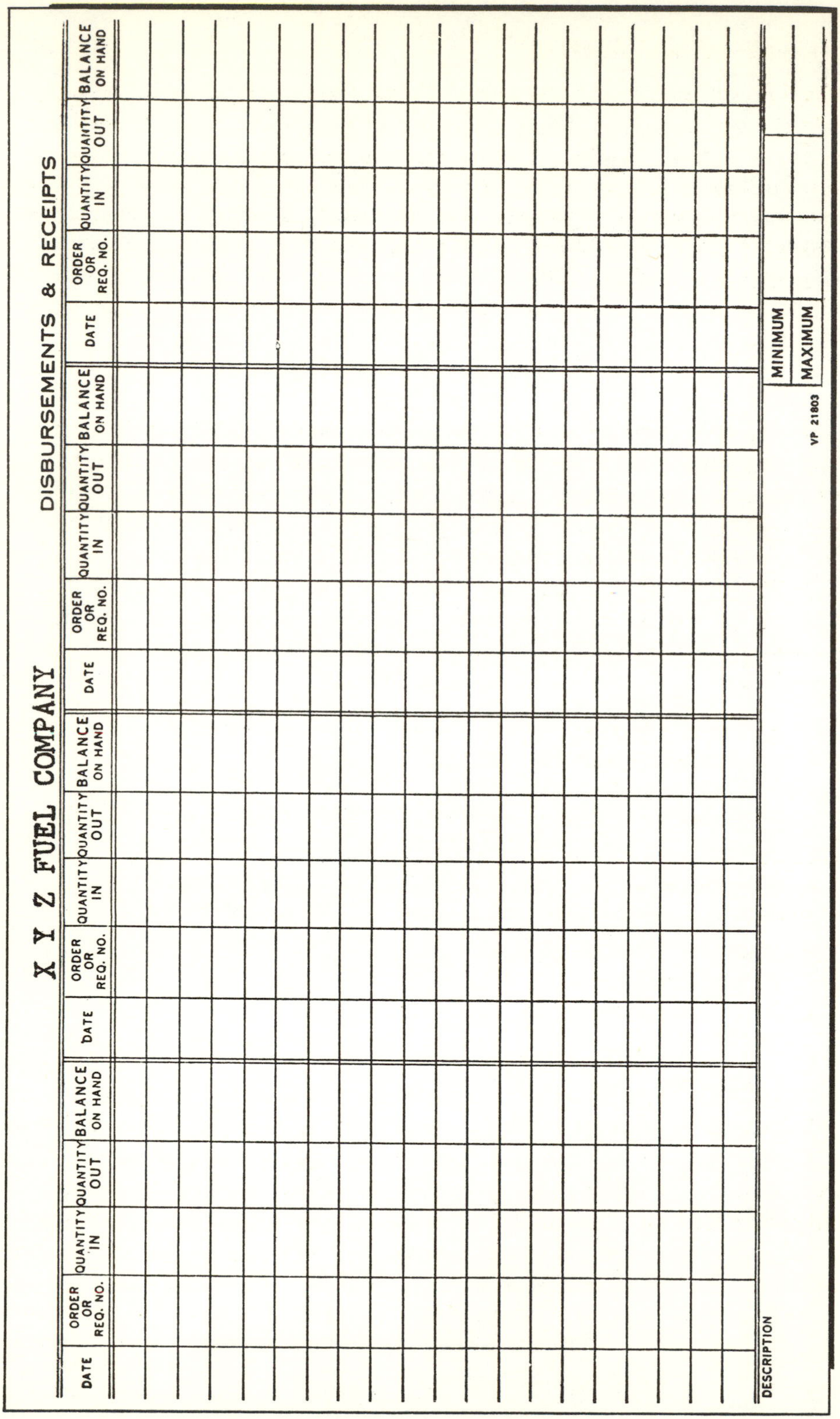

X Y Z FUEL COMPANY

DISBURSEMENTS & RECEIPTS

DATE	ORDER OR REQ. NO.	QUANTITY IN	QUANTITY OUT	BALANCE ON HAND	DATE	ORDER OR REQ. NO.	QUANTITY IN	QUANTITY OUT	BALANCE ON HAND	DATE	ORDER OR REQ. NO.	QUANTITY IN	QUANTITY OUT	BALANCE ON HAND	DATE	ORDER OR REQ. NO.	QUANTITY IN	QUANTITY OUT	BALANCE ON HAND

DESCRIPTION

MINIMUM	
MAXIMUM	

VP 21803

* COURTESY OF SHAWMUT PRESS, CHELSEA, MASSACHUSETTS

Figure 7: Service Department Inventory Card

charged to the proper departments. Credit Department salaries are maintained separately from office salaries; the same with Sales Department salaries. Such a separation enables management to pinpoint departmental expenses more accurately. The net payroll account is cleared through the checkbook. Need for a separate payroll account is, therefore, eliminated. There are other methods for payroll handling, but the one presented here is comprehensive and adequate.

Reports to Management

The reports to management consist of balance sheet, profit and loss statement, and supporting schedules including analysis of supplies. The frequency of these reports depends on management. The general rule calls for statements each month and more detailed information at the end of the fiscal year. Supporting schedules would include the following:

1. Analysis of accounts
   a. Accounts Receivable
   b. Exchange
   c. Investments
   d. Prepaid Expense
   e. Accounts Payable
   f. Notes Payable
2. Gross Profit
3. Purchases
4. Plant Expense
5. Oil Delivery Expense—Light and Heavy
6. Oil Burner Service Expense
7. General Overhead
8. Sales Expense.

Cash flow and ratio schedules would also be required from time to time. An illustration of an oil delivery expense schedule is shown in Figure 8.

References to these schedules are noted in the body of the statements.

The cost of sales schedule is an intricate part of the profit and loss statement. It is computed by adding purchases to opening inventory and deducting ending inventory. The profit and loss statement itself is shown in Figure 9 and reflects comparisons of the current year with one or more previous years.

X Y Z FUEL COMPANY

Oil Delivery Expense

For the Fiscal Year Ended June 30, 19--

Oil Shippers Salary

Drivers Wages

Pension Fund

Health and Welfare

Supplies

Insurance

Depreciation-Delivery Trucks

Tires and Tubes

Gas and Oil

Registrations

Excise Tax

Highway use tax

Truck Parts

Stationery

Truck Maintenance

Miscellaneous

Figure 8: Oil Delivery Expense Schedule

X Y Z FUEL COMPANY

Profit and Loss Statement

For the Fiscal Year Ended June 30, 19

Sales

    Less - cost of sales (Schedule)

Gross Profit

    Less Operating Expenses

        Plant Expense (Schedule #4)

        Oil Delivery Expense (Schedule #5)

        Service Department Expense (Schedule #6)

        General Expense (Schedule #7)

        Sales Expense (Schedule #8)

        Provision for Bad Debts

        Life Insurance Expense

        Discounts Allowed

Total Operating Expenses

Operating Profit

Add - Other Income

        Discounts received

        Bad Debts recovered

        Interest earned

Total Other Income

    Net Profit

        Less - Provision for Federal and State Taxes

Final Net Profit

Figure 9: Profit and Loss Statement

29

Fuel Oil (Bulk Distributors)

BY WILLIAM J. TIBBETTS

Public Accountant, Medford, Massachusetts; President and Director, M. J. Arnold Company, Inc., Boston; Treasurer and Director, Peerless Corporation, Newburyport, Massachusetts; Comptroller and Director, Glenco Oil Corporation, Charlestown, Massachusetts; Comptroller, Herbert McCarthy Oil Company, Inc., Stoneham, Massachusetts; Internal Auditor, Union Oil Company of Boston, Revere, Massachusetts

In this chapter, only inland fuel operations will be discussed. Distribution operations from the oil wells through the deep water terminal will not be considered, since they cannot be categorized as small or medium-sized business. Neither will retail fuel distribution be treated. This latter phase is to be found in another chapter of the "Portfolio".

Characteristics of the Business That Affect the Accounting System

The inland bulk fuel terminal is a storage plant located inland from the ocean, equipped with tanks (either above or below ground, depending on local Fire Department regulations). The retailer procures the product at this terminal, so that time-consuming and costly transportation to the deep water terminal is eliminated.

Fuel products, also known as heating oils, include kerosene (range oil or No. 1 oil), fuel oil (furnace oil or No. 2 oil), and bunker oils (heavy oil, or No. 4, No. 5, or No. 6 oil). Inland bulk plants do not generally handle bunker oils because of technical difficulties in their storage and transportation.

FUNCTIONAL CHARACTERISTICS OF THE BUSINESS

The seasonal nature of the business calls for fiscal closings at any time other than during the heating season, which normally extends from October through May. Because sizable Accounts Receivable and Accounts Payable are necessary in bulk plant operation, the books of account are always kept on an accrual basis.

Since World War II competition in the fuel oil business has been ever increasing. Discharged servicemen, rebelling against obeying military commands and with funds available to them from Federal and state governments, decided to establish their own businesses. A popular guide line in selecting a commercial field was "Businesses having an appeal to children and embodying necessaries of life always prosper." Both the retail and wholesale fuel oil trade received a considerable share of these new businessmen.

Competition in the heating oil field at all levels is extremely keen. Suppliers offer extra inducements to customers to maintain their gallonage volume. Unusual credit extension, painting of delivery equipment, loaning of delivery equipment, extension of management and accounting services, participation in cooperative promotional activities, etc., are common fringe benefits offered by competitors.

PRINCIPAL ACCOUNTING PROBLEMS

Inventory is the big factor confronting the inland bulk plant operator. Accountants—knowledgeable people on many subjects—are aware that petroleum products expand with heat and contract with cold. In this section we need not be concerned with these variances. They average out over the annual period. Product is sold, billed, and delivered year round to the bulk plant distributor at a converted temperature of 60 degrees. In the peak season the product is not stored long enough for any variations to affect inventory. In the slow seasons, inventory gains of small percentage will develop in the warm months, and losses of similar inconsequence will result in the cooler months.

"Stick measuring" is the process of taking a physical inventory of liquid products. A graduated stick is inserted into the top of the storage tank and lowered until the stick touches the bottom. Upon removal the resulting wet mark appearing on the stick provides the inches of product stored in the tank. These inches are converted to gallonage by referring to a calibration table. Many bulk plants of modern design are equipped with Petrometers, which are visual gauges showing the gallonage contained in the tank. Storing sufficient product during the peak seasons to satisfy the need of retailers requires hourly attention. Storing maximum product in the off season when prices are low and maintaining minimum inventories before prices are reduced are a profit and loss skill of themselves.

The accountant's greatest service to the inland bulk plant operator (and to himself) is to establish a perpetual inventory system to meet these inventory needs. The system described in this chapter should lend itself to daily reconciliation with physical inventories.

Functional Organization

Skilled personnel are *not* a requirement in the bulk distribution of fuel oil products. Tanker trucks or rail tanks bring the product to the plant. Oil is then discharged through use of pumps into storage tanks. Loading into retailers' trucks from the storage tanks is accomplished by pumps. The product passes through meters which record on a ticket the individual gallonage sale. Personnel familiar with the intake and output pumps of the storage plant can handle the mechanical operation of the plant.

A simple form, the Daily Summary of Operations (Figure 1), is prepared by the "pump man" to record meter readings, physical inventory, sales volume (gallonage and dollar value), receipts of the product (with supplier, trucker, or rail tank noted), and reconciliation of inventory or sales differences noted.

Principles and Objectives of the Accounting System

"Factoring" or "bank borrowing" by pledging Accounts Receivable to meet credit commitments to suppliers is a routine consideration of this business. Each sale to the retailer exceeds the $100 to $200 range, and several sales a day to each retailer are customary. For these reasons another vital

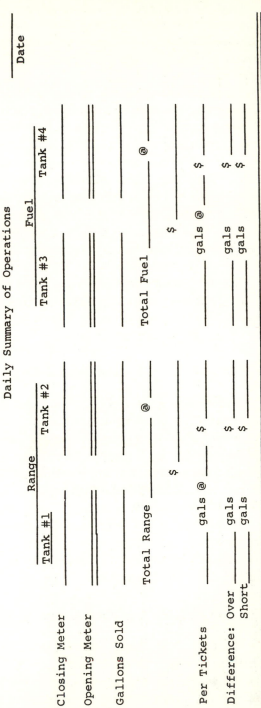

INLAND BULK TERMINAL
Daily Summary of Operations

	Range		Fuel		Date
	Tank #1	Tank #2	Tank #3	Tank #4	
Closing Meter					
Opening Meter					
Gallons Sold					
Total Range	____ gals @ ____				
	$ ____				
Total Fuel			____ gals @ ____		
			$ ____		
Per Tickets	____ gals		____ gals		
	$ ____		$ ____		
Difference: Over	____ gals		____ gals		
Short	____ gals $ ____		____ gals $ ____		

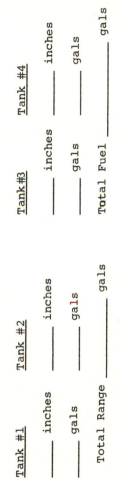

Inventory	Range	Fuel		Purchases Trucker or RR	Ticket No.	Gals.
On Hand at Opening	___ gals	___ gals		___	___	___
Add: Purchases				___	___	___
	___ gals	___ gals		___	___	___
Deduct: Sales	___ gals	___ gals		___	___	___
On Hand at Closing	___ gals	___ gals		___	___	___
Physical Inventory	___ gals	___ gals		___	___	___
Difference: Over	___ gals	___ gals		___	___	___
Short	___ gals	___ gals		___	___	___

PHYSICAL INVENTORY CLOSING

Tank #1 ___ inches   Tank #2 ___ inches   Tank#3 ___ inches   Tank #4 ___ inches
        ___ gals   ___ gals   ___ gals   ___ gals

Total Range ___ gals   Total Fuel ___ gals

Figure I: Daily Summary of Operations

part of the business is the billing and collection of Accounts Receivable. An Analysis of Current Aged Accounts Receivable (Figure 3) is necessary at least monthly; oftentimes a particular situation will require this report more frequently. No further elaboration is necessary on a routine report of this type.

Classification of Accounts and Books of Accounts

The General ledger, if arranged in the sequence of the following chart of accounts, facilitates preparation of interim reports. The trial balance can be taken by adding machine tape, then completed in financial statement form, so that the formal trial balance is eliminated.

BALANCE SHEET ACCOUNTS.

ASSETS

Current assets

1 Cash in Bank
2 Accounts Receivable
3 Loans Payable—Pledged
   Receivables
5 Due from Suppliers
10 Inventory

Fixed assets

15 Land
16 Buildings, Racks & Equipment
16A Allowance for Depreciation
17 Storage Tanks
17A Allowance for Depreciation
18 Furniture & Fixtures
18A Allowance for Depreciation

Prepaid expense

19 Unexpired Insurance
20 Other Prepayments

LIABILITIES

Current liabilities

31 Payroll Taxes Accrued and
    Withheld
32 Real Estate Taxes Payable
33 Accrued Federal and State
    Income Taxes
34 Accounts Payable

NET WORTH

40 Capital Stock
45 Retained Earnings

INCOME AND EXPENSE ACCOUNTS.

INCOME

Sales

50 Sales of Range—Fuel

Cost of sales

51 Purchases of Range—Fuel
55 Freight—Trucking In

60 Inventory Fluctuation

OPERATING EXPENSE

70 Wages
71 Payroll Taxes
75 Depreciation
80 Utilities
81 Insurance
82 Interest

83 Office Wages and Expenses
84 Professional Fees
85 Repairs and Maintenance
90 Taxes other than Payroll
95 Miscellaneous Expenses

OTHER INCOME AND EXPENSE

100 Sales Discounts and Allowances
105 Purchase Discounts
106 Additional Allowances
200 Profit or Loss

BOOKS AND FORMS PECULIAR TO THE BUSINESS

The full set of basic books includes the Cash Receipts journal, Cash Disbursements journal, Sales journal, Purchases book, General journal, General ledger, Accounts Receivable and Accounts Payable subsidiary ledgers, and the Individual Employee's Payroll records. An Expense or Voucher register is not necessary if expense items are expensed in the Cash Disbursements book. Product invoices and freight invoices are recorded in the Purchase book.

ACCOUNTS PECULIAR TO THE BUSINESS

Inventory Fluctuation (No. 60) represents the difference (gain or loss) between the inventory value appearing in the General ledger as the opening entry for the year, and the value of the physical inventory at the end of the report period.

Additional Allowances (No. 106) is unique to this business. This account records extra amounts offered by suppliers to terminal operators to meet competition; or they are offered as an inducement for purchasing when storage facilities of deep water terminals are saturated. This account is treated as other income rather than as a reduction of purchases. By keeping these figures out of Cost of Sales, the gross margin lends itself to a facile double check. Bulk plant margins (sales less purchases less freight) produce similar averages per gallon month after month. Variances can be traced to inventory appreciation or depreciation due to temperature (see discussion under the section titled Principal Accounting Problems) or freight differentials.

Peculiarities of Procedures

In preparing the income and expense statement directly from the General ledger, rather than from the formal trial balance, the usual Cost of Sales entry is replaced by purchases plus freight plus or minus Inventory Fluctuation (No. 60).

Using the Daily Summary of Operations form (Figure 1), the sales entry is prepared as follows:

Sales of Range Oil — Ticket gallonages × unit price = $ Sales
Sales of Fuel Oil — Ticket gallonages × unit price = $ Sales

The month's sales are simply an adding machine taping of this information.

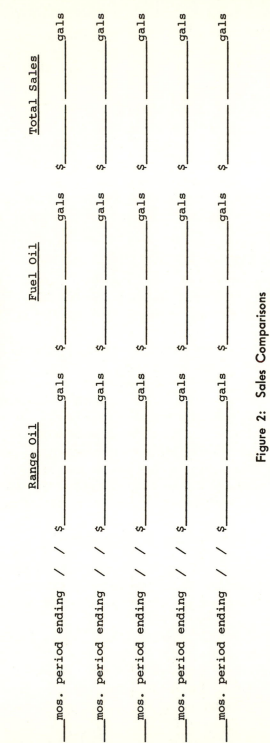

Figure 2: Sales Comparisons

ACCOUNTS RECEIVABLE AGING COMPARISONS

Date	Receivables	Current	30 Days	60 Days	90 Days	120 Days	Prior
	100%	%	%	%	%	%	%
	100%	%	%	%	%	%	%
	100%	%	%	%	%	%	%
	100%	%	%	%	%	%	%
	100%	%	%	%	%	%	%

Figure 3: Analysis of Current Aged Accounts Receivable

The Purchases column is used to check suppliers' invoices before posting the Purchase book and Accounts Payable subsidiary.

The Inventory reconciliation is used to reflect accumulative gains or losses of product per the books for the year.

Time and Payroll System

A routine procedure. Any payroll system preferred by the accountant for preparing required returns and recording individual earnings of employees may be used.

Reports to Management

The previously mentioned factoring or bank borrowing is a routine requirement of fuel oil distribution in bulk. It follows, therefore, that frequent financial reports (often monthly) be filed with loaning institutions. Among them is a Sales Comparisons report (Figure 2), a detailed comparison of gallonage and dollar value for the previous five years.

An evaluation of the Sales Comparisons report indicates that gallonage figures show management the gains or losses in business volume by comparison with other years. The dollar sales figures can explain increases or decreases in Accounts Receivable and Accounts Payable due to fluctuation in the unit prices.

Another report required frequently is the Analysis of Current Aged Accounts Receivable (Figure 3) with comparative agings at the same period for five years and the comparative percentages.

Evaluating this report for the accountant is not necessary. However, management can save considerable amounts in factoring costs and interest charges if this report is properly used. The desire for gallonage increases should be braked by cautioning the client that "sales are not sales until they have been collected."

The inland fuel terminal operator, like other seasonal business owners, smiles when the weather favors his particular enterprise. As the department store owner has his fat financial season at Christmas, the beach vendor loves the hot, sunny day, so the extreme cold weather pleases the fuel terminal operator.

Working with a "mills" per gallon gross margin, volume gallonage is essential. By establishing a system which constantly serves as a check on inventory, facilitates daily billing of sales, and provides immediate preparation of financial statements, the accountant supplies data at the time it is needed to the owner for the successful control of his business.

30

Funeral Directors

BY HAROLD J. COOK

Principal, H. J. Cook & Associates, Alma, Michigan; former Instructor in accounting and business subjects at Ferris Institute, Alma College, and Alma High School

Characteristics of the Business That Affect the Accounting System

"I certainly don't want to have any business with you!" is the stock remark of a person just introduced to a mortician. His business is probably the least understood of any, because most people don't want to think about, or talk about, the need for this service. Though we may treat him like the plague, all of us, at some time, will become his customer.

The business of the mortician is intricate, combining, as it does, the professional service of a licensed embalmer, the friendly and sympathetic assistance of a guiding director, and the diplomatic merchandising of caskets and paraphernalia. Numerous accommodations are usually performed by the establishment, such as obtaining burial permits, notifying relatives and the newspapers, and planning with the clergyman for services in the home, the church, the funeral establishment, and at the grave. Additional services in-

559

clude the securing of death certificate, arrangements for music, the receipt and placement of floral offerings, and last, but not least, the reception and ushering for family and friends. The funeral home has a chapel, a preparatory laboratory, and a casket selection room. The mortician's equipment usually includes a hearse, a flower car, limousines, and an ambulance as rolling stock. There are preparatory equipment and supplies, backdrop equipment, office equipment, furniture and fixtures, printing equipment and supplies, and real property. This multitude of tasks and expenses calls for a complete and detailed analysis to insure good financial control.

FUNCTIONAL CHARACTERISTICS OF THE BUSINESS

This business trends toward operation as a partnership because of the prevalence of father and son combinations. In many of the smaller towns the funeral home is run in conjunction with a furniture store, another reason for so many partnerships.

Records of the majority of the businesses are kept on a calendar-year basis. There could probably be a natural business year established, ending in the summer. Ordinarily there are more deaths in the winter months due to an increase in communicable diseases, winter accidents, etc. Therefore, if an accountant is interested in closing records during a naturally slow period, he would choose a fiscal-year basis terminating in June or July.

The profession of morticians does not experience competition, as it is generally understood in the business world. In the smaller towns, with populations up to about 4,000, there is usually only one mortuary. As a rule it is an old, well-established business that has been handed down through the family. Under such circumstances it is most difficult for a newcomer to become "competition," as it seems to be a human trait for a family to use the same mortician firm which has handled previous family funerals.

In cities, where competition does exist, it is a different type from that pertaining to merchandising of appliances, groceries, service stations, and so on. Morticians in these places must meet competitors in much the same manner as does a physician, an attorney, or a dentist. That is, he cannot openly advertise his wares and services, but relies on the appearance of his establishment, his social contacts in clubs, civic organizations, church, charity work, and personal recommendations by word-of-mouth from satisfied clients. The personality of a mortician and his "public relations" know-how serve as effective tools of competition.

Over the past decade union negotiators have placed increasing emphasis upon future contingencies. As a result, life insurance, hospitalization, old age insurance, retirement pensions, and annuities have become more common for the average person. Along with this foresightedness has been born a pre-arranged funeral plan. This is just another means of protecting the family's future. The plan provides for arrangement of the future service in a calm, businesslike manner; protects the family against sentimental over-spending; removes the possibility of a heavy burden falling on inexperienced or youthful shoulders.

PRINCIPAL ACCOUNTING PROBLEMS

The principal accounting problem is that of maintaining records to re-flect income and expenses as they relate to the many facets of the business. A departmental breakdown is a requisite in order to establish the fees and selling prices for caskets, vaults, clothing, and funeral and ambulance serv-ices. Actually a mortician's classification falls more into the category of a service, such as performed by an attorney or other professional men. There-fore, a funeral director's principal concern is the billing for services perform-ed. To arrive at a justifiable fee, all fixed overhead costs must be known, and to them all variable expenses and costs are added. The system to be de-scribed can be easily adapted either to a small, sole proprietorship opera-tion or a larger corporation.

As a result of recent best sellers which criticized the "high cost of dying," many more funeral directors are pricing complete service classifications. Using this method, established prices include the casket, embalming, burial permits, hearse, limousines, newspaper publications, use of the chapel, etc. Thus extra costs are listed separately. These would concern such items as organists and singers, shipment of remains to a distant city, extra flowers, candles, pallbearers, or even clothing for the deceased.

There are often instances where death occurs in one locality, with the funeral services and burial elsewhere. In these cases the relatives will prefer individual-item pricing from one mortician or both. Whatever pricing sys-tem is used, the state and local sales tax situation should be investigated, as it varies considerably from state to state. For example, in the state of Cali-fornia, the unit sale price is totaled and is 50 percent taxable at 4 percent. There the law provides that the sale total must include casket chosen, em-balming charge, hearse and one limousine, ambulance charge for bringing remains from place of death, flower car for transportation of floral offerings from funeral chapel to cemetery, burial permits, and death certificate fees. In Michigan it is permissible to include the casket, everything directly con-nected to it, and the services in a lump sum figure which is then 50 percent taxable at 4 percent. The vault and any clothing are listed separately on the invoice and are 100 percent taxable at 4 percent. Sales are required to be re-ported on an accrual basis.

Some states do not have any tax-exempt transactions or deductions as explained above. In all instances, to protect himself and his client the accountant should research his own state sales tax handbook or consult the area state sales tax auditors.

Functional Organization

At least two activities, funeral services and ambulance services, should be departmentalized. In larger operations there is often one man or a department responsible for the preparatory laboratory which covers embalming, death certificates, etc. Another man or department is in charge of the actual funeral arrangements of services and family welfare.

Principles and Objectives of the Accounting System

The purpose of this chapter is a dual one; i.e., to explain how to set up a system of record keeping for the mortician, and the use of the resulting system as a tool through which he can guide and measure his operations to be certain that he is accomplishing his objective.

The primary objective of a good accounting system is to make the business more effective in its operations, not only from its service to the public but also in its service to management towards strengthening the entrepreneur's financial stability. By utilizing the information thus provided, a norm can be established against which profits and efficiency can be measured.

Classification of Accounts and Books of Accounts

The following chart of accounts is standard for all departments. A departmental number may be prefixed to these codes. Basically, this chart of accounts consists primarily of the familiar, standard asset, liability, net worth, income, and expense accounts. However, there are several areas that contain new and different accounts. It is these differences which require further comment. The account numbers are more or less patterned after the age-old traditional numbering for assets, liabilities, etc. These numbers can be changed to coincide with those more or less standardized upon for EDP centers, local practitioners' established account numbers, or for any other reason.

BALANCE SHEET ACCOUNTS.

ASSETS

Current assets

100 Petty Cash

105 Cash in Bank
110 Investment in Stocks, Bonds
111-115 (for readily marketable
              securities)

120 Accounts Receivable—Funerals
121 Accounts Receivable—
Ambulance
122 Accounts Receivable—Other
120R Estimated Uncollectible
Accounts
125 Notes Receivable
126 (for nonbusiness accounts
or notes)
130 Finance Company Reserve
131 Cash Accommodation
Advances
140 Inventory—Caskets
141 Inventory—Vaults
142 Inventory—Boxes, Urns
143 Inventory—Clothing
144 Inventory—Embalming
Supplies
145 Inventory—Operating Supplies

Other current assets

150 Prepaid Insurance
151 Prepaid Interest
152 Prepaid Rent
153 Prepaid Taxes
154 Prepaid Postage Meter
155 Prepaid Miscellaneous
156 Exchange Checks
157 Deposits for Utilities
158 Cash Surrender Value—
Life Insurance Policies
159 Trust Funds for
Pre-arrangements

Property and equipment

160 Land
161 Buildings
161R Allowance for Depreciation
165 Building Additions and
Improvements
165R Allowance for Depreciation
170 Land Improvements (Parking)
170R Allowance for Depreciation
175 Leasehold Improvements
175R Allowance for Depreciation

180 Automobiles
180R Allowance for Depreciation
185 Funeral-Chapel Equipment and
Fixtures
185R Allowance for Depreciation
190 Office Furniture and Fixtures
190R Allowance for Depreciation
195 Goodwill
196 Corporate Organization Costs
196R Allowance for Amortization of
Organization Costs

LIABILITIES

Current liabilities

200 Notes Payable—Secured
201 Notes Payable—Unsecured
202 Notes Payable—Others
210 Accounts Payable—Trade
211 Accounts Payable—Other

Employee payroll deductions

215.1 FICA
215.2 Income Tax—Federal
215.3 Income Tax—State
215.4 Income Tax—City
215.5 Pension Plan

Accrued payroll taxes

220.1 FICA
220.2 Unemployment—Federal
220.3 Unemployment—State
225 Accrued Payroll
230 Accrued Interest
235 Accrued Expenses—
Miscellaneous
240 Accrued Sales and Use Tax
241 Accrued Property Taxes
242 Accrued Licenses
243 Accrued Taxes—Miscellaneous
245 Accrued Profit-Sharing Plan
250 Income Taxes

Long-term liabilities

260 Chattel Mortgages Payable

265 Notes Payable—Miscellaneous
270 Trust Fund Deposits—
    Pre-arrangements
275 Real Estate Mortgage

301 . . . ., Drawing
305 . . . ., Capital
306 . . . ., Drawing
350 Profit and Loss

NET WORTH

Sole proprietorship or partnership

300 . . . ., Capital

Corporation

300 Capital Stock
305 Paid-In Surplus
310 Earned Surplus

INCOME AND EXPENSE ACCOUNTS.

REVENUE

400 Funeral Sales—Caskets
405 Funeral Sales—Services Only
410 Funeral Sales—Vaults
415 Funeral Sales—Merchandise
430 Funeral Sales—Accommoda-
    tion Charges Billed
435 Funeral Sales—Auto Services
440 Ambulance
445 Fees from Other Funeral
    Homes
450 Fees—Miscellaneous
460 Commissions
470 Miscellaneous (Equipment
    Rental)
499 Discounts and Allowances

Cost of sales and services

500 Purchases—Caskets
505 Purchases—Vaults
510 Purchases—Boxes, Urns
515 Purchases—Clothing and
    Other Merchandise
520 Purchases—Embalming
    Supplies
525 Purchases—Operating
    Supplies
530 Advances on Accommodations
535 Freight and Express
550 Wages—Officers (Owner or
    Partners)
555 Wages—Managers
560 Wages—Others

575 Fees to Other Funeral Homes
585 Outside Services (Sublet)

EXPENSES

Operating expenses

600 Wages
605 Heat, Light, and Water
606 Insurance—Building
607 Insurance—Fleet
608 Insurance—Other
610 Rent—Buildings
611 Rent—Automobiles
612 Rent—Other
615 Repairs—Buildings
616 Repairs—Automobiles
617 Repairs—Equipment
620 Snow Removal
630 Supplies—Janitorial
631 Supplies—Uniforms and
    Laundry
632 Supplies—Miscellaneous
633 Supplies—Gas, Oil, and Grease
640 Taxes—Licenses
641 Taxes—Real Property
642 Taxes—Sales and Use
650 Depreciation—Building,
    Improvements, etc.
660 Depreciation—Leasehold
    Improvements
665 Depreciation—Automobiles
670 Depreciation—Funeral-Chapel
    Equipment

Administrative expenses

700 Wages—Clerical
705 Advertising
710 Bad Debts
715 Donations
716 Dues and Subscriptions
717 Employee Welfare
718 Employee Profit Sharing
720 Insurance—Liability
721 Insurance—Compensation
722 Insurance—Group
723 Insurance—Officers Life
725 Legal and Audit
730 Miscellaneous
735 Postage
740 Repairs—Office Equipment
745 Supplies—Office
750 Taxes—Payroll
751 Taxes—Property
752 Taxes—Business
753 Taxes—Miscellaneous
755 Telephone and Telegraph
760 Travel and Entertainment—
        Promotion
761 Travel and Entertainment—
        Conventions
762 Travel and Entertainment—
        Other
765 Amortization—Organization
        Expense
770 Depreciation—Office Furniture
        and Fixtures

NONOPERATING INCOME

800 Discounts Earned
810 Interest Earned
820 Miscellaneous Income
830 Gain/Loss on Sale of Capital
        Assets

NONOPERATING EXPENSE

900 Interest Expense
910 Finance Charges
920 Miscellaneous
930 Federal Income Tax (Corpora-
        tion Only)

ACCOUNTS PECULIAR TO THE BUSINESS

Cash Accommodation Advances. Account No. 131 is charged for those items which are handled as a special service to the family of the deceased and for which the family reimburses the mortician. Usually these items are of an even exchange nature or in accounting terms, a contra transaction.

Prepaid Postage Meter. Account No. 154 is similar to a Petty Cash account. A predetermined, standard amount is maintained in the postage meter. On the last day of each month, a check is written to bring the meter back to this fixed amount. In this manner the records will reflect the actual postage expense for any period.

Exchange Checks (No. 156). This is comparable to a Cash account. Frequently, to settle their account a family will turn over an insurance check in an amount greater than the funeral bill. Accounts Receivable is credited for the correct amount to balance it out, and the excess is credited to No. 156. When a check is drawn to refund the difference to the family, it is charged to this account. Its use is a safety factor in that expense or income accounts are not employed for any differences; and until this account has a zero balance, it is known there is a pending contra transaction.

Trust Funds for Pre-arrangements (No. 159). Here cash is represented in a special bank account which is an advance deposit for a funeral to be conducted in the future (upon the death of the depositor). These funds cannot be co-mingled with the regular working capital of the business. In this special savings account their safety to the depositor is guaranteed by the Federal Deposit Insurance Corporation. The funds are deferred income and should not be reflected in the income accounts at the time of deposit.

A separate account for each individual pre-arrangement is recommended. The account is banked in the name of the individual making the pre-arrangement, with the funeral director acting and named as trustee. The bank can be chosen by the individual, not the funeral director, and interest accrues to the account of the individual. Thus the money belongs to the indivdual, and the accruing interest helps to cover possible cost increases that may develop between completion of the pre-arrangement plan and the time that the individual dies. In addition it sometimes happens that the pre-arrangement plan is not used. The person may die in some distant location, or it is possible his funeral may be arranged for and carried out by someone who does not know of the pre-arranged plan. In such cases funds paid in advance under a pre-arrangement plan must be turned over by the funeral director to the estate of the deceased.

Land Improvements. Account No. 170 is charged for any expense incurred in developing a parking area, entrance, or exit for the use of customers. This would include tree removal, bulldozing, grading, drains, blacktopping, curbs, etc.

Trust Fund Deposits, Pre-arrangements. No. 270 reflects income; for example, interest on any advance deposits made in Account No. 159. The depositor should account for and pay any taxes involved on such income.

Funeral Sales-Accommodation Charges Billed. Account No. 430 is credited for any items billed which are of a reimbursement nature. Such items should not be considered as sales income but merely as an offsetting or contra transaction that will wash itself out when the entire cycle is completed. See account Nos. 131 and 530.

Cost of Sales-Advances on Accommodations. Account No. 530 is charged for any nonprofit, reimbursement expense item which cannot be considered a true operating cost or expense. As with account No. 430 above, it is merely an offsetting or contra transaction. If account Nos. 430 and 530 are treated as contra and nonoperating income and expense accounts, account No. 131 would not be needed.

Snow Removal. Account No. 620 would only be used by the more northerly located businesses. With the acquisition of parking areas, it has become necessary to hire commercial operators and equipment to clear the areas of snow.

BOOKS AND FORMS PECULIAR TO THE BUSINESS

A standard, double-entry system with its built-in checks and balances is the only acceptable method of accounting.

Invoices. Income transactions may be invoiced on a standard body, pre-numbered sales invoice, printed in quadruplicate. Each sheet of the four-part, snap-out invoice has distribution printed at the bottom of the form; i.e., customer's copy, numerical file, alphabetical file.

Most morticians, however, seem to feel that each funeral bill should be typed separately (original and three copies) on letterhead stationery. The reason is that two funerals are seldom alike in the services and merchandise provided; so that individual pricing (or the listing of items under a composite price) and itemization of extra services and their costs must be shown. In addition the consensus seems to be that a commercially printed form is not desirable under the circumstances.

The original letter (or invoice) and the quadruplicate go to the customer. The duplicate copy forms a part of the numerical file. The invoices may be prepunched, or the letters individually punched, and placed in a post binder in numerical sequence as soon as the bill is made up. The numerical file then becomes the source document for recording in the Sales journal. All numbers must be accounted for in the numerical file. If through some error a number is not used, the duplicate copy is labeled "void" and placed in numerical sequence in the post binder. In this way positive control of all bills or invoices is provided.

The triplicate copy forms an alphabetical, customer's file. Reference is often made to this copy for price comparisons, under varying circumstances. A widow may request the same casket and service as her deceased husband's best friend or business acquaintance had a year or two previously. Children may want to duplicate the same casket and service for their father, that he provided for their mother. If there is much of a time lapse in such circumstances, then costs are likely to have increased considerably during the period. By having the alphabetical file as a reference, the funeral director can compare and point out the areas of increase to justify the higher price now being charged for the same service. This file also provides a pattern of the family's buying habits. Provision for both a numerical and an alphabetical file makes it simple to find information about a billing that a customer might question.

Sales and Cash Receipts. The Sales journal and the Cash Receipts journal are a combination unit (Figure 1). All sales are invoiced and recorded nu-

CASH RECEIPTS AND SALES JOURNAL

DATE	SOLD TO OR RECEIVED FROM	INVOICE NO.	CASH DR.	BANK DR.	DISC. & ALLOW.	ACCTS. RECEIVABLE DR.	ACCTS. RECEIVABLE CR.	INCOME 400	INCOME 405	INCOME 410	INCOME 415
Jan 3	John Smith	101				4000		35000			
6	John Smith	102				104000			20000	15000	6500
6	Chiff Study Club	103	1500								
10	John Smith	—	102960		1040		104000				
10	Amy Jenke	—	5000				5000				
11	Deposited		(154460)	154460							

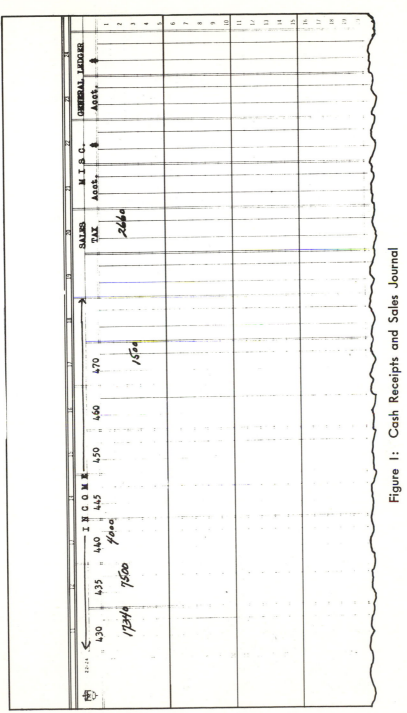

Figure 1: Cash Receipts and Sales Journal

merically in the Sales journal; therefore, the only distribution required for cash is a credit to Accounts Receivable.

After the invoices are recorded in the Sales journal, the amounts appearing under Accounts Receivable debit are posted to an individual Accounts Receivable ledger for each customer (Figure 2). Likewise, for any payments recorded in the Cash Receipts journal, the amounts appearing under Accounts Receivable credit are posted to this same ledger card. The ledger card, instead of the more familiar ledger sheet, is used; besides serving its purpose as a history of the customer's paying pattern and his total billings, it can be photocopied and sent as a statement, if desired.

Window envelopes should be ordered to match the ledger card being used. By properly folding the photocopied ledger card, it can be inserted in the envelope with the customer's address showing, and thereby the costly and time-consuming job of addressing envelopes can be eliminated.

All cash is deposited in the checking account. The various items making up the deposit are recorded on a duplicate deposit slip. The duplicate copy, after certification by the bank teller, is recorded in the Cash Receipts journal (Figure 1). After being recorded, the bank deposit slip is filed in chronological sequence.

The Check register (Figure 3) also serves a dual role. Most of the time bills are paid as they are received. In a few instances the checkbook is held open for a few days into the next month, and disbursements made for the preceding month are then recorded in the period to which they pertain. The small amount of payables that are left are recorded at the month end after all checks are recorded. By using any one or a combination of the above methods of handling payables, it is not necessary to maintain a separate Purchase journal.

Experience with both types of checks, the ordinary, three-to-a page with stubs remaining in the checkbook and the voucher check (Figure 4), shows that the voucher check is preferred by everyone involved. Where an outside accountant is engaged to maintain the Check register, a quadruplicate voucher check is used. The original, naturally, is issued to the payee. The duplicate copy, prepunched, forms the numerical and chronological file, serves as the check stub, and is used in recording to the Check register (Figure 3). The triplicate copy of the voucher check is stapled to the paid bill, and both are filed in the vendor's file. Any time a question arises about a paid bill and the file is pulled, the complete history of the transaction is available—original invoice, bill of lading, check number, date paid, etc.

The quadruplicate copy of the check is used by the outside accountant. The person typing the check codes each transaction with the proper account

A B C FUNERAL HOME
123 Main St.
Anytown, Michigan

Mr. John Jones
3333 Jasper Ave.
Anytown, Michigan

A-1000-03L

DATE	DESCRIPTION	CHARGES	CREDITS	BALANCE	✓
		BALANCE FORWARD ▶			
1-7-	Inv 3479	40 00		40 00	
1-11-	" 3486	1157 60		1197 60	
3-10-	CR 37		1197 60	— • —	

Figure 2: Customer's Ledger Card

DATE	PAID TO OR PURCHASED FROM	CHECK NO.	INVOICE NO.	BANK CR.	OAB CR.	WdDG CR.	MISC ACCOUNTS CR.	ACCOUNTS PAYABLE DR.	WAGES Acct.	$
Jan 8	ABC Mfg Co	1176		230000						
8	Leonard Lewis	1177		10250						
8	Amy Mfg Co	1178		8650				86500		
8	Rodney Smith	1179		7820	396	784				9000
31	Amy Mfg Co	—	A678				9000			

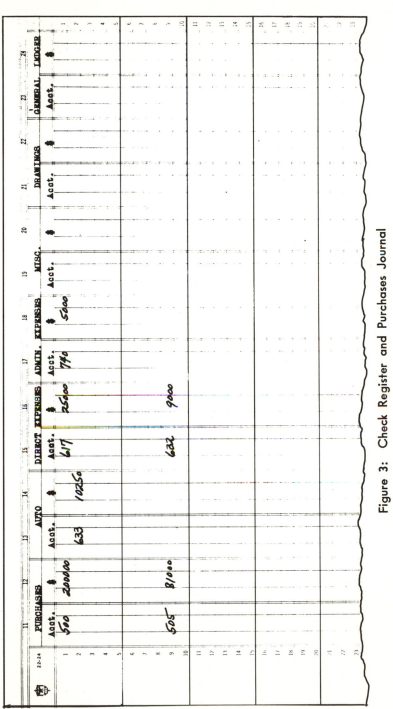

Figure 3: Check Register and Purchases Journal

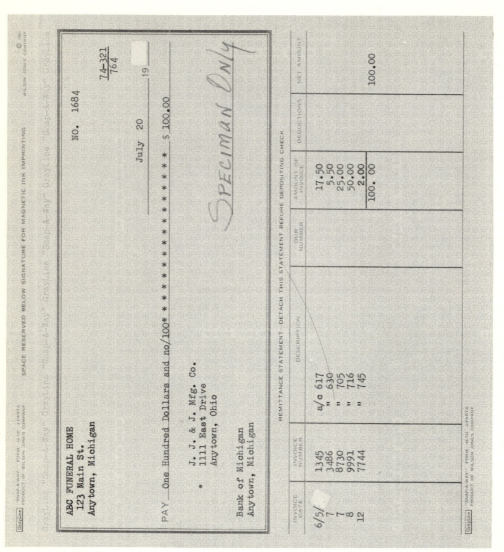

Figure 4:   Voucher Check

number. With these stubs, all coded, the accountant can prepare the Check register in his own office.

There has just recently become available a small, reasonably priced Source Data Capturing device. One model (Figure 5) can be electronically intercoupled through a typewriter. As a check or invoice is typed, a visually verified punch card is obtained as a by-product of any typing operation. The unit eliminates the transmittal of a source document to the Key Punch Department for card punching and verification. In addition it saves the time and cost of having the source document punched and verified in the Key Punch Department.

Time and Payroll System

All employees keep a weekly time card which they sign and turn in to the bookkeeper each week. The time card then becomes the basis for computing employee gross wages. After they are determined, the computations for Social Security and income tax are completed. By subtracting these two deductions (plus any other deductions such as hospital insurance, etc.), the net pay is arrived at.

An individual earnings record must be kept for each employee. This earnings record accumulates the weekly pay information so that at the end of each month, or quarter, the records can be balanced and reconciled with the General ledger accounts. These earnings records form the basis for preparing all state and Federal payroll reports each quarter and the annual wage statements.

Cost and Departmental Accounting

In the average operation, it is difficult to departmentalize wages. Usually the labor is performed by the owner plus one employee or the two owners, in case of partnership. In each instance the two men perform such a multiple series of intermixed duties (embalming, driving the ambulance, contacting ministers and newspapers, conducting the services, etc.) that it would be nearly impossible to departmentalize their time accurately.

In a larger firm each employee is hired to do a specific job; driving the ambulance, working in laboratory embalming, or performing other services necessary. In this case it is easy to departmentalize the wage expense. Frequently a man or two work a portion of each day on two or more distinct jobs. In that case, each keeps a separate time card for each job. From these cards the bookkeeper can charge to the proper department the exact expense incurred by it.

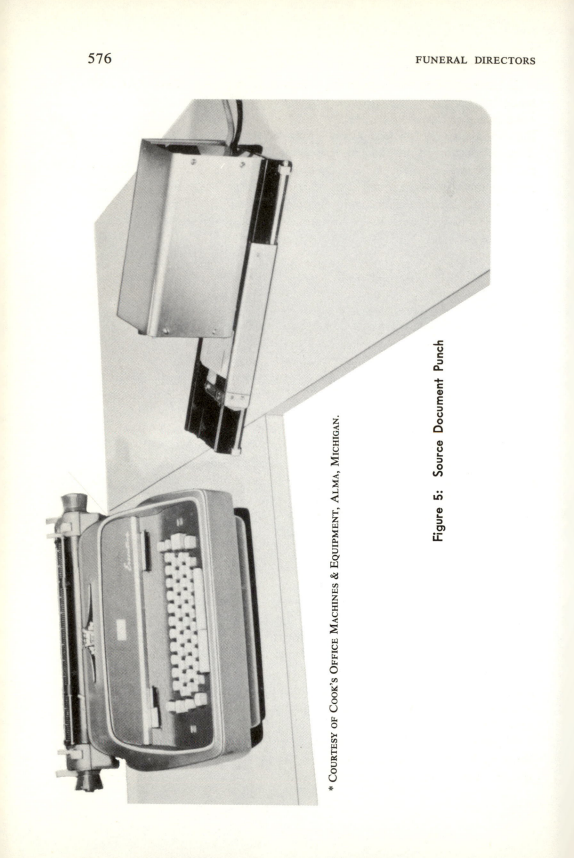

* COURTESY OF COOK'S OFFICE MACHINES & EQUIPMENT, ALMA, MICHIGAN.

Figure 5:   Source Document Punch

The average funeral director, who must keep his establishment open for business 24 hours a day, incurs operational overhead expenses that are the same dollarwise whether he handles one funeral a day, or none for a week. His expenses of maintenance do not vary much, so his profit is most often determined annually by the number of funerals he handles, with the same basic expenses. Thus his sales volume will not directly establish an average annual profit, but his fixed expense will establish a fixed annual overhead cost.

Incoming invoices are coded by the person who ordered the merchandise or incurred the expense. When the invoices are paid or set up as a payable, distribution is then made to the department involved, as indicated by the precoded invoice.

The numerical copy of the customer's invoice is also coded by the person originating the invoice. When this invoice is recorded in the Sales journal, it is easy for the bookkeeper to make distribution to the account and the department involved.

Time-Saving Ideas

One of the biggest time savers is the use of a ledger card for Accounts Receivable plus photostatic copies of the cards mailed as statements. The detailed explanation may be found under the section, Books and Forms Peculiar to the Business, and in Figure 2.

If four or more individuals are employed, an investigation of a payroll pegboard system should be considered. There are several versions on the market now, and they are becoming more reasonably priced. One system, the lowest priced set available, is not a true pegboard, but does embody all its principles (Figure 6).

The foregoing explanations illustrate how time is saved and accuracy gained as a by-product. At the same time the bookkeeper fills in the hours, earnings, deductions, and net pay on the individual earnings record; completion of the employee's earnings statement and the payroll summary sheet is made at one writing by use of carbons.

Utilization of a one-time carbon, snap-out voucher check, as described in the discussion of Figure 4, also saves much time. At one writing are completed the original, the stub (figuratively speaking), and as many other duplicate copies as required. This one-time writing eliminates the necessity of repeatedly copying the same figures and thereby automatically guarantees accuracy.

Because the inventory requirements are not excessive, as to the different items carried in stock, a mortuary lends itself readily to a perpetual inventory system. A very reasonably priced, visible card-type system (Figure 7) is

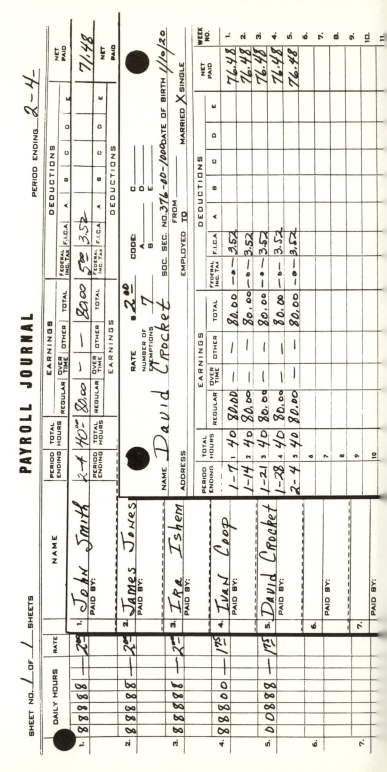

PAYROLL JOURNAL

SHEET NO. 1 OF 1 SHEETS   PERIOD ENDING 2-4-

DAILY HOURS	NAME	RATE	PERIOD ENDING	TOTAL HOURS	REGULAR	OVER TIME	OTHER	TOTAL	FEDERAL INC. TAX	F.I.C.A	A	B	C	D	E	NET PAID
							EARNINGS					DEDUCTIONS				
1. 88888	John Smith	2.00	2-4	40	80.00	-	-	80.00	5.00	3.52						71.48
PAID BY:																
2. 88888	James Jones	2.00														
PAID BY:																
3. 88888	Ira Ishem	2.00														
PAID BY:																
4. 88800	Ivan Coop	1.75														
PAID BY:																
5. 00888	David Crockett	1.75														
PAID BY:																
6.																
PAID BY:																
7.																
PAID BY:																

NAME David Crockett

RATE $2.00   CODE: A   B   C   D   E

NUMBER OF EXEMPTIONS 1

SOC. SEC. NO. 376-00-1000   DATE OF BIRTH 1/10/20

MARRIED   X SINGLE

EMPLOYED FROM ___ TO ___

ADDRESS

PERIOD ENDING	TOTAL HOURS	REGULAR	OVER TIME	OTHER	TOTAL	FEDERAL INC. TAX	F.I.C.A	A	B	C	D	E	NET PAID	WEEK NO.
			EARNINGS					DEDUCTIONS						
1-7	40	80.00	-	-	80.00	-0-	3.52						76.48	1.
1-14	40	80.00	-	-	80.00	-0-	3.52						76.48	2.
1-21	40	80.00	-	-	80.00	-0-	3.52						76.48	3.
1-28	40	80.00	-	-	80.00	-0-	3.52						76.48	4.
2-4	40	80.00	-	-	80.00	-0-	3.52						76.48	5.
														6.
														7.
														8.
														9.
														10.
														11.

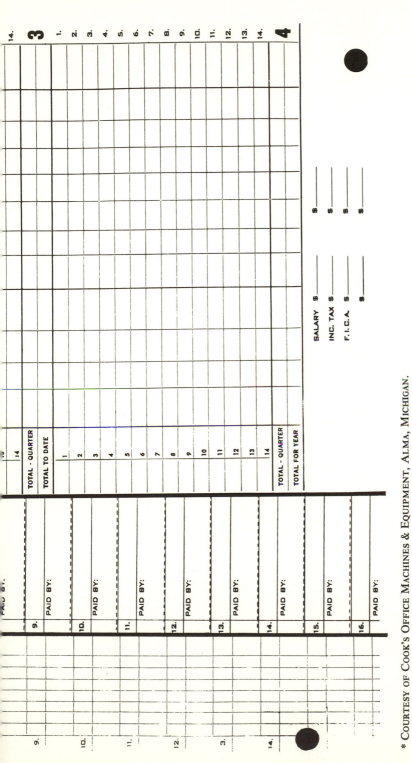

Figure 6: Pegboard Payroll System

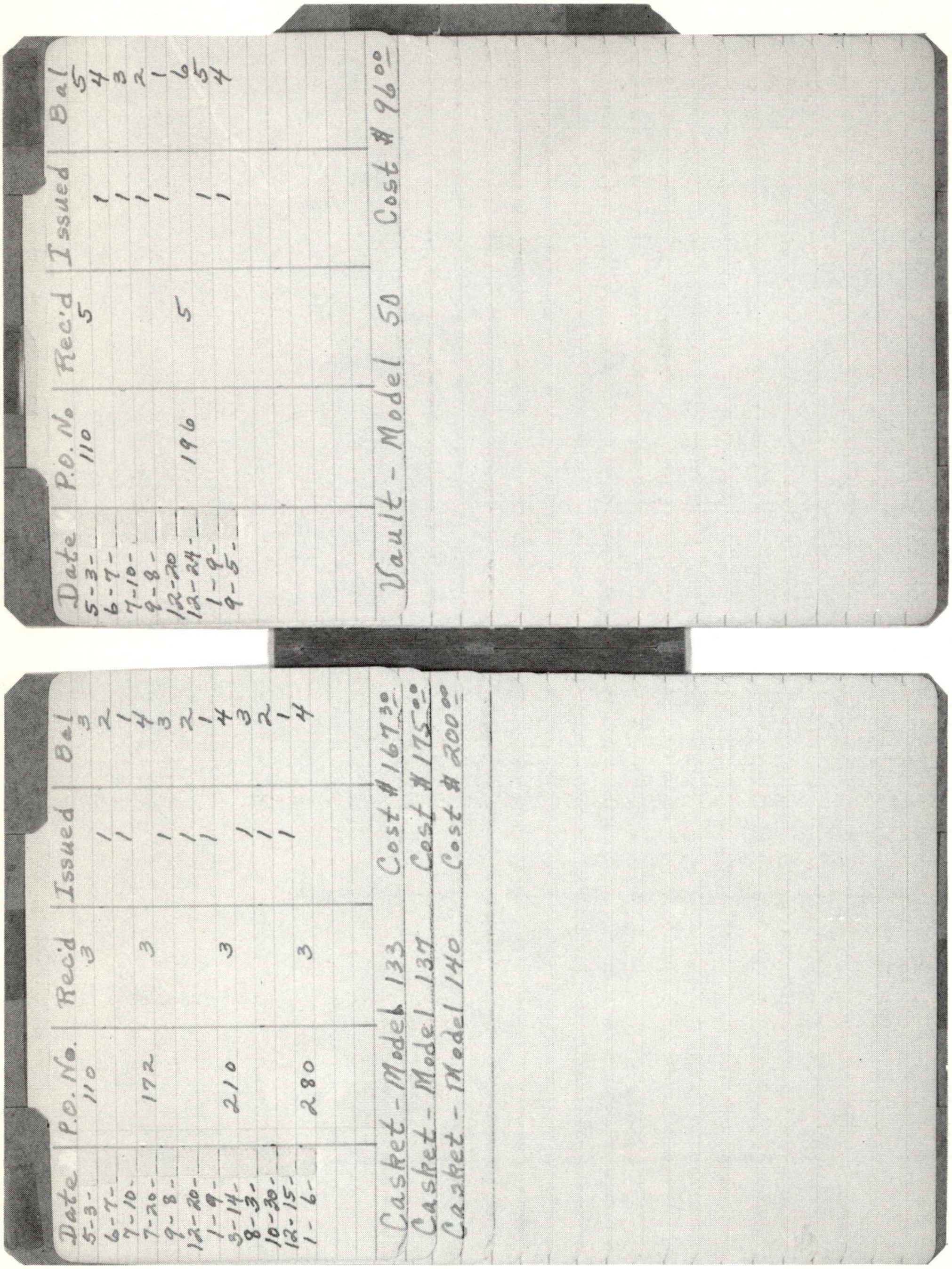

Date	P.O. No	Rec'd	Issued	Bal
5-3-	110	5		5
6-7-			1	4
7-10-			1	3
9-8-			1	2
12-20			1	1
12-24-	196	5		6
1-9-			1	5
9-5-			1	4

Vault - Model 50 Cost # 96.00

Date	P.O. No.	Rec'd	Issued	Bal
5-3-	110	3		3
6-7-			1	2
7-10-			1	1
7-20-	172	3		4
9-8-			1	3
12-20-			1	2
1-9-			1	1
5-14-	210	3		4
8-3-			1	3
10-30-			1	2
12-15-			1	1
1-6-	280	3		4

Casket - Model 133 Cost # 167.30
Casket - Model 137 Cost # 175.00
Casket - Model 140 Cost # 200.00

* Courtesy of Cook's Office Machines & Equipment, Alma, Michigan.

Figure 7: Visible Perpetual Inventory System

available. With this system, a separate card is made for each item on inventory. The card carries information as to vendor, description, model, cost, etc. As new purchases are received, the quantity is added to the card. As sales are made, they are subtracted from the balance shown on the card. In this manner the exact quantity of any item in stock is always known. This system gives an accurate monthly inventory at cost for the accountant's monthly operating statements. The records, once established, will also provide a guide for future purchases.

All accountants are familiar with a standard, loose-leaf General ledger book. However, one company is now manufacturing a spiral bound book that replaces the old General ledger. In this unit, called "The Compact" (Figure 8), all account titles are copied at the left side of the two-page spread under the heading, Name of Account. The beginning trial balance is then recorded in the columns provided. Columns are also provided for each book of original entry: Check register, Purchase journal (if used), Sales journal, Cash receipts, etc. At month end, when all journals have been balanced, the total for each journal is posted in its appropriate column opposite the account affected. All columns are then added across, and the month-end trial balance is done.

Reports to Management

Monthly financial reports include the following four: Profit and loss statement, balance sheet, statement of surplus (corporations only), and statement of source of funds and their application.

The profit and loss statement is prepared in such form each month to reflect results of operations for the current month and year to date, with both percentage and dollar figures. The format can be standard in nature, as patterned after any generally accepted pro forma operating statement.

The balance sheet, the statement of surplus, and the statement of source of funds are all of standard accounting procedure format. With this combination of reports the mortician controls the reins to the successful management of his business. By analyzing the information set forth in these statements, comparing current statements with those of the preceding year, or years, and with averages as set forth by his trade associations, the funeral director will obtain financial and operating ratios and all other information necessary to carry on a profitable business enterprise.

POSTINGS FOR MONTH OF *January* 19

#	Name of Account	Trial Balance Dr.	Trial Balance Cr.	Check Register Dr.	Check Register Cr.	Purchase Journal Dr.	Purchase Journal Cr.	Cash Receipts Dr.	Cash Receipts Cr.
1	Petty Cash	11224							
2	Bank	297415			176130			201167	
3	Accounts Receivable	567234							
4	Notes Receivable	70000							
5	Mdse. Inventory	2145228							
6	Prepaid Insurance	66939							
7	Land	200000							
8	Buildings	1448350							
9	Delivery Equipment	605958							
10	Furniture & Fixtures	2120020							
11	Office Equipment	248833							
12	Shop Equipment	64576							
13	Res. for Depr—Bldg		72417						
14	" " —Del. Eq		131077						
15	" " —F & F.		546449						
16	" " —Off.Eq.		7451						
17	" " —Shop Eq.		17483						
18	Accrued Blue Cross		6268						
19	FICA		3854						
20	" Withholding		8242						
21	Accounts Payable		244000						
22	Mortgage " – Bldg		2863069						
23	Notes " –C.N.Bank		47869						
24	H. Moore, Capital		491531						
25	W. J. Moore, Capital		1439319						
26	W. J. Moore, Drawing	459404							
27	Cash-Over & Short	34488							
28	Rtd Sales & Al-Retail	76578							
29	" & All-Wsle	306984							
30	Sales Discounts	3033							
31	Sales-Retail, Road		307834						
32	" " Store		2575792						
33	" Shop Labor		55310						
34	" Wsale-Road		1292099						
35	" —Store		3563015						
36	Other Income		6000						
37	Purchase Discount		85867						
38		10056							

	40	41	42	43	44	45	46	47	48	49	50	51	52	53	54	55	56	57	58	59	60	61	62	63	64	65	66	67	68	69	70	71	72	73	74	75	76	77	78
40																																							
41 Depreciation																																							- 0 -
42 Donations																																							2000
43 Dues & Subscriptions																																							12150
44 Employees Welfare																																							6933
45 Freight In																																							2960
46 Insurance																																							75746
47 Interest Expense																																							4316
48 Legal & Audit																																							33500
49 Postage																																							5837
50 Purchases																																							4195465
51 Rent																																							180440
52 Repairs - Bldgs																																							14424
53 " - Equip																																							5518
54 " - Trucks																																							- 0 -
55 Road Expense																																							- 0 -
56 Snow & Trash Removal																																							7003
57 Supplies - Office																																							24853
58 " - Shop																																							3459
59 " - Store																																							5653
60 Taxes - Property																																							51892
61 " - B.A.T.																																							8582
62 " - M.E.S.C.																																							16097
63 " - Licenses																																							4570
64 " - Misc.																																							500
65 " - Payroll																																							35175
66 " - Sales																																							97604
67 Telephone																																							73919
68 Travel & Entm't.																																							79752
69 Utilities																																							65367
70 Wages																																							985860
71																																							
72 Total																																						1327314 6	1327314 6

Figure 8: "Compact" General Ledger

(cont. on next page)

POSTINGS FOR MONTH OF *January* 19 ___

Sales Journal   General Journal

Do Not Detach (See Over)

TRIAL BALANCE

DR.	CR.	DR.	CR.	DR.	CR.	DR.	CR.		DATE DR.	CR.
1								1		
2								2	324 52	
3								3		
4								4		
5								5		
6								6		
7								7		
8								8		
9								9		
10								10		
11								11		
12								12		
13								13		
14								14		
15								15		
16								16		
17								17		
18								18		
19								19		
20								20		
21								21		
22								22		
23								23		
24								24		
25								25		
26								26		
27								27		
28								28		
29								29		
30								30		
31								31		
32								32		
33								33		
34								34		
35								35		
36								36		
37								37		
38								38		

"Correct" General Ledger (cont.)

31

Furniture Dealers

BY W. F. SHELTON

Accountant, Louisburg, North
Carolina

Characteristics of the Business That Affect the Accounting System

The mainstay of the average-sized furniture store is large items such as tables, dressers, divans, chairs, and suites of furniture. However, management also offers to customers such smaller pieces as ottomans and lamps. In addition, the display of draperies, bedding, carpeting, tapestries, pictures, and mirrors provides another drawing card. Often the concern will sell appliances, but the actual handling of this type of sales and service from an accounting viewpoint is found in a separate chapter of this volume.

Usually the store sells no used furniture. New furniture sales are lost when new merchandise is displayed next to used items. Sometimes as a service to customers the store will accept used furniture in trade. Disposal of these acquisitions is then accomplished through a subsidiary of the dealer's No. 1 store or via the facilities of a used furniture store.

The small home furnishings business is most likely to be a sole proprietorship, but the system of accounts will be readily adaptable to a partnership or a corporation by changing the accounts in the net worth section of the balance sheet.

FUNCTIONAL CHARACTERISTICS OF THE BUSINESS

As a rule, the calendar year is preferred as the fiscal period. Where furniture sales are affected seasonally, as in a farming area, the use of a fiscal year ending on a date other than December 31 may be desirable.

Most families buy groceries on the average of once or twice a week but purchase furniture only once or twice a year, if that often. Thus the grocery store has a high volume of traffic and daily sales, while the furniture mart is a low-traffic store. Markups ordinarily provide an excellent margin of profit from sales.

Because the average furniture sale runs higher in dollar volume than in many other lines of business, the modern dealer in home furnishings must pay special attention to the financing of Accounts Receivable.

ACCOUNTING PROBLEMS

Some of the Accounts Receivable will be carried by the small furniture store, but most of its installment contracts will be sold to commercial installment banks. Accounting problems stem principally from the necessity of proper handling of Accounts Receivable and installment paper.

A minor problem of a furniture store is generated when installment payments are made at the store on notes actually owed by customers to the bank. While collection of these payments is a bit worrisome to the staff, store managers like having the additional traffic. Quite often new sales are made from impulse buying, and customers may "add on" to their installment contracts.

The best procedure is to keep a separate receipt book for payments received for others, and thus provide an extra check against accuracy in forwarding payment to the bank. The account, Installment Collections on Pledged Accounts Receivable, takes both credits and debits to show passage of these payments through the business to the bank.

Principles and Objectives of the Accounting System

Like any other accounting system, the principal aims are to keep management intelligently informed on all phases of operation and to record accurately the transactions of the business. For smaller furniture stores, statements summarizing financial operations are best compiled on a comparative basis and should be provided monthly.

Detailed current inventory records are important to the operator of a furniture store, for he must order merchandise well in advance of probable sale dates. He also will need facts as a basis for determining whether it is more profitable to retain his Accounts Receivable or to discount (sell) them as installment paper to a commercial installment bank. He may discover that it is more profitable to sell the accounts for working capital, particularly to increase his inventory, rather than to tie up too much of his capital in receivables.

Classification of Accounts and Books of Accounts

A typical chart of accounts for the business follows.

BALANCE SHEET ACCOUNTS.

ASSETS

Current Assets	Debits from	Credits from
101 Office Fund	Cash Disbursements Journal	Petty cash vouchers
102 Cash Register Fund	Sales Journal	Cash Receipts Journal
105 Bank	Cash Receipts Journal	Cash Disbursements Journal
Marketable Securities		
111 Stocks	Cash Disbursements Journal	Cash Receipts Journal
Receivables		
121 Cash Sales Clearing	Sales Journal	Cash Receipts Journal
122 Accounts Receivable	Accounts Receivable File	Cash Receipts Journal
122R Allowance for Doubtful Accounts	General Journal	General Journal
125 Contracts Receivable	General Journal	Cash Receipts Journal
126 Notes Receivable	General Journal	Cash Receipts Journal

Inventories

131 New Furniture	Purchases Journal	General Journal
132 New Appliances	Purchases Journal	General Journal
133 Rugs & Draperies	Purchases Journal	General Journal
134 Bedding & Linen	Purchases Journal	General Journal
135 Crockery & China	Purchases Journal	General Journal
136 Used Furniture	Purchases Journal	General Journal
137 Used Appliances	Purchases Journal	General Journal
138 Repair Material	Purchases Journal	General Journal
139 Service Labor	Purchases Journal	General Journal

Other Current Assets

148 Due from Finance Companies	Sales Journal	Cash Receipts Journal

Fixed Assets

161 Land	Cash Disbursements Journal	Cash Receipts Journal
162 Buildings	Cash Disbursements Journal	Cash Receipts Journal
162R Allowance for Depreciation	General Journal	General Journal
163 Store Fixtures & Equipment	Cash Disbursements Journal	Cash Receipts Journal
163R Allowance for Depreciation	General Journal	General Journal
165 Motor Vehicles	Cash Disbursements Journal	Cash Receipts Journal
165R Allowance for Depreciation	General Journal	General Journal
167 Office Furniture & Equipment	Cash Disbursements Journal	Cash Receipts Journal
167R Allowance for Depreciation	General Journal	General Journal

Deferred Charges

181 Prepaid Insurance	Cash Disbursements Journal	General Journal
182 Prepaid Taxes	Cash Disbursements Journal	General Journal
189 Other Deferred Charges	Cash Disbursements Journal	General Journal

Other Assets

| 191 | Deposits (Rent. Utilities, etc.) | Cash Disbursements Journal | General Journal |

LIABILITIES

Current Liabilities

201	Notes Payable	Cash Disbursements Journal	General Journal
205	Contracts Payable	Cash Disbursements Journal	General Journal
206	Accounts Payable	Cash Disbursements Journal	General Journal
211	Sales Tax Payable	Cash Disbursements Journal	General Journal
213	Finance Charges	Cash Disbursements Journal	General Journal
221	Employee Payroll Deductions	Cash Disbursements Journal	General Journal
	2211 Social Security Taxes	Cash Disbursements Journal	General Journal
	2212 State Disability Insurance	Cash Disbursements Journal	General Journal
	2213 Federal Income Tax Withheld	Cash Disbursements Journal	General Journal
	2214 State Income Tax Withheld	Cash Disbursements Journal	General Journal
	2215 City Income Tax Withheld	Cash Disbursements Journal	General Journal
222	Employer Payroll Taxes Payable	Cash Disbursements Journal	General Journal
	2221 Social Security Taxes	Cash Disbursements Journal	General Journal
	2222 Federal Social Security Taxes	Cash Disbursements Journal	General Journal
	2223 State Social Security Taxes	Cash Disbursements Journal	General Journal
225	Accrued Payroll	Cash Disbursements Journal	General Journal
226	Accrued General Taxes	Cash Disbursements Journal	General Journal

Fixed Liabilities

261 Unearned Finance Charges	Cash Disbursements Journal	General Journal
262 Deferred Profit On Installment Sales	Cash Disbursements Journal	General Journal

NET WORTH

Sole Proprietorship or Partnership

291 Capital		General Journal
2911 Partner A	General Journal	General Journal
2912 Partner B	General Journal	General Journal
292 Drawing		
2921 Partner A	General Journal	General Journal
2922 Partner B	General Journal	General Journal
299 Profit & Loss	General Journal	General Journal

Corporate accounts

291 Capital	General Journal	General Journal
298 Retained Earnings	General Journal	General Journal
299 Profit & Loss	General Journal	General Journal

INCOME AND EXPENSE ACCOUNTS. REVENUES

Sales

301 New Furniture	General Journal	Sales Journal
302 New Appliances	General Journal	Sales Journal
303 Rugs & Draperies	General Journal	Sales Journal
304 Bedding & Linen	General Journal	Sales Journal
305 Crockery & China	General Journal	Sales Journal
306 Used Furniture	General Journal	Sales Journal
307 Used Appliances	General Journal	Sales Journal
308 Repair Material	General Journal	Sales Journal
309 Service Labor	General Journal	Sales Journal

Income

321 Finance Charges Earned	General Journal	Sales Journal

Cost of Sales

401 New Furniture	Sales Journal	Cash Disbursements Journal

402 New Appliances	Sales Journal	Cash Disbursements Journal
403 Rugs & Draperies	Sales Journal	Cash Disbursements Journal
404 Bedding & Linen	Sales Journal	Cash Disbursements Journal
405 Crockery & China	Sales Journal	Cash Disbursements Journal
406 Used Furniture	Sales Journal	Cash Disbursements Journal
407 Used Appliances	Sales Journal	Cash Disbursements Journal
408 Repair Material	Sales Journal	Cash Disbursements Journal
409 Service Labor	Sales Journal	Cash Disbursements Journal

Cost of Income

421 Interest Cost	General Journal	General Journal

EXPENSES

Salaries and Wages

11 Supervision Wages	Cash Disbursements Journal	Cash Receipts Journal
12 Clerical Salaries	Cash Disbursements Journal	Cash Receipts Journal
13 Sales Salaries & Commissions	Cash Disbursements Journal	Cash Receipts Journal
16 Indirect Labor	Cash Disbursements Journal	Cash Receipts Journal

Supplies

21 Stationery & Office Supplies	Cash Disbursements Journal	Cash Receipts Journal
22 Postage	Cash Disbursements Journal	Cash Receipts Journal
23 Operating Supplies	Cash Disbursements Journal	Cash Receipts Journal
24 Motor Vehicle Supplies	Cash Disbursements Journal	Cash Receipts Journal

Utilities & Services

31 Heat, Light & Water	Cash Disbursements Journal	Cash Receipts Journal

| 33 Telephone & Telegraph | Cash Disbursements Journal | Cash Receipts Journal |
| 34 Laundry & Cleaning | Cash Disbursements Journal | Cash Receipts Journal |

Taxes

| 41 General Taxes | Cash Disbursements Journal | Cash Receipts Journal |
| 43 Payroll Taxes | Cash Disbursements Journal | Cash Receipts Journal |

Insurance

51 General	Cash Disbursements Journal	Cash Receipts Journal
52 Retirement Plan	Cash Disbursements Journal	Cash Receipts Journal
53 Compensation	Cash Disbursements Journal	Cash Receipts Journal
54 Group Insurance	Cash Disbursements Journal	Cash Receipts Journal

Depreciation

62 Buildings	General Journal	General Journal
63 Store Fixtures & Equipment	General Journal	General Journal
65 Motor Vehicles	General Journal	General Journal
67 Office Furniture & Equipment	General Journal	General Journal

Repairs & Maintenance

72 Buildings	Cash Disbursements Journal	Cash Receipts Journal
73 Store Fixtures & Equipment	Cash Disbursements Journal	Cash Receipts Journal
75 Motor Vehicles	Cash Disbursements Journal	Cash Receipts Journal
77 Office Furniture & Equipment	Cash Disbursements Journal	Cash Receipts Journal

Other

| 81 Advertising | Cash Disbursements Journal | Cash Receipts Journal |
| 82 Losses On Bad Accounts | Cash Disbursements Journal | Cash Receipts Journal |

83 Donations	Cash Disbursements Journal	Cash Receipts Journal
84 Dues & Subscriptions	Cash Disbursements Journal	Cash Receipts Journal
85 Professional Services	Cash Disbursements Journal	Cash Receipts Journal
86 Travel & Entertainment	Cash Disbursements Journal	Cash Receipts Journal
87 Rentals	Cash Disbursements Journal	Cash Receipts Journal
88 Freight, Express, & Outside Delivery	Cash Disbursements Journal	Cash Receipts Journal
99 Unclassified	Cash Disbursements Journal	Cash Receipts Journal

OTHER INCOME

601 Cash Discounts Taken	Purchases Journal
602 Interest Earned	Sales Journal
605 Sale of Junk	Sales Journal
608 Cash Over	Cash Receipts Journal
609 Miscellaneous Income	Cash Receipts Journal

DEDUCTIONS FROM INCOME

651 Cash Discounts Allowed	Sales Journal
652 Interest Expense	General Journal
658 Cash Short	Cash Disbursements Journal
659 Miscellaneous Losses	General Journal

A large number of installment contracts moving through the business should certainly require a Contracts in Transit account. An asset account, it is debited with the amount of an installment contract when the contract is sent to the bank and credited when the money for the contract is received from the bank.

In many cases, the installment bank may hold back part of the store's sales proceeds until it is presumed that the account has been paid out. This is handled by means of the Due from Finance Companies account.

The funds in this account are presumed to stay with the installment bank at a certain percentage of the total of all the store's installment accounts outstanding. This presumably protects the bank against customer defaults, and acts as a guarantee that the customer will "pay out." It should be understood that the installment bank, when it takes such mortgages from the store, takes them upon the basis of "with recourse." Basically, this means that in the event of default, the defaulted amount may either be deducted from the amounts credited and held in the store's installment account or a defaulted account may be paid by the store itself by check. It is generally true that the store pays off defaulted balances. Then through its own means, the store seeks to collect or repossess the merchandise on the original conditional sales contract.

In the preparation of informational breakdowns for management as corollaries to financial statements, selling and delivery expense accounts, for example, could be easily adapted to fit into the Cost of Sales section of the financial statement. "Other Income" and "Other Expense" headings for a yearly financial statement would appear at the bottom of the statement.

They would modify the "Net Income from Sales" to give a "Net Income from Operations." The reason for this procedure is that installment earnings, collections of previously charged-off bad accounts, carrying charges, etc., are not directly connected with the sale of furniture. Too, interest and other charges not directly concerned with selling furniture technically are not considered chargeable against "Net Income from Sales."

BOOKS AND FORMS PECULIAR TO THE BUSINESS

Basic books are a General journal and a General ledger, plus an indexed card file for Accounts Receivable. These basic books may be amplified by the Purchases journal, Sales journal, Cash Receipts journal, and Cash Disbursements journal. If a business does not want to use the indexed card file, then an Accounts Receivable book would be maintained. The needs of management and the size of the business would be determining factors.

The usual precautions should be observed in making posting markings on papers of original entry. It is suggested that a Continuous Register form (Figure 1) be used to build a Daily Sales and Cash Report (Figure 3).

Sales of merchandise are generally written on the Continuous Register form. These forms are attached together and serially numbered in order that complete audit control may be maintained. It is not necessary to go into detail concerning types of sales forms used since many kinds are available. However, it is best if the form used produces numbered duplicates and if required by the business, numbered triplicates. Even if the sale is a credit sale, it should be written up on the firm's principal sales record, whether it be a Continuous Register form or a serially numbered sales book.

Powell Business Equipment Company

127 Sunset Ave.   TELEPHONE 446-6815   P. O. Box 567
                         ROCKY MOUNT, N. C.

CUSTOMER'S ORDER NO.				DATE			
							196___
NAME							
ADDRESS							

SOLD BY	CASH	C. O. D.	CHARGE	ON ACCT.	MDSE. RETD.	PAID OUT	

QUANTITY	DESCRIPTION	PRICE	AMOUNT
		Tax	
		Total	

ALL claims and returned goods MUST be accompanied by this bill

No. **10099**   Rec'd by

E14637   POWELL BUSINESS EQUIPMENT CO., ROCKY MOUNT, N. C.

No. **10099**   Rec'd by

E14632   POWELL BUSINESS EQUIPMENT CO., ROCKY MOUNT, N. C.

No. **10099**   Rec'd by

E14632   POWELL BUSINESS EQUIPMENT CO., ROCKY MOUNT, N. C.

* COURTESY POWELL BUSINESS EQUIPMENT COMPANY, ROCKY MOUNT, N.C.

Figure I: Continuous Register Form

The Continuous Register form and each cash receipt should bear two posting notations. The first notation should be made when the paper is used to work up the daily report. The second notation is made when the paper is posted to the proper Account Receivable. On a purely cash sale, the cash register receipt and the register sale form swap identification numbers for safety's sake, each showing the number of the other. A tape on each class of sales, plus another cumulative tape on the individual account postings, serves as a check on accuracy. A bank-stamped duplicate deposit slip, marked when entered, would also be an ideal paper of original entry. If a duplicate check system or a Cash Disbursements journal is not used, check stubs will provide sufficient information for posting cash expenditures.

Many firms will want to keep a perpetual inventory of merchandise on hand. This can be accomplished in several different ways, but it is preferable to employ a method which uses a Double Inventory card (Figure 2). The double-tag system works in this fashion: When the merchandise is received, the cost is entered in code on the display half of the tag and the cost in money is put on the inventory half. The latter half of the tag is removed and placed in the perpetual inventory file. Display half of the tag with tie strings remains on the item of merchandise; it is not removed until the merchandise is sold. When this tie-string portion of the tag is removed, the matching half of the tag is also removed from the inventory file and routed to the desk of management for possible reorder of the merchandise just sold. Some stores will attach the display half of the inventory tag either to the sales ticket or to the conditional sales contract, as the case may be. As for the inventory half of the tag, which has now reached the desk of the buyer, the latter may choose to keep this ticket in an inactive file to which he may refer at times to determine what kinds and types of merchandise are selling best. Perpetual inventory halves should also be kept for audit and for confirmation purposes.

When a cash sale is made, the cash sale notice should be entered on the Continuous Register form and a cash receipt issued showing the number of the sale form. When the sale is completed, a "Sold" tag and delivery instructions are placed on the item.

The Daily Sales and Cash Report (Figure 3) shows receipt of these payments and the deposit, along with the store funds in the store bank account.

The report may be used as a paper of original entry. Not only does this daily report indicate the beginning cash and closing cash amounts, but the other columns can give rise to daily sales entries and can help management keep a finger on collections made for finance companies. Use of this report, or a similar form, is recommended as an aid to internal control.

Peculiarities of Procedures

CASH RECEIPTS

It is not good practice to write money receipts on the Continuous Register form nor the receipts of merchandise taken in trade. Cash receipts should always be written on a printed duplicate receipt. It is good procedure to note on the Continuous Register form the number of the cash receipt which shows a down payment or which shows receipt of merchandise in trade. A cash receipts form may be used in receiving merchandise in trade with no amount shown on the cash line, but the receipt will show only the value and type of merchandise received in trade.

RECEIVABLES

Often the sale of furniture on an installment contract presents the knottiest problems. One of the headaches for store salespeople is the figuring and adding on of bank interest and carrying charges. Another is efforts which must be made to collect on defaulted contracts; and if that is impossible, to repossess the merchandise.

The handling of an installment contract may be illustrated by following through such a sale:

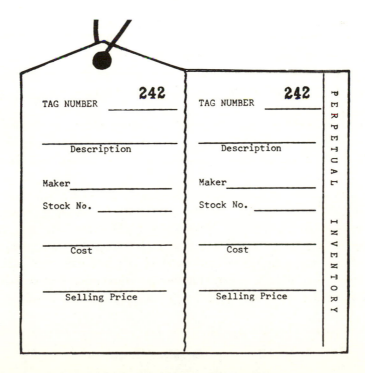

Figure 2: Double Inventory Card

Day _____ Date

DAILY SALES AND CASH REPORT

_____

Register cash-beginning $ _____

Cash sales $ _____   _____

Credit sales   _____

TOTAL SALES   _____

Other Income-credit $ _____

Other Income-cash   _____

TOTAL OTHER INCOME   _____

Collections for finance company   _____

Collections-accounts receivable   _____

Cash-short__over___   _____

Closing cash   _____

DEPOSIT_____   _____
        (date)   (slip no.)

CASH FORWARD
                                         _____

Signed_____

Figure 3: Daily Sales and Cash Report

a. John Doe buys $500 worth of furniture.

b. Salesman writes the sale on a Continuous Register form charging the entire sale to Mr. Doe.

c. A cash receipt for a $50 down payment is issued to Mr. Doe.

d. An installment contract and a recourse note are made up by the salesman and signed by Mr. Doe.

e. Salesman includes bank charges and interest at the proper place on the contract, known as a conditional sales contract.

f. The contract and note are sent to the installment bank.

g. The bank issues to the store a check for $405—holding back $45 in the Due from Finance Companies account.

h. The $405 is receipted in and credited to Mr. Doe's account against his balance owed of $450.

i. Bookkeeper then journalizes an entry which clears Mr. Doe's account of the balance of $45 and sets this amount into the Due from Finance Companies account.

Most banks allow stores to participate in their earnings on such contracts. But whatever system is used by the bank, the bookkeeper should not originate income from this source except by definite information from the bank. These earnings are credited to Other Income. These amounts, like the holdback, are placed in the Due from Finance Companies account.

The bank periodically totals the store's contingent liabilities and if the installment reserves are more than the bank's requirements, a refund is made to the store by reducing the bank's holdback account of the store's receivables.

In the case of default, if efforts by the store and bank fail to secure collection, a repossession is in order. Some customers may permit a repossession of merchandise. But, the case often turns out to be "claim and delivery," which means the seller of the mortgaged merchandise seeks to recover the merchandise and defaulted payment. Action then must be initiated before a magistrate to secure the merchandise, although this does not involve accounting.

When collection efforts have failed, the store will receive from the bank a "recourse demand" or similar information, requesting payment of the defaulted contract.

It is customary for the store to pay off the balance of the defaulted contract less any prepayment discount the bank might make. This payoff, along with any magistrate or collection expenses, reopens Mr. Doe's account.

Sale of repossessed merchandise to the used furniture outlet would be a credit to Mr. Doe's account. The balance owed by Mr. Doe may be written off by either the direct or reserve method. The chart of accounts is set up for the reserve method.

A word of caution about repossessions: Tax law generally denies a bad debt deduction if repossessed merchandise is placed back into store inventory. If the store places such items back on its floor for sale, an approved method calls for a "purchase by repossession" of the amount owed by the customer. This purchase-by-repossession price of the merchandise becomes the purchase price of the merchandise then offered for resale. The loss, if any, is taken when the merchandise is inventoried at its actual value or sold at a price less than its repurchase cost.

To illustrate: Mr. Doe's account now carries a balance due of $350 consisting of the payoff to the bank and collection charges.

Method 1. The used furniture outlet takes the merchandise at $100. This is credited to the Doe account and the loss of $250 is written off as a bad debt.

Method 2. The $350 in the Doe account is written off by a $350 credit and a $350 debit to Purchase by Repossession; the items are then placed back on the sales floor. The items are sold for $100, and the $250 loss is thus incurred. The net income is thus properly reflected.

Method 3. In the event the merchandise has been so ill used as to be valueless, it is junked and a notation made in the Doe account to that effect. The bad debt write-off is then available to show the loss.

A store may choose to handle some of its own time payment contracts. If this is preferred, the beginning of the installment sale follows the same steps as illustrated, but the store is the recipient of the note and the conditional sales contract.

Generally, the customer's Accounts Receivable card is used until the account is paid out. The sale is handled on the books like any credit sale. Carrying charges and interest credits are shown under Other Income.

INVENTORY

Good procedure requires that a perpetual inventory be kept. Perhaps the most practical inventory system is the one using the double tag as previously described and illustrated in Figure 2.

At the end of the fiscal period, the perpetual inventory half of the tags in the file can be audited and a total quickly made from these tags. However, sufficient actual counts should be carried out and the perpetual inventory half of the tags compared with a number of the tags on merchandise to make sure that the perpetual inventory is correct. The total of these tags should always be the value of the unsold merchandise at cost. While the purchase price should be coded on the half of the tag that is attached to the merchandise, the perpetual inventory half that is filed should bear the cost price in dollars and cents. This makes totaling the inventory for interim financial statements a matter of a few minutes' work with an adding machine.

Time and Payroll System

There is nothing unusual in the time and payroll system for a furniture store. Extra promotional activities on the part of the store, however, may call for special handling. A sales bonus program, for example, would require that the bookkeeper run through the sales slips and set up the necessary additional earnings for each salesclerk.

Reports to Management

Preparation of a monthly profit and loss statement and balance sheet should be on a comparative basis under the headings of "This Year to Date" and "Last Year to Date". Of course, the actual year would be specified.

Installment Sales Taxation

The Treasury Department and most state income tax laws permit a corporation, a partnership, and a sole proprietorship to pay income taxes on that portion of installment sales actually collected. In the event the "Installment Sales" method of reporting income is desired, the proper procedure, described and illustrated, can be found in a Treasury Department publication (No. 334), "Tax Guide for Small Business."

32

Garages

BY TOM A. BRIGHAM

Certified Public Accountant,
Normal, Illinois

Characteristics of the Business That Affect the Accounting System

Garages may be classified in a number of ways. They may be grouped by the specialty of repair work rendered, usually in one of three major areas: (1) Auto repair shops, which specialize in mechanical adjustments to the auto; these shops normally take care of all general repairs to the operating portion of the auto, (2) Body repair shops, which make repairs to the auto body but not to the mechanical portions of the car, (3) Specialty shops, whose specialized automotive services cover such items as transmission repairs, tune-up, muffler, and seat covers.

A second category classifies garages as franchised or independent. Franchised garages, the largest group, are those affiliated with automotive manufacturers. These shops specialize in servicing the cars sold by their dealership, but they will also service other makes of vehicles. In recent years there

has been an increasing number of franchises granted in the area of specialized automotive services. Those garages which are not franchised are normally considered to be independent.

In almost all instances, the customer initially brings his car to the shop
and requests that an estimate be made of the service to be performed. Using
a system of standard cost, the manager of the shop or the estimator prepares
an itemized list (Figure 1) of the services to be required. Usually the services
are categorized under parts and labor.

Often the Job Order Ticket (Figure 2), described later, is used for this
purpose. In some instances the estimator may ask the customer to sign the
authorization.

In many states and municipalities this division of cost by labor or parts
is essential because of the structure of the tax laws. Frequently a sales or use
tax is required on the parts but not on the labor or other services rendered.

FUNCTIONAL CHARACTERISTICS OF THE BUSINESS

The accounting year of the garage business may be a calendar year or
other fiscal period. In cases of franchised units, the fiscal year is often determined by the parent organization. In these instances, most franchisees must
comply not only with the fiscal year as set forth by the franchise but with
certain specific accounting systems and practices as well. In fact, in many

Estimate Variance				
Ticket Number_____			Estimator_____	
	Actual	Estimate	Over Under	Reason
Labor				
Parts				
Other				

Figure 1: Estimate Variance

of the specialized shops a part of the franchise fee is collected for performing all of the accounting functions for the franchisee.

PRINCIPAL ACCOUNTING PROBLEMS

In most specialized shops, the original estimate is prepared either by the manager or by an experienced estimator. Its purpose is to let the customer know not only the approximate cost of the service, but also to help him decide whether or not he would like the service to be rendered. The problem that often develops is that the actual cost of the service is recorded by a mechanic or other nonoffice worker as he performs the service. Therefore, a word of caution would be well taken. Each person who is charged with the responsibility of recording costs should know that the bill given to the customer is based upon figures placed there by the mechanic. Any errors on his part, either of timekeeping or reporting prices of the various parts, would be reflected in an erroneous statement to the customer. Perhaps in no other business is the accounting information gathered from documents where the person filling out the sales ticket is so far removed from the accounting function.

Functional Organization

Departmental organization of garages normally includes sections for repair, specialized tool work, parts, and accounting. If the shop is franchised, it is possible there may be an Accessory or a Parts Department available for use by the general public or other shops. In this instance the garage serves as a wholesaler for the parts of that specific auto manufacturer or other franchiser.

Principles and Objectives of the Accounting System

Since the two major sources of income in this type of business derive from the sale of parts and labor, the original Repair Order or Sales Slip (Figure 2) should show the amount separately for these two classifications. This is particularly important in those states which have a different tax or rate base applied to these separate categories. In addition to accounting for income, it is essential that each job should be separately priced and compared with the estimate for that job so that any substantial differences can be noted. If overhead is applied as part of the cost factor, it is normally considered to be a fixed amount or percent based on each dollar of material or labor supplied.

SPECIFIC OBJECTIVES OF THE SYSTEM

Specifically, the objectives of this accounting system are much the same as for any business. These are to provide careful records of income and related direct cost. In addition to the normal income and expenses, businesses of this type are particularly concerned with deviations from the standard cost. Standard costs normally are supplied by an outside agency which specializes in preparing standard or job costs. This information can be further used in revising estimates in the future.

Classification of Accounts and Books of Accounts

BALANCE SHEET ACCOUNTS.

ASSETS

Current assets

1001 Cash
1002 Petty Cash
1003 Change Fund
1004 Bank
1005 Accounts Receivable
1006 Notes Receivable
1010 Inventory
    1011 Parts
    1012 Accessories (if applicable)
    1013 Work in Process
    1014 Other

Fixed assets

1101 Equipment—Shop
    1112 Allowance for Depreciation—Shop Equipment
1102 Equipment—Office
    1113 Allowance for Depreciation—Office Equipment

1103 Equipment—Service
    1114 Allowance for Depreciation—Service Equipment
1104 Real Estate
1105 Furniture
    1115 Allowance for Depreciation—Furniture

Other assets

1120 Prepaid Expenses

LIABILITIES

Current liabilities

2001 Payroll Taxes Withheld
2005 Accrued Taxes
2010 Accounts Payable
2011 Notes Payable
2012 Other Accruals

NET WORTH

3001 Capital Stock
3002 Retained Earnings
3003 Profit or Loss

INCOME AND EXPENSE ACCOUNTS.

INCOME

Sales

4001 Labor

4002 Parts—Counter Sales
4003 Parts—Repair Orders
4004 Accessories
4005 Other

EXPENSES

5001 Advertising	5009 Meetings
5002 Salaries—Managers	5010 Dues and Subscriptions
5003 Salaries—Mechanics	5011 Postage and Office Supplies
5004 Salaries—Other Service	5013 Rent
5005 Salaries—Office	5014 Telephone
5006 Utilities	5015 Depreciation, Shop Equipment
5007 Maintenance	5016 Depreciation, Office Equipment
5008 Insurance	5017 Depreciation, Service Equipment
	5018 Depreciation, Furniture
	5019 Taxes (categorized)

BOOKS AND FORMS PECULIAR TO THE BUSINESS

The Repair Order (Figure 2) provides the original or source document for all sales except over-the-counter sales of parts. The Sales journal should provide columns appropriate for each classification of work performed. The usual classifications would be materials, labor, and supplies. In the case of a specialized shop or one which has multifunctions, the Sales journal would be expanded to provide a column for each of the appropriate types of sales. The repair orders are entered chronologically in the Sales journal. It is usually a good idea to provide the cost column for each type of sales. This procedure allows comparison by each repair order to see how far the actual cost deviated from the estimate and how much gross profit was made on each sale. The columns can be totaled monthly and posted in the usual manner.

The Check register and General journal for garages do not differ materially from other types of businesses. In fact, other special journals or ledgers, such as Accounts Receivable, etc., would not be unusual in any way. The use of other journals or ledgers would depend upon the volume and needs of the specific garage.

ACCOUNTS PECULIAR TO THE BUSINESS

Normally there should be several inventory accounts so that a running inventory of various parts may be kept. The actual number of inventory accounts would vary with the specialized type of business, but usual classifications are made for parts inventory, supply inventory, gas, oil, etc., and an inventory account for the work in process. If the garage is that of a franchised auto dealer, there frequently will be special accounts for service performed on used cars or make-ready costs on new cars. The major accounting record, as mentioned previously, is the customer Repair Order (Figure 2). This form normally is prepared in triplicate. The original serves as the customer invoice, the duplicate is retained for the accounting office, and the triplicate is used by the mechanic or other person performing the service.

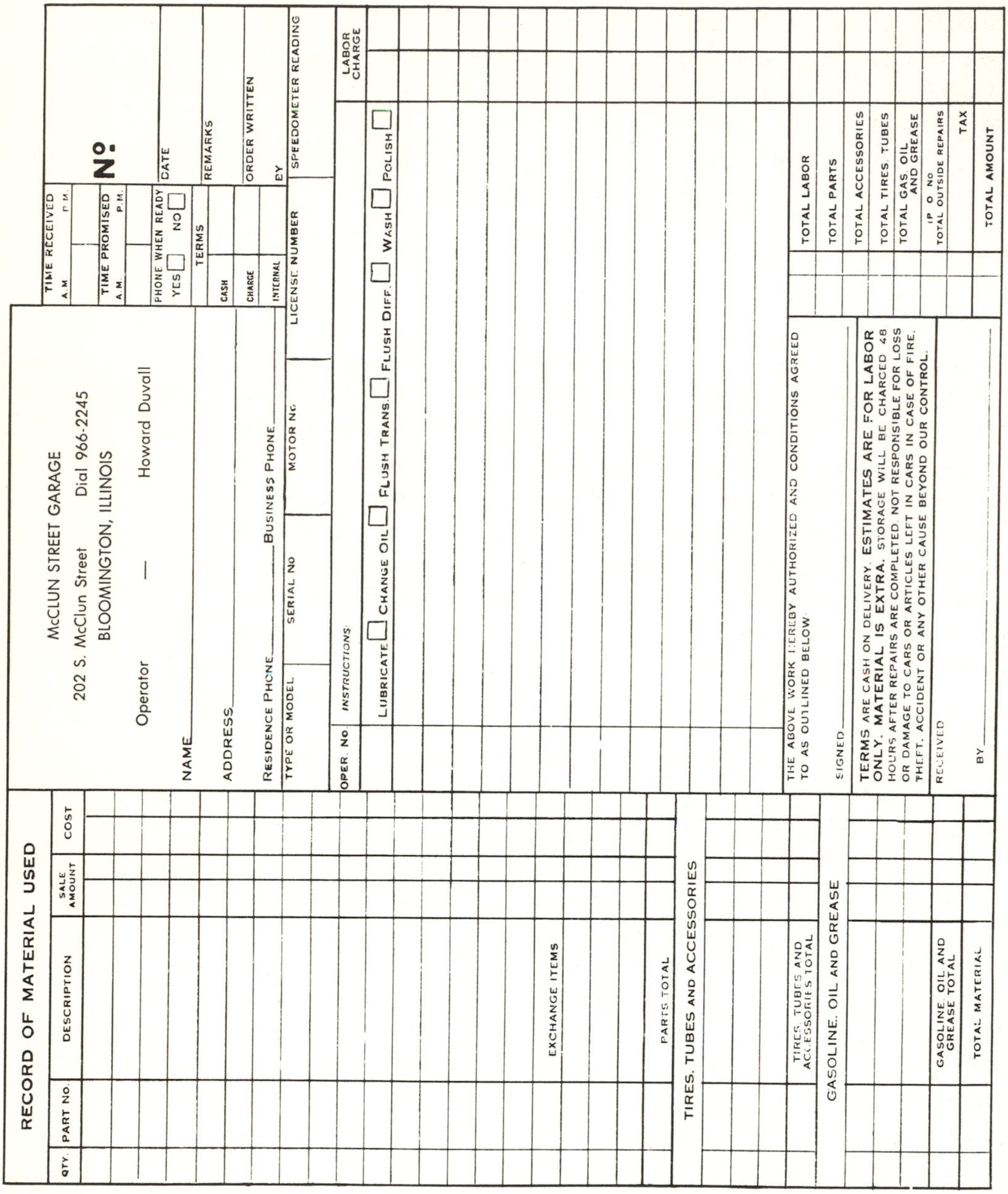

RECORD OF MATERIAL USED

QTY.	PART NO.	DESCRIPTION	SALE AMOUNT	COST
		EXCHANGE ITEMS		
		PARTS TOTAL		
		TIRES, TUBES AND ACCESSORIES		
		TIRES, TUBES AND ACCESSORIES TOTAL		
		GASOLINE, OIL AND GREASE		
		GASOLINE, OIL AND GREASE TOTAL		
		TOTAL MATERIAL		

McCLUN STREET GARAGE
202 S. McClun Street Dial 966-2245
BLOOMINGTON, ILLINOIS

Operator — Howard Duvall

TIME RECEIVED A.M. P.M.
TIME PROMISED A.M. P.M.
No
DATE

PHONE WHEN READY YES ☐ NO ☐
TERMS CASH CHARGE INTERNAL
REMARKS
ORDER WRITTEN BY

NAME
ADDRESS
RESIDENCE PHONE BUSINESS PHONE

TYPE OR MODEL	SERIAL NO	MOTOR NO	LICENSE NUMBER	SPEEDOMETER READING

OPER. NO. INSTRUCTIONS: LABOR CHARGE

LUBRICATE ☐ CHANGE OIL ☐ FLUSH TRANS. ☐ FLUSH DIFF. ☐ WASH ☐ POLISH ☐

THE ABOVE WORK HEREBY AUTHORIZED AND CONDITIONS AGREED TO AS OUTLINED BELOW:

SIGNED ____

TERMS ARE CASH ON DELIVERY. ESTIMATES ARE FOR LABOR ONLY. MATERIAL IS EXTRA. STORAGE WILL BE CHARGED 48 HOURS AFTER REPAIRS ARE COMPLETED. NOT RESPONSIBLE FOR LOSS OR DAMAGE TO CARS OR ARTICLES LEFT IN CARS IN CASE OF FIRE, THEFT, ACCIDENT OR ANY OTHER CAUSE BEYOND OUR CONTROL.

RECEIVED
BY ____

TOTAL LABOR
TOTAL PARTS
TOTAL ACCESSORIES
TOTAL TIRES, TUBES
TOTAL GAS, OIL AND GREASE
(P. O. NO.) TOTAL OUTSIDE REPAIRS
TAX
TOTAL AMOUNT

* Courtesy of McClun Street Garage, Bloomington, Illinois.

Figure 2: Repair Order

These forms are usually either prenumbered by the printer or numbered prior to being sent to the Service Department. In this manner the Accounting Department may keep track of each repair order to see that none of them is misplaced. The usual procedure is to record the Repair Order at the end of each day.

Peculiarities of Procedures

SALES-RECEIVABLES CYCLE

Recording of the repair order is the usual start of recording of sales. In addition, any over-the-counter sales would be recorded at this time. The form which is frequently used for counter sales is the simple continuous form which is ejected after each use. The third copy is frequently retained in the box for use by the Accounting Department with the original going to the customer. If there is a large number of counter sales, it may be desirable to have some classification of types of sales included in the Sales journal.

As a matter of course, sales are collected in cash at the time the service is rendered. Partly because of the mechanics-lien laws of many states, garages insist that cash be paid for their services prior to letting any car leave the premises. If financing is necessary, it is frequently arranged through a local bank or finance company; thereby the possibility of bad debts is reduced as well as the accounting cost.

ACCOUNTS PAYABLE CYCLE

There is no major deviation in the Accounts Payable procedure for garages as compared with other businesses.

Time and Payroll System

One unique feature of garages is that mechanics and other service personnel are usually paid a percentage of the services charged to customers. This means that frequently it is not necessary to have any timekeeping procedure other than the regular job order tickets (Figure 2). These repair orders would also serve if personnel are reimbursed on a piece-work basis. Office and other nonservice personnel timekeeping procedures are essentially the same as in all other businesses.

Cost Accounting and Departmental Accounting

Flat-Rate Manual. Most automotive repair businesses use a flat-rate manual. This manual provides a ready source of standard charges for repairs.

CONTACT _____ ZONE # _____ P'MARKED _____ REC'D _____ THRU _____ EXCL _____ DUAL _____ B C _____ O L _____ PASS _____ TRK _____ TOTAL _____

FINANCIAL STATEMENT

PAGE 1

COVERING PERIOD FROM _____ THRU _____
DEALER _____
ADDRESS _____

ASSETS	ACCT. NO.	AMOUNT
CURRENT ASSETS		
CASH		
Petty	200	
On Hand	201	
In Bank	202	
CONTRACTS IN TRANSIT	205	
TOTAL CASH AND CONTRACTS (LINES 3 TO 7 INC.)		
RECEIVABLES		
Customer Notes—Not Due	210	
Customer Notes—Past Due	210	
Customer Accounts—Not Due	220	
Customer Accounts—Past Due	220	
TOTAL CUSTOMER RECEIVABLES		
LESS: Allowance for Doubtful Accounts	340	
NET CUSTOMER RECEIVABLES		
Memo (CAR AND TRUCK NOTES IN ACCT. 210 $___ / CAR AND TRUCK ACCTS. IN ACCT. 220 $___)		
Accounts Payable Debit Balances	300	
TOTAL RECEIVABLES (LINES 16, 17, & 20 INC.)		
INVENTORIES		
★ Demonstrators (Cars) (Trucks)	230	
★ New Cars ( )	231	
★ New Trucks ( )	237	
★ Used Cars ( )	240	
★ Used Trucks ( )	241	
Parts	242	
Accessories	243	
Gas, Oil and Grease	244	
Paint and Body Shop Materials	245	
Sublet Repairs	246	
Work in Process—Labor	247	
Miscellaneous Assets Received in Trade	248	

LINE NO.	LIABILITIES	ACCT. NO.	AMOUNT
1	**CURRENT LIABILITIES**		
2	**ACCOUNTS PAYABLE**		
3	Trade Creditors	300	
4	Accounts Receivable Credit Balances	220	
5	Customer Deposits	220	
6			
7			
8	**NOTES PAYABLE**		
9	New Cars, Trucks and Demonstrators	310	
10	Others	314	
11			
12	Memo (NOTES PAYABLE SECURED BY CUSTOMER NOTES IN ACCT. 210 $___)		
13			
14			
15	**ACCRUED LIABILITIES**		
16	Interest	320	
17	Payroll	321	
18	Insurance	322	
19	Taxes—Payroll	323	
20	Taxes—Sales	324	
21	Taxes—Other than Payroll, Sales and Income	325	
22	Income Taxes—Previous Year	326	
23	Income Taxes—Current Year	327	
24	Bonuses—Employes	328	
25	Bonuses—Owners	329	
26	Pension Fund	330	
27	Other	331	
28			
29	TOTAL CURRENT LIABILITIES (LINES 3 TO 28 INC.)		
30			
31			
32	**LONG TERM DEBT**		
33	TOTAL (LINES 29 TO 32 INC.)	334	
34	MORTGAGES PAYABLE	335	
35			
36	TOTAL LIABILITIES (LINES 33 TO 35 INC.)		
37			

Item	Acct. No.	Line	OWNED NET WORKING CAPITAL
Tires and Tubes	249	38	
Non-Automotive Merchandise	250	39	
		40	
		41	$
TOTAL INVENTORIES (LINES 23 TO 41 INC.)	260	42	ASSETS LINES 54 PLUS 55, MINUS LIABILITIES LINE 33
SECURITIES	261	43	**NET WORTH**
DISCOUNTS RECEIVABLE		44	
DUE FROM FINANCE COMPANIES	262	45	**CORPORATIONS ONLY**
FACTORY CLAIMS	263	46	CAPITAL STOCK — 360
INSURANCE COMMISSIONS RECEIVABLE	264	47	RETAINED EARNINGS — 370
PREPAID EXPENSES Taxes	270	48	
Insurance	271	49	
Rent	272	50	
Interest	273	51	DIVIDENDS — 375
Other	274	52	**PROPRIETORSHIPS OR PARTNERSHIPS**
TOTAL PREPAID EXPENSES (LINES 48 TO 52 INC.)		53	INVESTMENTS (LIST EACH PARTNER) — 380
TOTAL CURRENT ASSETS (LINES 8, 21, 42, 43, 44, 45, 46, 47 & 53 INC.)		54	
★ LEASE AND RENTAL UNITS ( )	277	55	
FIXED ASSETS—AUTO BUSINESS ONLY		56	

FIXED ASSETS	ACT. NO.	COST	ACCUMULATED DEPRECIATION	Line	
LAND	280			57	DRAWINGS (LIST EACH PARTNER) — 390
BLDGS. & IMPRVM.	281		351	58	
MACH. & SHOP EQ.	282		352	59	
PARTS & ACC. EQ.	283		353	60	
FURN. & FIXTURES	284		354	61	
SERVICE UNITS	285		355	62	
LEASEHOLDS	286		356	63	

MONTHLY	NEW UNITS	PROFIT OR LOSS
(Line 63)		
January (64)		
February (65)		
March (66)		
April (67)		
May (68)		
June (69)		399
July (70)		
August (71)		
September (72)		
October (73)		
November (74)		
December (75)		
TOTAL NEW UNITS (76)		

Item	Acct. No.	Line
★ MEMO—SERVICE UNITS: CARS ( ) TRUCKS ( )		64
		65
TOTAL—NET FIXED ASSETS (LINES 58 TO 65 INC.)		66
OTHER ASSETS		67
Deposits on Contracts	290	68
Life Insurance—Cash Value	291	69
Notes and Accounts Receivable—Officers	293	70
Advances to Employes	294	71
Other Notes and Accounts Receivable	295	72
Other Non-Franchise Assets	296	73
		74
		75
		76
TOTAL OTHER ASSETS (LINES 69 TO 76 INC.)		77 — TOTAL NET WORTH (LINES 46 TO 69 INC.)
TOTAL ASSETS (LINES 54, 55, 67 & 77)		78 — TOTAL LIABILITIES AND NET WORTH (LINES 36, 37 & 77)

USE
BINDER BRS-159
PENCIL CARBON PAPER CP-1590 (BLUE)
TYPEWRITER CARBON PAPER CP-1595 (BLACK)
TYPEWRITER CARBON PAPER CP-1595-B (BLUE)

★ BE SURE TO SHOW NUMBER OF UNITS

COURTESY OF GENERAL MOTORS CORPORATION, DETROIT, MICHIGAN, AND THE REYNOLDS & REYNOLDS COMPANY, DAYTON, OHIO.

Figure 3: Balance Sheet for Franchised Garage

The flat-rate manual provides a quick reference for jobs which are frequently done as well as for those which occur less frequently. In addition to being a handy reference for the estimator, it is possible for the experienced mechanic to profit directly by the fact that he can perform the service in less time than the rate manual allows and, therefore, earn more money than estimated. Conversely, management can use this standard cost as a measurement to determine the efficiency of all mechanics. At the end of each month, comparison of standard costs with actual costs by job, by department, and by the individual mechanic provides management with one of its essential reports.

In the case of specialized shops such as brake, muffler, or transmission, prices are frequently based on the fact that specialized service personnel are now able to perform the specific repair in less time than the amount quoted in the flat-rate manual. In this way the selling price can be reduced and the shop can operate on a volume basis.

Overhead. Overhead is normally applied to departments on the basis of their dollar sales or man hours. As an example, if indirect expenses total $10,000 and there are 5,000 hours of mechanics' time charged during the period, the overhead might be applied at the rate of $2.00 per hour. The amount of burden ($2.00) could be estimated from month to month and adjusted if any substantial deviation occurs. Administrative expenses would be distributed in the same manner.

Time-Saving Ideas

At the completion of the work there will be two copies of each work order in the Accounting Department—the regular accounting office copy and the one used by the mechanic. It is suggested that the accounting copy be used as a source document for all entries and that the mechanic's copy be filed separately by employee. At the end of each pay period, it is a simple matter to add total labor by employee for use in preparing the payroll.

Reports to Management

FINANCIAL REPORTS

As in most businesses, the income statement and the balance sheet should be prepared each month. For comparison purposes, a year-to-date figure should be included next to the figure for the previous year. An example of a balance sheet for a franchised garage is shown as Figure 3.

OPERATING REPORTS

The nature of the business requires that frequent comparison between the estimated cost of a job and the actual cost should be prepared. If possible, the comparison should be made each day; otherwise, a report should be compiled no less frequently than each month. Comparison should be figured between the estimated cost and the actual cost under categories of parts as well as labor. Comments should appear on this comparison giving the reason for variance from the estimate. It is desirable to have these reports accumulated not only by individual repair order but also by department and by man. In this way management can determine the effectiveness of each employee as well as any department.

33

Grocery Stores (Retail)

BY BEN STONER

**President, Ben Stoner Associates,
Springfield, Missouri**

Characteristics of the Business That Affect the Accounting System

Grocery stores of the small to medium size serve a neighborhood on a very personal basis. Over recent years these stores have changed from predominately a credit system with delivery service to cash and carry. This change was made possible by improved family transportation, and on the other hand was forced by competition with large supermarkets. By use of the better management techniques of modern merchandising, the smaller stores are successfully competing. Many of these stores are manager owned and -operated with limited employment of outside help. However, small corporations have come into being which operate several stores of this type.

Many of the small and medium-volume grocery stores do not operate butcher shops for cutting fresh meat. Some stores stock cured meats, while others add prepackaged fresh meats purchased from a local butcher. The accounting system described in this chapter is designed for those grocery stores which do not operate butcher shops. However, a slight alteration of the Purchase journal to handle purchases at cost only for the Butcher Shop Department makes the system applicable to include this operation on a cost basis. Periodic physical inventories of this department are required to provide operating statements.

FUNCTIONAL CHARACTERISTICS OF THE BUSINESS

The grocery business is not seasonal in total, yet it does have its low points of the year, generally December and January. In these months consumers are making heavy expenditures for holiday merchandise, and until the Christmas bills are paid, the grocery store suffers from retardation of sales. Competition from supermarkets has been discussed previously.

PRINCIPAL ACCOUNTING PROBLEMS

Grocery store operation requires accurate daily cash reports and tabulation of merchandise purchases and expense items. The daily reports of the manager must be kept up to date and bank deposits made accurately and on time. Purchases create a problem because of their great number and frequency.

Another accounting problem, which arises only under the retail system of inventory, is that of recording and tabulating price changes; however, a properly trained store manager can cope with this problem if changes are recorded immediately.

The importance of good accounting cannot be overstressed. One problem is that very few qualified merchant-managers have the ability, either temperamentally or technically, to keep the necessary records. A public accounting firm usually is better equipped to keep proper accounting records and advise on tax matters. Fees spent for this service will be repaid many times in more efficient operation and higher profits.

Functional Organization

In the manager-owned and -operated store the entrepreneur's duties cover many areas in which he needs to be adept if he is to succeed. He is the personnel and employment manager, the merchandising manager and buyer, the advertising and public relations manager, and the office clerk.

Managers and owners of small and medium-sized groceries are becoming aware of the fact that a good accounting service can relieve them of onerous, time-consuming detail and can also furnish them with factual statistical, operating information which allows them to compete and to make a good profit. An owner-manager thus relieved has more time to devote to actual operation of the business.

Typical organization of the small corporation operating more than one store calls for a general manager to handle employment, advertising, and merchandise planning. Under him is a store manager whose duty it is to carry out the policies and plans set forth by the general manager, to supervise personnel, and to prepare daily reports for the accounting firm or the store's Bookkeeping Department.

Deliveries received by the store are checked item by item before invoices are signed. The average grocery store will have 35 to 40 suppliers, some of whom deliver daily; others deliver several times a week while still others deliver weekly. Most deliveries are made by route salesmen who make up the invoice and display the merchandise. Route salesmen also price mark their merchandise where it is permitted by the labor unions.

Classification of Accounts and Books of Accounts

A flexible numbering system for the chart of accounts eliminates an enormous amount of writing and time spent by the clerks. The system should be simple, yet broad enough to include all the needs of the business it serves. Any one of several systems may be used; however, the following standard system has been successfully applied to every type of small business except department stores.

BALANCE SHEET ACCOUNTS.

ASSETS

Current assets (Nos. 1-29)

1 Bank
2 Petty Cash or Change Fund
4 Returned Checks
5 Accounts Receivable
11 Inventory
20 Prepaid Expense

Fixed assets

30 Machinery
31 Allowance for Depreciation, Machinery

LIABILITIES

Current liabilities

51 Accounts Payable
52 Notes Payable
53 Payroll Payable
60 FICA Tax Payable
61 Federal Withholding Tax
62 State Withholding Tax
63 State Unemployment Tax Payable
64 Federal Unemployment Tax Payable

Long-term liabilities

66 Mortgage Payable

NET WORTH

70-79   Capital Accounts
90-100 Profit and Loss

Income and expense accounts.
INCOME

101-109 Income	134 Accounting and Legal Fees
110-119 Purchases and Cost	135 Travel and Entertainment
of Sales	137 Donations
	139 Telephone
EXPENSES	140 Utilities
120 Payroll	141 Rent
122 Store Supplies	142 Insurance
123 Advertising	144 Miscellaneous General Expense
126 Equipment Rental	145 Depreciation, Machinery
127 Payroll Taxes	150 Gas and Oil, Business Vehicles
132 Taxes and Licenses	151 Repairs, Vehicles
133 Interest on Indebtedness	

Under Fixed assets, even numbers are used for the assets and odd numbers for Depreciation Allowances, etc.

Peculiarities of Procedures

PURCHASES-PAYABLES CYCLE

Invoices. As deliveries are made to the store, a clerk on duty will check each item on the invoice. In all but a very few instances the retail prices are entered and circled by the delivery driver. The exceptions are for grocery house items on which markup must be calculated by the manager to arrive at retail price. A Voucher Envelope (Figure 1) is made for each invoice. At the beginning of each week a "set" of envelopes is prepared, one for each regular supplier. After the merchandise is checked, an entry is made on the voucher to show the amount and the date. The voucher is stapled to the envelope in which the invoice is inserted.

Purchase Journal. An office clerk checks the invoices, envelope by envelope. He computes the retail price and posts it on the outside of each envelope (Figure 1). Invoice amounts are tallied with voucher entries, and the voucher is then totaled. If there is a cash discount, it is computed and deducted from this voucher total. Expense account codes are noted in the place of the retail price on items of expense.

The Purchase journal is posted as to cost and retail price by category of merchandise (Figure 2). Expense items are posted separately in columns 7 and 8.

When the week's posting is accomplished, each category is totaled at cost and cross-balanced with a control tape on the voucher totals. The retail price is totaled for each category and the markup percentage computed. It is convenient in accumulating these retail column totals to omit the cents (.00), a procedure which has little or no effect upon the percentage of markup.

The Weekly Retail Report (Figure 3) is now started by posting to lines 8 through 21 from the Purchase journal. All figures in this report are stated at retail unless otherwise indicated. Account totals only are posted monthly to the General ledger. Accounts Payable are credited monthly.

It has been found to be most convenient, through seven years of experience in five stores, for the Weekly Retail Report to be compiled by each Wednesday. Such a deadline makes it profitable and practical for its use in a weekly meeting of managers on Thursday afternoons.

Payment of Invoices. Once the Purchase journal is balanced, the vouchers

THE NEIGHBORHOOD GROCERY REMITTANCE VOUCHER TO: *ANY BREAD CO.*		WEEK ENDING *4/16*
DATE	**AMOUNT**	
4-10	10 | 00	
4-11	17 | 50	
4-12	19 | 25	
4-13	20 | 50	
4-14	12 | 02	
TOTAL COST	79 | 27	
TOTAL RETAIL *99.09* TOTAL COST *79.27* OR ACCT. NO.		

Figure 1: Remittance Voucher

Neighborhood Grocery

Purchase Journal

#	Total	Expense	Cost	Retail	Mark-UP $	Mark-UP %	Expense acct.	amt	8
1							143	3.00	
2							122	5.16	
3							140	97.11	
4							143	1.50	
							122	17.87	
5							122	40	
6									125
7	2838.24	125.04	2713.20	3493—	780—	22 34			
8							122	9.69	
9							122	1.44	
10							143	15.07	
11							143	1.50	
							122	2.28	
12							122	40	
13									30
14	2403.52	30.38	2373.14	3112—	739—	23 14			
15									
16	Month To Date			6605—	1519—	22 99			
17							122	22.10	
18							122	1.56	
19							140	14.13	
20							122	40	
21	2486.03	39.69	2446.34	3160—	714—	22 58	143	1.50	
22	PURCHASE RECAP								39
23			*	9765—	2233—	22 86			
24	ACCT.								
25	110 10.083.68								
	122 81.92								
26	140 111.24						122	12.72	
27	143 28.43						122	2.90	
							122	1.80	
							122	2.80	
28	Cr 51 10.305.27 *						143	1.50	
							143	4.36	
29	Entries for Gen. L.						122	40	
30	2577.48	26.48	2551.00	3318—	767—	23 11			
31									26
32	Month To Date			13,083—	3000—	22 23			
33									
34									
35									
36									

FORM 50-30
MULTIPLEX COLUMNAR

9	10	11	12	13	14	15	16	17	18 MADE IN U.S.A.
Non-Food		Cured		Fresh		Eggs		Produce	
cost	retail	cost	retail	cost	retail	cost	retail	cost	retail
2402	3002	8836	11132	464	512	14555	19379	8130	10928
20730	31015							2910	4410
23132		8836		464		14555		11040	
32⁰	34017	20⁶	11132	9³	512	24⁹	19379	28⁸	15338
850	1062	9145	11813	954	1049	11573	14834	9850	14297
16218	23842							3825	5641
420	700								
120	200								
17608		9145		954		11573		13675	
31⁹	25804	22⁵	11813	9¹	1049	21⁹	14834	31⁷	19938
407		179		15		262		247	
31⁹	598	21⁸	229	0	15	23⁴	342	29⁸	352
18374	27166	8199	10416	1392	1522	11035	14052	12930	18259
3802	4752							805	1249
22176		8199		1392		11035		13735	
30⁵	31918	21³	10416	8⁵	1522	21⁵	14052	29⁶	19508
628		261		29		372		384	
31⁴	917	21⁶	333	3⁴	30	22⁹	483	29⁸	547
12280	18312	12630	16185	458	498	9825	12606	11045	16722
1377	1721							2010	3123
13657		12630		458		9825		13055	
31⁸	20033	21⁹	16185	8⁹	498	22⁷	12606	34²	19845
766		387		34		470		515	
31⁴	1117	21⁸	495	2⁸	35	22⁸	609	30⁹	745

Figure 2: Purchase Journal

19	20	21	22	23	24	25	26	27	28
MULTIPLEX COLUMNAR									
Frozen Food		Candy		Tobacco		Pop		Bread	
cost	retail	cost	retail	cost	retail	cost	retail	cost	retail
3562	5280	596	861	768	960	890	980	7927	9908
		3950	5716	4165	5206	1216	1816	14880	18600
		3414	4420	37323	46302	1430	1908		
		1620	2240			4080	5245		
		3235	4171			2140	2822		
		1763	2580			3095	4326		
		5244	7848						
		2226	3180						
3562		22048		42256		12851		22807	
32.5	5280	28.8	30986	19.4	52468	24.8	17091	20.0	28508
6931	9486	3749	5416	27414	34038	1567	2114	6673	8915
		2455	3420			1160	1696	15420	20069
		3247	4212			3560	5358		
		1426	2060			1105	1740		
		3291	4308			3380	4016		
		826	1183			3670	5719		
6931		15044		27414		14442		22093	
26.9	9486	26.5	20599	19.4	34038	30.0	20643	23.7	28984
105		370		697		273		449	
29.0	148	28.5	516	19.4	865	27.5	377	21.9	575
3960	5688	959	1578	30281	37546	1495	1700	6359	7948
		640	936	630	750	1199	1450	15483	19353
		3110	3978			1986	2400		
		3800	5554	2401	3001	3712	4820		
		610	788			3360	3906		
		3390	4750	4747	5936				
		960	1320	129	160	3955	5159		
		2603	3418						
3960		16012		38190		15687		21842	
30.4	5688	27.9	22316	19.4	47393	19.3	19435	20.0	27301
145		531		1079		430		667	
29.3	205	28.1	739	19.4	1339	24.7	571	21.3	848
3395	5160	3580	4665	33168	41138	920	1020	6604	8255
		4544	6836	2364	2920	1475	2154	14831	18538
		2100	3000			1870	2332		
		3570	4974	1032	1280	3228	4609		
		805	1100			3180	3524		
		2653	3472			2970	4664		
		490	705						
3395		17742		36564		13643		21435	
34.2	5160	28.3	24752	19.4	45338	25.5	18303	20.0	26793
179		708		1445		566		881	
30.3	257	28.3	987	19.4	1792	24.7	754	21.0	1116

29 Cost (Cakes)	30 retail	31 cost (Milk)	32 retail	33 cost (Ice Cream)	34 retail	35 cost (Groceries)	retail	
807	1098	6931	7826	5255	6916	645	869	1
2388	3114	26733	31825	2556	2832	46363	56980	2
2697	3392	10876	12949					3
522	702							
1387	1896							
2809	4214							4
								5
106 10		44340		1811		47008		6
26^4	14416	15^7	52598	19^8	9748	18^7	57849	7
2062	2688	9045	10355	5326	6904	46357	58789	8
522	702	21472	25532	2150	2150	(1886)	(2670)	9
2969	4454	8405	10548					10
3209	4031							
2336	3162	(3000)	(3571)					11
468	624							12
11566		35922		7476		43471		13
26^4	15661	16^2	42864	20^3	9384	22^6	56119	14
222		802		153		905		15
26^4	301	16^8	955	19^8	191	20^5	1139	16
2401	3601	6476	7530	8698	11218	35770	46734	17
1478	1926							
348	468	21381	25453	1120	1300	390	438	18
3627	4560	7515	8946			236	372	19
1197	1644							20
1709	2268							21
10760		35372		9818		36396		22
25^6	14467	15$^?$	41929	21^5	12518	23^4	47544	23
330		1156		251		1269		24
26^4	446	15^8	1374	20^8	316	21^5	1614	25
2308	3462	22718	27045	5571	7484	53195	69042	26
2516	3282							
609	819	10754	12802	970	1064	840	1140	27
3658	4592	7194	8365					28
1431	1925							29
932	1248							30
11454		40666		6541		54035		31
25^3	15328	15^6	48212	23^8	8548	23^9	70182	32
445		1563		316		1809		33
25^8	599	15^9	1856	21^3	401	21^9	2316	34
								35
								36

Figure 2: Purchase Journal (cont.)

WEEKLY RETAIL REPORT
(.00 OMITTED)
ALL FIGURES ARE STATED AT RETAIL

Store: Neighborhood Grocery

Month _____ Week Ending _____

	9th Period				9th Period to Date			
	Last Year $	%	This Year $	%	Last Year $	%	This Year $	%
1. SALES	3,388		3,283		13,395		12,782	
2. PURCHASES	3,640	22.96	3,318	23.11	13,436	22.18	13,083	22.93
3. M.D.S. (Loss)	6	2.47	4	2.95	23	3.31	17	3.04
4. M.D.S. (Sale)	70		93		431		351	
5. GROSS PROFIT	674	19.89	659	20.07	2,575	19.22	2,568	20.09
6. INVENTORY	7,974		8,192		7,074		8,192	
7. INVENT.INCR (*DECR)	202		*82		*429		*147	

RETAIL PURCHASES

	9th Period				9th Period to Date			
	Last Year $	%	This Year $	%	Last Year $	%	This Year $	%
8. NON-FOODS	336	31.4	200	31.8	997	31.3	1,117	31.4
9. CURED MEATS	134	21.9	162	21.9	571	20.6	495	21.8
10. FRESH MEATS	9	6.0	5	8.0	48	6.2	35	2.8
11. POULTRY & EGGS	145	28.8	126	22.1	544	30.1	609	22.8
12. PRODUCE	301	28.7	198	34.2	960	27.5	745	30.9
13. FROZEN FOODS	82	31.4	52	34.2	201	29.3	257	30.3
14. CANDY & CHIPS	274	26.8	248	28.3	1,055	27.8	987	28.3
15. CIGARETTES & TOBAC.	409	20.0	453	19.4	1,715	18.8	1,792	19.4
16. SOFT DRINKS	249	24.0	183	25.5	920	25.0	754	24.9
17. BREAD	258	20.0	268	20.0	1,135	20.0	1,116	21.1
18. CAKES & DONUTS	141	22.0	153	25.3	587	24.3	599	25.7
19. MILK & BUTTER	581	15.5	482	15.6	2,181	15.5	1,856	15.7
20. ICE CREAM	96	19.8	85	23.6	470	18.5	401	21.2
21. GROCERIES	635	23.5	702	23.0	2,070	21.2	2,316	21.9

Figure 3: Weekly Retail Report

are pulled from the envelopes and checks written. The voucher is mailed with the check. If it is desired to pay invoices on a monthly basis, the envelopes are filed each week with vouchers attached. When payment is to be made, the vouchers are pulled and totaled by supplier; they are then recapped for a total to balance with the Purchase journal accumulated total, so that checks can be issued. All vouchers accompany the checks to explain payment.

CASH RECEIPTS AND DISBURSEMENTS

Petty Cash. Petty cash is handled on an imprest system, usually on a regular daily or weekly basis. Petty Cash Envelopes (Figure 4) are used to hold the paid bills. The date, the number of the reimbursement check, distribution of charges, and total amount are shown on the face of each envelope. At the close of each week, the envelopes are sent to the bookkeeper.

Checker's Daily Report. At the close of the working day, subtotals from the cash register are taken and posted to the Checker's Daily Report (Figure 5). All money, including checks, is counted and entered on this report. Include in this listing the amount of the petty cash expended to date since the last reimbursement as well as any coupons accepted in payment for merchandise.

From the total money and receipts is now subtracted the standard Change Fund amount which will remain constant. The result of this calculation is the amount to be deposited in the bank for the day. The net register reading computed in the subtotals mentioned above is compared with the bank deposit amount. This shows the cash over or short for the day.

Cash Receipts Journal. The Cash Receipts journal shown in Figure 6 is self-explanatory. The journal should be recapped weekly to obtain sales figures for the Retail Inventory ledger (Figure 7). At the close of the month the Cash journal becomes the basis for posting the General ledger in total by each account affected. Miscellaneous cash receipts are recorded in the proper column and recapped for posting to the General ledger on a monthly basis.

Cash Disbursements Journal. This is always a multicolumn journal in which all disbursement checks are posted and distributed to the various accounts. All purchases of merchandise and expense items handled through the Purchase journal are paid through Accounts Payable. Items such as Payroll, Rent, Utilities, etc., are distributed to the various accounts in the Cash Disbursements journal. Account totals only are posted to the General ledger each month.

No special problem arises from the General ledger, except that to facili-

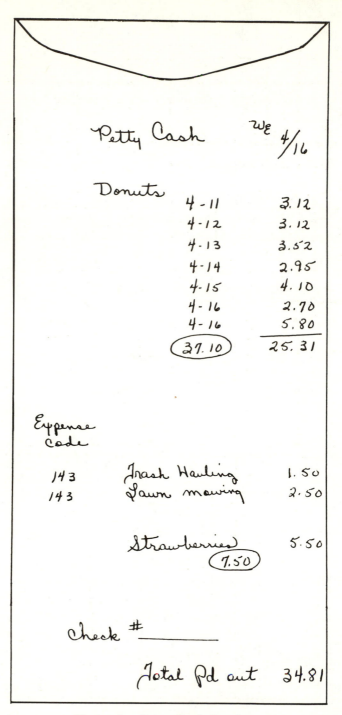

Figure 4: Petty Cash Envelope

CHECKERS DAILY REPORT

Name_____ Register No._____ Report No._____ Date_____ 19___

CASH AND SALES BALANCE		Transaction Counters	Departments	Amounts Shown On Register Totals	Voids and Refunds	Net Sales in Each Dept.
Pennies	1		GROCERY	15 / 16	27	33
Nickels	2		MEATS	17 / 18	28	34
Dimes	3		PRODUCE	19 / 20	29	35
Quarters	4			21	30	36
Halves	5			22	31	37
Silver Dollars	6			23		
Currency	7		TOTAL			38
Checks	8		Closing Total	24		
Paid Outs & Coupons	9		Beginning Total	25		
Total Cash	10		Tax Total	26		39
Change Fund (Sub)	11				32	
Today's Cash (Bank Deposit)	12	Total Items			Less Sales Tax (Sub)	40
Cash Register Totals	13				Net Sales (All Depts.)	41
Over Short	14					
Amount of Average Sale						

Group Totals

Figure 5: Checkers Daily Report

Neighborhood Grocery

April   Cash Receipts Journal

MULTIPLEX COLUMNAR

FORM 50-30

				Bank	Cash	over/short	Sales	Tax	Acct
1				6268	6268				#4
				48666	48666	26	47223	1417	
2				500	500				#4
				41130	41130	26	39906	1198	
3				500	500				#4
				38470	38470	15	37335	1120	
4				41324	41324	57	40065	1202	
5				40921	40921	24	39706	1191	
6				45891	45891	(09)	44563	1337	
7				49708	49708	16	48244	1448	
8	4-9			313378	313378	155	297042	8913	
9				238	238				#4
				67698	67698	(31)	65756	1973	
10				49022	49022	36	47559	1427	
11				49097	49097	08	47659	1430	
12				1886	1886				#51
				48300	48300	16	46877	1407	
13				47725	47725	61	46275	1389	
14				44554	44554	(11)	43267	1298	
15				44296	44296	(16)	43021	1291	
16	4-16			352816	352816	63	340414	10215	
17				45312	45312	62	43932	1318	
18				300	300				#4
				43761	43761	06	42480	1275	
19				45953	45953	(02)	44621	1339	
20				50495	50495	(23)	49046	1472	
21				47483	47483	(32)	46136	1384	
22				42722	42722	(09)	41486	1245	
23				46096	46096	(67)	44818	1345	
24	4-23			322122	322122	(75)	312519	9378	
25	April		*	49948	49948	38	48456	1453	
26				2200	2200				#4
				47853	47853	17	46443	1393	
27	#4 105.06			45671	45671	19	44322	1330	
28	#51 18.86			500	500				#4
				56643	56643	(18)	55010	1651	
29	123.92 *			45147	45147		43832	1315	
30	Recap of			42940	42940	01	41688	1251	
31	Misc. Credits			49944	49944	(31)	48519	1456	
32	4-30			340846	340846	26	328270	850	
33				1329162	1329162	169	1278245	38356	
34									
35									
36									

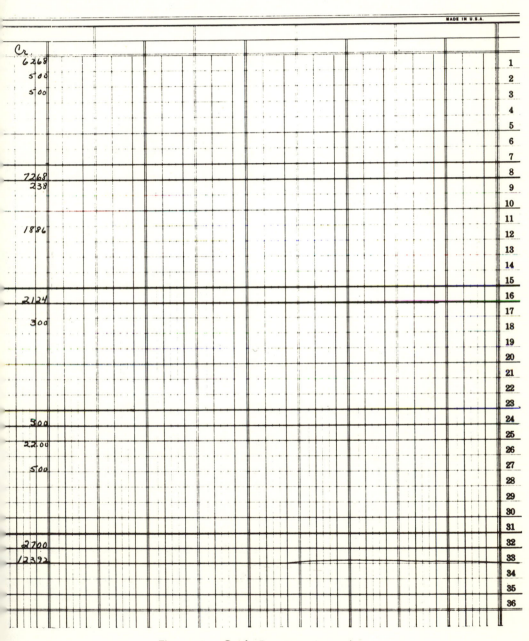

Figure 6: Cash Receipts Journal

Retail Inventory

Neighborhood Grocery

Column No. →	1	2 Purchase Cost	3 Retail	4 Mark up $	5 Up %	6 In C Res
1		105316	134374	31052	22⁷⁶	72
2		2373	3112	739	23⁷⁴	
3	6605 22⁹⁹					15 2
4	4/16	107689	139488	31791	22⁷⁹	74
5		2446	3160	714	22⁵⁹	
6	9165 22⁸⁶					15 2
7	4/23	110135	142648	32505	22⁸¹	76
8		2551	3318	767	23⁴⁴	
9	13083 22⁹³					15 2
10	4/30	112686	145966	33272	22⁷⁹	78
11		2531	3252	721	22¹⁷	
12		56	65	9		15 2
13	5/7	115273	149283	34002	22⁷⁸	80
14		2858	3708	850	22⁹³	
15	6960 22⁵³					15 2
16	5/14	118131	152991	34852	22⁷⁸	82
17		2777	3640	863	23⁷⁰	
18	10600 22⁹⁶	1	2	1		15 2
19	5/21	120909	156633	35716	22⁸⁰	84
20		3095	4044	950	23⁴⁹	
21	14644 23¹⁰					15 2
22	5/28	124004	160677	36666	22⁸¹	86
23		2379	3105	726	23³²	
24						15 2
25	6/4	126383	163782	37392	22⁸³	88
26	6764	2809	3659	850	2323	
27	23²⁹	20	20			15 2
28	6/11	129212	167461	38242	2283	90
29		2734	3573	839	23.48	
30	10337 23³⁶					15 2
31	6/18	131946	171034	39081	22⁹⁷	92
32		2826	3648	822	2253	
33	13985 23¹⁴					15 2
34	6/25	134772	174682	39903	2284	94
35						
36						

8	9	10	11	12	13	14	15	16	
Mark Cost	Down Retail	Mo to Date	Mo to Date		Sales Week	Gross $	Margin %	Inventory Retail	
	4041 ^{4}				122867	24096 ^{588}	19^{61}	8748	1
	83 ^{65}	172			3404	693	20^{35}		2
67.	87 ^{2}	181.2^{23}	6374				1281 20^{09}		3
	4128 ^{4}				126271	24789	19^{63}	8349	4
	86 ^{4}	258 ^{13}			3125	628	20^{02}		5
69.	90 ^{2}^{28}	271.2^{88}	9499				1909 20^{02}		6
	4218 ^{4}				129396	25417	19^{64}	8274	7
	93 ^{4}	351 ^{17}			3283	659	20^{07}		8
74.	97 ^{2}^{95}	368.30^4	12,782				2568 20^{09}		9
	4315				132679	26076	19^{65}	8192	10
	86 ^{4}				3388	687.	20^{27}		11
69.	90 ^{265}								12
	4405				136067	26763	19^{66}	8011	13
	122 ^{5}	213 ^{9}			3400	658.	19^{35}		14
101.	132 ^{2}^{88}	222.3^{22}	6788.				1345 19^{83}		15
	4537				139467	27421	19^{66}	8167	16
	120 ^{13}	333 ^{22}			3515.	684.	19^{45}		17
102.	133 ^{3}^{28}	355.3^{44}	10303				2029 19^{88}		18
	4670				142982	28105	19^{65}	8141	19
	187 ^{3}	520 ^{25}			3527.	643.	18^{23}		20
146.	190 ^{6}^{39}	545.3^{94}	13,830.				2673 19^{33}		21
	4860				146509	28748	19^{62}	8448	22
	60 ^{15}				3504.	737.	21^{03}		23
47.	62								24
	4922				150013	29485	19^{65}	7967	25
	87 ^{6}^{21}	147 ^{8}			3475.	707.	20^{34}		26
71.	93 ^{2}	155.2^{22}	6979.				1194 20^{62}		27
	5015				153488	30192	19^{67}	8058	28
	120 ^{11}	267 ^{19}			3606	713	19^{77}		29
100.	131 ^{3}^{62}	286.2^{78}	10585.	157094			2152 20^{37}		30
	5146 ^{7}					30905	19^{67}	7874	31
	110 ^{62}	377 ^{26}			3477	689	19^{81}		32
90.	117 ^{3}	403.2^{94}	14,062				2846 20^{03}		33
	5263				160571	31594	19^{67}	7908	34
									35
									36

Figure 7: Retail Inventory Ledger

tate posting and pulling operating statements, each expense account is carried as a General ledger account.

RETAIL INVENTORY

Retail Inventory Ledger (Figure 7). This type of ledger has long been used by department stores and other large retail outlets to facilitate fast and factual statistical data without the necessity of a physical inventory. In applying its use to the grocery store, there can be some modification without losing the total value. This type of record, properly maintained, is acceptable to the Internal Revenue Service and to insurance companies to prove value of inventory. Periodic physical inventories are taken to adjust the retail inventory on this record.

Figure 7 requires a detailed explanation which is best understood when column and line numbers are used in a formula for each column and on each line. In this way the training of clerks is facilitated, and errors in calculation which are difficult to spot thus tend to be eliminated. Lines 1 through 7 of the Weekly Retail Report (Figure 3) are posted from the record shown in Figure 7.

Retail Inventory Calculation. Columns and lines of Figure 7 are numbered for the convenience of instructing new clerks. Line 1 is a carry forward of the accumulated totals year to date.

Column 2—Line 2, Cost Purchases, from Purchase journal column 3, line 14.

Column 3—Line 2, Retail Purchases, from Purchase journal column 4, line 14.

Column 4—Line 2, Purchase Markup, is column 3 minus column 2 (column 5 of Purchase journal).

Column 5—Line 2, Markup Percentage, is column 4, line 2, divided by column 3, line 2 (column 6 of Purchase journal).

Column 6—Line 3, Cost of column 7, line 3, computed by applying the complement of the accumulated markup percentage (column 5, line 4) to the Retail Allowance (column 7, line 3).

Column 7—Line 3, Inventory Shortage Allowance for possible shortage. This is handled the same as a markdown.

Column 8—Line 3, Cost Markdown. This is computed by applying the complement of the accumulated markup percentage (column 5, line 4) to the Retail Markdowns (column 9, line 3).

Column 9—Line 2, Retail Markdowns for the week.

Column 10—Markdown percent to sales weekly.

Column 11—Line 3, Retail Markdowns, month to date, and percent to sales, month to date.

MARKDOWN REPORT

"DON'T GUESS ASK QUESTIONS"

MR. _____

STORE NO. _____

BEGINNING DATE _____

CLOSING DATE _____

ITEM	UNIT	ON HAND	RECD.	TOTAL	BAL. AFTER SALE	SOLD	REG. PRICE	SPEC. PRICE	PRICE DIFF.	AMT. OF LOSS

Figure 8: Markdown Report

Column 12—Line 3, Sales, month to date.

Column 13—Line 2, Sales for week from Cash Receipts journal (Figure 6, column 4, line 16).

Column 14—Line 2, Gross Margin for week. Computed by applying accumulated markup percentage (column 5, line 4) to Sales less column 6, line 3, and less column 8, line 3.

Column 15—Line 2, Gross Margin percent for the week (column 14, line 2, divided by column 13, line 2).

Column 16—Line 4, Retail Inventory, computed by using accumulated figures year to date on line 4 as follows: Column 3, line 4 (total beginning Retail Inventory, plus Retail Purchases to date) minus columns 7, 9, and 13, line 4, equals column 16, line 4.

The Markdown Report (Figure 8) is a special document that is needed to report retail price changes and to maintain the retail inventory at the correct figure. The total of this report is posted weekly to column 9 of the Retail Inventory ledger.

Every item to be sold at a reduction from the regular price will be listed on the Markdown Report and counted when the sale starts, then counted again when the sale ends.

Time and Payroll System

Usual procedures are followed.

Reports to Management

Any accounting system deserving of the name must first serve management by furnishing operating statistics of a current and timely nature. The greatest tendency of the accountant is to go into too great a volume of detail. Management then finds onerous the burden of assimilating the data because of lack of time or understanding.

A system for small or medium-sized grocery stores should provide two reports essential to good, clean, profitable operation, in terms that management can quickly comprehend. The first of these is the Weekly Retail Report (Figure 3). It is purely statistical in nature. The monthly Comparative Profit and Loss Statement (Figure 9) is of less value to management except insofar as expenses are concerned.

In the process of developing these two reports, use of the orderly procedures previously described will insure collection of information with the least possible work for operating personnel.

THE NEIGHBORHOOD GROCERY
Profit & Loss Statement
Period Ending April 19___
(Comparative .00 Omitted)

	Last Year		9th Month Fiscal This Year	
	Month	Year to Date	Month	Year to Date
SALES	13,381	106,428	12,782	132,682
Beginning Inventory	6,531	6,835	6,529	7,358
Purchases	10,422	85,443	10,058	104,233
Less Ending Inventory	6,198	6,198	6,415	6,415
Cost of Sales	10,755	86,080	10,172	105,176
Gross Profit	2,626	20,348	2,610	27,506
% to Sales	19.62	19.11	20.41	20.73
Expenses:				
Payroll	1,044	8,972	1,259	11,852
Executive	125	1,125	240	2,160
Store Supplies	95	624	82	794
Advertising	71	632	52	621
Taxes & Licenses	148	450	106	696
Interest	6	58	--	15
Acctg. & Legal	80	727	185	1,659
Utilities	97	1,013	111	1,043
Rent	125	1,125	125	1,125
Insurance	18	165	18	179
Maintenance	49	580	28	326
Miscellaneous	12	144	17	158
Depreciation	47	423	--	--
Total Expense	1,917	16,038	2,223	20,628
% to Sales	14.32	15.06	17.39	15.54
Net Profit	709	4,310	389	6,878
% to Sales	5.29	4.04	3.02	5.18

Figure 9: Profit and Loss Statement

The National Association of Retail Grocers is the leading trade association in the field and is supplemented by state and local associations. Management, no matter how small in scope, can obtain a great deal of assistance from these trade associations.

34

Hardware Dealers (Retail)

BY CHARLES F. BURGER

**Public Accountant, Lynbrook,
New York**

Characteristics of the Business That Affect the Accounting System

The outstanding characteristic of the retail hardware business is the complex inventory of many diversified lines of merchandise, including a large number of brand names. Purchases for resale may encompass such varied areas as plumbing, electrical, mill, roofing, and garden supplies; paints; tools, including power tools; housewares; contractor's and builder's hardware. Some dealers carry specialties such as unpainted furniture, car supplies, Christmas items, sportsware, artist's supplies, toys, interior decorating materials and accessories, greeting cards, and glassware. Other specialties, which must be carried in numerous forms, variety or colors, include mill supplies, paints, plumbing needs, etc.

The stock the dealer carries is adapted to the rural or urban location of the store and to the size of the community. In a rural area a hardware store would carry farm implements and supplies, in addition to the standard hardware merchandise. Customers are principally homeowners, industrial firms, and contractors. They are offered credit as a service, and catalogs are distributed to the hardware dealer's mailing list. A delivery service is necessary with its attendant requirement of proper records.

FUNCTIONAL CHARACTERISTICS OF THE BUSINESS

In line with the policy of wholesalers, retail hardware concerns use the calendar-year basis. There is no specific burst of seasonal activity, although there is some variation in the volume of business such as in the spring and fall seasons, which provide a little more activity than the rest of the year. Some of the merchandise is seasonal in character. These items would include gardening, water sport, heating, and snow tools.

Stiff competition from wholesalers in industrial hardware and other lines gives rise to the application of trade and quantity discounts. A separate discount is allowed to industrial concerns, contractors, real estate operators, apartment houses, and institutions.

To compete with chain and discount stores the retail hardware dealer must stock lower priced merchandise as well as top-quality items. Records of his sales volume are vital, and he must keep a finger on the pulse of gross profit ratios of his many departments.

PRINCIPAL ACCOUNTING PROBLEMS

The size of the dealer's inventory makes proper records and a good inventory control mandatory. There is also a considerable amount of seasonal stock; thus the owner must have specific and detailed records of past performance as guides for future purchases. If he overstocks, he is faced with the problem of storage until the next season.

The principal accounting problem, therefore, revolves around inventory control and the records required to establish and maintain a book inventory. Other problems consist of recording daily cash sales and charge sales and daily purchases of stock; recording merchandise on order and verifying merchandise received; checking prices with a price control list; keeping a payroll book and a record of part-time help available for Saturdays and during the spring and fall seasons; controlling overhead; making available credit control and credit ratings; maintaining an equipment rental record, and an insurance register for proper insurance coverage, as well as detailed inventory records which eliminate dead stock and assure proper turnover of merchandise. A practical record which would reflect cost and gross profit and also serve as an inventory control is illustrated in Figure 3.

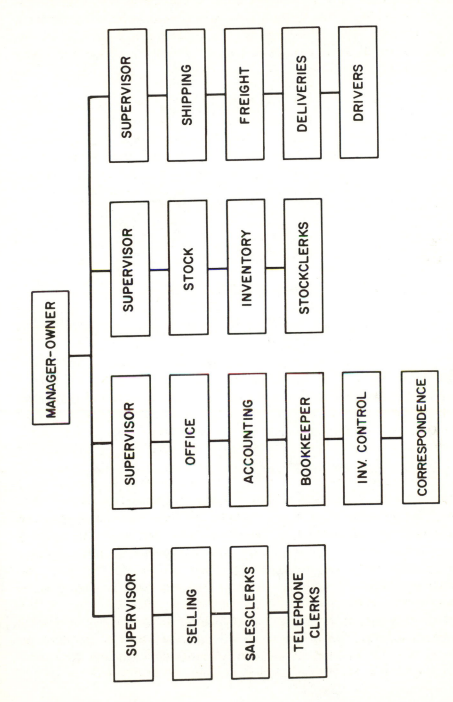

Figure I: Organizational Chart

Functional Organization

The diagram below of the organizational chart of a retail hardware store is self-explanatory.

Principles and Objectives of the Accounting System

A good accounting system furnishes the retail hardware dealer with a variety of benefits. It is used to:

1. Illustrate which items of merchandise are the most profitable, and thus help to keep inventory as low and as liquid as possible, yet adequate enough for the customers' needs.
2. Provide good cost and control records.
3. Show seasonal forecasts and sales forecasts.
4. Insure proper credit records.
5. Furnish data for the proper ordering of merchandise.
6. Control both full-time and part-time personnel.
7. Provide an accurate detailed General ledger and proper Accounts Receivable and Accounts Payable ledgers.

Of prime importance is the system's presenting management with a complete picture of volume, cost, expenses, liquidity of merchandise inventory, credit standing of customers, volume of merchandise sold by departments, and the ordering point of stock. The decision making by management depends on the accuracy and validity of the accounting reports.

Classification of Accounts and Books of Accounts

A chart of accounts for hardware dealers is similar to that of other merchandising business. A chart of accounts is shown below. It is quite detailed in order to cover as many transactions as might occur. The accounts for a smaller store would not need to be so elaborate and should, of course, be tailored to fit the requirements of the individual client. The major and the detailed accounts should be set up and used to meet the specific needs of the particular dealer.

Under expenses there is first a breakdown of the departmental expenses and then a breakdown of the details of the controlling expense accounts. A detailed code or chart of accounts of customers' Accounts Receivable should be established. All merchandise inventory should be coded in a logical, systematic, easily expandable way.

BALANCE SHEET ACCOUNTS.

ASSETS

Current assets

100 Cash
    101 Office Petty Cash Fund
    102 Cash Register Fund
    103 Cash in Bank
120 Receivables
    121 Cash Sales Clearing
    122 Accounts Receivable
        122.1 Merchandise
        122.2 Tool Rental
        122R Allowance for Bad
            Debts
    123 Installment Contracts
        Receivable
        123R Allowance for Bad
            Debts
    124 Notes Receivable
    125 Employees' Loans
    126 Advance Commissions
    127 Accrued Assets
130 Inventory
    131 Stock
        131.1 Electrical Supplies
        131.2 Garden
        131.3 Hardware Supplies,
            Tool
        131.4 Housewares
        131.5 Paint, paint supplies
        131.6 Plumbing and
            plumbing tools
        131.7 Carpenter tools
        131.8 Sporting goods
    132 Merchandise Stock—
        Implement shop
        132.1 Implements—New
        132.2 Implements—Used
        132.3 Parts and Acces-
            sories—Implements
        132.4 Service—Labor
140 Other Current Assets
    141 Prepaid Insurance
    142 Prepaid Taxes
    145 Accounts Receivable—Ex-
        ecutives, Employees, etc.

Fixed assets

160 Property and Equipment
    161 Land
    162 Buildings
    162R Allowance for
        Depreciation
    163 Furniture, Fixtures and
        Equipment
    163R Allowance for
        Depreciation
    164 Automobiles and Trucks
    164R Allowance for
        Depreciation
    165 Machinery and Equipment
        (Service Shop)
    165R Allowance for
        Depreciation
    166 Rental Tools
    166R Allowance for
        Depreciation
    167 Leasehold Improvements
    167R Allowance for
        Amortization
190 *Other Assets*
    191 Deposits—Rent, Utilities,
        etc.
    192 Other Assets

LIABILITIES

Current liabilities

200 Notes and Accounts Payable
    201 Notes Payable—Bank
    202 Notes Payable—Other
    205 Contracts Payable (less
        than one year)
    206 Accounts Payable
210 Taxes Payable
    211 Sales Tax Payable

220 Payroll Taxes Payable
   221 Federal Social Security Taxes
   222 State Social Security Taxes
   223 State Disability Insurance
   224 Income Tax Withheld (Federal)
   225 Income Tax Withheld (State)
   226 Income Tax Withheld (City)
   227 Accrued Payroll
   228 Accrued General Taxes
   229 Accrued Interest Payable
230 Other Current Liabilities and Deferred Income

Long-term debts

   241 Contracts Payable (longer than one year)
   242 Mortgages Payable

243-249 Other Long-Term Debts

NET WORTH

Corporate accounts

291 Capital Stock
   291.1 Capital Stock— Authorized
   291.2 Capital Stock— Unissued
298 Retained Earnings
299 Current Earnings

Sole proprietorship or partner- ship accounts

291 Capital
   291.1 Partner A
   291.2 Partner B
292 Drawing
   292.1 Partner A
   292.2 Partner B
299 Profit and Loss—Current

INCOME AND EXPENSE ACCOUNTS.
INCOME

Sales

   301 Electrical
   302 Garden
   303 Hardware
   304 Housewares
   305 Paint
   306 Plumbing
   307 Carpenters' Tools
   308 Sporting Goods
   309 Tool Rental
   311 Implements—New
   312 Implements—Used
   313 Parts and Accessories Implements
   314 Service—Labor

Cost of sales

Purchases
   401 Cost of Sales—Electrical

402 Cost of Sales—Garden
403 Cost of Sales—Hardware
404 Cost of Sales— Housewares
405 Cost of Sales—Paint
406 Cost of Sales—Plumbing
407 Cost of Sales—Carpen- ters' Tools
408 Cost of Sales—Sporting Goods
409 Cost of Sales—Tool Rental
411 Cost of Sales—Imple- ments—New
412 Cost of Sales—Imple- ments—Used
413 Cost of Sales—Parts and Accessories—Implements
414 Cost of Sales—Service Labor

EXPENSES

500 *Expenses—control*

    501 Expenses—Hardware Store
    502 Expenses—Implement Shop
    503 Expenses—Service Shop
    504 Expenses—Delivery
    505 Expenses—General and Administrative
    506 Expenses—Selling

Salaries and wages

    511 Salaries—Executive
    512 Salaries—Clerical-Office
    515 Salaries—Salesclerks
    517 Salaries—Mechanics
    519 Other Salaries and Wages —Stock Clerks-Delivery

Supplies

    521 Stationery and Printing— Office Supplies
    522 Operating Supplies
    525 Perishable Tools
    526 Operating Supplies— Service Shop
    527 Delivery Supplies

Utilities and services

    531 Heat, Light, and Water
    533 Telephone and Telegraph
    534 Cleaning

Taxes

    541 General
    543 Payroll

Insurance

    551 General
    552 Retirement Plan
    553 Compensation
    554 Group Insurance

Depreciation

    562 Buildings
    563 Furniture, Fixtures, and Equipment
    564 Automobiles and Trucks
    565 Machinery and Equipment (Service Shop)

Repair and maintenance

    572 Buildings
    573 Furniture, Fixtures, and Equipment
    574 Automobiles and Trucks
    575 Machinery and Equipment (Service Shop)
    576 Repair—Rental Tools

Selling expense

    581 Advertising
    582 Brochures and Catalogues
    583 Commissions
    584 Entertainment
    585 Freight Out
    586 Sales Expense (Meetings)
    587 Telephone and Telegraph
    588 Car Expense
    589 Window Display

Other

    591 Donations
    592 Dues and Subscriptions
    593 Professional Services
    594 Travel and Entertainment
    595 Rentals
    596 Gratis Material and Labor
    597 Miscellaneous Petty Cash
    598 General
    599 Losses on Bad Accounts

OTHER INCOME AND DEDUCTIONS

Other income

    601 Cash Discounts Taken
    602 Interest Earned
    608 Cash Over

609 Miscellaneous Income   652 Interest Expense

Deductions from income   658 Cash Short

651 Cash Discounts Allowed   659 Miscellaneous Losses

ACCOUNTS PECULIAR TO THE BUSINESS

A separate account in the Assets section labeled Employees' Loans (No. 125) insures proper control over repayment. Cost of Sales—Tool Rental (No. 409) covers the price of tools purchased for rental. Current Earnings (No. 299) is surplus of the immediate 12 months past; therefore, Retained Earnings (No. 298) refers to surplus of prior periods.

A comparison analysis of sales and purchases (Figure 2) is quite helpful. This record can be kept by the office staff on a weekly basis, since these figures are basic to the reports later described in Figure 4. The independent outside accountant can review these records monthly or quarterly, as needed.

Sales		**Purchases**	
Electrical		Electrical	
Garden		Garden	
Hardware		Hardware	
Housewares		Housewares	
Paint		Paint	
Plumbing		Plumbing	
Carpenter Tools		Carpenter Tools	
Sporting Goods		Sporting Goods	
Rental Tools		Rental Tools	
Others	———————	Others	———————
TOTAL	═══════	TOTAL	═══════

Figure 2. Analysis of Sales and Purchases Compared

Books and Forms Peculiar to the Business

Most of the books of account are those usual to any other business: Sales journal, Purchase journal, Cash Receipts journal, Cash Payments journal, Petty Cash journal, General journal, General ledger, Accounts Receivable ledger, and Accounts Payable ledger.

In addition, a hardware dealer might have a journal for equipment rental, one for inventory, and ledgers for equipment rental and for customer deposits payable. If he sells firearms, he would be required, in many states, to have a register of firearms sold.

Peculiarities of Procedures

SALES-RECEIVABLES CYCLE

Sales invoices are usually given at the time merchandise is sold and delivered, and a statement is prepared and sent once a month. Terms are usually 2 percent, 10 days; net, 30 days. The same procedure also applies to purchases from wholesalers and manufacturers.

CASH RECEIPTS

Receipt of money and checks is recorded daily from register tape which should be made by department, if possible.

CASH DISBURSEMENTS

These transactions are accomplished through the Petty Cash journal. The imprest system is preferable.

Time and Payroll System

For the average retail hardware store a regular time and payroll book may be used. If this is kept systematically, all the information which may at any time be required will be available. One example might refer to part-time help; a notation could be made at time of employment to explain why part-time help was needed at that time. Under the history of the employees, a record could be inserted regarding the times when each particular part-time employee is available for work.

Departmental Accounting

A simple and efficient method of cost accounting in a retail hardware business is delineated in the illustrations and charts following.

The Combination Gross Profit and Inventory Control chart (Figure 3) provides for the proprietor a visual record control of the various departments. Weekly Sales items shown are the actual sales figures in each department, derived from the Daily Sales entries directly above. The Gross Profit is based on the standard percentage of Gross Profits in each department. The percentage can be adjusted to any peculiar variation which may be present in the particular client's business. The Gross Profit is stated in dollars. Cost of Sales is the Sales less the standard Gross Profit.

Expense in each department is based on the budget expense plan allocated by the volume of sales in each department. The expense budget is figured on past years' experience with adjustment of the present year's projected expenses. Net Profit in each department is the Gross Profit less the budget expenses in each department.

Periodically throughout the year the total budget expenses should be compared with the actual expenses incurred up to that time, so that any variation will be detected.

Daily Sales

	Elec.	Garden	Hdwe.	House-wares	Paint	Plmbg.	Carpenter Tools	Sporting Goods	Rental Tools	Others
M										
T										
W										
T										
F										
S										
Total										

Weekly Sales

	Elec.	Garden	Hdwe.	House-wares	Paint	Plmbg.	Carpenter Tools	Sporting Goods	Rental Tools	Others
1										
2										
3										
4										
5										
Total										

Cost of Sales
Gross Profit
Expenses
Net Profit

Monthly Sales

	Elec.	Garden	Hdwe.	House-wares	Paint	Plmbg.	Carpenter Tools	Sporting Goods	Rental Tools	Others
J										
F										
M										
A										
M										
J										
J										
A										
S										
O										
N										
D										
Total										

Monthly Purchases

	Elec.	Garden	Hdwe.	House-wares	Paint	Plmbg.	Carpenter Tools	Sporting Goods	Rental Tools	Others
J										
F										
M										
A										
M										
J										
J										
A										
S										
O										
N										
D										
Total										

Figure 3. Combination Gross Profit and Inventory Control

Entries in the Weekly Book Inventory Record (Figure 4) are made each week from a weekly record of purchases in each department. Cost of Sales in each department is obtained from the record of Weekly Sales as described in Figure 3. Each Inventory account can be balanced monthly or quarterly,

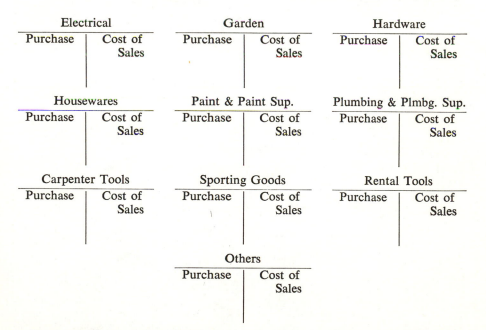

NOTE: Purchases are the actual purchases and Cost of Sales is the standard cost of sales based on the cost percentage in the retail hardware trade.

Figure 4. Weekly Book Inventory Record

if desired, and a new balance carried forward. Once a year the inventory record should be compared with an actual physical inventory count.

Time-Saving Ideas

Keep a record of extraordinary events that occur with reference to traffic, special occasions, weather, special sales, holiday periods, etc.

Compile a detailed mailing list with information about customers' preferences.

Maintain a record of customer inquiries and another of customer complaints.

Keep a record of new people moving into the area or buying homes in the area.

It is helpful to have a record of the credit history of the customer.

If a great volume of postings is involved in Accounts Receivable, use a punched-tape cash register.

For a larger hardware dealer, a data processing system would be ideal, especially for inventory control. The dealer could provide his own keypunch machine, and time could be rented from a service bureau.

BALANCE SHEET

Assets	Liabilities & Capital
Current Assets	Current Liabilities
Cash	Notes and Accounts Payable
Receivables	Other Current Liabilities
Inventory	Deferred Income
Other Current Assets	
Total Current Assets	Total Current Liabilities
Fixed Assets	Fixed Liabilities
Property and Equipment	Long Term Debts
Other Assets	
Total Fixed Assets	Total Fixed Liabilities
	Total Liabilities
	Capital
	Capital Stock and Net Worth
Total Assets	Total Liabilities and Capital

Figure 5. Balance Sheet (Condensed)

Reports to Management

The usual reports which the accountant should furnish to retail hardware store management are the balance sheet, profit and loss statement, analysis of sales, analysis of purchases, and profit and loss ratios. Other financial ratios could be provided as required.

For larger retailers, monthly statements would be given; for smaller concerns, quarterly statements would be adequate. If the need arises, analysis of accounts could be prepared for individual departments.

PROFIT AND LOSS STATEMENT

Sales
Cost of Sales
    Opening Inventory
    Purchases
    Closing Inventory
Total Cost of Sales
Gross Profit
    Less: Store Expenses
          Implement and Rental Tool Expenses
          Service Expense
          Selling Expense
          General and Administrative Expenses
Total Expenses
Net Profit on Sales
    Add: Other Income
    Deduct: Other Expenses
Net Profit before Income Tax
    Income Tax
Net Profit added to Surplus

Figure 6. Profit and Loss Statement (Condensed)

ANALYSIS OF TOTAL EXPENSES

1. Salaries and Wages
2. Supplies
3. Utilities and Services
4. Taxes
5. Insurance
6. Depreciation
7. Repairs and Maintenance
8. Selling
9. Others

TOTAL EXPENSES

Figure 7. Analysis of Total Expenses

For a typical retail hardware store, a condensed statement of the profit and loss ratio is shown below.

RETAIL HARDWARE STORES
Profit & Loss Ratios

	PERCENT
Sales	100.0
Cost of Sales	68.5
Gross Profits	31.5
Expenses	
Wages, including Owner, Salesclerks, etc.	18.5
Rent	3.0
All other Expenses	8.0
Total Expenses	29.5
Net Profit	2.0

Special Percent Ratios for Management

1. Current Year's Sales vs. Previous Year
2. Sales per Year per Person Employed
3. Merchandise Inventory per $10,000 of Sales
4. Average Stock Turn Times
5. Credit Sales
6. Average Accounts Receivable Collection

Special Percent Ratios for Credit Purposes

1. Average Capital Turn Times
2. Current Asset Ratio
3. Total Debt to Tangible Net Worth
4. Quick Asset Ratio
5. Turns of Working Capital

Figure 8. Profit and Loss Ratios

35

Hobby Supply Shops

BY R. RALPH KASMAN

Certified Public Accountant,
Trenton, New Jersey

Characteristics of the Business That Affect the Accounting System

The hobby supply shop came into being in the early Thirties when manufacturers of hobby products realized that they could not efficiently market their wares through outlets whose personnel were not conversant with the problems of the hobbyist. The major product at the time was the model railroad; fathers were (and continue to be) as interested in the construction of a model layout as their sons. The success of the hobby shop in those days was attributed to the fact that the depression of the Thirties created free time for many people and the hobby shop operator was merchandising one of the least expensive forms of leisure-time activity.

Soon model airplanes were added to the line of merchandise. The model flyers of the Thirties became the pilots of our war planes in the World War of the Forties.

Today the hobby supply store handles a vast array of handicraft products and materials for every shade of interest in the spectrum from children's blocks to geriatric-oriented bead designing.

FUNCTIONAL CHARACTERISTICS OF THE BUSINESS

The greatest volume of sales takes place in the seasonal Christmas period, but the hobby supply operator has endeavored to maintain the customer's interest throughout the year. After the Christmas rush, inventories are at their lowest ebb. The calendar year is therefore the logical fiscal year.

Since the 1950's, discounting has overtaken much of the retailing of this industry. The individual store proprietor has found it difficult to compete unless he, too, offers discounts to his customers. In order to compete with the harsh discounting of the large chain outlets, the small retailer must offer something *better* to his customers rather than something *cheaper*. This is usually accomplished by establishing a quality repair service on the premises. Such a service necessitates the creation of adequate records to reflect the cost of repair on each job handled.

PRINCIPAL ACCOUNTING PROBLEMS

Because of the discounting with which the hobby shop has become involved, a rigid surveillance over the gross profit percentage must be maintained. This requirement necessitates the preparation of monthly statements. For these statements to be meaningful, a physical inventory of merchandise should be taken every month, or if that is not feasible, at least every three months.

From time to time a new supplier in the industry enters the hobby field and finds it difficult to make inroads against the old-line products. To encourage acceptance by the retailer, he indulges in the consignment of his wares. A natural result is the requirement of proper record keeping of this pay-only-if-you-sell merchandise.

Functional Organization

Organization of the hobby shop is divided into four departments (see Figure 1).

Administration Department. All record keeping is done here including sales, purchasing, and the many other duties usually assigned to the "office."

Sales Department. This division, in addition to its selling function, is responsible for all promotion and advertising as well as public relations, when required. The department handles all customer inquiries regarding prices and availability of products not on hand. Comparison shopping is also part of its function.

Purchases Department. In addition to purchasing, the department is re-

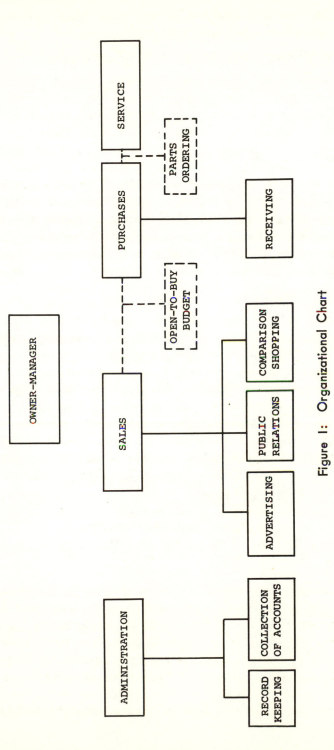

Figure I: Organizational Chart

sponsible for the receiving of merchandise. Policy must adhere to the open-to-buy budget which has been created in conjunction with the Sales Department. Purchases seeks out new products and endeavors to have them on hand at all times.

Service Department. Service personnel give estimates on repair jobs brought into the store and effect the repairs. Another responsibility is to insure that the inventory of parts and material is adequate.

Principles and Objectives of the Accounting System

Income. The hobby shop is in the retail family of business enterprises. As with most other members of this group, maintenance of a system to control a multitude of daily cash transactions is of great importance. The system should be so designed as to require as little excess bookkeeping as possible. Sales must be accumulated so that an accurate and complete record is available at all times. Charge sales must be distinguished from cash sales and a proper controlling account maintained for the receivables.

Costs. To control properly the availability of cost information, an up-to-date record of purchases is required. Of course, the Purchase journal would play an important role in the maintenance of a controlling account for accounts payable. In order that the bookkeeping system may reflect proper cost-of-goods-sold figures, a physical inventory is periodically required. The ideal would be once a month. By this means the gross profit percentage would be prepared every 30 days and the store operator would be cognizant of fluctuations from month to month.

Expenses. These items should be handled to reflect the accrual basis of accounting. Most small businesses can readily ascertain monthly accruals for insurance, depreciation, payroll taxes, and property taxes. If a Purchase journal is maintained and includes expense-item purchases as well as merchandise purchases, no other accruals would be required.

Classification of Accounts and Books of Accounts

BALANCE SHEET ACCOUNTS.

ASSETS

Current assets

101 Petty Cash
102 Cash Register Fund
103 Cash Operating Account
122 Accounts Receivable
123 Allowance for Uncollectible
      Accounts

131 Merchandise Inventory
138 Inventory of Display Items
143 Deferred Charges

Fixed assets

161 Land
162 Buildings
163 Allowance for Accumulated
      Depreciation

164 Fixtures and Equipment
165 Allowance for Accumulated Depreciation
166 Vehicles
167 Allowance for Accumulated Depreciation
168 Leasehold Improvements
169 Allowance for Accumulated Amortization

Other assets

172 Goodwill
191 Deposits on Rent and Utilities

LIABILITIES

Current liabilities

206 Accounts Payable—Regular
207 Accounts Payable—Dated
208 Trade Acceptances Payable
209 Notes Payable
227 Accrued Payroll Taxes
231 Accrued Expenses

Long-term liabilities

241 Mortgage Payable

NET WORTH

271 Owner's Capital

INCOME AND EXPENSE ACCOUNTS.

REVENUE

301 Sales of Merchandise—Cash
302 Sales of Merchandise—Charge
303 Sales of Repairs—Cash
305 Sales of Repairs—Charge

Cost of sales

401 Purchase of Resale Merchandise
402 Purchase of Repair Parts and Material
403 Labor for Repairs
404 Freight In

EXPENSES

501 Advertising
503 Bad Debts
504 Banking
507 Depreciation
509 Dues and Subscriptions
511 Insurance
513 Interest

514 Miscellaneous
521 Postage
523 Professional Services
524 Public Relations
525 Rent
526 Repairs and Maintenance
540 Salaries
541 Services
544 Supplies
551 Taxes—Payroll
552 Taxes—Property
553 Taxes—Licenses
560 Travel and Entertainment
571 Utilities

OTHER INCOME AND DEDUCTIONS

Other income

701 Discounts Earned

Other expenses

751 Discounts Given

ACCOUNTS PECULIAR TO THE BUSINESS

Petty Cash (No. 101). A very common item paid out of petty cash is freight-in. Inasmuch as the hobby center buys its wares from a multitude of suppliers, merchandise in small quantities is received almost daily.

Accounts Receivable (No. 122). Most hobby shops conduct their business on a cash basis. But organizations such as community centers and schools do request to be billed. The usual credit terms are net 30.

Inventory of Display Items (No. 138). Many hobby store proprietors are proud of their ownership of a model railroad car or engine of an ancient vintage. It could be an expensive item which is not for sale.

Accounts Payable—Dated (No. 207). Normal practice requires the payment of bills within 30 days without discount. However, the industry has developed a "dated billing" procedure by which a proprietor may make a purchase in July or August, receive the merchandise shortly thereafter but be invoiced under date of the following December 10, payable within 30 days thereafter. This plan permits the merchandise to be on display and sold during the entire Christmas season, but it is paid for by the merchant after the major seasonal proceeds are available.

Notes Payable (No. 209). In many instances not all merchandise can be obtained on dated billing. Some manufacturers require payment within 30 days, even during the off season. Some hobby shop operators borrow money at their local banks. Such a note is repaid at the close of the seasonal surge in December.

Trade Acceptances Payable (No. 208). This account would reflect accounts payable items which have been converted by the completion of a draft drawn upon the purchaser by the seller and accepted by the purchaser for payment at a specific future time. The transaction is usually accomplished through the purchaser's bank.

Purchases (Nos. 401 and 402). The invoices received by the hobby shop indicate the retail price less 40 percent. This is a standard procedure in the industry. The merchant thereby can ascertain the retail price very readily just by referring to the invoice.

Public Relations (No. 524). The products sold by this industry are especially attractive to a large number of people. Hobby store operators might arrange to display a model train layout at a local bank during National Hobby Week or at some other public location. All expenses involved in such a display would be charged to this account.

Taxes—Licenses (No. 553). This account covers a mercantile license required by the particular locality. Some cities may not levy this sort of tax.

BOOKS AND FORMS PECULIAR TO THE BUSINESS

Any form of double-entry record keeping would be adaptable to the hobby shop.

The repair service requires a special sales ticket. This invoice (Figure 2) should include customer's name, address, and telephone number, a description of the item left for repair, and the charge for work to be accomplished

and parts furnished as well as the date promised. If the item should be
returned to the manufacturer for repair or because of original defect, the
ticket should be so noted.

Peculiarities of Procedures

SALES-RECEIVABLES CYCLE

Charge sales are written upon a prenumbered sales ticket. These tickets
are then recorded in the Sales journal in chronological order. Care is taken to
assure that all numbered tickets are accounted for. Each charge ticket must
be approved for credit by the store or sales manager before the merchandise
leaves the premises.

Postings are made from the Sales journal to the Accounts Receivable
ledger maintained in alphabetical order. Cash received on account is also
posted to the Accounts Receivable ledger. At the end of each month the
total of the balances in the ledger is compared with the controlling account
in the General ledger. (See section on Time-Saving Ideas for use of pegboard
system for Accounts Receivable handling.)

```
┌─────────────────────────────────────────────────────────────┐
│                      REPAIR  INVOICE                          │
│                                                               │
│                  PENNRIDGE  HOBBY  SHOP                        │
│                    131  RIDGE  AVENUE                          │
│                   PERKASIE, PA.  15432                         │
│                                                               │
│     NAME _____  # _____           │
│                                                               │
│     ADDRESS _____  DATE _____           │
│                                                               │
│     CITY _____  PHONE ___            │
│     ┌──────────┬──────────────────┬─────────────┐             │
│     │   UNIT   │       ITEM       │    PRICE     │             │
│     ├──────────┼──────────────────┼─────────────┤             │
│     │          │                  │             │             │
│     ├──────────┼──────────────────┼─────────────┤             │
│     │          │                  │             │             │
│     ├──────────┼──────────────────┼─────────────┤             │
│     │          │                  │             │             │
│     ├──────────┴──────────────────┼─────────────┤             │
│     │          TOTAL              │             │             │
│     └────────────────────────────┴─────────────┘             │
│                                                               │
│     REPAIR ____ REPLACE PARTS ___ RETURN-MFG ___              │
│                                                               │
└─────────────────────────────────────────────────────────────┘
```

* COURTESY OF PENNRIDGE HOBBY SHOP, PERKASIE, PENNSYLVANIA.

Figure 2: Repair Invoice

PURCHASES-PAYABLES CYCLE

When shipments of merchandise are received, the Purchasing Department checks the merchandise against the original order, approves the price and quantities, and forwards the approved invoice to the Administrative Department. Here the extensions are checked and the total recorded in a purchase book. Postings are made from the latter to individual accounts in the Accounts Payable ledger. Checks are written periodically to pay off these accounts with discount being taken when at all possible. Disbursements are posted to each ledger account as paid. At the end of each month the total of the balances in the Accounts Payable ledger is compared with the controlling account in the General ledger. (See section labeled Time-Saving Ideas for use of pegboard systems for Accounts Payable handling.)

CASH RECEIPTS AND DISBURSEMENTS

Cash sales are rung on the cash register, and the tape receipt produced is given to the customer. Each salesclerk is assigned a separate drawer in the cash register. At the close of the day the cash in each drawer is individually reconciled with the Cash Register Daily Report (Figure 3) totals which are produced when the register is closed out for the day. Petty cash expenditures may come from any salesclerk's drawer after prior approval of the voucher by the sales manager. Refunds due customers for merchandise returned may be handled by any salesclerk after prior approval of the sales manager. A petty cash voucher may be used for this purpose.

Time and Payroll System

Most states require that employees' hours be kept on a daily basis. In a large organization a time clock would be a feasible method to account for hours worked; however, most hobby dealers have a small number of employees and find sufficient a time book in which hours are recorded by hand on a daily basis. Hours are accumulated for the week, and deductions calculated in the same book. A payroll check is then written and recorded on the Employees' Earnings Record (Figure 4).

Another method (Figure 5) illustrates the simultaneous preparation of a payroll check, the employees' earning card, and the Cash Disbursements (Payroll) journal.

Time-Saving Ideas

At the point of sale a cash register will save a great deal of time. The modern store uses the register not only as a repository for cash but also

DAILY REPORT

DATE

	NET READINGS		ADJUSTMENTS		REGISTER READINGS
* DEPT. 1					
* DEPT. 2					
* DEPT. 3					
* DEPT. 4					
* TAX					
TOTAL SALES (ADD)					
* CASH SALES					
* PAID ON ACCOUNT					
TOTAL CASH RECEIVED					
PAID OUT (SUBTRACT)					
NET CASH CALLED FOR					
CASH IN DRAWER					
OVER OR SHORT					
PREVIOUS ACCOUNTS RECEIVABLE TOTAL					
* TODAY'S CHARGES (ADD)					
TOTAL					
* TODAY'S PAID ON ACCOUNT					
TOTAL					
ADJUSTMENTS					
PRESENT ACCOUNTS RECEIVABLE TOTAL					
* TODAY'S PREVIOUS BALANCE PICKUP TOTAL					

CASH PAID OUT	MISC. EXPENSES		MERCHANDISE PURCHASES			
TO WHOM PAID	EXPLANATION	AMOUNT	DEPT. 1	DEPT. 2	DEPT. 3	DEPT. 4

* INDICATES MACHINE TOTAL

NCR B-5240

* COURTESY OF NATIONAL CASH REGISTER COMPANY, DAYTON, OHIO.

Figure 3: Cash Register Daily Report

Time for the

Week Ending _____ 19__

NO.	NAMES	REGISTRATION NUMBER	S	M	T	W	T	F	S	TOTAL TIME	RATE	AMOUNT OF WAGES	OTHER EARNINGS	TOTAL EARNINGS	DEDUCTIONS				AMOUNT PAID
															WITHHOLD-ING TAX	O. A. B.			

Figure 4: Employees' Earning Record

NAME FRED BURDON CLOCK NUMBER DEPT.

STREET 11Y S. BROAD STR SOC. SEC. NUMBER 13Y-5Y-9/1Y ☐ M. ☐ F.

CITY PERKASIE, PA YEAR 19YX PHONE NO. DATE STARTED 10-17-XX DATE LEFT

RECORD OF PAY RATE CHANGES

DATE	RATE
10-7-XX	2.00/hr

TIME WK'D.	PAY PERIOD ENDING	TO THE ORDER OF	GROSS AMOUNT	DEDUCTIONS		NET AMOUNT	CHECK NUMBER
				INCOME TAX	SOC. SEC.		
40	10/17/XX	Fred Burdon	80 00	-0-	3 36 -0-	76 64	3403
40	10/4/X	Fred Burdon	80 00	-0-	3,36 -0-	76 64	3407

DEDUCTION AMOUNTS

Figure 5: One-Write Payroll and Cash Disbursements Record

Employee's Earnings Card

(insert under checks in Figure 5—Payroll Checks and Journal)

* COURTESY OF SAFEGUARD BUSINESS SYSTEMS CORPORATION, LANSDALE, PENNYSLVANIA.

* Courtesy of Safeguard Business Systems Corporation, Lansdale, Pennsylvania.

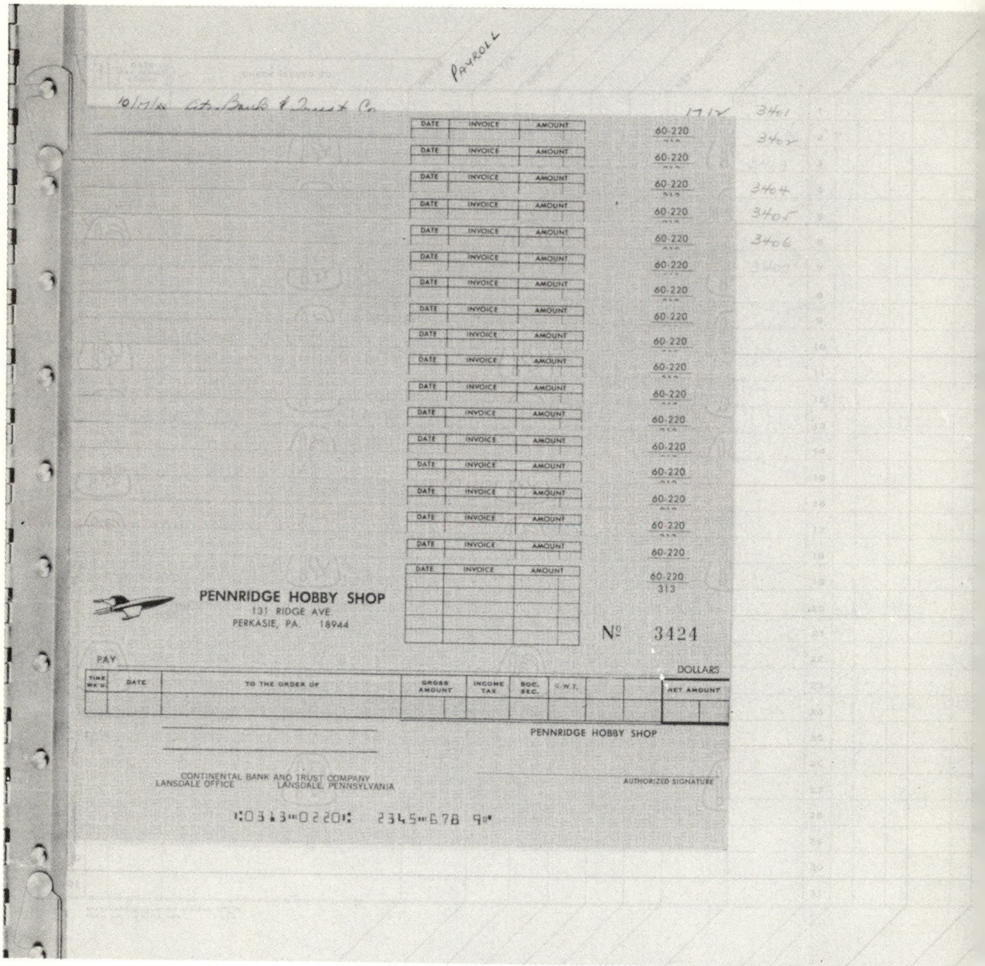

Figure 5: One-Write Payroll and Cash Disbursement Record (cont.)

Payroll Checks and Journal

Insert Employees Earnings Card under check

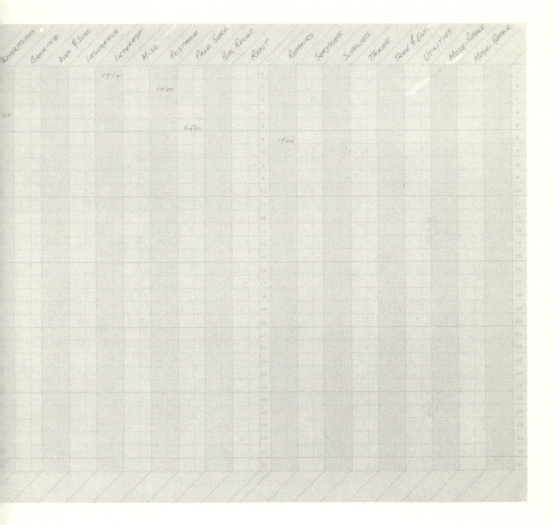

Figure 5: One-Write Payroll and Cash Disbursements Record (cont.)

Journal

as a means to departmentalize sales. Charge sales are segregated from cash sales by means of different register keys and a controlling account maintained over Accounts Receivable. Many cash registers print out at the end of the day the total of each category of transaction.

A Daily Report (Figure 3) is used when totaling the cash register drawers at the end of the day. The sales manager uses the report as a check on each salesman's cash and also as a means of summarizing the day's activities. The complete report with the cash and petty cash vouchers are sent to the Administrative Department where the cash is prepared for deposit. The petty cash vouchers and the report are summarized and an entry made in the Sales journal to reflect the day's activity.

Another device which saves time is the pegboard (one-write) method of bookkeeping. Through the use of carbon paper (or carbonless paper) an effective system can be maintained with little effort. Because most hobby stores are small retail endeavors, this multiple-record principle has been most helpful.

The system functions in this manner: Each day's sales transactions are recorded on a Sales journal sheet to accumulate cash and charge sales, as well as to record the breakdown of merchandise and service sales. Charge sales are controlled by keeping an accounts receivable control system with individual customer's cards for each charge account. A charge sale entry on the Sales journal sheet is simultaneously recorded on the customer's card by the technique of carbonless paper. Purchases are recorded in a Purchase journal and on the payable ledger cards simultaneously in the same manner.

The Cash Disbursement register is produced by means of a carbon strip on the back of each check written. This method saves a great deal of effort in the bookkeeping process. No checkbook stub need be written and no envelope addressed since a window envelope is used for mailing.

Reports to Management

Each month a comparative profit and loss statement is prepared. Percentages of each item to gross sales are an important ingredient of the statement. Through the use of these figures management may quickly ascertain if the gross profit percentage has been maintained and if all other expenses are in line. Periodically a balance sheet is prepared, no less often than at three-month intervals.

36

Home Appliance Dealers

BY LAURENCE T. KING

Assistant Professor of Accounting, Western New England College, Springfield, Massachusetts; Public Accountant, Massachusetts and New York

Characteristics of the Business That Affect the Accounting System

The home appliance store is usually a small retail establishment. There are nearly 20,000 such stores in the United States, engaged primarily in selling television sets, refrigerators, washers, radios, record players, air conditioners, dryers, ranges, freezers, and a variety of smaller household appliances such as electric irons, percolators, hot plates, and vacuum cleaners.

Annual sales by home appliance stores are in the vicinity of $3 billion. The business provides employment for nearly 80,000 people. The number of stores has diminished in recent years, but the trend of sales per establishment has been upward. Although major household appliances, the so-called "white goods," account for more than half of these sales, substantial revenue is generated by other products. Television is the largest contributor of all; radios, hi-fi and record players follow closely after refrigerators and washers on the industry-wide customer preference list.

A lesser, but often significant, source of sales consists of the small electrical kitchenware-houseware items already mentioned. Many stores also sell such nonappliance items as furniture, musical instruments, auto accessories and hardware, referred to in the trade as "odd-ball" lines.

Not all home appliance dealers offer product service as an adjunct to sales. Many find that servicing provides an effective competitive weapon, leads to new business, and brings in additional profit. Others take the view that the advantages of in-store appliance servicing are not sufficient to justify the cost of training and equipping technicians; these dealers prefer to contract with specialized appliance repair shops or to use manufacturer-owned service facilities to perform this function.

FUNCTIONAL CHARACTERISTICS OF THE BUSINESS

Competition and Price Policies. The battle for the consumer dollar is waged aggressively by home appliance dealers, especially in the larger metropolitan areas. Medium-sized and small stores must contend with keen competition from discount houses, chain stores, and department stores. Retail stores operated by public utility companies which sell electric and gas appliances for household use, also enter into the somewhat crowded competitive picture.

Market conditions are changing as new methods of retailing develop. These challenges have been met by the more efficient dealers; the less efficient have failed to survive in the changing scene, which accounts for the declining trend in total number of appliance stores. It takes the right combination of personality, initiative, sales ability, management skill, location, merchandise, and capital to succeed.

Appliance manufacturers and dealers have traditionally spent large sums on national and local advertising. Appliance stores, in an effort to maintain high sales volume, resort to a wide variety of price policies and promotional activities. Selling expense is traditionally a substantial element of operating costs.

A direct result of one promotional activity is the large volume of trade-in appliances which the typical dealer must accept if he is to compete successfully for new business. The dealer must figure reasonable trade-in values so he will not cut his margins too closely. He also has the problem of what to do with the traded items. Allowances should be based on what the dealer can expect to realize from the sale of the used appliance, either as-is or after repair. High trade-ins offered on any other basis must obviously be at the expense of reduced profit margins.

Capitalization. Undercapitalization is a significant problem for many home appliance stores, slowing modernization efforts and holding back expansion into newly developed high traffic areas. Retailers must update stocks continually with new products, model changes, and expanded product lines. Consumer demand for higher priced luxury items, including color TV and colored appliances, creates further mounting demands on capital. Although extended terms by suppliers and the growth of dealer floor plans have eased the burden, the cost of this type of credit has increased operating expense directly or through increased cost of merchandise.

Customer Credit and Financing. Sales of major appliances are normally made under long-term installment contracts which provide for payment of specific financing charges. Competitive practices of other stores may force a dealer to offer additional terms, such as 90-day installment contracts and 30- to 90-day open accounts. Conditional sales contracts, however, facilitate the great bulk of credit sales.

Most dealers finance through national or local finance companies or local banks. This type of financing presents no receivables problems for the dealer, with the exception of delinquent accounts when recourse plans are in force. However, as store volume grows, some dealers tend to assume gradually the responsibility of self-financing, long-term sales contracts, lured to some extent by added profits from carrying charges. These contracts increase permanently the volume of self-financed receivables the dealer must carry, enlarging his working capital requirements and his collection problems proportionately.

The same tendency exists in relation to 90-day installment contracts, which are frequently employed in used appliance sales. On the other hand, many dealers find that the cost of carrying their own receivables, in terms of added working capital requirements, bookkeeping and collection expense, far outweighs any competitive advantages involved; these dealers have learned to concentrate their resources on merchandising appliances and prefer to leave the financing function up to specialists.

Inventory Financing. The average dealer often finds it expedient to avail himself of "floor plan" financing arrangements offered by suppliers in respect to merchandise on display in the dealer's store. The dealer, under such a plan, makes a small down payment to the manufacturer or distributor on a number of models which he chooses to display in his salesrooms and executes a trust receipt note for the balance. The balance due on each item is paid off by the dealer as he sells the appliance, usually within six months.

Seasonal Nature of the Industry. The home appliance business is highly seasonal. Peak sales of refrigerators occur in the spring and summer months. Television, radio, hi-fi, and record player sales hit their high point in the fall and during the Christmas buying period. Since sales of home appliances and TV-radios are fairly sensitive to overall swings in the business cycle, both seasonal and annual sales for a particular store may fluctuate considerably from year to year.

Fiscal Period. The fiscal period used for accounting and reporting purposes in the home appliance business is, in most instances, the calendar year.

PRINCIPAL ACCOUNTING PROBLEMS

The foregoing discussion of functional characteristics of the home appliance business suggests some of the special accounting problems, which stem directly from these characteristics. Such problems involve (1) the primary need for segregating data pertaining to sales and cost of sales by major appliances, other appliances, used merchandise, parts and accessories, and service labor; (2) the requirement for close control over inventory and receivables inherent in a highly competitive, high-unit-cost type of retail business operated almost exclusively on credit terms; (3) the special accounting treatment which must be accorded transactions with financing institutions, relating to such items as reserves, repossessions, and collections; and (4) the need for accurate accounting for trade-ins and for losses resulting from repossessions and overallowances on trade-ins.

The intensity of competition in the trade with its narrowing effect on profit margins dictates an accounting system which facilitates comparisons of operating performance with industry-wide experience. The National Appliance and Radio-TV Dealers Association (NARDA) compiles an annual report of such statistics on a national basis for the benefit of its members. The operating data published by NARDA relate to both merchandise-plus-service firms and merchandise-only firms.

The chart of accounts outlined in this chapter is designed to cope adequately with the problems just enumerated.

Functional Organization

Like many other small and medium-sized business establishments, the typical home appliance store is rarely organized along clearly defined organizational or functional lines. There is often considerable overlapping of duties: salesmen shift between kitchen appliances and radio-TV; servicemen install new appliances as well as repair used ones; pickup and delivery involve both selling and service costs; accounting and credit and collections may be merged with general office functions and so on. Nevertheless, the basic functions common to most appliance stores dealing in both white goods and radio-TV can be identified as illustrated in Figure 1. The chart is considered generally descriptive of a typical store employing 10 to 15 persons and offering a full range of appliance service.

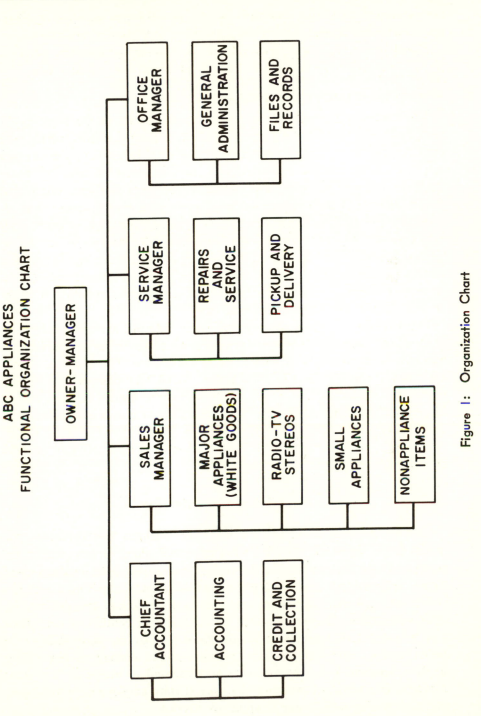

ABC APPLIANCES
FUNCTIONAL ORGANIZATION CHART

OWNER-MANAGER

CHIEF ACCOUNTANT — ACCOUNTING — CREDIT AND COLLECTION

SALES MANAGER — MAJOR APPLIANCES (WHITE GOODS) — RADIO-TV STEREOS — SMALL APPLIANCES — NONAPPLIANCE ITEMS

SERVICE MANAGER — REPAIRS AND SERVICE — PICKUP AND DELIVERY

OFFICE MANAGER — GENERAL ADMINISTRATION — FILES AND RECORDS

Figure 1: Organization Chart

Principles and Objectives of the Accounting System

Accounting for Revenue. Sales revenue should be accounted for by each major type of merchandise (refrigerators, television, radios, stereos, dryers, washers, and so forth). Separate records should reflect sales of used appliances.

Revenue from sales of small appliances and from nonappliance sales should likewise be segregated in the books of account.

Merchandise-plus-service firms need to maintain accurate records of revenue from service and repair work in order to measure the overall profitability of this function.

Accounting for Costs. The accounting system related to the cost of sales should be designed to accommodate charging revenue with the identified costs of the specific items sold. The sale of major appliance items particularly lends itself to this type of identification of costs with specific inventory items (i.e., to a perpetual inventory system). For sales of small appliances or certain nonappliance items it may be necessary to adopt some assumption with respect to the flow of costs that is to be associated with the movement of merchandise. This will require adaptation of the accounting system to the first-in-first-out, last-in-first-out, or weighted-average type of inventory valuation methods. The method chosen should, of course, be employed consistently.

Service and repair costs should be kept in sufficient detail to permit full recovery plus a profit in pricing individual jobs.

Accounting for Expense. Record keeping for expense should be so organized as to facilitate the matching of expense with revenue from each major source (sales and service), as well as proper allocation of expense related to overall administration of the business. Accounting for expense should be on a full accrual basis.

SPECIFIC OBJECTIVES OF THE SYSTEM

The specific objectives of the accounting system are to:

1. Measure income from sales, classified according to the various items and/or types of merchandise sold.
2. Measure the cost of merchandise sold, classified according to the breakdown of sales.
3. Reflect expenses related to solicitation and sale of merchandise.
4. Reflect expenses related to service, repair, installation, and delivery of merchandise.
5. Reflect expenses related to the general administration of the business.
6. Measure overall performance of the business and facilitate com-

parison of internal operating results on a year-to-year basis, as well as industry-wide comparisons with firms of similar size and sales volume.

Classification of Accounts and Books of Accounts

A typical home appliance dealer selling a normal line of white goods, radio-TV, stereos, record players and miscellaneous small appliances, including used appliances, and offering appliance repairs and service as an adjunct to sales, would have most, though not necessarily all, of the general ledger accounts appearing in the accompanying chart. The account numbers are illustrative only. They would, of course, vary in actual practice from one store to another.

Sales and cost of sales accounts included in the chart are broken down into "major appliances," "other appliances," "used merchandise," "parts and accessories," and "service labor." Additional refinement needed for internal operating purposes and for comparison with NARDA's cost-of-doing-business results can be accomplished by adding subsidiary accounts in whatever degree of analytical detail is required.

BALANCE SHEET ACCOUNTS.

ASSETS

Current assets

Cash and bank

101 Office Fund
102 Cash Register Fund
105 Bank—Commercial

Marketable securities

111 Stocks
112-119—(for other readily marketable securities)

Receivables

121 Cash Sales Clearing
122 Accounts Receivable
122R Estimated Uncollectible Accounts
125 Contracts Receivable
126 Notes Receivable

Inventories

131 Major Appliances
1311 Stoves
1312 Refrigerators and Freezers
1313 Washers and Dryers
1314 Radios and TV
1315 Other
132 Other Appliances
133 Used Merchandise (Trade-Ins)
134 Parts and Accessories
135 Service Labor in Process

Other current assets

141 Prepaid Insurance
142 Prepaid Taxes
143-149 Other Current Assets

Property and Equipment

*161 Land
*162 Buildings
*162R Accumulated Depreciation

* If leased premises are occupied, substitute the following accounts:

162 Leasehold Improvements
162R Accumulated Amortization

163 Shop Equipment and Tools
163R Accumulated Depreciation
164 Furniture and Fixtures
164R Accumulated Depreciation
165 Automobiles and Trucks
165R Accumulated Depreciation

Other assets

191 Finance Company Reserve

LIABILITIES

Current liabilities

Notes and accounts payable

201 Notes Payable
205 Contracts Payable (less than one year)
206 Accounts Payable
207 Customers' Deposits
211 Sales Tax Payable
221 Employee Payroll Deductions
    2211 Social Security Taxes (Old Age)
    2213 State Disability Insurance
    2214 Income Tax Withheld (Federal)
    2215 Income Tax Withheld (State)
    2216 Income Tax Withheld (City)
222 Employer Payroll Taxes Payable
    2221 Social Security Taxes (Old Age)
    2222 Federal Social Security Taxes (Unemployment)
    2223 State Social Security Taxes (Unemployment)

224 Due Finance Company on Repossessions
225 Accrued Payroll
226 Accrued General Taxes
227 Accrued Interest Payable
229 Other Accrued Liabilities

Other current liabilities

231 Finance Company Collections
232 Finance Charges

Long-term liabilities

241 Contracts Payable (longer than one year)
242 Mortgages Payable

Deferred income

261 Unearned Finance Charges

NET WORTH

Corporate accounts

291 Capital Stock
    2911 Capital Stock—Authorized
    2912 Capital Stock—Unissued
298 Retained Earnings
299 Profit and Loss—Current

NET WORTH

Sole proprietorship or partnership

291 Capital
    2911 Partner A
    2912 Partner B
292 Drawing
    2921 Partner A
    2922 Partner B
299 Profit and Loss—Current

INCOME AND EXPENSE ACCOUNTS.

INCOME

Sales

301 Major Appliances
302 Other Appliances
303 Used Merchandise (Trade-Ins)

304 Parts and Accessories
305 Service Labor

Cost of sales

401 Cost of Major Appliances
402 Cost of Other Appliances

403 Cost of Used Merchandise
404 Cost of Parts and Accessories
405 Cost of Service Labor

EXPENSES

500 Expenses (control)

Salaries and wages

511 Executive—Supervision
512 Clerical
513 Shop Wages
515 Sales Commissions

Supplies

521 Stationery and Postage
522 Operating Supplies
523 Gratis Material
524 Shop Supplies
525 Perishable Tools
527 Delivery Supplies

Utilities

531 Heat, Light, Water, and Power
533 Telephone and Telegraph
534 Laundry and Cleaning

Taxes

541 General
543 Payroll

Insurance

551 General
552 Retirement Plan
553 Compensation
554 Group Insurance

Depreciation

562 Buildings
563 Shop Equipment and Tools
564 Furniture and Fixtures
565 Automobiles and Trucks

Repairs and maintenance

572 Buildings
573 Shop Equipment and Tools
574 Furniture and Fixtures
575 Automobiles and Trucks

Other

581 Advertising
582 Losses on Bad Accounts
583 Donations
584 Dues and Subscriptions
585 Professional Services
587 Rentals
599 Unclassified

OTHER INCOME AND EXPENSE

Other income

601 Cash Discounts Taken
602 Interest Earned
603 Bonus on Contracts
609 Miscellaneous Gains

Other expense

651 Cash Discounts Allowed
652 Interest Expense
654 Losses on Repossessions
658 Overallowances on Trade-Ins
659 Miscellaneous Losses

BOOKS AND FORMS PECULIAR TO THE BUSINESS

The accounting system of the small to medium-sized home appliance dealer should include the following books of original entry: Sales journal, Purchases journal or Voucher register, Cash Receipts journal, Cash Disbursements journal, and General journal. The specialized columns to be included in these books will depend upon the specific requirements of the particular business in question. If a Voucher register is maintained, a Voucher System Check register will likewise be required.

The usual ledgers to which transactions are posted from the above described books of original entry are:

The General ledger, which controls all other ledgers and records and includes the complete record of assets, liabilities, capital, retained earnings, and the detailed revenue and expense accounts.

The Accounts and Contracts Receivable ledger, which is the detailed record of transactions with customers. This book comprises the subsidiary elements supporting the related General ledger accounts: Accounts Receivable (No. 122) and Contracts Receivable (No. 125).

The Accounts Payable ledger, or Voucher register, which is the detailed record of transactions with creditors.

The Stock ledger, which is the detailed record and perpetual inventory of all major appliances. Here are found pertinent facts concerning acquisition, location, and ultimate disposition of each individual item of merchandise by manufacturer's serial number.

A Payroll register, either of the pen-and-ink variety or one adapted for use with a bookkeeping machine, is normally maintained to provide statistical data needed to comply with Federal and state wages and hours, Social Security, and tax withholding requirements. The register is generally a supplementary memorandum record; its information is not posted directly to the accounts but is first recorded with a General journal entry, which is then posted.

ACCOUNTS PECULIAR TO THE BUSINESS

As suggested earlier, the chart of General ledger accounts provides accounts necessary for most home appliance dealers. It contains some accounts which may or may not be required; conversely it may need to be expanded to accommodate occasional transactions of an unusual nature. The chart provides the necessary flexibility for such expansion.

In most instances the titles assigned to the accounts are sufficiently self-explanatory to indicate their function. Brief comment on some of the accounts is offered to further clarify their use.

Service Labor in Process (No. 135). Where volume of repair work is sufficient to warrant, the dollar total of service labor applied to uncompleted jobs at the end of the accounting period may be inventoried and recorded in this account. An alternative procedure is to summarize labor costs reflected in job orders or on time cards at the end of the period and charge Cost of Service Labor (No. 405) directly with the total.

Finance Company Reserve (No. 191). This account reflects amounts withheld by financing agencies as a measure of protection against losses on contracts purchased from the dealer. Upon completion of payments by a customer, the portion of the reserve applicable to the customer's account is remitted to the dealer by the financing institution. Such remittances are recognized as revenue by the dealer and are credited to Bonus on Contracts (No. 603).

Due Finance Company on Repossessions (No. 224). This is a liability account which records the uncollectible balances on repossessed appliances which must be paid to the financing institution by the dealer. Losses on repossessions are charged to account No. 654.

Finance Company Collections (No. 231). Dealers frequently prefer to have customers make their installment payments on contracts at the store rather than directly to the financing agency. Such payments are properly recorded in this account pending ultimate transmittal to the finance company.

Unearned Finance Charges (No 261). Use of this account is appropriate for dealers who carry the financing of all or a large portion of their installment contracts. Contracts outstanding at the end of the accounting period are reviewed and a determination is made of deferred finance charges actually earned or realized. Account No. 261 is debited and No. 602, Interest Earned, is credited for the amount so determined.

Overallowances on Trade-Ins (No. 658). The use of trade-in allowances as a measure of the cost of used appliances occasionally tends to cause inflation of the inventory account, Used Merchandise (No. 133). A recommended solution is to charge the inventory with a reasonable cost value of the merchandise traded in and charge No. 658 with the excess allowance. This method highlights for management the extent to which overallowances are being granted. The balance of the overallowance account is normally reported as Other Expense. If the amount is substantial, however, a more realistic procedure would be to treat it as a special form of sales allowance and as a deduction in determining net sales of new appliances.

Gratis Material (No. 523). Charged to this account is the cost of parts and material used in repairing defective appliances without charge to the purchaser. Gratis work orders are summarized periodically and debited to this account. The Parts and Accessories inventory account and the applicable supplies expense accounts are credited as appropriate.

Peculiarities of Procedures

SALES-RECEIVABLES CYCLE

Cost of Sales. As already mentioned, sales of major appliances should be identified with specific items of inventory and charged to the cost of sales by a summary entry at the end of the period, debiting cost of sales and crediting the inventory account. Sales of other merchandise may be handled on the same basis, or they may be costed by the gross profit method (depending on the nature of the items), with periodic checks in the form of physical inventories.

Installment Sales. Most major appliance sales are made on the installment plan. In the majority of cases such conditional sales agreements are financed through commercial financing agencies or lending firms, with the dealer receiving the full invoice price* and the customer paying the invoice price plus financing charges to the financing institution. This method of handling poses no receivables problems for the dealer and amounts virtually to a cash sale.

When contracts are sold to or discounted by finance companies on a recourse basis, however, with guarantee of payment by the dealer in the event of default by the buyer, the nature and the amount of the contingent liability should be fully disclosed by appropriate footnote in the balance sheet.

If the dealer carries his own installment paper, he may choose either to credit current revenue with the total amount of the sale or he may elect to defer recognition of future installments as revenue until they are actually received, under the installment method. Either method is acceptable for income tax purposes. Use of the installment method requires the use of special forms and procedures if it is to be applied accurately.

Any finance charges collected in advance should be credited to Account 261, Unearned Finance Charges, and prorated over the life of the contract.

Trade-ins. Allowances granted on used merchandise traded in as part payment for new appliances should be related to the sale for which the allowance is made. Account 133, Used Merchandise (Trade-Ins), should be debited for the amount for which the dealer can reasonably expect to resell the item (industry trade-in blue books are available as a guide). As previously pointed out, any difference between this amount and the total allowance granted should be charged to Account 658, Overallowances on Trade-Ins.

Repossessions. When an appliance is repossessed it is usually necessary to reimburse the financing institution for the unpaid amount of the customer's contract less any adjustment of finance charges. The resale value of the returned merchandise is debited to Used Merchandise (No. 133). Any loss resulting from the repossession is charged to Losses on Repossessions (No. 654).

Other Receivables. Customer receivables resulting from sales on 30-, 60-, or 90-day accounts should be segregated from installment Accounts Receivable and handled in the normal manner. Such accounts will be subsidiary to Accounts Receivable (No. 122) in the General ledger.

---

* SOME FINANCING AGENCIES WITHHOLD A PORTION OF THE AMOUNT PAID FOR THE CONTRACT TO INSURE AGAINST LOSSES. SEE ACCOUNT NOS. 191 AND 603.

PURCHASES-PAYABLES CYCLE

Buying and inventory control are areas where home appliance dealers often get themselves into trouble—through overbuying, poor selection of merchandise, and inefficient control of inventory.

Dealers generally do their buying through distributors. Financing arrangements are often available which enable a reputable dealer to operate with a minimum of his own capital tied up in inventory. Many dealers have flooring lines of credit with financial institutions. In effect, under these plans the dealer obtains merchandise to sell by making a down payment of about 10 to 25 percent, depending on his credit reputation, the type of merchandise, and the ability to get a manufacturer or distributor repurchase agreement.

Some dealers get financing through finance companies controlled by the larger manufacturers. Financing under such an arrangement tends to be on even more liberal terms than those normally available. It is relatively easy for a dealer to become overstocked. Inventory should turn over 4 to 5½ times a year; levels of stocks should be based on potential sales rather than ease of financing inventory purchases.

Trust receipt purchase transactions with financial institutions are accounted for under Contracts Payable No. 205 (less than one year), since most become due within six months or when the merchandise is sold, whichever is earlier.

Trade accounts payable, notes payable, and long-term contracts payable present no unusual accounting difficulties and are handled normally. If the voucher system is used all such payments will be processed through the Voucher register.

CASH RECEIPTS AND DISBURSEMENTS

An adequate system of control should be devised for handling both cash receipts and cash disbursements. There should, of course, be the basic safeguard afforded by separation of duties in such a manner that the persons responsible for receiving or handling cash are not the same persons who make entries in the Cash journal or post to the accounts in which sources and uses of cash are recorded.

There should be the added safeguards against misappropriation provided by daily deposit of all cash receipts in the bank, intact, and the payment of all obligations by check.

A petty cash fund may be advisable, depending upon the volume of small cash purchases. If all cash receipts are deposited intact daily, a Cash Regisster Fund (No. 102) will also be required to insure availability of cash register change at the beginning of each business day.

All cash receipts are recorded in the Cash Receipts journal. A partial exception may occur in the case of cash sales. Since the Sales journal is frequently designed to accommodate the distribution of all sales, both cash and charge, either by classes of merchandise or by departments, the conventional Sales journal contains a cash sales debit column (sales distribution columns in the Cash journal are not desirable). The total of this column is debited to Account 121, Cash Sales Clearing. The balance of this account is in turn transferred to the Cash Receipts journal by a debit to Account 101, Cash on Hand, and a credit to Cash Sales Clearing.

It is usual practice for installment customers to make their payments to the dealer rather than to the financing agency. Such receipts are credited to Finance Company Collections (No. 231), and are promptly remitted to the finance company concerned.

Time and Payroll System

No unusual payroll problems are likely to be encountered in home appliance establishments. Some variation in detailed payroll procedures will be found among dealers, depending largely on the differing methods of compensating salesmen. Some dealers pay their salesmen a straight salary, some combine salary and commission, some may pay only commissions. The payment of a bonus in cash or in some other form may require special accounting handling, but none of these matters poses any serious difficulty.

A typical appliance store employing up to 15 people and keeping manual records may use one of the various "one writing", or posting board, payroll systems available commercially. These systems produce simultaneously a periodic payroll summary, a statement of earnings and deductions for each employee, and a payroll check. The savings in time and cost of payroll production afforded by use of these comparatively simple systems is considerable. They also meet requirements of all state and Federal laws applying to payroll records.

Cost Accounting and Departmental Accounting

Cost accounting. An appliance sale is unique. It is not consummated with satisfactory delivery of and payment for a product. Product service is generally stipulated in the sales contract and is, accordingly, a required function and responsibility of most appliance dealers.

If the function is performed by the dealer, rather than farmed out to a specialized appliance repair shop, then a simple but efficient job cost system will be needed to provide a basis for determining actual service costs and establishing service charges. Relevant costs consist of direct labor, materials

ABC APPLIANCES

No. _____
Customer Report No. _____

Date _____

1st Yr. War. ☐
2-5 Yr. War ☐
Out of War. ☐

SERVICE WORK ORDER

Name _____	Product _____
Address _____	Model No. _____
City _____	Serial No. _____
Phone _____	Date Inst. _____
Requested By _____	Promise Date _____

COMPLAINT: _____

_____

Work Performed: _____

PARTS USED

Part No.	Description	Am't	Acct'g.

	Total Material	
Prod. Time _____	Tax	
Unprod. Time _____	Labor	
Mileage _____		
Completed _____ Date	Total	
Incomplete _____ Date	Why _____	

Cash Rec'd. $ _____   Signed _____
      Amount   Technician

Figure 2: Service Work Order

ABC APPLIANCES
Income Statement
For the Year Ended December 31, 19___.

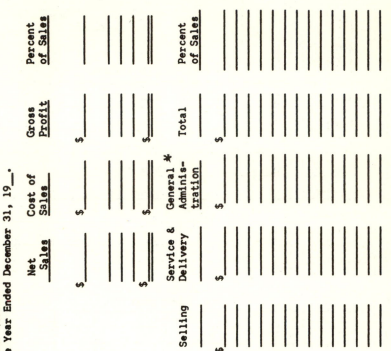

	Net Sales	Cost of Sales	Gross Profit	Percent of Sales
Revenues:				
Major appliances	$	$	$	
(Detail as necessary)				
Small appliances				
Other merchandise				
Service				
Total	$	$	$	

	Selling	Service & Delivery	General* Administration	Total	Percent of Sales
Operating Expenses:	$	$	$	$	
Executive salaries					
Clerical salaries					
Shop wages					
Sales commissions					
Stationery and postage					
Operating supplies					
Gratis material					
Shop supplies					
Perishable tools					
Delivery supplies					
Heat, light, water, and power					
Telephone and telegraph					
Laundry and cleaning					
Taxes					

100%

Insurance
Depreciation
Advertising
Losses on bad accounts
Donations
Dues and subscriptions
Professional services
Rent
Miscellaneous expense
      Totals

Percent of Sales:
   Net income from operations

Other Income and Deductions:
   Cash discounts taken
   Interest earned
   Bonus on contracts
   Miscellaneous other income
      Total other income

Other Expense:
   Cash discounts allowed
   Interest expense
   Losses on repossessions
   Over allowance on trade-ins
   Miscellaneous other expense
      Total other expense
            Net

Net Income

*Includes financial management

Figure 3: Income Statement

ABC APPLIANCES
Balance Sheet

December 31, 19--

ASSETS

Current assets:
  Cash in banks
  Cash on hand
  Marketable securities
  Accounts and contracts receivable
    Less: Allowance for doubtful accounts
  Prepaid expense
  Inventories:
    Major appliances
    Other appliances
    Used merchandise
    Parts and accessories

      Total current assets

	Cost	Accumulated Depreciation	Book Value
Plant assets:			
Land	$	$	$
Buildings			
Shop equipment and tools			
Furniture and fixtures			
Automobiles and trucks			
Total plant assets	$	$	

Deferred Charges
Other assets
Finance company reserve
    Total assets

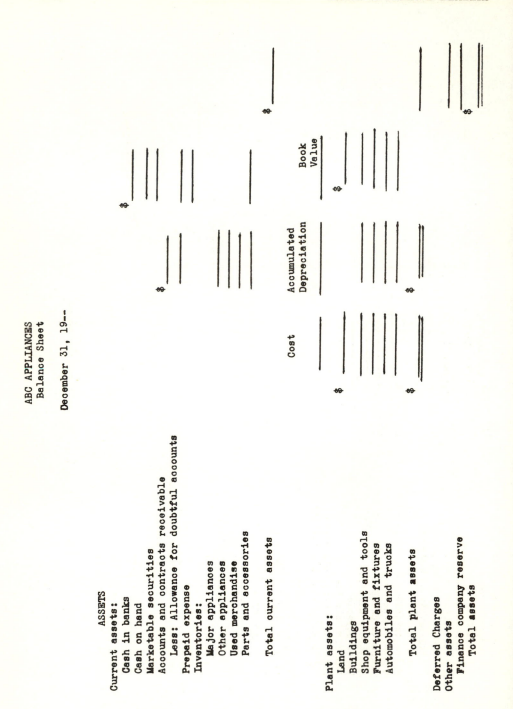

ABC APPLIANCES
Balance Sheet

December 31, 19___

LIABILITIES AND CAPITAL
Current liabilities:
  Notes payable $_____
  Contracts payable
  Accounts payable
  Customers deposits
  Taxes payable
  Salaries payable
  Finance company collections
    Total current liabilities $_____

Deferred credits:
  Unearned finance charges

Long term liabilities:
  Contracts payable* $_____
  Mortgage payable

    Total long term liabilities
    Total liabilities $_____

Capital
  (Single proprietorship, partnership or
  corporation capital accounts)

    Total liabilities and capital $_____

* Longer than one year

Figure 4: Balance Sheet

and parts, overhead, and credit charges. Mileage may also be a significant element of cost, depending on territory covered. Small and medium-sized dealers frequently record only labor and material and parts costs, using a percentage or some other factor for overhead in calculation of the price to be charged the customer. A common pricing policy, for example, is charging three times the cost of labor.

A sample Work Order form which will provide the necessary information for most service and repair jobs (including warranty status) is illustrated in Figure 2.

Departmental Accounting. The amount of statistical and analytical detail desired by appliance dealers for managerial purposes varies considerably and is based on size of the store, departmental organization, variety of merchandise offered and the individual preferences of the dealer-managers themselves.

Sales and cost of sales may be broken down by specific appliance items, such as television sets, refrigerators, washers, radios, stereos and so on; or a single category, "major appliances", may be established for all these products. Additional revenue and related cost of sales may be segregated under appropriate headings (such as "small appliances" or "other merchandise") in whatever degree of analytical detail is desired.

Expenses can be analyzed and allocated on some logical basis to each of the major functional areas suggested in Figure 1: Selling, service and delivery, general administration, and financial management. In a small or medium-sized appliance store this type of refinement may be considered impractical in view of the clerical costs involved. In such circumstances the conventional listing of expenses by control account titles included in the chart of accounts provides acceptable disclosure of the nature of expenses incurred for the business as a whole.

The classification of accounts suggested in this chapter is sufficiently flexible to accommodate analysis of revenue and expense on either a product or functional basis, as suggested above, and in virtually any degree of detail required. Some type of analysis along the lines indicated will be needed on a formal or informal basis at least once a year by those dealers who participate in the annual NARDA Cost-of-Doing-Business Survey.

Time-Saving Ideas

The saving in clerical work afforded by use of a commercially designed one-writing payroll system has already been discussed. The same bookkeeping economies can be achieved by use of a similar system (when volume of transactions does not require more sophisticated mechanical bookkeeping equipment) for cash disbursements and Accounts Payable. These simplified plans, which post all records simultaneously, provide to a very large extent the economies and accuracy of mechanized accounting methods without the need for either the expensive equipment or specially trained operators.

Use of data processing service bureaus may be found among medium-sized appliance dealers where volume of bookkeeping can justify the cost of punched-tape accounting equipment. In such instances accounting procedures will need to be adapted to the specific needs of the data processing center.

Use of ADP facilities is occasionally made by smaller firms as well. Original accounting documents, such as payrolls, invoices, and inventory data, are turned over to the data processing center which produces in completed form the analyses and operating statements required by the appliance dealer. Whatever sacrifice this procedure entails as a result of partial decentralization of the accounting function may be offset by increased accuracy, more timely operating results, and savings in personnel costs.

Reports to Management

The monthly reports to management, as a bare minimum, should be an income statement (Figure 3), a balance sheet (Figure 4), and a capital statement (Figure 5). Only the income statement requires special comment.

```
                                  ABC APPLIANCES
                                 Capital Statement

                          For the year ended December 31, 19__

                                                            $ _____
Capital, January 1, 19--
Net income for the year - Exhibit A          $ _____
Less withdrawals                               _____
Increase in capital                                           _____

   Capital, December 31, 19__                               $ _____
```

Figure 5: Capital Statement

Efficient operation of an appliance business calls for the inclusion in the income statement of the following:

1. Sales volume according to whatever classification breakdown
   the dealer may feel is needed.

2. Cost of sales and gross profit by each separate category, according to the sales classification breakdown.
3. Analysis of operating expenses as percentage of sales, individually and where appropriate or desirable, by departmental function.

The illustrative income statement incorporates all the above requirements. It may be condensed to include only those considered essential for a particular firm.